THE BEST POEMS OF
THE ENGLISH LANGUAGE

ALSO BY HAROLD BLOOM

Hamlet: Poem Unlimited (2003)

Genius: A Mosaic of One Hundred Exemplary Creative Minds (2002)

Stories and Poems for Extremely Intelligent Children of All Ages (2001)

How to Read and Why (2000)

Shakespeare: The Invention of the Human (1998)

Omens of Millennium (1996)

The Western Canon (1994)

The American Religion (1992)

The Book of J (1990)

Ruin the Sacred Truths (1989)

Poetics of Influence (1988)

The Strong Light of the Canonical (1987)

Agon: Towards a Theory of Revisionism (1982)

The Breaking of the Vessels (1982)

The Flight to Lucifer: A Gnostic Fantasy (1979)

Wallace Stevens: The Poems of Our Climate (1977)

Figures of Capable Imagination (1976)

Poetry and Repression (1976)

Kabbalah and Criticism (1975)

A Map of Misreading (1975)

The Anxiety of Influence (1973)

The Ringers in the Tower: Studies in Romantic Tradition (1971)

Yeats (1970)

Commentary to the Poetry and Prose of William Blake (1965)

Blake's Apocalypse (1963)

The Visionary Company (1961)

Shelley's Mythmaking (1959)

HarperCollins*Publishers*

The Best
Poems
of the
ENGLISH
LANGUAGE

FROM CHAUCER THROUGH FROST

Selected and with Commentary by

HAROLD BLOOM

HarperCollins books may be purchased for educational,
business, or sales promotional use.
For information, please write: Special Markets Department,
HarperCollins Publishers Inc., 10 East 53rd Street,
New York, NY 10022.

FIRST EDITION

Designed by Kate Nichols

Printed on acid-free paper

Library of Congress Cataloging-in-Publication Data

The best poems of the English language : from Chaucer through Frost /
selected and with commentary by Harold Bloom.—1st ed.
p.   cm.
Includes index.
ISBN 0-06-168647-6
ISBN 13: 978-0-06-168647-4

1. English poetry.   2. American poetry.   I. Bloom, Harold.
PR1175.B4566 2004
821.008—dc21
2003051104

08 09 10 NMSG/RRD 9 8 7 6 5 4 3 2 1

AUTHOR'S NOTE

FOR THE MOST PART, I have employed modernized texts, with only a few major exceptions: Chaucer, Spenser, Ralegh, Crashaw, and one or two others. Chaucer loses too much when we abandon his Middle English, while Spenser and Ralegh are deliberately archaic, as is Crashaw in his celebrations of Saint Teresa of Avila.

My introduction explains the concept and purpose of this book, but the center, for me, of my commentaries here is to be found in the essay "The Art of Reading Poetry."

The headnotes to poets and to poems vary greatly in length, and may sometimes appear disproportionate in regard to how fully the poets are represented. Thus, the discussions of Ezra Pound and of H. D. range widely, and give a total vision of their work. I have refrained from analyzing my selections from Shakespeare, as I do for Milton, because Shakespeare is more accessible to the common reader, while Milton requires mediation.

I acknowledge the debts owed to my research assistants: Brad Woodworth, Brett Foster, Deborah Kroplick, Jesse Zuba, and Stuart Watson. My wife, Jeanne, also aided in gathering together this volume.

Harold Bloom
Timothy Dwight College
Yale University
March 6, 2003

CONTENTS

INTRODUCTION

THOUGH ARRANGED CHRONOLOGICALLY, this vast book is intended for every kind of *personal* use, so that literary history is essentially irrelevant to its purposes, as are all considerations of political correctness and incorrectness. The best poems published by women before 1923 are here, chosen entirely on the basis of their aesthetic value. Poetry is in the first place poetry, a high and ancient art. It raises your consciousness of glory and of grief, of woe or wonder, as Shakespeare phrased it. Shakespeare spoke of "wonder-wounded hearers": they are the readers this volume seeks to serve.

My chronological limits are set by Geoffrey Chaucer, born around 1343, and Hart Crane, born in 1899. If poets born in the twentieth century were included here, many would be from Canada, the West Indies, Australia, New Zealand, and Africa, but because of the span covered, everyone here wrote in Great Britain or the United States.

I have included no poem or excerpt from a longer work that does not meet (in my judgment) the highest aesthetic and cognitive standards that poetry can exemplify. There are 108 poets represented in this book (aside from Anonymous), with about 24 given in something like their full abundance. Essentially, this is the anthology I've always wanted to possess. It reflects sixty years of deep and passionate reading, going back to my love of William Blake and Hart Crane, of William Shakespeare and John Milton, that vitalized my life from my twelfth year onward.

What is the use of great poetry for life? Wallace Stevens said that poetry was one of the enlargements of life. Oscar Wilde, marvelous critic and dramatist though a weak poet, remarked that all art was perfectly useless, an irony we need not literalize. Wilde knew, better than almost all of us, that Shakespeare, Michelangelo, and Mozart are superbly useful: they give the more difficult pleasures that can persuade us to abandon pleasures that are too easy, to adopt Shelley's formulation of the Sublime mode.

Ultimately, we seek out the best poems because something in many, if not most, of us quests for the transcendental and extraordinary, however secular, however well within the realm of the natural. We long, as Wordsworth wrote, for "something evermore about to be." The marvelous comes to us, when it comes, in very different forms: ideally in another person, but sometimes by an otherness in the self.

THE BEST POEMS OF
THE ENGLISH LANGUAGE

THE ART OF
READING POETRY

I

POETRY essentially is figurative language, concentrated so that its form is both expressive and evocative. Figuration is a departure from the literal, and the form of a great poem itself can be a trope ("turning") or figure. A common dictionary equivalent for "figurative language" is "metaphorical," but a metaphor actually is a highly specific figure, or turning from the literal. Kenneth Burke, a profound student of rhetoric, or the language of figures, distinguished four fundamental tropes: irony, synecdoche, metonymy, and metaphor. As Burke tells us, irony commits those who employ it to issues of presence and absence, since they are saying one thing while meaning something so different that it can be the precise opposite. We learn to wince when Hamlet says: "I humbly thank you" or its equivalent, since the prince generally is neither humble nor grateful.

We now commonly call synecdoche "symbol," since the figurative substitution of a part for a whole also suggests that incompletion in which something within the poem stands for something outside it. Poets frequently identify more with one trope than with the others. Among major American poets, Robert Frost (despite his mass reputation) favors irony, while Walt Whitman is the great master of synecdoche.

In metonymy, contiguity replaces resemblance, since the name or prime aspect of anything is sufficient to indicate it, provided it is near in space to what serves as substitute. Childe Roland, in Browning's remarkable monologue, is represented at the very end by the "slug-horn" or trumpet upon which he dauntlessly blows: "Childe Roland to the Dark Tower came."

Metaphor proper transfers the ordinary associations of one word to another, as when Hart Crane beautifully writes "peonies with pony manes," enhancing his metaphor by the pun between "peonies" and "pony." Or again Crane, most intensely metaphorical of poets, refers to the Brooklyn Bridge's curve as its "leap," and then goes on to call the bridge both harp and altar.

Figurations or tropes create meaning, which could not exist without them, and this making of meaning is largest in authentic poetry, where an excess or overflow emanates from figurative language, and brings about a condition of newness. Owen Barfield's *Poetic Diction: A Study in Meaning* is one of the best guides to this process, when he traces part of the poetic history of the English word "ruin."

The Latin verb *ruo*, meaning "rush" or "collapse," led to the substantive *ruina* for what had fallen. Chaucer, equally at home in French and English, helped to domesticate "ruin" as "a falling":

> Min is the ruine of the highe halles,
> The falling of the towers and of the walles.

One feels the chill of that, the voice being Saturn's or time's in "The Knight's Tale." Chaucer's disciple Edmund Spenser has the haunting line:

> The old ruines of a broken tower

My last selection in this book is Hart Crane's magnificent death ode, "The Broken Tower," in which Spenser's line reverberates. Barfield emphasizes Shakespeare's magnificence in the employment of "ruin," citing "Bare ruin'd choirs where late the sweet birds sang" from Sonnet 73, and the description of Cleopatra's effect upon her lover: "The noble ruin of her magic, Antony." I myself find even stronger the blind Gloucester's piercing outcry when he confronts the mad King Lear (IV, VI, 134–135):

> O ruin'd piece of nature! This great world
> Shall so wear out to nought.

Once Barfield sets one searching, the figurative power of "ruined" seems endless. Worthy of Shakespeare himself is John Donne, in his "A Nocturnal upon St. Lucy's Day," where love resurrects the poet to his ruin:

Study me then, you who shall lovers be
At the next world, that is, at the next spring:
    For I am every dead thing,
    In whom love wrought new alchemy.
      For his art did express
A quintessence even from nothingness,
From dull privations, and lean emptiness
He ruined me, and I am re-begot
Of absence, darkness, death; things which are not.

Barfield invokes what he rightly calls Milton's "terrific phrase": "Hell saw / Heaven ruining from Heaven," and then traces Wordsworth's allusive return to Milton. Rather than add further instances, I note Barfield's insight, that the figurative power of "ruin" depends upon restoring its original sense of *movement,* of rushing toward a collapse. One of the secrets of poetic rhetoric in English is to romance the etonym (as it were), to renew what Walter Pater called the "finer edges" of words.

2

LANGUAGE, to a considerable extent, is concealed figuration: ironies and synecdoches, metonymies and metaphors that we recognize only when our awareness increases. Real poetry is aware of and exploits these ruined tropes, though it is both a burden and a resource, for later poets in a tradition, that language ages into this wealth of figuration. The major poets of the twentieth century, in Britain and America, were those who could best exploit this equivocal richness: Thomas Hardy, W. B. Yeats, D. H. Lawrence, Robert Frost, T. S. Eliot, Wallace Stevens, and Hart Crane among them.

Eliot professed no use for Walter Pater, who nevertheless haunts his praxis both as poet and as critic, as in the superb "Preludes" from *Prufrock and Other Observations* (1917):

The conscience of a blackened street
Impatient to assume the world.

I am moved by fancies that are curled
Around these images, and cling:
The notion of some infinitely gentle
Infinitely suffering thing.

"Assume" goes back to the Latin *assumere*, meaning something like "take," and initially was used in English for receiving a person into association, as when heaven assumed a saint. Over time, "assume" began to mean "to take as being true"; thus Whitman tells his reader: "And what I assume you shall assume." Other meanings include "to put on oneself," as with a garment or insignia, or else "to simulate," a pretending to have. D. H. Lawrence wrote of houses "assuming the sun," perhaps remembering Hamlet's bitter advice to Gertrude: "Assume a virtue, if you have it not."

Eliot's blackened street, "impatient to assume the world," plays, I think, upon both Whitman and Hamlet. Yet the etymology, Pater's "finer edge of words," is renewed: by a dark irony, the street's "conscience" renders it impatient to take up the world even as heaven receives the blessed. "Conscience" comes from Latin *conscientia*, meaning "consciousness," and retains that significance sometimes in Shakespeare, as when the disguised Henry V observes: "I will speak my conscience of the King: I think he would not wish himself anywhere but where he is." Or we can remember Hamlet (as I suspect Eliot does): "Thus conscience doth make cowards of us all," whereas our "conscience" as moral awareness or sense of guilt is later in provenance, and is only secondary to Eliot's lines:

> The conscience of a blackened street
> Impatient to assume the world.

In a sustained, brilliant irony, Eliot imputes consciousness to the street, which in "assume" mistakes itself for heaven. Reflecting on the irony of his images, the poet has a notion of what heaven indeed might "assume": "some infinitely gentle / Infinitely suffering thing." Earlier in "Preludes," Eliot speaks to a waking soul:

> You had such a vision of the street
> As the street hardly understands;

I know nothing better by Eliot than the "Preludes." They so restored the strangeness of meaning that they became immensely fecund. *The Waste Land* founds its style upon them and so, in an intense agon with Eliot, does the lyrical genius of Hart Crane, who fought Eliot's vision yet could not resist Eliot's style and example, the "Preludes" in particular, where urban imagery is raised to an ironic glory.

3

GREATNESS in poetry depends upon splendor of figurative language and on cognitive power, or what Emerson termed "meter-making argument." Shakespeare is first among poets at representing thought, which pragmatically does not differ from *thinking in poetry*, a process not yet fully adumbrated. Angus Fletcher's *Colors of the Mind* can be recommended for its "conjectures on thinking in literature," which is the book's subtitle.

In Shakespeare, thought itself can be considered tragic or comic, or any shade between the two. Or, because of the Shakespearean detachment, so triumphant in the consciousness of Hamlet, we may hear what Wallace Stevens subtly termed "the hum of thoughts evaded in the mind." Clearly, poetic thinking takes place somewhat apart from philosophic thinking. There can be Epicurean poetry, or Platonic literature, in which concepts inform the work of the imagination, but most literary thinking is of a different kind.

Memory is crucial for all thought, but particularly so for poetic thinking. Poetic memory, as Fletcher suggests, allows *recognition,* which he regards as "the central modality of thinking, for literary purposes." "Recognition" here initially is Aristotle's *anagnorisis,* the recognition-scene toward which tragedy quests. Discovery can be a synonym for recognition, in this sense.

One definition of poetic power is that it so fuses thinking and remembering that we cannot separate the two processes. Can a poem, of authentic strength, be composed without remembering a prior poem, whether by the self or by another? Literary thinking relies upon literary memory, and the drama of recognition, in every writer, contains within it a moment of coming to terms with another writer, or with an earlier version of the self. Poetic thinking is contextualized by poetic influences, even in Shakespeare, most gifted of poets, who parodies Marlowe's *Jew of Malta* in *Titus Andronicus,* where Aaron the Moor attempts to overgo in villainy the sublime Barabas, the Marlovian Jew. Shakespeare's *Richard III* is more of an involuntary recollection of Marlowe, and it may be accurate to say that Shakespeare thinks less clearly through Richard III than he does through Aaron. But within two years, in *Richard II,* Shakespeare has so thought through Marlowe's influence (here of *Edward II*) that he audaciously mocks his precursor in what could be called Richard's recognition scene:

Give me that glass, and therein will I read.
No deeper wrinkles yet? Hath sorrow struck

So many blows upon this face of mine
And made no deeper wounds? O flatt'ring glass,
Like to my followers in prosperity,
Thou dost beguile me. Was this face the face
That every day under his household roof
Did keep ten thousand men? Was this the face
That like the sun did make beholders wink?
Is this the face which fac'd so many follies,
That was at last out-fac'd by Bolingbroke?
A brittle glory shineth in this face;
As brittle as the glory is the face,
                    [*Dashes the glass against the ground.*]
For there it is, crack'd in an hundred shivers.
Mark, silent king, the moral of this sport—
How soon my sorrow hath destroy'd my face.

The delighted audience, most of whom had attended Marlowe's *Dr. Faustus,* would have thrilled to Richard's triple-variant upon Faustus's ecstatic recognition of Helen of Troy, conjured up for him by Mephistopheles:

Was this the face that launched a thousand ships,
And burnt the topless towers of Ilium?

Here, Shakespearean thought triumphs over influence, as Marlowe returns from the dead, but only in the colors of Richard II's gorgeous rhetoric. Far subtler, Shakespeare in *The Tempest* gives us his anti-Faustus, Prospero, whose name is the Italian translation of the Latin Faustus, each "the favored one." The recognition scene in matured Shakespeare is one of a beautifully ironic self-recognition, a splendor of poetic thinking.

4

THE ART of reading poetry begins with mastering allusiveness in particular poems, from the simple to the very complex. We can start with quite short poems, like the lyrics of A. E. Housman (1859–1936). Here is his splendid "Epitaph on an Army of Mercenaries":

These, in the day when heaven was falling,
    The hour when earth's foundations fled,

Followed their mercenary calling
  And took their wages and are dead.

Their shoulders held the sky suspended;
  They stood, and earth's foundations stay;
What God abandoned, these defended,
  And saved the sum of things for pay.

Housman was a classical scholar, and his ultimate model here might be Simonides, the ancient Greek poet of epitaphs. Elsewhere in Housman, we are advised: "Shoulder the sky my lad, and drink your ale." Richard Wilbur, one of our best contemporary American poets, refers "and took their wages and are dead" to St. Paul's "the wages of sin is death." I think not, and cite instead Shakespeare's superb song from *Cymbeline:*

Fear no more the heat o' the Sun,
Nor the furious Winter's rages,
Thou thy worldly task hast done,
Home art gone, and ta'en thy wages.
Golden Lads, and Girls all must,
As Chimney-Sweepers come to dust.

At issue is how to determine the appropriateness of an allusion, and since great poetry is very nearly as allusive as it is figurative, the question of accuracy in tracing allusiveness is crucial. The echo here is far likelier to be of Shakespeare than of St. Paul, because the mercenaries are hardly being blamed, and the universalism of "Home art gone, and ta'en thy wages" therefore is more appropriate.

Wilbur more usefully finds "the sum of things," fled foundations, and heaven falling in two passages of Book IV of *Paradise Lost,* where Milton narrates the War in Heaven between the rebel angels and those who remain obedient to God:

                . . . horrid confusion leapt
Upon condition rose: and now all Heav'n
Had gone to wrack, with ruin overspread,
Had not th' Almighty Father where he sits
Shrin'd in his Sanctuary of Heav'n secure,
Consulting on the sum of things, foreseen
This tumult . . .
                        —LINES 668 FF.

Hell heard the unsufferable noise, Hell saw
Heav'n ruining from Heav'n, and would have fled
Affrighted, but strict Fate had cast too deep
Her dark foundations, and too fast had bound . . .
                        —LINES 867 FF.

But Housman, no Christian and a good Epicurean, makes these allusions ironic, since his mercenaries defended "What God abandoned," unlike the loyal angels, who followed Christ as he, at God's command, thrust the fallen angels out of Heaven. So we have a double lesson in allusiveness: is it accurate, and again is it itself figurative, as here?

Recognizing and interpreting allusions depends upon both the reader's learning and her tact. T. S. Eliot, in his charmingly outrageous and frequently unreliable "Notes" to *The Waste Land,* charts some of his allusions while evading others. His famous line—"I will show you fear in a handful of dust"—clearly alludes to the morbid young protagonist of Tennyson's *Maud,* who cries out to us: "And my heart is a handful of dust."

On a vaster scale, all of *The Waste Land,* but particularly Part V, "What the Thunder Said," is endlessly allusive to Walt Whitman's elegy "When Lilacs Last in the Dooryard Bloom'd." From "Lilacs" come Eliot's lilacs and other flowers, his unreal city, his triple self, the "third who always walks beside you," the maternal lamentation, the dead soldiers, and much more, but particularly the song of the hermit-thrush in the pine trees. Eliot's "Notes" refer the hermit-thrush to Chapman's *Handbook of Birdes in Eastern North America,* a somewhat hilarious evasion.

So profuse are the allusions to "Lilacs" in *The Waste Land* that we would forsake credulity to consider them accidental or even "unconscious." Allusion then can be a mode of evasion, or of warding off a precursor. Repressed reference is a defense against overinfluence. As forerunners, Eliot claimed Dante, Baudelaire, the rather minor Jules Laforgue, and Ezra Pound, his friend and mentor, but the authentic father was Walt Whitman, with a strong strain of Tennyson mixed in.

5

ALLUSION is only one strand in the relationship between later and earlier poems. More (in my judgment) than any other kind of imaginative literature, poetry brings its own past alive into its present. There is a benign haunting in poetic tradition, one that transcends the sorrows of influence, particularly the new poet's fear that there is little left for her or him to do. In truth, there is everything remaining to be thought and sung, provided an individual voice is attained.

Poetic voice is immensely difficult to define without examples. I give, almost at random, a sequence of major voices without (at first) identifying them:

1

Ay, but to die, and go we know not where;
To lie in cold obstruction, and to rot;
This sensible warm motion, to become
A kneaded clod; and the delighted spirit
To bathe in fiery floods, or to reside
In thrilling region of thick-ribbed ice;
To be imprison'd in the viewless winds
And blown with restless violence round about
The pendant world; or to be worse than worst
Of those that lawless and incertain thought
Imagine howling—'tis too horrible!
The weariest and most loathed wordly life
That age, ache, penury, and imprisonment
Can lay on nature is a paradise
To what we fear of death.

2

And that must end us, that must be our cure,
To be no more; sad cure; for who would lose,
Though full of pain, this intellectual being,
Those thoughts that wander through eternity,
To perish rather, swallowed up and lost
In the wide womb of uncreated night,
Devoid of sense and motion?

3

Not with more glories, in the ethereal plain,
The sun first rises o'er the purpled main,
Then issuing forth, the rival of his beams
Launched on the bosom of the silver Thames.
Fair nymphs and well-dressed youths around her shone,
But every eye was fixed on her alone.
On her white breast a sparkling cross she wore,
Which Jews might kiss, and infidels adore.

Her lively looks a sprightly mind disclose,
Quick as her eyes, and as unfixed as those:
Favours to none, to all she smiles extends,
Oft she rejects, but never once offends.
Bright as the sun, her eyes the gazers strike,
And, like the sun, they shine on all alike.
Yet graceful ease, and sweetness void of pride,
Might hide her faults, if belles had faults to hide:
If to her share some female errors fall,
Look on her face, and you'll forget 'em all.

4

I am made to sow the thistle for wheat; the nettle for a nourishing
    dainty
I have planted a false oath in the earth, it has brought forth a poison
    tree
I have chosen the serpent for a councellor & the dog
For a schoolmaster to my children
I have blotted out from light & living the dove & nightingale
And I have caused the earth worm to beg from door to door
I have taught the thief a secret path into the house of the just
I have taught pale artifice to spread his nets upon the morning
My heavens are brass my earth is iron my moon a clod of clay
My sun a pestilence burning at noon & a vapour of death in night

What is the price of Experience do men buy it for a song
Or wisdom for a dance in the street? No it is bought with the price
Of all that a man hath his house his wife his children
Wisdom is sold in the desolate market where none come to buy
And in the witherd field where the farmer plows for bread in vain

5

    Dust as we are, the immortal spirit grows
Like harmony in music; there is a dark
Inscrutable workmanship that reconciles
Discordant elements, makes them cling together
In one society. How strange that all
The terrors, pains, and early miseries,
Regrets, vexations, lassitudes interfused
Within my mind, should e'er have borne a part,
And that a needful part, in making up
The calm existence that is mine when I

Am worthy of myself! Praise to the end!
Thanks to the means which Nature deigned to employ;
Whether her fearless visitings, or those
That came with soft alarm, like hurtless light
Opening the peaceful clouds; or she may use
Severer interventions, ministry
More palpable, as best might suit her aim.

6
The woods decay, the woods decay and fall,
The vapours weep their burthen to the ground,
Man comes and tills the field and lies beneath,
And after many a summer dies the swan.
Me only cruel immortality
Consumes: I wither slowly in thine arms,
Here at the quiet limit of the world,
A white-haired shadow roaming like a dream
The ever-silent spaces of the East,
Far-folded mists, and gleaming halls of morn.

7
Yet each to keep and all, retrievements out of the night,
The song, the wondrous chant of the gray-brown bird,
And the tallying chant, the echo arous'd in my soul,
With the lustrous and drooping star with the countenance full of woe,
With the holders holding my hand nearing the call of the bird,
Comrades mine and I in the midst, and their memory ever to keep, for
the dead I loved so well,
For the sweetest, wisest soul of all my days and lands—and this for his
dear sake,
Lilac and star and bird twined with the chant of my soul,
There in the fragrant pines and the cedars dusk and dim.

8
Everything that man esteems
Endures a moment or a day.
Love's pleasure drives his love away,
The painter's brush consumes his dreams;
The herald's cry, the soldier's tread
Exhaust his glory and his might:
Whatever flames upon the night
Man's own resinous heart has fed.

9

There would still remain the never-resting mind,
So that one would want to escape, come back
To what had been so long composed.
The imperfect is our paradise.
Note that, in this bitterness, delight,
Since the imperfect is so hot in us,
Lies in flawed words and stubborn sounds.

We hear nine voices, all piercingly eloquent, and all making a difference to our consciousness that really is a difference. The first passage's
speaker, Claudio, in Shakespeare's *Measure for Measure* (III, I, 117–131),
faces execution, but while his cowardice (to call it that) is his own, there is
nothing in his eloquence that reflects his individual consciousness.
Instead, Shakespeare touches the universal with one of what we may call
his own voices: our fear of death scarcely could be more vividly expressed.

In the next passage, the fallen angel Belial, in Milton's grand Debate
in Hell (*Paradise Lost*, II, 145–151), may be echoing Claudio's lament as
he too fears extinction. Is this one of Milton's own accents? Anything but a
coward, the heroic, blind poet nevertheless allows Belial to catch a trace of
the poet's own dread of being ended before his great poem had been fully
composed.

With the third excerpt, we hear the exquisitely precise and modulated
voice of Alexander Pope (*The Rape of the Lock*, Canto II, 1–18). The gorgeous Belinda, universal flirt, is aptly portrayed as a sunrise, warm to all
but partial to none in particular. The Popean wit, Mozartean in its classical
playfulness, achieves apotheosis in a couplet that commends itself to
everyone:

On her white breast a sparkling cross she wore,
Which Jews might kiss, and infidels adore.

Pope's perfect pitch is answered by William Blake's prophetic tonalities in the fourth passage, the lament of Enion, the Earth Mother, in *The
Four Zoas* (Night II, p. 35, 1–15). In the accents of Zechariah 8:17 and Job
28:12–13, Blake speaks also in his own most authentic voice, as he himself
is both seller and farmer:

Wisdom is sold in the desolate market where none come to buy
And in the witherd field where the farmer plows for bread in vain

A different prophet, William Wordsworth, is heard in (5), from *The Prelude* I, 340–356, where Nature is exalted as subtlest of poetic teachers. The profound melancholia of Tennyson's Vergilian "Tithonus" sounds in (6), a lament for an immortality rendered useless by perpetual aging. Prophecy returns in (7), with the final lines of Walt Whitman's "When Lilacs Last in the Dooryard Bloom'd," where Whitman's elegiac, rocking threnody achieves a deep peace.

William Butler Yeats, his voice at its most oracular, is heard in (8), the final stanza of his "Two Songs from a Play," with its paradox beyond bitterness: "love's pleasure drives his love away." A final contrast is afforded by (9), where Wallace Stevens concludes his subtle "The Poems of Our Climate" with the somber realization: "The imperfect is our paradise." Yeats's voice is fierce, but Stevens's is very quiet, as he is the poet who listens for and somehow renders what lies beyond representation, "The hum of thoughts evaded in the mind."

6

WHAT MAKES one poem better than another? The question, always central to the art of reading poetry, is more crucial today than ever before, since extrapoetic considerations of race, ethnicity, gender, sexual orientation, and assorted ideologies increasingly constitute the grounds for judgment in the educational institutions and the media of the English-speaking world.

By concluding with Hart Crane, born in 1899, and by reprinting only half a dozen poems published after 1923, I have largely evaded our contemporary flight from all standards of aesthetic and cognitive value. Since there are no poems in this volume that are not among the best in the language, I will have to cite some bad or inadequate work not reprinted here in order to discuss how and why we legitimately should choose among poems.

One of the few gains from aging, at least for a critic of poetry, is that taste matures even as knowledge increases. As a younger critic, I tended to give my heart to the poetry of the Romantic tradition, doubtless spurred to polemics on its behalf by the distortions it suffered at the hands of T. S. Eliot and his New Critical academic followers: R. P. Blackmur, Allen Tate, Cleanth Brooks, W. K. Wimsatt among them. In my early seventies, I remain profoundly attached to the sequence that goes from Spenser through Milton on to the High Romantics (Blake, Wordsworth, Shelley,

Keats) and then to the continuators in Tennyson, Browning, Whitman, Dickinson, Yeats, Stevens, Lawrence, Hart Crane. With Chaucer and Shakespeare, these remain the poets I love best, but maturation has brought an almost equal regard for the tradition of Wit: Donne, Ben Jonson, Marvell, Dryden, Pope, Byron, and such modern descendants as Auden and Eliot (a secret Romantic, however).

I juxtapose two short poems, one of which is bad indeed, the other superb.

Alone

From childhood's hour I have not been
As others were—I have not seen
As others saw—I could not bring
My passions from a common spring—
From the same source I have not taken
My sorrow—I could not awaken
My heart to joy at the same tone—
And all I lov'd—*I* lov'd alone—
Then—in my childhood—in the dawn
Of a most stormy life—was drawn
From ev'ry depth of good and ill
The mystery which binds me still—
From the torrent, or the fountain—
From the red cliff of the mountain—
From the sun that 'round me rolled
In its autumn tint of gold—
From the lightning in the sky
As it pass'd me flying by—
From the thunder, and the storm—
And the cloud that took the form
(When the rest of Heaven was blue)
Of a demon in my view—

The Rhodora

On Being Asked, Whence Is the Flower?

In May, when sea-winds pierced our solitudes,
I found the fresh Rhodora in the woods,
Spreading its leafless blooms in a damp nook,

To please the desert and the sluggish brook.
The purple petals, fallen in the pool,
Made the black water with their beauty gay;
Here might the red-bird come his plumes to cool,
And court the flower that cheapens his array.
Rhodora! if the sages ask thee why
This charm is wasted on the earth and sky,
Tell them, dear, that if eyes were made for seeing,
Then Beauty is its own excuse for being:
Why thou wert there, O rival of the rose!
I never thought to ask, I never knew;
But, in my simple ignorance, suppose
The self-same Power that brought me there brought you.

Both are poems by Americans in the mid-nineteenth century, each better known for his other writings. The first, "Alone," is palpably Byronic, and closely imitates the noble lord's self-portrait in his *Lara:*

There was in him a vital scorn of all:
As if the worst had fallen which could befall,
He stood a stranger in this breathing world,
An erring spirit from another hurled;
A thing of dark imaginings, that shaped
By choice the perils he by chance escaped;
But 'scaped in vain, for in their memory yet
His mind would half exult and half regret.
With more capacity for love than earth
Bestows on most of mortal mould and birth,
His early dreams of good outstripped the truth,
And troubled manhood followed baffled youth;
With thought of years in phantom chase misspent,
And wasted powers for better purpose lent;
And fiery passions that had poured their wrath
In hurried desolation o'er his path,
And left the better feelings all at strife
In wild reflection o'er his stormy life;

Byron's narcissism is smooth and self-delighting; his disciple, Edgar Allan Poe, is self-pitying and metrically maladroit, and reminds us that Ralph Waldo Emerson called him "the jingle man." Both *Lara* and "Alone" are melodramatic, but Byron has the aristocratic flair to bring it off, while Poe's litany of "I"s and "my"s is pathetic in the context of torrent and fountain, cliff and mountain, rolling sun and flying lightning, thunder and storm and cloud. By the time Poe sees a demon in the cloud, the reader is wearied.

Poe's antithesis, Emerson, in "The Rhodora," declines to answer the question: "Whence is the Flower?" He does not know why this beautiful "rival of the rose" is placed so inexplicably. With Poe, because of the derivative echoes, we are compelled to remember Byron. With Emerson, a reader of Robert Frost will think of Frost, Emerson's professed disciple. Frost's powerful "The Wood-Pile" and "The Oven Bird" follow the pattern of "The Rhodora," where natural beauty wastes without purpose.

Emerson, with his tough sensibility, too easily can be misread. The only God that Emerson knew was a God within the self, and so the Power of the final line cannot be identified with a benign, external God. Out of context, "Beauty is its own excuse for being" could be confused with the Aestheticism of Oscar Wilde. But in the poem, the line means that beauty is a throwaway, as the wood-walking Emerson may be also, so far as the Power or Fate is concerned.

The diction in "The Rhodora" is assured and confident, and its figurative stance approaches an ironic edge, over which Emerson declines to cross. His "simple ignorance" wants to be taken literally, but "The Rhodora" is too adroit for that.

There *are* a few good poems by Poe, but they too are derivative. "Israfel" is haunted by Shelley's "To a Skylark," while "The City in the Sea" rewrites Byron's "Darkness." How can one tell the difference between involuntary echoing and controlled allusiveness? That is a difficult question to answer, since only the cumulative experience of reading poetry could render a reply accessible.

Sometimes a poet will show his awareness of an allusion through the process of revision. Here are the two versions of the first stanza of Edwin Arlington Robinson's superb incantation "Luke Havergal":

Go to the western gate, Luke Havergal,—
There where the vines cling crimson on the wall,—
And in the twilight wait for what will come.
The wind will moan, the leaves will whisper some—
Whisper of her, and strike you as they fall;
But go, and if you trust her she will call.
Go to the western gate, Luke Havergal—
Luke Havergal.

Go to the western gate, Luke Havergal,
There where the vines cling crimson on the wall,

And in the twilight wait for what will come.
The leaves will whisper there of her, and some,
Like flying words, will strike you as they fall;
But go, and if you listen she will call.
Go to the western gate, Luke Havergal—
Luke Havergal.

The modification is from: "The wind will moan, the leaves will whisper some— / Whisper of her, and strike you as they fall" to: "The leaves will whisper there of her, and some, / Like flying words, will strike you as they fall." Certainly the second version is even more eloquent, and the allusion to Shelley's "Ode to the West Wind" is rendered unmistakable. Shelley's figuration, in which dead leaves and words fuse, kindles Robinson's revision:

Drive my dead thoughts over the universe
Like withered leaves to quicken a new birth!
And, by the incantation of this verse,

Scatter, as from an unextinguished hearth
Ashes and sparks, my words among mankind!

Where are the flying words in Robinson's poem? "Trust" is altered to "listen" in the next line, and at the poem's conclusion the leaves are "dead words." Robinson strengthens his poem by making the allusion clearer. This dramatic lyric is chanted by Luke Havergal, rather than by Robinson, which helps the poet transmute Shelley's prophetic outcry into a highly individual litany for lost love.

The poetic excellence of "Luke Havergal" partly ensues from rhetorical control, the verbal equivalent of personal self-confidence. A faltering of voice mars, and can destroy, any poem whatsoever. Sustained and justified pride of performance is a frequent attribute of the best lyric poetry. Generally it is more appropriate that the pride be implicit, but there is a particular pleasure for the attentive reader when a poet justifies self-referentiality as Shelley does in the fifty-fifth and final stanza of *Adonais,* his elegy for John Keats:

The breath whose might I have invoked in song
Descends on me; my spirit's bark is driven,
Far from the shore, far from the trembling throng
Whose sails were never to the tempest given;
The massy earth and spherèd skies are riven!

I am borne darkly, fearfully, afar;
Whilst, burning through the inmost veil of Heaven,
The soul of Adonais, like a star,
Beacons from the abode where the Eternal are.

Shelley welcomes the "destroyer and preserver" invoked in his own "Ode to the West Wind," which now powers his spirit (breath) for a final, cosmological voyage. To thus call upon a prior creation of one's own is to affirm an authentic poetic election. Keats, wonderfully pugnacious by temperament, confronts his fierce Muse, Moneta, in *The Fall of Hyperion,* and proudly emphasizes his solitary election:

I sure should see
Other men here; but I am here alone.

The preternatural confidence of poetic election is unsurpassed in Walt Whitman, who at the start of section 25, *Song of Myself,* achieves apotheosis:

Dazzling and tremendous how quick the sun-rise would kill me,
If I could not now and always send sun-rise out of me.

We also ascend dazzling and tremendous as the sun,
We found our own O my soul in the calm and cool of the day-break.

My voice goes after what my eyes cannot reach,
With the twirl of my tongue I encompass worlds and volumes of
    worlds.

The play upon "quick" is superb, since it means both "speed" and "life." A perpetual American sunrise, Walt Whitman here also alludes to Jehovah, who walks in the Garden of Eden before the heat of the day. What makes Whitman the best of all American poets—except for his one rival, Emily Dickinson—is harmonic balance. At his greatest, he is flawless, with no false notes. Who could improve even a single phrase of the concluding section of *Song of Myself* ?

The spotted hawk swoops by and accuses me, he complains of my gab
    and my loitering.

I too am not a bit tamed, I too am untranslatable,
I sound my barbaric yawp over the roofs of the world.

The last scud of day holds back for me,
It flings my likeness after the rest and true as any on the shadow'd
    wilds,
It coaxes me to the vapor and the dusk.

I depart as air, I shake my white locks at the runaway sun,
I effuse my flesh in eddies, and drift it in lacy jags.

I bequeath myself to the dirt to grow from the grass I love,
If you want me again look for me under your boot-soles.

You will hardly know who I am or what I mean,
But I shall be good health to you nevertheless,
And filter and fibre your blood.

Failing to fetch me at first keep encouraged,
Missing me one place search another,
I stop somewhere waiting for you.

There is nothing "free" about this verse: in measure and phrase, it has that quality of the *inevitable* that is central to great poetry. "Inevitable," in this context, takes its primary meaning, phrasing that cannot be avoided, that *must be,* rather than the secondary meaning of "invariable" or "predictable." Indeed, the difference between those meanings is a pragmatic test for distinguishing between the best poems and merely imitative verses. "If you want me again look for me under your boot-soles" is unavoidable wording, while Poe's "In there stepped a stately Raven of the saintly days of yore" is woefully predictable.

The two kinds of "inevitability" are also two modes of the memorable. I can chant Poe by the yard, from memory, because it is jack-in-the-box verse, mechanical and repetitive. But when I possess a great poem by memory, it is because the work is inevitable, perfectly fulfilled and fulfillable. In the better mode of the memorable, cognition is a vital element in possession. Thus, I tend to recite Tennyson's superb dramatic monologue "Ulysses" to myself, on days when I have to battle depression or adversity, or just the consequences of old age. Frequently, I ask classes to read and reread "Ulysses" out loud to themselves while thinking and rethinking it through. What could be more inevitable, in the grand sense of what must be?

There lies the port; the vessel puffs her sail:
There gloom the dark broad seas. My mariners,
Souls that have toiled, and wrought, and thought with me—

That ever with a frolic welcome took
The thunder and the sunshine, and opposed
Free hearts, free foreheads—you and I are old;
Old age hath yet his honour and his toil;
Death closes all: but something ere the end,
Some work of noble note, may yet be done,
Not unbecoming men that strove with Gods.
The lights begin to twinkle from the rocks:
The long day wanes: the slow moon climbs: the deep
Moans round with many voices. Come, my friends,
'Tis not too late to seek a newer world.
Push off, and sitting well in order smite
The sounding furrows; for my purpose holds
To sail beyond the sunset, and the baths
Of all the western stars, until I die.
It may be that the gulfs will wash us down:
It may be we shall touch the Happy Isles,
And see the great Achilles, whom we knew.
Though much is taken, much abides; and though
We are not now that strength which in old days
Moved earth and heaven; that which we are, we are;
One equal temper of heroic hearts,
Made weak by time and fate, but strong in will
To strive, to seek, to find, and not to yield.

"Though much is taken, much abides": that seems to me the essence of positive inevitability of phrasing. When Ben Jonson remarked bitterly of Shakespeare, "He never blotted a line—would he had blotted many!," he testified to Shakespeare's uncanny power of unavoidable rather than predictable phrasing. Tennyson's Ulysses is overtly Shakespearean throughout his monologue, until in the final lines he begins to sound like Milton's quite Shakespearean Satan. In Shakespeare, more than in any other poet in English, we continually receive the impression of a control over phrasemaking so great that everything in the mind that is out of control finds itself organized by the inevitability of the power to phrase. John Keats, enraptured by this Shakespearean capability, seems to have associated it with Coleridge's Organic analogue, as when Keats observes that if a poem does not come as naturally as leaves to a tree, then it had better not come at all. The notion that Shakespeare and nature are everywhere the same is a false though poignant one. And yet that tribute to Shakespeare helps illuminate the idea of inevitability as unavoidable wording rather than merely predictable diction.

Matthew Arnold thought that this inevitability of great poetry could be clarified by the citation of "touchstones," brief passages of Homer, Dante, Shakespeare, and Milton against which other poems could be tested. But Arnold deliberately chose to be imprecise when he spoke of his touchstones as possessing "a high poetic stamp of diction and movement." That "movement" palpably is Arnold's own trope, as "inevitability" is mine, and does not illumine the question of how great poetry is to be recognized. A contrast of the true sense of "inevitability"—the unavoidable as opposed to the invariable—may take us closer to answering the question than the Arnoldian reliance upon the "movement" of touchstones, though *any* quotation from great poetry is bound to be a kind of touchstone, however we intend it.

The ancient idea of the Sublime, as set forth by the Hellenistic critic we call "Longinus," seems to me the origin of my expectation that great poetry will possess an inevitability of phrasing. Longinus tells us that in the experience of the Sublime we apprehend a greatness to which we respond by a desire for identification, so that we will become what we behold. Loftiness is a quality that emanates from the realm of aspiration, from what Wordsworth called a sense of something evermore *about to be*.

7

"INEVITABILITY," unavoidable phrasing, seems to me, then, a crucial attribute of great poetry. But how can a reader tell, for herself, whether a poem she has never seen before possesses the quality of authentic poetry? As you read a poem, there should be several questions in your mind. What does it mean, and how is that meaning attained? Can I judge how good it is? Has it transcended the history of its own time and the events of the poet's life, or is it now only a period piece?

I want to take as test case one of the great but truly difficult poems of the twentieth century, Hart Crane's *Voyages* II:

> —And yet this great wink of eternity,
> Of rimless floods, unfettered leewardings,
> Samite sheeted and processioned where
> Her undinal vast belly moonward bends,
> Laughing the wrapt inflections of our love;
>
> Take this Sea, whose diapason knells
> On scrolls of silver snowy sentences,
> The sceptered terror of whose sessions rends

As her demeanors motion well or ill,
All but the pieties of lovers' hands.

And onward, as bells off San Salvador
Salute the crocus lustres of the stars,
In these poinsettia meadows of her tides,—
Adagios of islands, O my Prodigal,
Complete the dark confessions her veins spell.

Mark how her turning shoulders wind the hours,
And hasten while her penniless rich palms
Pass superscription of bent foam and wave,—
Hasten, while they are true,—sleep, death, desire,
Close round one instant in one floating flower.

Bind us in time, O Seasons clear, and awe.
O minstrel galleons of Carib fire,
Bequeath us to no earthly shore until
Is answered in the vortex of our grave
The seal's wide spindrift gaze toward paradise.

The first draft of this visionary lyric was begun in April 1924, three months away from Hart Crane's twenty-fifth birthday, and in the early ecstatic phase of his love for a Danish sailor, Emil Oppfer. This second Voyage is part of a sequence of six, printed complete at the very end of this volume. Let us commence with a very close reading of Hart Crane's lyric, before considering its contexts in Crane's life and works, and in the poetic tradition he accepted and sought to extend: Shakespeare, Marlowe, Blake, Shelley, Melville, Whitman, Dickinson, and his immediate precursor, the early T. S. Eliot, with whose work he had an agonistic relationship, as I think Wallace Stevens and William Carlos Williams did also.

The *Voyages* are poems of intense erotic fulfillment set in the Caribbean, where Crane had sojourned in summertime, with his grandmother, on the Isle of Pines, since he was fifteen. At thirty-two, returning to New York City from a Guggenheim year in Mexico City, Crane drowned himself in the Caribbean, but *Voyages* II was composed seven years before. "Sleep, death, desire / Close round one instant in one floating flower" has taken on, for some, the authority of prophecy.

The initial line: "—And yet this great wink of eternity" plays against the final line of *Voyages* I: "The bottom of the sea is cruel." Whether we are to find flirtation in the Caribbean's wink is unclear; it is, after all, a sig-

nal from eternity, ordinarily hardly an erotic possibility. John Keats had
said to his silent Grecian urn that it teased us out of thought, as did eternity. Yet for Hart Crane the great wink emanates from a maternal sea that
is at least equivocal, if not invasive, in regard to the young men who have
become lovers. Floods with no rim or horizon, leewardings wholly free, as
though the wind's direction were open forever; these intimate an available
female presence beyond flirtation, dangerous because she incarnates the
Oedipal trespass. Sheeted in samite, the medieval rich, golden, silk garment of Tennysonian temptresses, the Caribbean passes by as in an
undine's procession. The sea's swell, bending upward to the moon's pull,
is the vast belly of a water demoness in search of a soul. Ambiguously
maternal, does she laugh with or at the young men's "wrapt inflections"?
Crane, by "inflections," appears to mean "motions," the rival "bendings"
of the young men, rather than any pitch of voice, in love's expression.
"Wrapt," a Lewis Carrollian or Joycean portmanteau word, pertains to
rapt embraces yet also to the sea's wrapping, the context through which
the lovers sail.

At fifteen, Hart Crane had read Shelley, and two poems seem to have
lingered in him: the early quest-vision, *Alastor,* and the late elegy for
Keats, *Adonais. Alastor* evidently suggested the voyage motif to Crane,
while *Adonais* inspired the rhapsodic "Atlantis" canto of Crane's epic, *The
Bridge,* where Atlantis is stationed last but was the first section of the
poem to be composed. *Alastor* was written when the twenty-three-year-
old Shelley mistakenly thought he was dying of consumption. His friend,
the ironic novelist Thomas Love Peacock (*Nightmare Abbey, Headlong
Hall*) said that he restored the young, vegetarian poet to health by feeding
him a steady diet of well-peppered muttonchops. Before this Peacockian
firming-up, Shelley had sent his surrogate, a nameless young poet, upon a
vast wandering through the ruins of the ancient world, and into an erotic
quasi-dream union with a mysterious beauty in the "vale of Cashmir" (now
much disputed between India and Pakistan). After the lady vanishes, the
Poet searches for her, eventually sailing off in a little shallop upon what
appears to be the Black Sea, which Shelley associated with death, night,
and the mothering aspect of nature.

Shelley thus inaugurated what would become more an American than
an English poetic motif, the fourfold figuration that finally fuses night,
death, the mother, and the sea in a sequence of American poets from Walt
Whitman though Hart Crane, Wallace Stevens, T. S. Eliot, and beyond.
Losing the visionary beloved, Shelley's Poet laments the mutual spell of
sleep, death, desire:

                                    Alas! Alas!
Were limbs, and breath, and being indetermined
Thus treacherously? Lost, lost, forever lost,
In the wide pathless desert of dim sleep,
That beautiful shape? Does the dark gate of death
Conduct to thy mysterious paradise,
O Sleep? Does the bright arch of rainbow clouds,
And pendent mountains seen in the calm lake,
Lead only to a black and watery depth,
While death's blue vault, with loathliest vapours hung
Where every shade which the foul grave exhales
Hides its dead eye from the detested days,
Conducts, O Sleep, to thy delightful realms?

This deliciously unhealthy passage surprisingly makes death the gate
to an erotic paradise of dream in sleep, a variant upon Hamlet's soliloquy
that meditates upon the "sleep of death." Behind Shelley's speculation, as
Crane seems to have known, perhaps through reading P. D. Ouspensky's
Tertium Organum in 1923, was the Hellenistic myth of Hermes Tris-
megistus, reputed author of the *Poimandres*, where Divine Man falls into
the ocean that is the cosmos of love, sleep, and death:

> When the man saw in the water the form like himself as it was in
> nature, he loved it and wished to inhabit it; wish and action came
> in the same moment, and he inhabited the unreasoning form.
> Nature took hold of her beloved, hugged him all about and
> embraced him, for they were lovers.
>   . . . although man is above the cosmic framework, he became a
> slave within it . . . love and sleep are his masters.
>
> —TRANS. B. P. COPENHAVEN

Like the Hermetic and Shelleyan falls into love and sleep, Crane's
lovers are knowingly narcissistic, and the mockingly maternal sea punishes
them for it. "Take this Sea," Crane cries to his lover, and it is difficult to
mark the limits of that "take." In a poem so initially intense as this, it
almost seems as though Crane invites Oppfer to join him in the act of
Oedipal violation. If the undinal vast mother is being embraced, all her
attributes are menacing. Her diapason, the full range of her outpouring
sound, *knells* (proclaims by the tolling of bells) on the scrolls of silver
snowy sentences, the Caribbean's shifting surfaces, and "sentences" must
mean court judgments as well as the lines of *Voyages* II, a reading confirmed by the brilliant "The sceptred terror of her sessions *rends*," a hint of

an Orphic *sparagmos* that she could willfully inflict, depending upon our interpretation of her ambiguous countenance and its ambivalent gestures. There is a wonderful pathos in "all but the pieties of lovers' hands," but that sets the question of how we are to visualize the lovers. Do they hold hands in a Shelleyan boat, braving the Caribbean, or are we to see them as afloat, hand in hand, carried by the sea itself?

Though we must not literalize this superbly organized procession of images, both visualizations are possible, the boat voyage, of course, likelier. The third stanza exemplifies this: Crane and Oppfer sail onward, hearing a different voice of bells, whether of a sunken city or of long-submerged Spanish galleons, and these bells *salute* both sky and sea as visions of fresh growth, crocus lustres, and poinsettia meadows. In an ecstasy of sexual knowing, Crane cries aloud with preternatural eloquence:

> Adagios of islands, O my Prodigal,
> Complete the dark confessions her veins spell.

To salute Oppfer as "my Prodigal" is overtly Whitmanian, taking the beloved comrade not as extravagantly wasteful but as one who gives in abundance, with homoerotic profusion of being. Crane himself explained "Adagios of islands" as the slow, rocking motion a small boat made as it sailed though closely arrayed islets. It is not clear whether "adagios" refers to a slow musical movement or a deliberate *pas de deux,* here erotic, because of the passionate reference to the closing lines of section 21 of *Song of Myself,* where Whitman proclaims:

> Prodigal, you have given me love—
>   therefore I to you give love!
> O unspeakable passionate love.

Directly after, at the start of section 22, Whitman erotically encounters the sea:

> You Sea! I resign myself to you also—I guess what you mean,
> I behold from the beach your crooked inviting fingers,
> I believe you refuse to go back without feeling of me,
> We must have a turn together, I undress, hurry me out of sight of the
>   land,
> Cushion me soft, rock me in billowy drowse,
> Dash me with amorous wet, I can repay you.

There is no overt anxiety here, or in Whitman's Oedipal trespass in "When Lilacs Last in the Dooryard Bloom'd":

> *Dark mother always gliding near with soft feet,*
> *Have none chanted for thee a chant of fullest welcome?*
> *Then I chant it for thee, I glorify thee above all,*
> *I bring thee a song that when thou must indeed come, come*
> *   unfalteringly.*
>
> *Approach strong deliveress,*
> *When it is so, when thou hast taken them I joyously sing the dead,*
> *Lost in the loving floating ocean of thee,*
> *Laved in the flood of thy bliss O death.*

Crane's mother-sea, the Caribbean, is far more equivocal in what seems to be the joined passion of the male lovers and the undine, where the homoerotic adagios "Complete the dark confessions her veins spell." But whose confessions are these?

The sea holds the sceptre, and the confessions are those of the lovers, under her spell, but also spelled by her veins (imagistically, foam) in the sentences of her scrolls. Certainly, the ambivalently maternal sea is again the center in the fourth stanza:

> Mark how her turning shoulders wind the hours,
> And hasten while her penniless rich palms
> Pass superscription of bent foam and wave,—
> Hasten, while they are true,—sleep, death, desire,
> Close round one instant in one floating flower.

A superscription is something written above or inside something else. But to pass superscription is to make such writing into another judgmental sentence, and here the term set is time itself. The sea's turning shoulders form a timepiece, and Crane urges his lover to mark this in a double sense: to notice and to indicate for memory. The "penniless rich palms" are the mother's, awarding nothing and everything, and they are also palm trees floating in the "bent foam and wave." Crane, who makes even his syntax figurative, does not clarify the antecedent of "they" in "Hasten while they are true." Are they the sea's palms or, more likely, "sleep, death, desire"? As in Shelley or in Hermetic writing, we fall into the narcissistic mirror of the sea, and sleep, death, and love fuse together. "Hasten" means to abandon the adagio phase of lovemaking, so as to achieve culmination: "Close round one instant in one floating flower," which may imply that what Shelley called "the boat of my desire" is now both exalted and reduced to the state of palm fronds floating in the sea. If the boat is still there, it is very frail indeed, and pragmatically voyaging has been transformed into floating in the sea:

> Bind us in time, O Seasons clear, and awe.
> O minstrel galleons of Carib fire,
> Bequeath us to no earthly shore until
> Is answered in the vortex of our grave
> The seal's wide spindrift gaze toward paradise.

The guiding genius of the poem here at the close is Melville rather than Whitman, and the end of Captain Ahab's voyage haunts the conclusion of Crane's and Oppfer's. "The seal's wide spindrift [which is wind-blown sea spray] gaze toward paradise" has a yearning for the mother in it, recalling the young seals who, in Chapter 126 of *Moby-Dick*, cry out because they have become separated from their dams. As Ahab goes on to his doom, "lovely leewardings" are associated with "something else than common land, more palmy than the palms." William Blake is also invoked in this ultimate stanza, since the "vortex of our graves" refers to his conceptual image of the "vortex," which closes the perceptual gap between subject and object.

Crane prays to "Seasons clear, and awe," probably in Emily Dickinson's sense of "awe," the name she gave to her love for Judge Otis Lord, and which she associated with Eternity. The prayer to be covenanted or bound in time, and the "minstrel galleons of Carib fire" may go back to the bells off San Salvador. The prayer is suicidal, prophesying Crane's leap into the Caribbean seven years later, since the bodies of the lovers are not to be washed ashore until the seal's longing gaze for the lost mother is answered "in the vortex of our grave," which in the Blakean sense of vortex intimates a resurrection, in which subject and object, spirit and body, unite again. And yet the tonalities of this concluding stanza are not suicidal, because desire is exalted over sleep and death. "Bind us" remains the dominant yearning, and the celebration of erotic completion continues to be ecstatic.

Voyages II revels in an absolute cognitive music, making enormous demands upon me, which it justifies by what I have termed "inevitability" in phrasing, measure, and rhythm. Like Coleridge's "Kubla Khan" and Keats's Great Odes, Crane's supreme lyric binds us both in and out of time.

8

HART CRANE is a difficult great poet, but very good, even great, poetry need not be overtly difficult. A. E. Housman is a clear instance, and there are many others. There are also difficult poets who at first look easy, but are not. Walt Whitman proclaims his accessibility, but his best poems are subtle, evasive, Hermetic, and call for a heightened awareness of the nuances of figuration.

Difficulty in great poetry can be of several, very different, kinds. Sustained allusiveness, as in the learned poetry of John Milton and Thomas Gray, demands a very high level of reader's literacy. Cognitive originality, the particular mark of Shakespeare and of Emily Dickinson, requires enormous intellectual agility as the reader's share. Personal mythmaking, as in William Blake and William Butler Yeats, at first can seem obscure, but the coherence of Blakean and Yeatsian myth yields to familiarity.

I think that poetry at its greatest—in Dante, Shakespeare, Donne, Milton, Blake—has one broad and essential difficulty: it is the true mode for expanding our consciousness. This it accomplishes by what I have learned to call *strangeness*. Owen Barfield was one of several critics to bring forth *strangeness* as a poetic criterion. For him, as for Walter Pater before him, the Romantic added strangeness to beauty: Wallace Stevens, a part of this tradition, has a Paterian figure cry out: "And there I found myself more truly and more strange." Barfield says: "It must be a strangeness of *meaning*," and then makes a fine distinction:

> It is not correlative with wonder; for wonder is our reaction to things which we are conscious of not quite understanding, or at any rate of understanding less than we had thought. The element of strangeness in beauty has the contrary effect. It arises from contact with a different kind of *consciousness* from our own, different, yet not so remote that we cannot partly share it, as indeed, in such a connection, the mere word "contact" implies. Strangeness, in fact, arouses wonder when we do not understand: aesthetic imagination when we do.

Consciousness is the central term here. As Barfield intimates, consciousness is to poetry what marble is to sculpture: the material that is being worked. Words are figurations of consciousness: metaphorical of consciousness, the poet's words invite us to share in a strangeness. "A felt change in consciousness" is one of Barfield's definitions of the poetic effect, and I relate this to what fascinates me most in the greatest Shake-spearean characters—Falstaff, Hamlet, Iago, Lear, Cleopatra—the extraordinary changes that come about when they *overhear* themselves. As James Wood remarks, actually they become conscious of listening to Shakespeare, because in overhearing themselves, what they are hearing is Shakespeare. They become themselves more truly and more strange, because they are "free artists of themselves" (Hegel's tribute to them).

The work of great poetry is to aid *us* to become free artists of ourselves. Even Shakespeare cannot make me into Falstaff or Hamlet, but all great poetry asks us to be possessed by it. To possess it by memory is a start, and to augment our consciousness is the goal. The art of reading poetry is an authentic training in the augmentation of consciousness, perhaps the most authentic of healthy modes.

GEOFFREY CHAUCER

1343–1400

I AM ARCHAIC ENOUGH to prefer the now unfashionable phrase "the English Renaissance" to the current "Early Modern Europe." The Elizabethan poets saw themselves as the children of Geoffrey Chaucer, and they were wise in thus recognizing their authentic father. Spenser presented himself as the rebirth of Chaucer, while Shakespeare, with preternatural shrewdness, took from Chaucer precisely what Ovid and Marlowe could not give him, personalities distinct from one another, and from the poet's self-consciousness. What Shakespeare avoided in Chaucer was the poet's overt self-awareness, in which Spenser was Chaucer's particular heir.

Chaucer had formidable precursors, but in Italian—Dante, Petrarch, Boccaccio—though mediated through the French. The best poetry in English, until this day, is by Chaucer and Shakespeare, with Milton a strong third, though an inevitable level below the creators of the Wife of Bath and of Falstaff. Milton's representations, even of Eve, Adam, and Samson, cannot be regarded as personalities. Satan is almost a personality, but he necessarily lacks mortality, without which we cannot recognize ourselves in one another. Adam and Eve, before the Fall, are demigods; after it, they are first quarrelsome children, and then poignantly homeless ones. For women and men, we turn still primarily to Chaucer and to Shakespeare.

During his final fifteen years, Chaucer worked at *The Canterbury Tales,* bequeathing it to us as a grand torso: "The lyfe so short, the craft so long to lerne," as he wrote elsewhere. Knowingly, Chaucer is the first great poet in English, emulating the classical writers, and the Italian and French, but creating the rhetorical and imaginative art of the English language, once and for all. Shakespeare refined and expanded Chaucer's art of poetry, but frequently in ways profoundly Chaucerian. When the Wife of Bath and the Pardoner overhear their own testimonies, they do not will to change, which will be the Shakespearean difference.

It is a mistake to translate Chaucer's Middle English into our vernacular, since then we lose his cognitive music. The essential glosses are in the right-hand margins in this book, and scarcely should slow readers down, since they average fewer than one per line. Pronunciation should be no obstacle, as no one can be quite certain of Chaucer's own pronunciation. By and large, his short vowels probably resembled ours, and his long ones (at line's end, or spelled doubled) generally would have sounded closer to French or Italian, as we now hear them. I myself was taught to read Chaucer by the late Helge Kökeritz, a Swedish medievalist at Yale, and to this day when I recite Chaucer or read him out loud, my friends and students tell me I sound like a character in an Ingmar Bergman movie.

This book begins with considerable selections from the "General Prologue" to *The Canterbury Tales*, and from the prologues of the Wife of Bath and the Pardoner. Chaucer the Pilgrim, who narrates the "General Prologue," is an extraordinary ironist whose ironies, as G. K. Chesterton observed, are so large that they are hard to see. Every one of his fellow pilgrims appears to evoke Chaucer's admiration, but it is clearly dangerous to take Chaucer the Pilgrim as being Geoffrey Chaucer the Poet. Indeed, his self-portrait as Pilgrim is his most ironical representation, and very likely is a delicious parody of Dante the Pilgrim in *The Inferno,* not a very Chaucerian poem.

Chaucer, like Shakespeare after him, had a natural genius for comedy, and again like Shakespeare, Chaucer was skeptical that language can be made to express the truth. And just as much as Shakespeare, Chaucer was wary of moral judgments. We may know how *we* feel about the Pardoner or Iago, but we will never know what Chaucer and Shakespeare felt in regard to them.

Shakespeare's own inwardness remains an enigma that defeats us; the best of writers chose to reveal himself only through the totality of a world. Chaucer anticipates Shakespeare, and yet chooses to present himself, *within his poem,* as a gullible appreciation of all vitality, however morally dubious it appears. Chronologically, Chaucer is a contemporary of Shakespeare's Falstaff, since Henry IV was the last English king that Chaucer served. Falstaff's demolition of "honor" might have charmed Chaucer, but would not have pleased his Knight in the "General Prologue." Though Chaucer the Pilgrim admires the Knight, his appreciation of the Wife of Bath is even more intense, and he reacts with enormous gusto to his riffraff: Miller, Manciple, Reeve, Summoner, and Pardoner.

I once thought that Chaucer, like his admirer Chesterton, celebrated a world he knew to be prematurely archaic. It seems now to me that Chaucer was too wise for such study of the nostalgias. Every era always seems to be waning: we are a less secure nation and world, since September 11, 2001. Yet I think it not Chaucerian to observe that we may have seen the best of our time. What marks Chaucer, and Shakespeare, is their immediacy and their vitalism: the Wife of Bath and Falstaff have had their world as in their time.

From The Canterbury Tales

from The General Prologue

Whan that Aprill with his shoures sote˃	*sweet showers*
The droghte˃ of Marche hath perced to the rote,˃	*dryness / root*
And bathed every veyne˃ in swich licour,˃	*vein / such moisture*
Of which vertu˃ engendred is the flour;	*By power of which*
5 Whan Zephirus˃ eek with his swete breeth	*the west wind*
Inspired˃ hath in every holt˃ and heeth˃	*Breathed into / wood / heath*
The tendre croppes,˃ and the yonge sonne	*sprouts*
Hath in the Ram his halfe cours y-ronne;	
And smale fowles˃ maken melodye,	*birds*
10 That slepen al the night with open yë˃—	*eye(s)*
So priketh hem Nature in hir corages—	
Than longen˃ folk to goon˃ on pilgrimages,	*Then long / go*
And palmeres for to seken straunge strondes,	
To ferne halwes,˃ couthe˃ in sondry londes;	*far-off shires / known*
15 And specially, from every shires ende	
Of Engelond to Caunterbury they wende,	
The holy blisful martir for to seke,˃	*seek*
That hem hath holpen,˃ whan that they were seke.˃	*helped / sick*
Bifel˃ that, in that seson on a day,	*It befell*
20 In Southwerk at the Tabard˃ as I lay˃	*(an inn) / lodged*
Redy to wenden˃ on my pilgrimage	*depart*
To Caunterbury with ful devout corage,˃	*heart*
At night was come into that hostelrye˃	*inn*
Wel nyne and twenty in a companye	
25 Of sondry folk, by aventure˃ y-falle˃	*chance / fallen*

In felawshipe, and pilgrims were they alle,
That toward Caunterbury woldenʳ ryde.   *wished to*
The chambresʳ and the stables weren wyde,ʳ   *bedrooms / spacious*
And wel we weren esedʳ atte beste.ʳ   *made comfortable / in the best (ways)*
30 And shortly, whan the sonne was toʳ reste,   *at*
So hadde I spoken with hem everichonʳ   *each and every one*
That I was of hir felawshipe anon,
And made forwardʳ erly for to ryse,   *agreement*
To take oure wey, ther as I yow devyse.ʳ   *(will) tell*
35 But natheles,ʳ whyl I have tyme and space,   *nevertheless*
Er that I ferther in this tale pace,ʳ   *pass on*
Me thinketh it acordaunt to resoun
To telle yow al the condicioun
Of ech of hem, so as it semed me,ʳ   *seemed to me*
40 And whicheʳ they weren, and of what degree,ʳ   *what / status*
And eek in what arrayʳ that they were inne;   *clothing*
And at a knight than wolʳ I first biginne.   *will*
A KNIGHT ther was, and that a worthy man,
That froʳ the tyme that he first bigan   *from*
45 To ryden out,ʳ he loved chivalrye,   *ride (on expeditions)*
Trouthe and honour, fredom and curteisye.
Ful worthy was he in his lordes werre,ʳ   *war(s)*
And thertoʳ hadde he riden, no man ferre,ʳ   *in such / further*
As wel in Cristendom as in hethenesse,ʳ   *in pagan lands*
50 And evere honoured for his worthinesse.
At Alisaundreʳ he was whan it was wonne;   *Alexandria*
Ful ofte tyme he hadde the bord bigonneʳ   *headed the table*
Aboven alle naciouns in Pruce.ʳ   *Prussia*
In Lettow hadde he reysed and in Ruce,
55 No Cristen man so ofte of his degree.ʳ   *rank*
In Gernadeʳ at the segeʳ eek hadde he beʳ   *Granada / siege / been*
Of Algezir,ʳ and riden in Belmarye.ʳ   *Algeciras / Benmarin (in Morocco)*
At Lyeysʳ was he and at Satalye,ʳ   *Ayas / Adalia (both in Asia Minor)*
Whan they were wonne; and in the Grete Seeʳ   *Mediterranean*
60 At many a noble armeeʳ hadde he be.   *armed expedition*
At mortal batailles hadde he been fiftene,
And foughten for oure feith at Tramisseneʳ   *Tlemcen (in Algeria)*
In listesʳ thryes,ʳ and ay slayn his foo.ʳ   *tournaments / thrice / foe*
This ilkeʳ worthy knight hadde been also   *same*
65 Somtyme with the lord of Palatye,ʳ   *Palatia*
Ageynʳ another hethen in Turkye;   *Against*
And everemore he hadde a sovereyn prys.ʳ   *reputation*
And though that he were worthy, he was wys,ʳ   *prudent*

And of his port> as meke as is a mayde.　*deportment*
70　He nevere yet no vileinye> ne sayde　*rudeness*
In al his lyf, unto no maner wight.>　*any sort of person*
He was a verray,> parfit,> gentil> knight.　*true / perfect / noble*
But for to tellen yow of his array,
His hors> were gode, but he was nat gay.>　*horses / brightly dressed*
75　Of fustian> he wered> a gipoun>　*rough cloth / wore / tunic*
Al bismotered with> his habergeoun,>　*stained by / coat of mail*
For he was late y-come> from his viage,>　*recently come / expedition*
And wente for to doon> his pilgrimage.　*make*
　　With him ther was his sone, a young SQUYER,
80　A lovyere, and a lusty bacheler,
With lokkes crulle, as they were leyd in presse.
Of twenty yeer of age he was, I gesse.
Of> his stature he was of evene lengthe,>　*In / average height*
And wonderly delivere,> and of greet strengthe.　*agile*
85　And he hadde been somtyme in chivachye>　*on expeditions*
In Flaundres,> in Artoys,> and Picardye,>　*Flanders / Artois / Picardy*
And born him wel, as of so litel space,
In hope to stonden> in his lady> grace.　*stand / lady's*
Embrouded> was he, as it were a mede>　*Embroidered / meadow*
90　Al ful of fresshe floures, whyte and rede.
Singinge he was, or floytinge,> al the day;　*fluting (whistling?)*
He was as fresh as is the month of May.
Short was his gowne, with sleves longe and wyde.
Wel coude> he sitte on hors, and faire ryde.　*knew how to*
95　He coude songes make and wel endyte,>　*compose verse*
Juste> and eek daunce, and wel purtreye> and wryte.　*Joust / draw*
So hote> he lovede that by nightertale>　*hotly / at night*
He sleep> namore> than dooth a nightingale.　*slept / no more*
Curteys he was, lowly, and servisable,
100　And carf> biforn his fader at the table.　*carved (meat)*

　·　·　·

　　A good WYF was ther of bisyde BATHE,>　*from near Bath*
445　But she was somdel> deef, and that was scathe.>　*somewhat / a pity*
Of clooth-making she hadde swiche an haunt,>　*such practiced skill*
She passed> hem of Ypres and of Gaunt.　*surpassed*
In al the parisshe wyf ne was ther noon
450　That to the offringe> bifore hir sholde goon;>　*offering in church / go*
And if ther dide, certeyn so wrooth> was she,　*angry*
That she was out of alle charitee.
Hir coverchiefs> ful fyne were of ground;>　*kerchiefs / texture*

I dorste˃ swere they weyeden˃ ten pound   *would dare / weighed*

455 That on a Sonday weren upon hir heed.

Hir hosen˃ weren of fyn scarlet reed,   *hose*

Ful streite y-teyd,˃ and shoos ful moiste˃ and newe.   *tightly tied / soft*

Bold was hir face, and fair, and reed of hewe.˃   *hue*

She was a worthy womman al hir lyve:

460 Housbondes at chirche dore she hadde fyve,

Withouten˃ other companye in youthe—   *Not to mention*

But therof nedeth nat to speke as nouthe˃—   *at present*

And thryes˃ hadde she been at Jerusalem.   *thrice*

She hadde passed many a straunge streem:

465 At Rome she hadde been, and at Boloigne,˃   *Boulogne (France)*

In Galice at Seint Jame, and at Coloigne;

She coude˃ muchel of wandringe by the weye.˃   *knew / along the road(s)*

Gat-tothed˃ was she, soothly for to seye.   *Gap-toothed*

Upon an amblere˃ esily˃ she sat,   *saddle-horse / comfortably*

470 Y-wimpled˃ wel, and on hir heed an hat   *Covered with a wimple*

As brood as is a bokeler or a targe;

A foot-mantel˃ aboute hir hipes large,   *outer skirt*

And on hir feet a paire of spores˃ sharpe.   *spurs*

In felawschipe wel coude she laughe and carpe.˃   *talk*

475 Of remedyes of love she knew per chaunce,˃   *as it happened*

For she coude˃ of that art the olde daunce.˃   *knew / (steps of the) dance*

    A good man was ther of religioun,

And was a povre PERSOUN˃ of a toun,   *poor parson*

But riche he was of holy thoght and werk.

480 He was also a lerned man, a clerk,˃   *scholar*

That Cristes gospel trewely wolde preche;

His parisshens˃ devoutly wolde he teche.   *parishioners*

Benigne˃ he was, and wonder˃ diligent,   *Kindly / very*

And in adversitee ful pacient,

485 And swich he was y-preved ofte sythes.

Ful looth˃ were him to cursen˃ for his tithes,   *loath / excommunicate*

But rather wolde he yeven,˃ out of doute,˃   *give / there is no doubt*

Unto his povre parisshens aboute

Of˃ his offring, and eek of his substaunce.˃   *From / income*

490 He coude in litel thing han suffisaunce.

Wyd was his parisshe, and houses fer asonder,

But he ne lafte˃ nat, for reyn ne˃ thonder,   *ceased / nor*

In siknes nor in meschief,˃ to visyte   *misfortune*

˙The ferreste in his parisshe, muche and lyte,

495 Upon his feet, and in his hand a staf.

This noble ensample˃ to his sheep he yaf,˃   *example / gave*

That first he wroghte,> and afterward he taughte.   *did (what was right)*
Out of the gospel he tho> wordes caughte,>   *those / took*
And this figure> he added eek therto,   *metaphor, image*
500 That if gold ruste, what shal iren> do?   *iron*
For if a preest be foul,> on whom we truste,   *corrupted*
No wonder is a lewed man to ruste;
And shame it is, if a preest take keep,>   *heed (it)*
A shiten shepherde and a clene sheep.
505 Wel oghte a preest ensample for to yive,>   *give*
By his clennesse, how that his sheep sholde live.
He sette nat his benefice to hyre,
And leet> his sheep encombred in the myre,   *left*
And ran to London unto Seynte Poules>   *St. Paul's cathedral*
510 To seken him a chaunterie for soules,
Or with a bretherhed to been withholde,

. . .

With him ther rood a gentil PARDONER
670 Of Rouncival, his freend and his compeer,>   *companion*
That streight was comen fro the court of Rome.
Ful loude he song,> "Com hider,> love, to me."   *sang / hither*
This somnour bar to> him a stif burdoun,>   *accompanied / sturdy bass*
Was nevere trompe> of half so greet a soun.>   *trumpet / sound*
675 This pardoner hadde heer> as yelow as wex,>   *hair / wax*
But smothe it heng,> as dooth a strike of flex;>   *hung / bunch of flax*
By ounces> henge his lokkes that he hadde,   *In thin strands*
And therwith> he his shuldres overspradde;>   *with it / covered*
But thinne it lay, by colpons> oon and oon;   *in small bunches*
680 But hood, for jolitee,> wered> he noon,   *sportiveness / wore*
For it was trussed> up in his walet.>   *packed / pouch*
Him thoughte he rood al of the newe jet;
Dischevele, save his cappe, he rood al bare.
Swiche glaringe eyen> hadde he as an hare.   *staring eyes*
685 A vernicle hadde he sowed on his cappe.
His walet lay biforn> him in his lappe,   *in front of*
Bretful of pardoun comen from Rome al hoot.
A voys he hadde as smal as hath a goot.>   *goat*
No berd hadde he, ne nevere sholde have,
690 As smothe it was as it were late shave:>   *recently shaved*
I trowe> he were a gelding or a mare.   *believe*
But of his craft, fro Berwik into Ware,
Ne was ther swich another pardoner.
For in his male> he hadde a pilwe-beer,>   *bag / pillowcase*

695   Which that he seyde was Oure Lady veyl.˃   *Our Lady's veil*
     He seyde he hadde a gobet˃ of the seyl˃   *piece / sail*
     That seynt Peter hadde, whan that he wente˃   *walked*
     Upon the see, til Jesu Crist him hente.˃   *took hold of*
     He hadde a croys˃ of latoun,˃ ful of stones,˃   *cross / metal / gems*
700   And in a glas˃ he hadde pigges bones.   *glass container*
     But with thise relikes,˃ whan that he fond   *relics*
     A povre person dwellinge upon lond,
     Upon a˃ day he gat him more moneye   *In one*
     Than that the person gat in monthes tweye.˃   *two*
705   And thus, with feyned flaterye and japes,˃   *tricks*
     He made the person and the peple his apes.˃   *fools*
     But trewely to tellen, atte laste,˃   *after all*
     He was in chirche a noble ecclesiaste.˃   *preacher*
     Wel coude he rede a lessoun or a storie,˃   *religious tale*
710   But alderbest˃ he song˃ an offertorie;   *best of all / sang*
     For wel he wiste,˃ whan that song was songe,   *knew*
     He moste preche, and wel affyle˃ his tonge   *make smooth*
     To winne silver, as he ful wel coude—
     Therefore he song the murierly˃ and loude.   *more merrily*

from The Wife of Bath's Prologue

     "My fourthe housebonde was a revelour˃—   *reveler, rioter*
     This is to seyn, he hadde a paramour˃—   *mistress*
455   And I was yong and ful of ragerye,˃   *wantonness, passion*
     Stiborn˃ and strong, and joly as a pye.˃   *Stubborn / magpie*
     Wel coude I daunce to an harpe smale,
     And singe, y-wis,˃ as any nightingale,   *truly*
     Whan I had dronke a draughte of swete wyn.
460   Metellius, the foule cherl, the swyn,˃   *swine*
     That with a staf birafte˃ his wyf hir lyf   *bereft*
     For she drank wyn, thogh˃ I hadde been his wyf,   *if*
     He sholde nat han daunted˃ me fro drinke!   *frightened*
     And after wyn on Venus moste˃ I thinke,   *must*
465   For al so siker˃ as cold engendreth˃ hayl,˃ *surely / engenders / hail*
     A likerous mouth moste han a likerous tayl.
     In wommen vinolent˃ is no defence˃—   *full of wine / resistance*
     This knowen lechours by experience.
       But, Lord Crist! whan that it remembreth me˃   *I think*
470   Upon my yowthe, and on my jolitee,˃   *gaiety*
     It tikleth˃ me aboute myn herte rote.˃   *tickles / heart's root*

Unto this day it dooth myn herte bote^   *good*
That I have had my world as in my tyme.
But age, allas! that al wol envenyme,^   *poison*
475 Hath me biraft^ my beautee and my pith.^   *bereft of / vigor*
Lat go,^ farewel! the devel go therwith!   *Let it go*
The flour is goon, ther is namore to telle:
The bren,^ as I best can, now moste I selle;   *bran, husks*
But yet to be right mery wol I fonde.^   *try*
480 Now wol I tellen of my fourthe housbonde.
        I seye, I hadde in herte greet despyt^   *malice*
That he of any other^ had delyt.   *other woman*
But he was quit,^ by God and by Seint Joce!   *repaid*
I made him of the same wode^ a croce^—   *wood / cross*
485 Nat of my body in no foul^ manere,   *unclean*
But certeinly, I made folk swich chere^   *such good cheer*
That in his owene grece^ I made him frye   *grease*
For angre and for verray^ jalousye.   *pure*
By God, in erthe^ I was his purgatorie,   *on earth*
490 For which I hope his soule be in glorie.
For God it woot,^ he sat ful ofte and song^   *knows / sang*
Whan that his shoo^ ful bitterly him wrong.^   *shoe / hurt*
Ther was no wight,^ save^ God and he, that wiste^   *person / except / knew*
In many wyse^ how sore^ I him twiste.^   *ways / sorely / tormented*
495 He deyde whan I cam fro^ Jerusalem,   *from (a pilgrimage to)*
And lyth y-grave under the rode-beem,
Al^ is his tombe noght so curious^   *Although / elaborate*
As was the sepulcre of him Darius,
Which that Appelles wroghte subtilly;^   *made skillfully*
500 It nis but wast to burie him preciously.
Lat him^ farewel, God yeve his soule reste!   *May he*
He is now in the grave and in his cheste.^   *coffin*
        Now of my fifthe housbond wol I telle—
God lete his soule nevere come in helle!
505 And yet was he to me the moste shrewe.^   *worst rascal*
That fele^ I on my ribbes al by rewe,^   *feel / in a row*
And evere shal unto myn ending-day.
But in oure bed he was so fresh and gay,
And therwithal so wel coude he me glose^   *cajole, flatter*
510 Whan that he wolde han my *bele chose*,^   *pretty thing*
That thogh he hadde me bet^ on every boon,^   *beaten / bone*
He coude winne agayn my love anoon.^   *at once*
I trowe^ I loved him beste for that he   *believe*
Was of his love daungerous^ to me.   *standoffish, grudging*

515 We wommen han, if that I shal nat lye,
In this matere a queynte fantasye:>   *an odd fancy*
Wayte what> thing we may nat lightly have,   *Whatever*
Therafter wol we crye al day and crave.
Forbede us thing,> and that desyren we;   *something*
520 Prees on> us faste,> and thanne wol we flee.   *Crowd, pursue / hard*
With daunger> oute> we al oure chaffare:>   *haughtiness / set out / wares*
Greet prees> at market maketh dere> ware,   *press, crowd / expensive*
And to> greet cheep> is holde at litel prys.>   *too / a bargain / worth*
This knoweth every womman that is wys.
525   My fifthe housbonde, God his soule blesse!
Which that I took for love and no richesse,
He som tyme> was a clerk> of Oxenford,>   *once / scholar / Oxford*
And had left scole, and wente at hoom to bord>   *to board at home*
With my gossib,> dwellinge in oure toun—   *gossip, intimate friend*
530 God have hir soule! hir name was Alisoun.
She knew myn herte and eek> my privetee>   *also / secrets*
Bet> than oure parisshe preest, so moot I thee!>   *Better / as I may thrive*
To hire biwreyed> I my conseil> al,   *disclosed / thoughts*
For had myn housebonde pissed on a wal,
535 Or doon a thing that sholde han cost his lyf,
To hire and to another worthy wyf,
And to my nece,> which that I loved weel,   *niece*
I wolde han told his conseil> every deel.>   *secrets / (in) every detail*
And so I dide ful often, God it woot,>   *knows*
540 That made his face ful often reed and hoot
For verray> shame, and blamed himself for> he   *pure / because*
Had told to me so greet a privetee.>   *secret*
     And so bifel> that ones> in a Lente>—   *it happened / once / at Lent*
So often tymes I to my gossib wente,
545 For evere yet I lovede to be gay,
And for to walke in March, Averille,> and May,   *April*
Fro hous to hous, to here> sondry talis>—   *hear / various tales*
That Jankin clerk> and my gossib dame Alis   *Jankin (the) clerk*
And I myself into the feldes> wente.   *fields*
550 Myn housbond was at London al that Lente:
I hadde the bettre leyser> for to pleye,   *leisure, opportunity*
And for to see, and eek> for to be seye>   *also / seen*
Of lusty folk. What wiste I wher my grace
Was shapen for to be, or in what place?
555 Therefore I made my visitaciouns,>   *visits*
To vigilies and to processiouns,
To preching eek and to thise pilgrimages,

To pleyes> of miracles, and mariages,   *(stage-)plays*

And wered upon> my gaye scarlet gytes.>   *wore / gowns*

560 Thise wormes, ne thise motthes,> ne thise mytes,>   *moths / mites*

Upon my peril, frete hem never a deel;

And wostow> why? for> they were used weel.   *knowest thou / because*

    Now wol I tellen forth what happed> me.   *befell*

I seye that in the feeldes walked we,

565 Til trewely we hadde swich daliance,

This clerk and I, that of my purveyance>   *by my foresight*

I spak to him and seyde him how that he,

If I were widwe,> sholde wedde me.   *a widow*

For certeinly, I sey for no bobance,>   *not as a boast*

570 Yet was I nevere withouten purveyance>   *(future) provision*

Of> mariage, n'of> othere thinges eek.   *Concerning / nor concerning*

I holde a mouses herte nat worth a leek>   *leek, onion*

That hath but oon hole for to sterte> to,   *run*

And if that faille,> thanne is al y-do.>   *fails / done for*

575   I bar him on honde> he hadde enchanted me—   *made him believe*

My dame> taughte me that soutiltee>—   *mother / subtlety, trick*

And eek I seyde I mette> of him al night: *dreamed*

He wolde han slayn> me as I lay up-right,>   *wanted to slay / face-up*

And al my bed was ful of verray> blood;   *real*

580 But yet I hope that he shal do me good,

For blood bitokeneth gold, as me was taught.

And al was fals—I dremed of it right naught,

But as> I folwed ay> my dames lore>   *But / ever / teaching*

As wel of> this as of othere thinges more.   *concerning*

585   But now sire, lat me see, what I shal seyn?

Aha! by God, I have my tale ageyn.

    Whan that my fourthe housbond was on bere,>   *(his) bier*

I weep algate, and made sory chere

As wyves moten,> for it is usage,>   *must / the custom*

590 And with my coverchief> covered my visage;>   *kerchief / face*

But for that> I was purveyed of> a make,>   *because / provided with / mate*

I wepte but smal,> and that I undertake.>   *little / declare*

    To chirche was myn housbond born> a-morwe>   *borne / in the morning*

With> neighebores, that for him maden sorwe;   *By*

595 And Jankin oure clerk was oon of tho.>   *them*

As> help me God! whan that I saugh> him go>   *So / saw / walk*

After the bere, me thoughte he hadde a paire

Of legges and of feet so clene> and faire,   *neat*

That al myn herte I yaf> unto his hold.>   *gave / possession*

600 He was, I trowe,> twenty winter old,   *believe*

And I was fourty, if I shal seye sooth;>   *tell the truth*
But yet I hadde alwey a coltes tooth.
Gat-tothed I was, and that bicam me weel;
I hadde the prente of Seynte Venus seel.
605 As help me God, I was a lusty> oon,   *vigorous*
And faire, and riche, and yong, and wel bigoon;>   *well-off*
And trewely, as myne housbondes tolde me,
I had the beste *quoniam* mighte be.
For certes, I am al Venerien
610 In felinge, and myn herte is Marcien:
Venus me yaf> my lust, my likerousnesse,>   *gave / lecherousness*
And Mars yaf me my sturdy hardinesse;>   *boldness*
Myn ascendent was Taur, and Mars therinne.
Allas! allas! that evere love was sinne!
615 I folwed ay> myn inclinacioun   *ever*
By vertu of my constellacioun;
That made me I coude noght withdrawe>   *withhold*
My chambre of Venus from a good felawe.>   *companion*
Yet have I Martes> mark upon my face,   *Mars's*
620 And also in another privee> place.   *secret*
For, God so wis be my savacioun,>   *salvation*
I ne loved nevere by no discrecioun,>   *with any wisdom*
But evere folwede myn appetyt:
Al> were he short or long,> or blak or whyt,   *Whether / tall*
625 I took no kepe, so that he lyked me,
How pore he was, ne eek> of what degree.>   *nor / social rank*
    What sholde I seye but, at the monthes ende,
This joly clerk Jankin, that was so hende,>   *pleasant*
Hath wedded me with greet solempnitee,>   *ceremony*
630 And to him yaf> I al the lond> and fee>   *gave / land / property*
That evere was me yeven> therbifore.   *given (by earlier husbands)*
But afterward repented me> ful sore;>   *I regretted it / deeply*
He nolde suffre nothing of my list.
By God, he smoot> me ones> on the list>   *hit / once / ear*
635 For that> I rente> out of his book a leef,>   *Because / tore / leaf, page*
That of the strook myn ere wex al deef.
Stiborn> I was as is a leonesse,>   *Stubborn / lionness*
And of my tonge a verray jangleresse,>   *real ranter*
And walke I wolde, as I had doon biforn,
640 From hous to hous, although he had it sworn.
For which he often tymes wolde preche,
And me of> olde Romayn gestes> teche,   *from / Roman stories*
How he Simplicius Gallus lefte his wyf,

And hire forsook for terme⟩ of al his lyf,   *the duration*
645 Noght but for open-heveded he hir say
Lokinge out at his dore upon a day.
     Another Romayn tolde he me by name,
That, for⟩ his wyf was at a someres game⟩   *because / summer's revel*
Withoute his witing,⟩ he forsook hire eke.⟩   *knowledge / also*
650 And thanne wolde he upon⟩ his Bible seke   *in*
That ilke⟩ proverbe of Ecclesiaste⟩   *same / Ecclesiasticus*
Wher he comandeth and forbedeth faste⟩   *firmly*
Man shal nat suffre⟩ his wyf go roule⟩ aboute;   *allow / to go roaming*
Thanne wolde he seye right thus, withouten doute:
655 'Whoso that⟩ buildeth his hous al of salwes,⟩   *Whoever / willow twigs*
And priketh⟩ his blinde hors over the falwes,⟩   *spurs / fallow (ploughed) land*
And suffreth⟩ his wyf to go seken halwes,⟩   *allows / shrines*
Is worthy to been hanged on the galwes!'⟩   *gallows*
But al for noght; I sette noght an hawe⟩   *haw (hawthorn berry)*
660 Of his proverbes n'of his olde sawe,⟩   *saw, proverb*
Ne I wolde nat of⟩ him corrected be.   *by*
I hate him that⟩ my vices telleth me,   *the one who*
And so do mo,⟩ God woot,⟩ of us than I.   *more / knows*
This made him with me wood⟩ al outrely:⟩   *mad / completely*
665 I nolde noght forbere him in no cas.
     Now wol I seye yow sooth,⟩ by Seint Thomas,   *tell you the truth*
Why that I rente⟩ out of his book a leef,⟩   *tore / leaf*
For which he smoot⟩ me so that I was deef.   *struck*
     He hadde a book that gladly, night and day,
670 For his desport⟩ he wolde rede alway.   *amusement*
He cleped it Valerie and Theofraste,
At which book he lough⟩ alwey ful faste.⟩   *laughed / strongly*
And eek ther was somtyme⟩ a clerk⟩ at Rome,   *once / scholar*
A cardinal, that highte⟩ Seint Jerome,   *was called*
675 That made a book agayn Jovinian;
In which book eek ther was Tertulan,
Crisippus, Trotula, and Helowys,
That was abbesse nat fer fro Parys;⟩   *Paris*
And eek the Parables⟩ of Salomon,   *Proverbs*
680 Ovydes Art,⟩ and bokes many on,⟩   *Ovid's Art (of Love) / a one*
And alle thise were bounden in o⟩ volume.   *one*
And every night and day was his custume,
Whan he hadde leyser⟩ and vacacioun⟩   *leisure / free time*
From other worldly occupacioun,
685 To reden on this book of wikked⟩ wyves.   *wicked*
He knew of hem mo⟩ legendes and lyves   *more*

Than been˃ of gode wyves in the Bible.   *there are*
For trusteth wel, it is an impossible˃   *impossibility*
That any clerk wol speke good of wyves,
690 But if˃ it be of holy seintes lyves,   *Unless*
Ne of noon other womman never the mo.˃   *in any way*
Who peyntede the leoun, tel me, who?
By God, if wommen hadde writen stories,
As clerkes han withinne hir oratories,˃   *chapels, studies*
695 They wolde han writen of men more wikkednesse
Than all the mark˃ of Adam may redresse.   *sex*
The children of Mercurie and of Venus
Been in hir wirking˃ ful contrarious:˃   *actions / contrary*
Mercurie loveth wisdom and science,˃   *knowledge*
700 And Venus loveth ryot˃ and dispence;˃   *revelry / spending*
And, for˃ hire diverse disposicioun,   *because of*
Ech˃ falleth in otheres exaltacioun,˃   *Each / moment of highest ascent*
And thus, God woot, Mercurie is desolat˃   *without influence*
In Pisces wher Venus is exaltat,˃   *in her greatest influence*
705 And Venus falleth ther˃ Mercurie is reysed;˃   *there where / has risen*
Therfore no womman of˃ no clerk is preysed.   *by*
The clerk, whan he is old, and may noght do
Of Venus werkes worth˃ his olde sho˃—   *to the value of / shoe*
Thanne sit he doun and writ in his dotage
710 That wommen can nat kepe hir mariage!
      But now to purpos why I tolde thee
That I was beten˃ for a book, pardee.˃   *beaten / by God*
Upon a night Jankin, that was our syre,˃   *lord, husband*
Redde on his book as he sat by the fyre
715 Of Eva˃ first, that for hir wikkednesse   *Eve*
Was al mankinde broght to wrecchednesse,
For which that Jesu Crist himself was slayn,
That boghte us with his herteblood agayn.
Lo, here expres˃ of womman may ye finde   *specifically*
720 That womman was the los˃ of all mankinde.   *destruction*
      Tho˃ redde he me how Sampson loste his heres:˃   *Then / hair(s)*
Slepinge, his lemman˃ kitte˃ hem˃ with hir sheres,   *lover / cut / it (them)*
Thurgh whiche tresoun loste he bothe his yën.˃   *eyes*
      Tho˃ redde he me, if that I shal nat lyen,   *Then*
725 Of Hercules and of his Dianyre,˃   *Deianira*
That caused him to sette himself afyre.˃   *on fire*
      Nothing forgat he the sorwe and the wo
That Socrates had with hise wyves two—
How Xantippa caste pisse upon his heed:

730 This sely⸃ man sat stille, as⸃ he were deed;   *poor / as if*
He wyped his heed; namore dorste⸃ he seyn   *dared*
But 'Er⸃ that thonder stinte,⸃ comth a reyn.'⸃   *Before / ceases / rain, shower*
　　Of Phasipha that was the quene of Crete—
For shrewednesse⸃ him thoughte the tale swete—   *Out of cursedness*
735 Fy! spek namore, it is a grisly thing,
Of hire horrible lust and hir lyking.⸃   *desire*
　　Of Clitermistra, for hire lecherye,
That falsly made hire housbond for to dye,
He redde it with ful good devocioun.
740 　　He tolde me eek for what occasioun
Amphiorax at Thebes loste his lyf.
Myn housbond hadde a legende of his wyf,
Eriphilem, that⸃ for an ouche⸃ of gold   *Eryphile, who / brooch*
Hath prively⸃ unto the Grekes told   *secretly*
745 Wher that hir housbonde hidde him in a place,
For which he hadde at Thebes sory grace.⸃   *ill fortune*
　　Of Lyvia tolde he me, and of Lucye.
They bothe made hir housbondes for to dye,
That oon for love, that other was for hate.
750 Lyvia hir housbond, on an even⸃ late,   *evening*
Empoysoned⸃ hath, for that she was his fo.⸃   *Poisoned / foe*
Lucya, likerous,⸃ loved hire housbond so,   *lecherous*
That, for⸃ he sholde alwey upon hire thinke,   *so that*
She yaf⸃ him swich a manere⸃ love-drinke,   *gave / such a kind of*
755 That he was deed er⸃ it were by the morwe;⸃   *before / morning*
And thus algates⸃ housbondes han sorwe.   *in every way*
　　Thanne tolde he me how oon Latumius
Compleyned unto his felawe⸃ Arrius,   *companion*
That in his gardin growed swich a⸃ tree   *a certain*
760 On which he seyde how that his wyves three
Hanged hemself⸃ for herte despitous.⸃   *themselves / spiteful*
'O leve⸃ brother,' quod this Arrius,   *dear*
'Yif⸃ me a plante⸃ of thilke⸃ blissed tree,   *Give / slip / that same*
And in my gardin planted shal it be!'
765 　　Of latter date, of wyves hath he red
That somme han slayn hir housbondes in hir bed,
And lete hir lechour⸃ dighte⸃ hire al the night   *lecher, lover / lie with*
Whyl that the corps lay in⸃ the floor up-right.⸃   *on / face-up*
And somme han drive⸃ nayles⸃ in hir brayn⸃   *driven / nails / brain*
770 Whyl that they slepte, and thus they han hem slayn.
Somme han hem yeve⸃ poysoun in hire drinke.   *given*
He spak more harm than herte may bithinke,⸃   *imagine*

And therwithal> he knew of mo> proverbes | *in addition / more*
Than in this world ther growen gras or herbes.> | *plants*
775 'Bet is,'> quod he, 'thyn habitacioun | *Better it is (that)*
Be with a leoun or a foul dragoun,
Than with a womman usinge for> to chyde. | *accustomed*
Bet is,' quod he, 'hye in> the roof abyde> | *high on / to stay*
Than with an angry wyf doun in the hous;
780 They been so wikked and contrarious> | *contradictory*
They haten that> hir housbondes loveth ay.'> | *what / ever*
He seyde, 'A womman cast> hir shame away, | *casts*
Whan she cast of> hir smok;> and forthermo,> | *off / smock, underdress / furthermore*
'A fair> womman, but> she be chaast also, | *beautiful / unless*
785 Is lyk a gold ring in a sowes> nose.' | *sow's*
Who wolde wene,> or who wolde suppose> | *think / imagine*
The wo that in myn herte was, and pyne?> | *suffering*
        And whan I saugh> he wolde nevere fyne> | *saw / finish*
To reden on this cursed book al night,
790 Al sodeynly> three leves> have I plight> | *suddenly / pages / plucked*
Out of his book, right> as he radde,> and eke> | *just / read / also*
I with my fist so took> him on the cheke | *hit*
That in oure fyr he fil> bakward adoun. | *fell*
And he upstirte> as dooth a wood leoun,> | *jumped up / mad lion*
795 And with his fist he smoot> me on the heed | *struck*
That in> the floor I lay as> I were deed. | *(So) that on / as if*
And when he saugh> how stille that I lay, | *saw*
He was agast,> and wolde han fled his way, | *frightened*
Til atte laste out of my swogh> I breyde:> | *swoon, faint / started up*
800 'O! hastow> slayn me, false theef?'> I seyde, | *hast thou / criminal*
'And for my land thus hastow mordred> me? | *murdered*
Er> I be deed, yet wol I kisse thee.' | *Before*
        And neer he cam, and kneled faire> adoun, | *courteously*
And seyde, 'Dere suster Alisoun,
805 As> help me God, I shall thee nevere smyte;> | *So / strike*
That I have doon, it is thyself to wyte.
Foryeve> it me, and that I thee biseke'>— | *Forgive / beseech*
And yet eftsones> I hitte him on the cheke | *again*
And seyde, 'Theef! thus muchel> am I wreke.> | *much / avenged*
810 Now wol I dye: I may no lenger speke.'
But atte laste, with muchel care and wo,
We fille acorded> by us selven two. | *came to an agreement*
He yaf me al> the brydel> in myn hond, | *completely / bridle*
To han the governance> of hous and lond, | *direction*
815 And of his tonge and of his hond also;

And made him brenne his book anon right tho.
And whan that I hadde geten unto me,>   *gotten for myself*
By maistrie,> al the soveraynetee,>   *mastery / supremacy, sovereignty*
And that he seyde, 'Myn owene trewe wyf,
820   Do as thee lust> the terme> of al thy lyf;   *please / (to the) end*
Keep> thyn honour, and keep eek myn estaat>—   *Preserve / public position*
After that day we hadden never debaat.>   *contention*
God help me so, I was to him as kinde
As any wyf from Denmark unto Inde,>   *India*
825   And also> trewe, and so was he to me.   *equally as*
I prey to God that sit> in magestee,>   *who sits / majesty*
So blesse his soule for his> mercy dere!   *by his*
Now wol I seye my tale, if ye wol here."

from The Pardoner's Prologue

The Introduction

                      .   .   .

"By corpus bones! but> I have triacle,>   *unless / medicine*
Or elles a draught of moyste> and corny> ale,   *fresh / malty*
Or but> I here anon> a mery tale,   *unless / at once*
Myn herte is lost for pitee of this mayde.
5   Thou bel amy,> thou Pardoner," he seyde,   *sweet friend*
"Tel us som mirthe or japes> right anon."   *jokes*
     "It shall be doon," quod> he, "by Seint Ronyon!   *said*
But first," quod he, "heer at this ale-stake>   *tavern sign*
I wol both drinke and eten> of a cake."   *eat*
10   But right anon thise gentils gonne to crye,
"Nay! lat him telle us of no ribaudye;>   *ribaldry*
Tel us som moral thing, that we may lere>   *learn*
Som wit,> and thanne wol we gladly here.">   *Something instructive / listen*
"I graunte,> y-wis,"> quod he, "but I mot> thinke   *agree / certainly / must*
15   Upon som honest> thing whyl that I drinke."   *decent, decorous*

The Prologue

"Lordinges," quod he, "in chirches whan I preche,
I peyne me> to han an hauteyn> speche,   *take pains / elevated*
And ringe it out as round as gooth> a belle,   *sounds*
For I can al by rote> that I telle.   *know all by memory*
20   My theme> is alwey oon,> and evere was—   *text / always the same*
Radix malorum est Cupiditas.

First I pronounce⟩ whennes⟩ that I come, — *proclaim / whence, from where*
And thanne my bulles shewe I, alle and somme.⟩ — *one and all*
Oure lige lordes seel on my patente,⟩ — *license*
That shewe I first, my body⟩ to warente,⟩ — *person / authorize*
That no man be so bold, ne preest ne clerk,⟩ — *neither priest nor scholar*
Me to destourbe of Cristes holy werk;
And after that thanne telle I forth my tales.
Bulles of popes and of cardinales,
Of patriarkes,⟩ and bishoppes I shewe, — *heads of churches*
And in Latyn I speke a wordes fewe,
To saffron with my predicacioun,
And for to stire⟩ hem to devocioun. — *stir*
Thanne shewe I forth my longe cristal stones,⟩ — *glass cases*
Y-crammed ful of cloutes⟩ and of bones— — *rags*
Reliks been they, as wenen they echoon.
Thanne have I in latoun a sholder-boon
Which that was of an holy Jewes shepe.
'Goode men,' seye I, 'tak of my wordes kepe:⟩ — *heed*
If that this boon be wasshe⟩ in any welle, — *washed, dunked*
If cow, or calf, or sheep, or oxe swelle,⟩ — *swell (up)*
That any worm hath ete, or worm y-stonge,
Tak water of that welle, and wash his tonge,
And it is hool⟩ anon;⟩ and forthermore, — *healed / at once*
Of pokkes⟩ and of scabbe and every sore — *pox*
Shal every sheep be hool,⟩ that of this welle — *healed*
Drinketh a draughte. Tak kepe⟩ eek⟩ what I telle: — *heed / also*
If that the good-man that the bestes⟩ oweth⟩ — *animals / owns*
Wol every wike,⟩ er⟩ that the cok him croweth, — *week / before*
Fastinge,⟩ drinken of this welle a draughte— — *(While) fasting*
As thilke⟩ holy Jewe oure eldres taughte— — *that same*
His bestes and his stoor⟩ shal multiplye. — *stock*
And, sires, also it heleth⟩ jalousye: — *heals*
For though a man be falle in jalous rage,
Let maken with this water his potage,
And nevere shal he more his wyf mistriste,⟩ — *mistrust*
Though he the sooth⟩ of hir defaute⟩ wiste⟩— — *truth / erring / should know*
Al⟩ had she taken⟩ preestes two or three. — *Even if / taken (as lovers)*
Heer is a miteyn⟩ eek, that ye may see: — *mitten*
He that his hond wol putte in this miteyn,
He shal have multiplying of his greyn⟩ — *grain*
Whan he hath sowen, be it whete⟩ or otes,⟩ — *wheat / oats*
So that he offre pens, or elles grotes.
Goode men and wommen, o⟩ thing warne⟩ I yow: — *one / tell*

65	If any wight> be in this chirche now,	*person*
	That hath doon sinne horrible, that he	
	Dar> nat for shame of it y-shriven be,	*Dare*
	Or any womman, be she yong or old,	
	That hath y-maked hir housbonde cokewold,>	*a cuckold*
70	Swich> folk shul have no power ne no grace	*Such*
	To offren> to my reliks in this place.	*To offer (money)*
	And whoso findeth him out of swich blame,>	*not deserving such blame*
	He wol com up and offre a> Goddes name,	*make an offering in*
	And I assoille> him by the auctoritee>	*(will) absolve / authority*
75	Which that by bulle y-graunted was to me.'	
	By this gaude> have I wonne,> yeer> by yeer,	*trick / earned / year*
	An hundred mark sith I was pardoner.	
	I stonde lyk a clerk> in my pulpet,	*scholar*
	And whan the lewed> peple is doun y-set,	*ignorant, unlearned*
80	I preche, so as ye han herd bifore,	
	And telle an hundred false japes> more.	*tricks, stories*
	Thanne peyne I me> to strecche forth the nekke,	*I take pains*
	And est and west upon the peple I bekke>	*nod*
	As doth a dowve,> sittinge on a berne.>	*dove / in a barn*
85	Myn hondes and my tonge goon so yerne>	*rapidly*
	That it is joye to see my bisinesse.	
	Of avaryce and of swich> cursednesse	*such*
	Is al my preching, for> to make hem free>	*in order / generous*
	To yeven hir pens, and namely unto me.	
90	For myn entente> is nat but for to winne,>	*intention / profit*
	And nothing> for correccioun of sinne:	*not at all*
	I rekke> nevere, whan that they ben beried,>	*care / buried*
	Though that hir soules goon a-blakeberied!	
	For certes,> many a predicacioun>	*certainly / sermon*
95	Comth ofte tyme of yvel> entencioun:	*evil*
	Som for plesaunce> of folk and flaterye,	*the entertainment*
	To been avaunced by ypocrisye,	
	And som for veyne glorie,> and som for hate.	*vainglory*
	For whan I dar non other weyes debate,	
100	Than wol I stinge him with my tonge smerte>	*sharp*
	In preching, so that he shal nat asterte>	*leap up (to protest)*
	To been> defamed falsly, if that he	*At being*
	Hath trespased to> my brethren or to me.	*wronged*
	For, though I telle noght his propre> name,	*own*
105	Men shal wel knowe that it is the same	
	By signes and by othere circumstances.	
	Thus quyte> I folk that doon us displesances;>	*requite / offenses*

Thus spitte I out my venim under hewe⸱   *hue, coloring*
Of holynesse, to semen⸱ holy and trewe.   *seem*
110   But shortly⸱ myn entente I wol devyse:⸱   *briefly / describe*
I preche of no thing but for coveityse.⸱   *out of covetousness*
Therfore my theme is yet, and evere was,
Radix malorum est cupiditas.
Thus can I preche agayn⸱ that same vyce   *against*
115 Which that I use,⸱ and that is avaryce.   *practice*
But though myself be gilty in that sinne,
Yet can I maken other folk to twinne⸱   *part*
From avaryce, and sore⸱ to repente.   *ardently*
But that is nat my principal entente:
120 I preche nothing but for coveityse.
Of this matere⸱ it oughte y-nogh suffyse.   *subject*
    Than telle I hem ensamples many oon⸱   *examples many a one*
Of olde stories longe tyme agoon,⸱   *past*
For lewed⸱ peple loven tales olde;   *unlearned*
125 Swich⸱ thinges can they wel reporte⸱ and holde.⸱   *Such / repeat / remember*
What, trowe ye, the whyles I may preche
And winne⸱ gold and silver for⸱ I teche,   *obtain / because*
That I wol live in povert⸱ wilfully?⸱   *poverty / willingly*
Nay, nay, I thoghte⸱ it nevere, trewely!   *considered*
130 For I wol preche and begge in sondry⸱ londes;   *various*
I wol nat do no labour with myn hondes,
Ne make baskettes, and live therby,
By cause I wol nat beggen ydelly.⸱   *without profit*
I wol non of the Apostles counterfete:⸱   *imitate*
135 I wol have money, wolle,⸱ chese, and whete,   *wool*
Al⸱ were it yeven of⸱ the povereste page,⸱   *Even if / given by / servant*
Or of⸱ the povereste widwe⸱ in a village,   *by / poorest widow*
Al sholde hir children sterve for famyne.
Nay! I wol drinke licour⸱ of the vyne,   *liquor, wine*
140 And have a joly wenche in every toun.
But herkneth,⸱ lordinges, in conclusioun: *listen*
Youre lyking is that I shall telle a tale.
Now have I dronke a draughte of corny⸱ ale,   *malty*
By God, I hope I shal yow telle a thing
145 That shal by resoun⸱ been at⸱ youre lyking.   *with reason / to*
For though myself be a ful vicious⸱ man,   *evil, vice-ridden*
A moral tale yet I yow telle can,
Which I am wont to preche for to winne.
Now holde youre pees,⸱ my tale I wol beginne."   *peace*

WILLIAM DUNBAR

1460–1520

THE FIRST GREAT Scottish poet, Dunbar served King James IV of
Scotland, whose court was highly cultured. A priest as well as a court poet
or "maker," Dunbar acknowledged Chaucer's influence. Elsewhere essentially a satirist, Dunbar is profoundly poignant in his lament for his fellow
makers, with its powerful refrain, *Timor Mortis conturbat me,* "The fear
of death bewilders me." Facing a severe illness in 1508, Dunbar salutes
his dead precursors, Chaucer above all, but "the Monk of Bury," John
Lydgate, and John Gower as well. A litany then peals forth, as Dunbar
remembers all of his Scottish poetic forerunners.

What always abides in my memory from "Lament for the Makers" is
the vision of "the babe full of benignity" snatched by death from his loving
mother.

There is a remarkable "Lament for the Makers" by W. S. Merwin that
brings Dunbar's poem up-to-date.

❧   ❧   ❧

Lament for the Makers

I that in heill⌐ was and gladness	*health*
Am trublit⌐ now with great sickness	*afflicted*
And feblit⌐ with infirmitie.	*enfeebled*
Timor Mortis conturbat me.	
Our plesance⌐ here is all vain glory,	*pleasure*
This fals world is but transitory,	
The flesh is bruckle,⌐ the Feynd is slee.⌐	*frail / wily*
Timor Mortis conturbat me.	
The state of man does change and vary,	
Now sound, now sick, now blyth, now sary,⌐	*sad*
Now dansand⌐ merry, now like to die.	*dancing*
Timor Mortis conturbat me.	
No state in erd⌐ here standis sicker;	*earth*
As with the wynd wavis the wicker	

So wavis this world's vanitie.
    Timor Mortis conturbat me.

Unto the death> gois all estatis,   *to death*
Princis, prelatis,> and potestatis,>   *prelates / potentates*
Baith> rich and poor of all degree.   *both*
20   *Timor Mortis conturbat me.*

He takis the knichtis> in to field>   *knights / in battle*
Enarmit> under helm and scheild;   *fully armed*
Victor he is at all mellie.
    Timor Mortis conturbat me.

That strong unmerciful tyrand>   *tyrant*
Takis, on the motheris breast sowkand,> *sucking*
The babe full of benignitie.>   *innocence*
    Timor Mortis conturbat me.

He takis the campion> in the stour,> *champion / conflict*
30 The captain closit> in the toure,> *enclosed / tower*
The lady in bour> full of bewtie.   *bower*
    Timor Mortis conturbat me.

He sparis no lord for his piscence,>   *power*
Na clerk> for his intelligence;   *scholar*
His awful straik> may no man flee. *terrible stroke*
    Timor Mortis conturbat me.

Art magicianis and astrologgis,>   *astrologers*
Rethoris, logicianis, and theologgis,
Them helpis no conclusionis slee.
40   *Timor Mortis conturbat me.*

In medecine the most practicianis,
Leechis, surrigianis,> and physicianis, *doctors, surgeons*
Themself from Death may not supplee.> *beg off*
    Timor Mortis conturbat me.

I see that makaris> amang the laif> *poets / rest*
Playis here their pageant, syne> gois to graif;> *soon / grief*
Sparit> is nocht> their facultie.   *spared / not*
    Timor Mortis conturbat me.

He has done petuously˃ devour   *frighteningly*
50   The noble Chaucer, of makaris flour,
The Monk of Bury, and Gower, all three.
   Timor Mortis conturbat me.

The good Sir Hew of Eglintoun,
And eik Heriot, and Wintoun,
He has tane˃ out of this cuntrie.˃   *taken / country*
   Timor Mortis conturbat me.

That scorpion fell˃ has done infeck˃   *terrible / infected*
Maister John Clerk, and James Affleck,
Fra ballat˃-making and tragedie.   *poem*
60   *Timor Mortis conturbat me.*

Holland and Barbour he has berevit;˃   *bereft*
Alas! that he not with us levit˃   *left*
Sir Mungo Lockart of the Lee.
   Timor Mortis conturbat me.

Clerk of Tranent eik˃ he has tane,   *also*
That made the Anteris˃ of Gawaine;   *adventures*
Sir Gilbert Hay endit has he.
   Timor Mortis conturbat me.

He has Blind Harry and Sandy Traill
70   Slain with his schour˃ of mortal˃ hail,   *shower / deadly*
Quhilk˃ Patrick Johnstoun might nocht flee.   *which*
   Timor Mortis conturbat me.

He has reft˃ Merseir his endite,˃   *bereft / poetry*
That did in luve˃ so lively write,   *love*
So short, so quick, of sentence hie.
   Timor Mortis conturbat me.

He has tane Rowll of Aberdene,
And gentill Rowll of Corstorphine;
Two better fallowis˃ did no man see.   *companions*
80   *Timor Mortis conturbat me.*

In Dunfermline he has done roune˃   *talked*
With Maister Robert Henrysoun;
Sir John the Ross enbrast˃ has he.   *embraced*
   Timor Mortis conturbat me.

And he has now tane, last of aw,⸍   *all*
Good gentil Stobo and Quintin Shaw,
Of quhom all wichtis hes pitie.
    Timor Mortis conturbat me.

Good Maister Walter Kennedy
90 In point of Death lies verily;
Great ruth⸍ it were that so shuld be.   *pity*
    Timor Mortis conturbat me.

Sen he has all my brether tane,
He will nocht let me live alane;⸍   *alone*
Of force⸍ I man⸍ his next prey be.   *necessarily / must*
    Timor Mortis conturbat me.

Since for the Death remeid⸍ is none,   *remedy*
Best is that we for Death dispone,
After our death that live may we.
100   *Timor Mortis conturbat me.*
    C. 1508

| PETRARCHAN POETRY |

WHAT WE REGARD as English Renaissance poetry has an immediate Italian source, just as Chaucer found an origin in Dante and Boccaccio. Sir Thomas Wyatt journeyed to Italy in 1526–1527 and returned with a deep passion for Petrarch's sonnets. Wyatt's versions of Petrarch are mostly very free, with very mixed metrics, and yet they began a new poetry in English, since Petrarch's poetics had inaugurated what, in retrospect, seems the art of the unsaid, vastly developed in the ironies of Chaucer and the extraordinary ellipses of Shakespeare, in his plays as in his sonnets. John Freccero says of Petrarch's self-portrait that it is precisely immortal:

> Because it is a composite of lyric instances, the portrait has no temporality; only the most naive reader would take it for authentic autobiography. For the same reasons, it is immune from the ravages of time, a mood given a fictive *durée* by the temporality of the

reader, or a score to be performed by generations of readers from the Renaissance to the Romantics.

Shrewdly, Freccero adds that the adulterous nature of Petrarch's passion takes its counterpart from the anxiety of influence: love and poetry alike must be stolen, or at least revised by the lover-poet's own creative misunderstanding, even as Petrarch had to revise his overwhelming forerunner, Dante.

Wyatt was not a revisionist, but a transmitter, like his friend and disciple, Henry Howard, Earl of Surrey, who took blank verse into English, again from the Italian. Sir Philip Sidney, beloved for his personality and chivalry, might have been the first major poet of the English Renaissance but for his death in battle at the age of thirty-two, a Protestant hero fighting for Holland's freedom from Spain.

Spenser was a crucial influence upon English poetry throughout the long span from John Milton through William Butler Yeats, but now, alas, is read only by a few scholars. To common readers in the twenty-first century, Spenser seems baroque: difficult, remote, even archaic. Yet, after a half-century of loving Spenser's poetry, he seems to me difficult to categorize but not to read. Though not a dramatic poet, his personality can seem as enigmatic and withdrawn as Shakespeare's. A Protestant visionary, mythopoeic and even apocalyptic, he is also as worldly as his friend Ralegh.

It is a disservice now to consider his national romance, *The Faerie Queene,* as an allegory, since the term frightens common readers away. It is better to think of Spenser as a Romantic symbolist, two centuries ahead of the era of Shelley and Keats, both profoundly influenced by him. I have included a selection of the nine-line stanzas of Book III, Canto VI of *The Faerie Queene:* the highly original myth of the Garden of Adonis. To phrase it as simply as possible, the myth of Adonis in Spenser celebrates the continuities of human and natural existence while confronting also the burden of mortality, the presence of Time in the earthly paradise. All human forms survive and maintain their identity, and yet the individual consciousness must touch its limit, and die. Spenser's vision of the Garden of Adonis is celebratory, and yet is shadowed by the negative, the waning and evanescence of our desires.

Spenser had a particular genius both for elegy and for celebration. His great elegy is "Astrophel," his eloquently measured lament for the heroic Sir Philip Sidney, but "Astrophel" is outdone by the two great marriage songs, *Epithalamion,* composed for the poet's own second marriage, and *Prothalamion,* for the double wedding of the Earl of Worcester's daughters. Spenser's lyric achievement, like his accomplishment in visionary romance, strongly affected Milton, but reverberated more forcefully in Shelley, Keats, and Tennyson.

SIR THOMAS WYATT

1503–1542

Whoso List to Hunt

Whoso list to hunt, I know where is an hind,
 But as for me alas, I may no more—
 The vain travail hath wearied me so sore,
 I am of them that farthest cometh behind.
Yet may I, by no means, my wearied mind
 Draw from the deer, but as she fleeth afore,
 Fainting I follow. I leave off therefore,
 Since in a net I seek to hold the wind.
Who list her hunt, I put him out of doubt,
 As well as I, may spend his time in vain.
 And graven with diamonds in letters plain
There is written her fair neck round about:
 '*Noli me tangere,* for Caesar's I am,
 And wild for to hold, though I seem tame.'
FROM MS. 1913

They Flee from Me

They flee from me, that sometime did me seek,
With naked foot stalking in my chamber.
I have seen them, gentle, tame, and meek,
That now are wild, and do not remember
That sometime they put themselves in danger
To take bread at my hand, and now they range,
Busily seeking with a continual change.

Thanked be Fortune it hath been otherwise,
Twenty times better; but once in special,
10   In thin array, after a pleasant guise,
When her loose gown from her shoulders did fall,
And she me caught in her arms long and small,
And therewith all sweetly did me kiss
And softly said, "Dear heart, how like you this?"

It was no dream, I lay broad waking.
But all is turned, thorough my gentleness,
Into a strange fashion of forsaking;
And I have leave to go, of her goodness,
And she also to use newfangleness.
20   But since that I so kindely am served,
I fain would know what she hath deserved.

FROM MS. 1913

SIR PHILIP SIDNEY

1554–1586

from Astrophel and Stella

I

Loving in truth, and fain in verse my love to show,
That she, dear she, might take some pleasure of my pain,
Pleasure might cause her read, reading might make her know,
Knowledge might pity win, and pity grace obtain,
I sought fit words to paint the blackest face of woe:
Studying inventions fine, her wits to entertain,
Oft turning others' leaves, to see if thence would flow
Some fresh and fruitful showers upon my sunburned brain.
But words came halting forth, wanting Invention's stay;
10   Invention, Nature's child, fled stepdame Study's blows;
And others' feet still seemed but strangers in my way.
Thus, great with child to speak, and helpless in my throes,
    Biting my truant pen, beating myself for spite:
    "Fool," said my Muse to me, "look in thy heart, and write!"

LXXI

Who will in fairest book of Nature know
How virtue may best lodged in beauty be,
Let him but learn of love to read in thee,
Stella, those fair lines which true goodness show.
There shall he find all vices' overthrow,
Not by rude force, but sweetest sovereignty
Of reason, from whose light those night-birds fly,
That inward sun in thine eyes shineth so.
And, not content to be perfection's heir
10   Thyself, dost strive all minds that way to move,
Who mark in thee what is in thee most fair.
So while thy beauty draws the heart to love,
    As fast thy virtue bends that love to good.
    But, ah, Desire still cries, "Give me some food."
1591

EDMUND SPENSER

1552–1599

. . . if the whole man be trained perfectly, and his mind calm, consistent, and powerful, the vision which comes to him is seen as in a perfect mirror, serenely, and in consistence with the rational power; but if the mind be imperfect and ill trained, the vision is seen as in a broken mirror, with strange distortions and discrepancies, all the passions of the heart breathing upon it in cross ripples, till hardly a trace of it remains unbroken. So that, strictly speaking, the imagination is never governed; it is always the ruling and Divine power. . . . And thus *Illiad, The Inferno,* the *Pilgrim's Progress,* the *Faerie Queene,* are all of them true dreams; only the sleep of the men to whom they came was the deep, living sleep which God sends, with a sacredness in it, as of death, the revealer of secrets.

— RUSKIN

I

OF ALL THE MAJOR POETS in English, Edmund Spenser is, at this time, the least read and, in proportion to his merits, the least valued. As a living presence in the poetry of the last sixty or so years he is scarcely to be felt, for since the death of Yeats the English-speaking world has had no poet even in part·educated by Spenser, no poetry directly affected by *The Faerie Queene*. Spenser has been abandoned to the academies, and within them he has become increasingly peripheral. When the critical sensibility that prevailed in Britain and America during the second half of the twentieth century turned to Spenser, it found little in him to justify the eminence he had held for three hundred years. His long poem was dismissed as the product of the will usurping the work of the imagination. The Shakespearean critic Derek Traversi may be taken as representative of still prevalent (though waning) taste when he judged Spenser to have made "splendid pieces of rhetorical decoration" devoid of deep personal content, and to have mastered a style which "tends irresistibly to become an instrument of disintegration, furthering the dissolution of the declared moral intention into mere rhythmical flow." The distance between such a verdict and an accurate judgment of Spenser's achievement is so great that a lover of Spenser's poetry is compelled to resist a reaction into overpraise of "the Prince of Poets in his time." One is tempted to maintain that a reader who cannot apprehend Spenser's voice as being, at its best, the voice of poetry itself is not capable of reading adequately any poetry whatsoever. But too much rhetoric of that dismissing kind has been used by critics; admirers of Spenser, of Milton, of Blake and Wordsworth and Shelley, have been assured, all too frequently, that the life of English poetry was elsewhere, and that the Romantic and mythopoeic tradition was an aberration. It was curiously necessary for the admirers of metaphysical verse to deprecate everything in English poetry that was most unlike Donne, but the poetry of Spenser and the tradition he inaugurated are too firmly central to require any polemic against a rival tradition.

John Hughes, who edited the works of Spenser in 1715, remarked of *The Faerie Queene* that "the chief merit of this Poem consists in that surprizing Vein of fabulous Invention, which runs thro it." We no longer commend poets specifically for their invention, but that seemed the essence of poetry from the Renaissance critics through Dr. Johnson and on into the Romantic period. The manner in which the invention was handled received only equal weight with the rarity of the fictive matter itself in Renaissance criticism, but gradually has come (in modern criticism) to crowd out the proper valuing of invention. In a period of revived mythopoeic poetry, the age of Yeats and Rilke, the poets were attended as exegetes by rhetorical critics, many of them hostile to the autonomy demanded by the inventive faculty, the mythopoeic power that Spenser possessed in greater measure than any poet in English except for Blake.

Hughes observed that "Spenser's Fable, tho often wild, is . . . always emblematical," and commended his poet for thus turning romance to the uses of allegory. The conventions of romance and the problematical nature of allegory have alike provided barriers between Spenser and many modern readers, but the poet's artistry as a romantic allegorist is informed by the exuberance of his invention. To consider Spenser under the arbitrary divisions of romance, allegory, and mythmaking, as I shall now proceed to do, is to endanger the integrity of his sustained vision, but one of the virtues of reading and discussing Spenser is to be taught a healthy fear of discursive reduction, of the organized translation of poetry into prose that criticism can so easily become. Yet one learns also, more from Spenser than from any poet, that all criticism of poetry tends toward allegorizing, and that the consciously allegorical poet is not content to abandon the reader and critic without a guide.

W. L. Renwick has said of Spenser that "we must regard his work as part of a cultural movement of European extent, as fruit of general and not merely personal experience." Certainly any attempt to understand the genesis of Spenser's poetry and that poetry's intentions must look on it as Renwick suggests, yet Spenser in his best poetry stands very much apart from his fellow poets of Renaissance Europe. There are very crucial elements in his poetry that make it more akin in certain ways to Blake and Shelley and Keats, writing two hundred years later, than to Ariosto and Du Bellay and Sidney, all of whom influenced him. To account for the emergence of those elements is perhaps not possible, since an imagination as full and powerful as Spenser's is strictly not accountable; we can see what it was and where it went but may never surmise its origins. Scholars of the history of ideas and historical critics of poetry think otherwise, but they tend to read all poetry by allegorizing it into concepts, on the implied assumption that the minds of great poets work as theirs do. It must be granted that Spenser thought of himself as being, among other things, a philosophical poet. Philosophically he was eclectic and richly confused, in the fortunate manner of his time, which could still believe in the ultimate unity of all knowledge, pagan and Christian, natural and revealed. The intricate tangle of his conceptual borrowings is a delight to the source hunter but irrelevant to a reader who seeks what a poet alone can give her. Again, Spenser conceived of his poetic function as being a uniquely national one; he wished to write an English poem that would match if not surpass the classical epic of Homer and of Vergil and the contemporary romance of Ariosto and of Tasso. The thrust toward national identity and international greatness that typified Elizabethan aspiration at its most intense is a vital component in Spenser's conscious poetic purpose. But where his poem is most national, most the work of the courtier, it is least interesting as a poem, and hopelessly mired in now disheartening historical allegory, which Dr. Johnson's "common reader" can safely ignore.

Yeats, who knew better, but was moved by an understandable Irish grudge against Spenser, spoke of him as "the first poet struck with remorse, the first poet who gave his heart to the State." Insofar as *The Faerie Queene* so gives its heart, it ceases to be a poem and does fasten its knights and ladies "with allegorical nails to a big barn door of common sense, of merely practical virtue," as Yeats maintained. But Spenser never gave all his heart to anything less than that imaginative vision in which the unattainable ideals of Protestant humanism were displaced into a poetic world where all good things and their dialectical counterparts were made simultaneously possible. Yeats was more accurate about Spenser and the value of his poetry when he realized how Spenser's visions, supposedly forgotten, "would rise up before me coming from I knew not where." Yeats's best criticism of Spenser is in his own poetry, where he makes use of him, as when "The Ruins of Time" and the *Prothalamion,* together with certain stanzas in *The Faerie Queene,* help form "Leda and the Swan" and "The Wild Swans at Coole." More is to be learned about what is most relevant to us in Spenser's poetry by seeing how it was used by Drayton, Milton, Blake, Shelley, Keats, Tennyson, and Yeats than by reading the bulk of past and present Spenserian criticism. There have been excellent Spenser critics, from Hughes and Thomas Warton to C. S. Lewis and Northrop Frye, but the extraordinary sense in which Spenser is truly the poet's poet is best brought out in a great poem like Shelley's "The Witch of Atlas," where the world of *The Faerie Queene* is relied upon as being the universe of poetry itself.

To understand the unique nature of Spenser's poetry is to understand also something vital about how poets influence one another; indeed, the study of Spenser's poetry is the best introduction available to the fascinating problem of what there is about poetry that can bring more poetry into being, for no poet has made so many other men into poets as Spenser has. What so many poets have learned from Spenser is not a style of writing but a mode of poetry and a sense of the poet's self-recognition in regard to his own poem. The mode is that of the poem as heterocosm, the other or possible world of the poem as it exists in relation to the too-probable world of the reader. Coleridge acutely noted "the marvellous independence and true imaginative absence of all particular space or time in *The Faerie Queene*. It is in the domain neither of history nor geography; it is ignorant of all artificial boundary, all material obstacles; it is truly in land of Faery, that is, of mental space." Dante comes closest to Spenser in creating such a world, but Dante's three worlds are categorical and sharply distinguished from one another. The persuasiveness of Spenser's imagined world is in the treachery of its boundaries; its heavens and hells, purgatories and earthly paradises, undergo a continual transmemberment, yet its appearances are either supremely delusive or absolutely truthful, and no honest reader could tell the difference between one and the other on the basis of imagistic vividness. What Spenser had, better, I think, than any poet before or since, was the power to project both the object of desire and the shape of nightmare with equal imaginative freedom. That power gives its possessor the control of the literary realm of romance or idealized narrative, a domain with a potential ranging from the most primordial and almost childlike to the most sophisticated of perspectives. Romance, Northrop Frye suggestively states, is the Mythos of Summer, the narrative of quest for a lost paradise, the proper story for the man of whom Wallace Stevens could say: "He had studied the nostalgias." So have we all, and when we find ourselves most impatient of romance, we are most susceptible to it, rejecting the wish but falling somehow into its fulfilling dream. Between the invaluable chaos of nostalgia and the achieved form of romance only the capable imagination can mediate, and the fully capable imagination must be uninhibited. Why Spenser's liberty to imagine existed at all we cannot know, but we can see how the circumstances of his life and time conspired to make him more free than his greater disciple, Milton, ever came to be.

Spenser, like Milton after him, is a Protestant poet, and the Spenserian tradition in English poetry has been a Protestant one, with a progressive movement to what could be called the visionary left wing: radical in politics, individualist in religion, and insisting upon the unsupported imagination as its own warrant. The movement in religion is from the moderate Puritanism of Spenser, with its prophetic strain conflicting with a residue of medieval sacramentalism, to the prophetic self-identification of Milton on to the displaced Protestantism of Romantic mythmaking: the naturalistic humanism of Keats, the natural supernaturalism (as M. H. Abrams terms it) of Wordsworth, the apocalyptic vitalism of Blake, and the despairing yet heroic agnosticism of the prophetic Shelley, most Spenserian of them all in the effect of his major poems. In our own time the

Spenserian and Romantic tradition is directly manifested in Yeats's eclectic "system" of belief, and indirectly in the American late Romanticism of Wallace Stevens (who returns to Wordsworth and Keats) and of Hart Crane, very much the Shelley of our age and the legitimate claimant to the sad dignity of being the Last Romantic. Extreme as this statement is, *Notes Towards a Supreme Fiction* and *The Bridge* are Spenserian poems, for the conception of the poem pointing to itself as a poem in *Notes* and the quest of the poet in *The Bridge* are both in lineal descent from *The Faerie Queene*. Crane trapped in the purgatorial maze of "The Tunnel" seems a symbolic figure far removed from Spenser's knight lost in the labyrinth of Error's wood, but the kinship is clear enough when we consider the binding figures in the middle of the tradition, the young poets of Shelley's *Alastor* and Keats's *Endymion* questing through the baffling mazes of the natural world. Stevens, meditating in his subtle variations on the theme of "the origin of the major man," and uncovering at last "how simply the fictive hero becomes the real," seems far indeed from Spenser laboring "to fashion a gentleman or noble person in vertuous and gentle discipline," but again the connecting link is in the Romantic tradition, in Blake's fictive hero, Los, the refiner in imaginative fire who labors to humanize man, or in Wordsworth's attempt through poetry to fashion a man in the nobility of a reciprocal generosity with nature.

Spenser and Milton were Christian humanists and, except for Wordsworth in his poetic decline, this can scarcely be said of any of their poetic descendants, but the lineage remains not only clear but illuminatingly inevitable in its progression. The Protestant aesthetic shifts from tradition to innovation in Milton's poetry, but the process can be traced earlier in *The Faerie Queene,* although certainly more ambiguously. Spenser did not allow himself to be inhibited either by the fear that a universal symbolism founded on sacramentalism might betray him into Catholic poetry or that his own fictive covering might obscure the truths of Scriptural revelation. No one else has so cheerfully and astonishingly compounded pagan mythology, Christian symbolism, and personal mythmaking while remaining centrally in a main doctrinal tradition of Christianity.

Spenser had the humanist belief that classical thought and poetic form did not conflict with Christian truth; for him all myths merged, as all mirrored a unity of truth. Yet his personal attitude toward mythology is confusing because his sense of history is poetically pragmatic; he seems to seek the relevant, the story he can use, whether it arouses his unrivaled powers for sensual description or because it might illuminate his allegory of sanctification, and usually because it can do both. The golden world seemed past to him, and although he heralded the greatest single period of English poetry, he evidently had as dark a view of his country's immediate literary prospects as any unimaginative moralist might have assumed. Like Sidney, Spenser believed that a poet shared in the creativity of God, and therefore believed also in the poet's responsibility to bring his creation into a meaningful relationship with the moral order of God's creation. Such a belief led Spenser into the writing of allegory, and finally into the ambitious enterprise of his allegorical epic-romance.

Much recent prejudice against *The Faerie Queene* is simply a prejudice against all allegory whatsoever. Works that declare themselves overtly as simply allegories, like *The Pilgrim's Progress*, now tend to go unread, while complex allegorists like Dante, Blake, and Melville are studied frequently, as if they had not consciously modulated the contexts in which their meanings were to be interpreted. Allegory is now associated for many with mere moralizing, while symbolism has the prestige of the legitimate about it. The Romantic descendants of Spenser, from Blake to Yeats, are partially responsible for this curious confusion. Blake was a great critic, but his distinction between "Allegory & Vision" was not a very happy one: "Fable or Allegory are a totally distinct & inferior kind of poetry. Vision or Imagination is a Representation of what Eternally Exists, Really & Unchangeably." Indeed, he could not rest in his own distinction, for his own poetry fits his earlier and positive use of the word: "Allegory address'd to the Intellectual powers, while it is altogether hidden from the Corporeal Understanding, is My Definition of the Most Sublime Poetry." On this definition, a proper defense of Spenser's poetry, as well as Blake's, can and should be made. The "Corporeal Understanding" is Blake's phrase for any empirical approach that is not open to vision or imaginative apprehension. What Blake means by "the Intellectual powers" is everything the reader's mind is capable of bringing to self-integration as the reader experiences the poem. If the poem falls short of the reader's potential for wholeness, the reader will learn it in time, but patience and goodwill are necessities if the effort is to be made.

Edwin Honig usefully finds "the allegorical quality in a twice-told tale written in rhetorical, or figurative, language and expressing a vital belief." So broad a way of approaching allegory seems the best antidote to the modern suspicion of allegory, a distrust reducing a complex relation between image and idea to the simple deception of an image masking an idea. For allegory in Spenser is neither a discourse in disguised ideas nor a pattern of familiar events deliberately (and momentarily) distorted. Spenser's allegory, in its totality and frequently in its details, reverberates into further meanings by its capability and adequacy as a poem, its strength in self-containment and completeness. *The Faerie Queene* is a more diffuse work than *Paradise Lost* or Blake's *Jerusalem,* more diffuse even than *Finnegans Wake* (with which it curiously has much in common), but the manner of its metaphoric extension justifies the seeming lack of cohesiveness. For Spenser begins with sustained allegory and ends (he died before conclusion) with an imagined world, a world containing as many of the total possibilities of literature within it as any other professed allegory up to his own time. His apocalyptic Book I may be his master-piece, but I pass over it here so as to consider the centers of vision else-where in his great romance.

2

THE ARTISTIC COMPLETENESS of Book I compels Spenser to an altogether fresh start in Book II, in which the literary context shifts from the Bible to the classical epic and the theme from experience in the order of grace to experience in the order of nature. Sir Guyon, the quester in Book II, exemplifies heroic virtue more directly and fully than Saint George could ever represent sanctification, since the classical virtues are wholly within the natural realm. Tough Guyon is spared the fearful purgations of Spenser's first hero, his triumph is necessarily a less definitive one, and the disinterested reader of poetry is rather less likely to be unequivocal in appreciating that triumph, the overthrow of the sensual delights of Acrasia and her Bower of Bliss.

Frequently noted is the clear parallel in narrative structure between the first two books, usefully explained by the contrast between the two orders, nature and grace. The knight of faith, guided by a veiled but still effectual truth, overcomes his earlier opponents but falls victim (through his own credulity) to deception and is tempted by an irrevocable despair. The knight of temperance, guided by an invulnerable and moderate wis-dom, undergoes temptation but resists it, and falls only through natural exhaustion. Roused again, his awakened nature accomplishes an ethical triumph without direct heavenly aid, unlike the knight of faith who must be rescued by grace, and then refreshed by it in the climactic battle.

Where Book I is dominated by scenes of struggle climaxing in the strife between death and resurrection, the actual battles in Book II are of only secondary importance. The first event in Book I is the Red Cross Knight's victory over Error; the parallel event in Book II is a fight that does not take place, as Guyon recognizes the error of his wrath before fully attacking the Red Cross Knight. Guyon already has the temperate virtues, and needs only to realize them by bringing them into activity in response to a wide range of temptations. By doing so, he becomes the prototype of Milton's Christ in *Paradise Regained,* for his is the task of a Hercules greater than the Herculean heroes of classical epic. Guyon and Milton's Christ must transform a passive consciousness of heroic virtue into an active awareness that knows itself fully because it becomes more itself in the act of confronting temptation. Guyon is, of course, only a man, and fortunately for the poem he can be tempted, although one sometimes wishes he could be tempted to a greater degree of dramatic indecisiveness as he quests remorselessly on.

The quest of Book II begins with the powerful episode of Amavia and Mordant, both slain indirectly by the sexual witchery of Acrasia, a Circe-like enchantress. Guyon vows to avenge their death, and begins this process by attempting to care for Ruddymane, the infant abandoned by their self-destructiveness. The ineffectuality of merely natural means to accomplish fully any moral quest is shown immediately by Guyon's inability to wash the babe's hands free of guilty human blood, a frightening symbolic parody of the sacrament of baptism.

The image of the babe's bloody hands haunts the rest of Book II, for the babe's equivocal innocence is an epitome of how closely original sin and the possibility of natural virtue dwell together in the experiential world. The adventures of Guyon are a series of encounters between his temperate affections and the excessive humors leading to "outrageous anger" or lust, or excessive desire of any kind. In these encounters Guyon goes on foot, and his victories are indecisive, for he is more skilled at resisting evils than at abolishing them. Temperance, as Northrop Frye observes, is deliberately displayed as a pedestrian virtue, and Guyon is memorable for what he rightfully declines to do, until the very close of his book, when he acts to destroy the Bower of Acrasia.

The Cave of Mammon

The most remarkable instance of Guyon's passive heroism is Canto VII, the descent into the Cave of Mammon, an episode that renews the archetype of the classical hero's descent to Avernus, as in *Aeneid* VI. Parted from his moral guide, the prudent Palmer, Guyon undergoes a three-day trial in the underworld that seems essentially to be an initiation, a parallel experience to the Red Cross Knight's three-day fight with the dragon. This extraordinary mythmaking of the Cave of Mammon is to be read partly as the supreme instance in Book II of the negative virtue of temperate endurance, but the invention of Spenser is too absolute to be interpreted only in terms of moral intention.

Charles Lamb noted the dream atmosphere of the Mammon episode, and praised Spenser for a creation replete with violent transitions and incongruities "and yet the waking judgment ratifies them." The Mammon episode is vision and not dream, for the poetic content is manifest in the images, and not latent in a depth-pattern hidden from the imagination. Milton is the best guide to the Cave of Mammon and Bower of Bliss alike when he writes in *Areopagitica* that Guyon is brought through these places "that he might see and know, and yet abstain." Even Guyon must be purified by trial "and trial is by what is contrary." Guyon must "scout into the regions of sin and falsity," and so it is just and necessary that he accompany Mammon into the depths, even as Christ must undergo the temptations of Satan in *Paradise Regained.*

All through his ordeal Guyon is shadowed by a fiend who would rend him apart at the least yielding to temptation, a persuasive symbol of the spectral self, the dark aspect of nature that must be purged from every man. The silver stool which is Guyon's last temptation, "to rest thy weary person in the shadow coole," was suggestively related by the eighteenth-century editor Upton to the forbidden seat in the Eleusinian mysteries. Like Christ in the temptations of Satan, Guyon voluntarily submits to the blandishments of Mammon, and shows his heroism negatively, by a firm resistance. Guyon's is the Miltonic fortitude of patience, the virtue Adam must learn if he is to be saved. As a Christian knight, Guyon does not achieve the revelation granted to Saint George, but he does overtake the Homeric and Vergilian heroes by attaining to a perfect control over his own nature through a descent into the underworld. His achievement is heroic but not supernatural; it hesitates on the edge of the world of grace, but does not cross over into the revealed order. At the triumphant end of his ordeal Guyon faints, not because he has been in any way intemperate, but because he has carried his heroism to a verge of the natural condition, and has exhausted nature in doing so. He has not harrowed hell, but he has seen and known the mysteries of hell, and been saved from them by his abstinence. He falls out of his vision back into nature, and, as with Keats's Endymion, the first touch of earth again comes nigh to killing him. We are left with the dark splendor of his ordeal, a pattern directly relevant to our society as it was to Spenser's. What Guyon has rejected is what Spenser sought and what most men compulsively seek: a glory that shines beautifully because it is surrounded by darkness, a kingdom where the only wealth is death. The moral is an aesthetically powerful dimension of the myth, not only because it is universal but because it is observation rather than admonition. Spenser knew himself to be no Hercules, and Guyon's escape is not the victory of an Everyman. The strength of Spenser's fiction is in its deathly attraction; the reader is not Guyon. A knight of Temperance humanistically fulfills his nature, and faints into the light of every day. The necessarily intemperate reader yields to the imagination, which desires to be indulged. We remain to some extent in the Cave, not because it is the best of places, or even because we are overwhelmingly tempted, but because we are poor; we lack the only wealth, which is life.

The Bower of Bliss

Probably no section of *The Faerie Queene* so directly identifies its poet as Canto XII of Book II, the account of the voyage toward and the overthrow of Acrasia's Bower of Bliss. Hazlitt praised the "voluptuous pathos" of the Bower, and implied that what was most poetic in Spenser was most at home in the Bower. This is a partial truth and certainly more valuable than the moralistic insistence of many commentators that the Bower is altogether a degraded as well as a degrading place. The Bower is a "horrible enchantment," but an enchantment nevertheless.

The most persuasive modern enemy of the Bower is C. S. Lewis, who has severely insisted that Acrasia's garden is artificial rather than natural, as contrasted to the natural and spontaneous profusion of the Garden of Adonis. The Bower, again according to Lewis, shows the whole sexual nature in sterile suspension: "There is not a kiss or an embrace in the island: only male prurience and female provocation." To this, Lewis again contrasts the Garden of Adonis, with its teeming sexual life. On this reading, one has got to be something of a voyeur to be attracted by the Bower, to be delighted as our "wanton eies do peepe" at Acrasia and her naked damsels.

Lewis is reacting against those critics who have charged Spenser with "actual sensuality and theoretical austerity." Spenser is subtler and more varied in his art than either his moralistic attackers or defenders have been willing to notice. Part of the contrast between the Garden of Adonis and the Bower of Bliss is certainly due to the element of artifice in the Bower, yet the Bower remains very much within the natural world. Indeed, its natural beauty is what we as readers are first asked to notice, and precisely what Guyon must first resist. He wonders much "at the fayre aspect of that sweet place," but he does not suffer any delight "to sincke into his sence, nor mind affect." The Bower is nature *mixed* with art, as one might expect of any sophisticated sensuality. Some of its fruits are of burnished gold, yet its boughs hang always heavy with the ripeness of nature. Acrasia and her victim-lover are not caught by Guyon and the Palmer in the act of love, but it will not do to maintain that there are no embraces in the Bower. Acrasia is seen in the "langour of her late sweet toyle," and her spent lover sleeps in her arms in what is intended as a demonic parody of the sleep of Adonis, a vision that would be pointless if it testified only to "male prurience and female provocation." No; whatever the Bower is, it is scarcely a picture of the whole sexual nature in disease. Moral criticism of poetry is self-defeating if it denies Satan his heroic courage, Iago his serpentine insight, or Acrasia her genuine attractiveness, the fierce vigor of her unsanctified sexual nature, presented as its own self-justifying goal. Even the Peeping Tom element in the Bower, which is undeniable, is an equivocal element throughout the poem. Spenser's vision always points us in toward a center in any scene, sexual or otherwise; his is the art of the cynosure, and no poet has yielded so fully to the tyranny of the bodily eye. His heroes long to gaze upon a variety of glories, and to fulfill themselves in that vision. Acrasia's wanton damsels, inviting the gaze of Guyon, are a parody of the Faerie Queene's granting of herself in vision to Arthur, and more directly of all Spenser's exposed heroines upon whom we so delightedly spy.

Guyon is not more nor less natural than the Bower he overthrows, any more than his resistance to the temptations of Mammon is more or less natural than a surrender to the Cave's wealth would have been. It is because both Guyon and Acrasia are natural possibilities that Spenser is capable of bringing them into an imaginatively meaningful juxtaposition. What Guyon destroys is not evil in itself, but is rather a good that has luxuriated into dangerous excess because it has denied all context. Guyon is faithful to a context in which sexual love can humanize and not merely naturalize, but Acrasia's love robs men of their human nature. If the reader is more inclined toward naturalism than Spenser was, he still need not suspend his disbelief in Guyon's context, for Spenser's poem stands in its own right as a making, rather than as an adornment to a moral order complete without the imaginings of the poet. Acrasia is like Keats's Belle Dame or

Blake's maidens of the Crystal Cabinet or the Golden Net, weaving an enchantment horrible only because it pretends to offer a final reality or inmost form within sexual experience alone. The ruined quester becomes the beast of the field, or starves, or enters into a baffled state unable to comprehend his loss. Keats and Blake are more humanistic in their implications as to what a saving context might be, but the mythic pattern they give us is Spenserian.

There is a curious bitterness in the final stanzas of Book II, as Spenser confronts Guyon and the Palmer with the stubborn Gryll, who had been happy as a hog. It was for this Gryll's sake, as for his fellows', that Guyon and the Palmer had surpassed the voyages of Odysseus, had risked the terrors of the sea so magnificently set forth in the earlier stanzas of Canto XII. The temperate voyager has shown the power of a Hercules and the endurance of an Odysseus; with "rigor pittilesse" he has broken down a great work of mixed art and nature, sparing no part of "their goodly workmanship." Part of his immediate reward is the hoggish lament of a Gryll, and the incongruity of this response provokes the abruptness of the canto's end. If there is bitterness here, there is a sour humor as well. Spenser usually spares himself (and us) the Miltonic contempt for "the donghill kinde" of all-too-natural men, but he has something of the Miltonic horror at any forgetfulness of the excellence of man's creation. The Bower is finally seen as a complement to Mammon's Cave, as yet another instrumentality for the dehumanization of man. We are asked to believe that the fruit of Acrasia, eaten for its own sake, destroys as surely as the fruit of Proserpina's garden. There is a natural resistance to so harsh a judgment, within Spenser as within ourselves. Gryll is the warning made not to overcome that resistance but to offer a speaking picture that may trouble even the self-indulging imagination.

The Mutabilitie Cantos

It is in the *Two Cantos of Mutabilitie* that Spenser troubles his own imagination most, by the strongest of his pictures. The *Mutabilitie Cantos* were not published until 1609, a decade after Spenser's death. Though this greatest of poetic fragments was printed as Cantos VI and VII (and two stanzas of Canto VIII) of Book VII of *The Faerie Queene,* one is tempted to read it as a complete unit in itself, a finishing coda to the otherwise unfinished poem. Certainly the fragment's last two stanzas could not have begun anything; what they yearn for is finality, and they proclaim a poet's farewell to his art and his life.

Various commentators have traced (or thought they traced) the effect of Empedocles, of Lucretius, and of Bruno on the *Mutabilitie Cantos,* but Spenser is here more than ever inventive, dealing imaginatively with his own obsessional theme of change and decay in the phenomenal world. Probably he owes the debate form of the fragment to Chaucer's *Parlement of Foules,* but *Mutabilitie* is a very un-Chaucerian comedy, with a profound anguish underlying the ebullient surface.

C. S. Lewis has maintained that Spenser's Titaness Mutabilitie "despite her beauty, is an evil force," an enemy of Spenserian health and concord, and indeed an incarnation of corruption and sin, but this is an overreading through excessive simplification. Part of the immense power of Spenser's fragment is lost if the Titaness is denied all justice, however much of a shudder must accompany the dramatic sympathy. What is poetically most important about Mutabilitie is what we find most surprising— that Spenser has made her beautiful. This is part of our involuntary sympathy with her, and wins even Jove's momentary (and mistaken) indulgence. Another part is in the genesis of the Titanic myth itself; her claim through lineage is better than Jove's. But most crucial is that Mutabilitie is more human than the gods she challenges; if she is tainted by earthly sin, we of course are too, and her mounting up into the sphere of the moon has its Promethean element.

The corruption of Mutabilitie is primarily decay rather than sin, for morality is not very relevant to this fragment. If it were, then Jove might be given power over Mutabilitie, or his ultimate rule over her realm be implied. But Spenser, for once in *The Faerie Queene,* is not giving us a vision of possibility, but a lament of experience, and the phenomenal sway of Mutabilitie is an experiential truth. The beauty of Mutabilitie is part of that truth, as is the virtual identity of Mutabilitie and human existence itself. On a larger scale, we have some degree of involvement in Mutabilitie's quest against Cynthia, much as we desire the verdict to go against the rebel.

Yet even the verdict is ambiguous. The poetic synthesis of Spenser is indeed conceptually simpler, more sensuous, and more passionate than any philosophical resolution of the problem of change and decay could have been. One element in that synthesis is almost a palinode, which emerges most clearly in the two final stanzas, perhaps the most moving Spenser wrote. The close of Chaucer's *Troilus and Criseyde* provides a rough but useful parallel to Spenser's last stanzas, but the heavenly laughter of Troilus is what Spenser seeks, not what he has already found.

The metamorphic land of Faerie is by turns a humanized nature and a demonic labyrinth, but the land of the *Mutabilitie Cantos* is our generative world, neither redeemed nor doomed, but perpetually subject to alteration, some of it cyclic and expected, like that portrayed in the pageant of the months, but some portion totally unexpected, and running generally to the worse. On the simplest and most human level of his subject Spenser is complaining for all men, and the dignity of the universal is deeply invested in his tone. Proud Mutabilitie is unquestioned mistress of all mortal things; from her "all living wights have learned to die." When she turns her ambitions to the heavens she projects our deathly desires toward the eternal world, and menaces an orderly alteration with our disorderly and corrupt beauty. Spenser's uniqueness as a poet, which he bequeaths to Keats especially among his descendants, is in the sensuous immediacy of all his imagined worlds. Mutabilitie is descended from chaos and from earth, and so are we. She carries up with her to the moon's sphere the menace of chaos and the beauty of earth, and the supposed right of capability. The relation of poetry to morality has always been a troubled one, but it seems clear that energy and resolution are always poetic virtues, however unlawful or evil their means may be in actual existence. Spenser's aspiring Titaness has something of the vigor of Milton's greatest creation, the Satan of *Paradise Lost*, and something, in consequence, of Satan's aesthetic hold upon us.

Her appeal is made past Jove to "the god of Nature," who appears only through the veiled presence of his surrogate, Nature herself, perhaps suggested to Spenser by the Wisdom of Proverbs 8:22–31, brought forth by God "before his works of old." The judging voice of Spenser's Nature is his version of the voice of the Hebrew God, for Spenser was poetically subtler than Milton, and too involved in the glory of invention to risk a portrayal of God in His proper person. So Spenser's Nature, though a "great goddess," is not to be seen by us as being either man or woman, terror or beauty. Yet her shrouding garment burns with the light of the Transfiguration, and her words are to be respected as definitive by Mutabilitie herself.

The judgment of Nature turns the evidence of Mutabilitie against itself, and makes of phenomenal change and decay an emblem of faith, in reply to the skepticism of the insurgent Titaness: "But what we see not, who shall persuade?" Everything changes, yet but dilates being, for natural existence constantly, though gradually, works toward the revelation of a more human nature. Mutabilitie seeks more palpable sway, yet her desire is self-destructive, for time in Spenser as in Blake or Shelley is the mercy of eternity, and the agent of prophetic redemption. Spenser's humanism is liberated into an imaginative vitalism through Nature's assurances that states of being survive, though all things must endure change. The time that shall come, in bringing about the uncovering of all things, will bring also the perfection that reigns over change. Until that time comes, Nature vanishes, leaving Mutabilitie dominant in the lower world beneath the moon, and Jove as ordered change still reigning in the heavens above.

Had Spenser ended there, his fragment would have a curiously cold climax for so turbulent and piercing a work. The poet's voice at its most personal breaks into the poem, weighing the speech of Mutabilitie and desperately granting the pragmatic strength of her claim to all the human world. Renouncing the beauty and pride of the only life we can lead, he turns to the speech of Nature for some comfort, and the urgency of his prayer reverberates strangely against the humanism and love celebrated throughout his poem. Yet even here, as he prays for a sight of the eternal sabbath, he does not allow himself to denigrate the experience of living. All shall rest with God, but meanwhile "all that moveth doth in change delight." The pride of life is "so fading and so fickle" and must yield to "short time," but while it lasts it remains a "flowring pride."

Amoretti

Spenser's sonnet sequence, Amoretti (1595), is sometimes undervalued because it is read in juxtaposition to Shakespeare's, which it certainly influenced. Even the sequences of Sidney, Daniel, and Drayton all have some poems better than any single sonnet in the Amoretti, and Sidney's sequence has always had more admirers than Spenser's. Unlike Milton, Spenser does not show himself in his true dimensions in his minor poems (if we except the Epithalamion). The Spenserian voice is there, but sometimes we feel it badly needs the mythic atmosphere of Faerie if we are to hear it properly.

The rhyme scheme (ababbcbccdcdee) of the Amoretti may have been invented by Spenser himself; in any case, it is characteristic of him in its aural complexity. Characteristic also is the very individual love relationship that the sequence celebrates, a relationship that suggests the ideal portrayed in Books III and IV of The Faerie Queene. Spenser, all his deliberate Petrarchism aside, is surely dealing with his own love for Elizabeth Boyle, and the whole sequence moves toward the supreme joy of the Epi-

thalamion. Gentleness and loving esteem on the poet's side, good humor and intelligence on the lady's, are the qualities that overcome the conventional difficulties of courtship. The very sophisticated Spenserian sense of humor, frequently evident in *The Faerie Queene,* is ambiguously involved in this sonnet sequence, although difficult to isolate.

⋁   ⋁   ⋁

from The Faerie Queene: The Gardens of Adonis

29 She brought her to her joyous Paradize,
    Where most she wonnes,˃ when she on earth does dwel.   *lives*
    So faire a place, as Nature can devize:
    Whether in *Paphos,* or *Cytheron* hill,
    Or it in *Gnidus* be, I wote not well;
    But well I wote by tryall,˃ that this same   *experience*
    All other pleasant places doth excell,
    And callèd is by her lost lovers name
The *Gardin* of *Adonis,* farre renowmd by fame.

30 In that same Gardin all the goodly flowres,
    Wherewith dame Nature doth her beautifie,
    And decks the girlonds of her paramoures,
    Are fetcht: there is the first seminarie˃   *seed nursery*
    Of all things, that are borne to live and die,
    According to their kindes. Long worke it were,
    Here to account the endlesse progenie
    Of all the weedes,˃ that bud and blossome there;   *plants*
But so much as doth need, must needs be counted here.

31 It sited was in fruitfull soyle of old,
    And girt in with two walles on either side;
    The one of yron, the other of bright gold,
    That none might thorough˃ breake, nor overstride: *through*
    And double gates it had, which opened wide,
    By which both in and out men moten˃ pas;   *could*
    Th'one faire and fresh, the other old and dride:
    Old *Genius* the porter of them was,
Old *Genius,* the which a double nature has.

32 He letteth in, he letteth out to wend,˃   *go*
    All that to come into the world desire;

A thousand thousand naked babes attend
About him day and night, which do require,
That he with fleshly weedes would them attire:
Such as him list, such as eternall fate
Ordainèd hath, he clothes with sinfull mire,>   *flesh*
And sendeth forth to live in mortall state,
Till they againe returne backe by the hinder gate.

33   After that they againe returnèd beene,
     They in that Gardin planted be againe;
     And grow afresh, as they had never seene
     Fleshly corruption, nor mortall paine.
     Some thousand yeares so doen they there remaine;
     And then of him are clad with other hew,>   *forms*
     Or sent into the chaungefull world againe,
     Till thither they returne, where first they grew:
So like a wheele around they runne from old to new.

34   Ne needs there Gardiner to set, or sow,
     To plant or prune: for of their owne accord
     All things, as they created were, doe grow,
     And yet remember well the mightie word,
     Which first was spoken by th'Almightie lord,
     That bad them to increase and multiply:
     Ne doe they need with water of the ford,
     Or of the clouds to moysten their roots dry;
For in themselves eternall moisture they imply.>   *contain*

35   Infinite shapes of creatures there are bred,
     And uncouth> formes, which none yet ever knew,   *unknown, strange*
     And every sort is in a sundry> bed   *separate*
     Set by it selfe, and ranckt in comely rew:>   *row*
     Some fit for reasonable soules t'indew,>   *put on*
     Some made for beasts, some made for birds to weare,
     And all the fruitfull spawne of fishes hew
     In endlesse rancks along enraungèd were,
That seem'd the *Oceán* could not containe them there.

36   Daily they grow, and daily forth are sent
     Into the world, it to replenish more;
     Yet is the stocke not lessenèd, nor spent,
     But still remaines in everlasting store,

As it at first created was of yore,
For in the wide wombe of the world there lyes,
In hatefull darkenesse and in deepe horrore,
An huge eternal *Chaos*, which supplyes
The substances of natures fruitfull progenyes.

37 All things from thence doe their first being fetch,
    And borrow matter, whereof they are made,
    Which when as forme and feature it does ketch,ʾ   *take*
    Becomes a bodie, and doth then invadeʾ   *enter*
    The state of life, out of the grieslyʾ shade.   *ghastly*
    That substance is eterne, and bideth so,
    Ne when the life decayes, and forme does fade,
    Doth it consume, and into nothing go,
But chaungèd is, and often altred to and fro.

38 The substance is not chaunged, nor alterèd,
    But th'onlyʾ forme and outward fashión;ʾ   *only the / appearance*
    For every substance is conditioned
    To change her hew, and sundry formes to don,
    Meet for her temper and complexión:
    For formes are variable and decay,
    By course of kind,ʾ and by occasión;ʾ   *nature / accident*
    And that faire flowre of beautie fades away,
As doth the lilly fresh before the sunny ray.

39 Great enimy to it, and to all the rest,
    That in the *Gardin* of *Adonis* springs,
    Is wicked *Time*, who with his scyth addrest,ʾ   *equipped*
    Does mow the flowring herbes and goodly things,
    And all their glory to the ground downe flings,
    Where they doe wither, and are fowly mard:
    He flyes about, and with his flaggyʾ wings   *drooping*
    Beates downe both leaves and buds without regard,
Ne ever pittie may relent his malice hard.

40 Yet pittie often did the gods relent,
    To see so faire things mard, and spoylèd quight:
    And their great mother *Venus* did lament
    The losse of her deare brood, her deare delight:
    Her hart was pierst with pittie at the sight,
    When walking through the Gardin, them she spyde,

Yet no'teˀ she find redresse for such despight.   *knew not how to*
   For all that lives, is subject to that law:
All things decay in time, and to their end do draw.

41   But were it not, that *Time* their troubler is,
     All that in this delightfull Gardin growes,
     Should happie be, and have immortall bliss.
     For here all plentie, and all pleasure flowes,
     And sweet love gentle fits emongst them throwes,
     Without fell rancor, or fond gealosie;
     Franckly each paramourˀ his lemanˀ knowes.   *lover / mistress*
     Each bird his mate, ne any does envieˀ   *resent*
Their goodly meriment, and gay felicitie.

42   There is continuall spring, and harvest there
     Continuall, both meeting at one time:
     For both the boughes doe laughing blossomes beare,
     And with fresh colours decke the wanton Prime,ˀ   *spring*
     And eke attonce the heavy trees they clime,
     Which seeme to labour under their fruits lode:
     The whiles the joyous birdes make their pastime
     Emongst the shadie leaves, their sweet abode,
And their true loves without suspitionˀ tell abrode.   *fear*

43   Right in the middest of that Paradise,
     There stood a stately Mount, on whose round top
     A gloomy grove of mirtle trees did rise,
     Whose shadie boughes sharpe steele did never lop,
     Nor wicked beasts their tender buds did crop,
     But like a girlond compassèd the hight,
     And from their fruitfull sides sweet gum did drop,
     That all the ground with precious deaw bedight,
Threw forth most dainty odours, and most sweet delight.

44   And in the thickest covert of that shade,
     There was a pleasant arbour, not by art,
     But of the trees owne inclinationˀ made,   *bending*
     Which knitting theirranckeˀ braunches part to part,   *luxuriant*
     With wanton yvie twyne entrayld athwart,
     And Eglantine, and Caprifoleˀ emong,   *honeysuckle*
     Fashiond above within their inmost part,
     That netherˀ *Phœbus* beams could through them throng,   *neither*
Nor *Aeolus* sharp blast could worke them any wrong.

45   And all about grew every sort of flowre,
      To which sad lovers were transformed of yore;
      Fresh *Hyacinthus, Phœbus* paramoure,
      And dearest love,
      Foolish *Narcisse,* that likes the watry shore,
      Sad *Amaranthus,* made a flowre but late,
      Sad *Amaranthus,* in whose purple gore
      Me seemes I see *Amintas* wretched fate,
  To whom sweet Poets verse hath given endlesse date.

46   There wont faire *Venus* often to enjoy
      Her deare *Adonis* joyous company,
      And reape sweet pleasure of the wanton boy;
      There yet, some say, in secret he does ly,
      Lappèd in flowres and pretious spycery,
      By her hid from the world, and from the skill>   *knowledge*
      Of *Stygian* Gods,> which doe her love envy;   *gods of hell*
      But she her selfe, when ever that she will,
  Possesseth him, and of his sweetnesse takes her fill.

47   And sooth it seemes they say: for he may not
      For ever die, and ever burièd bee
      In balefull night, where all things are forgot;
      All be> he subject to mortalitie,   *even though*
      Yet is eterne in mutabilitie,
      And by succession made perpetuall,
      Transformèd oft, and chaungèd diverslie:
      For him the Father of all formes, they call;
  Therefore needs mote he live, that living gives to all.

48   There now he liveth in eternall blis,
      Joying his goddesse, and of her enjoyd:
      Ne feareth he henceforth that foe of his,
      Which with his cruell tuske him deadly cloyd:>   *pierced*
      For that wilde Bore, the which him once annoyd,>   *injured*
      She firmely hath emprisonèd for ay,
      That her sweet love his malice mote avoyd,
      In a strong rocky Cave, which is they say,
  Hewen underneath that Mount, that none him losen> may.   *loose*

49   There now he lives in everlasting joy,
      With many of the Gods in company,
      Which thither haunt,> and with the wingèd boy   *visit*

Sporting himselfe in safe felicity:
Who when he hoth with spoiles and cruelty
Ransackt the world, and in the wofull harts
Of many wretches set his triumphes hye,
Thither resorts, and laying his sad darts
Aside, with faire *Adonis* playes his wanton parts.

50   And his true love faire *Psyche* with him playes,
Faire *Psyche* to him lately reconcyld,
After long troubles and unmeet upbrayes,˃   *unsuitable reproaches*
With which his mother *Venus* her revyld,
And eke himselfe her cruelly exyld:
But now in stedfast love and happy state
She with him lives, and hath him borne a chyld,
Pleasure, that doth both gods and men aggrate,
Pleasure, the daughter of *Cupid* and *Psyche* late.

51   Hither great *Venus* brought this infant faire,
The younger daughter of *Chrysogonee*,
And unto *Psyche* with great trust and care
Committed her, yfosterèd to bee,
And trainèd up in true feminitee:
Who no lesse carefully her tenderèd,
Then her owne daughter *Pleasure*, to whom shee
Made her companion, and her lessonèd
In all the lore of love, and goodly womanhead.

52   In which when she to perfect ripenesse grew,
Of grace and beautie noble Paragone,˃   *model*
She brought her forth into the worldes vew,
To be th'ensample of true love alone,
And Lodestarre of all chaste affectióne,
To all faire Ladies, that doe live on ground.
To Faery court she came, where many one
Admyred her goodly haveour,˃ and found   *behavior*
His feeble hart wide launchèd˃ with loves cruell wound.   *pierced*

53   But she to none of them her love did cast,
Save to the noble knight Sir *Scudamore*,
To whom her loving hart she linkèd fast
In faithfull love, t'abide for evermore,
And for his dearest sake endurèd sore,
Sore trouble of an hainous enimy;

Who her would forcèd have to have forlore⁔   *abandoned*
  Her former love, and stedfast loialty,
As ye may elsewhere read that ruefull history.

Epithalamion

Spenser's hymn for his own marriage, *Epithalamion*, is clearly the finest of
his minor poems, and one of the supreme shorter poems in the language,
worthy to be considered with *Lycidas* and *Ode, Intimations of Immortality*, for, like them, it gives in concise form an epic poet's vision of achieved
peace. Milton finished *Paradise Lost*, and Wordsworth *The Prelude*,
although Wordsworth did not publish it. Spenser wrote only half of his
great poem, leaving us the *Mutabilitie* fragment and the previously published *Epithalamion* as possible indications of how he might have completed the design set forth in his letter to Ralegh.

Ultimately, any hymn celebrating Christian marriage derives from the
Song of Solomon, and from the exaltation of God's marriage to the land
and people in Isaiah. The rites of marriage, Mircea Eliade has shown,
repeat the archetypes of a divine marriage, in which heaven is united with
earth. Spenser takes pains both to associate his own marriage with the
union of Jove and Maia and to dissociate it from the ritual pattern attendant upon other couplings of Jove (with Alcmena, and with night). The
pattern (repeated by Dido and Aeneas in *Aeneid* VI, for instance) is one of
bringing together heaven and earth by storm, so as to renew the fertility of
earth even as the god takes his human bride. By rejecting storm as the
proper setting (lines 326–331) Spenser carefully removes part of the pagan
background he has invoked in the reference to Jove and Maia (lines
307–310). From the love of Jove for Maia came the creation of Hermes,
cleverest of gods, never violent, bearer of good fortune, god of shepherds
and the common people. Of all the gods, Hermes is the most protective,
and Spenser may have felt a prophetic need for protection, even as the
events gathered that were to lead to his death five years later.

The complexity of mythological reference is vital to *Epithalamion*, for
Spenser's poem is more than a joyous celebration, being also a sage and
serious vision of human concord and the end of man. The astonishingly
beautiful first stanza leads into its refrain by an identification of Spenser
and the primal poet Orpheus, who also sang his own marriage hymn, and
all but conquered death through song, almost bringing his bride back from

darkness into the light. The profound joy that is to come later in the poem, with the poet's descendants seen as overcoming death by joining the company of saints, will be the more triumphant for the dark implications of this first stanza. The Muses have their own mishaps, and Orpheus suffered a tragic *sparagmos,* a fate too possible for Spenser in wild Ireland. Out of these barely hinted anxieties the most beautiful of all refrains rises. Orpheus, bereft of his bride, sang to himself in the woods. Spenser, in expectation of his bride, begins to sing to himself, and the first woodland answer will be only the ringing of his echo. But the isolation ends in the next stanza, and the refrain subtly changes, as the woods now answer in echo to a song of joy and solace, sung to the bride by the companions of the wedding. It is as though the first stanza represented the predawn reflections of the poet-bridegroom, musing in Orphic strain. From the second stanza on, the world begins to wake, the morning comes, and with it the greater light of the bride's awakening. Stanza by stanza the world comes to a fuller life, until the bride is described in terms of Solomon's Song, and the temple gates are opened wide for the marriage ceremony.

After the celebration and the moving invocation of night, with its mythological references as mentioned earlier, the poem comes to rest in hushed stanzas of hopefulness and thanksgiving, centering on the rite of marriage as an *imitatio dei,* or renewal of creation. The integral wholeness of the creation is to be restored, and the bringing together again of earth and heaven to be accomplished, only through marriage and its progeny. If *The Faerie Queene* had ended with a marriage between Gloriana and Arthur, the hymn at their festival could not have surpassed Spenser's chant for his own bride, and the thematic significance of that hymn would have differed from this *Epithalamion* probably only in degree. The redemption of nature is through the imagination of concord, and that imagination has never expressed itself more definitely than in Spenser's "Song, made in lieu of many ornaments."

Epithalamion

Ye learnèd sisters which have oftentimes
Beene to me ayding, others to adorne:
Whom ye thought worthy of your gracefull rymes,
That even the greatest did not greatly scorne
To heare theyr names sung in your simple layes,
But joyèd in theyr prayse.
And when ye list> your owne mishaps to mourne, *choose*

Which death, or love, or fortunes wreck did rayse,
Your string could soone to sadder tenor turne,
10   And teach the woods and waters to lament
Your dolefull dreriment.⸲   *grief*
Now lay those sorrowfull complaints aside,
And having all your heads with girland crownd,
Helpe me mine owne loves prayses to resound,
Ne let the same of any be envide:⸲   *grudged*
So Orpheus did for his owne bride,
So I unto my selfe alone will sing,
The woods shall to me answer and my Eccho ring.

Early before the worlds light giving lampe,
20   His golden beame upon the hils doth spred,
Having disperst the nights unchearefull dampe,
Doe ye awake, and with fresh lusty hed,⸲   *vigor*
Go to the bowre of my belovèd love,
My truest turtle dove,
Bid her awake; for Hymen is awake,
And long since ready forth his maske to move,
With his bright Tead⸲ that flames with many a flake,⸲   *torch / spark*
And many a bachelor to waite on him,
In theyr fresh garments trim.
30   Bid her awake therefore and soone her dight,⸲   *dress*
For lo the wishèd day is come at last,
That shall for al the paynes and sorrowes past,
Pay to her usury⸲ of long delight: *interest*
And whylest she doth her dight,
Doe ye to her of joy and solace sing,
That all the woods may answer and your eccho ring.

Bring with you all the Nymphes that you can heare
Both of the rivers and the forrests greene:
And of the sea that neighbours to her neare,
40   Al with gay girlands goodly wel beseene.⸲   *provided*
And let them also with them bring in hand,
Another gay girland
For my fayre love of lillyes and of roses,
Bound truelove wize⸲ with a blew silke riband.   *in a love knot*
And let them make great store of bridale poses,
And let them eeke bring store of other flowers
To deck the bridale bowers.
And let the ground whereas⸲ her foot shall tread,   *where*

For feare the stones her tender foot should wrong
50   Be strewed with fragrant flowers all along,
And diapred⸳ lyke the discolorèd⸳ mead.   *strewn with flowers / multicolored*
Which done, doe at her chambre dore awayt,
For she will waken strayt,
The whiles doe ye this song unto her sing,
The woods shall to you answer and your Eccho ring.

Ye Nymphes of Mulla which with carefull heed,
The silver scaly trouts doe tend full well;
And greedy pikes which use therein to feed,
(Those trouts and pikes all others doo excell)
60   And ye likewise which keepe the rushy lake,
Where none doo fishes take,
Bynd up the locks the which hang scatterd light,
And in his waters which your mirror make,
Byhold your faces as the christall bright,
That when you come whereas my love doth lie,
No blemish she may spie.
And eke ye lightfoot mayds which keepe the deere,
That on the hoary mountayne use to towre,
And the wylde wolves which seeke them to devoure,
70   With your steele darts doo chace from comming neer
Be also present heere,
To helpe to decke her and to help to sing,
That all the woods may answer and your eccho ring.

Wake, now my love, awake; for it is time,
The Rosy Morne long since left Tithones bed,
All ready to her silver coche to clyme,
And Phœbus gins to shew his glorious hed.
Hark how the cheerefull birds do chaunt theyr laies
And carroll of loves praise.
80   The merry Larke hir mattins sings aloft,
The thrush replyes, the Mavis⸳ descant playes.   *thrush*
The Ouzell⸳ shrills, the Ruddock⸳ warbles soft,   *blackbird / robin*
So goodly all agree with sweet consent,
To this dayes merriment.
Ah my deere love why doe ye sleepe thus long,
When meeter were that ye should now awake,
T'awayt the comming of your joyous make,⸳   *mate*
And hearken to the birds lovelearnèd song,

The deawy leaves among.
90   For they of joy and pleasance to you sing,
That all the woods them answer and theyr eccho ring.

My love is now awake out of her dreame,
And her fayre eyes like stars that dimmèd were
With darksome cloud, now shew theyr goodly beams
More bright then Hesperus his head doth rere.
Come now ye damzels, daughters of delight,
Helpe quickly her to dight.
But first come ye fayre houres which were begot
In Joves sweet paradice, of Day and Night,
100   Which doe the seasons of the yeare allot,
And al that ever in this world is fayre
Doe make and still˃ repayre.   *ever*
And ye three handmayds of the Cyprian Queene,
The which doe still adorne her beauties pride,
Helpe to addorne my beautifullest bride:
And as ye her array, still throw betweene
Some graces to be seene,
And as ye use˃ to Venus, to her sing,   *do as a rule*
The whiles the woods shal answer and your eccho ring.

110   Now is my love all ready forth to come,
Let all the virgins therefore well awayt,
And ye fresh boyes that tend upon her groome
Prepare your selves; for he is comming strayt.
Set all your things in seemely good aray
Fit for so joyfull day,
The joyfulst day that ever sunne did see.
Faire Sun, shew forth thy favourable ray,
And let thy lifull˃ heat not fervent be   *life-bestowing*
For feare of burning her sunshyny face,
120   Her beauty to disgrace.
O fayrest Phœbus, father of the Muse,
If ever I did honour thee aright,
Or sing the thing, that mote thy mind delight,
Doe not thy servants simple boone refuse,
But let this day let this one day be myne,
Let all the rest be thine.
Then I thy soverayne prayses loud wil sing,
That all the woods shal answer and theyr eccho ring.

Harke how the Minstrels gin to shrill aloud
130   Their merry Musick that resounds from far,
The pipe, the tabor, and the trembling Croud,⟩   *fiddle*
That well agree withouten breach or jar.⟩   *discord*
But most of all the Damzels doe delite,
When they their tymbrels smyte,
And thereunto doe daunce and carrol sweet,
That all the sences they doe ravish quite,
The whyles the boyes run up and downe the street,
Crying aloud with strong confusèd noyce,⟩   *noise*
As if it were one voyce.
140   Hymen io Hymen, Hymen they do shout,
That even to the heavens theyr shouting shrill
Doth reach, and all the firmament doth fill,
To which the people standing all about,
As in approvance doe thereto applaud
And loud advaunce her laud,⟩   *praise*
And evermore they Hymen Hymen sing,
That al the woods them answer and theyr eccho ring.

Loe where she comes along with portly⟩ pace   *stately*
Lyke Phœbe from her chamber of the East,
150   Arysing forth to run her mighty race,
Clad all in white, that seemes a virgin best.
So well it her beseemes⟩ that ye would weene   *becomes*
Some angell she had beene.
Her long loose yellow locks lyke golden wyre,
Sprinckled with perle, and perling flowres a tweene,
Doe lyke a golden mantle her attyre,
And being crownèd with a girland greene,
Seeme lyke some mayden Queene.
Her modest eyes abashèd to behold
160   So many gazers, as on her do stare,
Upon the lowly ground affixèd are.
Ne dare lift up her countenance too bold,
But blush to heare her prayses sung so loud,
So farre from being proud.
Nathlesse doe ye still loud her prayses sing,
That all the woods may answer and your eccho ring.

Tell me ye merchants daughters did ye see
So fayre a creature in your towne before,
So sweet, so lovely, and so mild as she,

170   Adornd with beautyes grace and vertues store,
      Her goodly eyes lyke Saphyres shining bright,
      Her forehead yvory white,
      Her cheekes lyke apples which the sun hath rudded,⸗   *reddened*
      Her lips lyke cherryes charming men to byte,
      Her brest like to a bowle of creame uncrudded,⸗   *uncurdled*
      Her paps lyke lyllies budded,
      Her snowie necke lyke to a marble towre,
      And all her body like a pallace fayre,
      Ascending uppe with many a stately stayre,
180   To honors seat and chastities sweet bowre.
      Why stand ye still ye virgins in amaze,
      Upon her so to gaze,
      Whiles ye forget your former lay to sing,
      To which the woods did answer and your eccho ring.

      But if ye saw that which no eyes can see,
      The inward beauty of her lively spright,⸗   *spirit*
      Garnisht with heavenly guifts of high degree,
      Much more then would ye wonder at that sight,
      And stand astonisht lyke to those which red⸗   *saw*
190   Medusaes mazeful hed.
      There dwels sweet love and constant chastity,
      Unspotted fayth and comely womanhood,
      Regard of honour and mild modesty,
      There vertue raynes as Queen in royal throne,
      And giveth lawes alone.
      The which the base affections⸗ doe obay,   *passions*
      And yeeld theyr services unto her will,
      Ne thought of thing uncomely ever may
      Thereto approach to tempt her mind to ill.
200   Had ye once seene these her celestial threasures,
      And unrevealèd pleasures,
      Then would ye wonder and her prayses sing,
      That al the woods should answer and your echo ring.

      Open the temple gates unto my love,
      Open them wide that she may enter in,
      And all the postes adorne as doth behove,⸗   *as is fitting*
      And all the pillours deck with girlands trim,
      For to recyve this Saynt with honour dew,
      That commeth in to you.
210   With trembling steps and humble reverence,

She commeth in, before th'almighties vew,
Of her ye virgins learne obedience,
When so ye come into those holy places,
To humble your proud faces:
Bring her up to th'high altar, that she may
The sacred ceremonies there partake,
The which do endlesse matrimony make,
And let the roring Organs loudly play
The praises of the Lord in lively notes,
220   The whiles with hollow throates
The Choristers the joyous Antheme sing,
That al the woods may answere and their eccho ring.

Behold whiles she before the altar stands
Hearing the holy priest that to her speakes
And blesseth her with his two happy hands,
How the red roses flush up in her cheekes,
And the pure snow with goodly vermill stayne,
Like crimsin dyde in grayne,⸌   *thoroughly*
That even th'Angels which continually,
230   About the sacred Altare doe remaine,
Forget their service and about her fly;
Ofte peeping in her face that seemes more fayre,
The more they on it stare.
But her sad⸌ eyes still fastened on the ground,   *grave*
Are governèd with goodly modesty,
That suffers not one looke to glaunce awry,
Which may let in a little thought unsownd.
Why blush ye love to give to me your hand,
The pledge of all our band?⸌   *bond*
240   Sing ye sweet Angels, Alleluya sing,
That all the woods may answere and your eccho ring.

Now al is done; bring home the bride againe,
Bring home the triumph of our victory,
Bring home with you the glory of her gaine,⸌   *of gaining her*
With joyance bring her and with jollity.
Never had man more joyfull day then this,
Whom heaven would heape with blis.
Make feast therefore now all this live long day,
This day for ever to me holy is,
250   Poure out the wine without restraint or stay,
Poure not by cups, but by the belly full,

Poure out to all that wull,⟩   *want*
And sprinkle all the postes and wals with wine,
That they may sweat, and drunken be withall.
Crowne ye God Bacchus with a coronall,⟩   *garland*
And Hymen also crowne with wreathes of vine,
And let the Graces daunce unto the rest;
For they can doo it best:
The whiles the maydens doe theyr carroll sing,
260   To which the woods shal answer and theyr eccho ring.

Ring ye the bels, ye yong men of the towne,
And leave your wonted⟩ labors for this day: *usual*
This day is holy; doe ye write it downe,
That ye for ever it remember may.
This day the sunne is in his chiefest hight,
With Barnaby the bright,
From whence declining daily by degrees,
He somewhat loseth of his heat and light,
When once the Crab behind his back he sees.
270   But for this time it ill ordainèd was,
To chose the longest day in all the yeare,
And shortest night, when longest fitter weare:
Yet never day so long, but late⟩ would passe.   *at last*
Ring ye the bels, to make it weare away,
And bonefiers⟩ make all day,   *midsummer bonfires*
And daunce about them, and about them sing:
That all the woods may answer, and your eccho ring.

Ah when will this long weary day have end,
And lende me leave to come unto my love?
280   How slowly do the houres theyr numbers spend?
How slowly does sad Time his feathers move?
Hast thee O fayrest Planet to thy home
Within the Westerne fome:
Thy tyrèd steedes long since have need of rest.
Long though it be, at last I see it gloome,⟩   *darken*
And the bright evening star with golden creast
Appeare out of the East.
Fayre childe of beauty, glorious lampe of love
That all the host of heaven in rankes doost lead,
290   And guydest lovers through the nightes dread,
How chearefully thou lookest from above,
And seemst to laugh atweene thy twinkling light

As joying in the sight
Of these glad many which for joy doe sing,
That all the woods them answer and their eccho ring.

Now ceasse ye damsels your delights forepast;˃   *over*
Enough is it, that all the day was youres:
Now day is doen, and night is nighing fast:
Now bring the Bryde into the brydall boures.
300   Now night is come, now soone her disaray,
And in her bed her lay;
Lay her in lillies and in violets,
And silken courteins over her display,˃   *spread*
And odourd sheetes, and Arras˃ coverlets.   *tapestry*
Behold how goodly my faire love does ly
In proud humility;
Like unto Maia, when as Jove her tooke,
In Tempe, lying on the flowry gras,
Twixt sleepe and wake, after she weary was,
310   With bathing in the Acidalian brooke.
Now it is night, ye damsels may be gon,
And leave my love alone,
And leave likewise your former lay to sing:
The woods no more shal answere, nor your eccho ring.

Now welcome night, thou night so long expected,
That long daies labour doest at last defray,˃   *pay for*
And all my cares, which cruell love collected,
Hast sumd in one, and cancellèd for aye:
Spread thy broad wing over my love and me,
320   That no man may us see,
And in thy sable mantle us enwrap,
From feare of perrill and foule horror free.
Let no false treason seeke us to entrap,
Nor any dread disquiet once annoy
The safety of our joy:
But let the night be calme and quietsome,
Without tempestuous storms or sad afray:
Lyke as when Jove with fayre Alcmena lay,
When he begot the great Tirynthian groome:
330   Or lyke as when he with thy selfe did lie,
And begot Majesty.
And let the mayds and yongmen cease to sing:
Ne let the woods them answer, nor theyr eccho ring.

Let no lamenting cryes, nor dolefull teares,
Be heard all night within nor yet without:
Ne let false whispers, breeding hidden feares,
Breake gentle sleepe with misconceivèd dout.
Let no deluding dreames, nor dreadful sights
Make sudden sad affrights;
340   Ne let housefyres, nor lightnings helpelesse⟩ harmes,   *incurable*
Ne let the Pouke, nor other evill sprights,
Ne let mischívous witches with theyr charmes,
Ne let hob Goblins, names whose sence we see not,
Fray us with things that be not,
Let not the shriech Oule, nor the Storke be heard:
Nor the night Raven that still⟩ deadly yels,   *ever*
Nor damnèd ghosts cald up with mighty spels,
Nor griesly vultures make us once affeard:
Ne let th'unpleasant Quyre of Frogs still⟩ croking   *always*
350   Make us to wish theyr choking.
Let none of these theyr drery accents sing;
Ne let the woods them answer, nor theyr eccho ring.

But let stil Silence trew night watches keepe,
That sacred peace may in assurance rayne,
And tymely sleep, when it is tyme to sleepe,
May poure his limbs forth on your pleasant playne,
The whiles an hundred little wingèd loves,
Like divers fethered doves,
Shall fly and flutter round about your bed,
360   And in the secret darke, that⟩ none reproves,   *when*
Their prety stealthes shal worke, and snares shal spread
To filch away sweet snatches of delight,
Conceald through covert night.
Ye sonnes of Venus, play your sports at will,
For greedy pleasure, carelesse of your toyes,⟩   *tricks*
Thinks more upon her paradise of joyes,
Then what ye do, albe it good or ill.
All night therefore attend your merry play,
For it will soone be day:
370   Now none doth hinder you, that say or sing,
Ne will the woods now answer, nor your Eccho ring.

Who is the same, which at my window peepes?
Or whose is that faire face, that shines so bright,
Is it not Cinthia, she that never sleepes,

But walkes about high heaven al the night?
O fayrest goddesse, do thou not envy
My love with me to spy:
For thou likewise didst love, though now unthought,>   *unremembered*
And for a fleece of woll, which privily,
380   The Latmian shephard once unto thee brought,
His pleasures with thee wrought.
Therefore to us be favorable now;
And sith of wemens labours thou hast charge,
And generation goodly dost enlarge,
Encline thy will t'effect our wishfull vow,
And the chast wombe informe with timely seed,
That may our comfort breed:
Till which we cease our hopefull hap> to sing,   *luck*
Ne let the woods us answere, nor our Eccho ring.

390   And thou great Juno, which with awful might
The lawes of wedlock still dost patronize,
And the religion> of the faith first plight>   *bond / pledged*
With sacred rites hast taught to solemnize:
And eeke for comfort often callèd art
Of women in their smart,>   *labor pains*
Eternally bind thou this lovely band,
And all thy blessings unto us impart.
And thou glad Genius, in whose gentle hand,
The bridale bowre and geniall bed remaine,
400   Without blemish or staine,
And the sweet pleasures of theyr loves delight
With secret ayde doest succour and supply,
Till they bring forth the fruitfull progeny,
Send us the timely fruit of this same night.
And thou fayre Hebe, and thou Hymen free,
Grant that it may so be.
Til which we cease your further prayse to sing,
Ne any woods shal answer, nor your Eccho ring.

And ye high heavens, the temple of the gods,
410   In which a thousand torches flaming bright
Doe burne, that to us wretched earthly clods,
In dreadful darknesse lend desirèd light;
And all ye powers which in the same remayne,
More then we men can fayne,
Poure out your blessing on us plentiously,

And happy influence upon us raine,
That we may raise a large posterity,
Which from the earth, which they may long possesse,
With lasting happinesse,
420   Up to your haughty pallaces may mount,
And for the guerdon of theyr glorious merit
May heavenly tabernacles there inherit,
Of blessèd Saints for to increase the count.
So let us rest, sweet love, in hope of this,
And cease till then our tymely joyes to sing,
The woods no more us answer, nor our eccho ring.

Song made in lieu of many ornaments,˃   *wedding presents*
With which my love should duly have bene dect,˃   *decked*
Which cutting off through hasty accidents,
430   Ye would not stay your dew time to expect,
But promist both to recompens,
Be unto her a goodly ornament,
And for short time an endlesse moniment.

     1595

Prothalamion

The relative coldness of *Prothalamion*, as compared to the warmly personal *Epithalamion*, might cause this lesser and later "Spousall Verse" to be undervalued. The *Prothalamion* is by intention a slighter poem than Spenser's song for his own bride, but its exquisite courtliness and appearance of easy power are unsurpassed in the expression of a deliberate and disciplined joy.

The occasion of the *Prothalamion* is a ceremony of betrothal, the mutually binding promises of human concord. Against the concord of nature at the poem's opening Spenser counterpoints his own "sullein care," the frustration of the courtier and his vain expectations. Walking forth along the Thames, the dejected poet eases his pain by observing the flowers as images of potential concord. The visions of the nymphs and the swans follow, to form the poem's substance, its imminent hope of actual concord, shining more brightly against the perpetually felt but subdued melancholy of the poet. The myth of river-marriage, although a convention, had a personal meaning for Spenser, who returns to it so often in his poetry. The teeming life in the Garden of Adonis, lavishly freshening human substance, finds its analogue in physical nature in the joining together of rivers, a cyclic renewal that can both suffer mutability and defiantly redeem time. In the *Prothalamion* the dark undersong tells of mutability—the poet's cares; the fall of his patron, "that great lord," Leicester; the decay through pride of the Templars—while the high song dominating the poem joyously acclaims a coming fruition, in the impending marriages, and in the burgeoning greatness of Essex. The emotional counterpoint is resolved in the famous and beautiful refrain, where the first line promises the consummation of joy and the second hints at a deferred turbulence, the world of troubles soon to come again upon the poetic celebrant of concord.

Prothalamion

1

Calme was the day, and through the trembling ayre,
Sweete breathing *Zephyrus* did softly play
A gentle spirit, that lightly did delay
Hot *Titans* beames, which then did glyster fayre:
5   When I whom sullein care,
Through discontent of my long fruitlesse stay
In Princes Court, and expectation vayne
Of idle hopes, which still doe fly away,
Like empty shaddowes, did aflict my brayne,
10 Walkt forth to ease my payne
Along the shoare of silver streaming *Themmes,*
Whose rutty Bancke, the which his River hemmes,
Was paynted all with variable flowers,
And all the meades adornd with daintie gemmes,
15 Fit to decke maydens bowres,
And crowne their Paramours,
Against the Brydale day, which is not long:
   Sweete *Themmes* runne softly, till I end my Song.

2

There, in a Meadow, by the Rivers side,
20 A Flocke of *Nymphes* I chaunced to espy,
All lovely Daughters of the Flood thereby,
With goodly greenish locks all loose untyde,
As each had bene a Bryde,

And each one had a little wicker basket,
25   Made of fine twigs entrayled curiously,
In which they gathered flowers to fill their flasket:
And with fine Fingers, cropt full feateously
The tender stalkes on hye.
Of every sort, which in that Meadow grew,
30   They gathered some; the Violet pallid blew,
The little Dazie, that at evening closes,
The virgin Lillie, and the Primrose trew,
With store of vermeil Roses,
To decke their Bridegromes posies,
35   Against the Brydale day, which was not long:
     Sweete *Themmes* runne softly, till I end my Song.

     3
With that I saw two Swannes of goodly hewe,
Come softly swimming downe along the Lee;
Two fairer Birds I yet did never see:
40   The snow which doth the top of *Pindus* strew,
Did never whiter shew,
Nor *Jove* himselfe when he a Swan would be
For love of *Leda*, whiter did appeare:
Yet *Leda* was they say as white as he,
45   Yet not so white as these, nor nothing neare;
So purely white they were,
That even the gentle streame, the which them bare,
Seem'd foule to them, and bad his billowes spare
To wet their silken feathers, least they might
50   Soyle their fayre plumes with water not so fayre,
And marre their beauties bright,
That shone as heavens light,
Against their Brydale day, which was not long:
     Sweete *Themmes* runne softly, till I end my Song.

     4
55   Eftsoones the *Nymphes*, which now had Flowers their fill,
Ran all in haste, to see that silver brood,
As they came floating on the Christal Flood,
Whom when they sawe, they stood amazed still,
Their wondring eyes to fill,
60   Them seem'd they never saw a sight so fayre,
Of Fowles so lovely, that they sure did deeme

Them heavenly borne, or to be that same payre
Which through the Skie draw *Venus* silver Teeme,
For sure they did not seeme
65   To be begot of any earthly Seede,
But rather Angels or of Angels breede:
Yet were they bred of *Somers-heat* they say,
In sweetest Season, when each Flower and weede
The earth did fresh aray,
70   So fresh they seem'd as day,
Even as their Brydale day, which was not long:
    Sweete *Themmes* runne softly till I end my Song.

5

Then forth they all out of their baskets drew,
Great store of Flowers, the honour of the field,
75   That to the sense did fragrant odours yield,
All which upon those goodly Birds they threw,
And all the Waves did strew,
That like old *Peneus* Waters they did seeme,
When downe along by pleasant *Tempes* shore
80   Scattred with Flowres, through *Thessaly* they streeme,
That they appeare through Lillies plenteous store,
Like a Brydes Chamber flore:
Two of those *Nymphes,* meane while, two Garlands bound,
Of freshest Flowres which in that Mead they found,
85   The which presenting all in trim Array,
Their snowie Foreheads therewithall they crownd,
Whil'st one did sing this Lay,
Prepar'd against that Day,
Against their Brydale day, which was not long:
90   Sweete *Themmes* runne softly till I end my Song.

6

Ye gentle Birdes, the worlds faire ornament,
And heavens glorie, whom this happie hower
Doth leade unto your lovers blisfull bower,
Joy may you have and gentle hearts content
95   Of your loves couplement:
And let faire *Venus,* that is Queene of love,
With her heart-quelling Sonne upon you smile,
Whose smile they say, hath vertue to remove
All Loves dislike, and friendships faultie guile
100   For ever to assoile.

Let endlesse Peace your steadfast hearts accord,
And blessed Plentie wait upon your bord,
And let your bed with pleasures chast abound,
That fruitfull issue may to you afford,
105   Which may your foes confound,
And make your joyes redound,
Upon your Brydale day, which is not long:
      Sweete *Themmes* run softly, till I end my Song.

      7

So ended she; and all the rest around
110   To her redoubled that her undersong,
Which said, their bridale daye should not be long.
And gentle Eccho from the neighbour ground,
Their accents did resound.
So forth those joyous Birdes did passe along,
115   Adowne the Lee, that to them murmurde low,
As he would speake, but that he lackt a tong,
Yeat did by signes his glad affection show,
Making his streame run slow.
And all the foule which in his flood did dwell
120   Gan flock about these twaine, that did excell
The rest, so far, as *Cynthia* doth shend
The lesser starres. So they enranged well,
Did on those two attend,
And their best service lend,
125   Against their wedding day, which was not long:
      Sweete *Themmes* run softly, till I end my song.

      8

At length they all to mery *London* came,
To mery London, my most kyndly Nurse,
That to me gave this Lifes first native sourse:
130   Though from another place I take my name,
An house of auncient fame.
There when they came, whereas those bricky towres,
The which on *Themmes* brode aged backe doe ryde,
Where now the studious Lawyers have their bowers,
135   There whylome wont the Templer Knights to byde,
Till they decayd through pride:
Next whereunto there standes a stately place,
Where oft I gayned giftes and goodly grace
Of that great Lord, which therein wont to dwell,

140 Whose want too well, now feeles my freendles case:
But Ah here fits not well
Olde woes but joyes to tell
Against the bridale daye which is not long:
 Sweete *Themmes* runne softly till I end my Song.

  9

145 Yet therein now doth lodge a noble Peer,
Great *Englands* glory and the Worlds wide wonder,
Whose dreadfull name, late through all *Spaine* did thunder,
And *Hercules* two pillors standing neere,
Did make to quake and feare:
150 Faire branch of Honor, flower of Chevalrie,
That fillest *England* with thy triumphes fame,
Joy have thou of thy noble victorie,
And endlesse happinesse of thine owne name
That promiseth the same:
155 That through thy prowesse and victorious armes,
Thy country may be freed from forraine harmes:
And great *Elisaes* glorious name may ring
Through al the world, fil'd with thy wide Alarmes,
Which some brave muse may sing
160 To ages following,
Upon the Brydale day, which is not long:
 Sweete *Themmes* runne softly till I end my Song.

  10

From those high Towers, this noble Lord issuing,
Like Radiant *Hesper* when his golden hayre
165 In th'*Ocean* billowes he hath Bathed fayre,
Descended to the Rivers open vewing,
With a great traine ensuing.
Above the rest were goodly to bee seene
Two gentle Knights of lovely face and feature
170 Beseeming well the bower of anie Queene,
With gifts of wit and ornaments of nature,
Fit for so goodly stature:
That like the twins of *Jove* they seem'd in sight,
Which decke the Bauldricke of the Heavens bright.
175 They two forth pacing to the Rivers side,
Received those two faire Brides, their Loves delight,
Which at th'appointed tyde,

Each one did make his Bryde,
Against their Brydale day, which is not long:
    Sweete *Themmes* runne softly, till I end my Song.

180

FINIS.

SIR WALTER RALEGH

1552–1618

EDMUND SPENSER, a great and elaborate poet, who wrongly seems too remote or baroque to some among us, was a friend and follower of the magnificent Sir Walter Ralegh—adventurer, courtier, soldier, and sailor, founder of the first colony in Virginia, prisoner in the Tower of London for thirteen years, and at sixty-six beheaded for treason by order of King James I. A marvelous sequence from *The Faerie Queen,* depicting the mythological Garden of Adonis, is in this book, as is an equally marvelous fragment from Ralegh's *The 11th: and last booke of the Ocean to Scinthia,* a great lament for the loss of Queen Elizabeth's love and favor:

> The blossumes fallen, the sapp gon from the tree,
> The broken monuments of my great desires,
> From thes so lost what may th' affections bee,
> What heat in Cynders of extinguisht fiers?
>
> Lost in the mudd of those hygh flowinge streames
> Which through more fayrer feilds ther courses bend,
> Slayne with sealf thoughts, amasde in fearfull dreams,
> Woes without date, discumforts without end,
>
> From frutfull trees I gather withred leues
> And glean the broken eares with misers hands,
> Who sumetyme did inioy the waighty sheves
> I seek faire floures amidd the brinish sand.

I rarely get out of my head: "The broken monuments of my great desires," a line universal in its plangency and wounded pride. John Aubrey, in his *Brief Lives* (left unpublished at his death in 1697), greatly admires Ralegh, but says that his blemish "was that he was damnable proud." Queen Elizabeth's "Shepherd of the Ocean" orchestrates his abandonment by Cynthia (Scinthia), the Virgin Queen in whose favor he had invested his "great desires."

Ralegh himself can seem more a narrative poem or stage tragedy than a historical personage. He is Shakespeare's only contemporary who can compete as a work of the imagination with Falstaff and Hamlet, Iago and Cleopatra. Ralegh could have been a great poet and a great statesman: he threw it all away and became a broken monument of his great desires.

Ralegh is the antithesis of Shakespeare: the Shepherd of the Ocean was the most charismatic personality of his era, outshining the equally tragic Earl of Essex. Shakespeare, even in the sonnets, represents himself as having no personality at all. This self-evasion has augmented the lunatic legions of the Oxfordians, who seem not to care that we have a few indubitable poems by Edward de Vere, 17th Earl of Oxford. These pale lyrics show that the great aristocrat could not write his way out of a paper bag. But nothing daunts the Oxfordians, not even the Earl's death in 1604, the year Shakespeare composed *Measure for Measure* and *Othello*. As for Shakespeare from 1605 to 1613, which includes *King Lear, Macbeth, Antony and Cleopatra, The Winter's Tale,* and *The Tempest,* the Oxfordians remain undaunted. The assiduous Earl left all these (and many more) in manuscript, and the wily Stratfordian pilfered them all!

Ralegh, that walking poem, was Elizabeth's favorite from 1583 through 1592, when she cast him out, supposedly for his feasting upon the Queen's Maids of Honor. Subsequently in and out of the Queen's grace, he suffered greatly under James I, who gave up inflicting fresh indignities upon Ralegh only by beheading him on false charges.

Time has restored Ralegh's honor, but not his poetry, unpublished until 1813, and then in an edition replete with work not his own. Accurate editions did not come until 1845 and 1870, which first printed *The Ocean to Cynthia.*

My anthology, *Best Poems,* adds to *The Ocean to Cynthia* the reply to Marlowe's "Passionate Shepherd." Superb and individual as Ralegh's poetry is, I urge that we take it as emblematic of poetry itself. Even if we had his lost work, Ralegh could not compete with his astounding contemporaries: Spenser and Marlowe, Donne and Jonson, setting aside Shakespeare, with whom no one (except Dante) could hope to contend. And yet the mystery of Ralegh's charisma gets into his poems, and shows us clearly one of the uses of great poetry: each of us, in turn, can find in it the broken monuments of her or his great desires.

✣   ✣   ✣

from The Ocean to Cynthia

XXIV

The 11th: and last booke of the Ocean to Scinthia

Sufficeth it to yow my ioyes interred,
In simpell wordes that I my woes cumplayne,
Yow that then died when first my fancy erred,
Ioyes vnder dust that never live agayne.

5   If to the liuinge weare my muse adressed,
Or did my minde her own spirrit still inhold,
Weare not my livinge passion so repressed,
As to the dead, the dead did thes vnfold,

Sume sweeter wordes, sume more becumming vers,
10 Should wittness my myshapp in hygher kynd,
But my loues wounds, my fancy in the hearse,
The Idea but restinge, of a wasted minde,

The blossumes fallen, the sapp gon from the tree,
The broken monuments of my great desires,
15 From thes so lost what may th' affections bee,
What heat in Cynders of extinguisht fiers?

Lost in the mudd of thos hygh flowinge streames
Which through more fayrer feilds ther courses bend,
Slayne with sealf thoughts, amasde in fearfull dreams,
20 Woes without date, discumforts without end,

From frutfull trees I gather withred leues
And glean the broken eares with misers hands,
Who sumetyme did inioy the waighty sheves
I seeke faire floures amidd the brinish sand.

25 All in the shade yeven in the faire soon dayes
Vnder thos healthless trees I sytt alone,

Wher ioyfull byrdds singe neather lovely layes
Nor Phillomen recounts her direfull mone.

No feedinge flockes, no sheapherds cumpunye
30   That might renew my dollorus consayte,
While happy then, while loue and fantasye
Confinde my thoughts onn that faire flock to waite;

No pleasinge streames fast to the ocean wendinge
The messengers sumetymes of my great woe,
35   But all onn yearth as from the colde stormes bendinge
Shrinck from my thoughts in hygh heauens and below.

Oh hopefull loue my obiect, and invention,
Oh, trew desire the spurr of my consayte,
Oh, worthiest spirrit, my minds impulsion,
40   Oh, eyes transpersant, my affections bayte,

Oh, princely forme, my fancies adamande,
Deuine consayte, my paynes acceptance,
Oh, all in onn, oh heaven on yearth transparant,
The seat of ioyes, and loues abundance!

45   Out of that mass of mirakells, my Muse,
Gathered thos floures, to her pure sences pleasinge,
Out of her eyes (the store of ioyes) did chuse
Equall delights, my sorrowes counterpoysinge.

Her regall lookes, my rigarus sythes suppressed,
Small dropes of ioies, sweetned great worlds of woes,
51   One gladsume day a thowsand cares redressed.
Whom Loue defends, what fortune overthrowes?

When shee did well, what did ther elce amiss?
When shee did ill what empires could haue pleased?
55   No other poure effectinge wo, or bliss,
Shee gave, shee tooke, shee wounded, shee apeased.

The honor of her loue, Loue still devisinge,
Woundinge my mind with contrary consayte,
Transferde it sealf sumetyme to her aspiringe
60   Sumetyme the trumpett of her thoughts retrayt;

To seeke new worlds, for golde, for prayse, for glory,
To try desire, to try loue seuered farr,
When I was gonn shee sent her memory
More stronge then weare ten thowsand shipps of warr,

65   To call mee back, to leue great honors thought,
To leue my frinds, my fortune, my attempte,
To leue the purpose I so longe had sought
And holde both cares, and cumforts in contempt.

Such heat in Ize, such fier in frost remaynde,
70   Such trust in doubt, such cumfort in dispaire,
Mich like the gentell Lamm, though lately waynde,
Playes with the dug though finds no cumfort ther.

But as a boddy violently slayne
Retayneath warmth although the spirrit be gonn,
75   And by a poure in nature moves agayne
Till it be layd below the fatall stone; . . .

．　　．　　．

XXV

***The end of the bookes, of the Oceans love to Scinthia, and the
beginninge of the 12 Boock, entreatinge of Sorrow***

My dayes delights, my springetyme ioies fordvnn,
Which in the dawne, and risinge soonn of youth
Had their creation, and weare first begunn,

Do in the yeveninge, and the winter sadd,
5   Present my minde, which takes my tymes accompt,
The greif remayninge of the ioy it had.

My tymes that then rann ore them sealves in thes,
And now runn out in others happines,
Bring vnto thos new ioyes, and new borne dayes.

10   So could shee not, if shee weare not the soonn,
Which sees the birth, and buriall, of all elce,
And holds that poure, with which shee first begvnn;

Levinge each withered boddy to be torne
By fortune, and by tymes tempestius,
15   Which by her vertu, once faire frute have borne,

Knowinge shee cann renew, and cann create
Green from the grovnde, and floures, yeven out of stone,
By vertu lastinge over tyme and date,

Levinge vs only woe, which like the moss,
20 Havinge cumpassion of vnburied bones
Cleaves to mischance, and vnrepayred loss.

For tender stalkes——

CECIL PAPERS 144, HATFIELD HOUSE

Answer to Marlowe

The Nimphs reply to the Sheepheard

If all the world and loue were young,
And truth in euery Sheepheards tongue,
These pretty pleasures might me moue,
To liue with thee, and be thy loue.

5   Time driues the flocks from field to fold,
When Riuers rage, and Rocks grow cold,
And Philomell becommeth dombe,
The rest complaines of cares to come.

The flowers doe fade, and wanton fieldes,
10 To wayward winter reckoning yeeldes,
A honny tongue, a hart of gall,
Is fancies spring, but sorrowes fall.

Thy gownes, thy shooes, thy beds of Roses,
Thy cap, thy kirtle, and thy poesies,
15 Soone breake, soone wither, soone forgotten:
In follie ripe, in reason rotten.

Thy belt of straw and Iuie buddes,
Thy Corall claspes and Amber studdes,
All these in mee no meanes can moue,
20 To come to thee, and be thy loue.

But could youth last, and loue still breede,
Had ioyes no date, nor age no neede,

Then these delights my minde might moue,
To liue with thee, and be thy loue.
ENGLANDS HELICON, 1600

CHIDIOCK TICHBORNE

1558–1586

A PLOTTER AGAINST Queen Elizabeth I, Tichborne was imprisoned in the Tower of London before his execution. Supposedly, he composed this in the Tower on the eve of execution. This became one of the most popular poems of the Age of Elizabeth, and several musical settings of it remain extant.

Its wide circulation, whoever wrote it, testified to its immediacy and its substantial pathos.

✦   ✦   ✦

Tichborne's Elegy

My prime of youth is but a frost of cares,
My feast of joy is but a dish of pain,
My crop of corn is but a field of tares,
And all my good is but vain hope of gain;
The day is past, and yet I saw no sun,
And now I live, and now my life is done.

My tale was heard and yet it was not told,
My fruit is fallen and yet my leaves are green,
My youth is spent and yet I am not old,
I saw the world and yet I was not seen;
My thread is cut and yet it is not spun,
And now I live, and now my life is done.

I sought my death and found it in my womb,
I looked for life and saw it was a shade,

I trod the earth and knew it was my tomb,
And now I die, and now I was but made;
My glass is full, and now my glass is run,
And now I live, and now my life is done.

  1586

ROBERT SOUTHWELL

1561–1595

THE REVEREND ROBERT SOUTHWELL, S.J., one of the most famous of Jesuit martyrs, went abroad to study at Douai, a gathering place for Catholic exiles, and then resided in Rome, where he was received into the Jesuit order. He heroically returned to England, to serve as a missionary priest, and worked in London, in several secret residences. Captured and jailed in 1592, he was convicted of treason and hanged in 1595. His poems were published posthumously.

Southwell is best when he meditates upon the Nativity, as in the poem "New Prince, New Pomp." His masterpiece in this mode is given here, the extraordinary "The Burning Babe," much admired by Ben Jonson, a severe critic.

⚘   ⚘   ⚘

The Burning Babe

As I in hoary winter's night stood shivering in the snow,
Surprised I was with sudden heat which made my heart to glow;
And lifting up a fearful eye to view what fire was near,
A pretty babe all burning bright did in the air appear;
Who, scorchèd with excessive heat, such floods of tears did shed
As though his floods should quench his flames which with his tears were fed.
"Alas," quoth he, "but newly born in fiery heats I fry,
Yet none approach to warm their hearts or feel my fire but I!
My faultless breast the furnace is, the fuel wounding thorns,

10 Love is the fire, and sighs the smoke, the ashes shame and scorns;
The fuel justice layeth on, and mercy blows the coals,
The metal in this furnace wrought are men's defiled souls,
For which, as now on fire I am to work them to their good,
So will I melt into a bath to wash them in my blood."
With this he vanished out of sight and swiftly shrunk away,
And straight I callèd unto mind that it was Christmas day.

1602

CHRISTOPHER MARLOWE

1564–1593

ONE CAN CHOOSE 1587 as an arbitrary date to begin the richest eighty years of poetry in English. Christopher Marlowe's *Tamburlaine* was then first performed, perhaps with Shakespeare in the audience, though we do not know when the greatest of poets first arrived in London: 1589 seems to me rather too late, even as an outward limit. The first three books of Spenser's *Faerie Queene* were published in 1590. In the early 1590s, Donne wrote many of the *Songs and Sonnets*, to be published only posthumously. By 1595, at the latest, Shakespeare was at his first full greatness, joined by Jonson at his strongest in *Volpone* (1606). The Tribe of Ben— disciples of the lyric and epigrammatic Jonson—included Robert Herrick, Thomas Carew, and Richard Lovelace. Andrew Marvell, a poetic party of one, wrote his lyrics by the 1650s, coming after the posthumous publication of George Herbert's poetry in 1633. Richard Crashaw and Henry Vaughan published by the 1650s. Milton's *Comus* was composed in 1634; *Paradise Lost,* dictated by the blind poet, was finished by 1665, seventy-eight years after Marlowe first shattered his London audiences.

Certainly, in the language's poetry, nothing else matches the period from 1587 to 1665 in England: Marlowe, Spenser, Shakespeare, Donne, Jonson, Marvell, Herbert, Milton. Eight great poets is an extraordinary panoply for eighty years. There is, as competition, only the extraordinary phenomenon of the High Romantics, six major poets in the brief span of twenty-five years from Blake's *Songs of Innocence* (1789) through the death of Byron in 1824. Shakespeare is the difference, transcending all others, as is Milton, outmeasuring even Blake and Wordsworth, Shelley and Keats.

Christopher Marlowe was as flamboyant and violent as Shakespeare (evidently) was colorless and peaceful. Only six years passed between the first part of *Tamburlaine the Great* and Marlowe's termination, with maximum prejudice, by Sir Francis Walsingham's secret service, the Elizabethan C.I.A. Even as an undergraduate, Marlowe operated abroad as Walsingham's agent against Catholic plotters who sought to eliminate Elizabeth. A street fighter, barely concealed heretic, and homosexual, Marlowe knew too much, and was too unstable to be trusted. Set up for a final tavern brawl, with three other agents, Marlowe died horribly of a dagger thrust to his eye. His presence haunts Shakespeare's plays long after his influence had been absorbed and transcended. I still maintain—though I have convinced no Shakespearean scholars—that Edmund in *King Lear* is Shakespeare's final vision of Marlowe.

I have given extracts from *Tamburlaine*. Marlowe unfolded, while Shakespeare developed. I do not think that Marlowe would have changed much, even had he been given the quarter-century of composition that Shakespeare enjoyed after his precursor's brutal death.

The chorus ends *Doctor Faustus* with what may be Marlowe's ironic self-elegy:

> Cut is the branch that might have grown full straight,
> And burnèd is Apollo's laurel bough,
> That sometime grew within this learnèd man.
> Faustus is gone: regard his hellish fall,
> Whose fiendful fortune may exhort the wise
> Only to wonder at unlawful things,
> Whose deepness doth entice such forward wits,
> To practice more than heavenly power permits.

❧   ❧   ❧

from Tamburlaine

30   TAMBURLAINE Now clear the triple region of the air,
    And let the Majesty of Heaven behold
    Their scourge and terror tread on emperors.
    Smile, stars that reign'd at my nativity,

And dim the brightness of their neighbour lamps;
Disdain to borrow light of Cynthia!
For I, the chiefest lamp of all the earth,
First rising in the east with mild aspect,
But fixed now in the meridian line,
Will send up fire to your turning spheres,
40   And cause the sun to borrow light of you.
My sword struck fire from his coat of steel
Even in Bithynia, when I took this Turk;
As when a fiery exhalation,
Wrapt in the bowels of a freezing cloud,
Fighting for passage, make[s] the welkin crack,
And casts a flash of lightning to the earth.
But ere I march to wealthy Persia,
Or leave Damascus and th' Egyptian fields,
As was the fame of Clymene's brain-sick son
50   That almost brent the axle-tree of heaven,
So shall our swords, our lances, and our shot
Fill all the air with fiery meteors.
Then, when the sky shall wax as red as blood,
It shall be said I made it red myself,
To make me think of naught but blood and war.

.   .   .

TAMBURLAINE   Black is the beauty of the brightest day;
The golden ball of heaven's eternal fire,
That danc'd with glory on the silver waves,
Now wants the fuel that inflam'd his beams,
And all with faintness and for foul disgrace,
He binds his temples with a frowning cloud,
Ready to darken earth with endless night.
Zenocrate, that gave him light and life,
Whose eyes shot fire from their ivory bowers,
10   And temper'd every soul with lively heat,
Now by the malice of the angry skies,
Whose jealousy admits no second mate,
Draws in the comfort of her latest breath,
All dazzled with the hellish mists of death.
Now walk the angels on the walls of heaven,
As sentinels to warn th' immortal souls
To entertain divine Zenocrate:
Apollo, Cynthia, and the ceaseless lamps
That gently look'd upon this loathsome earth,

20   Shine downwards now no more, but deck the heavens
To entertain divine Zenocrate:
The crystal springs, whose taste illuminates
Refined eyes with an eternal sight,
Like tried silver run through Paradise
To entertain divine Zenocrate:
The cherubins and holy seraphins,
That sing and play before the King of Kings,
Use all their voices and their instruments
To entertain divine Zenocrate:
And in this sweet and curious harmony,
The god that tunes this music to our souls
Holds out his hand in highest majesty
To entertain divine Zenocrate.
Then let some holy trance convey my thoughts
Up to the palace of th' empyreal heaven,
That this my life may be as short to me
As are the days of sweet Zenocrate.

.   .   .

TAMBURLAINE   Holla, ye pamper'd jades of Asia!
What, can ye draw but twenty miles a day,
And have so proud a chariot at your heels,
And such a coachman as great Tamburlaine,
But from Asphaltis, where I conquer'd you,
To Byron here, where thus I honour you?
The horse that guide the golden eye of heaven,
And blow the morning from their nostrils,
Making their fiery gait above the clouds,
10   Are not so honour'd in their governor
As you, ye slaves, in mighty Tamburlaine.
The headstrong jades of Thrace Alcides tam'd,
The King Ægeus fed with human flesh,
And made so wanton that they knew their strengths,
Were not subdu'd with valour more divine
Than you by this unconquer'd arm of mine.
To make you fierce, and fit my appetite,
You shall be fed with flesh as raw as blood,
And drink in pails the strongest muscadel.
20   If you can live with it, then live, and draw
My chariot swifter than the racking clouds;
If not, then die like beasts, and fit for naught
But perches for the black and fatal ravens.

Thus am I right the scourge of highest Jove;
And see the figure of my dignity,
By which I hold my name and majesty!

The Passionate Shepherd to His Love

Come live with me and be my love,
And we will all the pleasures prove
That valleys, groves, hills, and fields,
Woods, or steepy mountain yields.

And we will sit upon the rocks,
Seeing the shepherds feed their flocks,
By shallow rivers to whose falls
Melodious birds sings madrigals.

And I will make thee beds of roses
10   And a thousand fragrant posies,
A cap of flowers, and a kirtle
Embroidered all with leaves of myrtle.

A gown made of the finest wool
Which from our pretty lambs we pull;
Fair lined slippers for the cold,
With buckles of the purest gold;

A belt of straw and ivy buds,
With coral clasps and amber studs;
And if these pleasures may thee move,
20   Come live with me, and be my love.

The shepherd swains shall dance and sing
For thy delight each May morning:
If these delights thy mind may move,
Then live with me and be my love.

1599–1600

MICHAEL DRAYTON

1563–1631

A FRIEND OF SHAKESPEARE and Ben Jonson, Drayton is now remembered for his sequence of sonnets, *Idea,* one of which I include here. Yet Drayton, a follower of Edmund Spenser, was very nearly a major poet, and would have more readers now except for the imaginative richness of his era. To have Shakespeare, Marlowe, Spenser, Jonson, and Donne as one's contemporaries is an involuntary courtship of oblivion.

Drayton excelled in long, mythopoeic poems, the most ambitious being *Poly-Olbion* (1613). Probably his most memorable achievement is the highly Spenserian *The Muses' Elizium* (1630).

There is a Shakespearean immediacy in the famous sonnet "Since there's no help, come let us kiss and part," which may reflect a direct influence upon Drayton of Shakespeare's sonnets.

❧   ❧   ❧

from Idea

LVI

Since there's no help, come let us kiss and part;
Nay, I have done, you get no more of me,
And I am glad, yea glad with all my heart
That thus so cleanly I myself can free;
Shake hands forever, cancel all our vows,
And when we meet at any time again,
Be it not seen in either of our brows
That we one jot of former love retain.
Now at the last gasp of love's latest breath,
When, his pulse failing, Passion speechless lies,
When Faith is kneeling by his bed of death,
And Innocence is closing up his eyes,
   Now if thou wouldst, when all have given him over,
   From death to life thou mightst him yet recover.

1619

WILLIAM SHAKESPEARE

1564–1616

SHAKESPEARE, younger than Marlowe by only a few months, must have known him in the early 1590s in London, when they competed as playwrights, with Shakespeare at the start deeply shadowed by Marlowe. But we have little information, even anecdotal, to connect the two poets, and I hold to my surmise that Marlowe personally frightened the wary Shakespeare, who sensibly went the other way whenever his dangerous acquaintance came in sight.

Representing the world's best poet in any anthology is more than a challenge. I have confined myself to the elegy "The Phoenix and Turtle," extensive passages from five plays, plus a dozen sonnets, and five songs. I could not argue that this is the best of Shakespeare, but everything here is among the best. There is enough to show the Shakespearean difference, which is what most matters. It is arbitrary to divide Shakespeare's absolute supremacy into categories of any kind, but for brevity I designate three primary aspects of his power: cognitive originality, totally answerable style, and—the miracle—creation of utterly persuasive human personalities, here Hamlet and Lear in particular.

Shakespeare's language, and his men and women, have libraries devoted to them. His conceptual power has not sustained much commentary. David Hume and Ludwig Wittgenstein essentially denied it; you have to go back to Thomas Carlyle and Ralph Waldo Emerson to find something explicit in recognizing the uncanny originality of Shakespeare's mind. Their contemporary Kierkegaard catches the singularity of Shakespearean thought in a draft version of what became *The Sickness Unto Death:*

> The art of writing lines, replies, which express a passion with full tone and complete imaginative intensity, and in which you can none the less catch the resonance of its opposite—this is an art which no poet has practised except the unique poet Shakespeare.

The *resonance of the opposite:* it haunts every cadence of Hamlet; an ultimate insight had preceded Kierkegaard in Hegel, who said that only

Shakespeare's protagonists were "free artists of themselves." That freedom resonates the opposite, affirms the negation, at once undoing the self and enlarging its domain.

How can a poet *think* his characters into their own freedom? Shakespeare, with little precedent beyond Chaucer, practices an art of surprise, in which his characters can be as surprised as we are. When Milton's God says of Adam and Eve that he made them "sufficient to have stood but free to fall," I reflect that, for just once, that irate Schoolmaster of Souls is being Shakespearean. Othello and Macbeth certainly are sufficient to have stood but also more than free to fall. Shakespeare endows his people with the capacity to change, either through the will or with involuntary force. Either way, there is surprise, as the selfsame overhears itself and alters irrevocably.

Hamlet and Falstaff are original thinkers but their questionings and wit are not primarily what I mean by Shakespeare's cognitive gift. To have thought his way into *their* inwardness is Shakespeare's most startling originality. We now take it for granted after four centuries of being post-Shakespearean. But who—in play, novel, poem—can do what Shakespeare did, in creating so much human otherness? Of Shakespeare's contemporaries, Cervantes twice performed the miracle, with Don Quixote and Sancho Panza, two giant forms, while Montaigne created himself. The rich strangeness of Shakespeare gave us hundreds of personalities, each with his or her highly distinctive voice. So many separate selves seem scarcely possible as emanations from a single consciousness, itself a permanent enigma to us.

Shakespeare's influence upon the novel is larger even than that of Cervantes. The masters of the novel—from Jane Austen and Stendhal through Dickens, Tolstoy, Balzac, Dostoyevsky, Flaubert, Henry James, Proust, Joyce, Virginia Woolf—are obliged to be Shakespearean, with violent unwillingness on the part of Tolstoy, who found *King Lear* loathsome and unnatural. What Tolstoy resented is what Ben Jonson resisted, until Jonson read about half of Shakespeare's plays for the first time in helping to put together the First Folio in 1623, seven years after the death of his great friend and rival. "Nature herself, was proud of his designs" is Jonson's highest compliment, not to be bettered. The tradition since has identified Shakespeare with nature, which must be the true cause of Tolstoy's jealousy, since *after* Shakespeare, Tolstoy is unsurpassed in giving us the same complex illusion: that his representations are nature's own.

No representation, in language, actually can be natural, so the art of Shakespeare and of Tolstoy (and of Chaucer) is powerfully illusive in giving readers a sense that somehow we hear nature speaking. Wittgenstein particularly objected to the wide opinion that Shakespeare is lifelike, but then the great philosopher very fiercely insisted that Shakespeare primarily was "a creator of language." The creation of personality by Shakespeare irritated Wittgenstein, who preferred Tolstoy. An ever-growing inward self, which is the mark of Shakespearean representation, is not what Wittgenstein sought in literary language.

I am not always certain that any strong protagonist in Shakespeare ever bothers to listen to anyone else, because he or she is preoccupied with self-overhearing. They do it with another instance of the Shakespearean difference: we are wonder-wounded hearers, but they are startled by surprise, as when we cannot believe what we ourselves have said.

✧   ✧   ✧

The Phoenix and Turtle

Let the bird of loudest lay,
On the sole Arabian tree,
Herald sad and trumpet be,
To whose sound chaste wings obey.

5 But thou shriking harbinger,
Foul precurrer of the fiend,
Augur of the fever's end,
To this troop come thou not near.

From this session interdict
10 Every fowl of tyrant wing,
Save the eagle, feath'red king;
Keep the obsequy so strict.

Let the priest in surplice white,
That defunctive music can,
15 Be the death-divining swan,
Lest the requiem lack his right.

And thou treble-dated crow,
That thy sable gender mak'st
With the breath thou giv'st and tak'st,
20 'Mongst our mourners shalt thou go.

Here the anthem doth commence:
Love and Constancy is dead,
Phoenix and the Turtle fled
In a mutual flame from hence.

25 So they loved as love in twain
Had the essence but in one,
Two distincts, division none:
Number there in love was slain.

Hearts remote, yet not asunder;
30 Distance and no space was seen
'Twixt this Turtle and his queen:
But in them it were a wonder.

So between them love did shine,
That the Turtle saw his right
35 Flaming in the Phoenix' sight;
Either was the other's mine.

Property was thus appalled,
That the self was not the same;
Single nature's double name
40 Neither two nor one was called.

Reason, in itself confounded,
Saw division grow together,
To themselves yet either neither,
Simple were so well compounded:

45 That it cried, "How true a twain
Seemeth this concordant one!
Love hath reason, Reason none,
If what parts, can so remain."

Whereupon it made this threne
50 To the Phoenix and the Dove,
Co-supremes and stars of love,
As chorus to their tragic scene.

                    THRENOS

Beauty, Truth, and Rarity,
Grace in all simplicity,
55 Here enclos'd, in cinders lie.

Death is now the Phoenix' nest,
And the Turtle's loyal breast
To eternity doth rest.

Leaving no posterity,
60 'Twas not their infirmity,
It was married chastity.

Truth may seem, but cannot be,
Beauty brag, but 'tis not she,
Truth and Beauty buried be.

65 To this urn let those repair
That are either true or fair;
For these dead birds sigh a prayer.

from Hamlet

Hamlet. O that this too too sallied flesh would melt,
130 Thaw, and resolve itself into a dew!
Or that the Everlasting had not fix'd
His canon 'gainst [self-]slaughter! O God, God,
How [weary], stale, flat, and unprofitable
Seem to me all the uses of this world!
135 Fie on't, ah fie! 'tis an unweeded garden
That grows to seed, things rank and gross in nature
Possess it merely. That it should come [to this]!
But two months dead, nay, not so much, not two.
So excellent a king, that was to this
140 Hyperion to a satyr, so loving to my mother
That he might not beteem the winds of heaven
Visit her face too roughly. Heaven and earth,
Must I remember? Why, she should hang on him
As if increase of appetite had grown
145 By what it fed on, and yet, within a month—
Let me not think on't! Frailty, thy name is woman!—
A little month, or ere those shoes were old
With which she followed my poor father's body,
Like Niobe, all tears—why, she, [even she]—
150 O God, a beast that wants discourse of reason
Would have mourn'd longer—married with my uncle,
My father's brother, but no more like my father

Than I to Hercules. Within a month,
Ere yet the salt of most unrighteous tears
155   Had left the flushing in her galled eyes,
She married—O most wicked speed: to post
With such dexterity to incestious sheets,
It is not, nor it cannot come to good,
But break my heart, for I must hold my tongue.

Enter HORATIO, MARCELLUS, *and* BARNARDO.

   Hor. Hail to your lordship!
   Ham. I am glad to see you well.
161   Horatio—or I do forget myself.
   Hor. The same, my lord, and your poor servant ever.
   Ham. Sir, my good friend—I'll change that name with you.
And what make you from Wittenberg, Horatio?
165   Marcellus.
   Mar. My good lord.
   Ham. I am very glad to see you. [*To Barnardo.*] Good even, sir.—
But what, in faith, make you from Wittenberg?
   Hor. A truant disposition, good my lord.
170   *Ham.* I would not hear your enemy say so,
Nor shall you do my ear that violence
To make it truster of your own report
Against yourself. I know you are no truant.
But what is your affair in Elsinore?
175   We'll teach you to drink [deep] ere you depart.
   Hor. My lord, I came to see your father's funeral.
   Ham. I prithee do not mock me, fellow studient,
I think it was to [see] my mother's wedding.
   Hor. Indeed, my lord, it followed hard upon.
180   *Ham.* Thrift, thrift, Horatio, the funeral bak'd-meats
Did coldly furnish forth the marriage tables.
Would I had met my dearest foe in heaven
Or ever I had seen that day, Horatio!
184   My father—methinks I see my father.
   Hor. Where, my lord?
   Ham. In my mind's eye, Horatio.
   Hor. I saw him once, 'a was a goodly king.
   Ham. 'A was a man, take him for all in all,
I shall not look upon his like again.

   · · ·

   Ham. Now I am alone.
550   O, what a rogue and peasant slave am I!

Is it not monstrous that this player here,
But in a fiction, in a dream of passion,
Could force his soul so to his own conceit
That from her working all the visage wann'd,
555 Tears in his eyes, distraction in his aspect,
A broken voice, an' his whole function suiting
With forms to his conceit? And all for nothing,
For Hecuba!
What's Hecuba to him, or he to [Hecuba],
That he should weep for her? What would he do
561 Had he the motive and [the cue] for passion
That I have? He would drown the stage with tears,
And cleave the general ear with horrid speech,
Make mad the guilty, and appall the free,
565 Confound the ignorant, and amaze indeed
The very faculties of eyes and ears. Yet I,
A dull and muddy-mettled rascal, peak
Like John-a-dreams, unpregnant of my cause,
And can say nothing; no, not for a king,
570 Upon whose property and most dear life
A damn'd defeat was made. Am I a coward?
Who calls me villain, breaks my pate across,
Plucks off my beard and blows it in my face,
Tweaks me by the nose, gives me the lie i' th' throat
575 As deep as to the lungs? Who does me this?
Hah, 'swounds, I should take it; for it cannot be
But I am pigeon-liver'd, and lack gall
To make oppression bitter, or ere this
I should 'a' fatted all the region kites
580 With this slave's offal. Bloody, bawdy villain!
Remorseless, treacherous, lecherous, kindless villain!
Why, what an ass am I! This is most brave,
That I, the son of a dear [father] murthered,
Prompted to my revenge by heaven and hell,
Must like a whore unpack my heart with words,
586 And fall a-cursing like a very drab,
A stallion. Fie upon't, foh!
About, my brains! Hum—I have heard
That guilty creatures sitting at a play
590 Have by the very cunning of the scene
Been strook so to the soul, that presently
They have proclaim'd their malefactions:
For murther, though it have no tongue, will speak

With most miraculous organ. I'll have these players
595   Play something like the murther of my father
Before mine uncle. I'll observe his looks,
I'll tent him to the quick. If 'a do blench,
I know my course. The spirit that I have seen
May be a [dev'l], and the [dev'l] hath power
600   T' assume a pleasing shape, yea, and perhaps,
Out of my weakness and my melancholy,
As he is very potent with such spirits,
Abuses me to damn me. I'll have grounds
604   More relative than this—the play's the thing
Wherein I'll catch the conscience of the King.   *Exit.*

·   ·   ·

55   *Ham.*   To be, or not to be, that is the question:
Whether 'tis nobler in the mind to suffer
The slings and arrows of outrageous fortune,
Or to take arms against a sea of troubles,
And by opposing, end them. To die, to sleep—
60   No more, and by a sleep to say we end
The heart-ache and the thousand natural shocks
That flesh is heir to; 'tis a consummation
Devoutly to be wish'd. To die, to sleep—
To sleep, perchance to dream—ay, there's the rub,
65   For in that sleep of death what dreams may come,
When we have shuffled off this mortal coil,
Must give us pause; there's the respect
That makes calamity of so long life:
For who would bear the whips and scorns of time,
70   Th' oppressor's wrong, the proud man's contumely,
The pangs of despis'd love, the law's delay,
The insolence of office, and the spurns
That patient merit of th' unworthy takes,
When he himself might his quietus make
75   With a bare bodkin; who would fardels bear,
To grunt and sweat under a weary life,
But that the dread of something after death,
The undiscover'd country, from whose bourn
No traveller returns, puzzles the will,
80   And makes us rather bear those ills we have,
Than fly to others that we know not of?
Thus conscience does make cowards [of us all],

And thus the native hue of resolution
Is sicklied o'er with the pale cast of thought,
85   And enterprises of great pitch and moment
With this regard their currents turn awry,
And lose the name of action.

.   .   .

Ham. How all occasions do inform against me,
And spur my dull revenge! What is a man,
If his chief good and market of his time
35   Be but to sleep and feed? a beast, no more.
Sure He that made us with such large discourse,
Looking before and after, gave us not
That capability and godlike reason
To fust in us unus'd. Now whether it be
40   Bestial oblivion, or some craven scruple
Of thinking too precisely on th' event—
A thought which quarter'd hath but one part wisdom
And ever three parts coward—I do not know
Why yet I live to say, "This thing's to do,"
45   Sith I have cause, and will, and strength, and means
To do't. Examples gross as earth exhort me:
Witness this army of such mass and charge,
Led by a delicate and tender prince,
Whose spirit with divine ambition puff'd
50   Makes mouths at the invisible event,
Exposing what is mortal and unsure
To all that fortune, death, and danger dare,
Even for an egg-shell. Rightly to be great
Is not to stir without great argument,
55   But greatly to find quarrel in a straw
When honor's at the stake. How stand I then,
That have a father kill'd, a mother stain'd,
Excitements of my reason and my blood,
And let all sleep, while to my shame I see
60   The imminent death of twenty thousand men,
That for a fantasy and trick of fame
Go to their graves like beds, fight for a plot
Whereon the numbers cannot try the cause,
Which is not tomb enough and continent
65   To hide the slain? O, from this time forth,
My thoughts be bloody, or be nothing worth!   *Exit*

from Troilus and Cressida

    Ulysses. Troy, yet upon his bases, had been down,
And the great Hector's sword had lack'd a master,
But for these instances:
The specialty of rule hath been neglected,
And look how many Grecian tents do stand
80   Hollow upon this plain, so many hollow factions.
When that the general is not like the hive
To whom the foragers shall all repair,
What honey is expected? Degree being vizarded,
Th' unworthiest shows as fairly in the mask.
The heavens themselves, the planets, and this centre
86   Observe degree, priority, and place,
Insisture, course, proportion, season, form,
Office, and custom, in all line of order;
And therefore is the glorious planet Sol
90   In noble eminence enthron'd and spher'd
Amidst the other; whose med'cinable eye
Corrects the [ill aspects] of [planets evil],
And posts like the commandment of a king,
Sans check, to good and bad. But when the planets
95   In evil mixture to disorder wander,
What plagues and what portents, what mutiny!
What raging of the sea, shaking of earth!
Commotion in the winds! frights, changes, horrors
Divert and crack, rend and deracinate
100   The unity and married calm of states
Quite from their fixure! O, when degree is shak'd,
Which is the ladder of all high designs,
The enterprise is sick. How could communities,
Degrees in schools, and brotherhoods in cities,
105   Peaceful commerce from dividable shores,
The primogenity and due of birth,
Prerogative of age, crowns, sceptres, laurels,
But by degree stand in authentic place?
Take but degree away, untune that string,
And hark what discord follows. Each thing [meets]
111   In mere oppugnancy: the bounded waters
Should lift their bosoms higher than the shores,
And make a sop of all this solid globe;
Strength should be lord of imbecility,
115   And the rude son should strike his father dead;

Force should be right, or rather, right and wrong
(Between whose endless jar justice resides)
Should lose their names, and so should justice too!
Then every thing include itself in power,
120   Power into will, will into appetite,
And appetite, an universal wolf
(So doubly seconded with will and power),
Must make perforce an universal prey,
And last eat up himself. Great Agamemnon,
125   This chaos, when degree is suffocate,
Follows the choking,
And this neglection of degree it is
That by a pace goes backward with a purpose
It hath to climb. The general's disdain'd
130   By him one step below, he by the next,
That next by him beneath; so every step,
Exampled by the first pace that is sick
Of his superior, grows to an envious fever
Of pale and bloodless emulation,
135   And 'tis this fever that keeps Troy on foot,
Not her own sinews. To end a tale of length,
Troy in our weakness stands, not in her strength.

            .   .   .

      Ulyss. Time hath, my lord, a wallet at his back,
146   Wherein he puts alms for oblivion,
A great-siz'd monster of ingratitudes.
Those scraps are good deeds past, which are devour'd
As fast as they are made, forgot as soon
150   As done. Perseverance, dear my lord,
Keeps honor bright; to have done is to hang
Quite out of fashion, like a rusty mail
In monumental mock'ry. Take the instant way,
For honor travels in a strait so narrow,
155   Where one but goes abreast. Keep then the path,
For emulation hath a thousand sons
That one by one pursue. If you give way,
Or [hedge] aside from the direct forthright,
Like to an ent'red tide, they all rush by
160   And leave you [hindmost];
[Or like a gallant horse fall'n in first rank,
Lie there for pavement to the abject [rear],
O'errun and trampled on.] Then what they do in present,

Though less than yours in [past], must o'ertop yours;
165 For Time is like a fashionable host
That slightly shakes his parting guest by th' hand,
And with his arms outstretch'd as he would fly,
Grasps in the comer. The welcome ever smiles,
And farewell goes out sighing. Let not virtue seek
170 Remuneration for the thing it was;
For beauty, wit,
High birth, vigor of bone, desert in service,
Love, friendship, charity, are subjects all
To envious and calumniating Time.
175 One touch of nature makes the whole world kin,
That all with one consent praise new-born gawds,
Though they are made and moulded of things past,
And [give] to dust, that is a little gilt,
More laud than gilt o'erdusted.
180 The present eye praises the present object.
Then marvel not, thou great and complete man,
That all the Greeks begin to worship Ajax;
Since things in motion sooner catch the eye
[Than] what stirs not. The cry went once on thee,
185 And still it might, and yet it may again,
If thou wouldst not entomb thyself alive
And case thy reputation in thy tent,
Whose glorious deeds but in these fields of late
Made emulous missions 'mongst the gods themselves,
And drave great Mars to faction.

from Measure for Measure

5   *Duke.* Be absolute for death: either death or life
Shall thereby be the sweeter. Reason thus with life:
If I do lose thee, I do lose a thing
That none but fools would keep. A breath thou art,
Servile to all the skyey influences,
10 That dost this habitation where thou keep'st
Hourly afflict. Merely, thou art death's fool,
For him thou labor'st by thy flight to shun,
And yet run'st toward him still. Thou art not noble,
For all th' accommodations that thou bear'st
Are nurs'd by baseness. Thou'rt by no means valiant,
16 For thou dost fear the soft and tender fork

Of a poor worm. Thy best of rest is sleep,
And that thou oft provok'st, yet grossly fear'st
Thy death, which is no more. Thou art not thyself,
20   For thou exists on many a thousand grains
That issue out of dust. Happy thou art not,
For what thou hast not, still thou striv'st to get,
And what thou hast, forget'st. Thou art not certain,
For thy complexion shifts to strange effects,
25   After the moon. If thou art rich, thou'rt poor,
For like an ass, whose back with ingots bows,
Thou bear'st thy heavy riches but a journey,
And death unloads thee. Friend hast thou none,
For thine own bowels, which do call thee [sire],
30   The mere effusion of thy proper loins,
Do curse the gout, sapego, and the rheum
For ending thee no sooner. Thou hast nor youth nor age,
But as it were an after-dinner's sleep,
Dreaming on both, for all thy blessed youth
35   Becomes as aged, and doth beg the alms
Of palsied eld; and when thou art old and rich,
Thou hast neither heat, affection, limb, nor beauty,
To make thy riches pleasant. What's yet in this
That bears the name of life? Yet in this life
40   Lie hid moe thousand deaths; yet death we fear
That makes these odds all even.

      ·   ·   ·

    Claudio. Ay, but to die, and go we know not where;
To lie in cold obstruction, and to rot;
This sensible warm motion to become
120   A kneaded clod; and the delighted spirit
To bathe in fiery floods, or to reside
In thrilling region of thick-ribbed ice;
To be imprison'd in the viewless winds
And blown with restless violence round about
125   The pendant world; or to be worse than worst
Of those that lawless and incertain thought
Imagine howling—'tis too horrible!
The weariest and most loathed worldly life
That age, ache, [penury], and imprisonment
130   Can lay on nature is a paradise
To what we fear of death.

from King Lear

Enter LEAR [*mad, crowned with weeds and flowers*].

But who comes here?
81   The safer sense will ne'er accommodate
His master thus.
     Lear. No, they cannot touch me for [coining,] I am
the King himself.
85   *Edgar.* O thou side-piercing sight!
     Lear. Nature's above art in that respect. There's
your press-money. That fellow handles his bow like a
crow-keeper; draw me a clothier's yard. Look, look,
a mouse! Peace, peace, this piece of toasted cheese will
90   do't. There's my gauntlet, I'll prove it on a giant.
Bring up the brown bills. O, well flown, bird! i' th'
clout, i' th' clout—hewgh! Give the word.
     Edg. Sweet marjorum.
     Lear. Pass.
95   *Gloucester.* I know that voice.
     Lear. Ha! Goneril with a white beard? They
flatter'd me like a dog, and told me I had the white
hairs in my beard ere the black ones were there. To
say "ay" and "no" to every thing that I said! "Ay,"
100 and "no" too, was no good divinity. When the
rain came to wet me once, and the wind to make me
chatter, when the thunder would not peace at my
bidding, there I found 'em, there I smelt 'em out. Go
to, they are not men o' their words: they told me I was
105 every thing. 'Tis a lie, I am not ague-proof.
     Glou. The trick of that voice I do well remember;
Is't not the King?
     Lear. Ay, every inch a king!
When I do stare, see how the subject quakes.
I pardon that man's life. What was thy cause?
110 Adultery?
Thou shalt not die. Die for adultery? No,
The wren goes to't, and the small gilded fly
Does lecher in my sight.
Let copulation thrive; for Gloucester's bastard son
115 Was kinder to his father than my daughters
Got 'tween the lawful sheets.
To't, luxury, pell-mell, for I lack soldiers.

Behold yond simp'ring dame,
Whose face between her forks presages snow;
120 That minces virtue, and does shake the head
To hear of pleasure's name—
The fitchew nor the soiled horse goes to't
With a more riotous appetite.
Down from the waist they are Centaurs,
125 Though women all above;
But to the girdle do the gods inherit,
Beneath is all the fiends': there's hell, there's darkness,
There is the sulphurous pit, burning, scalding,
Stench, consumption. Fie, fie, fie! pah, pah!
130 Give me an ounce of civet; good apothecary,
Sweeten my imagination. There's money for thee.
    Glou. O, let me kiss that hand!
    Lear. Let me wipe it first, it smells of mortality.
    Glou. O ruin'd piece of nature! This great world
135 Shall so wear out to nought. Dost thou know me?
    Lear. I remember thine eyes well enough. Dost
thou squiny at me? No, do thy worst, blind Cupid, I'll
not love. Read thou this challenge; mark but the
139 penning of it.
    Glou. Were all thy letters suns, I could not see.
    Edg. [*Aside.*] I would not take this from report; it is,
And my heart breaks at it.
    Lear. Read.
144   *Glou.* What, with the case of eyes?
    Lear. O ho, are you there with me? No eyes in
your head, nor no money in your purse? Your eyes are
in a heavy case, your purse in a light, yet you see how
this world goes.
149   *Glou.* I see it feelingly.
    Lear. What, art mad? A man may see how this
world goes with no eyes. Look with thine ears; see
how yond justice rails upon yond simple thief. Hark
in thine ear: change places, and handy-dandy, which is
the justice, which is the thief? Thou hast seen a
155 farmer's dog bark at a beggar?
    Glou. Ay, sir.
    Lear. And the creature run from the cur? There
thou mightst behold the great image of authority: a
dog's obey'd in office.
160 Thou rascal beadle, hold thy bloody hand!

Why dost thou lash that whore? Strip thy own back,
Thou hotly lusts to use her in that kind
For which thou whip'st her. The usurer hangs the cozener.
Thorough tatter'd clothes [small] vices do appear;
165 Robes and furr'd gowns hide all. [Plate sin] with gold,
And the strong lance of justice hurtless breaks;
Arm it in rags, a pigmy's straw does pierce it.
None does offend, none, I say none, I'll able 'em.
Take that of me, my friend, who have the power
170 To seal th' accuser's lips. Get thee glass eyes,
And like a scurvy politician, seem
To see the things thou dost not. Now, now, now, now.
Pull off my boots; harder, harder—so.
    Edg. [*Aside.*] O, matter and impertinency mix'd,
175 Reason in madness!
    Lear. If thou wilt weep my fortunes, take my eyes.
I know thee well enough, thy name is Gloucester.
Thou must be patient; we came crying hither.
Thou know'st, the first time that we smell the air
180 We wawl and cry. I will preach to thee. Mark.

                [*Lear takes off his crown of weeds and flowers.*]

    Glou. Alack, alack the day!
    Lear. When we are born, we cry that we are come
To this great stage of fools.—This' a good block.
It were a delicate stratagem, to shoe
185 A troop of horse with felt. I'll put't in proof,
And when I have stol'n upon these son-in-laws,
Then kill, kill, kill, kill, kill, kill!

from The Tempest

Prospero. Ye elves of hills, brooks, standing lakes, and groves;
    And ye that on the sands with printless foot
    Do chase the ebbing Neptune, and do fly him
    When he comes back; you demi-puppets that
    By moonshine do the green sour ringlets make,
    Whereof the ewe not bites; and you whose pastime
    Is to make midnight mushrooms, that rejoice
40   To hear the solemn curfew; by whose aid—
    Weak masters though ye be—I have bedimmed
    The noontide sun, called forth the mutinous winds,
    And 'twixt the green sea and the azured vault

Set roaring war: to the dread rattling thunder
Have I given fire, and rifted Jove's stout oak
With his own bolt; the strong-based promontory
Have I made shake, and by the spurs plucked up
The pine and cedar: graves at my command
Have waked their sleepers, oped, and let 'em forth
50 By my so potent Art. But this rough magic
I here abjure; and, when I have required
Some heavenly music,—which even now I do,—
To work mine end upon their senses, that
This airy charm is for, I'll brake my staff,
Bury it certain fadoms in the earth,
And deeper than did ever plummet sound
I'll drown my book.   *Solemn music.*

Sonnets

XIX

Devouring Time, blunt thou the lion's paws,
And make the earth devour her own sweet brood;
Pluck the keen teeth from the fierce tiger's jaws,
And burn the long-lived phoenix in her blood;
Make glad and sorry seasons as thou fleet'st,
And do whate'er thou wilt, swift-footed Time,
To the wide world and all her fading sweets:
But I forbid thee one most heinous crime—
Oh carve not with thy hours my love's fair brow
10 Nor draw no lines there with thine ántique pen;
Him in thy course untainted do allow
For beauty's pattern to succeeding men.
    Yet do thy worst, old Time: despite thy wrong
    My love shall in my verse ever live young.

XXX

When to the sessions of sweet silent thought
I summon up remembrance of things past,
I sigh the lack of many a thing I sought,
And with old woes new wail my dear time's waste:
Then can I drown an eye, unused to flow,
For precious friends hid in death's dateless night,
And weep afresh love's long since cancelled woe,
And moan the expense of many a vanished sight:

Then can I grieve at grievances foregone,
10   And heavily from woe to woe tell o'er
The sad account of fore-bemoanèd moan,
Which I new pay as if not paid before.
      But if the while I think on thee, dear friend,
      All losses are restored and sorrows end.

LIII

What is your substance, whereof are you made,
That millions of strange shadows on you tend?
Since every one hath, every one, one shade,
And you, but one, can every shadow lend.
Describe Adonis, and the counterfeit
Is poorly imitated after you;
On Helen's cheek all art of beauty set,
And you in Grecian tires are painted new.
Speak of the spring and foison of the year:
10   The one doth shadow of your beauty show,
The other as your bounty doth appear,
And you in every blessèd shape we know.
      In all external grace you have some part,
      But you like none, none you for constant heart.

LV

Not marble, nor the gilded monuments
Of princes shall outlive this powerful rhyme;
But you shall shine more bright in these contents
Than unswept stone besmeared with sluttish time.
When wasteful war shall statues overturn,
And broils root out the work of masonry,
Nor Mars his sword nor war's quick fire shall burn
The living record of your memory.
'Gainst death and all oblivious enmity
10   Shall you pace forth: your praise shall still find room
Even in the eyes of all posterity
That wear this world out to the ending doom.
      So, till the judgment that yourself arise,
      You live in this, and dwell in lovers' eyes.

LXXIII

That time of year thou mayst in me behold
When yellow leaves, or none, or few, do hang
Upon those boughs which shake against the cold,

Bare ruined choirs where late the sweet birds sang:
In me thou see'st the twilight of such day
As after sunset fadeth in the west,
Which by and by black night doth take away,
Death's second self that seals up all in rest:
In me thou see'st the glowing of such fire
That on the ashes of his youth doth lie
As the death-bed whereon it must expire,
Consumed with that which it was nourished by:
    This thou perceivest, which makes thy love more strong
    To love that well which thou must leave ere long.

LXXXVI

Was it the proud full sail of his great verse,
Bound for the prize of all-too-precious you,
That did my ripe thoughts in my brain inhearse,
Making their tomb the womb wherein they grew?
Was it his spirit, by spirits taught to write
Above a mortal pitch, that struck me dead?
No, neither he, nor his compeers by night
Giving him aid, my verse astonishèd:
He, nor that affable familiar ghost
Which nightly gulls him with intelligence,
As victors of my silence cannot boast,
I was not sick of any fear from thence:
    But when your countenance filled up his line,
    Then lacked I matter; that enfeebled mine.

LXXXVII

Farewell—thou art too dear for my possessing,
And like enough thou knowest thy estimate:
The charter of thy worth gives thee releasing;
My bonds in thee are all determinate.
For how do I hold thee but by thy granting?
And for that riches where is my deserving?
The cause of this fair gift in me is wanting,
And so my patent back again is swerving.
Thy self thou gavest, thy own worth then not knowing;
Or me, to whom thou gavest it, else mistaking:
So thy great gift, upon misprision growing,
Comes home again on better judgment making.
    Thus have I had thee as a dream doth flatter:
    In sleep a king, but waking no such matter.

XCIV

They that have power to hurt and will do none,
That do not do the thing they most do show,
Who moving others are themselves as stone,
Unmovèd, cold, and to temptation slow;
They rightly do inherit heaven's graces,
And husband nature's riches from expense;
They are the lords and owners of their faces,
Others but stewards of their excellence.
The summer's flower is to the summer sweet,
Though to itself it only live and die;
But if that flower with base infection meet,
The basest weed outbraves his dignity:
    For sweetest things turn sourest by their deeds.
    Lilies that fester smell far worse than weeds.

CVII

Not mine own fears, nor the prophetic soul
Of the wide world dreaming on things to come
Can yet the lease of my true love control,
Supposed as forfeit to a cónfined doom.
The mortal moon hath her eclipse endured,
And the sad augurs mock their own presage;
Incertainties now crown themselves assured,
And peace proclaims olives of endless age.
Now with the drops of this most balmy time
My love looks fresh; and Death to me subscribes,
Since spite of him I'll live in this poor rhyme
While he insults o'er dull and speechless tribes:
    And thou in this shalt find thy monument
    When tyrants' crests and tombs of brass are spent.

CXVI

Let me not to the marriage of true minds
Admit impediments: love is not love
Which alters when it alteration finds,
Or bends with the remover to remove.
Oh no! it is an ever-fixèd mark
That looks on tempests and is never shaken;
It is the star to every wandering bark,
Whose worth's unknown although his height be taken.
Love's not Time's fool, though rosy lips and cheeks
Within his bending sickle's compass come;

Love alters not with his brief hours and weeks,
But bears it out even to the edge of doom.
    If this be error and upon me proved,
    I never writ, nor no man ever loved.

CXXI

'Tis better to be vile than vile esteemed,
When not to be receives reproach of being,
And the just pleasure lost which is so deemed
Not by our feeling but by others' seeing.
For why should others' false adulterate eyes
Give salutation to my sportive blood?
Or on my frailties why are frailer spies,
Which in their wills count bad what I think good?
No: I am that I am, and they that level
At my abuses reckon up their own;
I may be straight though they themselves be bevel;
By their rank thoughts my deeds must not be shown,—
    Unless this general evil they maintain:
    All men are bad and in their badness reign.

CXXIX

The expense of spirit in a waste of shame
Is lust in action; and till action, lust
Is perjured, murderous, bloody, full of blame,
Savage, extreme, rude, cruel, not to trust;
Enjoyed no sooner but despisèd straight;
Past reason hunted; and no sooner had,
Past reason hated, as a swallowed bait
On purpose laid to make the taker mad;
Mad in pursuit, and in possession so;
Had, having, and in quest to have, extreme;
A bliss in proof; and proved, a very woe;
Before, a joy proposed; behind, a dream.
    All this the world well knows, yet none knows well
    To shun the heaven that leads men to this hell.

CXXX

My mistress' eyes are nothing like the sun;
Coral is far more red than her lips' red;
If snow be white, why then her breasts are dun;
If hairs be wires, black wires grow on her head;
I have seen roses damasked, red and white,

But no such roses see I in her cheeks;
And in some perfumes is there more delight
Than in the breath that from my mistress reeks;
I love to hear her speak, yet well I know
10   That music hath a far more pleasing sound;
I grant I never saw a goddess go
(My mistress when she walks treads on the ground).
    And yet by heaven I think my love as rare
    As any she belied with false compare.

CXLIV

Two loves I have, of comfort and despair,
Which like two spirits do suggest me still:
The better angel is a man right fair,
The worser spirit a woman coloured ill.
To win me soon to hell, my female evil
Tempteth my better angel from my side,
And would corrupt my saint to be a devil,
Wooing his purity with her foul pride.
And whether that my angel be turned fiend
10   Suspect I may, yet not directly tell;
But being both from me, both to each friend,
I guess one angel in another's hell:
    Yet this shall I ne'er know, but live in doubt
    Till my bad angel fire my good one out.

Songs

Dirge

Fear no more the heat o' the sun
    Nor the furious winter's rages;
Thou thy worldly task hast done,
    Home art gone, and ta'en thy wages;
Golden lads and girls all must,
As chimney-sweepers, come to dust.

Fear no more the frown o' the great,
    Thou art past the tyrant's stroke;
Care no more to clothe and eat,
10   To thee the reed is as the oak:

The sceptre, learning, physic, must
All follow this and come to dust.

Fear no more the lightning flash,
    Nor the all-dreaded thunder-stone;
Fear not slander, censure rash;
    Thou hast finished joy and moan:
All lovers young, all lovers must
Consign to thee and come to dust.

No exorciser harm thee!
    Nor no witchcraft charm thee!
Ghost unlaid forbear thee!
    Nothing ill come near thee!
Quiet consummation have,
And renownèd be thy grave.

When That I Was and a Little Tiny Boy

When that I was and a little tiny boy,
    With hey, ho, the wind and the rain,
A foolish thing was but a toy,
    For the rain it raineth every day.

But when I came to man's estate,
    With hey, ho, the wind and the rain,
'Gainst knaves and thieves men shut their gate,
    For the rain it raineth every day.

But when I came, alas! to wive,
    With hey, ho, the wind and the rain,
By swaggering could I never thrive,
    For the rain it raineth every day.

But when I came unto my beds,
    With hey, ho, the wind and the rain,
With tosspots still had drunken heads,
    For the rain it raineth every day.

A great while ago the world begun,
    With hey, ho, the wind and the rain;

But that's all one, our play is done,
    And we'll strive to please you every day.

Autolycus' Song

When daffodils begin to peer,
    With heigh, the doxy over the dale!
Why, then comes in the sweet of the year
    For the red blood reigns in the winter's pale.

The white sheet bleaching on the hedge,
    With heigh, the sweet birds, O how they sing!
Doth set my pugging tooth on edge,
    For a quart of ale is a dish for a king.

The lark that tirra lirra chants,
10   With heigh, with heigh, the thrush and the jay!
Are summer songs for me and my aunts
    While we lie tumbling in the hay.

Autolycus As Peddler

Lawn as white as driven snow,
Cyprus black as e'er was crow,
Gloves as sweet as damask roses,
Masks for faces and for noses,
Bugle-bracelet, necklace amber,
Perfume for a lady's chamber,
Golden quoifs and stomachers
For my lads to give their dears,
Pins and poking sticks of steel
—What maids lack from head to heel.
Come buy of me, come; come buy, come buy,
Buy lads, or else your lasses cry.

THOMAS NASHE

1567–1601

A FIERCE ROISTERER, Thomas Nashe is best remembered for his splendid prose romance, *The Unfortunate Traveller* (1594), and for the pageant-like play *Summer's Last Will and Testament.*

Nashe's best poem, given here, is famous for its evocative third stanza, and testifies to the epidemics of plague that frequently closed the London theaters.

Some scholars find Moth in Shakespeare's *Love's Labour's Lost* to be an affectionate if sardonic portrait of Nashe. Page to Don Armado, Moth provokes Armado's splendid injunction: "Define, define, well-educated infant."

✙   ✙   ✙

Litany in Time of Plague

Adieu, farewell earth's bliss,
This world uncertain is:
Fond are life's lustful joys,
Death proves them all but toys,
None from his darts can fly.
I am sick, I must die.
            Lord, have mercy on us!

Rich men, trust not in wealth,
Gold cannot buy you health;
Physic himself must fade,
All things to end are made.
The plague full swift goes by.
I am sick, I must die.
            Lord, have mercy on us!

Beauty is but a flower
Which wrinkles will devour;
Brightness falls from the air,
Queens have died young and fair,

Dust hath closed Helen's eye.
I am sick, I must die.
   Lord, have mercy on us!

Strength stoops unto the grave,
Worms feed on Hector brave,
Swords may not fight with fate,
Earth still holds ope her gate.
Come! come! the bells do cry.
I am sick, I must die.
   Lord, have mercy on us!

Wit with his wantonness
Tasteth death's bitterness;
Hell's executioner
Hath no ears for to hear
What vain art can reply.
I am sick, I must die.
   Lord, have mercy on us!

Haste, therefore, each degree,
To welcome destiny.
Heaven is our heritage,
Earth but a player's stage;
Mount we unto the sky.
I am sick, I must die.
   Lord, have mercy on us!

 1600

| THOMAS CAMPION |

1567–1620

A SUPERB SONGWRITER, comparable to Shakespeare and Jonson, Campion was an immensely versatile individual, as adept a lawyer and physician as he was a lutanist and poet. His lyrics frequently follow classical models, and improve upon their originals.

✧   ✧   ✧

There Is a Garden in Her Face

There is a garden in her face
    Where roses and white lilies grow;
A heavenly paradise is that place,
    Wherein these pleasant fruits do flow.
There cherries grow which none may buy,
Till 'Cherry-ripe' themselves do cry.

These cherries fairly do enclose
    Of orient pearl a double row,
Which when her lovely laughter shows,
10   They look like rose-buds filled with snow;
Yet them no peer nor prince can buy,
Till 'Cherry-ripe' themselves do cry.

Her eyes like angels watch them still;
    Her brows like bended bows do stand,
Threatening with piercing shafts to kill
    All that presume with eye or hand
Those sacred cherries to come nigh,
Till 'Cherry-ripe' themselves do cry.
    1617

When to Her Lute Corinna Sings

When to her lute Corinna sings,
Her voice revives the leaden strings,
And doth in highest notes appear
As any challenged echo clear.
But when she doth of mourning speak,
Even with her sighs the strings do break.

And as her lute doth live or die,
Led by her passion, so must I.
For when of pleasure she doth sing,
10   My thoughts enjoy a sudden spring;
But if she doth of sorrow speak,
Even from my heart the strings do break.
    1601

When Thou Must Home to Shades of Under Ground

When thou must home to shades of under ground,
And there ariv'd, a newe admired guest,
The beauteous spirits do ingirt thee round,
White Iope, blith Hellen, and the rest,
To heare the stories of thy finisht love
From that smoothe toong whose musicke hell can move;

Then wilt thou speake of banqueting delights,
Of masks and revels which sweete youth did make,
Of Turnies and great challenges of knights,
And all these triumphes for thy beauties sake:
When thou hast told these honours done to thee,
Then tell, O tell, how thou didst murther me.

| JOHN DONNE |

1572–1631

JOHN DONNE CAN SEEM two poets, the charmed libertine of *Songs and Sonnets* and the master of devotional verse, but the same deep and versatile wit profoundly inhabits "The Ecstasy" and the Holy Sonnets and hymns. And yet "wit," in our current parlance, is a poor term for Donne's gifts. "Irony" differs from era to era, and from writer to writer. John Donne's ironies are close to Shakespeare's in that they focus meanings rather than exile them. It may be best to think of Donne's ironical wit as an instrument of discovery, akin to Shakespeare's ironically compassionate invention of personalities. "Wit" arguably meant intellect, but by the age of Shakespeare the word had modulated into creative mind or poetic intelligence. When we now speak of "wit," we tend to think of acute perception, or a quickness in apprehension.

Donne's wit inspired Ben Jonson to a certain ambivalence, which increased in Alexander Pope and his critical defender, Dr. Samuel Johnson. To this Neoclassical tradition, Donnean wit seemed ingenuity, even perverse abuse of metaphor. It is a charming irony that Donne was revived by the Romantics, from Coleridge through Browning and Arthur Symons, the irony being that T. S. Eliot belatedly "revived" Donne as an Eliotic anti-Romantic.

In an odd but clear sense, Donne's wit is pragmatic, always seeking a difference that truly will make a difference. There is thus no authentic divide between his libertine and his divine poetry. This allows the achievement of the two astonishing *Anniversaries,* baroque elegies written in 1610 to memorialize the death of Elizabeth Drury, a girl of high family whom actually Donne had never met. Ben Jonson said he had told Donne that these poems were blasphemous and profane: "if it had been written of the Virgin Mary it had been something: to which he answered, that he described the idea of a Woman, and not as she was."

Reading the *Anniversaries,* we hardly are given even the idea of a woman, but the progress of the soul, so memorably at times that Donne's dismissals of his natural faculties seem indisputable:

> Nor hear through labyrinths of ears, nor learn
> By circuit, or collections to discern.
> In heaven thou straight know'st all, concerning it,
> And what concerns it not, shalt straight forget.

You don't argue with Donne, however skeptical or naturalistic you may be. Eloquence and shrewdness in behalf of the invisible are not often so combined.

✣   ✣   ✣

Song

Goe, and catche a falling starre,
   Get with child a mandrake roote,
Tell me, where all past yeares are,
   Or who cleft the Divels foot,
Teach me to heare Mermaides singing,
Or to keep off envies stinging,
         And finde
         What winde
Serves to advance an honest minde.

If thou beest borne to strange sights,
   Things invisible to see,
Ride ten thousand daies and nights,

Till age snow white haires on thee,
Thou, when thou retorn'st, wilt tell mee
All strange wonders that befell thee,
       And sweare
       No where
Lives a woman true, and faire.

If thou findst one, let mee know,
   Such a Pilgrimage were sweet;
Yet doe not, I would not goe,
   Though at next doore wee might meet,
Though shee were true, when you met her,
And last, till you write your letter,
       Yet shee
       Will bee
False, ere I come, to two, or three.

A Nocturnal upon S. Lucy's Day, Being the Shortest Day

'Tis the year's midnight, and it is the day's,
Lucy's, who scarce seven hours herself unmasks,
   The sun is spent, and now his flasks
   Send forth light squibs, no constant rays;
     The world's whole sap is sunk:
The general balm the hydroptic earth hath drunk,
Whither, as to the bed's-feet, life is shrunk,
Dead and interred; yet all these seem to laugh,
Compared with me, who am their epitaph.

10 Study me then, you who shall lovers be
At the next world, that is, at the next spring:
   For I am every dead thing,
   In whom love wrought new alchemy.
     For his art did express
A quintessence even from nothingness,
From dull privations, and lean emptiness;
He ruined me, and I am re-begot
Of absence, darkness, death; things which are not.

All others, from all things, draw all that's good,
20 Life, soul, form, spirit, whence they being have;

I, by love's limbeck, am the grave
Of all, that's nothing. Oft a flood
   Have we two wept, and so
Drowned the whole world, us two; oft did we grow
To be two chaoses, when we did show
Care to aught else; and often absences
Withdrew our souls; and made us carcases.

But I am by her death (which word wrongs her)
Of the first nothing, the elixir grown;
   Were I a man, that I were one,
   I needs must know; I should prefer,
     If I were any beast,
Some ends, some means; yea plants, yea stones detest,
And love, all, all some properties invest;
If I an ordinary nothing were,
As shadow, a light, and body must be here.

But I am none; nor will my sun renew.
You lovers, for whose sake, the lesser sun
   At this time to the Goat is run
   To fetch new lust, and give it you,
     Enjoy your summer all;
Since she enjoys her long night's festival,
Let me prepare towards her, and let me call
This hour her virgil, and her eve, since this
Both the year's, and the day's deep midnight is.
   1633

The Ecstasy

Where, like a pillow on a bed,
   A pregnant bank swelled up, to rest
The violet's reclining head,
   Sat we two, one another's best;

Our hands were firmly cemented
   With a fast balm, which thence did spring,
Our eye-beams twisted, and did thread
   Our eyes, upon one double string;

So to intergraft our hands, as yet
10   Was all our means to make us one,
And pictures in our eyes to get
      Was all our propagatiòn.

As 'twixt two equal armies, Fate
      Suspends uncertain victory,
Our souls, (which to advance their state,
      Were gone out), hung 'twixt her, and me.

And whilst our souls negotiate there,
      We like sepulchral statues lay;
All day, the same our postures were,
20   And we said nothing, all the day.

If any, so by love refined,
      That he soul's language understood,
And by good love were grown all mind,
      Within convenient distance stood,

He (though he knew not which soul spake
      Because both meant, both spake the same)
Might thence a new concoction take,
      And part far purer than he came.

This ecstasy doth unperplex
30   (We said) and tell us what we love,
We see by this, it was not sex,
      We see we saw not what did move:

But as all several souls contain
      Mixture of things, they know not what,
Love, these mixed souls doth mix again,
      And makes both one, each this and that.

A single violet transplant,
      The strength, the colour, and the size,
(All which before was poor, and scant,)
40   Redoubles still, and multiplies.

When love, with one another so
      Interinanimates two souls,

That abler soul, which thence doth flow,
   Defects of loneliness controls.

We then, who are this new soul, know,
   Of what we are composed, and made,
For, th'atomies of which we grow,
   Are souls, whom no change can invade.

But O alas, so long, so far
50   Our bodies why do we forbear?
They are ours, though they are not we, we are
   The intelligences, they the sphere.

We owe them thanks, because they thus,
   Did us, to us, at first convey,
Yielded their forces, sense, to us,
   Nor are dross to us, but allay.

On man heaven's influence works not so,
   But that it first imprints the air,
So soul into the soul may flow,
60   Though it to body first repair.

As our blood labours to beget
   Spirits, as like souls as it can,
Because such fingers need to knit
   That subtle knot, which makes us man:

So must pure lovers' souls descend
   T'affections, and to faculties,
Which sense may reach and apprehend,
   Else a great prince in prison lies.

To our bodies turn we then, that so
70   Weak men on love revealed may look;
Love's mysteries in souls do grow,
   But yet the body is his book.

And if some lover, such as we,
   Have heard this dialogue of one,
Let him still mark us, he shall see
   Small change, when we are to bodies gone.
   1633

Hymn to God My God, in My Sickness

Since I am coming to that holy room,
    Where, with thy choir of saints for evermore,
I shall be made thy music; as I come
    I tune the instrument here at the door,
    And what I must do then, think now before.

Whilst my physicians by their love are grown
    Cosmographers, and I their map, who lie
Flat on this bed, that by them may be shown
    That this is my south-west discovery
10   *Per fretum febris,* by these strains to die,

I joy, that in these straits, I see my west;
    For, though their currents yield return to none,
What shall my west hurt me? As west and east
    In all flat maps (and I am one) are one,
    So death doth touch the resurrection.

Is the Pacific Sea my home? Or are
    The eastern riches? Is Jerusalem?
Anyan, and Magellan, and Gibraltàr,
    All straits, and none but straits, are ways to them,
20   Whether where Japhet dwelt, or Cham, or Shem.

We think that Paradise and Calvary,
    Christ's cross, and Adam's tree, stood in one place;
Look Lord, and find both Adams met in me;
    As the first Adam's sweat surrounds my face,
    May the last Adam's blood my soul embrace.

So, in his purple wrapped receive me Lord,
    By these his thorns give me his other crown;
And as to others' souls I preached thy word,
    Be this my text, my sermon to mine own,
Therefore that he may raise the Lord throws down.
    1635

A Hymn to God the Father

I

Wilt thou forgive that sin where I begun,
 Which is my sin, though it were done before?
Wilt thou forgive that sin, through which I run,
 And do run still: though still I do deplore?
  When thou hast done, thou hast not done,
   For I have more.

II

Wilt thou forgive that sin which I have won
 Others to sin? and, made my sin their door?
Wilt thou forgive that sin which I did shun
 A year, or two, but wallowed in a score?
  When thou hast done, thou hast not done,
   For I have more.

III

I have a sin of fear, that when I have spun
 My last thread, I shall perish on the shore;
But swear by thy self, that at my death thy son
 Shall shine as he shines now, and heretofore;
  And, having done that, thou hast done,
   I fear no more.

1633

| BEN JONSON |

1572–1637

BEN JONSON, born in the same year as Donne, survived him by six years, and divided with Donne the formative influence upon the next generation of poets, until the advent of John Milton. For us, now, Jonson lives in his three great comedies for the stage—*Volpone*, *The Alchemist*, and *Bartholomew Fair*—and as a lyrical and reflective poet. His frequently beautiful court masques tend now to be neglected, but the best of the twenty-eight read beautifully. The masques were, in a sense, collaborations with Inigo Jones, superb scenic designer and architect, whose showmanship frequently made Jonson unhappy. Coupled with the stage failure of his two Roman tragedies, *Catiline* and *Sejanus,* the effect of expostulating with Inigo Jones was to impel Jonson toward greater achievement in his own poems.

Jonson, in every respect that most matters, is about as unlike Donne as could be: most classical when most personal, and so always taking on the role of the poet proper, speaking or singing the ethical concerns of humankind to whoever is qualified to listen and to understand.

The history of the reception of Ben Jonson's poems is rather an enigma: though they inspired the marvelous Sons of Ben—Robert Herrick, Thomas Carew, Richard Lovelace, Thomas Randolph, William Cartwright, Sir John Suckling—and made possible the Augustan style of John Dryden and Alexander Pope, they never have garnered a general public. Today they are read by scholars only, a lamentable fate for a great poet, who now seems, like Edmund Spenser, to have become a poet's poet.

Spenser can seem almost too smooth, as it were, and too remote from our current concerns. Jonson had called John Donne "the first poet in the world in some things," but then had prophesied that Donne "for not being understood, would perish." That prophecy has not been fulfilled. Is it only an irony that Jonson, for being understood, has perished, except for his scholars?

The best of Jonson's songs, from masques and plays, are superb: elegant, dark, wise:

> Still to be neat, still to be dressed,
> As you were going to a feast;
> Still to be powdered, still perfumed—
> Lady, it is to be presumed,
> Though art's hid causes are not found,
> All is not sweet, all is not sound.
>
> Give me a look, give me a face,
> That makes simplicity a grace;
> Robes loosely flowing, hair as free:
> Such sweet neglect more taketh me
> Than all the adulteries of art;
> They strike mine eyes, but not my heart.

That "Lady, it is to be presumed" is one of the most withering lines in the language. Subtle and stoical, Jonson was also melancholic, and fought bravely against his own self-recognitions and tendency to despair. He compared himself to a broken compass, unable to complete the circle, and his life was frequently difficult. Art, for him, was hard work. To be Shakespeare's personal friend and rival poet-playwright was not an easy fate: "He was not of an age, but for all time!" Jonson's affectionate tribute was prophetic; he must have been aware that a poet's poet would never achieve such universality.

↓   ↓   ↓

To the Memory of My Beloved, the Author Mr. William Shakespeare:

and What He Hath Left Us

To draw no envy (Shakespeare) on thy name,
　　Am I thus ample to thy book, and fame,
While I confess thy writings to be such
　　As neither Man nor Muse can praise too much.
'Tis true, and all men's suffrage. But these ways
　　Were not the paths I meant unto thy praise:
For seeliest ignorance on these may light,
　　Which, when it sounds at best, but echoes right;
Or blind affection, which doth ne'er advance
10　　The truth, but gropes, and urgeth all by chance;
Or crafty malice might pretend this praise,
　　And think to ruin, where it seemed to raise.
These are, as some infamous bawd or whore,
　　Should praise a matron. What could hurt her more?
But thou art proof against them, and indeed
　　Above the ill fortune of them, or the need,
I therefore will begin. Soul of the age!
　　The applause! delight! the wonder of our stage!
My Shakespeare, rise; I will not lodge thee by
20　　Chaucer or Spenser, or bid Beaumont lie
A little further, to make thee a room:
　　Thou art a monument without a tomb,
And art alive still, while thy book doth live,
　　And we have wits to read, and praise to give.
That I not mix thee so, my brain excuses,
　　I mean with great, but disproportioned muses;
For, if I thought my judgment were of years,
　　I should commit thee surely with thy peers,

And tell, how far thou didst our Lyly outshine,
30   Or sporting Kyd, or Marlowe's mighty line.
And though thou hadst small Latin and less Greek,
   From thence to honour thee, I would not seek
For names; but call forth thundering Aeschylus,
   Euripides and Sophocles to us,
Paccuvius, Accius, him of Cordova dead,
   To life again, to hear thy buskin tread,
And shake a stage: Or, when thy socks were on,
   Leave thee alone, for the comparison
Of all that insolent Greece or haughty Rome
40   Sent forth, or since did from their ashes come.
Triumph, My Britain, thou hast one to show,
   To whom all scenes of Europe homage owe.
He was not of an age, but for all time!
   And all the muses still were in their prime,
When like Apollo he came forth to warm
   Our ears, or like a Mercury to charm!
Nature herself was proud of his designs,
   And joyed to wear the dressing of his lines!
Which were so richly spun and woven so fit,
50   As, since, she will vouchsafe no other wit:
The merry Greek, tart Aristophanes,
   Neat Terence, witty Plautus, now not please,
But antiquated, and deserted lie
   As they were not of nature's family.
Yet must I not give nature all: thy art,
   My gentle Shakespeare, must enjoy a part,
For though the poet's matter nature be,
   His art doth give the fashion; and that he
Who casts to write a living line, must sweat
60   (Such as thine are), and strike the second heat
Upon the muses' anvil, turn the same
   (And himself with it), that he thinks to frame,
Or for the laurel, he may gain a scorn;
   For a good poet's made, as well as born.
And such wert thou. Look how the father's face
   Lives in his issue; even so, the race
Of Shakespeare's mind, and manners brightly shines
   In his well turnèd, and true-filèd lines:
In each of which, he seems to shake a lance,
70   As brandished at the eyes of ignorance.
Sweet Swan of Avon! what a sight it were

To see thee in our waters yet appear,
And make those flights upon the banks of Thames,
   That so did take Eliza and our James!
But stay, I see thee in the hemisphere
   Advanced and made a constellation there!
Shine forth, thou star of poets, and with rage
   Or influence, chide, or cheer the drooping stage;
Which, since thy flight from hence, hath mourned like night,
80   And déspairs day, but for thy volume's light.

   1623

Song: To Celia

Come, my Celia, let us prove,
While we may, the sports of love;
Time will not be ours forever:
He, at length, our good will sever.
Spend not then his gifts in vain:
Suns that set may rise again;
But if once we lose this light,
'Tis with us perpetual night.
Why should we defer our joys?
10   Fame and rumour are but toys.
Cannot we delude the eyes
Of a few poor household spies?
Or his easier ears beguile,
So removèd by our wile?
'Tis no sin love's fruit to steal,
But the sweet theft to reveal:
To be taken, to be seen,
These have crimes accounted been.

   1606

Song: To Celia

Drink to me only with thine eyes,
   And I will pledge with mine;
Or leave a kiss but in the cup,
   And I'll not look for wine.
The thirst that from the soul doth rise
   Doth ask a drink divine:

But might I of Jove's nectar sup,
   I would not change for thine.
I sent thee, late, a rosy wreath,
10   Not so much honouring thee,
As giving it a hope that there
   It could not withered be.
But thou thereon didst only breathe
   And sent'st it back to me,
Since when it grows, and smells, I swear,
   Not of itself, but thee.
   1616

Clerimont's Song

Still to be neat, still to be dressed
As you were going to a feast;
Still to be powdered, still perfumed—
Lady, it is to be presumed,
Though art's hid causes are not found,
All is not sweet, all is not sound.

Give me a look, give me a face,
That makes simplicity a grace;
Robes loosely flowing, hair as free:
10 Such sweet neglect more taketh me
Than all the adulteries of art;
They strike mine eyes, but not my heart.

TOM O'BEDLAM'S SONG

THIS SEEMS TO ME the most magnificent Anonymous poem in the language, a "mad song" that surpasses Edgar's snatches of song in *King Lear* and the later lyrics in that genre by William Blake, Sir Walter Scott, and William Butler Yeats.

The manuscript commonplace book (roughly 1620) which preserved "Tom o' Bedlam's Song" is anonymous. So extraordinary is this chant that I cannot reread or recite it without thinking of Shakespeare. The poem is sophisticated and powerfully wrought, and is clearly marked by Shakespearean influence. Simply on the basis of its aesthetic splendor, it deserves to be Shakespeare's.

Released from the London asylum known as Bedlam (Bethlehem Hospital), Tom is a vagrant beggar, pleading with women for charity. Yet he seems more extravagant than vagrant, wandering beyond limits in order to break into a mode that is all but High Romantic vision.

↓   ↓   ↓

Tom o' Bedlam's Song

Anonymous

I

From the hag and hungry goblin
        That into rags would rend ye,
The spirit that stands by the naked man
        In the Book of Moons defend ye,
That of your five sound senses
        You never be forsaken
Nor wander from yourselves, with Tom,
        Abroad to beg your bacon.
While I do sing "Any food, any feeding
        Feeding, drink or clothing?"
Come dame or maid, be not afraid:
        Poor Tom will injure nothing.

II

Of thirty bare years have I
        Twice twenty been enraged,
And of forty been three times fifteen
        In durance soundly caged,
On the lordly lofts of Bedlam
        With stubble soft and dainty,
Brave bracelets strong, sweet whips ding-dong,
        And wholesome hunger plenty.
And now I sing "Any food, any feeding
        Feeding, drink or clothing?"
Come dame or maid, be not afraid:
        Poor Tom will injure nothing.

III

A thought I took for Maudlin
    With a cruse of cockle pottage—
A thing thus tall, sky bless you all!—
    When I fell into this dotage.
I've slept not since the Conquest,
    Ere then I never waked
Till the roguish boy of love where I lay
    Me found and stripped me naked.
And now I sing "Any food, any feeding
    Feeding, drink or clothing?"
Come dame or maid, be not afraid:
    Poor Tom will injure nothing.

IV

When I short have shorn my sow's-face
    And swigged my horny barrel,
At an oaken inn I impound my skin
    In a suit of gilt apparel.
The Moon's my constant mistress
    And the lovely owl my marrow,
The flaming drake and the night-crow make
    Me music to my sorrow.
While I do sing "Any food, any feeding
    Feeding, drink or clothing?"
Come dame or maid, be not afraid:
    Poor Tom will injure nothing.

V

The palsy plague my pulses
    If I prig your pigs or pullen,
Your culvers take, or matchless make
    Your Chanticlere or Solan!
When I want provant, with Humphry
    I sup, and when benighted
I repose in Paul's with waking souls
    Yet never am affrighted.
But I do sing "Any food, any feeding
    Feeding, drink or clothing?"
Come dame or maid, be not afraid:
    Poor Tom will injure nothing.

VI

I know more than Apollo,
　　For oft when he lies sleeping
I see the stars at bloody wars
　　And the wounded welkin weeping,
The moon embrace her shepherd
　　And the Queen of Love her warrior,
While the first doth horn the Star of Morn
　　And the next, the Heavenly Farrier.
While I do sing "Any food, any feeding
　　Feeding, drink or clothing?"
Come dame or maid, be not afraid:
　　Poor Tom will injure nothing.

VII

The gipsies, Snap and Pedro
　　Are none of Tom's comradoes;
The punk I scorn and the cut-purse sworn
　　And the roaring-boy's bravadoes:
The meek, the white, the gentle
　　Me handle, touch and spare not,
But those that cross Tom Rhinosceros
　　Do what the Panther dare not.
Although I sing "Any food, any feeding
　　Feeding, drink or clothing?"
Come dame or maid, be not afraid:
　　Poor Tom will injure nothing.

VIII

With an host of furious fancies
　　Whereof I am commander,
With a burning spear, and a horse of air
　　To the wilderness I wander.
By a knight of ghosts and shadows
　　I summoned am to Tourney,
Ten leagues beyond the wide world's end—
　　Methinks it is no journey.
Yet will I sing "Any food, any feeding
　　Feeding, drink or clothing?"
Come dame or maid, be not afraid:
　　Poor Tom will injure nothing.

JOHN CLEVELAND

1613–1658

CLEVELAND HAD CONSIDERABLE reputation in the 1650s as a kind of last stand of John Donne's metaphysical wit. Now forgotten except by scholars, Cleveland stays in my head for the splendid and rollicking "Mark Antony," at once an exuberant erotic exercise, and also a self-parody of metaphysical excess, of art's "ingeny" (wit). There is also a charming audacity in Cleveland's lyric, which brings out an element deliberately absent from Shakespeare's astonishing *Antony and Cleopatra*, where we are not allowed to see the Roman conqueror and the Egyptian queen alone together.

✢   ✢   ✢

Mark Antony

Whenas the nightingale chanted her vespers,
And the wild forester couched on the ground,
Venus invited me in the evening whispers
Unto a fragrant field with roses crowned,
　　Where she before had sent
　　My wishes' complement;
　　Unto my heart's content
　　Played with me on the green.
　　　Never Mark Antony
10　　Dallied more wantonly
　　　With the fair Egyptian Queen.

First on her cherry cheeks I mine eyes feasted,
Thence fear of surfeiting made me retire;
Next on her warmer lips, which when I tasted,
My duller spirits made active as fire.
　　Then we began to dart,
　　Each at another's heart,
　　Arrows that knew no smart,
　　Sweet lips and smiles between.
20　　Never Mark, &c.

Wanting a glass to plait her amber tresses,
Which like a bracelet rich deckèd mine arm,
Gaudier than Juno wears whenas she graces
Jove with embraces more stately than warm;
    Then did she peep in mine
    Eyes' humour crystalline;
    I in her eyes was seen,
    As if we one had been.
      Never Mark, &c.

30   Mystical grammar of amorous glances;
Feeling of pulses, the physic of love;
Rhetorical courtings and musical dances;
Numbering of kisses arithmetic prove;
    Eyes like astronomy;
    Straight-limbed geometry;
    In her art's ingeny
    Our wits were sharp and keen.
      Never Mark Antony
      Dallied more wantonly
40   With the fair Egyptian Queen.
    1647

JAMES SHIRLEY

1596–1666

JAMES SHIRLEY, a supporter of the Stuart cause, was a highly successful London dramatist until Parliament closed the theaters in 1642. He then fought for about two years in the royalist army, returning to London in 1644, to earn his living as a schoolmaster.

Life ended sadly for Shirley and his wife in 1666, when their house was consumed in the Great Fire of London. They died together only about two weeks later.

Shirley is now remembered only for the wonderful "Dirge" included here, which comes at the very end of his unreadable play *The Contention of Ajax and Ulysses* (1659).

I remember Robert Frost, at one of his readings, starting off by reciting Shirley's "Dirge" from memory, remarking that it was a favorite poem.

❧   ❧   ❧

Dirge

The glories of our blood and state
   Are shadows, not substantial things,
There is no armour against fate,
   Death lays his icy hand on Kings;
      Scepter and crown,
      Must tumble down,
And in the dust be equal made,
With the poor crooked scythe and spade.

Some men with swords may reap the field,
10   And plant fresh laurels where they kill,
But their strong nerves at last must yield,
   They tame but one another still;
      Early or late,
      They stoop to fate,
And must give up the murmuring breath,
When they, pale captives, creep to death.

The garlands wither on your brow,
   Then boast no more your mighty deeds;
Upon death's purple altar now,
20   See where the victor-victim bleeds,
      Your heads must come,
      To the cold tomb;
Only the actions of the just
Smell sweet, and blossom in their dust.
   1659

ROBERT HERRICK

1591–1674

HERRICK, a Londoner, returned there after Cambridge University and became one of the Tribe of Ben, the young poets who gathered around their oracle, Ben Jonson. Between 1629 and 1647, when the Cromwellians expelled him from his Devonshire parish, Herrick was a rather reluctant country clergyman, pining for the London literary life. This nostalgia may have made him into a better poet. Herrick charmingly transmutes his classical models—Horace, Catullus, the Greek Anthology—into a Devonshire pastoral poetry.

With the Restoration, Herrick returned to Devonshire in 1660, but wrote very little in the final phase of his long life. *Hesperides* (the golden apples of the sun gathered by Heracles), consisting of his secular amatory verse, was published together with *Noble Numbers*, his devotional poems, in 1648.

Rather unlike Donne, and also unlike some other poets of the Tribe of Ben, Herrick kept his amatory and religious poems strictly apart. The perpetual admonitions to virgins, to make much of time, are far more persuasive than the quite predictable devotional pieces, with the single exception of "The White Island, or Place of the Blessed." Herrick's masterpiece is the wonderful "Corinna's Going A-Maying," where the Devonshire context, the passionate urging of sexual fulfillment, and the classical poetics of Ben Jonson fuse perfectly. The poem's last stanza is particularly memorable, perhaps because Herrick implicitly understood that love, shadowed by mortality, is kindled into eroticism.

✣   ✣   ✣

To the Virgins, To Make Much of Time

Gather ye rosebuds while ye may,
    Old time is still a-flying;
And this same flower that smiles today,
    Tomorrow will be dying.

The glorious lamp of heaven, the sun,
    The higher he's a-getting,

The sooner will his race be run,
   And nearer he's to setting.

That age is best which is the first,
10   When youth and blood are warmer,
But being spent, the worse, and worst
   Times still succeed the former.

Then be not coy, but use your time,
   And while ye may, go marry:
For having lost but once your prime,
   You may forever tarry.
   1648

Upon Julia's Clothes

Whenas in silks my Julia goes,
Then, then (methinks) how sweetly flows
That liquefaction of her clothes.

Next, when I cast mine eyes and see
That brave vibration each way free,
O how that glittering taketh me!
   1648

Delight in Disorder

A sweet disorder in the dress
Kindles in clothes a wantonness:
A lawn about the shoulders thrown
Into a fine distraction:
An erring lace, which here and there
Enthralls the crimson stomacher:
A cuff neglectful, and thereby
Ribbands to flow confusèdly:
A winning wave (deserving note)
10 In the tempestuous petticoat:
A careless shoestring, in whose tie
I see a wild civility:
Do more bewitch me than when art
Is too precise in every part.
   1648

THOMAS CAREW

1594–1640

A DISCIPLE both of John Donne and of Ben Jonson, Carew was a courtier poet in the service of Charles I. The incredible richness of mid-seventeenth-century poetry sometimes obscures Carew's extraordinary gifts, which make him a stronger poet than the more popular Herrick or Lovelace. These gifts are psychological and rhetorical, and convey male sexual aggressivity more formidably than does any other poet since Shakespeare. One might speak of Carew, not in the terms of the "wit of love," but of the wit of male sexual drive, with its notorious tendency not to differentiate among women. A highly self-conscious Epicurean materialist, Carew was known as the "Oracle of Love," yet his honest reductiveness has little enough to do with love, and everything to do with desire and fulfillment.

Carew was the son of a well-known London lawyer, who later failed financially. The poet took up a diplomatic career, but it terminated, due to indiscretion on Carew's part. Fortunately, he won the patronage of Charles I, serving him at court, but, sadly, perished of prolonged illness at forty-five.

"A Rapture" is one of the finest erotic poems in the language, while the elegy on the death of John Donne is a deft tribute that uses Donne's characteristic turns of thought and paradoxical wit to praise the great poet and preacher. The song "Ask me no more where *Jove* bestowes" is as superbly rendered as the best songs of Ben Jonson, Carew's other master.

↓   ↓   ↓

A Rapture

I will enjoy thee now, my Celia, come,
And fly with me to Love's Elysium.
The giant, Honour, that keeps cowards out,
Is but a masquer, and the servile rout
Of baser subjects only bend in vain
To the vast idol; whilst the nobler train
Of valiant lovers daily sail between
The huge Colossus' legs, and pass unseen
Unto the blissful shore. Be bold and wise,

10 And we shall enter: the grim Swiss denies
Only to tame fools a passage, that not know
He is but form, and only frights in show
The duller eyes that look from far; draw near,
And thou shalt scorn what we were wont to fear.
We shall see how the stalking pageant goes
With borrowed legs, a heavy load to those
That made and bear him: not, as we once thought,
The seed of gods, but a weak model wrought
By greedy men, that seek to enclose the common,
20 And within private arms impale free woman.
   Come, then, and mounted on the wings of Love
We'll cut the flitting air, and soar above
The monster's head, and in the noblest seats
Of those blest shades quench and renew our heats.
There shall the Queens of Love and Innocence,
Beauty and Nature, banish all offence
From our close ivy-twines; there I'll behold
Thy barèd snow and thy unbraided gold;
There my enfranchised hand on every side
30 Shall o'er thy naked polished ivory slide.
No curtain there, though of transparent lawn,
Shall be before thy virgin-treasure drawn;
But the rich mine, to the inquiring eye
Exposed, shall ready still for mintage lie;
And we will coin young Cupids. There a bed
Of roses and fresh myrtles shall be spread
Under the cooler shade of cypress groves;
Our pillows of the down of Venus' doves,
Whereon our panting limbs we'll gently lay,
40 In the faint respites of our active play;
That so our slumbers may in dreams have leisure
To tell the nimble fancy our past pleasure,
And so our souls that cannot be embraced
Shall the embraces of our bodies taste.
Meanwhile the bubbling stream shall court the shore,
The enamoured chirping wood-choir shall adore
In varied tunes the Deity of Love;
The gentle blasts of western winds shall move
The trembling leaves, and through their close boughs breathe
50 Still music, whilst we rest ourselves beneath
Their dancing shade; till a soft murmur, sent
From souls entranced in amorous languishment,

Rouse us, and shoot into our veins fresh fire,
Till we in their sweet ecstasy expire.
   Then, as the empty bee, that lately bore
Into the common treasure all her store,
Flies 'bout the painted field with nimble wing,
Deflowering the fresh virgins of the spring,
So will I rifle all the sweets that dwell
60 In my delicious paradise, and swell
My bag with honey, drawn forth by the power
Of fervent kisses from each spicy flower.
I'll seize the rose-buds in their perfumed bed,
The violet knots, like curious mazes spread
O'er all the garden, taste the ripened cherry,
The warm firm apple, tipped with coral berry;
Then will I visit with a wandering kiss
The vale of lilies and the bower of bliss:
And where the beauteous region doth divide
70 Into two milky ways, my lips shall slide
Down those smooth alleys, wearing as I go
A tract for lovers on the printed snow;
Thence climbing o'er the swelling Apennine,
Retire into thy grove of eglantine,
Where I will all those ravished sweets distill
Through Love's alembic, and with chemic skill
From the mixed mass one sovereign balm derive,
Then bring that great elixir to thy hive.
   Now in more subtle wreaths I will entwine
80 My sinewy thighs, my legs and arms with thine;
Thou like a sea of milk shalt lie displayed,
Whilst I the smooth, calm ocean invade
With such a tempest, as when Jove of old
Fell down on Danaë in a storm of gold;
Yet my tall pine shall in the Cyprian strait
Ride safer at anchor, and unlade her freight:
My rudder with thy bold hand, like a tried
And skillful pilot, thou shalt steer, and guide
My bark into love's channel, where it shall
90 Dance, as the bounding waves do rise or fall.
Then shall thy circling arms embrace and clip
My willing body, and thy balmy lip
Bathe me in juice of kisses, whose perfume
Like a religious incense shall consume,
And send up holy vapours to those powers

That bless our loves and crown our sportful hours,
That with such halcyon calmness fix our souls
In steadfast peace, as no affright controls.
There no rude sounds shake us with sudden starts;
100   No jealous ears, when we unrip our hearts,
Suck our discourse in; no observing spies
This blush, that glance traduce; no envious eyes
Watch our close meetings; nor are we betrayed
To rivals by the bribèd chambermaid.
No wedlock bonds unwreathe our twisted loves;
We seek no midnight arbour, no dark groves
To hide our kisses: there the hated name
Of husband, wife, lust, modest, chaste or shame,
Are vain and empty words, whose very sound
110   Was never heard in the Elysian ground.
All things are lawful there that may delight
Nature or unrestrainèd appetite;
Like and enjoy, to will and act is one:
We only sin when Love's rites are not done.
    The Roman Lucrece there reads the divine
Lectures of Love's great master, Aretine,
And knows as well as Lais how to move
Her pliant body in the act of love.
To quench the burning ravisher, she hurls
120   Her limbs into a thousand winding curls,
And studies artful postures, such as be
Carved on the bark of every neighbouring tree
By learnèd hands, that so adorned the rind
Of those fair plants, which, as they lay entwined,
Have fanned their glowing fires. The Grecian dame,
That in her endless web toiled for a name
As fruitless as her work, doth there display
Herself before the youth of Ithaca,
And the amorous sport of gamesome nights prefer
130   Before dull dreams of the lost traveller.
Daphne hath broke her bark, and that swift foot
Which the angry gods had fastened with a root
To the fixed earth doth now unfettered run
To meet the embraces of the youthful Sun.
She hangs upon him like his Delphic lyre;
Her kisses blow the old, and breathe new fire;
Full of her god, she sings inspired lays,
Sweet odes of love, such as deserve the bays,

Which she herself was. Next her, Laura lies
140   In Petrarch's learnèd arms, drying those eyes
That did in such sweet smooth-paced numbers flow,
As made the world enamoured of his woe.
These, and ten thousand beauties more, that died
Slave to the tyrant, now enlarged deride
His cancelled laws, and for their time misspent
Pay into Love's exchequer double rent.
      Come then, my Celia, we'll no more forbear
To taste our joys, struck with a panic fear,
But will depose from his imperious sway
150   This proud usurper, and walk free as they,
With necks unyoked; nor is it just that he
Should fetter your soft sex with chastity,
Which Nature made unapt for abstinence;
When yet this false impostor can dispense
With human justice and with sacred right,
And, maugre both their laws, command me fight
With rivals or with emulous loves that dare
Equal with thine their mistress' eyes or hair.
If thou complain of wrong, and call my sword
160   To carve out thy revenge, upon that word
He bids me fight and kill, or else he brands
With marks of infamy my coward hands,
And yet religion bids from bloodshed fly,
And damns me for that act. Then tell me why
This goblin Honour, which the world adores,
Should make men atheists, and not women whores.
      1640

Song

Ask me no more where *Jove* bestowes,
When *June* is past, the fading rose:
For in your beauties orient deep,
These Flowers as in their causes sleep.

Ask me no more whither doe stray
The golden Atomes of the day:
For in pure love heaven did prepare
Those powders to inrich your hair.

Ask me no more whither doth hast
The Nightingale, when *May* is past:
For in your sweet dividing throat
She winters, and keeps warm her note.

Ask me no more where those starres light,
That downwards fall in dead of night:
For in your eyes they sit, and there,
Fixèd, become as in their sphere.

Ask me no more if East or West,
The Phenix builds her spicy nest:
For unto you at last she flyes,
And in your fragrant bosome dies.

RICHARD LOVELACE

1618–1658

LOVELACE, like Suckling, was a sacrifice to the cause of Stuart royalism, but is much the more considerable of the two poets. Sir William Lovelace, the poet's father, died in action, fighting for the Stuarts in Holland. At court, the young Lovelace came under the protection of Lord Goring, who in 1647 became one of the chiefs of the royalist army. In 1642, Lovelace was imprisoned by Parliament, and after his release was an exile in Holland and France until 1646. Parliament locked him up again from 1648 to 1649.

From 1649 until his death in 1658, Lovelace suffered a miserable existence in London, having ruined himself financially by his generous support of the Stuart cause. His strongest poem may be "The Grasshopper," but I do not include it here, because it requires elaborate historical commentary to be fully appreciated. Instead, I give three poems highly available to the common reader.

"La Bella Bona Roba" literally means a pleasantly plump young woman, but was a common expression for a whore. Lovelace, with outrageous charm, declares his preference for women not too slender. The same charm is present in his song to Lucasta, with its now notorious ending: "I could not love thee, dear, so much, / Loved I not honour more" and in the equally familiar song written from prison to Althea: "Stone walls do not a prison make, / Nor iron bars a cage."

After "The Grasshopper," Lovelace's most remarkable poem, to me, is "Love Made in the First Age." There the Cavalier poet uses the secular myth of the Golden Age, eloquently developed by the Roman poet Ovid, to give us a vision of unfallen sexuality, a somewhat outrageous one. The wit of the first stanza is altogether Lovelace's own: since seventeenth-century divines held that Hebrew was the original language, and since it is written from right to left, any English verbal courting is "backward." Ovid would have been startled to learn that Hebrew was the language of the Golden Age, but he might have enjoyed Lovelace's delicious version of sexuality without guilt.

↓   ↓   ↓

La Bella Bona Roba

I cannot tell who loves the skeleton
Of a poor marmoset, naught but bone, bone.
Give me a nakedness with her clothes on.

Such whose white-satin upper coat of skin,
Cut upon velvet rich incarnadin,
Has yet a body (and of flesh) within.

Sure it is meant good husbandry in men,
Who so incorporate with aery lean,
To repair their sides, and get their rib again.

10   Hard hap unto that huntsman that decrees
Fat joys for all his sweat, whenas he sees,
After his 'say, naught but his keeper's fees.

Then Love, I beg, when next thou takest thy bow,
Thy angry shafts, and dost heart-chasing go,
Pass rascal deer, strike me the largest doe.
    1649

Song

To Lucasta, Going to the Wars

Tell me not, sweet, I am unkind,
    That from the nunnery
Of thy chaste breast and quiet mind,
    To war and arms I fly.

True, a new mistress now I chase,
    The first foe in the field;
And with a stronger faith embrace
    A sword, a horse, a shield.

Yet this inconstancy is such
10   As you too shall adore;
I could not love thee, dear, so much,
    Loved I not honour more.
    1649

To Althea, from Prison

When Love with unconfinèd wings
    Hovers within my Gates;
And my divine *Althea* brings
    To whisper at the Grates:
When I lye tangled in her haire,
    And fetterd to her eye;
The *Gods* that wanton in the Aire,
    Know no such Liberty.

When flowing Cups run swiftly round
    With no allaying *Thames,*
Our carelesse heads with Roses bound,
    Our hearts with Loyall Flames;
When thirsty griefe in Wine we steepe,
    When Healths and draughts go free,
Fishes that tipple in the Deepe,
    Know no such Libertie.

When (like committed Linnets) I
    With shriller throat shall sing

The sweetnes, Mercy, Majesty,
   And glories of my KING;
When I shall voyce aloud, how Good
   He is, how Great should be;
     Inlargèd Winds that curle the Flood,
     Know no such Liberty.

Stone Walls doe not a Prison make,
   Nor Iron bars a Cage;
Mindes innocent and quiet take
   That for an Hermitage;
If I have freedome in my Love,
   And in my soule am free;
Angels alone that sore above,
   Injoy such Liberty.

SIR JOHN SUCKLING

1609–1641

THE SON OF A COMPTROLLER of the Household of James I, Suckling was raised in loyalty to the Stuarts, and died by his own hand in Paris at the age of thirty-two, in flight from the enemies of Charles I. A warrior as much as a poet, Suckling was a notorious gambler, and threw away his life as on a toss.

    The great English Romantic critic William Hazlitt is still Suckling's best critic:

> His compositions are almost all of them short and lively effusions of wit and gallantry, written in a familiar but spirited style, without much design or effort. . . . His Ballad on a Wedding is his masterpiece, and is indeed unrivaled in that class of composition, for the voluptuous delicacy of the sentiments, and the luxuriant richness of the images.

      ❧   ❧   ❧

Song

Why so pale and wan, fond lover?
　　Prithee, why so pale?
Will, when looking well can't move her,
　　Looking ill prevail?
5　　　Prithee, why so pale?

Why so dull and mute, young sinner?
　　Prithee, why so mute?
Will, when speaking well can't win her,
　　Saying nothing do't?
10　　　Prithee, why so mute?

Quit, quit, for shame; this will not move,
　　This cannot take her;
If of herself she will not love,
　　Nothing can make her:
15　　　The devil take her!

"Out upon it! I have loved"

Out upon it! I have loved
　　Three whole days together;
And am like to love three more,
　　If it prove fair weather.

5　Time shall molt away his wings
　　Ere he shall discover
In the whole wide world again
　　Such a constant lover.

But the spite on't is, no praise
10　　Is due at all to me:
Love with me had made no stay,
　　Had it any been but she.

Had it any been but she,
　　And that very very face,
15　There had been at least ere this
　　A dozen dozen in her place.

EDMUND WALLER

1606–1687

WALLER WAS A STUART POLITICIAN, accustomed from early days to wealth and power. In 1643, he was active in a royalist conspiracy to seize control of London. Apprehended by Parliament, Waller turned State's evidence, and informed on his associates, who were hanged. After a year's imprisonment in the Tower, he was banished from England.

Pardoned by Cromwell in 1651, Waller returned, and after the Restoration was elected to Parliament. Famous as a poet in his own day, he is now rightly passed over, except for the charming lyric included here.

✤   ✤   ✤

Song

Go lovely Rose,
Tell her that wastes her time and me,
That now she knows
When I resemble her to thee
How sweet and fair she seems to be.

Tell her that's young,
And shuns to have her graces spy'd
That hadst thou sprung
In desarts where no men abide,
Thou must have uncommended dy'd.

Small is the worth
Of beauty from the light retir'd;
Bid her come forth,
Suffer her self to be desir'd,
And not blush so to be admir'd.

Then die that she,
The common fate of all things rare
May read in thee;
How small a part of time they share,
That are so wondrous sweet and fair.

ANDREW MARVELL

1621–1678

ANDREW MARVELL is a unique poet, comparable to Jonson in lyric achievement, and as much an original as Donne. He is almost as private as Emily Dickinson. Like her, he chose to be unpublished in his own lifetime. A statesman, he served Cromwell, and continued to represent his native city of Hull after the Restoration.

Friend and admirer of John Milton, Marvell was no more Miltonic than he was Jonsonean or Donnean in his poetry. Critical admiration for Marvell began in the Romantic period with Charles Lamb and William Hazlitt and continued with Tennyson, achieving an apotheosis in T. S. Eliot. Since Eliot, Marvell has been another poet's poet, but a general audience has held fast to a few poems: "The Garden," "To His Coy Mistress," "The Definition of Love," and "An Horatian Ode upon Cromwell's Return from Ireland." Marvell is also immensely influential upon modern poetry; the greatest living American poet, John Ashbery, abounds in Marvellian allusions.

Marvell, despite his admiration for *Paradise Lost,* eloquently manifested in his dedicatory poem to the epic's second edition, essentially was cut off from his contemporaries, in literary rather than political terms. Eminently a thinker and imaginer for himself, Marvell is at once original and yet curiously central, so that he cannot be regarded as less than a major poet of an eminence equal to Donne's or Jonson's or George Herbert's.

Marvell is the most enigmatic, unclassifiable, and unaffiliated major poet in the language. It is finally unhelpful to call his poetry Metaphysical, Mannerist, Epicurean, Platonist, or Puritan, though all of those terms somehow are applicable. One of the most original poets in Western tradition, Marvell had no strong precursors, though Spenser may be near his hidden root. His poetry has a clear relation to the schools of Donne and Jonson, but is of neither, unlike that of such contemporaries as Randolph, Carew, and Lovelace. The distance from Milton, his greatest contemporary and the subject of one of his most admirable and admiring poems, is remarkable. His authentic affinities were with quite minor French poets who came after the Pléiade, Théophile de Viau (1590–1626) and Antoine-Girard de Saint-Amant (1594–1661).

Post-Pléiade French pastoralists can be said to have invented Marvell's lyric mode, but there is absolutely nothing Gallic about Marvell's own poetry. Nor are there Marvellian poets after Marvell. T. S. Eliot, though his essay on Marvell has been so influential, is a Tennysonian-Whitmanian elegist of the self, whose actual verse has more in common with that of William Morris than with Marvell.

Eliot's celebrated essay, still being exalted by Frank Kermode and others, is in fact quite bad, being replete with irrelevant assertions as to how much better a poet Marvell is than Shelley, Keats, Wordsworth, Tennyson, Browning, Hardy, and Yeats, all of whom lacked what Eliot "designated tentatively as wit, a tough reasonableness beneath the slight lyric grace." We learn also from Eliot that Marvell surpasses the "L'Allegro" and "Il Penseroso" of Milton, a judgment that might have provoked some amiable skepticism in Marvell himself. Poor William Morris, a poet not very relevant to Marvell's mode, is also dragged in for a drubbing, and Eliot concludes that Browning, whose "A Toccata of Galuppi's" may be the most maturely sophisticated shorter poem in the language, "seems oddly immature, in some way, beside Marvell." Two years after his 1921 essay on Marvell, Eliot changed his mind anyway, in a review of the Nonesuch Press edition of Marvell's *Miscellaneous Poems*, where we learn that Marvell, unlike Chaucer and Pope, is "fantastical," conceit-ridden, and is in any case not as great a poet as Bishop Henry King, author of the "Exequy," but not of much more that engages us now. Though Kermode is Eliot's declared inheritor as a Marvell critic, I find his general emphasis more useful than his precursor's:

> To conclude: Marvell is not a philosophical poet; in his role as poet he engaged his subjects as poetry, bringing to them a mind of great intelligence and intelligently ordered learning. Our knowledge of his religious and political thought helps us only a little more than our knowledge of his personal life (quick temper, preference for solitary drinking) and can be related to the substance of his poetry only very cautiously and generally (the power of a mind engaged but detached, the alertness, leaning on the wind). Negatively, we can learn a lot from other poetry, and from the nature and contemporary use of allegory (habitual intermittency defined by the cult of acuteness or wit, and the resonantly defined detail). Broad categories are misleading; using words such as "puritan," "Platonist," even such as "nature" and "wit," we must constantly discriminate: wit is not seventeenth-century property but an ancient instrument of poetry and of religion, nature an indescribably complex inheritance of assumptions and meanings.

My only dissent here would be to go a bit further; that Marvell was a bad-tempered, hard-drinking, lifelong bachelor and controversialist is more helpful knowledge than everything we know of his religion and politics, for the paradoxical reason that such a personality simply does not manifest itself in the poems, except perhaps for the satires. The Mower poems could have been written by a good-tempered married man who never touched alcohol and had little notion of religious and political quarrels. Yet they are at once absolutely idiosyncratic and personal, and totally universal in scope and emphasis, which is only to say that they are very great, very enigmatic lyric poems rather than philosophical tractates or scholarly investigations.

✤ ✤ ✤

To His Coy Mistress

Had we but world enough, and time,
This coyness, Lady, were no crime.
We would sit down, and think which way
To walk, and pass our long love's day.
Thou by the Indian Ganges' side
Shouldst rubies find; I by the tide
Of Humber would complain. I would
Love you ten years before the Flood,
And you should, if you please, refuse
Till the Conversion of the Jews.
My vegetable love should grow
Vaster than empires and more slow;
An hundred years should go to praise
Thíne eyes, and on thy forehead gaze;
Two hundred to adore each breast,
But thirty thousand to the rest;
An age at least to every part,
And the last age should show your heart.
For, Lady, you deserve this state,
Nor would I love at lower rate.
    But at my back I always hear
Time's wingéd chariot hurrying near;
And yonder all before us lie
Deserts of vast eternity.
Thy beauty shall no more be found,

Nor, in thy marble vault, shall sound
My echoing song; then worms shall try
That long-preserved virginity.
And your quaint honour turn to dust,
30 And into ashes all my lust:
The grave's a fine and private place,
But none, I think, do there embrace.
      Now therefore, while the youthful hue
Sits on thy skin like morning dew,
And while thy willing soul transpires
At every pore with instant fires,
Now let us sport us while we may,
And now, like amorous birds of prey,
Rather at once our time devour
40 Than languish in his slow-chapt power.
Let us roll all our strength and all
Our sweetness up into one ball,
And tear our pleasures with rough strife
Thorough the iron gates of life;
Thus, though we cannot make our sun
Stand still, yet we will make him run.

      1681

The Mower Poems

If Marvell is a poet's poet, then his lyrics and meditations have a particularly refreshing function for us right now, when poetry is studied as everything except poetry, be it politics, societal discontents, gender struggles,
historicisms, philosophies, psychologies, semiotics, or what you will. Good
critics, when once they still read poems as poems, accurately found in
Marvell the culmination of the European pastoral lyric that Theocritus had
inaugurated. Thomas G. Rosenmeyer, in his fine book on Theocritus, *The
Green Cabinet* (1969), concluded that in the pastoral mode, "the poem as
a whole is a trope, rather than any one portion of it." As a principle, this
seems truer even of Marvell than of Theocritus and Vergil. Marvell's
Mower poems are extended metaphors for a highly individual view of how
our fall caused nature's loss of value also, so that the wounding power of
sexual love became the wound that sexuality itself ended by being. William
Empson interpreted the Mower most grandly:

In these meadows he feels he has left his mark on a great territory, if not on everything, and as a typical figure he has mown all the meadows of the world; in either case Nature gives him regal and magical honors, and I suppose he is not only the ruler but the executioner of the daffodils—the Clown as Death.

In one aspect the pastoral Mower may be the Clown as Death, but in the enigmatic Mower poems this most original of Marvell's tropes cannot be uncovered once and for all. In "The Mower Against Gardens," the Mower ends by insisting that "the gods themselves with us do dwell," presumably because we are not altogether fallen any more than nature is, since "the sweet fields" still "to all dispense / A wild and fragrant innocence." This is very different from the extraordinary triad of "Damon the Mower," "The Mower to the Glowworms," and "The Mower's Song," all of them reliant upon a great text in Isaiah:

> The voice said, Cry. And he said, What shall I cry? All flesh is grass, and all the goodliness thereof is as the flower of the field:
> The grass withereth, the flower fadeth: because the spirit of the LORD bloweth upon it: surely the people is grass.
> The grass withereth, the flower fadeth: but the world of our God shall stand forever.
>
> —ISAIAH 40:6–8

In Walt Whitman, the grass becomes flesh, a metamorphosis in which Marvell preceded Whitman. Damon the Mower, stung by Juliana's scorching beams, attains involuntarily a congruence of inner qualities and outer emblems:

> Sharp like his scythe his sorrow was,
> And withered like his hopes the grass.

Marvell's Mower, absurdly enough, is both the ridiculous Polyphemus, the Cyclops of Theocritus, and, I suspect, the Adam Kadmon or unfallen God-Man of Kabbalistic and Hermetic tradition. That is, Damon is Adam, Adam both debased beneath and exalted beyond the Adam of Genesis. Damon is the Clown as Death, if you will, but he is (or was) also the Clown as a more abundant, preexistent life, not so much the Cyclops or Vergil's Corydon as the Platonic dream of a divine human before the crashing downward of a catastrophic creation. Marvell's more-than-ironic mode conveys mysteries only through an immensely sophisticated humor, edged by the reality principle of mortality. Ruth Nevo adroitly describes "Damon the Mower" as "a pastoral elegy for the quiet mind disturbed radically by desire unsatisfied," which sensibly leaves undefined whose mind that is, and how cosmological the desire may be. Geoffrey Hartman, sinuously seeking to match the subtle Marvell, finds the theme of the Mower poems in "the labor of hope," with "hope in nature frustrated by love or by the very strength of hope." Hartman's Mower is rather like the afflicted heroine of Wordsworth's "The Ruined Cottage"; what has been cultivated in hope is now destroyed in hope, as the end is hastened. The instrument of that hastening is death's scythe, which dominates the final three exquisite stanzas of this eleven-stanza lyric.

"The Mower Mown" might well have been the poem's title, except for its neglect of Damon in his self-apotheosis:

> I am the Mower Damon, known
> Through all the meadows I have mown.
> On me the morn her dew distills
> Before her darling daffodils.
> And, if at noon my toil me heat,
> The sun himself licks off my sweat.
> While, going home, the evening sweet
> In cowslip-water bathes my feet.

That does not seem to me the Clown as Death so much as the Clown as Hermetic Adam, living in a place very much his own, and even more his self, being at home all the time. We see Damon-Adam fall again in stanzas 9–11, and so lose his home, possibly forever.

The Mower Against Gardens

Luxurious man, to bring his vice in use,
    Did after him the world seduce,
And from the fields the flowers and plants allure,
    Where Nature was most plain and pure.
He first enclosed within the gardens square
    A dead and standing pool of air,
And a more luscious earth for them did knead,
    Which stupefied them while it fed.
The pink grew then as double as his mind;
10   The nutriment did change the kind.
With strange perfumes he did the roses taint;

And flowers themselves were taught to paint.
The tulip white did for complexion seek,
    And learned to interline its cheek;
Its onion root they then so high did hold,
    That one was for a meadow sold:
Another world was searched through oceans new,
    To find the *Marvel of Peru;*
And yet these rarities might be allowed
20   To man, that sovereign thing and proud,
Had he not dealt between the bark and tree,
    Forbidden mixtures there to see.
No plant now knew the stock from which it came;
    He grafts upon the wild the tame,
That the uncertain and adulterate fruit
    Might put the palate in dispute.
His green seraglio has its eunuchs too,
    Lest any tyrant him outdo;
And in the cherry he does Nature vex,
30   To procreate without a sex.
'Tis all enforced, the fountain and the grot,
    While the sweet fields do lie forgot,
Where willing Nature does to all dispense
    A wild and fragrant innocence;
And fauns and fairies do the meadows till
    More by their presence than their skill.
Their statues polished by some ancient hand,
    May to adorn the gardens stand;
But, howsoe'er the figures do excel,
40   The Gods themselves with us do dwell.
    1681

The Mower to the Glowworms

This extraordinary lyric, addressed by the fallen Mower to the luminaries of his severely shrunken world, is surely one of the most mysterious and beautiful poems in the language. I cannot reread it or recite it to myself without evoking the beautiful quatrains that Blake added to *The Gates of Paradise* when he reengraved the little Prophetic Book, addressing the quatrains "To The Accuser who is The God of This World" (see page 321.) But "The Mower to the Glowworms" has no Jobean associations, even if it too is a lost traveler's dream under the hill. "The grass's fall" is the fall of the flesh, and the third stanza might almost have been written by William Blake.

The first stanza of "The Mower's Song" recapitulates the last stanza here, when the Mower's mind is displaced, but the revision is in a finer tone:

> My mind was once the true survey
> Of all these meadows fresh and gay,
> And in the greenness of the grass
> Did see its hopes as in a glass;
> When Juliana came, and she
> What I do to the grass, does to my thoughts and me.

Juliana is the Charmer as Death, and the remainder of the poem centers itself upon the extraordinary revelations of that last line, Marvell's solitary and unique instance of a refrain. Damon, resenting the flowers, truly resents a green world that will survive his own now irretrievable fall. But his resentment is also an apocalyptic paradox, since his "revenge" of "one common ruin" is pragmatically a further riot of what Whitman calls the flag of the poet's disposition, out of hopeful green stuff woven. The heraldry of green will make the entire earth the Mower's tomb, but such a heraldry will bury the scythe and scyther alike, give death to Death, and perhaps herald the rebirth of Damon as Adam Kadmon, the Primal Man forever not to be mown down.

The Mower to the Glowworms

Ye living lamps, by whose dear light
The nightingale does sit so late,
And studying all the summer-night,
Her matchless songs does meditate;

Ye country comets, that portend
No war, nor prince's funeral,
Shining unto no higher end
Than to presage the grass's fall;

Ye glowworms, whose officious flame
10 To wand'ring mowers shows the way,
That in the night have lost their aim,
And after foolish fires do stray;

Your courteous lights in vain you waste,
Since Juliana here is come,
For she my mind hath so displaced
That I shall never find my home.

1681

The Garden

How vainly men themselves amaze
To win the palm, the oak, or bays;
And their uncessant labours see
Crowned from some single herb or tree:
Whose short and narrow-vergèd shade
Does prudently their toils upbraid;
While all flowers and all trees do close
To weave the garlands of repose.

Fair Quiet, have I found thee here,
And Innocence, thy sister dear!
Mistaken long, I sought you then
In busy companies of men.
Your sacred plants, if here below,
Only among the plants will grow.
Society is all but rude,
To this delicious solitude.

No white nor red was ever seen
So amorous as this lovely green.
Fond lovers, cruel as their flame,
Cut in these trees their mistress' name:
Little, alas, they know or heed
How far these beauties hers exceed!
Fair trees, wheresoe'er your barks I wound,
No name shall but your own be found.

When we have run our passion's heat,
Love hither makes his best retreat.
The gods, that mortal beauty chase,
Still in a tree did end their race:
Apollo hunted Daphne so,
Only that she might laurel grow;

And Pan did after Syrinx speed,
Not as a nymph, but for a reed.

What wondrous life in this I lead!
Ripe apples drop about my head;
The luscious clusters of the vine
Upon my mouth do crush their wine;
The nectarine and curious peach
Into my hands themselves do reach;
Stumbling on melons, as I pass,
40   Ensnared with flowers, I fall on grass.

Meanwhile the mind from pleasure less
Withdraws into its happiness;
The mind, that ocean where each kind
Does straight its own resemblance find;
Yet it creates, transcending these,
Far other worlds and other seas,
Annihilating all that's made
To a green thought in a green shade.

Here at the fountain's sliding foot,
50   Or at some fruit-tree's mossy root,
Casting the body's vest aside,
My soul into the boughs does glide:
There, like a bird, it sits and sings,
Then whets and combs its silver wings,
And, till prepared for longer flights,
Waves in its plumes the various light.

Such was that happy garden-state,
While man there walked without a mate:
After a place so pure and sweet,
60   What other help could yet be meet!
But 'twas beyond a mortal's share
To wander solitary there:
Two paradises 'twere in one
To live in paradise alone.

How well the skillful gardener drew,
Of flowers and herbs, this dial new;
Where, from above, the milder sun

Does through a fragrant zodiac run;
And, as it works, the industrious bee
70 Computes its time as well as we!
How could such sweet and wholesome hours
Be reckoned but with herbs and flowers!
   1681

An Horatian Ode upon Cromwell's Return from Ireland

The forward youth that would appear
Must now forsake his Muses dear,
   Nor in the shadows sing
   His numbers languishing:
'Tis time to leave the books in dust,
And oil th' unusèd armour's rust,
   Removing from the wall
   The corslet of the hall.
So restless Cromwell could not cease
10 In the inglorious arts of peace,
   But through adventurous war
   Urgèd his active star;
And like the three-forked lightning, first
Breaking the clouds where it was nursed,
   Did thorough his own side
   His fiery way divide.
For 'tis all one to courage high,
The emulous or enemy;
   And with such to inclose
20   Is more than to oppose.
Then burning through the air he went,
And palaces and temples rent;
   And Cæsar's head at last
   Did through his laurels blast.
'Tis madness to resist or blame
The force of angry heaven's flame;
   And, if we would speak true,
   Much to the man is due,
Who, from his private gardens, where
30 He lived reservèd and austere
   (As if his highest plot
   To plant the bergamot),

Could by industrious valour climb
To ruin the greatest work of time,
    And cast the kingdoms old
    Into another mould;
Though Justice against Fate complain,
And plead the ancient rights in vain;
    But those do hold or break,
40   As men are strong or weak.
Nature, that hateth emptiness,
Allows of penetration less,
    And therefore must make room
    Where greater spirits come.
What field of all the civil wars,
Where his were not the deepest scars?
    And Hampton shows what part
    He had of wiser art;
Where, twining subtle fears with hope,
50 He wove a net of such a scope
    That Charles himself might chase
    To Carisbrooke's narrow case,
That thence the Royal Actor borne
The tragic scaffold might adorn;
    While round the armèd bands
    Did clap their bloody hands.
He nothing common did, or mean,
Upon that memorable scene,
    But with his keener eye
60   The axe's edge did try;
Nor called the gods with vulgar spite
To vindicate his helpless right;
    But bowed his comely head
    Down, as upon a bed.
This was that memorable hour
Which first assured the forcèd power;
    So, when they did design
    The Capitol's first line,
A bleeding head, where they begun,
70 Did fright the architects to run;
    And yet in that the state
    Foresaw its happy fate.
And now the Irish are ashamed
To see themselves in one year tamed;

So much one man can do
   That does both act and know.
They can affirm his praises best,
And have, though overcome, confessed
   How good he is, how just,
80   And fit for highest trust,
Nor yet grown stiffer with command,
But still in the republic's hand—
   How fit is he to sway
   That can so well obey!
He to the Commons' feet presents
A kingdom for his first year's rents;
   And, what he may, forbears
   His fame, to make it theirs;
And has his sword and spoils ungirt,
90   To lay them at the public's skirt:
   So when the falcon high
   Falls heavy from the sky,
She, having killed, no more does search
But on the next green bough to perch;
   Where, when he first does lure,
   The falconer has her sure.
What may not, then, our isle presume,
While victory his crest does plume?
   What may not others fear,
100   If thus he crown each year?
A Cæsar he, ere long, to Gaul,
To Italy an Hannibal,
   And to all states not free
   Shall climactèric be.
The Pict no shelter now shall find
Within his party-coloured mind,
   But from this valour sad
   Shrink underneath the plaid;
Happy if in the tufted brake
110   The English hunter him mistake,
   Nor lay his hounds in near
   The Caledonian deer.
But thou, the war's and fortune's son,
March indefatigably on!
   And for the last effect,
   Still keep thy sword erect;
Besides the force it has to fright

The spirits of the shady night,
    The same arts that did gain
    A power must it maintain.

120

1681

GEORGE HERBERT

1593–1633

THERE ARE ONLY A FEW extraordinary devotional poets in the language, including Donne and the Victorians Gerard Manley Hopkins and Christina Rossetti. By any standard, George Herbert is the devotional poet proper in English, Donne being several other kinds of poet as well. Like Marvell, Hopkins, and Emily Dickinson, Herbert avoided publication in his own lifetime. But he arranged his book of poems, *The Temple*, knowing that it would be published soon after his death, at forty.

Without Donne's secular poetry, it would be hard to conceive of Herbert's sacred volume, since Herbert seems more aware of the erotic poems of Donne than of the hymns and Holy Sonnets. From Donne, Herbert takes an extraordinary ingenuity for the making of metaphor, but transfigures Donne's images into building blocks for *The Temple:*

> Doth poetry
> Wear Venus' livery? Only serve her turn?
> Why are not sonnets made of thee?

Samuel Johnson, more than a century later, in effect answers this by a fierce series of strictures against religious poetry, with Edmund Waller's *Divine Poems* as target:

> Contemplative piety, or the intercourse between God and the human soul, cannot be poetical. Man admitted to implore the mercy of his Creator, and plead the merits of his Redeemer, is already in a higher state than poetry can confer.
>   The essence of poetry is invention; such invention as, by producing something unexpected, surprises and delights. The topicks of devotion are few, and being few are universally known; but few

as they are, they can be made no more; they can receive no grace from novelty of sentiment, and very little from novelty of expression. . . .

Of sentiments purely religious, it will be found that the most simple expression is the most sublime. Poetry loses its lustre and its power, because it is applied to the decoration of something more excellent than itself. All that verse can do is to help the memory, and delight the ear, and for these purposes it may be very useful; but it supplies nothing to the mind. The ideas of Christian Theology are too simple for fiction, and too majestick for ornament; to recommend them by tropes and figures, is to magnify by a concave mirror the sidereal hemisphere.

For the fervent Dr. Johnson, this is a very painful matter indeed. Is he mistaken? I have never seen him refuted, and well remember that I could not induce my own Johnsonian teacher, the formidable Catholic New Critic William K. Wimsatt, to address himself to this argument that "the good and evil of eternity are too ponderous for the wings of wit." Dr. Johnson avoided George Herbert, who may be the only devotional poet in the language (besides Donne) inventive enough to answer the force of the Johnsonian assault. In Herbert, the poem discourses upon prayer, not at all a simple achievement, beautifully accomplished in "Prayer (1)":

> Prayer the Church's banquet, Angels' age,
>   God's breath in man returning to his birth,
>   The soul in paraphrase, heart in pilgrimage,
> The Christian plummet sounding heaven and earth;
> Engine against the Almighty, sinners' tower,
>   Reversed thunder, Christ-side-piercing spear,
>   The six-day's-world transposing in an hour,
> A kind of tune, which all things hear and fear;
> Softness, and peace, and joy, and love, and bliss,
>   Exalted manna, gladness of the best,
>   Heaven in ordinary, man well dressed,
> The milky way, the bird of paradise,
>   Church-bells beyond the stars heard, the soul's blood,
>   The land of spices; something understood.

This astonishing sonnet deploys some two dozen superb tropes, all images of prayer. That said, one notes it does not purport to be prayer, and so omits any predicate verb. Prayer ingeniously becomes a sequence of metaphors, several of them gustatory: banquet, manna, well dressed, the land of spices. Helen Vendler remarks on Herbert's tendency to reinvent his poems even while they are in process. That mode of wit, derived by Herbert from Donne, partly answers Dr. Johnson's strictures. The good and evil of eternity are paraphrased, postponed, danced from trope to trope, sounding heaven and earth.

ϟ   ϟ   ϟ

The Collar

I struck the board, and cried, "No more,
   I will abroad!
What? Shall I ever sigh and pine?
My lines and life are free, free as the road,
   Loose as the wind, as large as store.
     Shall I be still in suit?
Have I no harvest but a thorn
To let me blood, and not restore
What I have lost with cordial fruit?
10   Sure there was wine
Before my sighs did dry it; there was corn
   Before my tears did drown it.
   Is the year only lost to me?
     Have I no bays to crown it?
No flowers, no garlands gay? all blasted?
     All wasted?
   Not so, my heart: but there is fruit,
     And thou hast hands.
   Recover all thy sigh-blown age
20 On double pleasures: leave thy cold dispute
Of what is fit, and not. Forsake thy cage,
     Thy rope of sands,
Which petty thoughts have made, and made to thee
   Good cable, to enforce and draw,
     And be thy law,
   While thou didst wink and wouldst not see.
     Away; take heed:
     I will abroad.
Call in thy death's head there; tie up thy fears.
30   He that forbears
   To suit and serve his need,

    Deserves his load."
But as I raved and grew more fierce and wild
        At every word,
    Me thoughts I heard one calling, "Child!"
        And I replied, "My Lord."
    1633

Jordan (I)

Who says that fictions only and false hair
Become a verse? Is there in truth no beauty?
Is all good structure in a winding stair?
May no lines pass, except they do their duty
        Not to a true, but painted chair?

Is it no verse, except "enchanted groves"
And "sudden arbours" shadow coarse-spun lines?
Must "purling streams" refresh a lover's loves?
Must all be veiled, while he that reads, divines,
10   Catching the sense at two removes?
Shepherds are honest people: let them sing.
Riddle who list, for me, and pull for prime;
I envy no man's nightingale or spring;
Nor let them punish me with loss of rhyme,
        Who plainly say, "My God, My King."
    1633

Jordan (II)

When first my lines of heavenly joys made mention,
Such was their lustre, they did so excell,
That I sought out quaint words, and trim invention;
My thoughts began to burnish, sprout, and swell,
Curling with metaphors a plain intention,
Decking the sense, as if it were to sell.

Thousands of notions in my brain did run,
Offering their service, if I were not sped;
I often blotted what I had begun:
10   This was not quick enough, and that was dead.

Nothing could seem too rich to clothe the sun,
Much less those joys which trample on his head.

As flames do work and wind, when they ascend,
So did I weave my self into the sense.
But while I bustled, I might hear a friend
Whisper, "How wide is all this long pretense!
There is in love a sweetness ready penned:
Copy out only that, and save expense."
    1633

Church Monuments

While that my soul repairs to her devotion,
Here I entomb my flesh, that it betimes
Make take acquaintance of this heap of dust,
To which the blast of Death's incessant motion,
Fed with the exhalation of our crimes,
Drives all at last. Therefore I gladly trust

My body to this school, that it may learn
To spell his elements, and find his birth
Written in dusty heraldry and lines;
10 Which dissolution sure doth best discern,
Comparing dust with dust, and earth with earth.
These laugh at jet and marble, put for signs,

To sever the good fellowship of dust,
And spoil the meeting—what shall point out them,
When they shall bow and kneel and fall down flat
To kiss those heaps which now they have in trust?
Dear flesh, while I do pray, learn here thy stem
And true descent, that, when thou shalt grow fat,

And wanton in thy cravings, thou mayst know
20 That flesh is but the glass which holds the dust
That measures all our time, which also shall
Be crumbled into dust. Mark here below
How tame these ashes are, how free from lust,
That thou mayst fit thyself against thy fall.
    1633

Love (III)

Love bade me welcome: yet my soul drew back,
        Guilty of dust and sin.
But quick-eyed Love, observing me grow slack
        From my first entrance in,
Drew nearer to me, sweetly questioning,
        If I lacked any thing.

"A guest," I answered, "worthy to be here":
        Love said, "You shall be he."
"I the unkind, ungrateful? Ah my dear,
10   I cannot look on thee."
Love took my hand, and smiling did reply,
        "Who made the eyes but I?"

"Truth Lord, but I have marred them: let my shame
        Go where it doth deserve."
"And know you not," says Love, "who bore the blame?"
        "My dear, then I will serve."
"You must sit down," says Love, "and taste my meat":
        So I did sit and eat.

    1633

RICHARD CRASHAW

1612–1649

THIS EXTRAVAGANT and superb stylist is rightly considered the unique English representative of the Continental Baroque mode, of which the great sculptor was Bernini and the principal poet Giambattista Marino. Yet there is an English strain in Crashaw's devotional poems; he published two allied volumes called *Steps to the Temple,* in homage to George Herbert's posthumously printed *The Temple.*

    Richard Crashaw was the son of a Puritan preacher, but the poet himself became both a Royalist and a High Church enthusiast. In 1644, the

Puritan rebels dismissed him from his posts at Cambridge University, both his college fellowship and his curacy. Crashaw went into exile, first in Holland, then in Paris, and converted to Roman Catholicism. He then held minor clerical positions in Rome and finally in Loreto, where he may have died by deliberate poisoning.

Crashaw's best secular poem is "Music's Duel," which I urge readers to seek out. Here, I include one of his fiercely energetic celebrations of Saint Teresa of Avila, Carmelite nun of Spanish-Jewish background, whose mystical autobiography was available to the poet in an English version of 1642, published in Antwerp.

According to Crashaw himself, both of his tributes to Saint Teresa were composed while he was still a High Church Protestant. And yet they hardly could be more Spanish Catholic in their sensibility. Crashaw follows closely the English translation of Teresa's autobiography:

> It pleased our Blessed Lord, that I should have sometimes, this following Vision. I saw an Angell very neer me, towards my left side, and he appeared to me, in a Corporeall forme; though yet I am not want to see anie thing of that kind, but very rarely. For, though Angells be represented often to me, it is yet, without my seeing them, but only according to that other kind of Vision, whereof I spake before. But, in this Vision, our Lord was pleased, that I should see this Angell, after this other manner. He was not great; but rather little; yet withall, he was of very much beautie. His face was so inflamed, that he appeared to be of those most Superiour Angells, who seem to be, all in a fire; and he well might be of them, whome we call *Seraphins;* but as for me, they never tell me their names, or rankes; yet howsoever, I see thereby, that there is so great a difference in Heaven, between one Angell, and another, as I am no way able to expresse. I saw, that he had a long Dart of gold in his hand; and at the end of the iron below, me thought, there was a little fire; and I conceaved, that he thrust it, some severall times, through my verie Hart, after such a manner, as that it passed the verie inwards, of my Bowells; and when he drew it back, me thought, it carried away, as much, as it had touched within me; and left all that, which remained, wholy inflamed with a great love of Almightie God. The paine of it, was so excessive, that it forced me to utter those groanes; and the sauvitie, which that extremitie of paine gave, was also so very excessive, that there was no desiring at all, to be ridd of it; nor can the Soule then, receave anie contentment at all, in lesse, then God Almightie himself.

Anyone who has seen Bernini's superb sculpture of Saint Teresa's ecstasy at the church of Santa Maria della Salute in Rome will recognize Crashaw's powerful affinity with the Baroque, though Bernini did not complete the work until 1652, three years after the poet's death. Crashaw, in Rome, may have seen the sculpture in its unfinished form.

❧   ❧   ❧

The flaming Heart. Upon the booke and picture of *Teresa*. As she is usually expressed with a *Seraphim* beside her.

Well meaning Readers! you that come as Friends,
And catch the pretious name this piece pretends,
Make not so much hast to admire
That faire cheek't fallacie of fire.
5   That is a *Seraphim* they say,
And this the great *Teresia*.
Readers, be rul'd by me, and make,
Here a well plac't, and wise mistake.
You must transpose the picture quite,
10   And spell it wrong to reade it right;
Read *Him* for *Her,* and *Her* for *Him,*
And call the *Saint,* the *Seraphim.*
Painter, what did'st thou understand
To put her dart into his *Hand?*
15   See, even the yeares, and size of Him,
Shew this the Mother *Seraphim.*
This is the Mistrisse *Flame;* and duteous *hee*
Her happier *fire-works,* here, comes down to see.
O most poore spirited of men!
20   Had thy cold Pencill kist her Pen
Thou could'st not so unkindly err
To shew us this faint shade for Her.
Why man, this speakes pure mortall frame,
And mocks with Femall Frost Love's manly flame.
25   One would suspect thou mean'st to paint,
Some weake, inferior, *Woman Saint.*
But had thy pale-fac't purple tooke
Fire from the burning Cheekes of that *bright booke,*
Thou would'st on her have heap't up all
30   That could be form'd *Seraphicall.*

What e're this youth of fire wore faire,
Rosie Fingers, Radiant Haire,
Glowing cheekes, and glistring wings,
All those, faire and flagrant things,
35 But before All, that fierie Dart,
Had fill'd the *Hand* of this great *Heart.*
Do then as equall Right requires,
Since *his* the blushes be, and *hers* the fires,
Resume and rectifie thy rude designe,
40 Undresse thy *Seraphim* into *mine.*
Redeeme this injury of thy art,
Give *him* the *veyle,* give her the *Dart.*
Give *him* the *veyle,* that he may cover,
The red cheekes of a rivall'd Lover;
45 Asham'd that our world now can show
Nests of new *Seraphims* here below.
Give *her* the *dart,* for it is *she*
(Faire youth) shoot's both thy shafts and *thee.*
Say, all ye wise and well pierc't Hearts
50 That live, and dye amid'st Her darts,
What is't your tast-full spirits doe prove
In that rare Life of *her,* and Love?
Say and beare witnesse. Sends she not,
A *Seraphim* at every shot?
55 What *Magazins* of immortall armes there shine!
Heav'ns great *Artillery* in each *Love-span-line.*
Give then the *Dart* to *Her,* who gives the *Flame;*
Give *Him* the *veyle,* who kindly takes the shame.
But if it be the frequent *Fate*
60 Of worst faults to be *Fortunate;*
If all's *prescription;* and proud wrong,
Hearkens not to an humble song;
For all the *Gallantry* of *Him,*
Give me the suff'ring *Seraphim.*
65 His be the bravery of all those Bright things,
The glowing cheekes, the glittering wings,
The *Rosie* hand, the *Radiant Dart,*
Leave her alone the *flaming-Heart.*
Leave her that, and thou shalt leave her,
70 Not one loose shaft, but *loves* whole quiver.
For in *Love's* field was never found,
A nobler *Weapon* than a *wound.*

  Love's Passives, are his *activ'st* part,
  The *wounded* is the *wounding-heart.*
75 *O Heart!* the equall *Poise,* of *Love's* both *Parts,*
  Big alike with *wounds* and *Darts,*
Live in these conquering *leaves;* live all the same,
And walke through all tongues one triumphant flame.
Live here *great heart;* and Love, and dye, and kill,
80 And bleed, and wound, and yield, and conquer still.
Let this immortall Life, where e'er it comes,
Walke in a crowd of *Loves,* and *Martyrdomes.*
Let *Mystick Deaths* waite on't; and wise soules bee,
The *love-slaine-witnesses,* of this life of *Thee.*
85 O sweet incendiary! shew here thy art,
Upon this carcasse of a hard, cold, hart,
Let all thy scatter'd shafts of light, that play
Among the leaves of thy larg Books of day,
Combin'd against this *Brest* at once break in
90 And take away from me my self & sin,
This gratious Robbery shall thy bounty be;
And my best fortunes such fair spoiles of me.
O thou undanted daughter of desires!
By all thy dowr of *Lights & Fires;*
95 By all the eagle in thee, all the dove;
By all thy lives & deaths of love;
By thy large draughts of intellectuall day,
And by thy thirsts of love more large then they;
By all thy brim-fill'd Bowles of feirce desire
100 By the last Morning's draught of liquid fire;
By the full kingdome of that finall kisse
That seiz'd thy parting Soul, & seal'd thee his;
By all the heav'ns thou hast in him
(Fair sister of the *Seraphim!*)
105 By all of *Him* we have in *Thee;*
Leave nothing of my *Self* in me,
Let me so read thy life, that I
Unto all life of mine may dy.

HENRY VAUGHAN

1621–1695

AFTER THE INCOMPARABLE George Herbert, and John Donne's transcendental poems of faith, Henry Vaughan seems to me a devotional poet unmatched in the seventeenth century, original beyond the poignant contributions of Robert Southwell, Francis Quarles, Richard Crashaw, Thomas Traherne, and the American Edward Taylor.

A proud Welshman, Vaughan always was close to his twin brother, the Hermetic scholar-alchemist Thomas Vaughan. It is fascinating to trace the influence of Hermetism in Henry Vaughan's poetry, particularly since in Henry it remains a Christian Hermetism, quite unlike the heresies of the greatest of Renaissance legatees of the Hermetic corpus, Giordano Bruno.

Henry Vaughan, who studied both law and medicine, began his poetic career with a 1646 volume that was indebted to Ben Jonson. In 1648, the poet experienced a religious conversion, though he long had been both Royalist and Anglican. All his notable poetry was written from 1648 to 1655, totally under the acknowledged influence of George Herbert, in the two volumes called *Silex Scintillans* (*The Sparkling Flint*). In the last forty years of his life, Vaughan dwindled into a rather ordinary Welsh country doctor, and his later poems are drab.

The four poems included here cannot be said to share the powerful thinking-in-verse of John Donne and George Herbert, but they have something all their own, a unique difference from Vaughan's master, Herbert. Partly this is a question of voicing and pitch, but another portion emanates from Thomas Vaughan's cosmological blend of Neo-Platonism and Hermetism.

The most considerable of the poems reprinted here, "Cock-Crowing," is also the most Hermetist and difficult, at first, to comprehend. It turns upon the Hermetist image of the "seed" or "grain," which is akin to the spark or *pneuma* of ancient Gnosticism, a fragment of God concealed within the self, and so the best and oldest aspect of each individual.

❧   ❧   ❧

Peace

My Soul, there is a Countrie
    Far beyond the stars,
Where stands a winged Centrie
    All skilfull in the wars,
5 There above noise, and danger
    Sweet peace sits crown'd with smiles,
And one born in a Manger
    Commands the Beauteous files,
He is thy gracious friend,
10   And (O my Soul awake!)
Did in pure love descend
    To die here for thy sake,
If thou canst get but thither,
    There growes the flowre of peace,
15 The Rose that cannot wither,
    Thy fortresse, and thy ease;
Leave then thy foolish ranges;
    For none can thee secure,
But one, who never changes,
20   Thy God, thy life, thy Cure.

The World

I saw Eternity the other night
Like a great ring of pure and endless light,
    All calm as it was bright;
And round beneath it, Time in hours, days, years,
    Driven by the spheres
Like a vast shadow moved; in which the world
    And all her train were hurled.
The doting lover in his quaintest strain
    Did there complain;
10 Near him, his lute, his fancy, and his flights,
    Wit's sour delights;
With gloves and knots, the silly snares of pleasure,
    Yet his dear treasure,
All scattered lay, while he his eyes did pour
    Upon a flower.

The darksome statesman, hung with weights and woe
Like a thick midnight fog, moved there so slow,
   He did nor stay, nor go;
Condemning thoughts—like sad eclipses—scowl
20   Upon his soul,
And clouds of crying witnesses without
   Pursued him with one shout.
Yet digged the mole, and lest his ways be found,
   Worked under ground,
Where he did clutch his prey; but one did see
   That policy:
Churches and altars fed him, perjuries
   Were gnats and flies;
It rained about him blood and tears, but he
30   Drank them as free.

The fearful miser on a heap of rust
Sat pining all his life there, did scarce trust
   His own hands with the dust,
Yet would not place one piece above, but lives
   In fear of thieves.
Thousands there were as frantic as himself,
   And hugged each one his pelf;
The downright epicure placed heaven in sense,
   And scorned pretence;
40 While others, slipped into a wide excess,
   Said little less;
The weaker sort slight, trivial wares enslave,
   Who think them brave;
And poor, despised Truth sat counting by
   Their victory.

Yet some, who all this while did weep and sing,
And sing and weep, soared up into the ring;
   But most would use no wing.
Oh fools, said I, thus to prefer dark night
50   Before true light!
To live in grots and caves, and hate the day
   Because it shows the way;
The way, which from this dead and dark abode
   Leads up to God;
A way where you might tread the sun, and be

More bright than he!
But as I did their madness so discuss,
   One whispered thus,
"This ring the Bridegroom did for none provide,
60   But for His bride."

    JOHN 2:16–17

All that is in the world, the lust of the flesh, the lust of the eyes, and the
    pride of life, is not of the Father, but is of the world.
And the world passeth away, and the lusts thereof; but he that doeth the will
    of God abideth for ever.

    1650

"They are all gone into the world of light!"

They are all gone into the world of light!
   And I alone sit lingering here;
Their very memory is fair and bright
    And my sad thoughts doth clear.

It grows and glitters in my cloudy breast,
   Like stars upon some gloomy grove,
Or those faint beams in which this hill is dressed
    After the sun's remove.

I see them walking in an air of glory,
10   Whose light doth trample on my days:
My days, which are at best but dull and hoary,
    Mere glimmering and decays.

Oh holy hope, and high humility,
   High as the heavens above!
These are your walks, and you have showed them me
    To kindle my cold love.

Dear, beauteous death! the jewel of the just,
   Shining nowhere but in the dark,
What mysteries do lie beyond thy dust,
20   Could man outlook that mark!

He that hath found some fledged bird's nest, may know
    At first sight, if the bird be flown;
But what fair well or grove he sings in now,
      That is to him unknown.

And yet, as angels in some brighter dreams
    Call to the soul when man doth sleep,
So some strange thoughts transcend our wonted themes,
      And into glory peep.

If a star were confined into a tomb,
30   Her captive flames must needs burn there;
But when the hand that locked her up gives room,
      She'll shine through all the sphere.

Oh father of eternal life, and all
    Created glories under thee!
Resume thy spirit from this world of thrall
      Into true liberty.

Either disperse these mists, which blot and fill
    My pérspective still as they pass:
Or else remove me hence unto that hill
40   Where I shall need no glass.
    1655

Cock-Crowing

Father of lights! what sunny seed,
What glance of day hast thou confined
Into this bird? To all the breed
This busy ray thou hast assigned;
    Their magnetism works all night,
    And dreams of Paradise and light.

Their eyes watch for the morning-hue,
Their little grain, expelling night,
So shines and sings, as if it knew
10 The path unto the house of light.
    It seems their candle, howe'er done,
    Was tinned and lighted at the sun.

If such a tincture, such a touch,
So firm a longing can impour,
Shall thy own image think it much
To watch for thy appearing hour?
    If a mere blast so fill the sail,
    Shall not the breath of God prevail?

Oh thou immortal light and heat,
20 Whose hand so shines through all this frame,
That by the beauty of the seat,
We plainly see who made the same;
    Seeing thy seed abides in me,
    Dwell thou in it, and I in thee!

To sleep without thee is to die;
Yea, 'tis a death partakes of hell;
For where thou dost not close the eye
It never opens, I can tell.
    In such a dark, Egyptian border,
30   The shades of death dwell, and disorder.

If joys and hopes and earnest throes,
And hearts whose pulse beats still for light,
Are given to birds, who but thee knows
A love-sick soul's exalted flight?
    Can souls be tracked by any eye
    But his, who gave them wings to fly?

Only this veil which thou hast broke,
And must be broken yet in me,
This veil, I say, is all the cloak,
40 And cloud which shadows thee from me.
    This veil thy full-eyed love denies,
    And only gleams and fractions spies.

Oh take it off! make no delay,
But brush me with thy light, that I
May shine unto a perfect day,
And warm me at thy glorious eye.
    Oh take it off! or till it flee,
    Though with no lily, stay with me!
    1655

THOMAS TRAHERNE

1637–1674

THE POEMS OF THOMAS TRAHERNE, and his prose *Centuries of Meditations,* were not published until 1903–1908.

A shoemaker's son, Traherne was raised by a rich relative who financed his Oxford education. He became a rector and chaplain in the Church of England during the Stuart Restoration. Rather little is known about his life, or of his death at thirty-seven.

Traherne can be a somewhat clumsy poet, and his prose *Centuries* is consistently more eloquent than the poems. And yet Traherne survives his structured awkwardness, largely because his magical vision of childhood, influenced by Henry Vaughan's, retains a visionary force that does not fail. He represents the final ebbing-out of the devotional tradition of Donne and Herbert.

✣   ✣   ✣

Shadows in the Water

In unexperienced infancy
Many a sweet mistake doth lie:
Mistake though false, intending true;
A *seeming* somewhat more than *view;*
    That doth instruct the mind
    In things that lie behind,
And many secrets to us show
Which afterwards we come to know.

Thus did I by the water's brink
Another world beneath me think;
And while the lofty spacious skies
Reversèd there abused mine eyes,
    I fancied other feet
    Came mine to touch and meet;
As by some puddle I did play
Another world within it lay.

Beneath the water people drowned,
Yet with another heaven crowned,

In spacious regions seemed to go
20   Freely moving to and fro:
         In bright and open space
         I saw their very face;
Eyes, hands, and feet they had like mine;
Another sun did with them shine.

'Twas strange that people there should walk,
And yet I could not hear them talk;
That through a little watery chink,
Which one dry ox or horse might drink,
         We other worlds should see,
30   Yet not admitted be;
And other confines there behold
Of light and darkness, heat and cold.

I called them oft, but called in vain;
No speeches we could entertain:
Yet did I there expect to find
Some other world, to please my mind.
         I plainly saw by these
         A new Antipodes,
Whom, though they were so plainly seen,
40   A film kept off that stood between.

By walking men's reversed feet
I chanced another world to meet;
Though it did not to view exceed
A phantasm, 'tis a world indeed,
         Where skies beneath us shine,
         And earth by art divine
Another face presents below,
Where people's feet against ours go.

Within the regions of the air,
50   Compassed about with heavens fair,
Great tracts of land there may be found
Enriched with fields and fertile ground;
         Where many numerous hosts,
         In those far distant coasts,
For other great and glorious ends,
Inhabit, my yet unknown friends.

Oh ye that stand upon the brink,
Whom I so near me, through the chink,
With wonder see; what faces there,
60   Whose feet, whose bodies, do ye wear?
    I, my companions, see
    In you another me.
They seemed others, but are we;
Our second selves those shadows be.

Look how far off those lower skies
Extend themselves! scarce with mine eyes
I can them reach. Oh ye, my friends,
What secret borders on those ends?
    Are lofty heavens hurled
70   'Bout your inferior world?
Are ye the representatives
Of other peoples' distant lives?

Of all the playmates which I knew
That here I do the image view
In other selves, what can it mean?
But that below the purling stream
    Some unknown joys there be
    Laid up in store for me;
To which I shall, when that thin skin
Is broken, be admitted in.

FROM MS., PUB. 1903

| JOHN MILTON |

1608–1674

NO POET SINCE John Milton, in English, approaches his good eminence: not Blake, Wordsworth, Whitman, Dickinson, Yeats, Stevens.
Except for Shakespeare, no poet has been so influential. From John Dryden to T. S. Eliot, Milton has been a provocation and a shadow.

    In dedication to his vocation of becoming a great poet-prophet, Milton
has an intensity and drive that rivals Dante. Each desired both poetic

immortality and the redemption of his people. The imperial politics of Dante and the republican hopes of Milton alike came to ruin. For the last nineteen of his fifty-six years, Dante was an exile from Florence. At fifty-one, Milton, already totally blind for seven years, endured imprisonment, after suffering the strong possibility of dreadful public execution for defending regicide: hanging, being cut down alive, having one's private parts cut off, one's entrails ripped from the body, and only then being beheaded. The Florentines sentenced Dante to be burned alive; the English very nearly incurred the permanent disgrace of butchering their epic poet, who a decade later completed the composition of *Paradise Lost*. The world came close to possessing neither the *Commedia* nor *Paradise Lost*. When Franco's Fascists murdered Federico García Lorca, aged thirty-eight, they deprived Spain of its greatest lyric poet. The Tuscans and the Stuart royalists would have destroyed even greater aesthetic splendors.

John Milton is so large a form of thought, passion, and invention that his long sense of being a late developer can puzzle even his most informed admirers. On his twenty-fourth birthday (December 9, 1632), he composed a troubled sonnet:

> How soon hath time the subtle thief of youth,
>   Stol'n on his wing my three and twentieth year!
>   My hasting days fly on with full career,
>   But my late spring no bud or blossom shewth.
> Perhaps my semblance might deceive the truth,
>   That I to manhood am arrived so near,
>   And inward ripeness doth much less appear,
>   That some more timely-happy spirits endueth.
> Yet it be less or more, or soon or slow,
>   It shall be still in strictest measure even,
>   To that same lot, however mean or high,
> Toward which time leads me, and the will of heaven;
>   All is, if I have grace to use it so,
>   As ever in my great task-master's eye.

Milton already had written permanent poems, including "On the Morning of Christ's Nativity" and the matchless, rather Shakespearean, extended lyrics "L'Allegro" and "Il Penseroso." And yet he is perfectly serious in this sonnet, as only the most ambitious of all poets can be. One wonders just who those "more timely-happy spirits" could have been? Scholars have suggested two Cambridge contemporaries, the poet Thomas Randolph and Edward King, the clergyman whose drowning was to provide the occasion for Milton's magnificent elegy, *Lycidas,* five years later in 1637. Randolph, and still less King, were hardly Miltonic in poetic accomplishment. Yet the young Milton laments his supposed lack of "bud or blossom," despite the "L'Allegro"–"Il Penseroso" lyrical astonishments. There is no need to doubt the sincerity of this, but it shows considerable self-mystification on the poet's part.

"How Soon Hath Time" is, for Milton, a very minor poem, but its anxieties are revelations. Hidden in the sonnet is a Miltonic tension between knowing that he needed time for his massive gifts to mature and his fear that an untimely death might prevent that maturation. When, in the period from 1665 to 1669, the blind poet was able to finish and publish *Paradise Lost,* he won a great victory over fate and worldly defeat, comparable to Dante's successful completion of the *Commedia.* Milton's best biographer, Barbara Lewalski, usefully emphasizes that his epic is not a retreat into isolated spirituality: "It undertakes a strenuous project of educating readers in the virtues, values, and attitudes that make a people worthy of liberty."

Milton's greatest poetry was composed after he turned fifty-seven, an age neither Dante nor Shakespeare reached. Among modern poets, several also broke into a new splendor after that age: Thomas Hardy, W. B. Yeats, Wallace Stevens. But you would have to go back to Sophocles to find a paradigm for Milton's extraordinary late flowering in *Samson Agonistes,* which may well have been written after his sixtieth birthday. Poet-prophet as he was, Milton was accurate as to his own poetic career: "long choosing and beginning late."

Since *Paradise Lost* is the Protestant epic proper, the arch-heretical Milton has been subsumed by one Protestant orthodoxy or another for more than three centuries now. In precisely what sense is *Paradise Lost* a Christian poem? You can have a Protestant sensibility without being Christian, as Samuel Beckett demonstrated. The historian Christopher Hill opens onto the true scandal of Milton's supposed Christianity:

> Milton's virtual abandonment of the idea of sacrificial atonement,
> his failure to emphasize the miracles of the New Testament,
> including the incarnation, the resurrection, the ascension and pentecost, all make an approach verge on the secular.

The critic A. D. Nuttall goes even further, as I would, in questioning whether Milton at sixty-six, facing death, could still be termed a Christian. William Blake and Emily Dickinson were sects of one, and so was their heroic precursor, John Milton. Concerning Shakespeare's religion, we know absolutely nothing: was he secretly Catholic, Protestant, or nihilist? It does not matter, because the plays proclaim everything and nothing. Dante's Anglo-American scholars have assimilated him to Augustine and Aquinas; his Italian critics more sensibly emphasize his pride and individuality. As Dante, so Milton: no fiercer poetic selves ever existed.

I began this book's general commentary with an analysis of poetry as an *art of strangeness*, following the critics Walter Pater and Owen Barfield. Pater defined Romanticism as the adding of strangeness to beauty; Barfield characterizes authentic poetry as a strangeness of *meaning*. *Paradise Lost* becomes a stranger to me each time I reread it or recite it to myself. The poet-critic William Empson, in his splendid *Milton's God*, compared the unmatched English epic to archaic Benin (West African) sculpture: barbarously beautiful. Empson, Maoist and anti-Christian, felt that Milton had just barely managed to keep his temper with the poem's God. As a Gnostic Jew, in rebellion against normative Judaism and Christianity alike, I find Milton's God the principal blot upon an otherwise magnificent poem, whose strangeness makes such a God irrelevant and aesthetically inadequate, since there is nothing at all strange about the supposed God of *Paradise Lost*. He is self-righteous, irascible, and anxious: William Blake accurately termed him a Schoolmaster of Souls. You have to be a dogmatic Christian whose values are not aesthetic to find this God attractive.

Still, though he is called God, he is only a secondary representation of the divine in the poem. Christ, I hasten to add, is only tertiary. The primary transcendental agent in *Paradise Lost* is the Holy Spirit, *not* the third person in the Trinity, but the Inner Light of Protestant dissent, exalted by Milton's close friend Sir Henry Vane (martyred by the restored Stuarts), by the Muggletonians and other visionaries, and certainly by John Milton himself. In the *Christian Doctrine*, his posthumously published theology, Milton dutifully ranks the Son *over* the Holy Spirit. But what do we find in the rich strangeness of the poem? I hold to an observation I first printed many years ago, that the Christ of *Paradise Lost* is a kind of armored commander, a heavenly Rommel or Patton, who mounts his father's flaming chariot (*Merkabah* in Hebrew, which is also the name of the Israeli battle tank) and leads the angelic host in the fight that thrusts Satan and his host out of the skies into the depths of the abyss. The fire of the chariot ignites the falling demons, and the impact of Satan's legions upon the bottom of the deep creates Hell. Milton cannot have been unaware that his poem's Christ thus is the pragmatic creator of Hell.

If Milton lacks any central human and literary quality, it is the comic sense. What did he expect his Christian readers to make of the Miltonic Crucifixion?

> But to the Cross he nails thy enemies,
> The law that is against thee, and the sins
> Of all mankind, with him there crucified,
> Never to hurt them more who rightly trust
> In this his satisfaction; *so he dies,*
> *But soon revives . . .*
>   —Book XII, 415–420

My italics highlight six words, broken by an enjambment, which are all that this vast poem devotes to the death and resurrection of Jesus Christ. Milton's haste in getting Christ off the cross reflects profound uneasiness with the Incarnation, and with the Atonement. Why does he bother with the cross at all? But that brings us to the greatest mystery of *Paradise Lost* and its poet: how fully aware is he that there are two Gods in his epic, the static setter-of-limits and a dynamic deity of becoming, totally free of the Calvinist model?

Perhaps the most extraordinary aspect of *Paradise Lost* is that, by its close, Milton's God undergoes a metamorphosis, in which he has become one with the Holy Spirit who inspires and guides Milton's composition of the poem. A. D. Nuttall surprisingly observes: "The new God who emerges at the end of *Paradise Lost* is begotten of the Father, the tyrant." I dissent only from that "begotten": the second God emanates from Milton's Inner Light, the Holy Spirit that has made Milton her temple.

Angus Fletcher, whom I cited in my introductory commentary as an authority upon poetic thinking, terms *Paradise Lost* neither tragic nor Romantic, but *a suspension upon a threshold,* the border between life and death. The speed of light, always inward in Milton, is one with the speed of his poetic thinking. That speed *is* Milton's new God, and comes in the invocation to Book III, long before the epic's conclusion:

> Hail holy Light, offspring of Heav'n first-born,
> Or of th' Eternal coeternal beam
> May I express the unblamed? Since God is light,
> And never but in unapproachèd light
> Dwelt from eternity, dwelt in thee,
> Bright effluence of bright essence increate.

Or hear'st thou rather pure ethereal stream,
Whose fountain who shall tell? Before the sun,
Before the heavens thou wert, and at the voice
Of God, as with a mantle didst invest
The rising world of waters dark and deep.

Milton mingles allusions to the opening of the Gospel of John with Psalm 104 in these intricate eleven lines, which emphasize the Creation of Genesis 1, but with a difference that is Milton's own, based upon his lonely experience of creating his poem. We know that the blind prophet-bard composed at night, molding his marvelous verse-paragraphs, and then dictated them in the morning. His epic worships *light*, yet he knows only darkness. The poem is a drama for the theater of two minds, Milton's and the reader's. Most of us who encounter *Paradise Lost* can read it; we can see. I always have been fascinated by my blind students or other sightless auditors of Milton whom I have met through the years. They tend to know Milton through the ear, listening to readers or to recordings, though some have had access to *Paradise Lost* in Braille, at least in part. Milton assumes his reader can see, but the blind can have a peculiar affinity for his rich-sounding style.

Sometimes I close my own eyes and recite *Paradise Lost* out loud to myself, when alone, a habit I first practiced as a child, when I came to possess the poem by memory, that coming easy to me then. My experience can be only an approximation of my blind students', yet I come to share something of their sense of being domesticated in the sublime poem's warmth and light. I mean "sublime" in its precise literary sense: raised aloft, replete with power, which in Milton is disciplined wildness, that is, "wildness" in its meaning of "freedom."

Closing one's eyes and reciting aloud, say, the invocation to light that starts Book III, is to know directly the new God of *Paradise Lost,* not a tyrannical schoolmaster of souls but what Angus Fletcher calls the prolongation of the prophetic moment, the modulated breath that is the narrator's voice in Milton's epic. By "voice" I mean a Miltonic metaphor, an image of voice that features movements of rising to heights and falling to depths, movements incessant, almost obsessive, throughout the poem. I find it extraordinary to recite (or hear others recite) long passages of *Paradise Lost* while my eyes are closed, because the imagery of rising and falling takes on a boundless outline, the grand reverberation of Miltonic voice:

Him the Almighty Power
Hurled headlong flaming from th' ethereal sky

With hideous ruin and combustion down
To bottomless perdition, there to dwell
In adamantine chains and penal fire.

No single metaphor will serve for Milton's image of voice, the way "tally" splendidly serves as Walt Whitman's, but "fall" or "falling" does quite well. Of the poem's two falls, the angels' and men's, I hardly know which is rendered more gloriously. The first gives us Satan, the second deepens Eve, the two most interesting figures in Milton. I use "figure" advisedly, because Satan and Eve, and Adam, are not persons, as the Wife of Bath and Falstaff or the Pardoner and Iago are living personalities. After their fall, Eve and Adam are supposed to be representations of mortality, like ourselves, but Milton's art has more in common with Dante's than with Shakespeare's or Chaucer's. But then I do not know what either Shakespeare or Chaucer might have done with the hard task of representing mortal enigmas. I never feel that the reader *is* Eve or Adam, but for certain moments, in the darkness of voice, I can identify with Milton the prophet or with the sublime Satan.

Criticism from the start regarded Satan as a perversion of the heroic, but from childhood on I have agreed with Blake and Shelley, rather than with the editorializing Milton, who emerges frequently to damn his superbly rhetorical hero. If you love poetry, then you love Satan. Iago, an even greater creation, frightens me, but Iago is endless to meditation as a psychology, while Satan is closer to Melville's Captain Ahab in *Moby-Dick* or Judge Holden in Cormac McCarthy's *Blood Meridian,* three grand figurations but lacking the fascinations of Iago's personality. Though Satan is not a person, he is an extraordinary vision of consciousness, in Owen Barfield's sense of a "strangeness of meaning." In Shakespeare, consciousness seems almost an effortless given: Hamlet, Falstaff, Iago, Cleopatra all give us the impression that they apprehend more widely than we do. Milton's genius is of a different kind, again closer to Dante's than to Shakespeare's or Chaucer's. All consciousness in Milton is heroic, because it is somehow his own, whether Satanic or human, whether fallen or unfallen. In Shakespeare, we never know when consciousness is his own, even in the sonnets, because of their uncanny detachment. Milton's particular greatness is his transformation of his own profound passions, his hopes for the human, into an art absolutely personal and yet also near-universal.

Here, I want to describe Milton's particular genius for stationing himself in literary tradition, so as to make his forerunners into his descendants, and to overshadow his many actual poetic descendants, even when they possessed the genius of a Keats or a Shelley.

Milton was a learned poet, with extraordinary linguistic mastery: Hebrew, Greek, Latin, Italian, French, and other modern languages, including Dutch. In regard to the poetic riches of the past, Milton boldly attempted to subsume not less than everything. If there was a single flaw in his recondite awareness of every precedent and each precursor, it would be Shakespeare, most dangerous of influences. The only indeliberate allusions or unintended echoes of forerunners that I can uncover in *Paradise Lost* invariably turn out to be Shakespearean. Milton is adept at making himself seem early or first, and Homer, Vergil, Lucretius, Ovid, Camoëns, Tasso, Spenser, and even the Bible seem late, some of which I will demonstrate in regard to particular passages. Only the debt to Shakespeare could not be overcome: Satan's sense of Injured Merit is Iago's, and Belial in the Debate in Hell spookily echoes Claudio confronting the likelihood of death in *Measure for Measure*. Still, to be the foremost poet in the English language after the death of Shakespeare cannot be regarded as a defeat.

❧   ❧   ❧

Sonnets

XVII

When I consider how my light is spent,
    Ere half my days, in this dark world and wide,
    And that one talent which is death to hide
    Lodged with me useless, though my soul more bent
To serve therewith my maker, and present
    My true account, lest he, returning, chide.
    "Doth God exact day-labour, light denied?"
    I fondly ask; but Patience, to prevent
That murmur, soon replies: "God doth not need
10   Either man's work or his own gifts; who best
    Bear his mild yoke, they serve him best; his state
Is kingly—thousands at his bidding speed
    And post o'er land and ocean without rest:
    They also serve who only stand and wait."
    1652? 1673

XVIII

On the Late Massacre in Piedmont

Avenge, O Lord, thy slaughtered saints, whose bones
    Lie scattered on the Alpine mountains cold,
    Even them who kept thy truth so pure of old
    When all our fathers worshipped stocks and stones,
Forget not; in thy book record their groans
    Who were thy sheep, and in their ancient fold
    Slain by the bloody Piemontese that rolled
    Mother with infant down the rocks. Their moans
The vales redoubled to the hills, and they
    To heaven. Their martyred blood and ashes sow
    O'er all the Italian fields, where still doth sway
The triple tyrant, that from these may grow
    A hundredfold, who, having learnt thy way,
    Early may fly the Babylonian woe.
  1655 1673

XIX

Methought I saw my late espousèd saint
    Brought to me like Alcestis from the grave,
    Whom Jove's great son to her glad husband gave,
    Rescued from death by force, though pale and faint.
Mine, as whom washed from spot of child-bed taint
    Purification in the old Law did save,
    And such as yet once more I trust to have
    Full sight of her in heaven without restraint,
Came vested all in white, pure as her mind.
    Her face was veiled, yet to my fancied sight
    Love, sweetness, goodness in her person shined
So clear as in no face with more delight.
    But O as to embrace me she inclined,
    I waked, she fled, and day brought back my night.
  1658 1673

Lycidas

Dr. Samuel Johnson, my critical ideal, rejected *Lycidas* with wonderful vigor:

> Where there is leisure for fiction there is little grief . . . there is no nature, for there is nothing new. Its form is that of a pastoral, easy, vulgar, and therefore disgusting . . . With these trifling fictions are mingled the most awful and sacred truths, such as ought never to be polluted with such irreverend combinations.

Lycidas purports to be a monody bewailing the drowning of one Edward King, an acquaintance of Milton during their years together at Christ's College, Cambridge. King, a learned young man studying for the clergy, had written some Latin verses, but was no poet. Johnson was both massively right and dreadfully wrong: Milton was not flooded with grief, and was wholly concerned with the apprehension that he too might be cut off before he had composed what turned out to be *Paradise Lost*. Johnson's accusation of impiety is altogether accurate, from Johnson's own perspective, which was royalist and Anglican. Milton had served Cromwell, defended regicide, and was a veritable matrix of heresies.

Still, it disconcerts me that the strongest Western critic rejected the best poem of moderate length in English. I learn wariness from this, and from Johnson's unfortunate: "*Tristam Shandy* did not last." As always, one can build on Johnson: *Lycidas* awards itself ample "leisure for fiction." Allusive, mythological, elaborate—the poem is deliberate and artful, and I would think does just about everything that a poem *can* do. It is the central elegy in the language, and sets the pattern in which all those that come after are elegies for the self: Shelley's *Adonais*, Arnold's "Thyrsis," Swinburne's "Ave Atque Vale," Whitman's "When Lilacs Last in the Dooryard Bloom'd," Eliot's *The Waste Land*, Hart Crane's "The Broken Tower."

To fear the possibility of an early death primarily because it would thwart one's largest poetic ambitions is not unique to Milton among the greater poets, but I find no poem more obsessed with this anxiety than *Lycidas* is. Milton's mother died in 1637, the year of Edward King's drowning, and of the elegy's composition. His father, John Milton senior, evidently was closer to the poet, but we don't really know, since little is told us about the mother. *Lycidas* is no more an elegy for her than it is for Edward King, but the Orphic *sparagmos*, or rending-apart by the Maenads, seems to have a repressed, complex relation to her. The fate of Orpheus is a recurrent anxiety in Milton, from *Comus* through the invocation to Book VII of *Paradise Lost,* which emphasizes the Muse's inability to defend her son. In *Lycidas,* the lament for Orpheus is poignant and frightening:

> What could the Muse her self that Orpheus bore,
> The Muse her self, for her inchanting son
> Whom universal nature did lament,
> When by the rout that made the hideous roar
> His goary visage down the stream was sent,
> Down the swift Hebrus to the Lesbian shore.
>
> —LINES 58–63

The repetition of "the Muse her self" is emphatic: if informed by Milton's mother, this aptly confirms a recent absence, loss on some level of poetic consciousness. Milton, nearing thirty, was still living at home, on his parents' country estate in Horton, close by Windsor. The death of the mother necessarily is a larger matter than that of a college chum, and sets a more personal context for *Lycidas.*

The extraordinary opening lines of *Lycidas* are a complex irony, with the powerful surge of metric and rhetoric gesturing just the opposite of what supposedly is affirmed: that the poet Milton prematurely arrives to pluck the poetic crown of laurel, myrtle, and ivy. The repetition of "once more" refers back to the superb (but highly Shakespearean) *Comus,* and the irony touches a height in "shatter" with its palpable reference to the likely effect upon the reader of these strong lines:

> Yet once more, O ye laurels, and once more,
> Ye myrtles brown, with ivy never sear,
> I come to pluck your berries harsh and crude,
> And with forced fingers rude
> Shatter your leaves before the mellowing year.

Lycidas is the name of a shepherd in Theocritus, Vergil, and Sannazaro, though it is not clear why Milton selected precisely this name for a drowned poet. It *now* seems inevitable; yet Milton gives us no clue, though Frank Kermode notes a near-drowner of that name in Lucan's *Pharsalia.* For Milton, his Lycidas is all but identified with Orpheus, archetype of the drowned poet, which lurks in the irony of the second stanza:

> So may some gentle Muse
> With lucky words favour my destined urn,

And as he passes turn,
And bid fair peace be to my sable shroud.

Being male, the Muse here is a poet, whose "lucky" words will do for Milton what Milton does for Lycidas. "Lucky" means not just "auspicious" but "blessèd"; one remembers William Tyndale's Bible: "And the Lord was with Joseph, and he was a lucky fellow." Lycidas/King was unlucky, as Orpheus was. The irony centers in that word "So," where Milton means the opposite of what he says. The Orphic fate is that from which he swerves. There are no elegies for John Milton. Blind and disgraced as he was to be (his books burned by the public hangman), the poet of the national epic anticipated no laments.

Powerful as lines 1–24 are, the synecdochal 25–49 introduce the beauty of nature as a new element in the poem. My own time at Cambridge University returns to me, after a half-century, kindled by Milton's vision: "ere the high lawns appeared / Under the opening eyelids of the morn." The use of a "map of misreading" can be demonstrated here, as Milton antithetically completes the poem's opening movement. There is a kind of turning against the self, to balance the poet's refusal of the Orphic role. The "heavy change" finds nature's loss to all shepherd-poets in the loss of Lycidas, in a pathetic fallacy that Ruskin did not deplore:

> But O the heavy change, now thou art gone,
> Now thou art gone, and never must return!
> Thee, Shepherd, thee the woods, and desert caves,
> With wilde thyme and the gadding vine o'ergrown,
> And all their echoes mourn.
> The willows, and the hazel copses green
> Shall now no more be seen,
> Fanning their joyous leaves to thy soft lays.
> As killing as the canker to the rose,
> Or taint-worm to the weanling herds that graze,
> Or frost to flowers, that their gay wardrobe wear,
> When first the white-thorn blows;
> Such, Lycidas, thy loss to shepherd's ear.

The loss is to Milton's own ear, and symbolizes his dread of a similarly untimely disaster. Literally, echoes of poems are lost, but this is necessarily figurative, since what matters are the poems left unwritten. There is deliberate self-hurt in this lovely cognitive music, as the poem begins to be more overt as a late developer's lament.

The plangency grows more intense in the *kenosis,* or emptying-out of the poet's identity as a kind of mortal god, throughout the next two verse-paragraphs, lines 50–84. One of the monody's hidden elements, the recent death of Milton's mother, enters in the vision of Calliope, mother of Orpheus and leader of the Muses, since she represents epic or heroic poetry. I quote this again:

> What could the Muse her self that Orpheus bore,
> The Muse her self, for her inchanting son
> Whom universal nature did lament,
> When by the rout that made the hideous roar
> His goary visage down the stream was sent,
> Down the swift Hebrus to the Lesbian shore?

There is a movement of psychic regression here, all but universal in men whose mother, in dying, on some level of consciousness reminds them that in giving birth, she also gave mortality. A gathering sense of isolation and abandonment breaks through in the extraordinary verse-paragraph that follows; there the crucial metonymic displacement centers upon the poet's "trembling ears," plucked by Apollo as a sign of disfavor:

> Alas! what boots it with uncessant care
> To tend the homely slighted shepherd's trade,
> And strictly meditate the thankless Muse?
> Were it not better done as others use,
> To sport with Amaryllis in the shade,
> Or with the tangles of Neaera's hair?
> Fame is the spur that the clear spirit doth raise
> (That last infirmity of noble mind)
> To scorn delights, and live laborious days;
> But the fair guerdon when we hope to find,
> And think to burst out into sudden blaze,
> Comes the blind Fury with the abhorrèd shears,
> And slits the thin-spun life. "But not the praise,"
> Phoebus replied, and touched my trembling ears:
> "Fame is no plant that grows on mortal soil,
> Nor in the glistering foil
> Set off to the world, nor in broad rumour lies,
> But lives and spreads aloft by those pure eyes
> And perfect witness of all-judging Jove;
> As he pronounces lastly on each deed,
> Of so much fame in heaven expect thy meed.

Even in old age, I continue a lifelong habit of quoting to myself those deliciously erotic lines in which Milton's fascination with women's hair is immortalized, as it will be again with the portraits of Eve in *Paradise Lost* and of Dalila in *Samson Agonistes*. The vision of Atropos, inflexible and blind Fury, slitting Milton's "thin-spun life" is far more compelling than the bland comfort proffered by Apollo.

Lycidas mounts to its daemonic sublimity in the powerfully repressive prophecy of Saint Peter, where what is forgotten, purposively though with some evasions of consciousness, is Milton's own shattering fear of extinction before fame is won:

> "How well could I have spared for thee, young swain,
> Enow of such as for their bellies' sake
> Creep and intrude and climb into the fold!
> Of other care they little reckoning make
> Then how to scramble at the shearers' feast,
> And shove away the worthy bidden guest.
> Blind mouths! that scarce themselves know how to hold
> A sheep-hook, or have learned aught else the least
> That to the faithful herdman's art belongs!
> What recks it them? What need they? They are sped;
> And when they list, their lean and flashy songs
> Grate on their scrannel pipes of wretched straw.
> The hungry sheep look up, and are not fed,
> But swoln with wind, and the rank mist they draw,
> Rot inwardly, and foul contagion spread,
> Besides what the grim wolf with privy paw
> Daily devours apace, and nothing said;
> But that two-handed engine at the door
> Stands ready to smite once, and smite no more."

Historically, the religiously independent Milton denounces the English Church of Archbishop Laud, whose execution by an angry Parliament was to precede that of King Charles I. But the rhetorical excess of this remarkable passage retains its tang almost four centuries later. John Ruskin, in his *Sesame and Lilies*, made the classic explication of "blind mouths":

> A "Bishop" means "a person who sees." A "Pastor" means "person who feeds." The most unbishoply character a man can have is therefore to be blind. The most unpastoral is, instead of feeding, to want to be fed, to be a Mouth.

That "grim wolf," as everyone recognized, was the Roman Catholic Church, while no one ever agrees with anyone else on "that two-handed engine," which perhaps intimates only that men can and will end this evil with their own two hands.

Milton's grand *askesis,* or "sublimation," as Freud would have said, dominates the dramatic verse-paragraph, lines 132–164, with their extraordinary metaphor of the return of the pastoral Muse (Sicilian, in honor of Theocritus) in the form of a cascade of flowers: "To strew the laureate hearse where Lycid lies." Lovely as this bouquet is, Milton surpasses it in the knowingly "false surmise" which is an *askesis,* or self-limiting wound, in itself. That limitation allows the poet "the great Vision of the guarded mount":

> Ay me! whilst thee the shores, and sounding seas
> Wash far away, where'er thy bones are hurled,
> Whether beyond the stormy Hebrides,
> Where thou perhaps under the whelming tide
> Visit'st the bottom of the monstrous world;
> Or whether thou to our moist vows denied,
> Sleep'st by the fable of Bellerus old,
> Where the great vision of the guarded mount
> Looks toward Namancos and Bayona's hold:
> Look homeward, Angel, now, and melt with ruth;
> And, O ye dolphins, waft the hapless youth.

Milton's vision travels past Land's End (Bellerus) at the tip of Cornwall on to Mount St. Michael, the Cornish eminence traditionally guarded by the archangel Michael, looking toward the Spanish strongholds of Namancos and Bayona. In the great outcry to Michael: "Look homeward, Angel, now," Milton intimates what a prophet should anticipate, the slowly gathering ferment that will lead on to Cromwell and the Civil Wars.

The final movement of *Lycidas* is one of the supreme examples in poetry of a transumption or metaleptic reversal, a return of the Dead in the poet's own colors, establishing his own earliness and the belatedness of the tradition, audaciously even of Revelation:

> Weep no more, woeful Shepherds, weep no more,
> For Lycidas, your sorrow, is not dead,
> Sunk though he be beneath the watery floor;
> So sinks the day-star in the ocean bed,

And yet anon repairs his drooping head,
And tricks his beams, and with new-spangled ore
Flames in the forehead of the morning sky:
So Lycidas sunk low, but mounted high,
Through the dear might of him that walked the waves,
Where other groves and other streams along,
With Nectar pure his oozy locks he laves,
And hears the unexpressive nuptial song
In the blest kingdoms meek of joy and love.
There entertain him all the saints above,
In solemn troops and sweet societies
That sing, and singing in their glory move,
And wipe the tears for ever from his eyes.
Now, Lycidas the shepherds weep no more;
Henceforth thou art the Genius of the Shore,
In thy large recompense, and shalt be good
To all that wander in that perilous flood.

Lycidas is now the rising sun as well as the setting, resurrected: "Through the dear might of him that walked the waves." As "the Genius of the Shore," Lycidas will be Milton's guardian, preserving him for achievement in heroic poetry. The sacred nuptial song of Revelation 19:9 is subsumed by the images of Milton's monody. That permits the beautiful coda in which Milton as unknown poet ("uncouth swain") appears in perpetual earliness, ready to accomplish the still greater poems waiting for him beyond:

Thus sang the uncouth swain to the oaks and rills,
While the still morn went out with sandals grey;
He touched the tender stops of various quills,
With eager thought warbling his Doric lay.
And now the sun had stretched out all the hills,
And now was dropped into the western bay;
At last he rose, and twitched his mantle blue:
Tomorrow to fresh woods, and pastures new.

This is a different kind of sunset, an opening to fresh achievement, and a closure of the poetic past. The art of *Paradise Lost*, which will make Milton's epic primary, and Homer, Vergil, Tasso, Spenser secondary or tertiary, already is in play at the triumphant close of *Lycidas*.

Lycidas

In this monody the author bewails a learned friend, unfortunately drowned in his passage from Chester on the Irish Seas, 1637. And by occasion foretells the ruin of our corrupted clergy, then in their height.

Yet once more, O ye laurels, and once more,
Ye myrtles brown, with ivy never sere,
I come to pluck your berries harsh and crude,
And with forced fingers rude
Shatter your leaves before the mellowing year.
Bitter constraint, and sad occasion dear,
Compels me to disturb your season due:
For Lycidas is dead, dead ere his prime,
Young Lycidas, and hath not left his peer.
10 Who would not sing for Lycidas? He knew
Himself to sing, and build the lofty rhyme.
He must not float upon his watery bier
Unwept, and welter to the parching wind,
Without the meed of some melodious tear.
  Begin then, Sisters of the sacred well
That from beneath the seat of Jove doth spring,
Begin, and somewhat loudly sweep the string.
Hence with denial vain, and coy excuse,
So may some gentle Muse
20 With lucky words favour my destined urn,
And as he passes turn,
And bid fair peace be to my sable shroud.
For we were nursed upon the self-same hill,
Fed the same flock, by fountain, shade, and rill.
  Together both, ere the high lawns appeared
Under the opening eyelids of the morn,
We drove afield, and both together heard
What time the grey-fly winds her sultry horn,
Battening our flocks with the fresh dews of night,
30 Oft till the star that rose, at evening, bright
Toward heaven's descent had sloped his westering wheel.
Meanwhile the rural ditties were not mute,
Tempered to the oaten flute;
Rough Satyrs danced, and Fauns with cloven heel
From the glad sound would not be absent long,
And old Damaetas loved to hear our song.
  But O the heavy change, now thou art gone,

Now thou art gone, and never must return!
Thee, Shepherd, thee the woods and desert caves,
40 With wild thyme and the gadding vine o'ergrown,
And all their echoes mourn.
The willows and the hazel copses green
Shall now no more be seen
Fanning their joyous leaves to thy soft lays.
As killing as the canker to the rose,
Or taint-worm to the weanling herds that graze,
Or frost to flowers, that their gay wardrobe wear,
When first the white-thorn blows;
Such, Lycidas, thy loss to shepherd's ear.
50   Where were ye, Nymphs, when the remorseless deep
Closed o'er the head of your loved Lycidas?
For neither were ye playing on the steep
Where your old bards, the famous Druids, lie,
Nor on the shaggy top of Mona high,
Nor yet where Deva spreads her wizard stream.
Ay me, I fondly dream,
Had ye been there!—for what could that have done?
What could the Muse herself that Orpheus bore,
The Muse herself, for her enchanting son
60 Whom universal nature did lament,
When by the rout that made the hideous roar
His gory visage down the stream was sent,
Down the swift Hebrus to the Lesbian shore?
    Alas! what boots it with uncessant care
To tend the homely slighted shepherd's trade,
And strictly meditate the thankless Muse?
Were it not better done as others use,
To sport with Amaryllis in the shade,
Or with the tangles of Neaera's hair?
70 Fame is the spur that the clear spirit doth raise
(That last infirmity of noble mind)
To scorn delights, and live laborious days;
But the fair guerdon when we hope to find,
And think to burst out into sudden blaze,
Comes the blind Fury with the abhorrèd shears,
And slits the thin-spun life. "But not the praise,"
Phoebus replied, and touched my trembling ears:
"Fame is no plant that grows on mortal soil,
Nor in the glistering foil
80 Set off to the world, nor in broad rumour lies,

But lives and spreads aloft by those pure eyes
And perfect witness of all-judging Jove;
As he pronounces lastly on each deed,
Of so much fame in heaven expect thy meed."
    O fountain Arethuse, and thou honoured flood,
Smooth-sliding Mincius, crowned with vocal reeds,
That strain I heard was of a higher mood.
But now my oat proceeds,
And listens to the herald of the sea
90   That came in Neptune's plea.
He asked the waves, and asked the felon winds,
What hard mishap hath doomed this gentle swain?
And questioned every gust of rugged wings
That blows from off each beakéd promontory—
They knew not of his story,
And sage Hippotades their answer brings,
That not a blast was from his dungeon strayed;
The air was calm, and on the level brine
Sleek Panope with her all sisters played.
100 It was that fatal and perfidious bark,
Built in the eclipse, and rigged with curses dark,
That sunk so low that sacred head of thine.
    Next Camus, reverend sire, went footing slow,
His mantle hairy, and his bonnet sedge,
Inwrought with figures dim, and on the edge
Like to that sanguine flower inscribed with woe.
"Ah, who hath reft," quoth he, "my dearest pledge?"
Last came, and last did go,
The Pilot of the Galilean lake;
110 Two massy keys he bore of metals twain
(The golden opes, the iron shuts amain).
He shook his mitred locks, and stern bespake:
"How well could I have spared for thee, young swain,
Enow of such as for their bellies' sake
Creep and intrude and climb into the fold!
Of other care they little reckoning make
Than how to scramble at the shearers' feast,
And shove away the worthy bidden guest.
Blind mouths! that scarce themselves know how to hold
120 A sheep-hook, or have learned aught else the least
That to the faithful herdman's art belongs!
What recks it them? What need they? They are sped;
And when they list, their lean and flashy songs

Grate on their scrannel pípes of wretched straw.
The hungry sheep look up, and are not fed,
But swoln with wind, and the rank mist they draw,
Rot inwardly, and foul contagion spread,
Besides what the grim wolf with privy paw
Daily devours apace, and nothing said;
130   But that two-handed engine at the door
Stands ready to smite once, and smite no more."
       Return, Alphéus, the dread voice is past
That shrunk thy streams; return, Sicilian Muse,
And call the vales, and bid them hither cast
Their bells and flowerets of a thousand hues.
Ye valleys low where the mild whispers use
Of shades and wanton winds and gushing brooks,
On whose fresh lap the swart star sparely looks,
Throw hither all your quaint enamelled eyes,
140   That on the green turf suck the honied showers,
And purple all the ground with vernal flowers.
Bring the rathe primrose that forsaken dies,
The tufted crowtoe, and pale jessamine,
The white pink, and the pansy freaked with jet,
The glowing violet,
The musk-rose, and the well-attired woodbine,
With cowslips wan that hang the pensive head,
And every flower that sad embroidery wears.
Bid amaranthus all his beauty shed,
150   And daffadillies fill their cups with tears,
To strew the laureate hearse where Lycid lies.
For so to interpose a little ease,
Let our frail thoughts dally with false surmise;
Ay me! whilst thee the shores and sounding seas
Wash far away, where'er thy bones are hurled,
Whether beyond the stormy Hebrides,
Where thou perhaps under the whelming tide
Visit'st the bottom of the monstrous world;
Or whether thou, to our moist vows denied,
160   Sleep'st by the fable of Bellerus old,
Where the great Vision of the guarded mount
Looks toward Namancos and Bayona's hold:
Look homeward, Angel, now, and melt with ruth;
And, O ye dolphins, waft the hapless youth.
       Weep no more, woeful shepherds, weep no more,
For Lycidas, your sorrow, is not dead,

Sunk though he be beneath the watery floor;
So sinks the day-star in the ocean bed,
And yet anon repairs his drooping head,
170 And tricks his beams, and with new-spangled ore
Flames in the forehead of the morning sky:
So Lycidas sunk low, but mounted high,
Through the dear might of him that walked the waves,
Where other groves and other streams along,
With nectar pure his oozy locks he laves,
And hears the unexpressive nuptial song
In the blest kingdoms meek of joy and love.
There entertain him all the saints above,
In solemn troops and sweet societies
180 That sing, and singing in their glory move,
And wipe the tears for ever from his eyes.
Now, Lycidas, the shepherds weep no more;
Henceforth thou art the Genius of the Shore,
In thy large recompense, and shalt be good
To all that wander in that perilous flood.

    Thus sang the uncouth swain to the oaks and rills,
While the still morn went out with sandals grey;
He touched the tender stops of various quills,
With eager thought warbling his Doric lay.
190 And now the sun had stretched out all the hills,
And now was dropped into the western bay;
At last he rose, and twitched his mantle blue:
Tomorrow to fresh woods, and pastures new.

    1637   1645

from Paradise Lost

FROM BOOK I

Of man's first disobedience, and the fruit
Of that forbidden tree, whose mortal taste
Brought death into the world, and all our woe,
With loss of Eden, till one greater Man
Restore us, and regain the blissful seat,
Sing, heavenly Muse, that on the secret top
Of Oreb, or of Sinai, didst inspire
That shepherd who first taught the chosen seed
In the beginning how the heavens and earth

10   Rose out of Chaos; or if Sion hill
       Delight thee more, and Siloa's brook that flowed
       Fast by the oracle of God, I thence
       Invoke thy aid to my adventurous song,
       That with no middle flight intends to soar
       Above the Aonian mount, while it pursues
       Things unattempted yet in prose or rhyme.
       And chiefly thou, O Spirit, that dost prefer
       Before all temples the upright heart and pure,
       Instruct me, for thou knowest; thou from the first
20   Wast present, and with mighty wings outspread
       Dove-like sat'st brooding on the vast abyss
       And mad'st it pregnant: what in me is dark
       Illumine, what is low raise and support;
       That to the highth of this great argument
       I may assert eternal providence,
       And justify the ways of God to men.
           Say first, for heaven hides nothing from thy view,
       Nor the deep tract of hell, say first what cause
       Moved our grand parents in that happy state,
30   Favoured of heaven so highly, to fall off
       From their creator, and transgress his will
       For one restraint, lords of the world besides?
       Who first seduced them to that foul revolt?
       The infernal serpent; he it was whose guile,
       Stirred up with envy and revenge, deceived
       The mother of mankind, what time his pride
       Had cast him out from heaven, with all his host
       Of rebel angels, by whose aid aspiring
       To set himself in glory above his peers,
40   He trusted to have equalled the Most High,
       If he opposed; and with ambitious aim
       Against the throne and monarchy of God
       Raised impious war in heaven and battle proud
       With vain attempt. Him the Almighty Power
       Hurled headlong flaming from the ethereal sky
       With hideous ruin and combustion down
       To bottomless perdition, there to dwell
       In adamantine chains and penal fire,
       Who durst defy the omnipotent to arms.
50   Nine times the space that measures day and night
       To mortal men, he with his horrid crew
       Lay vanquished, rolling in the fiery gulf

Confounded though immortal. But his doom
Reserved him to more wrath; for now the thought
Both of lost happiness and lasting pain
Torments him; round he throws his baleful eyes,
That witnessed huge affliction and dismay
Mixed with obdúrate pride and steadfast hate.
At once as far as angels' ken he views
60   The dismal situation waste and wild:
A dungeon horrible, on all sides round
As one great furnace flamed, yet from those flames
No light, but rather darkness visible
Served only to discover sights of woe,
Regions of sorrow, doleful shades, where peace
And rest can never dwell, hope never comes
That comes to all; but torture without end
Still urges, and a fiery deluge, fed
With ever-burning sulphur unconsumed:
70   Such place eternal justice had prepared
For those rebellious, here their prison ordained
In utter darkness, and their portion set
As far removed from God and light of heaven
As from the centre thrice to the utmost pole.
O how unlike the place from whence they fell!
There the companions of his fall, o'erwhelmed
With floods and whirlwinds of tempestuous fire,
He soon discerns, and weltering by his side
One next himself in power, and next in crime,
80   Long after known in Palestine, and named
Beelzebub. To whom the arch-enemy,
And thence in heaven called Satan, with bold words
Breaking the horrid silence thus began:
    "If thou beest he . . . but O how fallen! how changed
From him, who in the happy realms of light
Clothed with transcendent brightness didst outshine
Myriads though bright—if he whom mutual league,
United thoughts and counsels, equal hope
And hazard in the glorious enterprise,
90   Joined with me once, now misery hath joined
In equal ruin: into what pit thou seest
From what highth fallen, so much the stronger proved
He with his thunder, and till then who knew
The force of those dire arms? Yet not for those,
Nor what the potent victor in his rage

Can else inflict, do I repent or change,
Though changed in outward lustre that fixed mind
And high disdain, from sense of injured merit,
That with the mightiest raised me to contend,
100 And to the fierce contention brought along
Innumerable force of spirits armed
That durst dislike his reign, and me preferring,
His utmost power with adverse power opposed
In dubious battle on the plains of heaven,
And shook his throne. What though the field be lost?
All is not lost; the unconquerable will,
And study of revenge, immortal hate,
And courage never to submit or yield:
And what is else not to be overcome?
110 That glory never shall his wrath or might
Extort from me. To bow and sue for grace
With suppliant knee, and deify his power—
Who from the terror of this arm so late
Doubted his empire—that were low indeed,
That were an ignominy and shame beneath
This downfall; since by fate the strength of gods
And this empyreal substance cannot fail,
Since through experience of this great event,
In arms not worse, in foresight much advanced,
120 We may with more successful hope resolve
To wage by force or guile eternal war
Irreconcilable to our grand foe,
Who now triumphs, and in the excess of joy
Sole reigning holds the tyranny of heaven."
    So spake the apostate Angel, though in pain,
Vaunting aloud, but racked with deep despair;
And him thus answered soon his bold compeer:
    "O Prince, O chief of many thronèd powers,
That led the embattled seraphim to war
130 Under thy conduct, and in dreadful deeds
Fearless, endangered heaven's perpetual king,
And put to proof his high supremacy,
Whether upheld by strength, or chance, or fate;
Too well I see and rue the dire event,
That with sad overthrow and foul defeat
Hath lost us heaven, and all this mighty host
In horrible destruction laid thus low,
As far as gods and heavenly essences

Can perish: for the mind and spirit remains
140   Invincible, and vigour soon returns,
Though all our glory extinct, and happy state
Here swallowed up in endless misery.
But what if he our conqueror (whom I now
Of force believe almighty, since no less
Than such could have o'erpowered such force as ours)
Have left us this our spirit and strength entire
Strongly to suffer and support our pains,
That we may so suffice his vengeful ire,
Or do him mightier service as his thralls
150   By right of war, whate'er his business be,
Here in the heart of hell to work in fire,
Or do his errands in the gloomy deep?
What can it then avail though yet we feel
Strength undiminished, or eternal being
To undergo eternal punishment?"
    Whereto with speedy words the arch-fiend replied:
"Fallen cherub, to be weak is miserable,
Doing or suffering: but of this be sure,
To do aught good never will be our task,
160   But ever to do ill our sole delight,
As being the contrary to his high will
Whom we resist. If then his providence
Out of our evil seek to bring forth good,
Our labour must be to pervert that end,
And out of good still to find means of evil;
Which ofttimes may succeed, so as perhaps
Shall grieve him, if I fail not, and disturb
His inmost counsels from their destined aim.
But see the angry victor hath recalled
170   His ministers of vengeance and pursuit
Back to the gates of heaven; the sulphurous hail
Shot after us in storm, o'erblown hath laid
The fiery surge, that from the precipice
Of heaven received us falling, and the thunder,
Winged with red lightning and impetuous rage,
Perhaps hath spent his shafts, and ceases now
To bellow through the vast and boundless deep.
Let us not slip the occasion, whether scorn
Or satiate fury yield it from our foe.
180   Seest thou yon dreary plain, forlorn and wild,
The seat of desolation, void of light,

Save what the glimmering of these livid flames
Casts pale and dreadful? Thither let us tend
From off the tossing of these fiery waves,
There rest, if any rest can harbour there,
And reassembling our afflicted powers,
Consult how we may henceforth most offend
Our enemy, our own loss how repair,
How overcome this dire calamity,
190   What reinforcement we may gain from hope;
If not, what resolution from despair."
—Thus Satan talking to his nearest mate
With head uplift above the wave, and eyes
That sparkling blazed; his other parts besides
Prone on the flood, extended long and large
Lay floating many a rood, in bulk as huge
As whom the fables name of monstrous size,
Titanian or Earth-born, that warred on Jove,
Briareos or Typhon, whom the den
200   By ancient Tarsus held, or that sea-beast
Leviathan, which God of all his works
Created hugest that swim the ocean stream:
Him haply slumbering on the Norway foam,
The pilot of some small night-foundered skiff,
Deeming some island, oft, as seamen tell,
With fixèd anchor in his scaly rind
Moors by his side under the lee, while night
Invests the sea, and wishèd morn delays:
So stretched out huge in length the arch-fiend lay
210   Chained on the burning lake; nor ever thence
Had risen or heaved his head, but that the will
And high permission of all-ruling heaven
Left him at large to his own dark designs,
That with reiterated crimes he might
Heap on himself damnation, while he sought
Evil to others, and enraged might see
How all his malice served but to bring forth
Infinite goodness, grace and mercy shown
On man by him seduced, but on himself
220   Treble confusion, wrath and vengeance poured.
    Forthwith upright he rears from off the pool
His mighty stature; on each hand the flames
Driven backward slope their pointing spires, and rolled
In billows, leave i' th' midst a horrid vale.

Then with expanded wings he steers his flight
Aloft, incumbent on the dusky air
That felt unusual weight, till on dry land
He lights, if it were land that ever burned
With solid, as the lake with liquid fire;
230 And such appeared in hue; as when the force
Of subterranean wind transports a hill
Torn from Pelorus, or the shattered side
Of thundering Aetna, whose combustible
And fuelled entrails thence conceiving fire,
Sublimed with mineral fury, aid the winds,
And leave a singèd bottom all involved
With stench and smoke: such resting found the sole
Of unblest feet. Him followed his next mate,
Both glorying to have scaped the Stygian flood
240 As gods, and by their own recovered strength,
Not by the sufferance of supernal power.
    "Is this the region, this the soil, the clime,"
Said then the lost archangel, "this the seat
That we must change for heaven, this mournful gloom
For that celestial light? Be it so, since he
Who now is sovereign can dispose and bid
What shall be right: farthest from him is best,
Whom reason hath equalled, force hath made supreme
Above his equals. Farewell, happy fields,
250 Where joy for ever dwells: hail, horrors! hail,
Infernal world! and thou, profoundest hell,
Receive thy new possessor: one who brings
A mind not to be changed by place or time.
The mind is its own place, and in itself
Can make a heaven of hell, a hell of heaven.
What matter where, if I be still the same,
And what I should be, all but less than he
Whom thunder hath made greater? Here at least
We shall be free; the Almighty hath not built
260 Here for his envy, will not drive us hence:
Here we may reign secure, and in my choice
To reign is worth ambition, though in hell:
Better to reign in hell than serve in heaven.
But wherefore let we then our faithful friends,
The associates and co-partners of our loss,
Lie thus astonished on the oblivious pool,
And call them not to share with us their part

In this unhappy mansion, or once more
With rallied arms to try what may be yet
270   Regained in heaven, or what more lost in hell?"
    So Satan spake, and him Beelzebub
Thus answered: "Leader of those armies bright,
Which but the omnipotent none could have foiled,
If once they hear that voice, their liveliest pledge
Of hope in fears and dangers, heard so oft
In worst extremes, and on the perilous edge
Of battle when it raged, in all assaults
Their surest signal, they will soon resume
New courage and revive, though now they lie
280   Grovelling and prostrate on yon lake of fire,
As we erewhile, astounded and amazed;
No wonder, fallen such a pernicious highth!"
    He scarce had ceased when the superior fiend
Was moving toward the shore; his ponderous shield,
Ethereal temper, massy, large, and round,
Behind him cast; the broad circumference
Hung on his shoulders like the moon, whose orb
Through optic glass the Tuscan artist views
At evening from the top of Fesole,
290   Or in Valdarno, to descry new lands,
Rivers or mountains in her spotty globe.
His spear, to equal which the tallest pine
Hewn on Norwegian hills, to be the mast
Of some great ammiral, were but a wand,
He walked with to support uneasy steps
Over the burning marl, not like those steps
On heaven's azure; and the torrid clime
Smote on him sore besides, vaulted with fire.
Nathless he so endured, till on the beach
300   Of that inflamèd sea, he stood and called
His legions, angel forms, who lay entranced,
Thick as autumnal leaves that strow the brooks
In Vallombrosa, where the Etrurian shades
High over-arched embower; or scattered sedge
Afloat, when with fierce winds Orion armed
Hath vexed the Red Sea coast, whose waves o'erthrew
Busiris and his Memphian chivalry,
While with perfidious hatred they pursued
The sojourners of Goshen, who beheld
310   From the safe shore their floating carcasses

And broken chariot wheels; so thick bestrown,
Abject and lost lay these, covering the flood,
Under amazement of their hideous change.
He called so loud that all the hollow deeps
Of hell resounded: "Princes, Potentates,
Warriors, the flower of heaven, once yours, now lost,
If such astonishment as this can seize
Eternal Spirits; or have ye chosen this place
After the toil of battle to repose
320   Your wearied virtue, for the ease you find
To slumber here, as in the vales of heaven?
Or in this abject posture have ye sworn
To adore the conqueror, who now beholds
Cherub and seraph rolling in the flood
With scattered arms and ensigns, till anon
His swift pursuers from heaven gates discern
The advantage, and descending tread us down
Thus drooping, or with linkèd thunderbolts
Transfix us to the bottom of this gulf?
330   Awake, arise, or be for ever fallen!"
        They heard, and were abashed, and up they sprung
Upon the wing, as when men wont to watch
On duty, sleeping found by whom they dread,
Rouse and bestir themselves ere well awake.
Nor did they not perceive the evil plight
In which they were, or the fierce pains not feel;
Yet to their general's voice they soon obeyed
Innumerable. As when the potent rod
Of Amram's son in Egypt's evil day
340   Waved round the coast, up called a pitchy cloud
Of locusts, warping on the eastern wind,
That o'er the realm of impious Pharaoh hung
Like night, and darkened all the land of Nile:
So numberless were those bad angels seen
Hovering on wing under the cope of hell
'Twixt upper, nether, and surrounding fires;
Till, as a signal given, the uplifted spear
Of their great Sultan waving to direct
Their course, in even balance down they light
350   On the firm brimstone, and fill all the plain;
A multitude, like which the populous North
Poured never from her frozen loins, to pass
Rhene or the Danaw, when her barbarous sons

Came like a deluge on the south, and spread
Beneath Gibraltar to the Libyan sands.
Forthwith from every squadron and each band
The heads and leaders thither haste where stood
Their great commander; godlike shapes and forms
Excelling human, princely dignities,
360 And powers that erst in heaven sat on thrones;
Though of their names in heavenly records now
Be no memorial, blotted out and razed
By their rebellion from the books of life.
Nor had they yet among the sons of Eve
Got them new names, till wandering o'er the earth,
Through God's high sufferance for the trial of man,
By falsities and lies the greatest part
Of mankind they corrupted to forsake
God their creator, and the invisible
370 Glory of him that made them to transform
Oft to the image of a brute, adorned
With gay religions full of pomp and gold,
And devils to adore for deities:
Then were they known to men by various names,
And various idols through the heathen world.

.   .   .

FROM BOOK III

Hail, holy Light, offspring of heaven first-born,
Or of the eternal coeternal beam
May I express thee unblamed? since God is light,
And never but in unapproachèd light
Dwelt from eternity, dwelt then in thee,
Bright effluence of bright essence increate.
Or hearest thou rather pure ethereal stream,
Whose fountain who shall tell? Before the sun,
Before the heavens thou wert, and at the voice
10 Of God, as with a mantle didst invest
The rising world of waters dark and deep,
Won from the void and formless infinite.
Thee I revisit now with bolder wing,
Escaped the Stygian pool, though long detained
In that obscure sojourn, while in my flight
Through utter and through middle darkness borne
With other notes than to the Orphéan lyre
I sung of Chaos and eternal Night,

Taught by the heavenly Muse to venture down
20   The dark descent, and up to reascend,
Though hard and rare. Thee I revisit safe,
And feel thy sovereign vital lamp; but thou
Revisit'st not these eyes, that roll in vain
To find thy piercing ray, and find no dawn;
So thick a drop serene hath quenched their orbs,
Or dim suffusion veiled. Yet not the more
Cease I to wander where the Muses haunt
Clear spring, or shady grove, or sunny hill,
Smit with the love of sacred song; but chief
30   Thee, Sion, and the flowery brooks beneath
That wash thy hallowed feet, and warbling flow,
Nightly I visit; nor sometimes forget
Those other two equalled with me in fate,
So were I equalled with them in renown,
Blind Thamyris and blind Maeonides,
And Tiresias and Phineus prophets old:
Then feed on thoughts that voluntary move
Harmonious numbers, as the wakeful bird
Sings darkling, and in shadiest covert hid
40   Tunes her nocturnal note. Thus with the year
Seasons return; but not to me returns
Day, or the sweet approach of even or morn,
Or sight of vernal bloom, or summer's rose,
Or flocks, or herds, or human face divine;
But cloud instead, and ever-during dark
Surrounds me, from the cheerful ways of men
Cut off, and for the book of knowledge fair
Presented with a universal blank
Of Nature's works to me expunged and razed,
50   And wisdom at one entrance quite shut out.
So much the rather thou, celestial Light,
Shine inward, and the mind through all her powers
Irradiate, there plant eyes, all mist from thence
Purge and disperse, that I may see and tell
Of things invisible to mortal sight.

.   .   .

FROM BOOK IV
O for that warning voice, which he who saw
The Apocalypse heard cry in heaven aloud,
Then when the dragon, put to second rout,

Came furious down to be revenged on men,
"Woe to the inhabitants on earth!" that now,
While time was, our first parents had been warned
The coming of their secret foe, and scaped,
Haply so scaped, his mortal snare; for now
Satan, now first inflamed with rage, came down,
10   The tempter ere the accuser of mankind,
To wreak on innocent frail man his loss
Of that first battle, and his flight to hell:
Yet not rejoicing in his speed, though bold,
Far off and fearless, nor with cause to boast,
Begins his dire attempt, which nigh the birth
Now rolling, boils in his tumultuous breast,
And like a devilish engine back recoils
Upon himself; horror and doubt distract
His troubled thoughts, and from the bottom stir
20   The hell within him, for within him hell
He brings, and round about him, nor from hell
One step no more than from himself can fly
By change of place. Now conscience wakes despair
That slumbered, wakes the bitter memory
Of what he was, what is, and what must be
Worse; of worse deeds worse sufferings must ensue.
Sometimes towards Eden which now in his view
Lay pleasant, his grieved look he fixes sad,
Sometimes towards heaven and the full-blazing sun,
30   Which now sat high in his meridian tower.
Then much revolving, thus in sighs began:
   "O thou that with surpassing glory crowned
Look'st from thy sole dominion like the god
Of this new world; at whose sight all the stars
Hide their diminished heads; to thee I call,
But with no friendly voice, and add thy name,
O sun, to tell thee how I hate thy beams
That bring to my remembrance from what state
I fell, how glorious once above thy sphere;
40   Till pride and worse ambition threw me down
Warring in heaven against heaven's matchless king.
Ah wherefore? He deserved no such return
From me, whom he created what I was
In that bright eminence, and with his good
Upbraided none; nor was his service hard.
What could be less than to afford him praise,

The easiest recompense, and pay him thanks,
How due! Yet all his good proved ill in me,
And wrought but malice; lifted up so high
50   I sdained subjection, and thought one step higher
Would set me highest, and in a moment quit
The debt immense of endless gratitude,
So burdensome still paying, still to owe;
Forgetful what from him I still received,
And understood not that a grateful mind
By owing owes not, but still pays, at once
Indebted and discharged; what burden then?
O had his powerful destiny ordained
Me some inferior angel, I had stood
60   Then happy; no unbounded hope had raised
Ambition. Yet why not? Some other power
As great might have aspired, and me though mean
Drawn to his part; but other powers as great
Fell not, but stand unshaken, from within
Or from without, to all temptations armed.
Hadst thou the same free will and power to stand?
Thou hadst. Whom hast thou then or what to accuse,
But heaven's free love dealt equally to all?
Be then his love accurst, since love or hate,
70   To me alike, it deals eternal woe.
Nay cursed be thou, since against his thy will
Chose freely what it now so justly rues.
Me miserable! which way shall I fly
Infinite wrath, and infinite despair?
Which way I fly is hell; myself am hell;
And in the lowest deep a lower deep
Still threatening to devour me opens wide,
To which the hell I suffer seems a heaven.
O then at last relent: is there no place
80   Left for repentance, none for pardon left?
None left but by submission; and that word
Disdain forbids me, and my dread of shame
Among the spirits beneath, whom I seduced
With other promises and other vaunts
Than to submit, boasting I could subdue
The omnipotent. Ay me, they little know
How dearly I abide that boast so vain,
Under what torments inwardly I groan;
While they adore me on the throne of hell,

90 With diadem and sceptre high advanced,
The lower still I fall, only supreme
In misery; such joy ambition finds.
But say I could repent and could obtain
By act of grace my former state; how soon
Would highth recall high thoughts, how soon unsay
What feigned submission swore: ease would recant
Vows made in pain, as violent and void.
For never can true reconcilement grow
Where sounds of deadly hate have pierced so deep;
100 Which would but lead me to a worse relapse
And heavier fall: so should I purchase dear
Short intermission bought with double smart.
This knows my punisher; therefore as far
From granting he, as I from begging peace.
All hope excluded thus, behold instead
Of us outcast, exiled, his new delight,
Mankind created, and for him this world.
So farewell hope, and with hope farewell fear,
Farewell remorse! All good to me is lost;
110 Evil, be thou my good; by thee at least
Divided empire with heaven's king I hold
By thee, and more than half perhaps will govern;
As man ere long, and this new world shall know."
  Thus while he spake, each passion dimmed his face
Thrice changed with pale, ire, envy, and despair,
Which marred his borrowed visage, and betrayed
Him counterfeit, if any eye beheld.

  . . .

FROM BOOK V

Now Morn her rosy steps in the eastern clime
Advancing, sowed the earth with orient pearl,
When Adam waked, so customed—for his sleep
Was airy light, from pure digestion bred,
And temperate vapours bland, which the only sound
Of leaves and fuming rills, Aurora's fan,
Lightly dispersed, and the shrill matin song
Of birds on every bough—so much the more
His wonder was to find unwakened Eve
10 With tresses discomposed, and glowing cheek,
As through unquiet rest. He on his side
Leaning half-raised, with looks of cordial love

Hung over her enamoured, and beheld
Beauty, which whether waking or asleep
Shot forth peculiar graces; then with voice
Mild, as when Zephyrus on Flora breathes,
Her hand soft touching, whispered thus: "Awake,
My fairest, my espoused, my latest found,
Heaven's last best gift, my ever new delight,
20   Awake, the morning shines, and the fresh field
Calls us; we lose the prime, to mark how spring
Our tended plants, how blows the citron grove,
What drops the myrrh, and what the balmy reed,
How Nature paints her colours, how the bee
Sits on the bloom extracting liquid sweet."
    Such whispering waked her, but with startled eye
On Adam, whom embracing, thus she spake:
    "O sole in whom my thoughts find all repose,
My glory, my perfection, glad I see
30   Thy face, and morn returned, for I this night—
Such night till this I never passed—have dreamed,
If dreamed, not as I oft am wont, of thee,
Works of day past, or morrow's next design,
But of offence and trouble, which my mind
Knew never till this irksome night. Methought
Close at mine ear one called me forth to walk
With gentle voice; I thought it thine. It said:
'Why sleep'st thou, Eve? Now is the pleasant time,
The cool, the silent, save where silence yields
40   To the night-warbling bird, that now awake
Tunes sweetest his love-laboured song; now reigns
Full-orbed the moon, and with more pleasing light
Shadowy sets off the face of things; in vain,
If none regard; heaven wakes with all his eyes,
Whom to behold but thee, Nature's desire,
In whose sight all things joy, with ravishment
Attracted by thy beauty still to gaze?'
I rose as at thy call, but found thee not;
To find thee I directed then my walk;
50   And on, methought, alone I passed through ways
That brought me on a sudden to the tree
Of interdicted knowledge. Fair it seemed,
Much fairer to my fancy than by day;
And as I wondering looked, beside it stood
One shaped and winged like one of those from heaven

By us oft seen; his dewy locks distilled
Ambrosia; on that tree he also gazed;
And *'O fair plant,'* said he, *'with fruit surcharged,*
Deigns none to ease thy load and taste thy sweet,
60   *Nor god, nor man; is knowledge so despised?*
Or envy, or what reserve forbids to taste?
Forbid who will, none shall from me withhold
Longer thy offered good, why else set here?'
This said he paused not, but with venturous arm
He plucked, he tasted; me damp horror chilled
At such bold words vouched with a deed so bold.
But he thus, overjoyed: *'O fruit divine,*
Sweet of thyself, but much more sweet thus cropped,
Forbidden here, it seems, as only fit
70   *For gods, yet able to make gods of men;*
And why not gods of men, since good, the more
Communicated, more abundant grows,
The author not impaired, but honoured more?
Here, happy creature, fair angelic Eve,
Partake thou also; happy though thou art,
Happier thou may'st be, worthier canst not be;
Taste this, and be henceforth among the gods
Thyself a goddess, not to earth confined,
But sometimes in the air, as we; sometimes
80   *Ascend to heaven, by merit thine, and see*
What life the gods live there, and such live thou.'
So saying, he drew nigh, and to me held,
Even to my mouth of that same fruit held part
Which he had plucked; the pleasant savoury smell
So quickened appetite that I, methought,
Could not but taste. Forthwith up to the clouds
With him I flew, and underneath beheld
The earth outstretched immense, a prospect wide
And various. Wondering at my flight and change
90   To this high exaltation, suddenly
My guide was gone, and I, methought, sunk down,
And fell asleep; but O how glad I waked
To find this but a dream!" Thus Eve her night
Related, and thus Adam answered sad:
    "Best image of myself and dearer half,
The trouble of thy thoughts this night in sleep
Affects me equally; nor can I like
This uncouth dream, of evil sprung, I fear;

Yet evil whence? In thee can harbour none,
100 Created pure. But know that in the soul
Are many lesser faculties that serve
Reason as chief; among these fancy next
Her office holds; of all external things,
Which the five watchful senses represent,
She forms imaginations, airy shapes,
Which reason joining or disjoining frames
All what we affirm or what deny, and call
Our knowledge or opinion; then retires
Into her private cell when nature rests.
110 Oft in her absence mimic fancy wakes
To imitate her; but misjoining shapes,
Wild work produces oft, and most in dreams,
Ill matching words and deeds long past or late.
Some such resemblances methinks I find
Of our last evening's talk in this thy dream,
But with addition strange; yet be not sad.
Evil into the mind of god or man
May come and go, so unapproved, and leave
No spot or blame behind; which gives me hope
120 That what in sleep thou didst abhor to dream,
Waking thou never wilt consent to do.
Be not disheartened then, nor cloud those looks
That wont to be more cheerful and serene
Than when fair morning first smiles on the world,
And let us to our fresh employments rise
Among the groves, the fountains, and the flowers
That open now their choicest bosomed smells
Reserved from night, and kept for thee in store."

.   .   .

FROM BOOK VII

Descend from heaven, Urania, by that name
If rightly thou art called, whose voice divine
Following, about the Olympian hill I soar,
Above the flight of Pegasean wing.
The meaning, not the name I call; for thou
Nor of the Muses nine, nor on the top
Of old Olympus dwell'st, but heavenly born,
Before the hills appeared or fountain flowed,
Thou with eternal wisdom didst converse,
10 Wisdom thy sister, and with her didst play

In presence of the almighty father, pleased
With thy celestial song. Up led by thee
Into the heaven of heavens I have presumed,
An earthly guest, and drawn empyreal air,
Thy tempering; with like safety guided down,
Return me to my native element,
Lest from this flying steed unreined (as once
Bellerophon, though from a lower clime)
Dismounted, on the Aleian field I fall,
20 Erroneous there to wander and forlorn.
Half yet remains unsung, but narrower bound
Within the visible diurnal sphere;
Standing on earth, not rapt above the pole,
More safe I sing with mortal voice, unchanged
To hoarse or mute, though fallen on evil days,
On evil days, though fallen, and evil tongues;
In darkness, and with dangers compassed round,
And solitude; yet not alone, while thou
Visit'st my slumbers nightly, or when morn
30 Purples the east. Still govern thou my song,
Urania, and fit audience find, though few.
But drive far off the barbarous dissonance
Of Bacchus and his revellers, the race
Of that wild rout that tore the Thracian bard
In Rhodope, where woods and rocks had ears
To rapture, till the savage clamour drowned
Both harp and voice; nor could the Muse defend
Her son. So fail not thou who thee implores;
For thou art heavenly, she an empty dream.

FROM BOOK IX

No more of talk where God or angel guest
With man, as with his friend, familiar used
To sit indulgent, and with him partake
Rural repast, permitting him the while
Venial discourse unblamed. I now must change
Those notes to tragic; foul distrust, and breach
Disloyal on the part of man, revolt,
And disobedience; on the part of heaven
Now alienated, distance and distaste,
10 Anger and just rebuke, and judgment given,
That brought into this world a world of woe,
Sin and her shadow Death, and misery,

Death's harbinger. Sad task, yet argument
Not less but more heroic than the wrath
Of stern Achilles on his foe pursued
Thrice fugitive about Troy wall; or rage
Of Turnus for Lavinia disespoused;
Or Neptune's ire or Juno's, that so long
Perplexed the Greek and Cytherea's son;
20   If answerable style I can obtain
Of my celestial patroness, who deigns
Her nightly visitation unimplored,
And dictates to me slumbering, or inspires
Easy my unpremeditated verse,
Since first this subject for heroic song
Pleased me long choosing, and beginning late;
Not sedulous by nature to indite
Wars, hitherto the only argument
Heroic deemed, chief maistry to dissect
30   With long and tedious havoc fabled knights
In battles feigned (the better fortitude
Of patience and heroic martyrdom
Unsung), or to describe races and games,
Or tilting furniture, emblazoned shields,
Impresses quaint, caparisons and steeds,
Bases and tinsel trappings, gorgeous knights
At joust and tournament; then marshalled feast
Served up in hall with sewers and seneschals;
The skill of artifice or office mean,
40   Not that which justly gives heroic name
To person or to poem. Me of these
Nor skilled nor studious, higher argument
Remains, sufficient of itself to raise
That name, unless an age too late, or cold
Climate, or years damp my intended wing
Depressed, and much they may, if all be mine,
Not hers who brings it nightly to my ear.
    The sun was sunk, and after him the star
Of Hesperus, whose office is to bring
50   Twilight upon the earth, short arbiter
'Twixt day and night, and now from end to end
Night's hemisphere had veiled the horizon round,
When Satan, who late fled before the threats
Of Gabriel out of Eden, now improved
In meditated fraud and malice, bent

On man's destruction, maugre what might hap
Of heavier on himself, fearless returned.
By night he fled, and at midnight returned
From compassing the earth, cautious of day,
60   Since Uriel, regent of the sun, descried
His entrance, and forewarned the Cherubim
That kept their watch; thence full of anguish driven,
The space of seven continued nights he rode

.   .   .

FROM BOOK XII

He ended, and they both descend the hill;
Descended, Adam to the bower where Eve
Lay sleeping ran before, but found her waked;
And thus with words not sad she him received:
610   "Whence thou return'st, and whither went'st, I know;
For God is also in sleep, and dreams advise,
Which he hath sent propitious, some great good
Presaging, since with sorrow and heart's distress
Wearied I fell asleep. But now lead on;
In me is no delay; with thee to go,
Is to stay here; without thee here to stay,
Is to go hence unwilling; thou to me
Art all things under heaven, all places thou,
Who for my wilful crime art banished hence.
620   This further consolation yet secure
I carry hence; though all by me is lost,
Such favour I unworthy am vouchsafed,
By me the promised seed shall all restore."
So spake our mother Eve, and Adam heard
Well pleased, but answered not; for now too nigh
The archangel stood, and from the other hill
To their fixed station, all in bright array
The Cherubim descended; on the ground
Gliding metéorous, as evening mist
630   Risen from a river o'er the marish glides,
And gathers ground fast at the labourer's heel
Homeward returning. High in front advanced,
The brandished sword of God before them blazed
Fierce as a comet; which with torrid heat,
And vapour as the Libyan air adust,
Began to parch that temperate clime; whereat

In either hand the hastening Angel caught
Our lingering parents, and to the eastern gate
Led them direct, and down the cliff as fast
640 To the subjected plain; then disappeared.
They, looking back, all the eastern side beheld
Of Paradise, so late their happy seat,
Waved over by that flaming brand, the gate
With dreadful faces thronged and fiery arms.
Some natural tears they dropped, but wiped them soon;
The world was all before them, where to choose
Their place of rest, and Providence their guide:
They hand in hand, with wandering steps and slow,
Through Eden took their solitary way.

    1658?–1665? 1667

from Samson Agonistes

    SEMICHORUS While their hearts were jocund and sublime,
1670 Drunk with idolatry, drunk with wine,
And fat regorged of bulls and goats,
Chanting their idol, and preferring
Before our living dread who dwells
In Silo, his bright sanctuary,
Among them he a spirit of frenzy sent,
Who hurt their minds,
And urged them on with mad desire
To call in haste for their destroyer;
They only set on sport and play
1680 Unweetingly importuned
Their own destruction to come speedy upon them.
So fond are mortal men
Fallen into wrath divine,
As their own ruin on themselves to invite,
Insensate left, or to sense reprobate,
And with blindness internal struck.
    SEMICHORUS But he, though blind of sight,
Despised and thought extinguished quite,
With inward eyes illuminated,
1690 His fiery virtue roused
From under ashes into sudden flame,
And as an evening dragon came,
Assailant on the perchèd roosts

And nests in order ranged
Of tame villatic fowl; but as an eagle
His cloudless thunder bolted on their heads.
So virtue, given for lost,
Depressed, and overthrown, as seemed,
Like that self-begotten bird
1700   In the Arabian woods embost,
That no second knows nor third,
And lay erewhile a holocaust,
From out her ashy womb now teemed,
Revives, reflourishes, then vigorous most
When most unactive deemed,
And though her body die, her fame survives,
A secular bird, ages of lives.
    MANOA Come, come, no time from lamentation now,
Nor much more cause; Samson hath quit himself
1710   Like Samson, and heroicly hath finished
A life heroic, on his enemies
Fully revenged; hath left them years of mourning,
And lamentation to the sons of Caphtor
Through all Philistian bounds. To Israel
Honour hath left, and freedom: let but them
Find courage to lay hold on this occasion;
To himself and father's house eternal fame;
And, which is best and happiest yet, all this
With God not parted from him, as was feared,
1720   But favouring and assisting to the end.
Nothing is here for tears, nothing to wail
Or knock the breast, no weakness, no contempt,
Dispraise, or blame, nothing but well and fair,
And what may quiet us in a death so noble.
Let us go find the body where it lies
Soaked in his enemies' blood, and from the stream
With lavers pure and cleansing herbs wash off
The clotted gore. I with what speed the while
(Gaza is not in plight to say us nay)
1730   Will send for all my kindred, all my friends,
To fetch him hence and solemnly attend
With silent obsequy and funeral train
Home to his father's house: there will I build him
A monument, and plant it round with shade
Of laurel ever green, and branching palm,
With all his trophies hung, and acts enrolled

In copious legend, or sweet lyric song.
Thither shall all the valiant youth resort,
And from his memory inflame their breasts
1740 To matchless valour and adventures high;
The virgins also shall on feastful days
Visit his tomb with flowers, only bewailing
His lot unfortunate in nuptial choice,
From whence captivity and loss of eyes.
   CHORUS All is best, though we oft doubt,
What the unsearchable dispose
Of highest wisdom brings about,
And ever best found in the close.
Oft he seems to hide his face,
1750 But unexpectedly returns
And to his faithful champion hath in place
Bore witness gloriously; whence Gaza mourns,
And all that band them to resist
His uncontrollable intent:
His servants he, with new acquist
Of true experience from this great event,
With peace and consolation hath dismissed,
And calm of mind, all passion spent.
   1647–1670?   1671

| JOHN DRYDEN |

1631–1700

"THE MIND CREATES no order of its own," in Martin Price's reading of Dryden's view, "but the mind can give shape to whatsoever of the order of charity can be made the world's concern." Pascal's order of charity transcends the orders of body and of mind, and rebukes philosophers and poets who would substitute their own cleverness for sacred wisdom. Dryden, Ancient and Modern, quested for both orders, mind and charity, and longed always for the spiritual authority he found at last in the Roman Catholic Church. His religious poems, though not the equal of his masterpieces, the political satire *Absalom and Achitophel,* and the mock-heroic satire *Mac Flecknoe* haunt us with a singular intensity, partly because they suggest that there is no such genre as the religious poem. Dryden teaches us, implicitly, that literature is both secular and sacred, either all secular or all sacred, with the supposed distinction being founded only upon social or political dialectics.

The underlying sadness of Dryden's professedly religious poems is akin to his somewhat concealed literary pessimisms. What we hear in the celebrated opening of *Religio Laici* is an ultimate sense of spiritual loss:

> Dim as the borrowed beams of moon and stars
> To lonely, weary, wandering travelers,
> Is Reason to the soul; and, as on high
> Those rolling fires discover but the sky,
> Not light us here, so Reason's glimmering ray
> Was lent, not to assure our doubtful way,
> But guide us upward to a better day.

The poet Walter Savage Landor remarked to the diarist Crabb Robinson that "nothing was ever written in hymn equal to the beginning of Dryden's *Religio Laici,*—the first eleven lines." What Landor caught was the curiously hymnlike harmony of Dryden's opening, a harmony somewhat at variance with the *dianoia* or thought-content of those first eleven lines. Dryden's faith is movingly revealed as a yearning for revelation, rather than as the revelation itself. The burden of the opening is to mediate between the Deists, who discard revelation, and the Fideists, who reject reason. Metaphorically, Dryden's Reason dissolves into the supernatural sun whose beams it has borrowed, but the tonal effect of the passage suggests a darker skepticism. The hymnlike strain rises to lament "our doubtful way," yet rises so strongly as to make equivocal Dryden's professed aim to keep to a middle way in religion.

How much, imagistically speaking, can Reason do for us, according to this passage? The moon and the planets together help little enough those "lonely, weary, wandering travelers" who do not seem to be traversing the best of all possible worlds. What reveals the sky does not illuminate us. "Dim," the poem's first word, sets the key for a cosmos where Aristotle himself cannot see the truths of creation, since here the philosophers are condemned to blind gropes and rash judgments. Reason perhaps stands in this passage like the proverbial glass we call half full or half empty depending upon our temperaments and circumstances.

Dryden will end his *Layman's Faith* with the dangerously bland assurances that "the things we must believe are few and plain," and that "points obscure are of small use to learn, / But common quiet is mankind's concern." Critically, we can acknowledge that the poem's opening was so mysteriously strong that no ending would have sufficed, but still no one ever has preferred the amiable close of *Religio Laici* to its illustrious opening. Something rich and strange in Dryden returns from repression in that immense beginning, and that something has one of its origins in Milton's *Paradise Lost,* particularly in the great invocation to Book III, where the blind prophet addresses the Holy Light:

> So much the rather thou, celestial Light,
> Shine inward, and the mind through all her powers
> Irradiate, there plant eyes, all mist from thence
> Purge and disperse, that I may see and tell
> Of things invisible to mortal sight.

It is this inwardness that is deliberately lacking in Dryden, whose dim celestial light shines as an external image. What refreshes us in Dryden, the lack of prophetic election or an egotistical sublime, at last estranges him from us also. He appeals to all varieties of historicism—old and new—but perhaps not to the deepest reader in each of us. And yet his limitations were knowing ones, wisely maintained at every point. Consider his famous lines on Milton, printed under the prophetic engraved portrait of the greatest modern epic writer in Tonson's folio edition of *Paradise Lost* in 1688.

> Three poets, in three distant ages born,
> Greece, Italy, and England, did adorn.
> The first in loftiness of thought surpassed,
> The next in majesty, in both the last:
> The force of Nature could no farther go;
> To make a third she join'd the former two.

The comparative superiority of Homer, joined to the stylistic eminence of Vergil, compels Nature to drive beyond her limits in making Milton, who is a more-than-natural force. Dryden knows himself to be in the unenviable position of being the first major and representative post-Miltonic poet. Milton has usurped the kingdom of poetry, more powerfully because more permanently than Cromwell, his chief of men, usurped the kingdom of Britain. Greatest of Ancients *and* of Moderns, Milton leaves Dryden only the middle way, and the middle voice:

All, all of a piece throughout:
Thy chase had a beast in view;
Thy wars brought nothing about;
Thy lovers were all untrue.
'Tis well an old age is out,
And time to begin a new.

ψ   ψ   ψ

from Religio Laici

or, a Layman's Faith

Dim as the borrowed beams of moon and stars
To lonely, weary, wandering travelers,
Is Reason to the soul; and, as on high
Those rolling fires discover but the sky,
Not light us here, so Reason's glimmering ray
Was lent, not to assure our doubtful way,
But guide us upward to a better day.
And as those nightly tapers disappear
When day's bright lord ascends our hemisphere;
10   So pale grows Reason at Religion's sight;
So dies, and so dissolves in supernatural light.
Some few, whose lamp shone brighter, have been led
From cause to cause, to nature's secret head;
And found that one first principle must be:
But what, or who, that universal He;
Whether some soul incompassing this ball,
Unmade, unmoved, yet making, moving all;
Or various atoms' interfering dance
Leapt into form (the noble work of chance);
20   Or this great all was from eternity;
Not even the Stagirite himself could see,
And Epicurus guessed as well as he:
As blindly groped they for a future state;
As rashly judged of providence and fate:
But least of all could their endeavours find
What most concerned the good of humankind;
For happiness was never to be found,
But vanished from 'em like enchanted ground.
One thought content the good to be enjoyed;
30   This every little accident destroyed:

The wiser madmen did for virtue toil,
A thorny or at best a barren soil;
In pleasure some their glutton souls would steep,
But found their line too short, the well too deep,
And leaky vessels which no bliss could keep.
Thus anxious thoughts in endless circles roll,
Without a centre where to fix the soul;
In this wild maze their vain endeavours end:
How can the less the greater comprehend?
40   Or finite reason reach Infinity?
For what could fathom God were more than He.
The Deist thinks he stands on firmer ground;
Cries: "Eúreka! the mighty secret's found:
God is that spring of good, supreme and best;
We, made to serve, and in that service blest.
If so, some rules of worship must be given,
Distributed alike to all by Heaven:
Else God were partial, and to some denied
The means his justice should for all provide.
50   This general worship is to *praise* and *pray*,
One part to borrow blessings, one to pay;
And when frail nature slides into offence,
The sacrifice for crimes is penitence.
Yet, since the effects of providence, we find,
Are variously dispensed to humankind;
That vice triumphs and virtue suffers here
(A brand that sovereign justice cannot bear),
Our reason prompts us to a future state,
The last appeal from fortune and from fate:
60   Where God's all-righteous ways will be declared,
The bad meet punishment, the good reward."
    Thus man by his own strength to heaven would soar,
And would not be obliged to God for more.
Vain, wretched creature, how art thou misled
To think thy wit these godlike notions bred!
These truths are not the product of thy mind,
But dropped from heaven, and of a nobler kind.
Revealed Religion first informed thy sight,
And Reason saw not, till Faith sprung the light.
70   Hence all thy natural worship takes the source:
'Tis revelation what thou thinkest discourse.
Else, how comest thou to see these truths so clear,
Which so obscure to heathens did appear?

Not Plato these, nor Aristotle found;
Nor he whose wisdom oracles renowned.
Hast thou a wit so deep, or so sublime,
Or canst thou lower dive, or higher climb?
Canst thou, by Reason, more of Godhead know
Than Plutarch, Seneca, or Cicero?
80 Those giant wits, in happier ages born,
(When arms and arts did Greece and Rome adorn)
Knew no such system; no such piles could raise
Of natural worship, built on prayer and praise,
To One Sole God:
Nor did remorse to expiate sin prescribe,
But slew their fellow creatures for a bribe:
The guiltless victim groaned for their offence,
And cruelty and blood was penitence.
If sheep and oxen could atone for men,
90 Ah! at how cheap a rate the rich might sin!
And great oppressors might Heaven's wrath beguile,
By offering his own creatures for a spoil!
   1682

· · ·

To the Memory of Mr. Oldham

Farewell, too little, and too lately known,
Whom I began to think and call my own:
For sure our souls were near allied, and thine
Cast in the same poetic mould with mine.
One common note on either lyre did strike,
And knaves and fools we both abhorred alike.
To the same goal did both our studies drive;
The last set out the soonest did arrive.
Thus Nisus fell upon the slippery place,
10 While his young friend performed and won the race.
O early ripe! to thy abundant store
What could advancing age have added more?
It might (what nature never gives the young)
Have taught the numbers of thy native tongue.
But satire needs not those, and wit will shine
Through the harsh cadence of a rugged line:
A noble error, and but seldom made,
When poets are by too much force betrayed.

Thy generous fruits, though gathered ere their prime,
20   Still showed a quickness; and maturing time
But mellows what we write to the dull sweets of rhyme.
Once more, hail and farewell; farewell, thou young,
But ah too short, Marcellus of our tongue;
Thy brows with ivy, and with laurels bound;
But fate and gloomy night encompass thee around.

   1684

Lines on Milton

Three poets, in three distant ages born,
Greece, Italy, and England did adorn.
The first in loftiness of thought surpassed,
The next in majesty, in both the last:
The force of Nature could no farther go;
To make a third, she joined the former two.

   1688

JOHN WILMOT, EARL OF ROCHESTER

1647–1680

IT IS DIFFICULT to think about the Restoration court of Charles II without falling into a fascination with John Wilmot, Earl of Rochester. In a circle of fierce libertines, the young Rochester was the leading and most witty of rakehells. Dying at thirty-three, he chose repentance and received Christian last rites.

Rochester's great poem is "A Satire Against Mankind," a characteristic expression of his Epicurean materialism. Because of its length, I represent him here by his charming "A Song of a young Lady, to her Ancient Lover." So witty is Rochester that the "Song" transcends its amiable outrageous-ness.

✹   ✹   ✹

A Song of a young Lady

To her Ancient Lover

1

Ancient Person, for whom I,
All the flattering Youth defy;
Long be it e're thou grow Old,
Aking, shaking, Crazy Cold.
But still continue as thou art,
Antient Person of my Heart.

2

On thy withered Lips and dry,
Which like barren Furrows lye;
Brooding Kisses I will pour,
Shall thy youthful Heat restore.
Such kind Show'rs in Autumn fall,
And a second Spring recall:
Nor from thee will ever part,
Antient Person of my Heart.

3

Thy Nobler part, which but to name
In our Sex wou'd be counted shame,
By Ages frozen grasp possest,
From his Ice shall be releast:
And, sooth'd by my reviving hand,
In former Warmth and Vigor stand.
All a Lover's wish can reach,
For thy Joy my Love shall teach:
And for thy Pleasure shall improve,
All that Art can add to Love.
Yet still I love thee without Art,
Antient Person of my Heart.

ALEXANDER POPE

1688–1744

I

DR. SAMUEL JOHNSON, the strongest critic in all the Western tradition (so far as I am able to judge), placed Pope ultimately in relation to Homer, greatest of precursors:

> [I]f the writer of the *Iliad* were to class his successors, he would assign a very high place to his translator, without requiring any other evidence of genius.

Elsewhere in *The Life of Pope,* Johnson insists that Pope's *Iliad* "is certainly the noblest version of poetry which the world has ever seen." Pope, most modern critics would agree, is the poet of *The Rape of the Lock, An Epistle to Dr. Arbuthnot,* some of the *Moral Essays,* the astonishing *Epistle to Augustus,* and, above all, *The Dunciad.* Translations, with rare exceptions, are for an age only. Yet what did Johnson hear when he read Pope's *Iliad?*

> Then thus to *Phoebus,* in the Realms above,
> Spoke from his Throne, the Cloud-compelling *Jove:*
> Descend my *Phoebus,* on the *Phrygian* Plain,
> And from the Fight convey *Sarpedon* slain;
> Then bathe his Body in the crystal Flood,
> With Dust dishonour'd, and deform'd with Blood:
> O'er all his Limbs *Ambrosial* Odours shed,
> And with Celestial Robes adorn the mighty Dead.
> To the soft Arms of silent *Sleep* and *Death;*
> They to his Friends the mournful Charge shall bear;
> His Friends a Tomb and Pyramid shall rear;
> These unavailing Rites he may receive,
> These, after Death, are All a God can give!

This is from *The Epistle of Sarpedon,* published with Pope's early *Pastorals* in 1709, and later incorporated into his complete version of the *Iliad.* It is not unrepresentative of Pope's Homer, and helps justify William Blake's savagery:

> Thus Hayley on his Toilette seeing the sope
> Cries Homer is very much improved by Pope

Still, it is unwise to dispute Johnson, and it is difficult to recall him ever praising a work so near to him in time as Pope's Homer, with anything like such unrestrained fervor:

> Pope searches the pages of Dryden for happy combinations of Delphick diction; but it will not be denied that he added much to what he found. He cultivated our language with so much diligence and art, that he has left in his *Homer* a treasure of poetical elegances to posterity. His version may be said to have tuned the English tongue; for since its appearance no writer, however deficient in other powers, has wanted melody. Such a series of lines so elaborately corrected, and so sweetly modulated, took possession of the publick ear; the vulgar was enamoured of the poem, and the learned wondered at the translation.

That Pope's Homer, rather than Spenser, Shakespeare, and Milton, "may be said to have tuned the English tongue" was not Johnson's eccentric judgment, but the verdict of his age. The Augustan critical mythology that culminated in Johnson had its remote origins in the tripartite division of much seventeenth-century poetry into the schools of Spenser, Donne, and Ben Jonson. The line from Jonson to Johnson may be called the Neoclassic, a version of literary history that has its most influential manifesto in Pope's early *Essay on Criticism,* regarded by Johnson as sufficient in itself to "have placed him among the first criticks and the first poets," another uncharacteristic burst of Johnsonian hyperbole, doubtless traceable to ideological exuberance. "But most by *Numbers* judge a Poet's Song," the youthful Pope persuasively intones, while urging us to "praise the *Easie Vigor* of a Line, / Where *Denham's* strength, and *Waller's* sweetness join."

Pope's own elected precursor, Dryden, caused him no more anxiety than Homer did, a judgment in which I am happy to concur with David B. Morris. Morris remarks that "there is no more profound kinship between Pope and Dryden than the belief that poetry advances by refining the achievement of the past." Yes, but how do you refine John Milton? Pope and Dr. Johnson alike handle Milton *in their own poetry* in ways very different from Pope's refinement of Dryden or Johnson's reliance upon Pope. The exquisite parodies of Milton in *The Rape of the Lock,* and the wonderfully grotesque Miltonic mock-sublimities of *The Dunciad,* are remarkable instances of the Nietzschean, daemonic dance of influence-as-parody, much more than they are mimetic or mercantile refinements. Milton and nature are hardly everywhere the same, and *Paradise Lost* is a difficult native resource to convert into trade.

"Refinement," as a poetic trope in the context of literary history, is too large to be confined to tuning diction or metric. In Dryden and Pope, refining the tradition meant extending the realm of Enlightenment, by continuing to dispel the empire of Enthusiasm. Theodicy without enthusiasm might be described as the project of Pope's *Essay on Man,* an admirable project doubtless, but perhaps not suited to the Muse. Here is the poem's conclusion:

> Say, shall my little bark attendant sail,
> Pursue the triumph and partake the gale?
> When statesmen, heroes, kings, in dust repose,
> Whose sons shall blush their fathers were thy foes,
> Shall then this verse to future age pretend
> Thou wert my guide, philosopher and friend?
> That urg'd by thee, I turn'd the tuneful art
> From sounds to things, from fancy to the heart;
> For Wit's false mirror held up Nature's light;
> Shew'd erring Pride, WHATEVER IS, IS RIGHT;
> That REASON, PASSION, answer one great aim;
> That true SELF-LOVE and SOCIAL are the same;
> That VIRTUE only makes our Bliss below;
> And all our Knowledge is OURSELVES TO KNOW.

The Muse here is the poet himself, trapped in the aesthetic impossibility of proclaiming that "WHATEVER IS, IS RIGHT." This poetic disaster, if it refines tradition, does so at an outrageous price. The *Essay on Man* has its scholarly defenders, but they praise as paradox what the great Johnson properly dismissed as principles it was not his business "to clear from obscurity, dogmatism, or falsehood." We do not esteem *Paradise Lost* for its theodicy. Those who praise *An Essay on Man* for its moral and spiritual wisdom, its absurd abasement of theodicy, have done Pope ill service.

Epistle to Augustus

If *An Essay on Man* is Pope at his most dubious, then the *Epistle to Augustus,* or *The First Epistle of the Second Book of Horace Imitated,* displays him at very nearly his strongest. No poet before or since has written a satire either so subtle or so delicious. King George II, whose name was George Augustus, was renowned alike for his military vainglory and his contempt for poetry. ("Leave such work to little Mr. Pope," he is reported to have said, "It is his trade.") Pope's revenge was at once decorous and perfect:

> While You, great Patron of Mankind, sustain
> The balanc'd World, and open all the Main;
> Your Country, chief, in Arms abroad defend,
> At home, with Morals, Arts, and Laws amend;
> How shall the Muse, from such a Monarch, steal
> An hour, and not defraud the Publick Weal?

George Augustus, or any monarch, could not ask for better. Unfortunately, he was inept at foreign policy ("sustain / The balanc'd World"), incapable of protecting British merchantmen from the marauding Spaniards ("open all the Main"), had just spent half a year abroad "in Arms," but those were the arms of his notorious German girlfriend, Amalie Sophie, and at home distinguished himself by the neglect of his duties, dislike of painting and literature, and the vigor of his performance with a harem of mistresses ("with Morals, Arts, and Laws amend").

Deftly, and with superb aplomb, Pope proceeds to destroy his victim and defend his own reputation:

> Oh! Could I mount on the Maeonian wing,
> Your Arms, your Actions, your Repose to sing!
> What seas you travers'd! and what fields you fought!
> Your Country's Peace, how oft, how dearly bought!
> How barb'rous rage subsided at your word,
> And Nations wonder'd while they dropp'd the sword!
> How, when you nodded, o'er the land and deep,
> Peace stole her wing, and wrapt the world in sleep;
> Till Earth's extremes your mediation own,
> And Asia's Tyrants tremble at your Throne—
> But Verse alas! your Majesty disdains;
> And I'm not used to Panegyric strains:
> The Zeal of Fools offends at any time,
> But most of all, the Zeal of Fools in ryme.
> Besides, a fate attends on all I write,
> That when I aim at praise, they say I bite.
> A vile Encomium doubly ridicules,

There's nothing blackens like the ink of fools;
If true, a woeful likeness, and if lyes,
"Praise undeserv'd is scandal in disguise:"
Well may he blush, who gives it, or receives;
And when I flatter, let my dirty leaves
(Like Journals, Odes, and such forgotten things
As Eusden, Philips, Settle, writ of Kings)
Cloath spice, line trunks, or flutt'ring in a row,
Befringe the rails of Bedlam and Sohoe.

Maeonian or Homeric mountings are necessary to sing of Achilles or Odysseus. Every line in the passage above is a mortal insult, George Augustus being what he was, but to acknowledge the insult would be to accept the truth. The grand movement of "Your Arms, your Actions, your Repose to sing!" is as fresh now as it was in 1737, and as applicable to President George W. Bush's repose as it was to George II's. "[W]hen I aim at praise, they say I bite," Pope protests, and we recognize that no satirist since in the language, from Byron to Waugh, is Pope's peer. But if that were the limit of Pope's satirical art, we would not be obliged to admit him among the strongest poets in the language. What makes him so formidable, a Milton among satirists, is *The Dunciad*, certainly the poetic masterpiece of its century.

The Rape of the Lock

The character of *Belinda,* as we take it in this third View, represents the Popish Religion, or the Whore of *Babylon;* who is described in the state this malevolent Author wishes for, coming forth in all her *Glory* upon the *Thames,* and overspreading the Nation with Ceremonies.

—A KEY TO THE LOCK

In April 1715, writing under the splendid name of Esdras Barnikelt, apothecary, Pope published *A Key to the Lock,* with the subtitle "Or a Treatise proving, beyond all Contradiction, the dangerous Tendency of a late Poem entitled *The Rape of the Lock* to Government and Religion." The continued use of the *Key* is to warn critics not to seek a key to Pope's mock-epic, which is to say, do not apply critical "methods" to one of the most poised and artful poems in Western literature.

Critics long have recognized that the genres of epic and mock-epic are not clearly distinct in or for Pope. *The Rape of the Lock* participates in the heroic mode rather more subtly than Pope's Homer does. The most surprising assertion as to this is the judgment of Reuben Brower:

> By inventing the sylphs Pope solved the almost impossible problems that the theorists set for the heroic poet. He is almost certainly the only modern poet to create a company of believable deities which are not simply the ancient classical divinities in modern dress, and which are not offensive to a Christian audience.

What makes Brower's remarks problematical centers in the phrase "offensive to a Christian audience," though "*believable* deities" also perhaps begs the question. Milton's angels remain Milton's, and the deities of late Shakespearean romance are persuasive (if not "believable") and offensive to no one. This is to cite only the greatest; examples are too profuse to be cataloged. Brower's true point, I think, was that Pope brilliantly exploited the shadowy ground between heroic and mock-heroic poetry. The play of allusions, splendidly studied by Brower, seems to me unlike the two fundamental modes set forth by John Hollander. Pope is neither like Donne nor his modernist followers, who give us a sense that baroque elaboration of metaphor is almost infinitely possible, nor is Pope like Milton and his Romantic followers, including such twentieth-century Romantics as W. B. Yeats and Wallace Stevens, who so station their allusions as to make further figuration almost redundant. In his own mode of refinement, Pope lightly but strongly intimates that more turnings of allusion always are possible, while charmingly insinuating that the elegance and justice of his tropes will constitute a proper haven for the amiable reader.

Martin Price calls *The Rape of the Lock* "the heroic-turned-artful." Belinda's world, on the epic scale, is second-best, even trivial, but "it is also a world of grace and delicacy." Charms replace heroic action, a substitution principally symbolized by the Rosicrucian machinery of the sylphs.

The only modification I would suggest to Price's superb observation is that the sylphs dialectically both travesty and yet surpass (in a knowingly limited but crucial way) the Homeric gods and the Miltonic angels, partly by shrewdly compounding both with the Shakespearean fairies, and with the specifically Ovidian elements in *A Midsummer Night's Dream*. Homer and Milton perhaps are not so much travestied by Pope as they are Shakespeareanized and Ovidianized. Instead of the sagacious Athena and the affable Archangel Raphael, we are given the sylphs who are Ovidian sophisticated flirts. Their sophistication is keen enough to be poetically dangerous. Let us take, as instance, the most flamboyant parody of the sacred Milton in Pope's poem:

> The Peer now spreads the glitt'ring *Forfex* wide,
> T'inclose the Lock; now joins it, to divide.
> Ev'n then, before the fatal Engine clos'd,
> A wretched *Sylph* too fondly interpos'd;
> Fate urg'd the Sheers, and cut the *Sylph* in twain,
> (But Airy Substance soon unites again):
> The meeting Points the sacred Hair dissever
> From the fair Head, for ever, and for ever!

That "wretched *Sylph*," as Pope's own note tells us, is suggested by the Miltonic blunder "of Satan cut asunder by the Angel Michael":

> but the sword
> Of Michael from the armoury of God
> Was given him tempered so, that neither keen
> Nor solid might resist that edge: it met
> The sword of Satan with steep force to smite
> Descending, and in half cut sheer, nor stayed,
> But with swift wheel reverse, deep entering shared
> All his right side; then Satan first knew pain,
> And writhed him to and fro convolved; so sore
> The griding sword with discontinuous wound
> Passed through him, but the ethereal substance closed
> Not long divisible, and from the gash
> A stream of nectarous humour issuing flowed
> Sanguine, such as celestial spirits may bleed,
> And all his armour stained ere while so bright.
> Forthwith on all sides to his aid was run
> By angels many and strong who interposed
> Defence, while others bore him on their shields
> Back to his chariot; where it stood retired
> From off the files of war; there they him laid
> Gnashing for anguish and despite and shame
> To find himself not matchless, and his pride
> Humbled by such rebuke, so far beneath
> His confidence to equal God in power.

> Yet soon he healed; for spirits that live throughout
> Vital in every part, not as frail man
> In entrails, heart or head, liver or reins,
> Cannot but by annihilating die;
> Nor in their liquid texture mortal wound
> Receive, no more than can the fluid air:
> All heart they live, all head, all eye, all ear,
> All intellect, all sense, and as they please,
> They limb themselves, and colour, shape or size
> Assume, as likes them best, condense or rare.

A comparison of the two passages will demonstrate Pope's triumph over the sublimely humorless Milton, who for once works entirely too hard to transume Homer and Vergil and Spenser. Michael's sword transcends the blade given by Astraea to Arthegall in Book V of *The Faerie Queene*, where it would pierce and cleave whatever came against it. More overtly, the Miltonic sword (out of the prophet Jeremiah's armory of God) greatly outdoes the armor of Aeneas, against which the sword of Turnus shattered into chunks. Satan is dreadfully chopped up, and like the Homeric gods, he can be wounded, and suffer pain, but he cannot be killed. Yet Homer's Ares, wounded in battle, is fiercely impressive, while not just Satan but the poet Milton loses dignity when we read "Yet soon he healed . . . ," because he is one of those spirits: "Nor in their liquid texture mortal wound / Receive, no more than can the fluid air."

Pope rather wickedly overgoes Milton by turning the entire cumbersome Satanic passage into one airy, parenthetical line, the superb throwaway of "(But Airy Substance soon unites again)," strikingly contrasted to the Ovidian mock-pathos of the couplet following. The fond Sylph and proud Satan soon heal, but Belinda's lock and Belinda's fair head are forever separated:

> The meeting Points the sacred Hair dissever
> From the fair Head, for ever, and for ever!

Outrageously moved as we are by "for ever, and for ever," we are compelled to award the palm to Pope over Milton, in this instance. The greatness of *The Rape of the Lock* is that it may be the only poem that seems to demand Mozartean comparisons, because it too is infinitely nuanced, absolutely controlled, and yet finally poignant in the highest degree.

The Dunciad

Johnson, perhaps up too close to the person, judged it as the text where "Pope's irascibility prevailed" and where "Pope confessed his own pain by his anger; but he gave no pain to those who had provoked him." Clearly, Johnson strongly misread *The Dunciad,* since he refused to believe that the poem's design was moral. He found in it "petulance and malignity enough," granted it some beauties, and condemned "the grossness of its images," which he rightly found Swiftian. Certainly a comparison of the savagery of *The Dunciad* with the compassion of *The Vanity of Human Wishes* will convince us that Johnson had a profounder moral intellect than Pope, and was much the better man, but *The Dunciad* is immensely the finer poem, beautifully eloquent and humane as *The Vanity of Human Wishes* remains.

Yet one can sympathize with Johnson's uneasiness at Pope's freedom in expressing a personal rancor in his masterwork. It is difficult to read *The Dunciad* as a refinement upon the poetic tradition. At his rhetorical best, Pope is not quite the embattled defender of Enlightened England he declared himself to be. His fear of universal madness, of the return of a nihilistic abyss, is more than a personal pathology or ideology. The parallel fear is actually more personal in Johnson, which may be the clue to his reservations about the poem. How rational a poem is *The Dunciad*? Compared to *Paradise Lost,* not very, must surely be the answer. The astonishing opening invokes Milton, thus enforcing a contrast at once dangerous and audaciously successful:

> Yet, yet a moment, one dim Ray of Light
> Indulge, dread Chaos, and eternal night!
> Of darkness visible so much be lent,
> As half to shew, half veil the deep intent.
> Ye Powers! whose Mysteries restored I sing,
> To whom Time bears me on his rapid wing,
> Suspend a while your force inertly strong,
> Then take at once the poet and the song.

Satan, viewing the horrible dungeon of hell, discovers:

> yet from those flames
> No light, but rather darkness visible

> Served only to discover rights of woe,
> Regions of sorrow, doleful shades, where peace
> And rest can never dwell, hope never comes
> That comes to all;

The cultural world is now hell, Pope avers, nor is he out of it. Dulness, a goddess as malevolent as Vergil's Juno, comes in all her majesty, to establish the Kingdom of the Dull upon earth, and her triumph is complete:

> Beneath her footstool, *Science* groans in chains,
> And *Wit* dreads exile, penalties, and pains.
> There foamed rebellious *Logic,* gagged and bound,
> There, stripped, fair *Rhetoric* languished on the ground;
> His blunted arms by *Sophistry* are borne,
> And shameless *Billingsgate* her Robes adorn.
> *Morality,* by her false guardians drawn,
> *Chicane* in furs, and *Casuistry* in lawn,
> Gasps, as they straiten at each end the cord,
> And dies, when Dulness gives her Page the word.
> Mad *Máthesis* alone was unconfined,
> Too mad for mere material chains to bind,
> Now to pure space lifts her ecstatic stare,
> Now running round the circle, finds it square.
> But held in tenfold bonds the *Muses* lie,
> Watched both by Envy's and by Flattery's eye:
> There to her heart sad Tragedy addrest
> The dagger wont to pierce the tyrant's breast;
> But sober History restrain'd her rage,
> And promised vengeance on a barbarous age.

This may have been justified in 1743; in 2003 it is simply the way things are. Every reader shudders (or should) as Pope ends the poem with a prophecy we continue to fulfill daily, even as we approach the domestication of a universal cultural disaster:

> Lo! thy dread empire, CHAOS! is restored;
> Light dies before thy uncreating word:
> Thy hand, great anarch! lets the curtain fall;
> And universal darkness buries all.

The Gospel of John, and Milton's variations upon it, are reversed as: "Light dies before thy uncreating word." Johnson, who dreaded something like this return to chaos, may have been too strongly affected by Pope's vision to have valued it properly. It cannot be an accident that Pope's most Miltonic moments come in the apocalyptic opening and close of Book IV of *The Dunciad*. The trouble at the core of Milton is also Pope's, whose relation to Milton was very unlike his relation to Dryden. Whatever the force of the poetic past was to Pope, that part of it he felt emanating from Milton was beyond refinement. "Darkness visible," the Miltonic legacy after all, returned as the inevitable trope for Pope's sense of what lay always beyond the possibilities of the Enlightenment.

from The Dunciad

from Book the Fourth

Yet, yet a moment, one dim ray of light
Indulge, dread Chaos, and eternal Night!
Of darkness visible so much be lent,
As half to show, half veil, the deep intent.
Ye Powers! whose mysteries restored I sing,
To whom Time bears me on his rapid wing,
Suspend a while your force inertly strong,
Then take at once the poet and the song.
    Now flamed the Dog-star's unpropitious ray,
10 Smote every brain and withered every bay;
Sick was the sun, the owl forsook his bower,
The moon-struck prophet felt the madding hour:
Then rose the seed of Chaos, and of Night,
To blot out order and extinguish light,
Of dull and venal a new world to mould,
And bring Saturnian days of lead and gold.
    She mounts the throne: her head a cloud concealed,
In broad effulgence all below revealed;
('Tis thus aspiring Dulness ever shines)
20 Soft on her lap her laureate son reclines.
    Beneath her footstool, *Science* groans in chains,
And *Wit* dreads exile, penalties, and pains.
There foamed rebellious *Logic*, gagged and bound,
There, stripped, fair *Rhetoric* languished on the ground;
His blunted arms by *Sophistry* are borne,
And shameless *Billingsgate* her robes adorn.
Morality, by her false guardians drawn,
Chicane in furs, and *Casuistry* in lawn,

Gasps, as they straiten at each end the cord,
30   And dies, when Dulness gives her Page the word.
Mad *Máthesis* alone was unconfined,
Too mad for mere material chains to bind,
Now to pure space lifts her ecstatic stare,
Now running round the circle, finds it square.
But held in tenfold bonds the *Muses* lie,
Watched both by Envy's and by Flattery's eye:
There to her heart sad Tragedy addrest
The dagger wont to pierce the tyrant's breast;
But sober History restrained her rage,
40   And promised vengeance on a barbarous age.
There sunk Thalia, nerveless, cold, and dead,
Had not her sister Satire held her head:
Nor couldst thou, Chesterfield! a tear refuse,
Thou weptst, and with thee wept each gentle Muse.
   When lo! a harlot form soft sliding by,
With mincing step, small voice, and languid eye;
Foreign her air, her robe's discordant pride
In patchwork fluttering, and her head aside.
By singing peers upheld on either hand,
50   She tripped and laughed, too pretty much to stand;
Cast on the prostrate Nine a scornful look,
Then thus in quaint recitativo spoke:
   "O *Cara! Cara!* silence all that train:
Joy to great Chaos! let Division reign:
Chromatic tortures soon shall drive them hence,
Break all their nerves, and fritter all their sense:
One trill shall harmonize joy, grief, and rage,
Wake the dull Church, and lull the ranting stage;
To the same notes thy sons shall hum, or snore,
60   And all thy yawning daughters cry, *encore*.
Another Phoebus, thy own Phoebus, reigns,
Joys in my jigs, and dances in my chains.
But soon, ah soon, rebellion will commence,
If music meanly borrows aid from sense:
Strong in new arms, lo! giant Handel stands,
Like bold Briareus, with a hundred hands;
To stir, to rouse, to shake the soul he comes,
And Jove's own thunders follow Mars's drums.
Arrest him, Empress; or you sleep no more—"
70   She heard, and drove him to the Hibernian shore.
   And now had Fame's posterior trumpet blown,

And all the nations summoned to the throne.
The young, the old, who feel her inward sway,
One instinct seizes, and transports away.
None need a guide, by sure attraction led,
And strong impulsive gravity of head:
None want a place, for all their centre found,
Hung to the goddess, and cohered around.
Not closer, orb in orb, conglobed are seen
80   The buzzing bees about their dusky queen.

.   .   .

     Next bidding all draw near on bended knees,
The Queen confers her *titles* and *degrees*.
Her children first of more distinguished sort,
Who study Shakespeare at the Inns of Court,
Impale a glowworm, or virtú profess,
570   Shine in the dignity of F.R.S.
Some, deep Freemasons, join the silent race
Worthy to fill Pythagoras's place:
Some botanists, or florists at the least;
Or issue members of an annual feast.
Nor passed the meanest unregarded; one
Rose a Gregorian, one a Gormogon.
The last, not least in honour or applause,
Isis and Cam made Doctors of her Laws.
     Then, blessing all, "Go, children of my care!
580   To practice now from theory repair.
All my commands are easy, short, and full:
My sons! be proud, be selfish, and be dull.
Guard my prerogative, assert my throne:
This nod confirms each privilege your own.
The cap and switch be sacred to his Grace;
With staff and pumps the Marquis lead the race;
From stage to stage the licensed Earl may run,
Paired with his fellow charioteer the sun;
The learnèd Baron butterflies design,
590   Or draw to silk Arachne's subtile line,
The Judge to dance his brother Sergeant call;
The Senator at cricket urge the ball;
The Bishop stow (pontific luxury!)
An hundred souls of turkeys in a pie;
The sturdy Squire to Gallic masters stoop,
And drown his lands and manors in a soup.

Others import yet nobler arts from France,
Teach kings to fiddle, and make senates dance.
Perhaps more high some daring son may soar,
600   Proud to my list to add one monarch more;
And nobly conscious, princes are but things
Born for first ministers, as slaves for kings,
Tyrant supreme! shall three estates command,
And MAKE ONE MIGHTY DUNCIAD OF THE LAND!"
    More she had spoke, but yawned—all nature nods:
What mortal can resist the yawn of gods?
Churches and chapels instantly it reached;
(St. James's first, for leaden Gilbert preached)
Then catched the schools; the Hall scarce kept awake;
610   The convocation gaped, but could not speak:
Lost was the nation's sense, nor could be found,
While the long solemn unison went round:
Wide, and more wide, it spread o'er all the realm;
Even Palinurus nodded at the helm:
The vapour mild o'er each committee crept;
Unfinished treaties in each office slept;
And chiefless armies dozed out the campaign;
And navies yawned for orders on the main.
    O Muse! relate (for you can tell alone,
620   Wits have short memories, and dunces none)
Relate, who first, who last resigned to rest;
Whose heads she partly, whose completely blessed;
What charms could faction, what ambition lull,
The venal quiet, and entrance the dull;
Till drowned was sense, and shame, and right, and wrong—
O sing, and hush the nations with thy song!

      ·   ·   ·

    In vain, in vain—the all-composing hour
Resistless falls: the Muse obeys the power.
She comes! she comes! the sable throne behold
630   Of *Night* primeval, and of *Chaos* old!
Before her, *Fancy's* gilded clouds decay,
And all its varying rainbows die away.
Wit shoots in vain its momentary fires,
The meteor drops, and in a flash expires.
As one by one, at dread Medea's strain,
The sickening stars fade off the ethereal plain;
As Argus' eyes by Hermes' wand opprest,

Closed one by one to everlasting rest;
Thus at her felt approach, and secret might,
640   *Art* after *Art* goes out, and all is night.
See skulking *Truth* to her old cavern fled,
Mountains of casuistry heaped o'er her head!
Philosophy, that leaned on Heaven before,
Shrinks to her second cause, and is no more.
Physic of *Metaphysic* begs defence,
And *Metaphysic* calls for aid on *Sense!*
See *Mystery* to *Mathematics* fly!
In vain! they gaze, turn giddy, rave, and die.
Religion blushing veils her sacred fires,
650   And unawares *Morality* expires.
Nor public flame, nor private, dares to shine;
Nor human spark is left, nor glimpse divine!
Lo! thy dread empire, CHAOS! is restored;
Light dies before thy uncreating word:
Thy hand, great anarch! lets the curtain fall;
And universal darkness buries all.

   1741   1743

| SAMUEL JOHNSON |

1709–1784

DR. JOHNSON, in my judgment still the principal Western literary critic, had enormous poetic potential, which his worship of Alexander Pope inhibited him from developing. Though Johnson was too discerning to group Pope with Homer, Shakespeare, and Milton, his three supreme poets, he loved Pope's poetry with the personal passion I myself bring to the reading of Wallace Stevens and Hart Crane.

I include here only Johnson's strongest poem, *The Vanity of Human Wishes.* Though Johnson forms the poem as a very free version of a satire of Juvenal, a fierce Roman ironist, the wisdom invoked is that of Ecclesiastes (Koheleth): "Vanity of vanities, all is vanity." Imagination, Johnson cautioned us, is always scheming to escape the pressures of reality. And yet some hope, however illusory, is necessary for all of us if we are to keep going on. In this emphasis, Johnson is one of Samuel Beckett's acknowledged precursors.

Son of a bookseller, Johnson was educated at Oxford, but independently read not less than everything of value available in his lifetime. A married schoolmaster unable to live on the periphery, Johnson went to London in 1737, working at first as a journalist. He achieved fame with his *Dictionary of the English Language* (1755), an astonishing one-man effort. But though known to his contemporaries as "Dictionary Johnson," he reached critical greatness with his essays in *The Rambler* and other periodicals, now best read in Walter Jackson Bate's *Selected Essays* (1968), and in the "Preface" to his edition of Shakespeare. His masterpiece is *The Lives of the Poets* (1779–1781), which sets the standard for the art of literary criticism.

James Boswell sought out Johnson in 1763, and the close friendship began that led to the best biography ever written, Boswell's *Life of Samuel Johnson* (1791), published seven years after the great critic's death. The biography is worthy of its subject, and should be read universally.

The Vanity of Human Wishes is rather difficult only because of the brilliance and economy of Johnson's phrasing. The power of his mind, to be experienced in all of his criticism, is here condensed into one massive formulation of the human dilemma. Johnson's perpetual relevance abides in his prudential wisdom, clearly evident in this major poem.

✙   ✙   ✙

The Vanity of Human Wishes

The Tenth Satire of Juvenal Imitated

Let observation with extensive view,
Survey mankind, from China to Peru;
Remark each anxious toil, each eager strife,
And watch the busy scenes of crowded life;
Then say how hope and fear, desire and hate,
O'erspread with snares the clouded maze of fate,
Where wavering man, betrayed by venturous pride,
To tread the dreary paths without a guide,
As treacherous phantoms in the mist delude,
10 Shuns fancied ills, or chases airy good;
How rarely reason guides the stubborn choice,
Rules the bold hand, or prompts the suppliant voice;
How nations sink, by darling schemes oppressed,

When vengeance listens to the fool's request.
Fate wings with every wish the afflictive dart,
Each gift of nature, and each grace of art,
With fatal heat impetuous courage glows,
With fatal sweetness elocution flows,
Impeachment stops the speaker's powerful breath,
20   And restless fire precipitates on death.
　　　But scarce observed, the knowing and the bold
Fall in the general massacre of gold;
Wide-wasting pest! that rages unconfined,
And crowds with crimes the records of mankind;
For gold his sword the hireling ruffian draws,
For gold the hireling judge distorts the laws;
Wealth heaped on wealth, nor truth nor safety buys,
The dangers gather as the treasures rise.
　　　Let history tell where rival kings command,
30   And dubious title shakes the madded land,
When statutes glean the refuse of the sword,
How much more safe the vassal than the lord;
Low skulks the hind beneath the rage of power,
And leaves the wealthy traitor in the Tower,
Untouched his cottage, and his slumbers sound,
Though confiscation's vultures hover round.
　　　The needy traveller, serene and gay,
Walks the wild heath, and sings his toil away.
Does envy seize thee? crush the upbraiding joy,
40   Increase his riches and his peace destroy;
Now fears in dire vicissitude invade,
The rustling brake alarms, and quivering shade,
Nor light nor darkness bring his pain relief,
One shows the plunder, and one hides the thief.
　　　Yet still one general cry the skies assails,
And gain and grandeur load the tainted gales;
Few know the toiling statesman's fear or care,
The insidious rival and the gaping heir.
　　　Once more, Democritus, arise on earth,
50   With cheerful wisdom and instructive mirth,
See motley life in modern trappings dressed,   ·
And feed with varied fools the eternal jest:
Thou who couldst laugh where want enchained caprice,
Toil crushed conceit, and man was of a piece;
Where wealth unloved without a mourner died,
And scarce a sycophant was fed by pride;

Where ne'er was known the form of mock debate,
Or seen a new-made mayor's unwieldy state;
Where change of favorites made no change of laws,
60   And senates heard before they judged a cause;
How wouldst thou shake at Britain's modish tribe,
Dart the quick taunt, and edge the piercing gibe.
Attentive truth and nature to descry,
And pierce each scene with philosophic eye.
To thee were solemn toys or empty show
The robes of pleasure and the veils of woe:
All aid the farce, and all thy mirth maintain,
Whose joys are causeless or whose griefs are vain.
　　Such was the scorn that filled the sage's mind,
70   Renewed at every glance on humankind;
How just that scorn ere yet thy voice declare,
Search every state, and canvass every prayer.
　　Unnumbered suppliants crowd Preferment's gate,
Athirst for wealth, and burning to be great;
Delusive Fortune hears the incessant call,
They mount, they shine, evaporate, and fall.
On every stage the foes of peace attend,
Hate dogs their flight, and insult mocks their end.
Love ends with hope, the sinking statesman's door
80   Pours in the morning worshipper no more;
For growing names the weekly scribbler lies,
To growing wealth the dedicator flies,
From every room descends the painted face,
That hung the bright Palladium of the place,
And smoked in kitchens, or in auctions sold,
To better features yields the frame of gold;
For now no more we trace in every line
Heroic worth, benevolence divine:
The form distorted justifies the fall,
90   And detestation rids the indignant wall.
　　But will not Britain hear the last appeal,
Sign her foes' doom, or guard her favourites' zeal?
Through Freedom's sons no more remonstrance rings,
Degrading nobles and controlling kings;
Our supple tribes repress their patriot throats,
And ask no questions but the price of votes;
With weekly libels and septennial ale,
Their wish is full to riot and to rail.
　　In full-blown dignity, see Wolsey stand,

100 Law in his voice, and fortune in his hand:
To him the church, the realm, their powers consign,
Through him the rays of regal bounty shine,
Turned by his nod the stream of honour flows,
His smile alone security bestows:
Still to new heights his restless wishes tower,
Claim leads to claim, and power advances power;
Till conquest unresisted ceased to please,
And rights submitted left him none to seize.
At length his sovereign frowns—the train of state
110 Mark the keen glance and watch the sign to hate.
Where'er he turns he meets a stranger's eye,
His suppliants scorn him and his followers fly;
At once is lost the pride of awful state,
The golden canopy, the glittering plate,
The regal palace, the luxurious board,
The liveried army and the menial lord.
With age, with cares, with maladies oppressed,
He seeks the refuge of monastic rest.
Grief aids disease, remembered folly stings,
120 And his last sighs reproach the faith of kings.
    Speak thou, whose thoughts at humble peace repine,
Shall Wolsey's wealth with Wolsey's end be thine?
Or livest thou now, with safer pride content,
The wisest justice on the banks of Trent?
For why did Wolsey near the steeps of fate,
On weak foundations raise the enormous weight?
Why but to sink beneath misfortune's blow,
With louder ruin to the gulfs below?
    What gave great Villiers to the assassin's knife,
130 And fixed disease on Harley's closing life?
What murdered Wentworth, and what exiled Hyde,
By kings protected, and to kings allied?
What but their wish indulged in courts to shine,
And power too great to keep, or to resign?
    When first the college rolls receive his name,
The young enthusiast quits his ease for fame;
Through all his veins the fever of renown
Burns from the strong contagion of the gown;
O'er Bodley's dome his future labours spread,
140 And Bacon's mansion trembles o'er his head.
Are these thy views? proceed, illustrious youth,
And virtue guard thee to the throne of Truth!

Yet should thy soul indulge the generous heat,
Till captive Science yields her last retreat;
Should Reason guide thee with her brightest ray,
And pour on misty Doubt resistless day;
Should no false Kindness lure to loose delight,
Nor Praise relax, nor Difficulty fright;
Should tempting Novelty thy cell refrain,
150 And Sloth effuse her opiate fumes in vain;
Should Beauty blunt on fops her fatal dart,
Nor claim the triumph of a lettered heart;
Should no Disease thy torpid veins invade,
Nor Melancholy's phantoms haunt thy shade;
Yet hope not life from grief or danger free,
Nor think the doom of man reversed for thee:
Deign on the passing world to turn thine eyes,
And pause awhile from letters to be wise;
There mark what ills the scholar's life assail,
160 Toil, envy, want, the patron, and the jail.
See nations slowly wise, and meanly just,
To buried merit raise the tardy bust.
If dreams yet flatter, once again attend,
Hear Lydiat's life, and Galileo's end.
     Nor deem, when learning her last prize bestows,
The glittering eminence exempt from foes;
See when the vulgar 'scape, despised or awed,
Rebellion's vengeful talons seize on Laud.
From meaner minds, though smaller fines content,
170 The plundered palace or sequestered rent;
Marked out by dangerous parts he meets the shock,
And fatal Learning leads him to the block:
Around his tomb let Art and Genius weep,
But hear his death, ye blockheads, hear and sleep.
     The festal blazes, the triumphal show,
The ravished standard, and the captive foe,
The senate's thanks, the gazette's pompous tale,
With force resistless o'er the brave prevail.
Such bribes the rapid Greek o'er Asia whirled,
180 For such the steady Romans shook the world;
For such in distant lands the Britons shine,
And stain with blood the Danube or the Rhine;
This power has praise that virtue scarce can warm,
Till fame supplies the universal charm.
Yet Reason frowns on War's unequal game,

Where wasted nations raise a single name,
And mortgaged states their grandsires' wreaths regret,
From age to age in everlasting debt;
Wreathes which at last the dear-bought right convey
190　To rust on medals, or on stones decay.
　　On what foundation stands the warrior's pride,
How just his hopes let Swedish Charles decide;
A frame of adamant, a soul of fire,
No dangers fright him, and no labours tire;
O'er love, o'er fear, extends his wide domain,
Unconquered lord of pleasure and of pain;
No joys to him pacific sceptres yield,
War sounds the trump, he rushes to the field;
Behold surrounding kings their power combine,
200　And one capitulate, and one resign;
Peace courts his hand, but spreads her charms in vain;
"Think nothing gained," he cries, "till nought remain,
On Moscow's walls till Gothic standards fly,
And all be mine beneath the polar sky."
The march begins in military state,
And nations on his eye suspended wait;
Stern Famine guards the solitary coast,
And Winter barricades the realms of Frost;
He comes, not want and cold his course delay;—
210　Hide, blushing Glory, hide Pultowa's day:
The vanquished hero leaves his broken bands,
And shows his miseries in distant lands;
Condemned a needy supplicant to wait,
While ladies interpose, and slaves debate.
But did not Chance at length for error mend?
Did no subverted empire mark his end?
Did rival monarchs give the fatal wound?
Or hostile millions press him to the ground?
His fall was destined to a barren strand,
220　A petty fortress, and a dubious hand;
He left the name, at which the world grew pale,
To point a moral, or adorn a tale.
　　All times their scenes of pompous woes afford,
From Persia's tyrant to Bavaria's lord.
In gay hostility, and barbarous pride,
With half mankind embattled at his side,
Great Xerxes comes to seize the certain prey,
And starves exhausted regions in his way;

Attendant Flattery counts his myriads o'er,
230   Till counted myriads soothe his pride no more;
Fresh praise is tried till madness fires his mind,
The waves he lashes, and enchains the wind;
New powers are claimed, new powers are still bestowed,
Till rude resistance lops the spreading god;
The daring Greeks deride the martial show,
And heap their valleys with the gaudy foe;
The insulted sea with humbler thoughts he gains,
A single skiff to speed his flight remains;
The incumbered oar scarce leaves the dreaded coast
240   Through purple billows and a floating host.
        The bold Bavarian, in a luckless hour,
Tries the dread summits of Cesarean power,
With unexpected legions bursts away,
And sees defenceless realms receive his sway;
Short sway! fair Austria spreads her mournful charms,
The queen, the beauty, sets the world in arms;
From hill to hill the beacons' rousing blaze
Spreads wide the hope of plunder and of praise;
The fierce Croatian, and the wild Hussar,
250   And all the sons of ravage crowd the war;
The baffled prince in honour's flattering bloom
Of hasty greatness finds the fatal doom,
His foes' derision, and his subjects' blame,
And steals to death from anguish and from shame.
        "Enlarge my life with multitude of days,"
In health, in sickness, thus the suppliant prays;
Hides from himself his state, and shuns to know,
That life protracted is protracted woe.
Time hovers o'er, impatient to destroy,
260   And shuts up all the passages of joy:
In vain their gifts the bounteous seasons pour,
The fruit autumnal, and the vernal flower,
With listless eyes the dotard views the store,
He views, and wonders that they please no more;
Now pall the tasteless meats and joyless wines,
And Luxury with sighs her slave resigns.
Approach, ye minstrels, try the soothing strain,
Diffuse the tuneful lenitives of pain:
No sounds, alas, would touch the impervious ear,
270   Though dancing mountains witnessed Orpheus near;
Nor lute nor lyre his feeble powers attend,

Nor sweeter music of a virtuous friend,
But everlasting dictates crowd his tongue,
Perversely grave, or positively wrong.
The still returning tale and lingering jest
Perplex the fawning niece and pampered guest,
While growing hopes scarce awe the gathering sneer,
And scarce a legacy can bribe to hear;
The watchful guests still hint the last offence,
280 The daughter's petulance, the son's expense,
Improve his heady rage with treacherous skill,
And mould his passions till they make his will.
    Unnumbered maladies his joints invade,
Lay siege to life, and press the dire blockade;
But unextinguished Avarice still remains,
And dreaded losses aggravate his pains;
He turns, with anxious heart and crippled hands,
His bonds of debt and mortgages of lands;
Or views his coffers with suspicious eyes,
290 Unlocks his gold, and counts it till he dies.
    But grant, the virtues of a temperate prime
Bless with an age exempt from scorn or crime;
An age that melts with unperceived decay,
And glides in modest innocence away;
Whose peaceful day Benevolence endears,
Whose night congratulating Conscience cheers;
The general favourite as the general friend:
Such age there is, and who shall wish its end?
    Yet even on this her load Misfortune flings,
300 To press the weary minutes' flagging wings:
New sorrow rises as the day returns,
A sister sickens, or a daughter mourns.
Now kindred Merit fills the sable bier,
Now lacerated Friendship claims a tear.
Year chases year, decay pursues decay,
Still drops some joy from withering life away;
New forms arise, and different views engage,
Superfluous lags the veteran on the stage,
Till pitying Nature signs the last release,
310 And bids afflicted worth retire to peace.
    But few there are whom hours like these await,
Who set unclouded in the gulfs of fate.
From Lydia's monarch should the search descend,
By Solon cautioned to regard his end,

In life's last scene what prodigies surprise,
Fears of the brave, and follies of the wise?
From Marlborough's eyes the streams of dotage flow,
And Swift expires a driveller and a show.
    The teeming mother, anxious for her race,
320 Begs for each birth the fortune of a face:
Yet Vane could tell what ills from beauty spring;
And Sedley cursed the form that pleased a king.
Ye nymphs of rosy lips and radiant eyes,
Whom Pleasure keeps too busy to be wise,
Whom Joys with soft varieties invite,
By day the frolic, and the dance by night,
Who frown with vanity, who smile with art,
And ask the latest fashion of the heart,
What care, what rules your heedless charms shall save,
330 Each nymph your rival, and each youth your slave?
Against your fame with fondness hate combines,
The rival batters, and the lover mines.
With distant voice neglected Virtue calls,
Less heard and less, the faint remonstrance falls;
Tired with contempt, she quits the slippery reign,
And Pride and Prudence take her seat in vain.
In crowd at once, where none the pass defend,
The harmless freedom and the private friend.
The guardians yield, by force superior plied;
340 By Interest, Prudence; and by Flattery, Pride.
Now Beauty falls betrayed, despised, distressed.
And hissing Infamy proclaims the rest.
    Where then shall Hope and Fear their objects find?
Must dull Suspense corrupt the stagnant mind?
Must helpless man, in ignorance sedate,
Roll darkling down the torrent of his fate?
Must no dislike alarm, no wishes rise,
No cries attempt the mercies of the skies?
Enquirer, cease, petitions yet remain,
350 Which heaven may hear; nor deem religion vain.
Still raise for good the supplicating voice,
But leave to heaven the measure and the choice,
Safe in his power, whose eyes discern afar
The secret ambush of a specious prayer.
Implore his aid, in his decisions rest,
Secure whate'er he gives, he gives the best.
Yet when the sense of sacred presence fires,

And strong devotion to the skies aspires,
Pour forth thy fervours for a healthful mind,
360 Obedient passions, and a will resigned;
For love, which scarce collective man can fill;
For patience sovereign o'er transmuted ill;
For faith, that panting for a happier seat,
Counts death kind Nature's signal of retreat:
These goods for man the laws of heaven ordain,
These goods he grants, who grants the power to gain;
With these celestial wisdom calms the mind,
And makes the happiness she does not find.

1748   1749

WILLIAM COLLINS

1721–1759

DR. SAMUEL JOHNSON disapproved of the poetry of William Collins, while intensely liking the poet as a person. Collins came to London in 1744, with many literary projects but no money, and was rescued by Johnson, who saved the improvident poet from debtor's imprisonment. Upon receiving a legacy, poor Collins yielded to his many depressions, becoming alcoholic and psychotic, and was confined. Johnson, in his *Lives of the Poets*, eloquently lamented his friend:

> Such was the fate of Collins, with whom I once delighted to converse, and whom I yet remember with tenderness.

Johnson, a great Neoclassical critic, who considered Pope the perfection of poetry, could not abide the pre-Romantic odes of Gray and Collins. I myself greatly admire several of Collins's most ambitious odes— *On the Poetical Character, To Fear, On the Popular Superstitions of the Highlands*—but these are rather too recondite and difficult for this anthology. Instead, I give Collins's two most popular poems, the poignant ode "How Sleep the Brave" and the exquisite "Ode to Evening," a Miltonic evocation of the evening star.

❧   ❧   ❧

Ode, Written in the beginning of the Year 1746

How sleep the Brave, who sink to Rest,
By all their Country's Wishes blest!
When *Spring,* with dewy Fingers cold,
Returns to deck their hallow'd Mold,
She there shall dress a sweeter Sod,
Than *Fancy's* Feet have ever trod.

By Fairy Hands their Knell is rung,
By Forms unseen their Dirge is sung;
There *Honour* comes, a Pilgrim grey,
To bless the Turf that wraps their Clay,
And *Freedom* shall a-while repair,
To dwell a weeping Hermit there!

Ode to Evening

If ought of Oaten Stop, or Pastoral Song,
May hope, chaste *Eve,* to sooth thy modest Ear,
    Like thy own solemn Springs,
    Thy Springs, and dying Gales,
O *Nymph* reserv'd, while now the bright-hair'd Sun
Sits in yon western Tent, whose cloudy Skirts,
    With Brede ethereal wove,
    O'erhang his wavy Bed:
Now Air is hush'd, save where the weak-ey'd Bat,
With short shrill Shriek flits by on leathern Wing,
    Or where the Beetle winds
    His small but sullen Horn,
As oft he rises 'midst the twilight Path,
Against the Pilgrim borne in heedless Hum:
    Now teach me, *Maid* compos'd,
    To breathe some soften'd Strain,
Whose Numbers stealing thro' thy darkning Vale,
May not unseemly with its Stillness suit,
    As musing slow, I hail
    Thy genial lov'd Return!

For when thy folding Star arising shews
His paly Circlet, at his warning Lamp
    The fragrant *Hours,* and *Elves*
    Who slept in Flow'rs the Day,
And many a *Nymph* who wreaths her Brows with Sedge,
And sheds the fresh'ning Dew, and lovelier still,
    The *Pensive Pleasures* sweet
    Prepare thy shadowy Car.
Then lead, calm *Vot'ress,* where some sheety Lake
Cheers the lone Heath, or some time-hallow'd Pile,
    Or up-land Fallows grey
    Reflect its last cool Gleam.
But when chill blustring Winds, or driving Rain,
Forbid my willing Feet, be mine the Hut,
    That from the Mountain's Side,
    Views Wilds, and swelling Floods,
And Hamlets brown, and dim-discover'd Spires,
And hears their simple Bell, and marks o'er all
    Thy Dewy Fingers draw
    The gradual dusky Veil.
While *Spring* shall pour his Show'rs, as oft he wont,
And bathe thy breathing Tresses, meekest *Eve!*
    While *Summer* loves to sport,
    Beneath thy ling'ring Light:
While sallow *Autumn* fills thy Lap with Leaves,
Or *Winter* yelling thro' the troublous Air,
    Affrights thy shrinking Train,
    And rudely rends thy Robes.
So long, sure-found beneath the Sylvan Shed,
Shall *Fancy, Friendship, Science,* rose-lip'd *Health,*
    Thy gentlest Influence own,
    And hymn thy fav'rite Name!

THOMAS GRAY

1716–1771

Elegy Written in a Country Churchyard

Roger Lonsdale, our leading authority on Thomas Gray, locates the *Elegy's* crucial meaning in the poet's transition from the first version, which concluded with the four rejected stanzas in the Eton Manuscript, to the familiar final version, revised into a less lucid but more poignant work. The first *Elegy* is essentially Vergilian and Horatian, a poem in praise of country retirement, with a moderately Christian conclusion, in which the comforts of heaven replace the abandoned vanities of the court and the city. Our *Elegy*, the second, is more Miltonic than Horatian, and centers upon the universal human desire to be remembered after death. As Lonsdale shrewdly remarks, Gray's crossing as he goes from first to second version is between two very different visions of the poet:

> The figure of the Poet is no longer urban, urbane, worldly, rational Augustan man among men, with his own place in society; what Gray dramatizes is the poet as outsider, with an uneasy consciousness of a sensibility and an imagination at once unique and burdensome.

Part of the burden of that imagination is the immensely rich heritage of Spenser, Shakespeare, and Milton. Unlike Vergil and Horace, Shakespeare and Milton are not safely remote for Gray. Lonsdale's copious notes to the *Elegy* record a complex allusive crossing from an Augustan *Elegy* to a highly dialectical *Elegy* of Sensibility, akin to the 1746 *Odes* of William Collins and the *Jubilate Agno* of Christopher Smart. After line 72 of the poem, the Eton Manuscript concluded with these splendid rejected stanzas:

> The thoughtless World to Majesty may bow
> Exalt the brave, & idolize Success
> But more to Innocence their Safety owe
> Than Power & Genius e'er conspired to bless

And thou, who mindful of the unhonour'd Dead
Dost in these Notes their artless Tale relate
By Night & lonely Contemplation led
To linger in the gloomy Walks of Fate

Hark how the sacred Calm, that broods around
Bids ev'ry fierce tumultuous Passion cease
In still small Accents whisp'ring from the Ground
A grateful Earnest of eternal Peace

No more with Reason & thyself at strife;
Give anxious Cares and endless Wishes room
But thro' the cool sequestered Vale of Life
Pursue the silent Tenour of thy Doom.

The sensibility that informs these eloquent quatrains is a touch too morbid, perhaps, to be Popean, but the Horatian mask of Pope, taken on whenever he supposedly longed for the garlands of repose, can be associated with this initial close of Gray's *Elegy*. Very different is the conclusion of the revised *Elegy*:

For who, to dumb forgetfulness a prey,
    This pleasing anxious being e'er resigned,
Left the warm precincts of the cheerful day,
    Nor cast one longing lingering look behind?

On some fond breast the parting soul relies,
    Some pious drops the closing eye requires;
Even from the tomb the voice of Nature cries,
    Even in our ashes live their wonted fires.

For thee, who mindful of the unhonoured dead
    Dost in these lines their artless tale relate;
If chance, by lonely contemplation led,
    Some kindred spirit shall inquire thy fate,

Haply some hoary-headed swain may say,
    "Oft have we seen him at the peep of dawn
Brushing with hasty steps the dews away
    To meet the sun upon the upland lawn.

"There at the foot of yonder nodding beech
    That wreathes its old fantastic roots so high,

His listless length at noontide would he stretch,
    And pore upon the brook that babbles by.

"Hard by yon wood, now smiling as in scorn,
    Muttering his wayward fancies he would rove;
Now drooping, woeful-wan, like one forlorn,
    Or crazed with care, or crossed in hopeless love.

"One morn I missed him on the customed hill,
    Along the heath and near his favourite tree;
Another came; nor yet beside the rill,
    Nor up the lawn, nor at the wood was he;

"The next, with dirges due, in sad array,
    Slow through the church-way path we saw him borne.
Approach and read (for thou canst read) the lay,
    Graved on the stone beneath yon agèd thorn."

THE EPITAPH

Here rests his head upon the lap of earth,
    A youth to fortune and to fame unknown;
Fair Science frowned not on his humble birth,
    And Melancholy marked him for her own.

Large was his bounty and his soul sincere;
    Heaven did a recompense as largely send:
He gave to Misery all he had, a tear;
    He gained from Heaven ('twas all he wished) a friend.

No farther seek his merits to disclose,
    Or draw his frailties from their dread abode,
(There they alike in trembling hope repose)
    The bosom of his Father and His God.

The echo of Milton's Belial, at the very start of this final sequence, seems to me the most decisive allusion in this perhaps most allusive of all poems in the language. Belial, much maligned by Milton himself, gives permanent expression to the intellectual's particular share in the universal dread of mortality:

            for who would lose,
Though full of pain, this intellectual being,

These thoughts that wander through eternity,
To perish rather, swallowed up and lost
In the wide womb of uncreated night,
Devoid of sense and motion?

— PARADISE LOST, Book II, lines 146–151

Belial echoes *Measure for Measure*'s Claudio, but Milton intellectualizes Claudio's fears by giving them a Senecan touch. Gray compounds Milton with Spenser and Lucretius, mingling a Spenserian use of "forgetfulness" as Sir Thomas Browne's sense of "oblivion" with Lucretian and Miltonic shining "precincts of light." The allusive effect is to center the fear of mortality within a specifically poetic area, which is the desire for immortality through one's own eloquence. That is why "Ev'n in our ashes live their wonted fires" refers us to Petrarch's Sonnet 170, with its prophecy of the poet's thought remaining full of sparks after his and Laura's deaths. Far more important is the agile allusion to Milton's *Lycidas* in lines 99–100, where Gray wants us to hear lines 25–26 of Milton's great elegy for the poetic self: "Together both, ere the high lawns appeared / Under the opening eyelids of the morn."

Is not Gray's *Elegy,* in the concluding movement of its revised version, the reticent Gray's version of *Lycidas*? What moves me most about the superb *Elegy* is the quality that, following Milton, it shares with so many of the major elegies down to Walt Whitman's grand dirges that culminated in "When Lilacs Last in the Dooryard Bloom'd." Call this quality the pathos of a poetic-death-in-life, the fear that one either has lost one's gift before life has ebbed or that one may lose life before the poetic gift has expressed itself fully. The strong pathos of Gray's *Elegy* achieves a central position in the antithetical tradition that truly mourns primarily a loss to the self.

Dr. Samuel Johnson had an acute apprehension of the anxiety of influence, yet he still read any new poet by the test of asking whether any new matter had been disclosed. Loathing Gray, Johnson nevertheless was compelled to the highest praise of Gray on encountering notions that seemed to him original:

The *Church-yard* abounds with images which find a mirrour in every mind, and with sentiments to which every bosom returns an echo. The four stanzas beginning *Yet even these bones,* are to me original: I have never seen the notions in any other place; yet he that reads them here, persuades himself that he has always felt them. Had Gray written often thus, it had been vain to blame, and useless to praise him.

Original *notions* which every reader has *felt,* or is persuaded he had felt; this is more difficult than the fame of Johnson's passage allows us to see. Was Johnson accurate in finding these stanzas original?

> Yet even these bones from insult to protect,
>   Some frail memorial still erected nigh,
> With uncouth rhymes and shapeless sculpture decked,
>   Implores the passing tribute of a sigh.
>
> Their names, their years, spelt by the unlettered Muse,
>   The place of fame and elegy supply;
> And many a holy text around she strews,
>   That teach the rustic moralist to die.
>
> For who, to dumb forgetfulness a prey,
>   This pleasing anxious being e'er resigned,
> Left the warm precincts of the cheerful day,
>   Nor cast one longing lingering look behind?
>
> On some fond breast the parting soul relies,
>   Some pious drops the closing eye requires;
> Even from the tomb the voice of Nature cries,
>   Even in our ashes live their wonted fires.

Swift, Pope's *Odyssey,* Milton's Belial, Lucretius, Ovid, and Petrarch are all among Gray's precursors here, for as an immensely learned poet, Gray rarely wrote without deliberately relating himself to every possible literary ancestor. Johnson was an immensely learned critic; why did he praise these stanzas for an originality they do not possess? A possible answer is that Johnson's own deepest anxieties are openly expressed in this passage, and to find a contemporary saying what one feels even more deeply than he does, and yet what one is inhibited from expressing oneself, is to be persuaded of more originality than exists. Gray's stanzas cry out for just that minimal and figurative immortality that the anxiety of influence denies us. Whenever the rugged Johnsonian sensibility finds fresh matter in literature, it is a safe assumption that Johnsonian repression is also involved in such finding. But, as Johnson is so universal a reader, he illustrates a tendency in many other readers, which is to be found most decisively by the notions we evade in our own minds. Johnson, who hated Gray's style, understood that in Gray's poetry the anxiety of style and the anxiety of influence had become indistinguishable, yet he forgave Gray for the one passage where Gray universalized the anxiety of self-preservation into a more general pathos. Writing on his poor friend Collins, Johnson has Gray in mind when he observes: "He affected the obsolete when it was not worthy of revival; and he puts his words out of the common order, seeming to think, with some later candidates for fame, that not to write prose is certainly to write poetry." Johnson seems to have so compounded the burden of originality and the problem of style that he could denounce style he judged vicious, and intend by the denunciation that no fresh matter was offered. So, despite seeming our opposite, when we neglect content and search for individuality of tone in a new poet, Johnson is very much our ancestor. By the 1740s, at the latest, the anxiety of style and the comparatively recent anxiety of influence had begun a process of merging that seems to have culminated during our last few decades.

✤   ✤   ✤

Elegy Written in a Country Churchyard

The curfew tolls the knell of parting day,
    The lowing herd wind slowly o'er the lea,
The ploughman homeward plods his weary way,
    And leaves the world to darkness and to me.

Now fades the glimmering landscape on the sight,
    And all the air a solemn stillness holds,
Save where the beetle wheels his droning flight,
    And drowsy tinklings lull the distant folds;

Save that from yonder ivy-mantled tower
10   The moping owl does to the moon complain
Of such, as wandering near her secret bower,
    Molest her ancient solitary reign.

Beneath those rugged elms, that yew-tree's shade,
    Where heaves the turf in many a mouldering heap,
Each in his narrow cell forever laid,
    The rude forefathers of the hamlet sleep.

The breezy call of incense-breathing morn,
    The swallow twittering from the straw-built shed,
The cock's shrill clarion or the echoing horn,
20   No more shall rouse them from their lowly bed.

For them no more the blazing hearth shall burn,
    Or busy housewife ply her evening care;
No children run to lisp their sire's return,
    Or climb his knees the envied kiss to share.

Oft did the harvest to their sickle yield;
    Their furrow oft the stubborn glebe has broke;
How jocund did they drive their team afield!
    How bowed the woods beneath their sturdy stroke!

Let not Ambition mock their useful toil,
30   Their homely joys and destiny obscure;
Nor Grandeur hear with a disdainful smile
    The short and simple annals of the poor.

The boast of heraldry, the pomp of power,
    And all that beauty, all that wealth e'er gave,
Awaits alike the inevitable hour:
    The paths of glory lead but to the grave.

Nor you, ye proud, impute to these the fault,
    If Memory o'er their tomb no trophies raise,
Where through the long-drawn aisle and fretted vault
40   The pealing anthem swells the note of praise.

Can storied urn or animated bust
    Back to its mansion call the fleeting breath?
Can Honour's voice provoke the silent dust,
    Or Flattery soothe the dull cold ear of Death?

Perhaps in this neglected spot is laid
    Some heart once pregnant with celestial fire;
Hands that the rod of empire might have swayed,
    Or waked to ecstasy the living lyre.

But Knowledge to their eyes her ample page,
50   Rich with the spoils of time, did ne'er unroll;
Chill Penury repressed their noble rage,
    And froze the genial current of the soul.

Full many a gem of purest ray serene,
    The dark unfathomed caves of ocean bear;

Full many a flower is born to blush unseen,
    And waste its sweetness on the desert air.

Some village Hampden, that with dauntless breast
    The little tyrant of his fields withstood;
Some mute inglorious Milton here may rest,
60   Some Cromwell, guiltless of his country's blood.

The applause of listening senates to command,
    The threats of pain and ruin to despise,
To scatter plenty o'er a smiling land,
    And read their history in a nation's eyes,

Their lot forbade; nor circumscribed alone
    Their growing virtues, but their crimes confined.
Forbade to wade through slaughter to a throne,
    And shut the gates of mercy on mankind;

The struggling pangs of conscious truth to hide,
70   To quench the blushes of ingenuous shame,
Or heap the shrine of Luxury and Pride
    With incense kindled at the Muse's flame.

Far from the madding crowd's ignoble strife,
    Their sober wishes never learned to stray;
Along the cool sequestered vale of life
    They kept the noiseless tenor of their way.

Yet even these bones from insult to protect,
    Some frail memorial still erected nigh,
With uncouth rhymes and shapeless sculpture decked,
80   Implores the passing tribute of a sigh.

Their name, their years, spelt by the unlettered Muse,
    The place of fame and elegy supply;
And many a holy text around she strews,
    That teach the rustic moralist to die.

For who, to dumb forgetfulness a prey,
    This pleasing anxious being e'er resigned,
Left the warm precincts of the cheerful day,
    Nor cast one longing lingering look behind?

On some fond breast the parting soul relies,
90   Some pious drops the closing eye requires;
Even from the tomb the voice of Nature cries,
    Even in our ashes live their wonted fires.

For thee, who mindful of the unhonoured dead
    Dost in these lines their artless tale relate;
If chance, by lonely contemplation led,
    Some kindred spirit shall inquire thy fate,

Haply some hoary-headed swain may say,
    "Oft have we seen him at the peep of dawn
Brushing with hasty steps the dews away
100   To meet the sun upon the upland lawn.

"There at the foot of yonder nodding beech
    That wreathes its old fantastic roots so high,
His listless length at noontide would he stretch,
    And pore upon the brook that babbles by.

"Hard by yon wood, now smiling as in scorn,
    Muttering his wayward fancies he would rove;
Now drooping, woeful-wan, like one forlorn,
    Or crazed with care, or crossed in hopeless love.

"One morn I missed him on the customed hill,
110   Along the heath and near his favourite tree;
Another came; nor yet beside the rill,
    Nor up the lawn, nor at the wood was he;

"The next, with dirges due, in sad array,
    Slow through the church-way path we saw him borne.
Approach and read (for thou canst read) the lay,
    Graved on the stone beneath yon agèd thorn."

THE EPITAPH
Here rests his head upon the lap of earth,
    A youth to fortune and to fame unknown;
Fair Science frowned not on his humble birth,
120   *And Melancholy marked him for her own.*

Large was his bounty and his soul sincere;
    Heaven did a recompense as largely send:

He gave to Misery all he had, a tear;
He gained from Heaven ('twas all he wished) a friend.

No farther seek his merits to disclose,
Or draw his frailties from their dread abode,
(There they alike in trembling hope repose)
The bosom of his Father and His God.
1742–1750   1751

CHRISTOPHER SMART

1722–1771

OF THE SIGNIFICANT poets of the later eighteenth century, sometimes termed the Age of Sensibility to distinguish it from the Augustan Age of Pope and Swift, a high proportion went mad. Like William Collins and William Cowper, Christopher Smart rarely is discussed without reference to his clinical insanity.

Smart, a poet of immense promise, left Pembroke College, Cambridge, when he was overwhelmed by debts, and began a literary career in London. He broke down in 1757, and spent several years in asylums, during which he wrote his astonishing *Jubilate Agno*, which was not to be published until 1939. His magnificent extended lyric, *A Song to David*, was composed and published in 1763, when he was released. I reluctantly omit it here because it is over five hundred lines, and give instead the most famous passage from *Rejoice in the Lamb* (*Jubilate Agno*).

Smart never could escape the stigma of madness, which prevented *A Song to David* and other later works from receiving the esteem they deserved. He died in debtor's prison, a melancholy end that haunts me whenever I reread *Jubilate Agno* and *A Song to David*.

The great chant from the *Jubilate*, "For I Will Consider my Cat Jeoffry," is superbly poignant, as it celebrates Smart's asylum companion. At certain moments, here and elsewhere in *Jubilate Agno*, Smart becomes a precursor of William Blake:

For he is of the tribe of Tiger.
For the Cherub Cat is a term of the Angel Tiger.

✢   ✢   . ✢

from Jubilate Agno

from Fragment B1

Let Elizure rejoice with the Partridge, who is a prisoner of state and is proud
    of his keepers.
For I am not without authority in my jeopardy, which I derive inevitably
    from the glory of the name of the Lord.
Let Shedeur rejoice with Pyrausta, who dwelleth in a medium of fire, which
    God hath adapted for him.
For I bless God whose name is Jealous—and there is a zeal to deliver us
    from everlasting burnings.
Let Shelumiel rejoice with Olor, who is of a goodly savour, and the very look
    of him harmonizes the mind.
For my existimation is good even amongst the slanderers and my memory
    shall arise for a sweet savour unto the Lord.
Let Jael rejoice with the Plover, who whistles for his live, and foils the marks-
    men and their guns.
For I bless the PRINCE of PEACE and pray that all the guns may be nailed
    up, save such as are for the rejoicing days.

from Fragment B2

For I will consider my Cat Jeoffry.
For he is the servant of the Living God duly and daily serving him.
For at the first glance of the glory of God in the East he worships in his way.
700   For is this done by wreathing his body seven times round with elegant quick-
    ness.
For then he leaps up to catch the musk, which is the blessing of God upon
    his prayer.
For he rolls upon prank to work it in.
For having done duty and received blessing he begins to consider himself.
For this he performs in ten degrees.
For first he looks upon his fore-paws to see if they are clean.
For secondly he kicks up behind to clear away there.
For thirdly he works it upon stretch with the fore-paws extended.
For fourthly he sharpens his paws by wood.
For fifthly he washes himself.
710   For sixthly he rolls upon wash.

For seventhly he fleas himself, that he may not be interrupted upon the beat.

For eighthly he rubs himself against a post.

For ninthly he looks up for his instructions.

For tenthly he goes in quest of food.

For having considered God and himself he will consider his neighbour.

For if he meets another cat he will kiss her in kindness.

For when he takes his prey he plays with it to give it a chance.

For one mouse in seven escapes by his dallying.

For when his day's work is done his business more properly begins.

720   For he keeps the Lord's watch in the night against the adversary.

For he counteracts the powers of darkness by his electrical skin and glaring
    eyes.

For he counteracts the Devil, who is death, by brisking about the life.

For in his morning orisons he loves the sun and the sun loves him.

For he is of the tribe of Tiger.

For the Cherub Cat is a term of the Angel Tiger.

For he has the subtlety and hissing of a serpent, which in goodness he sup-
    presses.

For he will not do destruction if he is well-fed, neither will he spit without
    provocation.

For he purrs in thankfulness, when God tells him he's a good Cat.

For he is an instrument for the children to learn benevolence upon.

730   For every house is incomplete without him and a blessing is lacking in the
    spirit.

For the Lord commanded Moses concerning the cats at the departure of the
    Children of Israel from Egypt.

For every family had one cat at least in the bag.

For the English Cats are the best in Europe.

For he is the cleanest in the use of his fore-paws of any quadruped.

For the dexterity of his defence is an instance of the love of God to him
    exceedingly.

For he is the quickest to his mark of any creature.

For he is tenacious of his point.

For he is a mixture of gravity and waggery.

For he knows that God is his Saviour.

740   For there is nothing sweeter than his peace when at rest.

For there is nothing brisker than his life when in motion.

For he is of the Lord's poor and so indeed is he called by benevolence
    perpetually—Poor Jeoffry! poor Jeoffry! the rat has bit thy throat.

For I bless the name of the Lord Jesus that Jeoffry is better.

For the divine spirit comes about his body to sustain it in complete cat.

For his tongue is exceeding pure so that it has in purity what it wants in
    music.

For he is docile and can learn certain things.
For he can set up with gravity which is patience upon approbation.
For he can fetch and carry, which is patience in employment.
For he can jump over a stick which is patience upon proof positive.
750   For he can spraggle upon waggle at the word of command.
For he can jump from an eminence into his master's bosom.
For he can catch the cork and toss it again.
For he is hated by the hypocrite and miser.
For the former is afraid of detection.
For the latter refuses the charge.
For he camels his back to bear the first notion of business.
For he is good to think on, if a man would express himself neatly.
For he made a great figure in Egypt for his signal services.
For he killed the Icneumon-rat very pernicious by land.
760   For his ears are so acute that they sting again.
For from this proceeds the passing quickness of his attention.
For by stroking of him I have found out electricity.
For I perceived God's light about him both wax and fire.
For the electrical fire is the spiritual substance, which God sends from
    heaven to sustain the bodies both of man and beast.
For God has blessed him in the variety of his movements.
For, though he cannot fly, he is an excellent clamberer.
For his motions upon the face of the earth are more than any other
    quadruped.
For he can tread to all the measures upon the music.
For he can swim for life.
770   For he can creep.
    1756–1763   1939

WILLIAM COWPER

1731–1800

COWPER'S EARLY CAREER as a lawyer led to stress that he could not
withstand, and his prior attacks of acute melancholia culminated in total
breakdown in 1763. Convinced that he was damned, he attempted suicide.
During his stay at an asylum, he experienced religious conversion to evangelical faith.

Retiring to the countryside, Cowper composed a long poem, *The Task*, of considerable aesthetic merit. But *The Task* is little read now, and Cowper is remembered mostly for his portrayals of his own ongoing mental crisis. The strongest of these poems is "The Castaway," founded upon the narrative of George Anson, an admiral in the British navy during its wars with Spain. A sailor is swept overboard in the Atlantic, while Anson's ship is battered by a storm. The parallel between the drowned sailor and the melancholic Cowper is deferred until the final stanza, where it bursts forth with amazing eloquence, so inspirited that we wonder how much greatness was lost to us through Cowper's madness:

> No voice divine the storm allayed,
>   No light propitious shone;
> When, snatched from all effectual aid,
>   We perished, each alone:
> But I beneath a rougher sea,
> And whelmed in deeper gulfs than he.

❧   ❧   ❧

The Castaway

Obscurest night involved the sky,
    The Atlantic billows roared,
When such a destined wretch as I,
    Washed headlong from on board,
Of friends, of hope, of all bereft,
His floating home for ever left.

No braver chief could Albion boast
    Than he with whom he went,
Nor ever ship left Albion's coast,
10   With warmer wishes sent.
He loved them both, but both in vain,
Nor him beheld, nor her again.

Not long beneath the whelming brine,
    Expert to swim, he lay;
Nor soon he felt his strength decline,
    Or courage die away;
But waged with death a lasting strife,
Supported by despair of life.

He shouted: nor his friends had failed
20   To check the vessel's course,
But so the furious blast prevailed,
        That, pitiless perforce,
They left their outcast mate behind,
And scudded still before the wind.

Some succour yet they could afford;
        And, such as storms allow,
The cask, the coop, the floated cord,
        Delayed not to bestow.
But he (they knew) nor ship, nor shore,
30 Whate'er they gave, should visit more.

Nor, cruel as it seemed, could be
        Their haste himself condemn,
Aware that flight, in such a sea,
        Alone could rescue them;
Yet bitter felt it still to die
Deserted, and his friends so nigh.

He long survives who lives an hour
        In ocean, self-upheld;
And so long he, with unspent power,
40   His destiny repelled;
And ever, as the minutes flew,
Entreated help, or cried, "Adieu!"

At length, his transient respite past,
        His comrades, who before
Had heard his voice in every blast,
        Could catch the sound no more.
For then, by toil subdued, he drank
The stifling wave, and then he sank.

No poet wept him: but the page
50   Of narrative sincere,
That tells his name, his worth, his age,
        Is wet with Anson's tear.
And tears by bards or heroes shed
Alike immortalize the dead.

I therefore purpose not, or dream,
    Descanting on his fate,
To give the melancholy theme
    A more enduring date:
But misery still delights to trace
60   Its semblance in another's case.

No voice divine the storm allayed,
    No light propitious shone;
When, snatched from all effectual aid,
    We perished, each alone:
But I beneath a rougher sea,
And whelmed in deeper gulfs than he.

    1799   1803

| ROBERT BURNS |

1759–1796

THOUGH HE HAS BECOME the national poet of Scotland, Burns had a difficult life, and died before the onset of middle years, worn out by the struggle to establish a literary career. Like the English Romantic John Clare, Robert Burns was an authentic peasant-poet, though unlike Clare he avoided madness, only to yield to alcoholism.

Popular as he is (all over the world), Burns is a subtle ironist, who cultivates a mask of the natural man even as he writes poems of high sophistication, three of which are included here.

"Address to the Deil" charmingly salutes Satan, in both his Miltonic and his Scottish folk guises, while the even more pungent "Holy Willie's Prayer" exposes the hypocrisies of evangelical Calvinism in Burn's Scotland.

The stirring "Scots Wha Hae" is the ultimate poem of Scottish nationalism, but also has the subtle undersong of Burns's left-wing support of the French Revolution.

        ⇓   ⇓   ⇓

Address to the Deil

O Prince! O Chief of many thronèd powers!
That led the embattled seraphim to war.

MILTON

O thou! whatever title suit thee,
Auld Hornie, Satan, Nick, or Clootie,
Wha in yon cavern grim an' sootie,
          Closed under hatches,
Spairges about the brunstane cootie,
          To scaud poor wretches!

Hear me, auld Hangie, for a wee,
An' let poor damnèd bodies be;
I'm sure sma' pleasure it can gie,
          Even to a deil,
To skelp an' scaud poor dogs like me,
          An' hear us squeel.

Great is thy power, an' great thy fame;
Far kend an' noted is thy name;
An' tho' von lowan heugh's thy hame,
          Thou travels far;
An' faith! thou's neither lag nor lame,
          Nor blate nor scaur.

Whyles, ranging like a roarin lion
For prey, a' holes an' corners tryin;
Whyles on the strong-winged tempest flyin,
          Tirlan the kirks;
Whyles, in the human bosom pryin,
          Unseen thou lurks.

I've heard my reverend graunie say,
In lanely glens ye like to stray;
Or where auld ruined castles grey
          Nod to the moon,
Ye fright the nightly wanderer's way,
          Wi' eldritch croon.

When twilight did my graunie summon,
To say her prayers, douce, honest woman!

Aft yont the dyke she's heard you bumman,
      Wi' eerie drone;
Or, rustlin, thro' the boortrees coman,
      Wi' heavy groan.

Ae dreary, windy, winter night,
The stars shot down wi' sklentan light,
Wi' you mysel I gat a fright
      Ayont the lough;
Ye, like a rash-buss stood in sight
      Wi' waving sugh.

The cudgel in my nieve did shake,
Each bristled hair stood like a stake,
When, wi' an eldritch, stoor quaick, quaick,
      Amang the springs,
Awa ye squattered, like a drake,
      On whistling wings.

Let warlocks grim, an' withered hags,
Tell how wi' you on ragweed nags,
They skim the muirs, an' dizzy crags,
      Wi' wicked speed;
And in kirk-yards renew their leagues,
      Owre howcket dead.

Thence countra wives, wi' toil an' pain,
May plunge an' plunge the kirn in vain;
For, oh! the yellow treasure's taen
      By witching skill;
An' dawtit, twal-pint Hawkie's gaen
      As yell's the bill.

Thence mystic knots mak great abuse
On young guidmen, fond, keen, an' crouse;
When the best wark-lume i' the house,
      By cantraip wit,
Is instant made no worth a louse,
      Just at the bit.

When thowes dissolve the snawy hoord,
An' float the jinglin icy boord,
Then water-kelpies haunt the foord,

70   By your direction,
An' nighted travellers are allured
        To their destruction.

An' aft your moss-traversing spunkies
Decoy the wight that late an' drunk is:
The bleezan, curst, mischievous monkies
        Delude his eyes,
Till in some miry slough he sunk is,
        Ne'er mair to rise.

When Masons' mystic word an' grip
80 In storms an' tempests raise you up,
Some cock or cat your rage maun stop,
        Or, strange to tell!
The youngest brother ye wad whip
        Aff straught to hell.

Lang syne, in Eden's bonie yard,
When youthfu' lovers first were paired,
An' all the soul of love they shared,
        The raptured hour,
Sweet on the fragrant flowery swaird,
90   In shady bower:

Then you, ye auld, snick-drawing dog!
Ye cam to Paradise incog,
An' played on man a cursed brogue
        (Black be you fa'!),
An' gied the infant warld a shog,
        'Maist ruin'd a'.

D'ye mind that day, when in a bizz,
Wi' reekit duds, an' reestit gizz,
Ye did present your smoutie phiz
100   'Mang better folk,
An' sklented on the man of Uz
        Your spitefu' joke?

An' how ye gat him i' your thrall,
An' brak him out o' house an' hal',
While scabs an' botches did him gall
        Wi' bitter claw,

An' lowsed his ill-tongued, wicked scawl,
          Was warst ava?

But a' your doings to rehearse,
110   Your wily shares an' fechtin fierce,
Sin' that day Michael did you pierce,
          Down to this time,
Wad ding a' Lallan tongue, or Erse,
          In prose or rhyme.

An' now, auld Cloots, I ken ye're thinkan,
A certain Bardie's rantin, drinkin,
Some luckless hour will send him linkan,
          To your black pit;
But faith! he'll turn a corner jinkan,
120   An' cheat you yet.

But fare you weel, auld Nickie-ben!
O wad ye tak a thought an' men'!
Ye aiblins might—I dinna ken—
          Still hae a stake:
I'm wae to think upo' yon den,
          Even for your sake!
     1785–1786   1786

Holy Willie's Prayer

And send the godly in a pet to pray.
          POPE

O Thou, wha in the heavens dost dwell,
Wha, as it pleases best thysel,
Sends ane to heaven an' ten to hell,
          A' for thy glory,
And no for ony guid or ill
          They've done afore thee!

I bless and praise thy matchless might,
Whan thousands thou hast left in night,
That I am here afore thy sight,
10   For gifts an' grace
A burnin an' a shinin light,
          To a' this place.

What was I, or my generation,
That I should get sic exaltation?
I, wha deserved most just damnation
    For broken laws
Five thousand years 'fore my creation,
    Thro' Adam's cause!

When from my mither's womb I fell,
20 Thou might hae plunged me deep in hell,
To gnash my gums and weep and wail.
    In burnin lakes,
Where damnèd devils roar and yell,
    Chained to their stakes.

Yet I am here, a chosen sample,
To show thy grace is great an' ample;
I'm here a pillar in thy temple,
    Strong as a rock,
A guide, a buckler, and example
30   To a' thy flock.

O Lord, thou kens what zeal I bear,
When drinkers drink, an' swearers swear,
And singin here and dancin there,
    Wi' great an' sma':
For I am keepit by thy fear
    Free frae them a'.

But yet, O Lord! confess I must,
At times I'm fashed wi' fleshy lust;
An' sometimes too, in warldly trust,
40   Vile self gets in;
But thou remembers we are dust,
    Defiled wi' sin.

O Lord! yestreen, thou kens, wi' Meg—
Thy pardon I sincerely beg;
O! may't ne'er be a livin plague
    To my dishonour,
An' I'll ne'er lift a lawless leg
    Again upon her.

Besides I farther maun allow,
50   Wi' Leezie's lass, three times I trow—
But, Lord, that Friday I was fou,
                When I cam near her,
Or else, thou kens, the servant true
                Wad ne'er hae steered her.

May be thou lets this fleshly thorn
Beset thy servant e'en and morn
Lest he owre high and proud should turn,
                Cause he's sae gifted;
If sae, thy han' maun e'en be borne,
60   Until thou lift it.

Lord, bless thy chosen in this place,
For here thou hast a chosen race;
But God confound their stubborn face,
                And blast their name,
What bring thy elders to disgrace
                An' public shame!

Lord, mind Gau'n Hamilton's deserts,
He drinks, an' swears, an' plays at cartes,
Yet has sae mony takin arts
70   Wi' great and sma',
Frae God's ain priest the people's hearts
                He steals awa'.

An' when we chastened him therefore,
Thou kens how he bred sic a splore
As set the warld in a roar
                O' laughin at us;
Curse thou his basket and his store,
                Kail an' potatoes.

Lord, hear my earnest cry an' prayer,
80   Against that Presbyt'ry o' Ayr;
Thy strong right hand, Lord, mak it bare
                Upo' their heads;
Lord, weigh it down, and dinna spare,
                For their misdeeds!

O Lord my God, that glib-tongued Aiken,
My vera heart and saul are quakin,
To think how we stood sweatin, shakin,
   An' pissed wi' dread,
While he, wi' hingin lips and snakin,
90   Held up his head.

Lord, in thy day of vengeance try him;
Lord, visit him wha did employ him,
And pass not in thy mercy by them,
   Nor hear their prayer;
But, for thy people's sake, destroy them,
   And dinna spare!

But, Lord, remember me and mine
Wi' mercies temp'ral and divine,
That I for grace an' gear may shine
100   Excelled by nane;
And a' the glory shall be thine,
   Amen, Amen!
  1785 1789

Scots Wha Hae

Robert Bruce's Address to His Army, Before the Battle of Bannockburn

Scots, wha hae wi' Wallace bled,
Scots, wha Bruce has aften led,
Welcome to your gory bed,
  Or to victorie.

Now's the day, and now's the hour;
See the front o' battle lour;
See approach proud Edward's power—
  Chains and slaverie!

Wha will be a traitor knave?
10 Wha can fill a coward's grave?
Wha sae base as be a slave?
  Let him turn and flee!

Wha for Scotland's king and law
Freedom's sword will strongly draw,

Freeman stand, or freeman fa'?
    Let him follow me!

By oppression's woes and pains!
By your sons in servile chains!
We will drain our dearest veins,
20   But they *shall* be free!

Lay the proud usurpers low!
Tyrants fall in every foe!
Liberty's in every blow!
    Let us do—or die!

1793 1794

WILLIAM BLAKE

1757–1827

BLAKE WAS BORN in London on November 28, 1757, into the family of a hosier. He had no formal education, but was apprenticed to an engraver, James Basire. In 1782 he married Catherine Boucher; the marriage was childless, and went through intense difficulties, particularly in early 1793, when Blake complained bitterly of her sexual jealousy, but eventually the relationship became serene and very close. Blake died on a Sunday evening, August 12, 1827, Catherine by his side, and by all accounts he died majestically, a fulfilled and happy man.

There were almost no outward events in Blake's life. He was not a professional poet or man of letters, but earned his living, sometimes very precariously, as an engraver. Insofar as he had any public reputation during his lifetime, it was as a failed, eccentric painter. But some of his lyrics were known and admired by Coleridge and other literary men, and his paintings were valued by some of the better artists of his time. Almost unknown, however, were what are widely (and rightly) now regarded as his most important achievement, a series of visionary poems culminating in three brief or foreshortened epics, works demonstrating probably the greatest conceptual power ever to appear among poets.

Blake, for all his gifts, is not a poet of the eminence of Chaucer, Shakespeare, or Milton, yet he gives his readers not only what can be expected from a great poet, but a profundity of schematized psychological insight comparable to Freud's, and a disciplined intellectual inventiveness comparable to Hegel's. His difficulty for readers, and his unique value, is that he offers even more than that, for he is, as he insisted, a prophet, in the precise sense that Isaiah and Ezekiel (he would have added Milton) are prophetic poets. His poems, which are always poems, are astonishingly ambitious, even for the Romantic Age, into which he survived. They propose nothing less than to teach us how to live, and to explain to us what has made it so hard to live as fully human rather than merely natural beings.

Blake, a self-taught London radical Protestant, was more than deeply read in the King James Bible, and in Milton. In the Talmudic phrase, he had "eaten those books," and they account for all but an insignificant part of his literary tradition, and indeed of his knowledge. Much scholarship has wasted itself, from Yeats to the present moment, in attempting to trace Blake's ideas and images to a large number of arcane traditions. But Blake was a very impatient reader, except of the Bible and Milton, and though he glanced at anything he encountered, he would have snorted at the suggestion that he give serious effort to the study of alchemy, mysticism, theosophy, esoteric forms of Neo-Platonism, occult "science," latter-day Gnosticisms, or any of the crankeries that have elicited respectful concentration from some of his scholarly pursuers.

To comprehend Blake, his reader needs to understand how Blake read the Bible and Milton, or as Blake might have said, how to read poetry. For Blake was primarily an intellectual revisionist, even as Nietzsche, Marx, Freud, in the longest perspective, seem most important as revisionists of the European Enlightenment. Blake, like the major Romantics after him, sought to correct the Enlightenment, and not to abolish it. He had no quarrel with reason itself but only with inadequate accounts of reason, and he refused to distinguish between "the intellectual powers" and what he called "the Real Man the Imagination," whose most complete expression was in the arts of poetry and painting. The Bible, whose degree of historical validity was quite irrelevant to Blake, represented for him the Great Code of Art, the total form of what he called the Divine Vision, which he believed to have been so obscured by the nightmare of history as to be all but totally darkened in his own time.

Most of what currently passes for movements of human liberation would have been condemned by Blake as what he bitterly called Druidism, taking the name from what he judged to have been the native British version of natural religion. All of Blake's work is based on a firm distinction between what is imaginative and what is merely natural in us, with the natural rejected, cast out beyond the balance of what Blake termed "contraries." The revolt of youth-as-youth Blake saw as a cyclic self-defeat, the sad destiny of the eternal rebel he called Orc. The revolt of women-as-women (as exemplified in his acquaintance Mary Wollstonecraft) he judged also as doomed to the perpetual failure of natural cycle, for all natural women, like all natural men, were subject to what he named the Female Will, always rampant in nature. The revolt of the heart against the head (as represented by Rousseau) he pungently characterized as "reasoning from the loins in the unreal forms of Beulah's Night," Beulah being a lower paradise of illusory appearances. D. H. Lawrence, a lesser Blake, inveighed against "sex in the head," following Blake's prophecy, but proceeded, like so many since, to reason from the loins, hardly a more humanizing procedure, in Blake's view.

Blake's view was what he himself always termed Vision or Intellectual Vision, which he took ironic care to distinguish from the literalism of the natural eye, and from the chemistry of the natural mind. He saw with the eye of the imagination, and without the aid of artificial paradises of any kind whatsoever. His visions are what Ezekiel and Milton saw, and what he believed all of us could see, by the hard efforts of poetry and painting, or of learning to apprehend the poets and the painters, and so to re-create their worlds after them. He hoped to rescue English culture from what he interpreted as its decadence, by restoring poetry to what it had been in Milton and the Renaissance writers before Milton, and by raising English painting to what it had never been, the spiritual art of Michelangelo and Raphael.

Yet Blake's own genius was curiously divided. As poet and as painter he excels as a caricaturist, an intellectual satirist, and a master of a new kind of vitalizing but ironic parody, which first triumphs in *The Marriage of Heaven and Hell*. Where he wished most to excel was in the Sublime of Milton and Michelangelo, and here his achievement was only partial, though larger in poetry than in painting. His painting was anachronistic in a somewhat crippling sense, and his failure to understand Rubens and Rembrandt was more self-defeating than it need have been. In his Sublime poetry, he is least successful where he is most directly Miltonic, and rather closer to the highest kind of accomplishment when he is even more Hebraic than Milton is. But there, too, his stature is lessened when he is read in direct juxtaposition with the Bible. His own true Sublime comes in another mode, a Northern one, in the tradition of the Icelandic Eddas, and in the less strenuous but still Miltonic eighteenth-century English tradition of James Thomson, Thomas Gray, William Collins, and William Cowper, the poets of Sensibility, as recent scholarly criticism has begun to call them. After Milton, Blake felt closer to Cowper than to any other English poet, and though he read, admired, and (very complexly) protested Wordsworth's poetry, he always was more comfortable with an ode like Gray's *The Progress of Poesy* than with one like "Intimations of Immortality."

The Miltonizing poets of Sensibility failed, in Blake's opinion, because they were not sane enough to overthrow a worldview Blake regarded as totally mad, and which he associated with Bacon, Newton, and Locke in metaphysics and with Dryden, Pope, Dr. Johnson, and Sir Joshua Reynolds in the arts. This worldview is so savagely caricatured by Blake that we need to be very wary about accepting his version of it as being in any way adequate to those thinkers and artists. But Blake was no more unjust than the Augustan satirists were, from their almost opposite points of departure. Blake was politically of the permanent Left, like Shelley in the next generation, and to him the Augustan trinity of Reason, Nature, and Society was a three-headed beast or triple whore responsible for the sufferings of the lower classes of England, out of whom he had come and with whom he defiantly remained. The Revolution did not come to England, the repression of Pitt did its work well, and Blake learned the joyless wisdom of public timidity. He secretly raged, in his notebooks and his poems, but he accurately said of his outward obedience: "I am hid." When he did speak his mind, he suffered for it, whether in defying patrons or in angrily throwing a soldier out of his garden. The first brought on Jobean trials of poverty for himself and his loyal, suffering wife, and the second brought on him the ordeal of trial for treason (he was acquitted, but the terror of the experience is intense throughout his greatest poem, *Jerusalem*). Too profound a consciousness to accept any easy explanations for the torments of his fellows and himself, Blake prophetically indicted the English conservative cultural tradition in its totality. In his gathering vision all fit together: the theology of the English state church, the political theory of Burke, the deistic natural religion which he believed the church only pretended to oppose, the poetics of Pope and the aesthetics of Reynolds, the philosophy of Locke, the physics of Newton, the morality of Bacon. The aggregate of all this, quite unfairly but wholly unforgettably, Blake fused together as the Accuser of Sin, the spectral torturer of English man, of Albion. His mature poetry became an attempt to identify, with final clarity, this Accuser, in the belief that to know the clear outline of error, particularly within the self, is to make its destruction inevitable.

To achieve this identification, Blake tried several times to organize his vision so as to tell a comprehensive story of how mankind fell into its present condition, what that condition was, and how mankind was to be freed from all conditions, particularly from the confining context of nature. We begin to apprehend Blake when we realize that for him "human nature" is a wholly unacceptable phrase, an absolute contradiction, or, as he said, "an impossible absurdity." What was human about us, Blake insisted, was the imagination; what was natural about us had to be redeemed by the imagination, or else it would destroy us. The imagination, to Blake, was not a faculty, however glorious, but was the Real Man, the unfallen unity we had been and must become again.

Blake's story is too complex and long for this introduction. But it is crucial, as we begin to read Blake, that we ask why he made his story so difficult for us. Though several major poets since Blake have invented mythologies, and though there are mythopoeic elements in all major poets, Blake's myths are the most formidable and complete in the language. Northrop Frye, probably Blake's best critic, has insisted that Blake's poetic procedures were as central as any poet's, and this may be so; yet the experience of most common readers seems to tell them otherwise. What can be made explicit to the idiot, Blake said, was not worth his care, and so he addressed a sublime allegory to the intellectual powers. But need his address have been so solitary a one? Could he have been more direct and immediate, as apparently he was in his earlier work, or is there a convincing inner necessity in his initially strange procedures? Did a voice crying in the wilderness of 1790 to 1810, the years of his major works, have to cry aloud in so subtly complex a language that it seems always to need translation for even willing auditors?

There are no certain answers, yet one can be ventured, by comparing Blake's poetry to that of his older contemporary Cowper, and his younger contemporary Wordsworth. Cowper is so Milton-haunted that he never fully finds his own voice, and so afflicted by a sense of worthlessness and damnation that he scarcely can find his way past fear and trembling. When we read Cowper, if we read acutely and sympathetically, we are very moved, but what moves us is the pathos of Cowper's predicament, and his helplessness at breaking out of it. Blake's was a fierce spirit, akin to the greatest dissenters that the "inner light" tradition of Protestantism has produced among the English. He would not allow himself to be a victim or a latecomer, like the poets of Sensibility before him, and so he resolved to break through every net, external and internal, that had blocked his precursors from joining themselves to Milton's greatness, even the net of Milton himself.

Wordsworth, born thirteen years after Blake, was also a titanic individuality, a consciousness fierce enough not to accept victimization by history and circumstances, or even by Milton, whom he revered quite as much as Cowper and Blake did. But Wordsworth chose another way, not a personal mythology, but a demythologizing so radical that it enabled him to create modern poetry, if any single figure can be said to have done so. He is ultimately a more difficult poet than Blake, if "difficult" means problematic, as it should. Once a reader has mastered Blake's initial complexities, he goes on encountering vast profundities, but his way is clear before him. A little way into Wordsworth, the reader begins to encounter enormous and legitimate obscurities and dark passages, whereas Blake gives almost too continuous and directing a light. For Blake is not only more systematic than Wordsworth, he is also far closer than Wordsworth to English Renaissance poetry, and necessarily far less modern, however you want to interpret "modern." It is one of the disturbing paradoxes about Blake that, lifelong rebel though he was, his mature work increasingly seems conservative in the longest perspectives we can achieve. An enemy of the rationalists, he was a great rationalizer; an exploder of the mythologies, he remythologized so extensively as to help preserve the cultural life of many phenomena he wished to bury. Though he has been reclaimed for the latest movements of social, political, and artistic revolt from late nineteenth-century England down to this present moment, he is further away from any and all of us than he is from the Enlightenment he prophesied against.

Blake could or would not do what Hazlitt rightly said Wordsworth had done: begin anew on a tabula rasa ("clean slate") of poetry, almost as though none had been written before him. *Jerusalem,* at first reading, may baffle or repel an unprepared contemporary reader, but so does Ezekiel, and so does John Milton. Poetry meant too much to Blake to abandon the main continuities of what it had been; poetry meant a great deal to Wordsworth, but nature meant more. Yet to Blake, nature was a hindrance, not action, and so no part of him. He undertook the immense task of his mythologizing so as to begin the preservation of man by the preservation of poetry, in a form still fundamentally recognizable as a major creation of the English Renaissance. Though, in his own terms, he did not fail, and on any terms he became one of the half dozen or so poets in the language, he did not succeed as Wordsworth was to succeed. Blake became the last epic poet in the old sense of epic. It was left for Wordsworth to become a new kind of poet, one which, perhaps to our sorrow, is necessarily with us still.

The Marriage of Heaven and Hell

This is Blake's manifesto, his declaration of spiritual independence, and his version of what it means to rise in the body at thirty-three, the age at which Christ died. Deliberately, Blake makes it the entryway into the canon of his mature work, his highly organized story of how man and the universe got into their present sorry condition, and his prophecy of what should be done by every man who wishes to work free of a merely natural or given condition.

The central element in this prose poem is Blake's presentation of his dialectic, his imaginative but still rational process of arriving at truth through the progression of contraries, opposites which are not negations or denials but partial truths. What makes *The Marriage* initially a little difficult is that its rhetoric of presentation and its complex and experimental literary form embody a dialectical argument, so that the shock value of the work goes beyond its actually quite restrained wisdom. Commenting on Emanuel Swedenborg (Swedish theologian and mystic, 1688–1772) in 1788, Blake wrote: "Good and Evil are here both Good and the two contraries Married"; Blake's contraries replace Swedenborg's "correspondences," which are mutually absorbing categories, identities between the spiritual and natural worlds. By "marriage" Blake means that the contraries are to be reconciled, but are not to absorb or subsume one another. Blake was never Swedenborgian, but may have believed him to be a fellow visionary, until by reading more of Swedenborg, he came to know better. In another 1788 comment on Swedenborg, Blake wrote: "Heaven and Hell are born Together," meaning that Swedenborg never knew this, since that onetime rebel against Calvinism had embraced the doctrine of Predestination. Blake begins and largely continues as though he were on the "Devil's," or imaginative rebel's, side, and certainly he is more in that camp than among "Angels," or the timidly orthodox, but his final stance transcends any upsurge of energy and desire. Just as the states of Innocence and of Experience satirize each other, so the contraries of Devil and Angel satirically reveal each other's limitations.

The Marriage, then, is an intellectual satire, but it is also a qualified prophecy of an apocalypse that may be imminent. Rabelais (whom Blake never read) provides the closest analogue to Blake's tone, with the difference that Blake finds in his contemporary time of troubles the presages of the promised end. Not so much the French Revolution but the English reaction against the spread of revolution is Blake's starting point.

Songs of Innocence and of Experience

There are twenty-one copies of *Songs of Innocence*, and twenty-seven of the combined work, but no separate copies at all of *Songs of Experience*. Blake therefore was willing to have *Songs of Innocence* read separately (he continued to issue it after he had combined the two groups) but not the contrary work. These are works in illuminated printing, engraved after a process of Blake's own invention, in which he applied words and pictures to copper plates, and then etched surrounding surfaces away. The colors of inks and the tints and washes, some translucent, some opaque, vary from copy to copy.

Together with some early tracts, Blake's *Songs of Innocence* and *Book of Thel* begin his deliberate canon of engraved works. The first drafts of three of the *Songs of Innocence* are to be found in a satirical context in the early prose fragment *An Island in the Moon*, and satire of a very subtle kind is crucial throughout the combined work, in which Innocence and Experience are so juxtaposed as to demonstrate each other's inadequacies.

The *Songs of Innocence* are indeed "of" and not "about" the state of innocence. There is much critical debate about Blake's Innocence, and little that is definitive can be said about it. The reader should know that the root meaning of "innocence" is "harmlessness"; the derived meanings, "guiltlessness" and "freedom from sin." But Blake uses the word to mean "inexperience" as well, which is a very different matter. As the contrary of Experience, Innocence cannot be reconciled with it within the context of natural existence. Implicit in the contrast between the two states is a distinction Blake made between "unorganized innocence," unable to sustain experience, and an organized kind which could. On the manuscript of *The Four Zoas*, he jotted down: "*Unorganized Innocence: An Impossibility. Innocence dwells with Wisdom, but never with Ignorance.*"

Since Innocence and Experience are states of the soul through which we pass, neither is a finality, both are necessary, and neither is wholly preferable to the other. Not only are they satires upon each other, but they exist in a cyclic relation as well. Blake does not intend us to see Innocence as belonging to childhood and Experience to adulthood, which would be not only untrue but also uninteresting.

The relation of the matched pairs of poems, where they exist, does not appear to be schematic, but varies from instance to instance. The matching of "The Divine Image" and "The Human Abstract" seems to be the crucial one, since it shows the widest possibilities of the relationship, and demonstrates vividly what readers are too likely to forget, which is that Innocence satirizes Experience just as intensely as it itself is satirized by Experience, and also that any song of either state is also a kind of satire upon itself.

ᵛ   ᵛ   ᵛ

The Sick Rose

O Rose thou art sick.
The invisible worm,
That flies in the night
In the howling storm:

Has found out thy bed
Of crimson joy:
And his dark secret love
Does thy life destroy.

1794

The Tyger

Tyger Tyger, burning bright,
In the forests of the night;
What immortal hand or eye,
Could frame thy fearful symmetry?

In what distant deeps or skies
Burnt the fire of thine eyes!
On what wings dare he aspire?
What the hand, dare sieze the fire?

And what shoulder, & what art,
Could twist the sinews of thy heart?

And when thy heart began to beat,
What dread hand? & what dread feet?

What the hammer? what the chain,
In what furnace was thy brain?
What the anvil? what dread grasp,
Dare its deadly terrors clasp?

When the stars threw down their spears
And water'd heaven with their tears:
Did he smile his work to see?
20 Did he who made the Lamb make thee?

Tyger, Tyger burning bright,
In the forests of the night:
What immortal hand or eye,
Dare frame thy fearful symmetry?
                1793   1794

Ah! Sun-flower

Ah Sun-flower! weary of time,
Who countest the steps of the Sun:
Seeking after that sweet golden clime
Where the travellers journey is done.

Where the Youth pined away with desire,
And the pale Virgin shrouded in snow:
Arise from their graves and aspire,
Where my Sun-flower wishes to go.
                1794

London

I wander thro' each charter'd street,
Near where the charter'd Thames does flow.
And mark in every face I meet
Marks of weakness, marks of woe.

In every cry of every Man,
In every Infants cry of fear,

In every voice: in every ban,
The mind-forg'd manacles I hear

How the Chimney-sweepers cry
10 Every blackning Church appalls,
And the hapless Soldiers sigh,
Runs in blood down Palace walls

But most thro' midnight streets I hear
How the youthful Harlots curse
Blasts the new-born Infants tear
And blights with plagues the Marriage hearse.

    1793   1794

The Mental Traveller

Like "The Crystal Cabinet," this poem exists in a fair copy manuscript that Blake may have intended for engraving. Both poems are highly finished, economical, complex ballads, and seem to be deliberate experiences at telling versions of Blake's myths without using a technical vocabulary or private personages. "The Mental Traveller" foreshadows the entire Orc-Urizen cycle, and is perhaps the bleakest of Blake's comprehensive accounts of fallen existence. Yeats acknowledged its influence upon his mythological book *A Vision.* Few poems in the language do so much so grandly and so grimly in just over a hundred lines.

The poem may be described, briefly, as a report upon a grotesque planet given by a being alien to it, who cannot understand the horrors he sees. He describes two cycles moving in opposite directions, and out of phase with each other. The natural cycle (symbolized by the female) is moving backward, the human (symbolized by the male) forward. There are only two personages in the poem, but they move through several phases, and phantoms of earlier phases sometimes linger. The human cycle moves between an infant Orc and an aged, beggared Urizen, and then back again. The natural sequence is Tirzah (Nature-as-Necessity), Vala (Nature-as-Temptress), and Rahab (Nature-as-Destroyer), and then back again.

      ✦   ✦   ✦

The Mental Traveller

I traveld thro' a Land of Men
A Land of Men & Women too
And heard & saw such dreadful things
As cold Earth wanderers never knew

For there the Babe is born in joy
That was begotten in dire woe
Just as we Reap in joy the fruit
Which we in bitter tears did sow

And if the Babe is born a Boy
10   He's given to a Woman Old
Who nails him down upon a rock
Catches his shrieks in cups of gold

She binds iron thorns around his head
She pierces both his hands & feet
She cuts his heart out at his side
To make it feel both cold & heat

Her fingers number every Nerve
Just as a Miser counts his gold
She lives upon his shrieks & cries
20   And she grows young as he grows old

Till he becomes a bleeding youth
And she becomes a Virgin bright
Then he rends up his Manacles
And binds her down for his delight

He plants himself in all her Nerves
Just as a Husbandman his mould
And she becomes his dwelling place
And Garden fruitful seventy fold

An aged Shadow soon he fades
30   Wandring round an Earthly Cot
Full filled all with gems & gold
Which he by industry had got

And these are the gems of the Human Soul
The rubies & pearls of a lovesick eye
The countless gold of the akeing heart
The martyrs groan & the lovers sigh

They are his meat they are his drink
He feeds the Beggar & the Poor
And the wayfaring Traveller
40   For ever open is his door

His grief is their eternal joy
They make the roofs & walls to ring
Till from the fire on the hearth
A little Female Babe does spring

And she is all of solid fire
And gems & gold that none his hand
Dares stretch to touch her Baby form
Or wrap her in his swaddling-band

But She comes to the Man she loves
50   If young or old or rich or poor
They soon drive out the aged Host
A Beggar at anothers door

He wanders weeping far away
Untill some other take him in
Oft blind & age-bent sore distrest
Until he can a Maiden win

And to allay his freezing Age
The Poor Man takes her in his arms
The Cottage fades before his sight
60   The Garden & its lovely Charms

The Guests are scatterd thro' the land
For the Eye altering alters all
The Senses roll themselves in fear
And the flat Earth becomes a Ball

The Stars Sun Moon all shrink away
A desert vast without a bound

And nothing left to eat or drink
And a dark desart all around

The honey of her Infant lips
70 The bread & wine of her sweet smile
The wild game of her roving Eye
Does him to Infancy beguile

For as he eats & drinks he grows
Younger & younger every day
And on the desart wild they both
Wander in terror & dismay

Like the wild Stag she flees away
Her fear plants many a thicket wild
While he pursues her night & day
80 By various arts of Love beguild

By various arts of Love & Hate
Till the wide desart planted oer
With Labyrinths of wayward Love
Where roams the Lion Wolf & Boar

Till he becomes a wayward Babe
And she a weeping Woman Old
Then many a Lover wanders here
The Sun & Stars are nearer rolld

The trees bring forth sweet Extacy
90 To all who in the desart roam
Till many a City there is Built
And many a pleasant Shepherds home

But when they find the frowning Babe
Terror strikes thro the region wide
They cry the Babe the Babe is Born
And flee away on Every side

For who dare touch the frowning form
His arm is witherd to its root
Lions Boars Wolves all howling flee
100 And every Tree does shed its fruit

And none can touch that frowning form
Except it be a Woman Old
She nails him down upon the Rock
And all is done as I have told
    1803? 1863

The Crystal Cabinet

The Maiden caught me in the Wild
Where I was dancing merrily
She put me into her Cabinet
And Lockd me up with a golden Key

This Cabinet is formd of Gold
And Pearl & Crystal shining bright
And within it opens into a World
And a little lovely Moony Night

Another England there I saw
10   Another London with its Tower
Another Thames & other Hills
And another pleasant Surrey Bower

Another Maiden like herself
Translucent lovely shining clear
Threefold each in the other closd
O what a pleasant trembling fear

O what a smile a threefold Smile
Filld me that like a flame I burnd
I bent to Kiss the lovely Maid
20   And found a Threefold Kiss returnd

I strove to sieze the inmost Form
With ardor fierce & hands of flame
But burst the Crystal Cabinet
And like a Weeping Babe became

A weeping Babe upon the wild
And Weeping Woman pale reclind
And in the outward air again
I filld with woes the passing Wind
    1803? 1863

from The Four Zoas

[Song of Enion]

I am made to sow the thistle for wheat; the nettle for a nourishing dainty
I have planted a false oath in the earth, it has brought forth a poison tree
I have chosen the serpent for a councellor & the dog
For a schoolmaster to my children
I have blotted out from light & living the dove & nightingale
And I have caused the earth worm to beg from door to door
I have taught the thief a secret path into the house of the just
I have taught pale artifice to spread his nets upon the morning
My heavens are brass my earth is iron my moon a clod of clay
10   My sun a pestilence burning at noon & a vapour of death in night

What is the price of Experience do men buy it for a song
Or wisdom for a dance in the street? No it is bought with the price
Of all that a man hath his house his wife his children
Wisdom is sold in the desolate market where none come to buy
And in the witherd field where the farmer plows for bread in vain

It is an easy thing to triumph in the summers sun
And in the vintage & to sing on the waggon loaded with corn
It is an easy thing to talk of patience to the afflicted
To speak the laws of prudence to the houseless wanderer

PAGE 36
To listen to the hungry ravens cry in wintry season
When the red blood is filld with wine & with the marrow of lambs
It is an easy thing to laugh at wrathful elements
To hear the dog howl at the wintry door, the ox in the slaughter house moan
To see a god on every wind & a blessing on every blast
To hear sounds of love in the thunder storm that destroys our enemies house
To rejoice in the blight that covers his field, & the sickness that cuts off his
    children
While our olive & vine sing & laugh round our door & our children bring
    fruits & flowers

Then the groan & the dolor are quite forgotten & the slave grinding at the
    mill
10   And the captive in chains & the poor in the prison, & the soldier in the field
When the shatterd bone hath laid him groaning among the happier dead

It is an easy thing to rejoice in the tents of prosperity
Thus could I sing & thus rejoice, but it is not so with me!
   1796–1807?   1893

from Milton

[The Vision of Beulah]

There is a place where Contrarieties are equally True
This place is called Beulah. It is a pleasant lovely Shadow
Where no dispute can come. Because of those who Sleep.
Into this place the Sons & Daughters of Ololon descended
With solemn mourning into Beulahs moony shades & hills
Weeping for Milton: mute wonder held the Daughters of Beulah
Enrapturd with affection sweet and mild benevolence

Beulah is evermore Created around Eternity; appearing
To the Inhabitants of Eden, around them on all sides.
10 But Beulah to its Inhabitants appears within each district
As the beloved infant in his mothers bosom round incircled
With arms of love & pity & sweet compassion. But to
The Sons of Eden the moony habitations of Beulah,
Are from Great Eternity a mild & pleasant Rest.

And it is thus Created. Lo the Eternal Great Humanity
To whom be Glory & Dominion Evermore Amen
Walks among all his awful Family seen in every face
As the breath of the Almighty, such are the words of man to man
In the great Wars of Eternity, in fury of Poetic Inspiration,
20 To build the Universe stupendous: Mental forms Creating

But the Emanations trembled exceedingly, nor could they
Live, because the life of Man was too exceeding unbounded
His joy became terrible to them, they trembled & wept
Crying with one voice. Give us a habitation & a place
In which we may be hidden under the shadow of wings
For if we who are but for a time, & who pass away in winter

Behold these wonders of Eternity we shall consume
But you O our Fathers & Brothers, remain in Eternity

But grant us a Temporal Habitation. do you speak
30   To us; we will obey your words as you obey Jesus
The Eternal who is blessed for ever.& ever. Amen

So spake the lovely Emanations; & there appeard a pleasant
Mild Shadow above: beneath: & on all sides round,

PLATE 31

Into this pleasant Shadow all the weak & weary
Like Women & Children were taken away as on wings
Of dovelike softness, & shadowy habitations prepared for them
But every Man returnd & went still going forward thro'
The Bosom of the Father in Eternity on Eternity
Neither did any lack or fall into Error without
A Shadow to repose in all the Days of Happy Eternity

Into this pleasant Shadow Beulah, all Ololon descended
And when the Daughters of Beulah heard the lamentation
10   All Beulah wept, for they saw the Lord coming in the Clouds.
And the Shadows of Beulah terminate in rocky Albion.
And all Nations wept in affliction Family by Family
Germany wept towards France & Italy: England wept & trembled
Towards America: India rose up from his golden bed:
As one awakend in the night: they saw the Lord coming
In the Clouds of Ololon with Power & Great Glory!

And all the Living Creatures of the Four Elements, wail'd
With bitter wailing: these in the aggregate are named Satan
And Rahab: they know not of Regeneration, but only of Generation
20   The Fairies, Nymphs, Gnomes & Genii of the Four Elements
Unforgiving & unalterable: these cannot be Regenerated
But must be Created, for they know only of Generation
These are the Gods of the Kingdoms of the Earth: in contrarious
And cruel opposition: Element against Element, opposed in War
Not Mental, as the Wars of Eternity, but a Corporeal Strife
In Los's Halls continual labouring in the Furnaces of Golgonooza
Orc howls on the Atlantic: Enitharmon trembles: All Beulah weeps

Thou hearest the Nightingale begin the Song of Spring;
The Lark sitting upon his earthly bed: just as the morn
30   Appears; listens silent; then springing from the waving Corn-field! loud
He leads the Choir of Day! trill, trill, trill, trill,

Mounting upon the wings of light into the Great Expanse:
Reecchoing against the lovely blue & shining heavenly Shell:
His little throat labours with inspiration; every feather
On throat & breast & wings vibrates with the effluence Divine
All Nature listens silent to him & the awful Sun
Stands still upon the Mountain looking on this little Bird
With eyes of soft humility, & wonder love & awe.
Then loud from their green covert all the Birds begin their Song
40   The Thrush, the Linnet & the Goldfinch, Robin & the Wren
Awake the Sun from his sweet reverie upon the Mountain:
The Nightingale again assays his song, & thro the day,
And thro the night warbles luxuriant; every Bird of Song
Attending his loud harmony with admiration & love.
This is a Vision of the lamentation of Beulah over Ololon!

Thou percievest the Flowers put forth their precious Odours!
And none can tell how from so small a center comes such sweets
Forgetting that within that Center Eternity expands
Its ever during doors, that Og & Anak fiercely guard[.]
50   First eer the morning breaks joy opens in the flowery bosoms
Joy even to tears, which the Sun rising dries; first the Wild Thyme
And Meadow-sweet downy & soft waving among the reeds.
Light springing on the air lead the sweet Dance: they wake
The Honeysuckle sleeping on the Oak: the flaunting beauty
Revels along upon the wind; the White-thorn lovely May
Opens her many lovely eyes: listening the Rose still sleeps
None dare to wake her. soon she bursts her crimson curtaind bed
And comes forth in the majesty of beauty; every Flower:
The Pink, the Jessamine, the Wall-flower, the Carnation
60   The Jonquil, the mild Lilly opes her heavens! every Tree,
And Flower & Herb soon fill the air with an innumerable Dance
Yet all in order sweet & lovely, Men are sick with Love!
Such is a Vision of the lamentation of Beulah over Ololon

from Jerusalem

The Emanation of the Giant Albion

PLATE 10
        [The Spectre of Urthona]
Shuddring the Spectre howls. his howlings terrify the night

He stamps around the Anvil, beating blows of stern despair
He curses Heaven & Earth, Day & Night & Sun & Moon
He curses Forest Spring & River, Desart & sandy Waste
Cities & Nations, Families & Peoples, Tongues & Laws
Driven to desperation by Los's terrors & threatning fears

Los cries, Obey my voice & never deviate from my will
30   And I will be merciful to thee: be thou invisible to all
To whom I make thee invisible, but chief to my own Children
O Spectre of Urthona: Reason not against their dear approach
Nor them obstruct with thy temptations of doubt & despair[.]
O Shame O strong & mighty Shame I break thy brazen fetters
If thou refuse, thy present torments will seem southern breezes
To what thou shalt endure if thou obey not my great will.

The Spectre answer'd. Art thou not ashamd of those thy Sins
That thou callest thy Children? lo the Law of God commands
That they be offered upon his Altar: O cruelty & torment
40   For thine are also mine! I have kept silent hitherto,
Concerning my chief delight: but thou hast broken silence
Now I will speak my mind! Where is my lovely Enitharmon
O thou my enemy, where is my Great Sin? She is also thine
I said: now is my grief at worst: incapable of being
Surpassed: but every moment it accumulates more & more
It continues accumulating to eternity! the joys of God advance
For he is Righteous: he is not a Being of Pity & Compassion
He cannot feel Distress; he feeds on Sacrifice & Offering:
Delighting in cries & tears & clothed in holiness & solitude
50   But my griefs advance also, for ever & ever without end
O that I could cease to be! Despair! I am Despair
Created to be the great example of horror & agony: also my
Prayer is vain I called for compassion: compassion mockd[,]
Mercy & pity threw the grave stone over me & with lead
And iron, bound it over me for ever: Life lives on my
Consuming: & the Almighty hath made me his Contrary
To be all evil, all reversed & for ever dead: knowing
And seeing life, yet living not; how can I then behold
And not tremble; how can I be beheld & not abhorrd

60   So spoke the Spectre shuddring, & dark tears ran down his shadowy face
Which Los wiped off, but comfort none could give! or beam of hope
Yet ceasd he not from labouring at the roarings of his Forge
With iron & brass Building Golgonooza in great contendings

Till his Sons & Daughters came forth from the Furnaces
At the sublime Labours, for Los compelld the invisible Spectre

from The Gates of Paradise

[Epilogue]
To The Accuser who is
The God of This World

Truly My Satan thou art but a Dunce
And dost not know the Garment from the Man
Every Harlot was a Virgin once
Nor canst thou ever change Kate into Nan

Tho thou art Worshipd by the Names Divine
Of Jesus & Jehovah: thou art still
The Son of Morn in weary Nights decline
The lost Travellers Dream under the Hill
    1818?

WILLIAM WORDSWORTH

1770–1850

BORN NEAR, and raised in, the English Lake District, Wordsworth was left alone with the visible world at an unnaturally early age. Though he had three brothers and a sister, Dorothy, to whom he was closer than ever he would be to anyone else, he still had to sustain the death of his mother when he was just eight, and of his father when he was thirteen.

From 1787 to 1791 Wordsworth attended St. John's College, Cambridge, where his record was undistinguished. In the summer of 1790 he went on a walking tour of the Alps and France (see *The Prelude* VI) and observed France at the height of its revolutionary hopefulness, which he shared. He returned to France and lived there for a turbulent year (November 1791 to December 1792), during which time he associated himself with the moderate faction of the Revolution, fell in love with Annette Vallon, and fathered their daughter, Caroline. Abandoning both mother and child, and his political friends, he returned to England, to spend five years troubled by guilt and remorse, not only about these near-betrayals, but concerning also his identity as Englishman and as poet. Though the continued presence of Dorothy (she never married) was an essential element in Wordsworth's recovery from this long crisis, the catalyst for his renovation was his best friend, Coleridge, whom he first met early in 1795. Coleridge gave Wordsworth rather more than he took, intellectually and poetically, but in return Wordsworth gave Coleridge something necessary out of his own massive (though still turbulent) emotional strength. Later in 1795 a friend's legacy enabled Wordsworth to free himself from financial burdens. By 1797 Wordsworth had surmounted his crisis, and in the almost-daily company of Coleridge was able to begin upon his mature and characteristic work, first published (anonymously) in 1798 as *Lyrical Ballads, With a Few Other Poems*. The ballads included Coleridge's *Rime of the Ancient Mariner*, and the other poems included "Tintern Abbey." Historically considered, this remains the most important volume of verse in English since the Renaissance, for it began modern poetry, the poetry of the growing inner self.

The birth of this self had preceded Wordsworth, and is located variously by different intellectual historians. It seems clear that the inner self was a Protestant creation, and that before Luther it was prefigured in Catholic thinkers as diverse as Savonarola and the meditative Thomas à Kempis, who wrote *The Imitation of Christ*. In Luther, though, the inner self achieves the kind of prominence that made a writer like Rousseau possible. As the inner self grew, landscape paradoxically began to enter European literature, for the inner self made landscape visible precisely through a devaluation of everything else that the self would not contain. The outer world moved more outward as the inner self grew more inward, until the estrangement between the two worlds produced the phenomenon of Rousseau's ecstatic nature worship. Confronting what had ceased to be a world in which he shared, Rousseau was moved by love and longing for what he had lost. The next and all-important step in poetry was taken by Wordsworth. It could be said that Wordsworth did for literature what Freud was to do for modern psychology, nearly a century later.

The immense burden of Wordsworth's poetry is the contradiction that he understood better than all his followers down to today: self-consciousness is essential for modern poetry, yet self-consciousness is the antagonist of poetry, the demon that needs to be exorcised. Before Wordsworth, poetry had a subject. After Wordsworth, its prevalent subject was the poet's own subjectivity. Before Wordsworth, any poet, professional or amateur, would in some sense choose a subject in order to write a poem. After Wordsworth, this is no longer true, and so a new poetry was born.

Hazlitt, in some ways a more acute critic of Wordsworth than Coleridge (because much more detached), reviewed *The Excursion* in 1814, and said of its poet: "He sees all things in himself," and added that his mind was "conversant only with itself and nature." Lecturing on the "living poets" in 1818, Hazlitt emphasized Wordsworth's astonishing originality, and simply observed that the poet "is his own subject." Rightly associating Wordsworth's poetical revolution with the French Revolution, Hazlitt nevertheless added the stern warning that a poet of Wordsworth's school necessarily manifested an "egotism [that] is in some respects a madness." Yet Wordsworth knew this better than Hazlitt did, as "Resolution and Independence" and *The Prelude* show.

What was Wordsworth's "healing power?" How does his best poetry work so as to save not only the poet himself in his own crises, but so as to have been therapeutic for the imagination of so many poets and readers since? Six generations have passed since Wordsworth experienced his Great Decade (1797–1807), and still the attentive and dedicated reader can learn to find in him the human art he teaches better than any poet before or since, including precursors greater than himself (but no successors, as yet, of his eminence). The art is simply what Keats, Shelley, Arnold, Emerson, and others called it: how to feel. Wordsworth, by a primordial power uncanny in its depths, educates the affective life of his reader. He teaches precisely what he knew he could teach: how to become, within severe limitations, a renovated spirit, free of crippling self-consciousness yet still enjoying the varied gifts of an awakened consciousness. He proposes to observe nature with an eye steadily on the object, and yet not to lose his freedom to the tyranny of the bodily eye, while also preserving the integrity of nature from our profane tendency to practice analysis upon it.

This is the primary Wordsworth of whom Matthew Arnold was the classical critic, the poet "Of blessed consolations in distress, / Of moral strength and intellectual powers, / Of joy in widest commonalty spread—." Arnold superbly located Wordsworth's healing effect in *power,* "the extraordinary power with which Wordsworth feels the joy offered to us in nature, the joy offered to us in the simple primary affections and duties . . . and renders it so as to make us share it." Like Tolstoy at his finest, like the great sages of Judaic and some aspects of Christian tradition, this Wordsworth hallows the commonplace, celebrates the common, human heart by which we live, and the nature that cares for and refreshes that heart.

But there is another Wordsworth, and he is a great poet also, though more problematic and far less heartening. Arnold turned away from the Miltonic, strong, sublime, non-Coleridgean side of Wordsworth, as the critic A. C. Bradley first demonstrated early in the twentieth century. Recent critics have followed Bradley in exploring Wordsworth's uneasiness with nature, his dark sense that nature was a hidden antagonist to the full, Miltonic development of his own imagination. The hidden story of *The Prelude* and of the great crisis poems of 1802 (e.g., "Resolution and Independence" and the "Intimations" ode) is largely concerned with this struggle, and the inability to resolve this conflict between questing self and adherence to nature may be the clue to Wordsworth's rapid, indeed catastrophic, decline after 1807, at the very latest.

Certainly the facts of Wordsworth's own mature biography do little to explain his poetic decay. He settled, with Dorothy, late in 1799, at Grasmere, not far from the beloved scenes of his boyhood. Coleridge settled nearby. Wordsworth married, happily, in 1802, but sorrows began to shadow him. His closest brother, John, drowned in 1805; the friendship with the increasingly unhappy Coleridge began to fade, and largely ended in a dreadful quarrel in 1810. Two of his children died in 1812, and the fear of his own mortality, always strong in him, necessarily augmented. He became outwardly well-off, politically a champion of the established order, and eminently orthodox in the Church of England. He iced over.

But the astonishing poems remained, and cannot die. In them, more than any other in the language before or since, we find ourselves, and this "we" is very nearly universal. The great poems do not champion any cause or urge any vision but one: to know ourselves, sincerely, in our own origins and in what we still are. The hiding places of every person's power, Wordsworth insisted, are in his own past, however painful that past might have been. To live life, and not death-in-life, Wordsworth gently but forcefully advises us to find the natural continuities between what we were and what we are. If he himself never quite became what he might have been, that does not matter. Though he himself could not sustain even the strength he attained, that also does not matter. What matters is that his poetry found a way of showing how much a natural man might do for himself, by the hard discipline of holding himself open both to imagination and to nature.

Tintern Abbey

Here, under Coleridge's direct influence, Wordsworth arrives at his myth of memory. Coming again into the presence of a remembered place, he attains a more complete understanding of his poetic self than he enjoyed before. What he persuades himself he has learned is a principle of reciprocity between himself and nature, a mutual generosity, an exchange of his disinterested love for nature's disinterested beauty. In the poet's recognition of this sharing, there comes into being a state of aesthetic contemplation, in which his will ceases to attempt to relate knowledge of the natural world to discursive knowledge of any kind. Nature is a reality to him, one that he will not murder by dissecting.

Yet this great poem is not a celebration, though it would like to be. It is almost a lament. Wordsworth wants the poem to be about renovation, about carrying the past alive into the present, and so being able to live on into the future with a full sense of continuity. "Tintern Abbey" is all the more powerful for breaking away from Wordsworth's intention. The poem's subject, despite the poet, is memory. Is the story he tells himself about memory a visionary lie? Though he is eager to review his covenant with nature, has he adequate cause to trust that nature will renew her past movements toward him?

The poem does not trust its own answers to these questions. What Emerson, following Coleridge, called the law of compensation now comes into operation. "Nothing is got for nothing," Emerson grimly observed. Wordsworth now *knows* consciously his love for nature, as he begins to know his bond to other men, but this knowing is darkened by shadows of mortality. An urgency enters the second half of the poem, as the poet begins to press for evidences of continuity with the ardors of his earlier self. Simply, he seeks what in religion is called salvation, but his earlier quest is displaced into a wholly naturalistic context. He knows only nature and his own mind; he remembers that nature gave him a more direct joy than he now has, and farther back there was a time when he knew himself only in union with nature. Desperately, he affirms that nature will not betray him, but the deep reverberations of this seminal poem hint distinctly at how troubled he is.

✣   ✣   ✣

Lines

Composed a Few Miles Above Tintern Abbey
On Revisiting the Banks of the Wye During a Tour. July 13, 1798

Five years have passed; five summers, with the length
Of five long winters! and again I hear
These waters, rolling from their mountain-springs
With a soft inland murmur.—Once again
Do I behold these steep and lofty cliffs,
That on a wild secluded scene impress
Thoughts of more deep seclusion; and connect
The landscape with the quiet of the sky.
The day is come when I again repose
10 Here, under this dark sycamore, and view
These plots of cottage-ground, these orchard-tufts,
Which at this season, with their unripe fruits,
Are clad in one green hue, and lose themselves
'Mid groves and copses. Once again I see
These hedge-rows, hardly hedge-rows, little lines
Of sportive wood run wild: these pastoral farms,
Green to the very door; and wreaths of smoke
Sent up, in silence, from among the trees!
With some uncertain notice, as might seem
20 Of vagrant dwellers in the houseless woods,
Or of some Hermit's cave, where by his fire
The Hermit sits alone.

                    These beauteous forms,
Through a long absence, have not been to me
As is a landscape to a blind man's eye:
But oft, in lonely rooms, and 'mid the din
Of towns and cities, I have owed to them
In hours of weariness, sensations sweet,
Felt in the blood, and felt along the heart;
And passing even into my purer mind,
30 With tranquil restoration:—feelings too
Of unremembered pleasure: such, perhaps,
As have no slight or trivial influence
On that best portion of a good man's life,
His little, nameless, unremembered, acts

Of kindness and of love. Nor less, I trust,
To them I may have owed another gift,
Of aspect more sublime; that blessed mood
In which the burthen of the mystery,
In which the heavy and the weary weight
40 Of all this unintelligible world,
Is lightened:—that serene and blessed mood,
In which the affections gently lead us on,—
Until, the breath of this corporeal frame
And even the motion of our human blood
Almost suspended, we are laid asleep
In body, and become a living soul:
While with an eye made quiet by the power
Of harmony, and the deep power of joy,
We see into the life of things.
                        If this
50 Be but a vain belief, yet, oh! how oft—
In darkness and amid the many shapes
Of joyless daylight; when the fretful stir
Unprofitable, and the fever of the world,
Have hung upon the beatings of my heart—
How oft, in spirit, have I turned to thee,
O sylvan Wye! thou wanderer through the woods,
How often has my spirit turned to thee!

        And now, with gleams of half-extinguished thought,
With many recognitions dim and faint,
60 And somewhat of a sad perplexity,
The picture of the mind revives again:
While here I stand, not only with the sense
Of present pleasure, but with pleasing thoughts
That in this moment there is life and food
For future years. And so I dare to hope,
Though changed, no doubt, from what I was when first
I came among these hills; when like a roe
I bounded o'er the mountains, by the sides ·
Of the deep rivers, and the lonely streams,
70 Wherever nature led: more like a man
Flying from something that he dreads than one
Who sought the thing he loved. For nature then
(The coarser pleasures of my boyish days,
And their glad animal movements all gone by)
To me was all in all.—I cannot paint

What then I was. The sounding cataract
Haunted me like a passion: the tall rock,
The mountain, and the deep and gloomy wood,
Their colours and their forms, were then to me
80   An appetite; a feeling and a love,
That had no need of a remoter charm,
By thought supplied, nor any interest
Unborrowed from the eye.—That time is past,
And all its aching joys are now no more,
And all its dizzy raptures. Not for this
Faint I, nor mourn nor murmur; other gifts
Have followed; for such loss, I would believe,
Abundant recompense. For I have learned
To look on nature, not as in the hour
90   Of thoughtless youth; but hearing oftentimes
The still, sad music of humanity,
Nor harsh nor grating, though of ample power
To chasten and subdue. And I have felt
A presence that disturbs me with the joy
Of elevated thoughts; a sense sublime
Of something far more deeply interfused,
Whose dwelling is the light of setting suns,
And the round ocean and the living air,
And the blue sky, and in the mind of man:
100   A motion and a spirit, that impels
All thinking things, all objects of all thought,
And rolls through all things. Therefore am I still
A lover of the meadows and the woods,
And mountains; and of all that we behold
From this green earth; of all the mighty world
Of eye, and ear,—both what they half create,
And what perceive; well pleased to recognize
In nature and the language of the sense
The anchor of my purest thoughts, the nurse,
110   The guide, the guardian of my heart, and soul
Of all my moral being.
            Nor perchance,
If I were not thus taught, should I the more
Suffer my genial spirits to decay:
For thou art with me here upon the banks
Of this fair river; thou my dearest Friend,
My dear, dear Friend; and in thy voice I catch
The language of my former heart, and read

My former pleasures in the shooting lights
Of thy wild eyes. Oh! yet a little while
120   May I behold in thee what I was once,
My dear, dear Sister! and this prayer I make,
Knowing that Nature never did betray
The heart that loved her; 'tis her privilege,
Through all the years of this our life, to lead
From joy to joy: for she can so inform
The mind that is within us, so impress
With quietness and beauty, and so feed
With lofty thoughts, that neither evil tongues,
Rash judgments, nor the sneers of selfish men,
130   Nor greetings where no kindness is, nor all
The dreary intercourse of daily life,
Shall e'er prevail against us, or disturb
Our cheerful faith, that all which we behold
Is full of blessings. Therefore let the moon
Shine on thee in thy solitary walk;
And let the misty mountain-winds be free
To blow against thee: and, in after years,
When these wild ecstasies shall be matured
Into a sober pleasure; when thy mind
140   Shall be a mansion for all lovely forms,
Thy memory be as a dwelling-place
For all sweet sounds and harmonies; oh! then,
If solitude, or fear, or pain, or grief,
Should be thy portion, with what healing thoughts
Of tender joy wilt thou remember me.
And these my exhortations! Nor, perchance—
If I should be where I no more can hear
Thy voice, nor catch from thy wild eyes these gleams
Of past existence—wilt thou then forget
150   That on the banks of this delightful stream
We stood together; and that I, so long
A worshipper of Nature, hither came
Unwearied in that service: rather say
With warmer love—oh! with far deeper zeal
Of holier love. Nor wilt thou then forget,
That after many wanderings, many years
Of absence, these steep woods and lofty cliffs,
And this green pastoral landscape, were to me
More dear, both for themselves and for thy sake!

1798   1798

The Lucy Poems

"Strange fits of passion have I known:"

Strange fits of passion have I known:
And I will dare to tell,
But in the Lover's ear alone,
What once to me befell.

When she I loved looked every day
Fresh as a rose in June,
I to her cottage bent my way,
Beneath an evening-moon.

Upon the moon I fixed my eye,
10 All over the wide lea;
With quickening pace my horse drew nigh
Those paths so dear to me.

And now we reached the orchard-plot;
And, as we climbed the hill,
The sinking moon to Lucy's cot
Came near, and nearer still.

In one of those sweet dreams I slept,
Kind Nature's gentlest boon!
And all the while my eyes I kept
20 On the descending moon.

My horse moved on; hoof after hoof
He raised, and never stopped:
When down behind the cottage roof,
At once, the bright moon dropped.

What fond and wayward thoughts will slide
Into a Lover's head!
'O mercy!' to myself I cried,
'If Lucy should be dead!'

1799   1800

"She dwelt among the untrodden ways"

She dwelt among the untrodden ways
    Beside the springs of Dove,
A Maid whom there were none to praise
    And very few to love:

A violet by a mossy stone
    Half hidden from the eye!
—Fair as a star, when only one
    Is shining in the sky.

She lived unknown, and few could know
10   When Lucy ceased to be;
But she is in her grave, and, oh,
    The difference to me!
    1799   1800

"Three years she grew in sun and shower,"

Three years she grew in sun and shower,
Then Nature said, 'A lovelier flower
On earth was never sown;
This Child I to myself will take;
She shall be mine, and I will make
A Lady of my own.

'Myself will to my darling be
Both law and impulse: and with me
The Girl, in rock and plain,
10 In earth and heaven, in glade and bower,
Shall feel an overseeing power
To kindle or restrain.

'She shall be sportive as the fawn
That wild with glee across the lawn
Or up the mountain springs;
And hers shall be the breathing balm,
And hers the silence and the calm
Of mute insensate things.

'The floating clouds their state shall lend
20 To her; for her the willow bend;
Nor shall she fail to see
Even in the motions of the Storm
Grace that shall mould the Maiden's form
By silent sympathy.

'The stars of midnight shall be dear
To her; and she shall lean her ear
In many a secret place
Where rivulets dance their wayward round,
And beauty born of murmuring sound
30 Shall pass into her face.

'And vital feelings of delight
Shall rear her form to stately height,
Her virgin bosom swell;
Such thoughts to Lucy I will give
While she and I together live
Here in this happy dell.'

Thus Nature spake—The work was done—
How soon my Lucy's race was run!
She died, and left to me
40 This heath, this calm, and quiet scene;
The memory of what has been,
And never more will be.

    1799   1800

"A slumber did my spirit seal;"

A slumber did my spirit seal;
   I had no human fears:
She seemed a thing that could not feel
   The touch of earthly years.

No motion has she now, no force;
   She neither hears nor sees;
Rolled round in earth's diurnal course,
   With rocks, and stones, and trees.

    1799   1800

"I travelled among unknown men,"

I travelled among unknown men,
    In lands beyond the sea;
Nor, England! did I know till then
    What love I bore to thee.

'Tis past, that melancholy dream!
    Nor will I quit thy shore
A second time; for still I seem
    To love thee more and more.

Among thy mountains did I feel
    The joy of my desire;
And she I cherished turned her wheel
    Beside an English fire.

Thy mornings showed, thy nights concealed,
    The bowers where Lucy played;
And thine too is the last green field
    That Lucy's eyes surveyed.

1801   1807

Resolution and Independence

More even than "Tintern Abbey" and the "Intimations of Immortality" ode, this is the archetype that sets the pattern for the modern crisis-lyric, the poem through and in which a poet saves himself for poetry, and by implication for life. In a secularized epiphany or "privileged moment," as Walter Pater was to call it (Wordsworth's own phrase for it, in *The Prelude*, is "spots of time"), the poet receives the equivalent of a "peculiar grace," a "something given" that redeems the time, that allows renovation to begin. Coleridge in Chapter XXII of his *Biographia Literaria* says: "Indeed this fine poem is *especially* characteristic of the author. There is scarce a defect or excellence in his writings of which it would not present a specimen." Something of the defects can be studied in the mad reflecting-glasses of the poem's two greater parodies, Lewis Carroll's "The White Knight's Ballad" and Edward Lear's "Incidents in the Life of My Uncle Arly."

    Wordsworth based the poem on an actual meeting with an old leech-gatherer, and wrote a strong commentary on his poetic intentions in a letter written to Sara Hutchinson on June 14, 1802 (while the poem was still being composed). She had disliked the latter part of the draft she had read. Wordsworth defended his poem with considerable passion:

> I describe myself as having been exalted to the highest pitch of the delight by the joyousness and beauty of Nature and then as depressed, even in the midst of these beautiful objects, to the lowest dejection and despair. A young Poet in the midst of the happiness of Nature is described as overwhelmed by the thought of the miserable reverses which have befallen the happiest of all men, viz Poets—I think of this till I am so deeply impressed by it, that I consider the manner in which I was rescued from my dejection and despair almost as an interposition of Providence. . . . It is in the character of the old man to tell his story in a manner which an *impatient* reader must necessarily feel as tedious. But Good God! Such a figure, in such a place, a pious self-respecting, miserably infirm old man telling such a tale!

Resolution and Independence

I

There was a roaring in the wind all night;
The rain came heavily and fell in floods;
But now the sun is rising calm and bright;
The birds are singing in the distant woods;
Over his own sweet voice the Stock-dove broods;
The Jay makes answer as the Magpie chatters;
And all the air is filled with pleasant noise of waters.

II

All things that love the sun are out of doors;
The sky rejoices in the morning's birth;
The grass is bright with rain-drops;—on the moors
The hare is running races in her mirth;
And with her feet she from the plashy earth
Raises a mist; that, glittering in the sun,
Runs with her all the way, wherever she doth run.

III

I was a Traveller then upon the moor;
I saw the hare that raced about with joy;

I heard the woods and distant waters roar;
Or heard them not, as happy as a boy:
The pleasant season did my heart employ:
My old remembrances went from me wholly;
And all the ways of men, so vain and melancholy.

IV

But, as it sometimes chanceth, from the might
Of joy in minds that can no further go,
As high as we have mounted in delight
In our dejection do we sink as low;
To me that morning did it happen so;
And fears and fancies thick upon me came;
Dim sadness—and blind thoughts, I knew not,
    nor could name.

V

I heard the sky-lark warbling in the sky;
And I bethought me of the playful hare:
Even such a happy Child of earth am I;
Even as these blissful creatures do I fare;
Far from the world I walk, and from all care;
But there may come another day to me—
Solitude, pain of heart, distress, and poverty.

VI

My whole life I have lived in pleasant thought,
As if life's business were a summer mood;
As if all needful things would come unsought
To genial faith, still rich in genial good;
But how can He expect that others should
Build for him, sow for him, and at his call
Love him, who for himself will take no heed at all?

VII

I thought of Chatterton, the marvellous Boy,
The sleepless Soul that perished in his pride;
Of Him who walked in glory and in joy
Following his plough, along the mountain-side:
By our own spirits are we deified:
We Poets in our youth begin in gladness;
But thereof come in the end despondency
    and madness.

VIII

50   Now, whether it were by peculiar grace,
A leading from above, a something given,
Yet it befell that, in this lonely place,
When I with these untoward thoughts had striven,
Beside a pool bare to the eye of heaven
I saw a Man before me unawares:
The oldest man he seemed that ever wore grey hairs.

IX

As a huge stone is sometimes seen to lie
Couched on the bald top of an eminence;
Wonder to all who do the same espy,
60   By what means it could thither come, and whence;
So that it seems a thing endued with sense:
Like a sea-beast crawled forth, that on a shelf
Of rock or sand reposeth, there to sun itself;

X

Such seemed this Man, not all alive nor dead,
Nor all asleep—in his extreme old age:
His body was bent double, feet and head
Coming together in life's pilgrimage;
As if some dire constraint of pain, or rage
Of sickness felt by him in times long past,
70   A more than human weight upon his frame had cast.

XI

Himself he propped, limbs, body, and pale face,
Upon a long grey staff of shaven wood:
And, still as I drew near with gentle pace,
Upon the margin of that moorish flood
Motionless as a cloud the old Man stood,
That heareth not the loud winds when they call;
And moveth all together, if it move at all.

XII

At length, himself unsettling, he the pond
Stirred with his staff, and fixedly did look
80   Upon the muddy water, which he conned,
As if he had been reading in a book:
And now a stranger's privilege I took;

And, drawing to his side, to him did say,
'This morning gives us promise of a glorious day.'

XIII

A gentle answer did the old Man make,
In courteous speech which forth he slowly drew:
And him with further words I thus bespake,
'What occupation do you there pursue?
This is a lonesome place for one like you.'
90   Ere he replied, a flash of mild surprise
Broke from the sable orbs of his yet-vivid eyes.

XIV

His words came feebly, from a feeble chest,
But each in solemn order followed each,
With something of a lofty utterance drest—
Choice word and measured phrase, above the reach
Of ordinary men; a stately speech;
Such as grave Livers do in Scotland use,
Religious men, who give to God and man their dues.

XV

He told, that to these waters he had come
100   To gather leeches, being old and poor:
Employment hazardous and wearisome!
And he had many hardships to endure:
From pond to pond he roamed, from moor to moor;
Housing, with God's good help, by choice or chance;
And in this way be gained an honest maintenance.

XVI

The old Man still stood talking by my side;
But now his voice to me was like a stream
Scarce heard; nor word from word could I divide;
And the whole body of the Man did seem
110   Like one whom I had met with in a dream;
Or like a man from some far region sent,
To give me human strength, by apt admonishment.

XVII

My former thoughts returned: the fear that kills;
And hope that is unwilling to be fed;

Cold, pain, and labour, and all fleshly ills;
And mighty Poets in their misery dead.
—Perplexed, and longing to be comforted,
My question eagerly did I renew,
'How is it that you live, and what is it you do?'

XVIII

120 He with a smile did then his words repeat;
And said that, gathering leeches, far and wide
He travelled; stirring thus about his feet
The waters of the pools where they abide.
'Once I could meet with them on every side;
But they have dwindled long by slow decay;
Yet still I persevere, and find them where I may.'

XIX

While he was talking thus, the lonely place,
The old Man's shape, and speech—all troubled me:
In my mind's eye I seemed to see him pace
130 About the weary moors continually,
Wandering about alone and silently.
While I these thoughts within myself pursued,
He, having made a pause, the same discourse renewed.

XX

And soon with this he other matter blended,
Cheerfully uttered, with demeanour kind,
But stately in the main; and when he ended,
I could have laughed myself to scorn to find
In that decrepit Man so firm a mind.
'God,' said I, 'be my help and stay secure;
140 I'll think of the Leech-gatherer on the lonely moor!'

1802   1807

Ode: Intimations of Immortality from Recollections of Early Childhood

It has been maintained, with justice, that after Milton's *Lycidas* this is the most important shorter poem in the language; certainly it has been one of the most influential upon poets coming after Wordsworth. The Great

Ode's effect can be traced in Coleridge, Shelley, Keats, Byron, Clare, Tennyson, Browning, Arnold, Hopkins, Swinburne, and Yeats, among many others, and in American poetry throughout the entire succession that moves between Emerson and Wallace Stevens.

Lionel Trilling succinctly observed that the Ode is not about growing old, but about growing up, with its mingling of painful loss and hard-won gain. Whether, and in what sense, the Ode is also a poem about mortality (rather than about immortality at all) is in perpetual dispute. Wordsworth himself said that "this poem rests entirely upon two recollections of childhood: one that of a splendour in the objects of sense which is passed away; and the other an indisposition to bend to the law of death, as applying to our own particular case." The poet's more general comment on the poem is of great value:

> Two years at least passed between the writing of the first four stanzas and the remaining part. To the attentive and competent reader the whole sufficiently explains itself, but there is no harm in adverting here to particular feelings or experiences of my own mind on which the structure of the poem partly rests. Nothing was more difficult for me in childhood than to admit the notion of death as a state applicable to my own being . . . it was not so much from the source of animal vivacity that my difficulty came as from a sense of the indomitableness of the spirit within me. I used to brood over the stories of Enoch and Elijah, and almost to persuade myself that, whatever might become of others, I should be translated in something of the same way to heaven. With a feeling congenial to this, I was often unable to think of external things as having external existence, and I communed with all that I saw as something not apart from, but inherent in, my own immaterial nature. Many times while going to school have I grasped at a wall or a tree to recall myself from this abyss of idealism to the reality. At that time I was afraid of such processes. In later periods of life I have deplored, as we have all reason to do, a subjugation of an opposite character, and have rejoiced over the remembrances, as is expressed in the lines, "obstinate questionings," etc. To that dreamlike vividness and splendour which invest objects of sight in childhood, everyone, I believe, if he would look back, could bear testimony. . . .

Though Wordsworth goes on to deny that the Ode argues for the preexistence of the soul, his denial is ambivalent, since he asserts that there is nothing in the Christian revelation to contradict it. Despite scholarly tradition, which has found "sources" for the Ode in Plato's *Phaedrus* and his *Phaedo*, it is well to remember that Wordsworth actually denied any Platonic influence.

Structurally, the Ode is in three parts, with stanzas I through IV stating the problem of Wordsworth's sense of loss, and stanzas V through VIII and IX through XI giving contrary reactions to that sense. Trilling's comment has justly attained a kind of classical status:

> That there should be ambivalence in Wordsworth's response to this diminution is quite natural, and the two answers, that of stanzas V–VIII and that of stanzas IX–XI, comprise both the resistance to and the acceptance of growth. Inevitably we resist change and turn back with passionate nostalgia to the stage we are leaving. Still, we fulfill ourselves by choosing what is painful and difficult and necessary, and we develop by moving toward death. In short, organic development is a hard paradox which Wordsworth is stating in the discrepant answers of the second part of the Ode.

Ode

Intimations of Immortality from Recollections of Early Childhood

The Child is father of the Man;
And I could wish my days to be
Bound each to each by natural piety.
PAULÒ MAJORA CANAMUS

I

There was a time when meadow, grove, and stream,
The earth, and every common sight,
    To me did seem
    Apparelled in celestial light,
The glory and the freshness of a dream.
It is not now as it hath been of yore;—
    Turn wheresoe'er I may,
    By night or day,
The things which I have seen I now can see no more.

II

10
    The Rainbow comes and goes,
    And lovely is the Rose,
    The Moon doth with delight

Look around her when the heavens are bare;
      Waters on a starry night
      Are beautiful and fair;
   The sunshine is a glorious birth;
   But yet I know, where'er I go,
That there hath past away a glory from the earth.

   III
Now, while the birds thus sing a joyous song,
     And while the young lambs bound
       As to the tabor's sound,
To me alone there came a thought of grief:
A timely utterance gave that thought relief,
     And I again am strong:
The cataracts blow their trumpets from the steep;
No more shall grief of mine the season wrong;
I hear the Echoes through the mountains throng,
The Winds come to me from the fields of sleep,
      And all the earth is gay;
            Land and sea
     Give themselves up to jollity,
      And with the heart of May
    Doth every Beast keep holiday;—
      Thou Child of Joy,
Shout round me, let me hear thy shouts, thou happy Shepherd-boy!

   IV
Ye blessèd Creatures, I have heard the call
   Ye to each other make; I see
The heavens laugh with you in your jubilee;
   My heart is at your festival,
     My head hath its coronal,
The fulness of your bliss, I feel—I feel it all.
    Oh evil day! if I were sullen
    While Earth herself is adorning,
     This sweet May-morning,
   And the Children are culling
     On every side,
    In a thousand valleys far and wide,
    Fresh flowers; while the sun shines warm,
And the Babe leaps up on his Mother's arm:—
    I hear, I hear, with joy I hear!
    —But there's a Tree, of many, one,

A single Field which I have looked upon,
Both of them speak of something that is gone:
            The Pansy at my feet
            Doth the same tale repeat:
Whither is fled the visionary gleam?
Where is it now, the glory and the dream?

        V

Our birth is but a sleep and a forgetting:
The Soul that rises with us, our life's Star,
60   Hath had elsewhere its setting,
                And cometh from afar:
            Not in entire forgetfulness,
            And not in utter nakedness,
But trailing clouds of glory do we come
            From God, who is our home:
Heaven lies about us in our infancy!
Shades of the prison-house begin to close
            Upon the growing Boy,
                    But He
70   Beholds the light, and whence it flows,
            He sees it in his joy;
The Youth, who daily farther from the east
            Must travel, still is Nature's Priest,
            And by the vision splendid
            Is on his way attended;
At length the Man perceives it die away,
And fade into the light of common day.

        VI

Earth fills her lap with pleasures of her own;
Yearnings she hath in her own natural kind,
80   And, even with something of a Mother's mind,
            And no unworthy aim,
            The homely Nurse doth all she can
To make her Foster-child, her Inmate Man,
            Forget the glories he hath known,
And that imperial palace whence he came.

        VII

Behold the Child among his new-born blisses,
A six years' Darling of a pigmy size!
See, where 'mid work of his own hand he lies,

Fretted by sallies of his mother's kisses,
90 With light upon him from his father's eyes!
See, at his feet, some little plan or chart,
Some fragment from his dream of human life,
Shaped by himself with newly-learned art;
   A wedding or a festival,
   A mourning or a funeral;
    And this hath now his heart,
    And unto this he frames his song:
    Then will he fit his tongue
To dialogues of business, love, or strife;
100   But it will not be long
    Ere this be thrown aside,
    And with new joy and pride
The little Actor cons another part;
Filling from time to time his 'humorous stage'
With all the Persons, down to palsied Age,
That Life brings with her in her equipage;
   As if his whole vocation
   Were endless imitation.

  VIII
Thou, whose exterior semblance doth belie
110   Thy Soul's immensity;
Thou best Philosopher, who yet dost keep
Thy heritage, thou Eye among the blind,
That, deaf and silent, read'st the eternal deep,
Haunted for ever by the eternal mind,—
   Mighty Prophet! Seer blest!
   On whom those truths do rest,
Which we are toiling all our lives to find,
In darkness lost, the darkness of the grave;
Thou, over whom thy Immortality
120 Broods like the Day, a Master o'er a Slave,
A Presence which is not to be put by;
Thou little Child, yet glorious in the might
Of heaven-born freedom on thy being's height,
Why with such earnest pains dost thou provoke
The years to bring the inevitable yoke,
Thus blindly with thy blessedness at strife?
Full soon thy Soul shall have her earthly freight,
And custom lie upon thee with a weight,
Heavy as frost, and deep almost as life!

IX

130
        O joy! that in our embers
        Is something that doth live,
        That nature yet remembers
        What was so fugitive!
The thought of our past years in me doth breed
Perpetual benediction: not indeed
For that which is most worthy to be blest;
Delight and liberty, the simple creed
Of Childhood, whether busy or at rest,
With new-fledged hope still fluttering in his breast:—

140
        Not for these I raise
        The song of thanks and praise;
    But for those obstinate questionings
    Of sense and outward things,
    Fallings from us, vanishings;
    Blank misgivings of a Creature
Moving about in worlds not realized,
High instincts before which our mortal Nature
Did tremble like a guilty Thing surprised:
    But for those first affections,

150
    Those shadowy recollections,
    Which, be they what they may,
Are yet the fountain light of all our day,
Are yet a master light of all our seeing;
    Uphold us, cherish, and have power to make
Our noisy years seem moments in the being
Of the eternal Silence; truths that wake,
    To perish never;
Which neither listlessness, nor mad endeavour,
    Nor Man nor Boy,

160
Nor all that is at enmity with joy,
Can utterly abolish or destroy!
    Hence in a season of calm weather
    Though inland far we be,
Our Souls have sight of that immortal sea
    Which brought us hither,
    Can in a moment travel thither,
And see the Children sport upon the shore,
And hear the mighty waters rolling evermore.

X

Then sing, ye Birds, sing, sing a joyous song!
170   And let the young Lambs bound
          As to the tabor's sound!
We in thought will join your throng,
        Ye that pipe and ye that play,
        Ye that through your hearts today
        Feel the gladness of the May!
What though the radiance which was once so bright
Be now for ever taken from my sight,
        Though nothing can bring back the hour
Of splendour in the grass, of glory in the flower;
180   We will grieve not, rather find
        Strength in what remains behind;
        In the primal sympathy
        Which having been must ever be;
        In the soothing thoughts that spring
        Out of human suffering;
        In the faith that looks through death,
In years that bring the philosophic mind.

XI

And O, ye Fountains, Meadows, Hills, and Groves,
Forebode not any severing of our loves!
190 Yet in my heart of hearts I feel your might;
I only have relinquished one delight
To live beneath your more habitual sway.
I love the Brooks which down their channels fret,
Even more than when I tripped lightly as they;
The innocent brightness of a new-born Day
        Is lovely yet;
The Clouds that gather round the setting sun
Do take a sober colouring from an eye
That hath kept watch o'er man's mortality;
200 Another race hath been, and other palms are won.
Thanks to the human heart by which we live,
Thanks to its tenderness, its joys, and fears,
To me the meanest flower that blows can give
Thoughts that do often lie too deep for tears.

    1802–1804   1807

The Solitary Reaper

Behold her, single in the field,
Yon solitary Highland Lass!
Reaping and singing by herself;
Stop here, or gently pass!
Alone she cuts and binds the grain,
And sings a melancholy strain;
O listen! for the Vale profound
Is overflowing with the sound.

No Nightingale did ever chaunt
10   More welcome notes to weary bands
Of travellers in some shady haunt,
Among Arabian sands:
A voice so thrilling ne'er was heard
In spring-time from the Cuckoo-bird,
Breaking the silence of the seas
Among the farthest Hebrides.

Will no one tell me what she sings?—
Perhaps the plaintive numbers flow
For old, unhappy, far-off things,
20   And battles long ago:
Or is it some more humble lay,
Familiar matter of today?
Some natural sorrow, loss, or pain,
That has been, and may be again?

Whate'er the theme, the Maiden sang
As if her song could have no ending;
I saw her singing at her work,
And o'er the sickle bending:—
I listened, motionless and still;
30   And, as I mounted up the hill,
The music in my heart I bore,
Long after it was heard no more.

      1805   1807

The Prelude

The first version of this internalized romance was completed in 1805, but Wordsworth refused to publish the poem, and resented Coleridge's publication of "To William Wordsworth," the poem giving his reactions at having heard Wordsworth read aloud this major work. Wordsworth revised it over several decades, and the 1850 version, published posthumously, is rhetorically superior to the 1805 text, and is the source of the substantial selections that follow. Yet Wordsworth's reasons for declining publication were not stylistic. "The Poem to Coleridge," as he always called it (the title *The Prelude* was chosen by his widow), is the summation of his earlier self, the central poem of his Great Decade (1797–1807). The poet aged very quickly, and only a double handful of strong poems came out of the second half of his life. Though he would not have accepted such a judgment, something in him was unable to confront his own earlier self. He could not abandon *The Prelude,* but also he could not live with it as a public presence. Perhaps his sense of survival compelled him to keep the poem to himself, as a talisman against death. With Wordsworth, massive simplicity is usually the accurate formula for understanding; perhaps he just did not want to be reminded, or have others reminded, of how much he had lost.

The Prelude is not a "confessional" poem, as is so much recent verse in America. Its subject is subjectivity, and the poet maps the growth of his consciousness in the faith that he is wholly representative of the best potentialities of mankind. Unlike St. Augustine, whose crises were resolved by the realization he was hardly alone in the universe, but shared it with God as well as with other men, Wordsworth is essentially alone with the universe. If *The Prelude* is a religious poem, then the religion is not quite Christianity, though it is certainly closer to Christianity than to the natural religion of eighteenth-century England or of Rousseau. The God of *The Prelude* is neither nature nor Wordsworth's imagination but an unnamed third presence which, at crucial moments, can subsume both. Yet *The Prelude* is not a quest after that presence, or a quest after nature. It is, like some works of Ruskin and Proust and Beckett after it, a search for lost time, a journey seeking a remembered world. That world belonged to imagination, and Wordsworth finds it again by returning to a perception that was also creation, a way of thinking that was a way of recognition.

The persistent theme of *The Prelude* is the power of the poet's mind over the universe it inhabits. This power is so great that it could be saved for the discipline of poetry, Wordsworth believed, only because nature worked to subdue and chasten it. Wordsworth feared the strength of his own imagination, and showed himself the terror of such strength in figures like Margaret and the Solitary of *The Excursion,* and in the dream-figure of the Arab in Book V of *The Prelude.* His imagination pressed for autonomy, as against nature, and would have been wholly and dangerously free of nature had Wordsworth yielded to it. He did not, but this did not make him only a nature poet, as *The Prelude* shows throughout. The poem's theme, like that of "Tintern Abbey," is not the humanizing of nature (a more Coleridgean ambition) and not the naturalizing of the human imagination (Arnold's interpretation of Wordsworth). The poet knows he is wholly apart from nature, once he is mature, but he confronts in nature presences from whom he fears (and cannot accept) estrangement. His theme is the tempering of imagination by nature, an educational process that leads to renovation, and to a balanced power of imagining that neither yields to a universe of decay nor seeks (as Blake did) to burn through that universe.

from The Prelude

Or, Growth of a Poet's Mind
An Autobiographical Poem

from Book First

INTRODUCTION — CHILDHOOD
AND SCHOOL-TIME

O there is blessing in this gentle breeze,
A visitant that while it fans my cheek
Doth seem half-conscious of the joy it brings
From the green fields, and from yon azure sky.
Whate'er its mission, the soft breeze can come
To none more grateful than to me; escaped
From the vast city, where I long had pined
A discontented sojourner: now free,
Free as a bird to settle where I will.
What dwelling shall receive me? in what vale
Shall be my harbour? underneath what grove
Shall I take up my home? and what clear stream
Shall with its murmur lull me into rest?
The earth is all before me. With a heart
Joyous, nor scared at its own liberty,
I look about; and should the chosen guide

Be nothing better than a wandering cloud,
I cannot miss my way. I breathe again!
Trances of thought and mountings of the mind
20   Come fast upon me: it is shaken off,
That burthen of my own unnatural self,
The heavy weight of many a weary day
Not mine, and such as were not made for me.
Long months of peace (if such bold word accord
With any promises of human life),
Long months of ease and undisturbed delight
Are mine in prospect; whither shall I turn,
By road or pathway, or through trackless field,
Up hill or down, or shall some floating thing
30   Upon the river point me out my course?

· · ·

Was it for this
270   That one, the fairest of all rivers, loved
To blend his murmurs with my nurse's song,
And, from his alder shades and rocky falls,
And from his fords and shallows, sent a voice
That flowed along my dreams? For this, didst thou,
O Derwent! winding among grassy holms
Where I was looking on, a babe in arms,
Make ceaseless music that composed my thoughts
To more than infant softness, giving me
Amid the fretful dwellings of mankind
280   A foretaste, a dim earnest, of the calm
That Nature breathes among the hills and groves.
When he had left the mountains and received
On his smooth breast the shadow of those towers
That yet survive, a shattered monument
Of feudal sway, the bright blue river passed
Along the margin of our terrace walk;
A tempting playmate whom we dearly loved.
Oh, many a time have I, a five years' child,
In a small mill-race severed from his stream,
290   Made one long bathing of a summer's day;
Basked in the sun, and plunged and basked again
Alternate, all a summer's day, or scoured
The sandy fields, leaping through flowery groves
Of yellow ragwort; or when rock and hill,
The woods, and distant Skiddaw's lofty height,

Were bronzed with deepest radiance, stood alone
Beneath the sky, as if I had been born
On Indian plains, and from my mother's hut
Had run abroad in wantonness, to sport
300   A naked savage, in the thunder shower.

from Book Sixth

Yet still in me with those soft luxuries
Mixed something of stern mood, an under-thirst
Of vigour seldom utterly allayed.
560   And from that source how different a sadness
Would issue, let one incident make known.
When from the Vallais we had turned, and clomb
Along the Simplon's steep and rugged road,
Following a band of muleteers, we reached
A halting-place, where all together took
Their noon-tide meal. Hastily rose our guide,
Leaving us at the board; awhile we lingered,
Then paced the beaten downward way that led
Right to a rough stream's edge, and there broke off;
570   The only track now visible was one
That from the torrent's further brink held forth
Conspicuous invitation to ascend
A lofty mountain. After brief delay
Crossing the unbridged stream, that road we took,
And clomb with eagerness, till anxious fears
Intruded, for we failed to overtake
Our comrades gone before. By fortunate chance,
While every moment added doubt to doubt,
A peasant met us, from whose mouth we learned
580   That to the spot which had perplexed us first
We must descend, and there should find the road,
Which in the stony channel of the stream
Lay a few steps, and then along its banks;
And, that our future course, all plain to sight,
Was downwards, with the current of that stream.
Loth to believe what we so grieved to hear,
For still we had hopes that pointed to the clouds,
We questioned him again, and yet again;
But every word that from the peasant's lips
590   Came in reply, translated by our feelings,
Ended in this,—*that we had crossed the Alps.*

Imagination—here the Power so called
Through sad incompetence of human speech,
That awful Power rose from the mind's abyss
Like an unfathered vapour that enwraps,
At once, some lonely traveller, I was lost;
Halted without an effort to break through;
But to my conscious soul I now can say—
'I recognise thy glory': in such strength
600 Of usurpation, when the light of sense
Goes out, but with a flash that has revealed
The invisible world, doth greatness make abode,
There harbours; whether we be young or old,
Our destiny, our being's heart and home,
Is with infinitude, and only there;
With hope it is, hope that can never die,
Effort, and expectation, and desire,
And something evermore about to be.
Under such banners militant, the soul
610 Seeks for no trophies, struggles for no spoils
That may attest her prowess, blest in thoughts
That are their own perfection and reward,
Strong in herself and in beatitude
That hides her, like the mighty flood of Nile
Poured from his fount of Abyssinian clouds
To fertilise the whole Egyptian plain.

.   .   .

from Book Fourteenth

It was a close, warm, breezeless summer night,
Wan, dull, and glaring, with a dripping fog
Low-hung and thick that covered all the sky;
But, undiscouraged, we began to climb
The mountain-side. The mist soon girt us round,
And, after ordinary travellers' talk
With our conductor, pensively we sank
Each into commerce with his private thoughts:
Thus did we breast the ascent, and by myself
20 Was nothing either seen or heard that checked
Those musings or diverted, save that once
The shepherd's lurcher, who, among the crags,
Had to his joy unearthed a hedgehog, teased
His coiled-up prey with barkings turbulent.

This small adventure, for even such it seemed
In that wild place and at the dead of night,
Being over and forgotten, on we wound
In silence as before. With forehead bent
Earthward, as if in opposition set
30 Against an enemy, I panted up
With eager pace, and no less eager thoughts.
Thus might we wear a midnight hour away,
Ascending at loose distance each from each,
And I, as chanced, the foremost of the band;
When at my feet the ground appeared to brighten,
And with a step or two seemed brighter still;
Nor was time given to ask or learn the cause,
For instantly a light upon the turf
Fell like a flash, and lo! as I looked up,
40 The Moon hung naked in a firmament
Of azure without cloud, and at my feet
Rested a silent sea of hoary mist.
A hundred hills their dusky backs upheaved
All over this still ocean; and beyond,
Far, far beyond, the solid vapours stretched,
In headlands, tongues, and promontory shapes,
Into the main Atlantic, that appeared
To dwindle, and give up his majesty,
Usurped upon far as the sight could reach.
50 Not so the ethereal vault; encroachment none
Was there, nor loss; only the inferior stars
Had disappeared, or shed a fainter light
In the clear presence of the full-orbed Moon,
Who, from her sovereign elevation, gazed
Upon the billowy ocean, as it lay
All meek and silent, save that through a rift—
Not distant from the shore whereon we stood,
A fixed, abysmal, gloomy, breathing-place—
Mounted the roar of waters, torrents, streams
60 Innumerable, roaring with one voice!
Heard over earth and sea, and, in that hour,
For so it seemed, felt by the starry heavens.

.   .   .

430   Oh! yet a few short years of useful life,
And all will be complete, thy race be run,

Thy monument of glory will be raised;
Then, though (too weak to tread the ways of truth)
This age fall back to old idolatry,
Though men return to servitude as fast
As the tide ebbs, to ignominy and shame
By nations sink together, we shall still
Find solace—knowing what we have learnt to know,
Rich in true happiness if allowed to be
440   Faithful alike in forwarding a day
Of firmer trust, joint labourers in the work
(Should Providence such grace to us vouchsafe)
Of their deliverance, surely yet to come.
Prophets of Nature, we to them will speak
A lasting inspiration, sanctified
By reason, blest by faith: what we have loved,
Others will love, and we will teach them how;
Instruct them how the mind of man becomes
A thousand times more beautiful than the earth
450   On which he dwells, above this frame of things
(Which, 'mid all revolution in the hopes
And fears of men, doth still remain unchanged)
In beauty exalted, as it is itself
Of quality and fabric more divine.

  1799–1805   1850

SAMUEL TAYLOR COLERIDGE

1772–1834

COLERIDGE, the youngest of fourteen children of a country clergyman, was a precocious and lonely child, almost a changeling in his own family. Early a dreamer and (as he said) a "character," he suffered the loss of his father (who had loved him best) when he was only nine. At Christ's Hospital in London, soon after his father's death, he found an excellent school that gave him the intellectual nurture he needed, as well as a lifelong friend in the future essayist Charles Lamb. Early a poet, he fell deeply in love with Mary Evans, a schoolfellow's sister, but nothing came of it.

At Jesus College, Cambridge, Coleridge started well, but temperamentally he was not suited to academic discipline, and failed of distinction. Fleeing Cambridge, and much in debt, he enlisted in the cavalry under the immortal name of Silas Tomkyn Comberbacke, but kept falling off his horse. Though he proved useful to his fellow dragoons at writing love letters, he was good for little else but stable-cleaning, and the cavalry allowed his brothers to buy him out. He returned to Cambridge, but his characteristic guilt impeded academic labor, and when he abandoned Cambridge in 1794 he had no degree.

A penniless young poet, radical in politics, original in religion, he fell in with the then equally radical bard Robert Southey, remembered today as the Conservative Laureate constantly savaged in Byron's satirical verse. Like our contemporary communards, the two poetical youths projected what they named a Pantisocracy. With the right young ladies, and other choice spirits, they would found a communistic agrarian-literary settlement on the banks of the Susquehanna in exotic Pennsylvania. At Southey's urging, Coleridge made a Pantisocratic engagement to the not very brilliant Miss Sara Fricker, whose sister Southey was to marry. Pantisocracy died at birth, and Coleridge in time woke up to find himself unsuitably married, the largest misfortune of his life.

He turned to Wordsworth, whom he had met early in 1795. Coleridge's poetry influenced Wordsworth's, and helped Wordsworth attain his characteristic mode. It is not too much to say that Coleridge's poetry disappeared into Wordsworth's. We remember *Lyrical Ballads* (1798) as Wordsworth's book, yet about a third of it (in length) was Coleridge's, and "Tintern Abbey," the crown of the volume except for *The Ancient Mariner,* is immensely indebted to Coleridge's "Frost at Midnight." Nor is there much evidence of Wordsworth's admiring or encouraging his friend's poetry. Toward *The Ancient Mariner* he was always very grudging, and he was discomfited (but inevitably so) by both "Dejection: An Ode" and "To William Wordsworth." Selfless where Wordsworth's poetry was concerned, Coleridge had to suffer his closest friend's neglect of Coleridge's own poetic ambitions.

This is not an easy matter to be fair about, since literature necessarily is as much a matter of personality as it is of character. Coleridge, like Keats (and to certain readers, Shelley) is lovable. Byron is at least always fascinating, and Blake in his lonely magnificence is a hero of the imagination.

But Wordsworth's personality, like Milton's or Dante's, does not stimulate affection for the poet in the common reader. Coleridge has, as Walter Pater observed, a "peculiar charm"; he seems to lend himself to myths of failure, which is astonishing when the totality of his work is contemplated.

Yet it is his life, and his self-abandonment of his poetic ambitions, that continue to convince us that we ought to find in him parables of the failure of genius. His best poetry was all written in the year and a half in which he saw Wordsworth daily (1797–1798); yet even it, with the single exception of *The Ancient Mariner,* is fragmentary. The pattern of his life is fragmentary also. When he received an annuity from the Wedgwood family, he left Wordsworth and Dorothy to study language and philosophy in Germany (1798–1799). Soon after returning, his miserable middle years began, though he was only twenty-seven. He moved near the Wordsworths again, and fell in love, permanently and unhappily, with Sara Hutchinson, whose sister Mary was to become Wordsworth's wife in 1802. His own marriage was hopeless, and his health rapidly deteriorated, perhaps for psychological reasons. To help endure the pain he began to drink laudanum, liquid opium, and thus contracted an addiction he never entirely cast off. In 1804, seeking better health, he went to work in Malta, but returned two years later in the worst condition of his life. Separating from his wife, he moved to London, and began another career as lecturer, general man of letters, and periodical editor, while his miseries augmented. The inevitable quarrel with Wordsworth in 1810 was ostensibly reconciled in 1812, but real friendship was not reestablished until 1828.

From 1816 on, Coleridge lived in the household of a physician, James Gillman, so as to be able to keep working, and thus avoid total breakdown. Prematurely aged, his poetry over, Coleridge entered into a major last phase as critic and philosopher, upon which his historical importance depends; but this, like his earlier prose achievements, is beyond the scope of an introduction to his poetry. It remains to ask, what was his achievement as a poet, and extraordinary as that was, why did his poetry effectively cease after about 1807? Wordsworth went on with poetry after 1807, but mostly very badly. The few poems Coleridge wrote from the age of thirty-five on are powerful but occasional. Did the poetic will fail in him, since his imaginative powers remained always fresh?

Coleridge's large poetic ambitions included the writing of a philosophic epic on the origin of evil, and a sequence of hymns to the sun, moon, and elements. These high plans died, slowly but definitively, and were replaced by the dream of a philosophic *opus maximum,* a huge work of synthesis that would reconcile German Idealist philosophy with the orthodox truths of Christianity. Though only fragments of this work were ever written, much was done in its place: speculations on theology, political theory, and criticism that had a profound influence on conservative British thought in the Victorian period, and in quite another way on the American Transcendentalism led by Emerson and Theodore Parker.

Coleridge's actual achievement as poet divides into two diverse groups, remarkable because they are almost simultaneous. The daemonic group, necessarily more famous, is the triad of *The Ancient Mariner,* "Christabel," and "Kubla Khan." The conversational group includes the conversation-poems proper, of which "The Eolian Harp" and "Frost at Midnight" are the most important, as well as the irregular ode "Dejection" and "To William Wordsworth." The late fragments "Limbo" and "Ne Plus Ultra" mark a kind of return to the daemonic mode. To have written only nine poems that really matter, for a poet of Coleridge's gifts, is a sorrow, but the uniqueness of the two groups partly compensates for the slenderness of the canon.

The daemonic poems break through the orthodox censor set up by Coleridge's moral fears of his own imaginative impulses. Unifying the group is a magical quest-pattern which intends as its goal a reconciliation between the poet's self-consciousness and a higher order of being, associated with divine forgiveness, but this reconciliation fortunately lies beyond the border of all these poems. The Mariner attains a state of purgation, but cannot get beyond that process: Christabel is violated by Geraldine, but this too is a purgation, rather than damnation, as her absolute innocence is her only flaw. Coleridge himself, in the most piercing moment in his poetry, is tempted to assume the state of an Apollo-rebirth, the youth with flashing eyes and floating hair in "Kubla Khan," but he withdraws from his vision of a poet's paradise, judging it to be only another purgatory.

The conversational group, though so immensely different in mode, speaks more directly of an allied theme: the desire to go home, not to the past, but to what Hart Crane beautifully called "an improved infancy." Each of these poems, like the daemonic group, verges upon a kind of vicarious and purgatorial atonement, in which Coleridge must fail or suffer so that someone he loves may succeed or experience joy. There is a subdued implication that somehow the poet will yet be accepted into a true home this side of the grave, if he can perfect an atonement.

Where Wordsworth, in his primordial power, masters the subjective world, and aids his readers in the difficult art of feeling, Coleridge deliberately courts defeat by his own subjectivity, and is content to be confessional. But, though he cannot help us to feel, as Wordsworth does, he gives us to understand how deeply felt his own sense of reality is. Though in a way his poetry is a testament of defeat, a yielding to the anxiety of influence, and to the fear of self-glorification, it is one of the most enduringly poignant of such testaments that literature affords us.

The Rime of the Ancient Mariner

First published in *Lyrical Ballads,* this is the revised version, to which the marginal glosses were added in 1816; Coleridge's most helpful comment on the poem was recorded in 1830, in reply to the celebrated Bluestocking, Mrs. Barbauld, who had objected that the poem lacked a moral: "I told her that in my own judgement the poem had too much; and that the only, or chief fault, if I might say so, was the obtrusion of the moral sentiment so openly on the reader as a principle or cause of action in a work of pure imagination. It ought to have had no more moral than the *Arabian Nights'* tale of the merchant's sitting down to eat dates by the side of a well and throwing the shells aside, and lo! a genie starts up and says he *must* kill the aforesaid merchant *because* one of the date shells had, it seems, put out the eye of the genie's son."

   The Ancient Mariner has a power that is beyond any moral sentiments whatsoever. It cannot be said that the Mariner has been purged or saved by his terrible experiences. Indeed, he has become eternally doomed to keep telling his own story. There is a repetition-compulsion in this, on his part, but certainly not on Coleridge's. It is scarcely possible to say what the inner relation of Coleridge to his masterpiece might be. The poem's high point comes when the Mariner blesses the water snakes, moved by their vitality and beauty. This blessing is unaware of itself, in the Mariner, but certainly not in Coleridge.

ᴠ   ᴠ   ᴠ

The Rime of the Ancient Mariner

In Seven Parts

> Facile credo, plures esse Naturas invisibiles quam visibiles in rerum universitate. Sed horum omnium familiam quis nobis enarrabit? et gradus et cognationes et discrimina et singulorum munera? Quid agunt? quae loca habitant? Harum rerum notitiam semper ambivit ingenium humanum, nunquam attigit. Juvat, interea, non diffiteor, quandoque in animo, tanquam in tabula, majoris et melioris mundi imag-

inem contemplari: ne mens assuefacta hodiernae vitae minutiis se contrahat nimis,
et tota subsidat in pusillas cogitationes. Sed veritati interea invigilandum est,
modusque servandus, ut certa ab incertis, diem a nocte, distinguamus.

T. BURNET, *ARCHAEOL. PHIL.* P. 68

Argument

How a Ship having passed the Line was driven by storms to the cold Country
towards the South Pole; and how from thence she made her course to the tropical Latitude of the Great Pacific Ocean; and of the strange things that befell;
and in what manner the Ancyent Marinere came back to his own Country.

PART I

*An ancient
Mariner meet-
eth three Gal-
lants bidden
to a wedding-
feast, and
detaineth one.*

It is an ancient Mariner,
And he stoppeth one of three.
'By thy long grey beard and glittering eye,
Now wherefore stopp'st thou me?

'The Bridegroom's doors are opened wide,
And I am next of kin;
The guests are met, the feast is set:
May'st hear the merry din.'

10

He holds him with his skinny hand,
'There was a ship,' quoth he.
'Hold off! unhand me, grey-beard loon!'
Eftsoons his hand dropped he.

*The Wedding-
Guest is spell-
bound by the
eye of the old
seafaring man,
and con-
strained to
hear his tale.*

He holds him with his glittering eye—
The Wedding-Guest stood still,
And listens like a three years' child:
The Mariner hath his will.

The Wedding-Guest sat on a stone:
He cannot choose but hear;
And thus spake on that ancient man,

20

The bright-eyed Mariner.

'The ship was cheered, the harbour cleared,
Merrily did we drop
Below the kirk, below the hill,
Below the lighthouse top.

*The Mariner
tells how the
ship sailed
southward
with a good
wind and fair
weather, till it
reached the
line.*

'The Sun came up upon the left,
Out of the sea came he!
And he shone bright, and on the right
Went down into the sea.

30

'Higher and higher every day,
Till over the mast at noon—'
The Wedding-Guest here beat his breast,
For he heard the loud bassoon.

*The Wedding-
Guest heareth
the bridal
music; but
the Mariner
continueth
his tale.*

The bride hath paced into the hall,
Red as a rose is she;
Nodding their heads before her goes
The merry minstrelsy.

The Wedding-Guest he beat his breast,
Yet he cannot choose but hear;
And thus spake on that ancient man,
The bright-eyed Mariner.

40

*The ship
driven by a
storm toward
the south pole.*

'And now the STORM-BLAST came, and he
Was tyrannous and strong:
He struck with his o'ertaking wings,
And chased us south along.

'With sloping masts and dipping prow,
As who pursued with yell and blow
Still treads the shadow of his foe,
And forward bends his head,
The ship drove fast, loud roared the blast,
And southward aye we fled.

50

'And now there came both mist and snow,
And it grew wondrous cold:
And ice, mast-high, came floating by,
As green as emerald.

*The land of
ice, and of
fearful sounds
where no
living thing
was to be seen.*

'And through the drifts the snowy clifts
Did send a dismal sheen:
Nor shapes of men nor beasts we ken—
The ice was all between.

'The ice was here, the ice was there,
60   The ice was all around:
It cracked and growled, and roared and howled,
  Like noises in a swound!

Till a great
sea-bird,   'At length did cross an Albatross,
called the   Thorough the fog it came;
Albatross,   As if it had been a Christian soul,
came through   We hailed it in God's name.
the snow-fog,
and was
received with   'It ate the food it ne'er had eat,
great joy and   And round and round it flew.
hospitality.   The ice did split with a thunder-fit;
70   The helmsman steered us through!

And lo! the   'And a good south wind sprung up behind;
Albatross   The Albatross did follow,
proveth a bird   And every day, for food or play,
of good omen,   Came to the mariner's hollo!
and followeth
the ship as it
returned
northward   'In mist or cloud, on mast or shroud,
through fog   It perched for vespers nine;
and floating   Whiles all the night, through fog-smoke white,
ice.   Glimmered the white Moon-shine.'

The ancient   'God save thee, ancient Mariner!
Mariner   From the fiends, that plague thee thus!—
80 *inhospitably*   Why lookest thou so?'—'With my cross-bow
killeth the   I shot the ALBATROSS.'
pious bird of
good omen.

    PART II
The Sun now rose upon the right:
  Out of the sea came he,
Still hid in mist, and on the left
  Went down into the sea.

And the good south wind still blew behind,
  But no sweet bird did follow,
Nor any day for food or play
90   Came to the mariners' hollo!

His shipmates   And I had done a hellish thing,
cry out against   And it would work 'em woe:

the ancient Mariner, for killing the bird of good luck.

For all averred, I had killed the bird
That made the breeze to blow.
'Ah wretch!' said they, 'the bird to slay,
That made the breeze to blow!'

But when the fog cleared off, they justify the same, and thus make themselves accomplices in the crime.

Nor dim nor red, like God's own head,
The glorious Sun uprist:
Then all averred, I had killed the bird
That brought the fog and mist.
'Twas right, said they, such birds to slay,
That bring the fog and mist.

The fair breeze continues; the ship enters the Pacific Ocean, and sails northward, even till it reaches the line.

The fair breeze blew, the white foam flew,
The furrow followed free;
We were the first that ever burst
Into that silent sea.

Down dropped the breeze,
    the sails dropped down,
'Twas sad as sad could be;
And we did speak only to break
The silence of the sea!

The ship hath been suddenly becalmed.

All in a hot and copper sky,
The bloody Sun, at noon,
Right up above the mast did stand,
No bigger than the Moon.

Day after day, day after day,
We stuck, nor breath nor motion;
As idle as a painted ship
Upon a painted ocean.

And the Albatross begins to be avenged.

Water, water, every where,
And all the boards did shrink;
Water, water, every where,
Nor any drop to drink.

The very deep did rot: O Christ!
That ever this should be!
Yea, slimy things did crawl with legs
Upon the slimy sea.

About, about, in reel and rout
The death-fires danced at night;
The water, like a witch's oils,
130   Burnt green, and blue and white.

A Spirit had
followed them;   And some in dreams assurèd were
one of the in-   Of the Spirit that plagued us so;
visible inhabi-   Nine fathom deep he had followed us
tants of this   From the land of mist and snow.
planet, neither
departed souls nor angels; concerning whom the learned Jew, Josephus, and the Platonic
Constantinopolitan, Michael Psellus, may be consulted. They are very numerous, and there
is no climate or element without one or more.

And every tongue, through utter drought,
Was withered at the root;
We could not speak, no more than if
We had been choked with soot.

The shipmates,
in their sore   Ah! well a-day! what evil looks
140 *distress, would*   Had I from old and young!
fain throw the   Instead of the cross, the Albatross
whole guilt on   About my neck was hung.
the ancient
Mariner: in sign whereof they hang the dead sea-bird round his neck.

PART III
There passed a weary time. Each throat
Was parched, and glazed each eye.
A weary time! a weary time!
How glazed each weary eye,
The ancient   When looking westward, I beheld
Mariner   A something in the sky.
beholdeth a
sign in the ele-
ment afar off.   At first it seemed a little speck,
150   And then it seemed a mist;
It moved and moved, and took at last
A certain shape, I wist.

A speck, a mist, a shape, I wist!
And still it neared and neared:
As if it dodged a water-sprite,
It plunged and tacked and veered.

At its nearer   With throats unslaked, with black lips baked
approach, it   We could nor laugh nor wail;
seemeth him   Through utter drought all dumb we stood!

160   *to be a ship;*   I bit my arm, I sucked the blood,
and at a dear   And cried, A sail! a sail!
ransom he
freeth his
speech from   With throats unslaked, with black lips baked
the bonds of   Agape they heard me call:
thirst.   Gramercy! they for joy did grin,
A flash of joy;   And all at once their breath drew in,
As they were drinking all.

And horror   See! see! (I cried) she tacks no more!
follows. For   Hither to work us weal;
can it be a   Without a breeze, without a tide,
ship that
170   *comes onward*   She steadies with upright keel!
without wind
or tide?

The western wave was all a-flame.
The day was well nigh done!
Almost upon the western wave
Rested the broad bright Sun;
When that strange shape drove suddenly
Betwixt us and the Sun.

It seemeth   And straight the Sun was flecked with bars,
him but the   (Heaven's Mother send us grace!)
skeleton of   As if through a dungeon-grate he peered
a ship.   With broad and burning face.
180

Alas! (thought I, and my heart beat loud)
And its ribs   How fast she nears and nears!
are seen as   Are those *her* sails that glance in the Sun,
bars on the   Like restless gossameres?
face of the
setting Sun.

The Spectre-   Are those *her* ribs through which the Sun
Woman and   Did peer, as through a grate?
her Death-   And is that Woman all her crew?
mate, and no   Is that a DEATH? and are there two?
other on   Is DEATH that woman's mate?
board the
skeleton ship.

190   *Like vessel,*   *Her* lips were red, *her* looks were free,
like crew!   Her locks were yellow as gold:
Death and   Her skin was as white as leprosy,
Life-in-Death   The Night-mare LIFE-IN-DEATH was she,
have diced for   Who thicks man's blood with cold.
the ship's
crew, and she

(the latter)
winneth the
ancient
Mariner.

The naked hulk alongside came,
And the twain were casting dice;
'The game is done! I've won! I've won!'
Quoth she, and whistles thrice.

No twilight
within the
courts of the
Sun.

200

The Sun's rim dips; the stars rush out:
At one stride comes the dark;
With far-heard whisper, o'er the sea,
Off shot the spectre-bark.

At the rising
of the Moon,

We listened and looked sideways up!
Fear at my heart, as at a cup,
My life-blood seemed to sip!
The stars were dim, and thick the night,
The steersman's face by his lamp gleamed white;
From the sails the dew did drip—

210

Till clomb above the eastern bar
The hornèd Moon, with one bright star
Within the nether tip.

One after
another,

One after one, by the star-dogged Moon,
Too quick for groan or sigh,
Each turned his face with a ghastly pang,
And cursed me with his eye.

His shipmates
drop down
dead.

Four times fifty living men,
(And I heard nor sigh nor groan)
With heavy thump, a lifeless lump,
They dropped down one by one.

220

But Life-in-
Death begins
her work on
the ancient
Mariner.

The souls did from their bodies fly,—
They fled to bliss or woe!
And every soul, it passed me by,
Like the whizz of my cross-bow!

PART IV

The Wedding-
Guest feareth
that a Spirit
is talking to
him;

'I fear thee, ancient Mariner!
I fear thy skinny hand!
And thou art long, and lank, and brown,
As is the ribbed sea-sand.

'I fear thee and thy glittering eye,
And thy skinny hand, so brown.'—

230   *But the ancient*   Fear not, fear not, thou Wedding-Guest!
       Mariner as-   This body dropped not down.
       sureth him of
       his bodily life,
       and proceed-   Alone, alone, all, all alone,
       eth to relate   Alone on a wide wide sea!
       his horrible   And never a saint took pity on
       penance.   My soul in agony.

       He despiseth
       the creatures   The many men, so beautiful!
       of the calm,   And they all dead did lie:

       And envieth   And a thousand thousand slimy things
       that they   Lived on; and so did I.
       should live,
       and so many
240   *lie dead.*   I looked upon the rotting sea,
                            And drew my eyes away;
                            I looked upon the rotting deck,
                            And there the dead men lay.

                            I looked to heaven, and tried to pray;
                            But or ever a prayer had gusht,
                            A wicked whisper came, and made
                            My heart as dry as dust.

                            I closed my lids, and kept them close,
                            And the balls like pulses beat;
250   For the sky and the sea, and the sea and the sky
                            Lay like a load on my weary eye,
                            And the dead were at my feet.

       But the curse   The cold sweat melted from their limbs,
       liveth for him   Nor rot nor reek did they:
       in the eye of   The look with which they looked on me
       the dead men.   Had never passed away.

                            An orphan's curse would drag to hell
                            A spirit from on high;
                            But oh! more horrible than that
260   Is the curse in a dead man's eye!
                            Seven days, seven nights, I saw that curse,
                            And yet I could not die.

       In his lone-   The moving Moon went up the sky,
       liness and   And no where did abide:

fixedness he
yearneth
towards the
journeying
Moon, and the
stars that still
sojourn, yet
still move
onward; and
every where
the blue sky
belongs to

Softly she was going up,
And a star or two beside—

Her beams bemocked the sultry main,
Like April hoar-frost spread;
But where the ship's huge shadow lay,
The charmèd water burnt alway
A still and awful red.

270

them, and is their appointed rest, and their native country and their own natural homes, which they enter
unannounced, as lords that are certainly expected and yet there is a silent joy at their arrival.

By the light
of the Moon
he beholdeth
God's crea-
tures of the
great calm.

Beyond the shadow of the ship,
I watched the water-snakes:
They moved in tracks of shining white,
And when they reared, the elfish light
Fell off in hoary flakes.

Within the shadow of the ship
I watched their rich attire:
Blue, glossy green, and velvet black,
They coiled and swam; and every track
Was a flash of golden fire.

280

Their beauty
and their
happiness.

O happy living things! no tongue
Their beauty might declare:
A spring of love gushed from my heart,

He blesseth
them in his
heart.

And I blessed them unaware:
Sure my kind saint took pity on me,
And I blessed them unaware.

The spell
begins to
break.

The self-same moment I could pray;
And from my neck so free
The Albatross fell off, and sank
Like lead into the sea.

290

PART V

Oh sleep! it is a gentle thing,
Beloved from pole to pole!
To Mary Queen the praise be given!
She sent the gentle sleep from Heaven,
That slid into my soul.

*By grace of
the holy
Mother, the
ancient
Mariner is
refreshed with
rain.*

The silly buckets on the deck,
That had so long remained,
I dreamt that they were filled with dew;
And when I awoke, it rained.

*He heareth
sounds and
seeth strange
sights and
commotions in
the sky and
the element.*

My lips were wet, my throat was cold,
My garments all were dank;
Sure I had drunken in my dreams,
And still my body drank.

I moved, and could not feel my limbs:
I was so light—almost
I thought that I had died in sleep,
And was a blessèd ghost.

And soon I heard a roaring wind:
It did not come anear;
But with its sound it shook the sails,
That were so thin and sere.

The upper air burst into life!
And a hundred fire-flags sheen,
To and fro they were hurried about!
And to and fro, and in and out,
The wan stars danced between.

And the coming wind did roar more loud,
And the sails did sigh like sedge;
And the rain poured down from one black cloud;
The Moon was at its edge.

The thick black cloud was cleft, and still
The Moon was at its side:
Like waters shot from some high crag,
The lightning fell with never a jag,
A river steep and wide.

*The bodies of
the ship's crew
are inspired
and the ship
moves on.*

The loud wind never reached the ship,
Yet now the ship moved on!
Beneath the lightning and the Moon
The dead men gave a groan.

They groaned, they stirred, they all uprose,
Nor spake, nor moved their eyes;
It had been strange, even in a dream,
To have seen those dead men rise.

The helmsman steered, the ship moved on;
Yet never a breeze up-blew;
The mariners all 'gan work the ropes,
Where they were wont to do;
They raised their limbs like lifeless tools—
We were a ghastly crew.

The body of my brother's son
Stood by me, knee to knee:
The body and I pulled at one rope,
But he said nought to me.

'I fear thee, ancient Mariner!'
Be calm, thou Wedding-Guest!
'Twas not those souls that fled in pain,
Which to their corses came again,
But a troop of spirits blest:

For when it dawned—they dropped their arms,
And clustered round the mast;
Sweet sounds rose slowly through their mouths,
And from their bodies passed.

Around, around, flew each sweet sound,
Then darted to the Sun;
Slowly the sounds came back again,
Now mixed, now one by one.

Sometimes a-dropping from the sky
I heard the sky-lark sing;
Sometimes all little birds that are,
How they seemed to fill the sea and air
With their sweet jargoning!

And now 'twas like all instruments,
Now like a lonely flute;
And now it is an angel's song,
That makes the heavens be mute.

340

350

360

But not by the souls of the men, nor by daemons of earth or middle air, but by a blessed troop of angelic spirits, sent down by the invocation of the guardian saint.

It ceased; yet still the sails made on
A pleasant noise till noon,
A noise like of a hidden brook
In the leafy month of June,

370

That to the sleeping woods all night
Singeth a quiet tune.

Till noon we quietly sailed on,
Yet never a breeze did breathe:
Slowly and smoothly went the ship,
Moved onward from beneath.

*The lonesome
Spirit from
the south-pole
carries on the
ship as far as
the Line, in
obedience to
the angelic
troop, but still
requireth
vengeance.*

Under the keel nine fathom deep,
From the land of mist and snow,
The spirit slid: and it was he
That made the ship to go.

380

The sails at noon left off their tune,
And the ship stood still also.

The Sun, right up above the mast,
Had fixed her to the ocean:
But in a minute she 'gan stir,
With a short uneasy motion—
Backwards and forwards half her length
With a short uneasy motion.

Then like a pawing horse let go,
She made a sudden bound:

390

It flung the blood into my head,
And I fell down in a swound.

*The Polar
Spirit's fellow-
daemons, the
invisible
inhabitants of
the element,
take part in
his wrong;
and two of
them relate,
one to the
other, that
penance long
and heavy for
the ancient
Mariner hath
been accorded
to the Polar*

How long in that same fit I lay,
I have not to declare;
But ere my living life returned,
I heard and in my soul discerned
Two voices in the air.

400

'Is it he?' quoth one, 'Is this the man?
By him who died on cross,
With his cruel bow he laid full low
The harmless Albatross.

'The spirit who bideth by himself
In the land of mist and snow,

Spirit, who returneth southward.

He loved the bird that loved the man
Who shot him with his bow.'

The other was a softer voice,
As soft as honey-dew:
Quoth he, 'The man hath penance done,
And penance more will do.'

PART VI
FIRST VOICE
'But tell me, tell me! speak again,
Thy soft response renewing—
What makes that ship drive on so fast?
What is the ocean doing?'

SECOND VOICE
'Still as a slave before his lord,
The ocean hath no blast;
His great bright eye most silently
Up to the Moon is cast—

'If he may know which way to go;
For she guides him smooth or grim.
See, brother, see! how graciously
She looketh down on him.'

FIRST VOICE
'But why drives on that ship so fast,
Without or wave or wind?'

The Mariner hath been cast into a trance; for the angelic power causeth the vessel to drive northward faster than human life could endure.

SECOND VOICE
'The air is cut away before,
And closes from behind.

'Fly, brother, fly! more high, more high!
Or we shall be belated:
For slow and slow that ship will go,
When the Mariner's trance is abated.'

The supernatural motion is retarded; the Mariner awakes, and his penance begins anew.

I woke, and we were sailing on
As in a gentle weather:
'Twas night, calm night, the moon was high;
The dead men stood together.

410

420

430

All stood together on the deck,
For a charnel-dungeon fitter:
All fixed on me their stony eyes,
That in the Moon did glitter.

The pang, the curse, with which they died,
Had never passed away:
440   I could not draw my eyes from theirs,
Nor turn them up to pray.

The curse is   And now this spell was snapped: once more
finally ex-   I viewed the ocean green,
piated.   And looked far forth, yet little saw
Of what had else been seen—

Like one, that on a lonesome road
Doth walk in fear and dread,
And having once turned round walks on,
And turns no more his head;
450   Because he knows, a frightful fiend
Doth close behind him tread.

But soon there breathed a wind on me,
Nor sound nor motion made:
Its path was not upon the sea,
In ripple or in shade.

It raised my hair, it fanned my cheek
Like a meadow-gale of spring—
It mingled strangely with my fears,
Yet it felt like a welcoming.

460   Swiftly, swiftly flew the ship,
Yet she sailed softly too:
Sweetly, sweetly blew the breeze—
On me alone it blew.

And the   Oh! dream of joy! is this indeed
ancient   The light-house top I see?
Mariner   Is this the hill? is this the kirk?
beholdeth his   Is this mine own countree?
native
country.

We drifted o'er the harbour-bar,
And I with sobs did pray—

470
O let me be awake, my God!
Or let me sleep alway.

The harbour-bay was clear as glass,
So smoothly it was strewn!
And on the bay the moonlight lay,
And the shadow of the Moon.

The rock shone bright, the kirk no less,
That stands above the rock:
The moonlight steeped in silentness
The steady weathercock.

480
And the bay was white with silent light,
Till rising from the same,
The angelic spirits leave the dead bodies,
Full many shapes, that shadows were,
In crimson colours came.

A little distance from the prow
And appear in their own forms of light.
Those crimson shadows were:
I turned my eyes upon the deck—
Oh, Christ! what saw I there!

Each corse lay flat, lifeless and flat,
And, by the holy rood!
490
A man all light, a seraph-man,
On every corse there stood.

This seraph-band, each waved his hand:
It was a heavenly sight!
They stood as signals to the land,
Each one a lovely light;

This seraph-band, each waved his hand,
No voice did they impart—
No voice; but oh! the silence sank
Like music on my heart.

500
But soon I heard the dash of oars,
I heard the Pilot's cheer;
My head was turned perforce away
And I saw a boat appear.

The Pilot and the Pilot's boy,
I heard them coming fast:
Dear Lord in Heaven! it was a joy
The dead men could not blast.

I saw a third—I heard his voice:
It is the Hermit good!
He singeth loud his godly hymns
That he makes in the wood.
He'll shrieve my soul, he'll wash away
The Albatross's blood.

PART VII

The Hermit of the Wood,

This Hermit good lives in that wood
Which slopes down to the sea.
How loudly his sweet voice he rears!
He loves to talk with marineres
That come from a far countree.

He kneels at morn, and noon, and eve—
He hath a cushion plump:
It is the moss that wholly hides
The rotted old oak-stump.

The skiff-boat neared: I heard them talk,
'Why, this is strange, I trow!
Where are those lights so many and fair,
That signal made but now?'

Approacheth the ship with wonder.

'Strange, by my faith!' the Hermit said—
'And they answered not our cheer!
The planks looked warped! and see those sails,
How thin they are and sere!
I never saw aught like to them,
Unless perchance it were

'Brown skeletons of leaves that lag
My forest-brook along;
When the ivy-tod is heavy with snow,
And the owlet whoops to the wolf below,
That eats the she-wolf's young.'

'Dear Lord! it hath a fiendish look—
(The Pilot made reply)
540   I am a-feared'—'Push on, push on!'
Said the Hermit cheerily.

The boat came closer to the ship,
But I nor spake nor stirred;
The boat came close beneath the ship,
And straight a sound was heard.

The ship
suddenly
sinketh.

Under the water it rumbled on,
Still louder and more dread:
It reached the ship, it split the bay;
The ship went down like lead.

550   *The ancient*
Mariner is
saved in the
Pilot's boat.

Stunned by that loud and dreadful sound,
Which sky and ocean smote,
Like one that hath been seven days drowned
My body lay afloat;
But swift as dreams, myself I found
Within the Pilot's boat.

Upon the whirl, where sank the ship,
The boat spun round and round;
And all was still, save that the hill
Was telling of the sound.

560   I moved my lips—the Pilot shrieked
And fell down in a fit;
The holy Hermit raised his eyes,
And prayed where he did sit.

I took the oars: the Pilot's boy,
Who now doth crazy go,
Laughed loud and long, and all the while
His eyes went to and fro.
'Ha! ha!' quoth he, 'full plain I see,
The Devil knows how to row.'

570   And now, all in my own countree,
I stood on the firm land!
The Hermit stepped forth from the boat,
And scarcely he could stand.

*The ancient
Mariner
earnestly
entreateth the
Hermit to
shrieve him;
and the
penance of
life falls on
him.*

'O shrieve me, shrieve me, holy man!'
The Hermit crossed his brow.
'Say quick,' quoth he, 'I bid thee say—
What manner of man art thou?'

580

Forthwith this frame of mine was wrenched
With a woeful agony,
Which forced me to begin my tale;
And then it left me free.

*And ever and
anon through
out his future
life an agony
constraineth
him to travel
from land to
land;*

Since then, at an uncertain hour,
That agony returns:
And till my ghastly tale is told,
This heart within me burns.

I pass, like night, from land to land;
I have strange power of speech;
That moment that his face I see,
I know the man that must hear me:
To him my tale I teach

590

What loud uproar bursts from that door!
The wedding-guests are there:
But in the garden-bower the bride
And bride-maids singing are:
And hark the little vesper bell,
Which biddeth me to prayer!

O Wedding-Guest! this soul hath been
Alone on a wide wide sea:
So lonely 'twas, that God himself
Scarce seemèd there to be.

600

O sweeter than the marriage-feast,
'Tis sweeter far to me,
To walk together to the kirk
With a goodly company!—

To walk together to the kirk,
And all together pray,
While each to his great Father bends,
Old men, and babes, and loving friends
And youths and maidens gay!

610 *And to teach,*
by his own
example, love
and reverence
to all things
that God
made and
loveth.

Farewell, farewell! but this I tell
To thee, thou Wedding-Guest!
He prayeth well, who loveth well
Both man and bird and beast.

He prayeth best, who loveth best
All things both great and small;
For the dear God who loveth us,
He made and loveth all.

The Mariner, whose eye is bright,
Whose beard with age is hoar,
620 Is gone: and now the Wedding-Guest
Turned from the bridegroom's door.

He went like one that hath been stunned,
And is of sense forlorn:
A sadder and a wiser man,
He rose the morrow morn.

1797–1798   1798

Kubla Khan

Coleridge's amazing fragment, "Kubla Khan," was the result of an opium dream, and we can discount his charming fiction of the person from Porlock whose intrusion caused the poet to forget the remaining lines. Among Coleridge's many abortive visions was the desire to write an epic on the fall of Jerusalem to the Romans, and "Kubla Khan" may be a relic of this ambition. However, other matters clearly got into the mix, including another borrowing from Purchas, which describes the Old Man of the Mountain, whose earthly paradise was a training ground for assassins sent forth against his enemies.

Kubla Khan

Or, a Vision in a Dream. A Fragment.

The following fragment is here published at the request of a poet of great and deserved celebrity, and, as far as the Author's own opinions are concerned, rather as a psychological curiosity, than on the ground of any supposed *poetic* merits.

In the summer of the year 1797, the Author, then in ill health, had retired to a lonely farmhouse between Porlock and Lindon, on the Exmoor confines of Somerset and Devonshire. In consequence of a slight indisposition, an anodyne had been prescribed, from the effects of which he fell asleep in his chair at the moment that he was reading the following sentence, or words of the same substance, in 'Purchas's Pilgrimage': 'Here the Khan Kubla commanded a palace to be built, and a stately garden thereunto. And thus ten miles of fertile ground were inclosed with a wall.' The Author continued for about three hours in a profound sleep at least of the external senses, during which time he has the most vivid confidence, that he could not have composed less than from two to three hundred lines; if that indeed can be called composition in which all the images rose up before him as *things*, with a parallel production of the correspondent expressions, without any sensation or consciousness of effort. On awaking he appeared to himself to have a distinct recollection of the whole, and taking his pen, ink, and paper, instantly and eagerly wrote down the lines that are here preserved. At this moment he was unfortunately called out by a person on business from Porlock, and detained by him above an hour, and on his return to his room, found, to his no small surprise and mortification, that though he still retained some vague and dim recollection of the general purport of the vision, yet, with the exception of some eight or ten scattered lines and images, all the rest had passed away like the images on the surface of a stream into which a stone has been cast, but alas! without the after restoration of the latter!

      Then all the charm
Is broken—all that phantom-world so fair
Vanishes, and a thousand circlets spread,
And each mis-shape[s] the other. Stay awhile,
Poor youth! who scarcely dar'st life up thine eyes—
The stream will soon renew its smoothness, soon
The visions will return! And lo, he stays,
And soon the fragments dim of lovely forms
Come trembling back, unite, and now once more
The pool becomes a mirror.
    [FROM *THE PICTURE; OR, THE LOVER'S RESOLUTION*, LINES 91–100]

Yet from the still surviving recollections in his mind, the Author has frequently purposed to finish for himself what had been originally, as it were, given to him. Σαμερον αδιον ασω [Αὔριον ἄδιον ἄοω 1834]: but the tomorrow is yet to come.

In Xanadu did Kubla Khan
A stately pleasure-dome decree:
Where Alph, the sacred river, ran

Through caverns measureless to man
 Down to a sunless sea.
So twice five miles of fertile ground
With walls and towers were girdled round:
And there were gardens bright with sinuous rills,
Where blossomed many an incense-bearing tree;
10 And here were forests ancient as the hills,
Enfolding sunny spots of greenery.

But oh! that deep romantic chasm which slanted
Down the green hill athwart a cedarn cover!
A savage place! as holy and enchanted
As e'er beneath a waning moon was haunted
By woman wailing for her demon-lover!
And from this chasm, with ceaseless turmoil seething,
As if this earth in fast thick pants were breathing,
A mighty fountain momently was forced:
20 Amid whose swift half-intermitted burst
Huge fragments vaulted like rebounding hail,
Or chaffy grain beneath the thresher's flail:
And 'mid these dancing rocks at once and ever
It flung up momently the sacred river.
Five miles meandering with a mazy motion
Through wood and dale the sacred river ran,
Then reached the caverns measureless to man,
And sank in tumult to a lifeless ocean:
And 'mid this tumult Kubla heard from far
30 Ancestral voices prophesying war!
 The shadow of the dome of pleasure
  Floated midway on the waves;
 Where was heard the mingled measure
  From the fountain and the caves.
It was a miracle of rare device,
A sunny pleasure-dome with caves of ice!

 A damsel with a dulcimer
 In a vision once I saw:
 It was an Abyssinian maid,
40 And on her dulcimer she played,
 Singing of Mount Abora.
 Could I revive within me
  Her symphony and song,
 To such a deep delight 'twould win me,

That with music loud and long,
I would build that dome in air,
That sunny dome! those caves of ice!
And all who heard should see them there,
And all should cry, Beware! Beware!
His flashing eyes, his floating hair!
Weave a circle round him thrice,
And close your eyes with holy dread,
For he on honey-dew hath fed,
And drunk the milk of Paradise.

50 (margin)

    1798   1816

Christabel

This is perhaps best read as a sequence of fragments, or four poems linked together only partly by subject and partly by the striking way in which Christabel openly admits Geraldine, in what certainly appears to be a mutual sexual seduction.

    Coleridge said that the poem was "founded on the notion, that the virtuous of this world save the wicked," and he remarked also that, in composing "Christabel," he was haunted by lines from Richard Crashaw's "A Hymn to the Name and Honour of the Admirable Saint Teresa": "Since 'tis not to be bad at home / She'll travel to a martyrdom. / No home for her confesses she, / But where she may a martyr be." But in the fragments as they stand, there are no indications that Geraldine will be redeemed by the sexual sacrifice of Christabel.

from Christabel

Preface by Coleridge

The first part of the following poem was written in the year 1797, at Stowey, in the country of Somerset. The second part, after my return from Germany, in the year 1800, at Keswick, Cumberland. It is probable that if the poem had been finished at either of the former periods, or if even the first and second part had been published in the year 1800, the impression of its originality would have been much greater than I dare at present expect. But for this I have only my own indolence to blame. The dates are mentioned for the exclusive purpose of precluding charges of plagiarism or servile imitation from myself. For there is amongst us a set of critics, who seem to hold, that every possible thought and image is traditional; who have no notion that there are such things as fountains in the world, small as well as great; and who would therefore charitably derive every rill they behold flowing, from a perforation made in some other man's tank. I am confident, however, that as far as the present poem is concerned, the celebrated poets whose writings I might be suspected of having imitated, either in particular passages, or in the tone and the spirit of the whole, would be among the first to vindicate me from the charge, and who, on any striking coincidence, would permit me to address them in this doggerel vision of two monkish Latin hexameter.

'Tis mine and it is likewise yours;
But an if this will not do;
Let it be mine, good friend! for I
Am the poorer of the two.

    I have only to add that the metre of "Christabel" is not, properly speaking, irregular, though it may seem so from its being founded on a new principle: namely, that of counting in each line the accents, not the syllables. Though the latter may vary from seven to twelve, yet in each line the accents will be found to be only four. Nevertheless, this occasional variation in number of syllables is not introduced wantonly, or for the mere ends of convenience, but in correspondence with some transition in the nature of the imagery or passion.

PART I
'Tis the middle of night by the castle clock,
And the owls have awakened the crowing cock;
Tu—whit!——Tu—whoo!
And hark, again! the crowing cock,
How drowsily it crew.
Sir Leoline, the Baron rich,
Hath a toothless mastiff bitch;
From her kennel beneath the rock
She maketh answer to the clock,
Four for the quarters, and twelve for the hour;
Ever and aye, by shine and shower,
Sixteen short howls, not over loud;
Some say, she sees my lady's shroud.

Is the night chilly and dark?
The night is chilly, but not dark.
The thin grey cloud is spread on high,
It covers but not hides the sky.

The moon is behind, and at the full;
And yet she looks both small and dull.
20   The night is chill, the cloud is grey:
'Tis a month before the month of May,
And the Spring comes slowly up this way.

The lovely lady, Christabel,
Whom her father loves so well,
What makes her in the wood so late,
A furlong from the castle gate?
She had dreams all yesternight
Of her own betrothèd knight;
And she in the midnight wood will pray
30   For the weal of her lover that's far away.

She stole along, she nothing spoke,
The sighs she heaved were soft and low,
And naught was green upon the oak
But moss and rarest mistletoe:
She kneels beneath the huge oak tree,
And in silence prayeth she.

The lady sprang up suddenly,
The lovely lady, Christabel!
It moaned as near, as near can be,
40   But what it is she cannot tell.—
On the other side it seems to be,
Of the huge, broad-breasted, old oak tree.

The night is chill; the forest bare;
Is it the wind that moaneth bleak?
There is not wind enough in the air
To move away the ringlet curl
From the lovely lady's cheek—
There is not wind enough to twirl
The one red leaf, the last of its clan,
50   That dances as often as dance it can,
Hanging so light, and hanging so high,
On the topmost twig that looks up at the sky.

Hush, beating heart of Christabel!
Jesu, Maria, shield her well!
She folded her arms beneath her cloak,

And stole to the other side of the oak.
    What sees she there?

There she sees a damsel bright,
Dressed in a silken robe of white,
60   That shadowy in the moonlight shone:
The neck that made that white robe wan,
Her stately neck, and arms were bare;
Her blue-veined feet unsandaled were,
And wildly glittered here and there
The gems entangled in her hair.
I guess, 'twas frightful there to see
A lady so richly clad as she—
Beautiful exceedingly!

Mary mother, save me now!
70   (Said Christabel,) And who art thou?
The lady strange made answer meet,
And her voice was faint and sweet:—
Have pity on my sore distress,
I scarce can speak for weariness:
Stretch forth thy hand, and have no fear!
Said Christabel, How camest thou here?
And the lady, whose voice was faint and sweet,
Did thus pursue her answer meet:—

My sire is of noble line,
80   And my name is Geraldine:
Five warriors seized me yestermorn,
Me, even me, a maid forlorn:
They choked my cries with force and fright,
And tied me on a palfrey white.
The palfrey was as fleet as wind,
And they rode furiously behind.

They spurred amain, their steeds were white:
And once we crossed the shade of night.
As sure as Heaven shall rescue me,
90   I have no thought what men they be;
Nor do I know how long it is
(For I have lain entranced I wis)
Since one, the tallest of the five,
Took me from the palfrey's back,

A weary woman, scarce alive.
Some muttered words his comrades spoke:
He placed me underneath this oak;
He swore they would return with haste;
Whither they went I cannot tell—
I thought I heard, some minutes past,
Sounds as of a castle bell.
Stretch forth thy hand (thus ended she).
And help a wretched maid to flee.

Then Christabel stretched forth her hand,
And comforted fair Geraldine:
O well, bright dame! may you command
The service of Sir Leoline;
And gladly our stout chivalry
Will he send forth and friends withal
To guide and guard you safe and free
Home to your noble father's hall.

She rose: and forth with steps they passed
That strove to be, and were not, fast.
Her gracious stars the lady blest,
And thus spake on sweet Christabel:
All our household are at rest,
The hall as silent as the cell;
Sir Leoline is weak in health,
And may not well awakened be,
But we will move as if in stealth,
And I beseech your courtesy,
This night, to share your couch with me.

They crossed the moat, and Christabel
Took the key that fitted well;
A little door she opened straight,
All in the middle of the gate;
The gate that was ironed within and without,
Where an army in battle array had marched out.
The lady sank, belike through pain,
And Christabel with might and main
Lifted her up, a weary weight,
Over the threshold of the gate:
Then the lady rose again,
And moved, as she were not in pain.

So free from danger, free from fear,
They crossed the court: right glad they were.
And Christabel devoutly cried
To the lady by her side,
Praise we the Virgin all divine
140   Who hath rescued thee from thy distress!
Alas, alas! said Geraldine,
I cannot speak for weariness.
So free from danger, free from fear,
They crossed the court: right glad they were.

Outside her kennel, the mastiff old
Lay fast asleep, in moonshine cold.
The mastiff old did not awake,
Yet she an angry moan did make!
And what can ail the mastiff bitch?
150   Never till now she uttered yell
Beneath the eye of Christabel.
Perhaps it is the owlet's scritch:
For what can ail the mastiff bitch?

They passed the hall, that echoes still,
Pass as lightly as you will!
The brands were flat, the brands were dying,
Amid their own white ashes lying;
But when the lady passed, there came
A tongue of light, a fit of flame;
160   And Christabel saw the lady's eye,
And nothing else saw she thereby,
Save the boss of the shield of Sir Leoline tall,
Which hung in a murky old niche in the wall.
O softly tread, said Christabel,
My father seldom sleepeth well.

Sweet Christabel her feet doth bare,
And jealous of the listening air
They steal their way from stair to stair,
Now in glimmer, and now in gloom,
170   And now they pass the Baron's room,
As still as death, with stifled breath!
And now have reached her chamber door;
And now doth Geraldine press down
The rushes of the chamber floor.

The moon shines dim in the open air,
And not a moonbeam enters here.
But they without its light can see
The chamber carved so curiously,
Carved with figures strange and sweet,
180 All made out of the carver's brain,
For a lady's chamber meet:
The lamp with twofold silver chain
Is fastened to an angel's feet.

The silver lamp burns dead and dim;
But Christabel the lamp will trim.
She trimmed the lamp, and made it bright,
And left it swinging to and fro,
While Geraldine, in wretched plight,
Sank down upon the floor below.

190 O weary lady, Geraldine,
I pray you, drink this cordial wine!
It is a wine of virtuous powers;
My mother made it of wild flowers.

And will your mother pity me,
Who am a maiden most forlorn?
Christabel answered—Woe is me!
She died the hour that I was born.
I have heard the grey-haired friar tell
How on her death-bed she did say,
200 That she should hear the castle-bell
Strike twelve upon my wedding-day.
O mother dear! that thou wert here!
I would, said Geraldine, she were!

But soon with altered voice, said she—
'Off, wandering mother! Peak and pine!
I have power to bid thee flee.'
Alas! what ails poor Geraldine?
Why stares she with unsettled eye?
Can she the bodiless dead espy?
210 And why with hollow voice cries she,
'Off, woman, off! this hour is mine—
Though thou her guardian spirit be,
Off, woman, off! 'tis given to me.'

Then Christabel knelt by the lady's side,
And raised to heaven her eyes so blue—
Alas! said she, this ghastly ride—
Dear lady! it hath wildered you!
The lady wiped her moist cold brow,
And faintly said, ''tis over now!'

220   Again the wild-flower wine she drank:
Her fair large eyes 'gan glitter bright,
And from the floor whereon she sank,
The lofty lady stood upright:
She was most beautiful to see,
Like a lady of a far countree.

And thus the lofty lady spake—
'All they who live in the upper sky,
Do love you, holy Christabel!
And you love them, and for their sake
230   And for the good which me befel,
Even I in my degree will try,
Fair maiden, to requite you well.
But now unrobe yourself; for I
Must pray, ere yet in bed I lie.'

Quoth Christabel, So let it be!
And as the lady bade, did she.
Her gentle limbs did she undress,
And lay down in her loveliness.

But through her brain of weal and woe
240   So many thoughts moved to and fro,
That vain it were her lids to close;
So half-way from the bed she rose,
And on her elbow did recline
To look at the lady Geraldine.
Beneath the lamp the lady bowed,
And slowly rolled her eyes around;
Then drawing in her breath aloud,
Like one that shuddered, she unbound
The cincture from beneath her breast:
250   Her silken robe, and inner vest,
Dropped to her feet, and full in view,

Behold! her bosom and half her side——
A sight to dream of, not to tell!
O shield her! shield sweet Christabel!

Yet Geraldine nor speaks nor stirs;
Ah! what a stricken look was hers!
Deep from within she seems half-way
To lift some weight with sick assay,
And eyes the maid and seeks delay;
260   Then suddenly, as one defied,
Collects herself in scorn and pride,
And lay down by the Maiden's side!—
And in her arms the maid she took,
        Ah wel-a-day!
And with low voice and doleful look
These words did say:
'In the touch of this bosom there worketh a spell,
Which is lord of thy utterance, Christabel!
Thou knowest tonight, and wilt know tomorrow,
270   This mark of my shame, this seal of my sorrow;
      But vainly thou warrest,
        For this is alone in
      Thy power to declare,
        That in the dim forest
      Thou heardest a low moaning.
And foundest a bright lady, surpassingly fair;
And didst bring her home with thee in love
    and in charity,
To shield her and shelter her from the damp air.'

THE CONCLUSION TO PART I
It was a lovely sight to see
280   The lady Christabel, when she
Was praying at the old oak tree.
      Amid the jaggèd shadows
      Of mossy leafless boughs,
      Kneeling in the moonlight,
      To make her gentle vows;
Her slender palms together prest,
Heaving sometimes on her breast;
Her face resigned to bliss or bale—
Her face, oh call it fair not pale,

290   And both blue eyes more bright than clear,
      Each about to have a tear.

      With open eyes (ah woe is me!)
      Asleep, and dreaming fearfully,
      Fearfully dreaming, yet, I wis,
      Dreaming that alone, which is—
      O sorrow and shame! Can this be she,
      The lady, who knelt at the old oak tree?
      And lo! the worker of these harms,
      That holds the maiden in her arms,
300   Seems to slumber still and mild,
      As a mother with her child.

      A star hath set, a star hath risen,
      O Geraldine! since arms of thine
      Have been the lovely lady's prison.
      O Geraldine! one hour was thine—
      Thou'st had thy will! By tairn and rill,
      The night-birds all that hour were still.
      But now they are jubilant anew,
      From cliff and tower, tu—whoo! tu—whoo!
310   Tu—whoo! tu—woo! from wood and fell!

      And see! the lady Christabel
      Gathers herself from out her trance;
      Her limbs relax, her countenance
      Grows sad and soft; the smooth thin lids
      Close o'er her eyes; and tears she sheds—
      Large tears that leave the lashes bright!
      And oft the while she seems to smile
      As infants at a sudden light!

      Yea, she doth smile, and she doth weep,
320   Like a youthful hermitess,
      Beauteous in a wilderness,
      Who, praying always, prays in sleep.
      And, if she move unquietly,
      Perchance, 'tis but the blood so free
      Comes back and tingles in her feet.
      No doubt, she hath a vision sweet.
      What if her guardian spirit 'twere,
      What if she knew her mother near?

But this she knows, in joys and woes,
330   That saints will aid if men will call:
For the blue sky bends over all!
        1797   1798

THE CONCLUSION TO PART II

A little child, a limber elf,
Singing, dancing to itself,
A fairy thing with red round cheeks,
That always finds, and never seeks,
660   Makes such a vision to the sight
As fills a father's eyes with light;
And pleasures flow in so thick and fast
Upon his heart, that he at last
Must needs express his love's excess
With words of unmeant bitterness.
Perhaps 'tis pretty to force together
Thoughts so all unlike each other;
To mutter and mock a broken charm,
To dally with wrong that does no harm,
670   Perhaps 'tis tender too and pretty
At each wild word to feel within
A sweet recoil of love and pity.
And what, if in a world of sin
(O sorrow and shame should this be true!)
Such giddiness of heart and brain
Comes seldom save from rage and pain,
So talks as it's most used to do.
        1801   1816

Dejection: An Ode

> *Late, late yestreen I saw the new Moon,*
> *With the old Moon in her arms;*
> *And I fear, I fear, my Master dear!*
> *We shall have a deadly storm.*
>   BALLAD OF SIR PATRICK SPENCE

I

Well! If the Bard was weather-wise, who made
    The grand old ballad of Sir Patrick Spence,
        This night, so tranquil now, will not go hence

Unroused by winds, that ply a busier trade
Than those which mould yon cloud in lazy flakes,
Or the dull sobbing draft, that moans and rakes
Upon the strings of this Aeolian lute,
     Which better far were mute.
   For lo! the New-moon winter-bright!
10   And overspread with phantom light,
    (With swimming phantom light o'erspread
    But rimmed and circled by a silver thread)
I see the old Moon in her lap, foretelling
   The coming-on of rain and squally blast.
And oh! that even now the gust were swelling,
   And the slant night-shower driving loud and fast!
Those sounds which oft have raised me, whilst they awed,
    And sent my soul abroad,
Might now perhaps their wonted impulse give,
20 Might startle this dull pain, and make it move and live!

   II
A grief without a pang, void, dark, and drear,
   A stifled, drowsy, unimpassioned grief,
   Which finds no natural outlet, no relief,
     In word, or sigh, or tear—
O Lady! in this wan and heartless mood,
To other thoughts by yonder throstle wooed,
   All this long eve, so balmy and serene,
Have I been gazing on the western sky,
   And its peculiar tint of yellow green:
30 And still I gaze—and with how blank an eye!
And those thin clouds above, in flakes and bars,
That give away their motion to the stars;
Those stars, that glide behind them or between,
Now sparkling, now bedimmed, but always seen:
Yon crescent Moon, as fixed as if it grew
In its own cloudless, starless lake of blue;
I see them all so excellently fair,
I see, not feel, how beautiful they are!

   III
     My genial spirits fail;
40   And what can these avail
To lift the smothering weight from off my breast?
    It were a vain endeavour,

Though I should gaze forever
On that green light that lingers in the west:
I may not hope from outward forms to win
The passion and the life, whose fountains are within.

IV

O Lady! we receive but what we give,
And in our life alone does Nature live:
Ours is her wedding garment, ours her shroud!
50   And would we aught behold, of higher worth,
Than that inanimate cold world allowed
To the poor loveless ever-anxious crowd,
    Ah! from the soul itself must issue forth
A light, a glory, a fair luminous cloud
        Enveloping the Earth—
And from the soul itself must there be sent
    A sweet and potent voice, of its own birth,
Of all sweet sounds the life and element!

V

O pure of heart! thou needest not ask of me
60   What this strong music in the soul may be!
What, and wherein it doth exist.
This light, this glory, this fair luminous mist,
This beautiful and beauty-making power.
    Joy, virtuous Lady! Joy that ne'er was given,
Save to the pure, and in their purest hour,
Life, and Life's effluence, cloud at once and shower,
Joy, Lady! is the spirit and the power,
Which, wedding Nature to us, gives in dower
    A new Earth and new Heaven,
70   Undreamt of by the sensual and the proud—
Joy is the sweet voice, Joy the luminous cloud—
        We in ourselves rejoice!
And thence flows all that charms or ear or sight,
    All melodies the echoes of that voice,
All colours a suffusion from that light.

VI

There was a time when, though my path was rough,
    This joy within me dallied with distress,
And all misfortunes were but as the stuff
    Whence Fancy made me dreams of happiness:

80 For hope grew round me, like the twining vine,
And fruits, and foliage, not my own, seemed mine.
But now afflictions bow me down to earth:
Nor care I that they rob me of my mirth;
        But oh! each visitation
Suspends what nature gave me at my birth,
    My shaping spirit of Imagination.
For not to think of what I needs must feel,
    But to be still and patient, all I can;
And haply by abstruse research to steal
90   From my own nature all the natural man—
    This was my sole resource, my only plan:
Till that which suits a part infects the whole,
And now is almost grown the habit of my soul.

    VII
Hence, viper thoughts, that coil around my mind,
        Reality's dark dream!
I turn from you, and listen to the wind,
    Which long has raved unnoticed. What a scream
Of agony by torture lengthened out
That lute sent forth! Thou Wind, that rav'st without,
100   Bare crag, or mountain tairn, or blasted tree,
Or pine-grove whither woodman never clomb,
Or lonely house, long held the witches' home,
    Methinks were fitter instruments for thee,
Mad Lutanist! who in this month of showers,
Of dark-brown gardens, and of peeping flowers,
Makest Devils' yule, with worse than wintry song,
The blossoms, buds, and timorous leaves among.
    Thou Actor, perfect in all tragic sounds!
Thou mighty Poet, e'en to frenzy bold!
110   What tellest thou now about?
        'Tis of the rushing of an host in rout,
    With groans, of trampled men, with smarting wounds—
At once they groan with pain, and shudder with the cold!
But hush! there is a pause of deepest silence!
    And all that noise, as of a rushing crowd,
With groans, and tremulous shudderings—all is over—
    It tells another tale, with sounds less deep and loud!
        A tale of less affright,
        And tempered with delight,
120   As Otway's self had framed the tender lay,—

'Tis of a little child
Upon a lonesome wild,
Not far from home, but she hath lost her way:
And now moans low in bitter grief and fear,
And now screams loud, and hopes to make her mother hear.

VIII
'Tis midnight, but small thoughts have I of sleep:
Full seldom may my friend such vigils keep!
Visit her, gentle Sleep! with wings of healing,
    And may this storm be but a mountain-birth,
130 May all the stars hang bright above her dwelling,
        Silent as though they watched the sleeping Earth!
        With light heart may she rise,
        Gay fancy, cheerful eyes,
    Joy lift her spirit, joy attune her voice;
To her may all things live, from pole to pole,
Their life the eddying of her living soul!
    O simple spirit, guided from above,
Dear Lady! friend devoutest of my choice,
Thus mayest thou ever, evermore rejoice.

1802   1802

GEORGE GORDON, LORD BYRON

1788–1824

BYRON'S LIFE and personality are at least as fascinating as his poetry. No author before or since has enjoyed and suffered such notoriety, or had a literary and social influence so much out of proportion with his actual imaginative achievement, considerable as that was. Somehow Byron was at once a man of incredible personal beauty, and yet congenitally half-lame and incessantly struggling against a tendency to grow fat. The most brilliant conversationalist of his time, except for the incomparable Coleridge, he glorified solitude and at last attained it. Celebrated as the highest of

High Romantics (the only one to attain a European reputation, in part because he does not lose too much by translation, but primarily because of his life), he despised Romanticism, and insisted that English poetry all but died with the death of Pope. A virtual synonym for the greatest of lovers, he was passive toward women, sodomistic, sadomasochistic, fundamentally homosexual, and early disgusted with all sexual experience anyway. Outcast for his incest with his half-sister, he nevertheless seems to have gotten beyond narcissistic self-regard only in relation to her, yet she was in no way remarkable. A radical by the English standards of his day, and an active revolutionary in Italy, he was wholly skeptical as to the benefits of either reform or revolution. Acclaimed to this day as the martyr-hero of the Greek Revolution against the Turks, he despised the modern Greeks even as he financed, trained, and led them in rebellion. Apparently emancipated in religion, he was shocked by his closest friend Shelley's polemic against Christianity, could not rid himself of a Calvinistic temper, and inclined secretly toward Catholicism. A superb athlete and champion swimmer, he had to compel his reluctant, sluggish body to keep up with his restless spirit. To sum up: he was the most antithetical of men, and one of the most self-divided of poets.

Byron's father, widely known as a rakehell, died when the poet was three, leaving him with a neurotic, unstable mother and a governess who both seduced and chastised him. He attended Harrow, and Trinity College, Cambridge, where he had homosexual experiences. When his early lyrics, *Hours of Idleness* (1807), were attacked in *The Edinburgh Review,* Byron retaliated in his first satire, *English Bards and Scotch Reviewers* (1809). Returning from a grand tour of Iberia and Greece (1809–1811), he published his verse diary, *Childe Harold's Pilgrimage,* Cantos I and II, in 1812, and his true career began: "I awoke one morning and found myself famous." Enormous success in Regency society followed, including love affairs with Lady Oxford and with Caroline Lamb, who terrorized him to the extent that he sought refuge in marriage with Annabella Milbanke, a virtuous lady much given to mathematical interests, and, a very improbable choice on his part. A number of verse-tales (*Lara* is the best of them) enjoyed the same popularity as *Childe Harold,* and meanwhile Byron devoted himself also to the left wing of the Whig party. In eloquent speeches to the House of Lords he urged Catholic Emancipation and defended the "framebreakers," workers who had destroyed machines that had displaced them.

Though a daughter was born to Lady Byron, the marriage soon

became insupportable, evidently because of Byron's periodic rages, continued incest with his half-sister, and sodomistic demands on his highly conventional wife. They separated, amid much public scandal, and Byron, after encountering many social snubs, abandoned England for good in April 1816. He went to Geneva, and began his close friendship with Shelley, which lasted unbroken—though with strains—until Shelley drowned in 1822. Under Shelley's influence (and, paradoxically, Wordsworth's through Shelley) he wrote Canto III of *Childe Harold,* and entered on a new phase of his poetry. Moving to Italy in autumn 1817, he enjoyed an orgiastic season in Venice, involving many scores of women. During this time, he completed the second Romantic phase of his work, writing Canto IV of *Childe Harold* and finishing *Manfred,* which he had begun in Shelley's company. More important, he discovered his true mode in the poem *Beppo,* a light satire in ottava rima that soon led him to begin his masterpiece, *Don Juan.*

From 1819 until he left for Greece in 1823, Byron settled down in a domestic relationship with the Countess Teresa Guiccioli, joining her family in revolutionary plots against the Austrians, and following them to Pisa, where he was again in daily association with Shelley. To this time belong much the largest part of *Don Juan,* the brilliant satire *The Vision of Judgment,* and an effective, apocalyptic drama, *Cain* (a work difficult to represent by excerpts).

Weary of his life, Byron went to Greece to seek a soldier's death at thirty-six, and found it. He found also, though, a last, bitter, frustrated homosexual passion for his Greek page boy Loukas, and his final verses and letters betray profound self-disgust but an unwearied intelligence and quick humor. His death at Missolonghi in April 1824 saved him from middle age, and made his legend imperishable.

If we can put aside the phenomenon of Byronism, which flowered extravagantly all over Europe after so Romantic a death, we are left with two parts of Byron's accomplishment—*Don Juan* and everything else. Of the latter, there is clearly lasting value in a handful of lyrics, in aspects of *Childe Harold* III and IV, and of *Manfred,* and major achievement in *Cain* and in *The Vision of Judgment.* But, taken together, this is little compared with *Don Juan,* which only Shelley of Byron's contemporaries judged accurately and adequately, as being something wholly new and yet completely relevant to the Romantic Age.

↓   ↓   ↓

from Childe Harold's Pilgrimage, A Romaunt

from Canto the Fourth

CXXI

Oh Love! no habitant of earth thou art—
An unseen seraph, we believe in thee,
A faith whose martyrs are the broken heart,
But never yet hath seen, nor e'er shall see
The naked eye, thy form, as it should be;
The mind hath made thee, as it peopled heaven,
Even with its own desiring phantasy,
And to a thought such shape and image given,
As haunts the unquenched soul—parched—wearied—wrung—and riven.

CXXII

1090   Of its own beauty is the mind diseased,
And fevers into false creation:—where,
Where are the forms the sculptor's soul hath seized?—
In him alone. Can Nature show so fair?
Where are the charms and virtues which we dare
Conceive in boyhood and pursue as men,
The unreached Paradise of our despair,
Which o'er-informs the pencil and the pen,
And overpowers the page where it would bloom again?

CXXIII

Who loves, raves—'tis youth's frenzy; but the cure
1100   Is bitterer still; as charm by charm unwinds
Which robed our idols, and we see too sure
Nor worth nor beauty dwells from out the mind's
Ideal shape of such; yet still it binds
The fatal spell, and still it draws us on,
Reaping the whirlwind from the oft-sown winds;
The stubborn heart, its alchemy begun,
Seems ever near the prize,—wealthiest when most undone.

CXXIV

We wither from our youth, we gasp away—
Sick—sick; unfound the boon—unslaked the thirst,
1110   Though to the last, in verge of our decay,
Some phantom lures, such as we sought at first—
But all too late,—so are we doubly curst.

Love, fame, ambition, avarice—'tis the same,
Each idle—and all ill—and none the worst—
For all are meteors with a different name,
And Death the sable smoke where vanishes the flame.

CXXV

Few—none—find what they love or could have loved,
Though accident, blind contact, and the strong
Necessity of loving, have removed
1120 Antipathies—but to recur, ere long,
Envenomed with irrevocable wrong;
And Circumstance, that unspiritual god
And miscreator, makes and helps along
Our coming evils with a crutch-like rod,
Whose touch turns Hope to dust,—the dust we all have trod.

CXXVI

Our life is a false nature—'tis not in
The harmony of things,—this hard decree,
This uneradicable taint of sin,
This boundless upas, this all-blasting tree
1130 Whose root is earth, whose leaves and branches be
The skies which rain their plagues on men like dew—
Disease, death, bondage—all the woes we see—
And worse, the woes we see not—which throb through
The immedicable soul, with heart-aches ever new.

.   .   .

CXXXVII

But I have lived, and have not lived in vain:
My mind may lose its force, my blood its fire,
And my frame perish even in conquering pain;
But there is that within me which shall tire
Torture and Time, and breathe when I expire;
1230 Something unearthly which they deem not of,
Like the remembered tone of a mute lyre,
Shall on their softened spirits sink, and move
In hearts all rocky now the late remorse of love.

CXXXVIII

The seal is set.—Now welcome, thou dread power!
Nameless, yet thus omnipotent, which here

Walkest in the shadow of the midnight hour
With a deep awe, yet all distinct from fear;
Thy haunts are ever where the dead walls rear
Their ivy mantles, and the solemn scene
1240   Derives from thee a sense so deep and clear
That we become a part of what has been,
And grow unto the spot, all-seeing but unseen.

.   .   .

CLXIII
And if it be Prometheus stole from Heaven
1460   The fire which we endure, it was repaid
By him to whom the energy was given
Which this poetic marble hath arrayed
With an eternal glory—which, if made
By human hands, is not of human thought;
And Time himself hath hallowed it, nor laid
One ringlet in the dust—nor hath it caught
A tinge of years, but breathes the flame with which 'twas wrought.

CLXIV
But where is he, the Pilgrim of my song,
The being who upheld it through the past?
1470   Methinks he cometh late and tarries long.
He is no more—these breathings are his last;
His wanderings done, his visions ebbing fast,
And he himself as nothing:—if he was
Aught but a phantasy, and could be classed
With forms which live and suffer—let that pass—
His shadow fades away into Destruction's mass.

.   .   .

CLXXVII
Oh! that the Desert were my dwelling-place,
With one fair Spirit for my minister,
That I might all forget the human race,
And, hating no one, love but only her!
Ye Elements!—in whose ennobling stir
1590   I feel myself exalted—Can ye not
Accord me such a being? Do I err
In deeming such inhabit many a spot?
Though with them to converse can rarely be our lot.

CLXXVIII

There is a pleasure in the pathless woods,
There is a rapture on the lonely shore,
There is society where none intrudes,
By the deep Sea, and music in its roar:
I love not Man the less, but Nature more,
From these our interviews, in which I steal
1600   From all I may be, or have been before,
To mingle with the Universe, and feel
What I can ne'er express, yet can not all conceal.

CLXXIX

Roll on, thou deep and dark blue Ocean—roll!
Ten thousand fleets sweep over thee in vain;
Man marks the earth with ruin—his control
Stops with the shore;—upon the watery plain
The wrecks are all thy deed, nor doth remain
A shadow of man's ravage, save his own,
When, for a moment, like a drop of rain,
1610   He sinks into thy depths with bubbling groan,
Without a grave, unknelled, uncoffined, and unknown.

CLXXX

His steps are not upon thy paths,—thy fields
Are not a spoil for him,—thou dost arise
And shake him from thee; the vile strength he wields
For earth's destruction thou dost all despise,
Spurning him from thy bosom to the skies,
And sendest him, shivering in thy playful spray
And howling, to his Gods, where haply lies
His petty hope in some near port or bay,
1620   And dashest him again to earth:—there let him lay.

CLXXXI

The armaments which thunderstrike the walls
Of rock-built cities, bidding nations quake
And monarchs tremble in their capitals,
The oak leviathans, whose huge ribs make
Their clay creator the vain title take
Of lord of thee, and arbiter of war,—
These are thy toys, and, as the snowy flake,
They melt into thy yeast of waves, which mar
Alike the Armada's pride or spoils of Trafalgàr.

CLXXXII

1630　Thy shores are empires, changed in all save thee—
Assyria, Greece, Rome, Carthage, what are they?
Thy waters washed them power while they were free,
And many a tyrant since; their shores obey
The stranger, slave, or savage; their decay
Has dried up realms to deserts:—not so thou,
Unchangeable save to thy wild-waves' play;
Time writes no wrinkle on thine azure brow—
Such as creation's dawn beheld, thou rollest now.

CLXXXIII

Thou glorious mirror, where the Almighty's form
1640　Glasses itself in tempests; in all time,
Calm or convulsed—in breeze, or gale, or storm,
Icing the pole, or in the torrid clime
Dark-heaving;—boundless, endless, and sublime—
The image of Eternity—the throne
Of the Invisible; even from out thy slime
The monsters of the deep are made; each zone
Obeys thee; thou goest forth, dread, fathomless, alone.

CLXXXIV

And I have loved thee, Ocean! and my joy
Of youthful sports was on thy breast to be
1650　Borne, like thy bubbles, onward: from a boy
I wantoned with thy breakers—they to me
Were a delight; and if the freshening sea
Made them a terror—'twas a pleasing fear,
For I was as it were a child of thee,
And trusted to thy billows far and near,
And laid my hand upon thy mane—as I do here.

CLXXXV

My task is done—my song hath ceased—my theme
Has died into an echo; it is fit
The spell should break of this protracted dream.
1660　The torch shall be extinguished which hath lit
My midnight lamp—and what is writ, is writ,—
Would it were worthier! but I am not now
That which I have been—and my visions flit
Less palpably before me—and the glow
Which in my spirit dwelt is fluttering, faint, and low.

CLXXXVI

Farewell! a word that must be, and hath been—
A sound which makes us linger;—yet—farewell!
Ye! who have traced the Pilgrim to the scene
Which is his last, if in your memories dwell
A thought which once was his, if on ye swell
A single recollection, not in vain
He wore his sandal-shoon and scallop-shell;
Farewell! with *him* alone may rest the pain,
If such there were—with *you*, the moral of his strain!

1670

1817   1818

Don Juan

"This crammed, various creation renders the Romantic view of a world too large in all directions and too complex in its workings to be captured and arranged in any neat system of thought or formal pattern." This description by Alvin Kernan best characterizes the open universe of Byron's great satire, his only work that reflects both the immensity and the paradoxes of his own character and personality.

In reading a series of excerpts from *Don Juan,* we need not feel that we are betraying the poem, which is frankly digressive, unfinished and unfinishable (it would have gone on as long as Byron did), and unified only by the identity of the narrator with the poet himself. Byron is not Don Juan, and indeed Don Juan is scarcely a person, but rather a traditional hero of the picaresque mode, who remains unaltered by experience (no matter how violent) and remarkably passive in most of his love affairs. He is eminently seducible, this being his principal point of resemblance to his creator.

The best comments on the poem, in its own day, after Shelley's (he considered it the great poem of the age, superior to the work of Wordsworth and Goethe), were by Hazlitt, and of course, by Byron himself. Hazlitt accurately saw Byron's poetry as the record of "a mind preying upon itself." Despite the poem's fierce vitalism, it masks throughout a thoroughgoing transvaluation of values and a hopelessness as to the human condition. The poem's grand defense is Byron's own: "Confess, confess— you dog," he says to us as readers even as he exclaimed in a letter, "it may be bawdy but is it not good English? It may be profligate but is it not *life,* is it not the *thing*?"

The style, first used by him in the slight but charming *Beppo,* comes from the comic poets of the Italian Renaissance, Pulci and Boiardo in particular. Byron had been preceded in this adaptation by a contemporary, John Hookham Frere, but far outdoes Frere. In a deeper sense, the poem stems from English tradition, rather than Italian. Its true precursors are Samuel Butler, Swift, and Sterne.

from Don Juan

Difficile est propriè communia dicere.
                    HORACE

Dost thou think, because thou art virtuous, there shall be no more cakes and ale? Yes, by Saint Anne, and ginger shall be hot i' the mouth, too!
                    SHAKESPEARE, *TWELFTH NIGHT, OR WHAT YOU WILL*

Fragment
On the back of the Poet's MS. of Canto I

I would to heaven that I were so much clay,
    As I am blood, bone, marrow, passion, feeling—
Because at least the past were passed away—
    And for the future—(but I write this reeling,
Having got drunk exceedingly today,
    So that I seem to stand upon the ceiling)
I say—the future is a serious matter—
And so—for God's sake—hock and soda-water!

Dedication

I

Bob Southey! You're a poet—Poet-laureate,
    And representative of all the race,
Although 'tis true that you turned out a Tory at
    Last,—yours has lately been a common case,—
And now, my Epic Renegade! what are ye at?
    With all the Lakers, in and out of place?
A nest of tuneful persons, to my eye
Like 'four and twenty Blackbirds in a pye;

II

'Which pye being opened they began to sing'
    (This old song and new simile holds good),

'A dainty dish to set before the King,'
   Or Regent, who admires such kind of food;—
And Coleridge, too, has lately taken wing,
   But like a hawk encumbered with his hood,—
Explaining metaphysics to the nation—
I wish he would explain his Explanation.

III

You, Bob! are rather insolent, you know,
   At being disappointed in your wish
To supersede all warblers here below,
20   And be the only Blackbird in the dish;
And then you overstrain yourself, or so,
   And tumble downward like the flying fish
Gasping on deck, because you soar too high, Bob,
And fall, for lack of moisture quite a-dry, Bob!

IV

And Wordsworth, in a rather long *Excursion*
   (I think the quarto holds five hundred pages),
Has given a sample from the vasty version
   Of his new system to perplex the sages;
'Tis poetry—at least by his assertion,
30   And may appear so when the dog-star rages—
And he who understands it would be able
To add a story to the Tower of Babel.

V

You—Gentlemen! by dint of long seclusion
   From better company, have kept your own
At Keswick, and, through still continued fusion
   Of one another's minds, at last have grown
To deem as a most logical conclusion,
   That Poesy has wreaths for you alone:
There is a narrowness in such a notion,
40 Which makes me wish you'd change your
    lakes for ocean.

VI

I would not imitate the petty thought,
   Nor coin my self-love to so base a vice,
For all the glory your conversion brought,
   Since gold alone should not have been its price.

You have your salary; was't for that you wrought?
    And Wordsworth has his place in the Excise.
You're shabby fellows—true—but poets still,
And duly seated on the immortal hill.

VII

Your bays may hide the baldness of your brows—
50   Perhaps some virtuous blushes;—let them go—
To you I envy neither fruit nor boughs—
    And for the fame you would engross below,
The field is universal, and allows
    Scope to all such as feel the inherent glow:
Scott, Rogers, Campbell, Moore, and Crabbe, will try
'Gainst you the question with posterity.

VIII

For me, who, wandering with pedestrian Muses,
    Contend not with you on the wingèd steed,
I wish your fate may yield ye, when she chooses,
60   The fame you envy, and the skill you need;
And recollect a poet nothing loses
    In giving to his brethren their full meed
Of merit, and complaint of present days
Is not the certain path to future praise.

IX

He that reserves his laurels for posterity
    (Who does not often claim the bright reversion)
Has generally no great crop to spare it, he
    Being only injured by his own assertion;
And although here and there some glorious rarity
70   Arise like Titan from the sea's immersion,
The major part of such appellants go
To—God knows where—for no one else can know.

X

If, fallen in evil days on evil tongues,
    Milton appealed to the Avenger, Time,
If Time, the Avenger, execrates his wrongs,
    And makes the word 'Miltonic' mean 'sublime,'
He deigned not to belie his soul in songs,
    Nor turn his very talent to a crime;

He did not loathe the Sire to laud the Son,
80   But closed the tyrant-hater he begun.

XI

Think'st thou, could he—the blind Old Man—arise,
    Like Samuel from the grave, to freeze once more
The blood of monarchs with his prophecies,
    Or be alive again—again all hoar
With time and trials, and those helpless eyes,
    And heartless daughters—worn—and pale—and poor;
Would *he* adore a sultan? *he* obey
The intellectual eunuch Castlereagh?

XII

Cold-blooded, smooth-faced, placid miscreant!
90   Dabbling its sleek young hands in Erin's gore,
And thus for wider carnage taught to pant,
    Transferred to gorge upon a sister shore,
The vulgarest tool that Tyranny could want,
    With just enough of talent, and no more,
To lengthen fetters by another fixed,
And offer poison long already mixed.

XIII

An orator of such set trash of phrase
    Ineffably—legitimately vile,
That even its grossest flatterers dare not praise,
100   Nor foes—all nations—condescend to smile,—
Not even a sprightly blunder's spark can blaze
    From that Ixion grindstone's ceaseless toil,
That turns and turns to give the world a notion
Of endless torments and perpetual motion.

XIV

A bungler even in its disgusting trade,
    And botching, patching, leaving still behind
Something of which its masters are afraid,
    States to be curbed, and thoughts to be confined,
Conspiracy or Congress to be made—
110   Cobbling at manacles for all mankind—
A tinkering slave-maker, who mends old chains,
With God and man's abhorrence for its gains.

XV

If we may judge of matter by the mind,
    Emasculated to the marrow *It*
Hath but two objects, how to serve, and bind,
    Deeming the chain it wears even men may fit,
Eutropius of its many masters,—blind
    To worth as freedom, wisdom as to wit,
Fearless—because *no* feeling dwells in ice,
120 Its very courage stagnates to a vice.

XVI

Where shall I turn me not to *view* its bonds,
    For I will never *feel* them;—Italy!
Thy late reviving Roman soul desponds
    Beneath the lie this State-thing breathed o'er thee—
Thy clanking chain, and Erin's yet green wounds,
    Have voices—tongues to cry aloud for me.
Europe has slaves, allies, kings, armies still,
And Southey lives to sing them very ill.

XVII

Meantime, Sir Laureate, I proceed to dedicate,
130   In honest simple verse, this song to you.
And, if in flattering strains I do not predicate,
    'Tis that I still retain my 'buff and blue';
My politics as yet are all to educate:
    Apostasy's so fashionable, too,
To keep *one* creed's a task grown quite Herculean:
Is it not so, my Tory, Ultra-Julian?

VENICE, SEPTEMBER 16, 1818

from Canto the First

I

I want a hero: an uncommon want,
    When every year and month sends forth a new one,
Till, after cloying the gazettes with cant,
    The age discovers he is not the true one;
Of such as these I should not care to vaunt,
    I'll therefore take our ancient friend Don Juan—
We all have seen him, in the pantomime,
Sent to the devil somewhat ere his time.

.   .   .

V

Brave men were living before Agamemnon
 And since, exceeding valorous and sage,
A good deal like him too, though quite the same none;
 But then they shone not on the poet's page,
And so have been forgotten:—I condemn none,
 But can't find any in the present age
Fit for my poem (that is, for my new one);
So, as I said, I'll take my friend Don Juan.

VI

Most epic poets plunge 'in medias res'
 (Horace makes this the heroic turnpike road),
And then your hero tells, whene'er you please,
 What went before—by way of episode,
While seated after dinner at his ease,
 Beside his mistress in some soft abode,
Palace, or garden, paradise, or cavern,
Which serves the happy couple for a tavern.

VII

That is the usual method, but not mine—
 My way is to begin with the beginning;
The regularity of my design
 Forbids all wandering as the worst of sinning,
And therefore I shall open with a line
 (Although it cost me half an hour in spinning)
Narrating somewhat of Don Juan's father,
And also of his mother, if you'd rather.

On This Day I Complete My Thirty-sixth Year

'Tis time this heart should be unmoved,
 Since others it hath ceased to move:
Yet, though I cannot be beloved,
  Still let me love!

My days are in the yellow leaf;
 The flowers and fruits of love are gone;
The worm, the canker, and the grief
  Are mine alone!

The fire that on my bosom preys
10   Is lone as some volcanic isle;
No torch is kindled at its blaze—
        A funeral pile.

The hope, the fear, the jealous care,
     The exalted portion of the pain
And power of love, I cannot share,
        But wear the chain.

But 'tis not *thus*—and 'tis not *here*—
     Such thoughts should shake my soul, nor *now*,
Where glory decks the hero's bier,
20   Or binds his brow.

The sword, the banner, and the field,
     Glory and Greece, around me see!
The Spartan, borne upon his shield,
        Was not more free.

Awake! (not Greece—she is awake!) `
     Awake, my spirit! Think through *whom*
Thy life-blood tracks its parent lake,
        And then strike home!

Tread those reviving passions down,
30   Unworthy manhood!—unto thee
Indifferent should the smile or frown
        Of beauty be.

If thou regret'st thy youth, *why live?*
     The land of honourable death
Is here:—up to the field, and give
        Away thy breath!

Seek out—less often sought than found—
     A soldier's grave, for thee the best;
Then look around, and choose thy ground,
40   And take thy rest.

PERCY BYSSHE SHELLEY

1792–1822

SHELLEY WAS BORN on August 4, 1792, to a prosperous family of country gentry in Sussex. His radical religious and political vision began in his rebellion against the system at Eton. He was expelled from University College, Oxford, in March 1811, after a half a year in residence, during which he co-authored and published *The Necessity of Atheism.* Going up to London, he met Leigh Hunt, and other radicals, and eloped with Harriet Westbrook, he having just turned nineteen, she being sixteen. With the astonishing rapidity that always marked his life and his poetry ("I always go on until I am stopped and I never am stopped"), he announced himself to the Necessitarian philosopher-reformer William Godwin as a true disciple, journeyed to Ireland to agitate against the English government, published pamphlets, was shadowed by royal agents, privately printed his revolutionary poem *Queen Mab,* fathered a daughter upon Harriet and then abandoned her, again pregnant, to elope with Mary Godwin, the brilliant seventeen-year-old daughter of Godwin and the pioneer of women's liberation, the late Mary Wollstonecraft, who had died in giving birth to Mary Godwin.

In the autumn of 1815, fearing imminent death from tuberculosis (which he did not have), he wrote his first considerable poem, *Alastor,* in a Wordsworthian style but polemically directed against Wordsworth. In May 1816, Shelley left England, and went to Geneva, where his friendship with Byron began and where his genius found itself in composing the "Hymn to Intellectual Beauty" and "Mont Blanc." When he returned to England, in the autumn, Harriet drowned herself, which allowed him to legalize his union with Mary Godwin. In 1817, the Lord Chancellor Eldon refused Shelley custody of his two children by Harriet, on moral grounds. In March 1818, Shelley went into permanent Italian exile.

During his four Italian years, in his later twenties (his drowning came a month before his thirtieth birthday), Shelley wrote his sequence of major poems: *Julian and Maddalo, Prometheus Unbound, The Cenci, The Sensitive Plant, The Witch of Atlas, Epipsychidion, Adonais, Hellas,* the unfinished death-poem, *The Triumph of Life*, scores of magnificent lyrics, and the major prose essay, his *Defence of Poetry*. These years were turbulent with intense friendships, many love affairs, revolutionary politics, and deep reading and meditation. Personally all but selfless, invariably benevolent, Shelley was also gentle, urbane, and by most accounts the most lovable of human beings. Byron, a bitter judge of character, said of Shelley after his death that everyone else he knew seemed a beast in comparison. Nevertheless, Shelley was constantly reviled in England as an immoral atheist, an enemy of decency. A prominent English obituary trumpeted: "Shelley the Atheist is dead. Now he knows whether there is a Hell or not."

Shelley's posthumous poetic reputation is the most volatile and hardest-fought-over of the last 150 years. Eminent modern critics have agreed with one another that he is all but totally worthless, an opinion held in his own time by Charles Lamb, and developed later by Carlyle and Arnold. T. S. Eliot, F. R. Leavis, Allen Tate, and W. H. Auden are typical of the majority view in modern criticism that prevailed until recently. Their Shelley is a bad craftsman and an adolescent.

This is not even good nonsense. Shelley is a central influence upon Beddoes, Browning, Swinburne, Yeats, Shaw, and Hardy. His urbane control is the crucial element in his poetry. He is a superb craftsman, a lyrical poet without rival, and surely one of the most advanced skeptical intellects ever to write a poem. He can be seen as a blend of an English Pindar and an English Lucretius. His poetry has never had total appeal among literary people because it is idiosyncratic enough to be menacing. Also, to be honest, certain readers always will be alienated by Shelley's dissent in political, religious, and sexual matters. And yet he stands as the modern lyrical poet proper. The design of Shelley's poetry is remorseless quest for a world where Eros is triumphant. Shelley loved Plato's work but was no Platonist. Rather, he was a skeptic, who came to understand that head and heart could not be reconciled. An original religious temperament, Shelley created what could be termed a Protestant Orphism, a prophecy of human renovation in which fallen men would rise to "Man, one harmonious soul of many a soul, / Whose nature is its own divine control, / Where, all things flow to all, as rivers to the sea. . . ." As the poet aged, he saw more vividly that this hope could not be realized by reform or revolution (though he always remained on the extreme Left) but could come only through an overcoming of each natural selfhood by imagination. This sounds rather like Blake, but the two poets never met, and evidently never read each other. Shelley differs from Blake in not systemizing his myth of salvation, for his intellectual skepticism made him doubt profoundly his own idealizations.

There is, despite his courage, a pattern of deepening despair in the cycle of Shelley's poetry. From the dead end of *Alastor*, Shelley rose to the highly qualified hope of *Prometheus Unbound*, and then came full circle again to the natural defeat of imaginative quest in *Adonais* and in the unfinished but totally hopeless *The Triumph of Life*, which is not a *Purgatorio* but an *Inferno*. Shelley's heart, when he died, had begun to touch the limits of desire. A tough but subtle temperament, he had worn himself out, and was ready to depart.

❧   ❧   ❧

Prometheus Unbound

The Greek Orphic tradition maintained that the Titans, whom Zeus and the Olympian gods overthrew, were our ancestors. Hesiod said that the name "Titans" means "punished overreachers." Of these overreachers, Prometheus (whose name means "foresighted," "prophetic") is the most celebrated. Aeschylus, the Athenian tragic dramatist, wrote a trilogy on Prometheus, of which only the first play, *Prometheus Bound*, survives. In it, Zeus (Shelley's Jupiter) is a tyrant who tortures Prometheus, but the Titan has faults also, being prideful and unrestrained. The surviving fragments of Aeschylus's second play, *Prometheus Unbound*, indicate that Zeus is reforming himself, as he has partly restored the Titan, and has given up his threats to destroy mankind. He still seeks to induce Prometheus to reveal a fatal secret, known only to the Titan, which will destroy Olympian rule, the secret being that any child Zeus begets upon Thetis, a mortal woman, will rise eventually to destroy his father.

Shelley rejects the outcome of Aeschylus's lost second play, which reconciles Zeus and Prometheus, and which permits Zeus to be warned in time. Shelley's Romantic Prometheus never yields to Jupiter, but he ceases to hate Jupiter, and in doing so begins a process that destroys the High God, whom Shelley regards as being beyond redemption. This process is imaginatively difficult, but is undoubtedly the supreme poetic invention in Shelley's work. To understand it, a reader needs to clarify for himself the curious shape of Shelley's myth in the poem.

As in Blake's *The Four Zoas*, the postulate is that a unitary Man fell, and separated out into torturing and tortured components, and into male and female forms as well. Jupiter is not an ultimate evil, even though he would like to be; he is too limited, because he has been invented by his victim, Prometheus, and cannot survive long once Prometheus abandons hatred of his own invention. As for Prometheus himself, he is limited also, for though he contains the human imagination and sexual energy, he can only begin the process of freeing imagination and sexuality. To complete it he requires his spouse, Asia, who is again a limited being. Mostly she remains subject to nature and can best be thought of as that provisional strength in humanity (much celebrated by Wordsworth) that holds the natural world open to the love and beauty that hover perpetually just beyond the range of our senses.

Demogorgon is the lyrical drama's prime difficulty. Unlike the Demogorgon of Spenser, Milton, and Coleridge (see his fragment, "Limbo"), Shelley's daemon is not the pagan god of the abyss, but rather the god of skepticism, of our appalled but honest question: "What can we know?" He governs the turning-over of historical cycles, resembling in this the Marxist dialectic of history (Engels and Marx greatly admired Shelley's poem). He is also a parody of the descent of the Holy Spirit in some Christian accounts. His limitation is what most characterizes him, for he represents the imagelessness of ultimates, like the dread, morally unallied Power behind the ravine in Shelley's "Mont Blanc."

Prometheus Unbound transcends the limiting context of any particular time and becomes sharply relevant in any new time of troubles. Shelley, always a revolutionary, is not teaching quietism or acceptance. But he shows, in permanent ways, how difficult the path of regeneration is, and how much both the head and the heart need to purge in themselves if and when regeneration is ever to begin.

Ode to the West Wind

Preface by Shelley

This poem was conceived and chiefly written in a wood that skirts the Arno, near Florence, and on a day when that tempestuous wind, whose temperature is at once mild and animating, was collecting the vapours which pour down the autumnal rains. They began, as I foresaw, at sunset with a violent tempest of hail and rain, attended by that magnificent thunder and lightning peculiar to the Cisalpine regions.

The phenomenon alluded to at the conclusion of the third stanza is well known to naturalists. The vegetation at the bottom of the sea, of rivers, and of

lakes, sympathizes with that of the land in the change of seasons, and is consequently influenced by the winds which announce it.—

I

O wild West Wind, thou breath of Autumn's being,
Thou, from whose unseen presence the leaves dead
Are driven, like ghosts from an enchanter fleeing,

Yellow, and black, and pale, and hectic red,
Pestilence-stricken multitudes: O thou,
Who chariotest to their dark wintry bed

The wingèd seeds, where they lie cold and low,
Each like a corpse within its grave, until
Thine azure sister of the Spring shall blow

10   Her clarion o'er the dreaming earth, and fill
(Driving sweet buds like flocks to feed in air)
With living hues and odours plain and hill:

Wild Spirit, which art moving everywhere;
Destroyer and preserver; hear, oh, hear!

II

Thou on whose stream, mid the steep sky's commotion,
Loose clouds like earth's decaying leaves are shed,
Shook from the tangled boughs of Heaven and Ocean,

Angels of rain and lightning: there are spread
On the blue surface of thine aery surge,
20   Like the bright hair uplifted from the head

Of some fierce Maenad, even from the dim verge
Of the horizon to the zenith's height,
The locks of the approaching storm. Thou dirge

Of the dying year, to which this closing night
Will be the dome of a vast sepulchre,
Vaulted with all thy congregated might

Of vapours, from whose solid atmosphere
Black rain, and fire, and hail will burst: oh, hear!

III

Though who didst waken from his summer dreams
30   The blue Mediterranean, where he lay,
Lulled by the coil of his crystàlline streams,

Beside a pumice isle in Baiae's bay,
And saw in sleep old palaces and towers
Quivering within the wave's intenser day,

All overgrown with azure moss and flowers
So sweet, the sense faints picturing them! Thou
For whose path the Atlantic's level powers

Cleave themselves into chasms, while far below
The sea-blooms and the oozy woods which wear
40   The sapless foliage of the ocean, know

Thy voice, and suddenly grow grey with fear,
And tremble and despoil themselves: oh, hear!

IV

If I were a dead leaf thou mightest bear;
If I were a swift cloud to fly with thee;
A wave to pant beneath thy power, and share

The impulse of thy strength, only less free
Than thou, O uncontrollable! If even
I were as in my boyhood, and could be

The comrade of thy wanderings over Heaven,
50   As then, when to outstrip thy skiey speed
Scarce seemed a vision; I would ne'er have striven

As thus with thee in prayer in my sore need.
Oh, lift me as a wave, a leaf, a cloud!
I fall upon the thorns of life! I bleed!

A heavy weight of hours has chained and bowed
One too like thee: tameless, and swift, and proud.

V

Make me thy lyre, even as the forest is:
What if my leaves are falling like its own!
The tumult of thy mighty harmonies

60 Will take from both a deep, autumnal tone,
　　Sweet though in sadness. Be thou, Spirit fierce,
　　My spirit! Be thou me, impetuous one!

　　Drive my dead thoughts over the universe
　　Like withered leaves to quicken a new birth!
　　And, by the incantation of this verse,

　　Scatter, as from an unextinguished hearth
　　Ashes and sparks, my words among mankind!
　　Be through my lips to unawakened earth

　　The trumpet of a prophecy! O, Wind,
70 If Winter comes, can Spring be far behind?
　　　　1819   1820

The Two Spirits: An Allegory

FIRST SPIRIT
O thou, who plumed with strong desire
　　Wouldst float above the earth, beware!
A Shadow tracks thy flight of fire—
　　　　Night is coming!
　　Bright are the regions of the air,
And among the winds and beams
　　It were delight to wander there—
　　　　Night is coming!

SECOND SPIRIT
The deathless stars are bright above;
10　　If I would cross the shade of night,
Within my heart is the lamp of love,
　　　　And that is day!
　　And the moon will smile with gentle light
On my golden plumes where'er they move;
　　The meteors will linger round my flight,
　　　　And make night day.

FIRST SPIRIT
But if the whirlwinds of darkness waken
　　Hail, and lightning, and stormy rain;
See, the bounds of the air are shaken—

Night is coming!
20   The red swift clouds of the hurricane
Yon declining sun have overtaken,
The clash of the hail sweeps over the plain—
Night is coming!

SECOND SPIRIT
I see the light, and I hear the sound;
I'll sail on the flood of the tempest dark,
With the calm within and the light around
Which makes night day:
And thou, when the gloom is deep and stark,
30   Look from thy dull earth, slumber-bound,
My moon-like flight thou then mayst mark
On high, far away.

———

Some say there is a precipice
Where one vast pine is frozen to ruin
O'er piles of snow and chasms of ice
Mid Alpine mountains;
And that the languid storm pursuing
That wingèd shape, forever flies
Round those hoar branches, aye renewing
40   Its aery fountains.

Some say when nights are dry and clear,
And the death-dews sleep on the morass,
Sweet whispers are heard by the traveller,
Which make night day:
And a silver shape like his early love doth pass
Upborne by her wild and glittering hair,
And when he awakes on the fragrant grass,
He finds night day.
1820   1824

from Epipsychidion

[Three Sermons on Free Love]
Thy wisdom speaks in me, and bids me dare
Beacon the rocks on which high hearts are wrecked.
I never was attached to that great sect,

150 Whose doctrine is, that each one should select
Out of the crowd a mistress or a friend,
And all the rest, though fair and wise, commend
To cold oblivion, though it is in the code
Of modern morals, and the beaten road
Which those poor slaves with weary footsteps tread,
Who travel to their home among the dead
By the broad highway of the world, and so
With one chained friend, perhaps a jealous foe,
The dreariest and the longest journey go.

160   True Love in this differs from gold and clay,
That to divide is not to take away.
Love is like understanding, that grows bright,
Gazing on many truths; 'tis like thy light,
Imagination! which from earth and sky,
And from the depths of human fantasy,
As from a thousand prisms and mirrors, fills
The Universe with glorious beams, and kills
Error, the worm, with many a sun-like arrow
Of its reverberated lightning. Narrow
170 The heart that loves, the brain that contemplates,
The life that wears, the spirit that creates
One object, and one form, and builds thereby
A sepulchre for its eternity.

    Mind from its object differs most in this:
Evil from good; misery from happiness;
The baser from the nobler; the impure
And frail, from what is clear and must endure.
If you divide suffering and dross, you may
Diminish till it is consumed away;
180 If you divide pleasure and love and thought,
Each part exceeds the whole; and we know not
How much, while any yet remains unshared,
Of pleasure may be gained, of sorrow spared:
This truth is that deep well, whence sages draw
The unenvied light of hope; the eternal law
By which those live, to whom this world of life
Is as a garden ravaged, and whose strife
Tills for the promise of a later birth
The wilderness of this Elysian earth.

    .   .   .

[The Annihilation of Love]
Let us become the overhanging day,
The living soul of this Elysian isle,
540   Conscious, inseparable, one. Meanwhile
We two will rise, and sit, and walk together,
Under the roof of blue Ionian weather,
And wander in the meadows, or ascend
The mossy mountains, where the blue heavens bend
With lightest winds, to touch their paramour;
Or linger, where the pebble-paven shore,
Under the quick, faint kisses of the sea
Trembles and sparkles as with ecstasy,—
Possessing and possessed by all that is
550   Within that calm circumference of bliss,
And by each other, till to love and live
Be one:—or, at the noontide hour, arrive
Where some old cavern hoar seems yet to keep
The moonlight of the expired night asleep,
Through which the awakened day can never peep;
A veil for our seclusion, close as night's,
Where secure sleep may kill thine innocent lights;
Sleep, the fresh dew of languid love, the rain
Whose drops quench kisses till they burn again.
560   And we will talk, until thought's melody
Become too sweet for utterance, and it die
In words, to live again in looks, which dart
With thrilling tone into the voiceless heart,
Harmonizing silence without a sound.
Our breath shall intermix, our bosoms bound,
And our veins beat together; and our lips
With other eloquence than words, eclipse
The soul that burns between them, and the wells
Which boil under our being's inmost cells,
570   The fountains of our deepest life, shall be
Confused in Passion's golden purity,
As mountain-springs under the morning sun.
We shall become the same, we shall be one
Spirit within two frames, oh! wherefore two?
One passion in twin-hearts, which grows and grew,
Till like two meteors of expanding flame,
Those spheres instinct with it become the same,
Touch, mingle, are transfigured; ever still

Burning, yet ever inconsumable:
580   In one another's substance finding food,
Like flames too pure and light and unimbued
To nourish their bright lives with baser prey,
Which point to Heaven and cannot pass away:
One hope within two wills, one will beneath
Two overshadowing minds, one life, one death,
One Heaven, one Hell, one immortality,
And one annihilation . . .

    1821   1839

Adonais

Adonais is one of the major pastoral elegies, and, like the others, it both laments a dead poet and speculates darkly on its author's own possible fate. Shelley's poem is unique, partly for the extraneous reason that he mourns a poet of his own eminence, John Keats, but largely because of its scope and ambition, which transcend the limits of elegy. The last seventeen stanzas of *Adonais* are closer to their descendants, Yeats's "Sailing to Byzantium" and "Byzantium," than to their ancestors: the second-century (B.C.E.) Hellenic poems, Bion's "Lament for Adonis" and Moschus's "Lament for Bion," and the great English Renaissance elegies, Spenser's "Astrophel" for Sir Philip Sidney and Milton's *Lycidas* for Edward King. Bion mourns the death of Adonis, god of the vegetative year and lover of Venus. Moschus laments the untimely death of the mourner for Adonis, and the Renaissance elegists follow, though with astonishing departures in Milton's poem. But Shelley, in the last third of his poem, is not mourning at all. He struggles to attain a luminous self-recognition that will prepare him for his own death, which he accurately senses is coming shortly (only a year away), and he strives to secure also some vision of the state of being of poetry itself, in its border relations both to life and to death.

Adonais

An Elegy on the Death of John Keats, Author of Endymion, Hyperion, Etc.

    Ἀστὴρ πρὶν μὲν ἔλαμπες ἐνὶ ζωοῖσιν Ἑῷος·
    νῦν δὲ θανὼν λάμπεις Ἕσπερος ἐν φθιμένοις.
                          PLATO

I

I weep for Adonais—he is dead!
O, weep for Adonais! though our tears
Thaw not the frost which binds so dear a head!
And thou, sad Hour, selected from all years
To mourn our loss, rouse thy obscure compeers,
And teach them thine own sorrow, say: 'With me
Died Adonais; till the Future dares
Forget the Past, his fate and fame shall be
An echo and a light unto eternity!'

II

10   Where wert thou, mighty Mother, when he lay,
When thy Son lay, pierced by the shaft which flies
In darkness? where was lorn Urania
When Adonais died? With veilèd eyes,
'Mid listening Echoes, in her Paradise
She sate, while one, with soft enamoured breath,
Rekindled all the fading melodies,
With which, like flowers that mock the corse beneath,
He had adorned and hid the coming bulk of Death.

III

Oh, weep for Adonais—he is dead!
20   Wake, melancholy Mother, wake and weep!
Yet wherefore? Quench within their burning bed
Thy fiery tears, and let thy loud heart keep
Like his, a mute and uncomplaining sleep;
For he is gone, where all things wise and fair
Descend;—oh, dream not that the amorous Deep
Will yet restore him to the vital air;
Death feeds on his mute voice, and laughs at our despair.

IV

Most musical of mourners, weep again!
Lament anew, Urania!—He died,
30   Who was the Sire of an immortal strain,
Blind, old, and lonely, when his country's pride,
The priest, the slave, and the liberticide,
Trampled and mocked with many a loathèd rite
Of lust and blood; he went, unterrified,
Into the gulf of death; but his clear Sprite
Yet reigns o'er earth; the third among the sons of light.

V

Most musical of mourners, weep anew!
Not all to that bright station dared to climb;
And happier they their happiness who knew,
40   Whose tapers yet burn through that night of time
In which suns perished; others more sublime,
Struck by the envious wrath of man or god,
Have sunk, extinct in their refulgent prime;
And some yet live, treading the thorny road,
Which leads, through toil and hate, to Fame's serene abode.

VI

But now, thy youngest, dearest one, has perished—
The nursling of thy widowhood, who grew,
Like a pale flower by some sad maiden cherished,
And fed with true-love tears, instead of dew;
50   Most musical of mourners, weep anew!
Thy extreme hope, the loveliest and the last,
The bloom, whose petals nipped before they blew
Died on the promise of the fruit, is waste;
The broken lily lies—the storm is overpast.

VII

To that high Capital, where kingly Death
Keeps his pale court in beauty and decay,
He came; and bought, with price of purest breath,
A grave among the eternal.—Come away!
Haste, while the vault of blue Italian day
60   Is yet his fitting charnel-roof! while still
He lies, as if in dewy sleep he lay;
Awake him not! surely he takes his fill
Of deep and liquid rest, forgetful of all ill.

VIII

He will awake no more, oh, never more!—
Within the twilight chamber spreads apace
The shadow of white Death, and at the door
Invisible Corruption waits to trace
His extreme way to her dim dwelling-place;
The eternal Hunger sits, but pity and awe
70   Soothe her pale rage, nor dares she to deface
So fair a prey, till darkness, and the law
Of change, shall o'er his sleep the mortal curtain draw.

IX

Oh, weep for Adonais!—The quick Dreams,
The passion-winged Ministers of thought,
Who were his flocks, whom near the living streams
Of his young spirit he fed, and whom he taught
The love which was its music, wander not,—
Wander no more, from kindling brain to brain,
But droop there, whence they sprung; and mourn their lot
80   Round the cold heart, where, after their sweet pain,
They ne'er will gather strength, or find a home again.

X

And one with trembling hands clasps his cold head,
And fans him with her moonlight wings, and cries;
'Our love, our hope, our sorrow, is not dead;
See, on the silken fringe of his faint eyes,
Like dew upon a sleeping flower, there lies
A tear some Dream has loosened from his brain.'
Lost Angel of a ruined Paradise!
She knew not 'twas her own; as with no stain
90   She faded, like a cloud which had outwept its rain.

XI

One from a lucid urn of starry dew
Washed his light limbs as if embalming them;
Another clipped her profuse locks, and threw
The wreath upon him, like an anadem,
Which frozen tears instead of pearls begem;
Another in her wilful grief would break
Her bow and wingèd reeds, as if to stem
A greater loss with one which was more weak;
And dull the barbèd fire against his frozen cheek.

XII

100   Another Splendour on his mouth alit,
That mouth, whence it was wont to draw the breath
Which gave it strength to pierce the guarded wit,
And pass into the panting heart beneath
With lightning and with music: the damp death
Quenched its caress upon his icy lips;
And, as a dying meteor stains a wreath
Of moonlight vapour, which the cold night clips,
It flushed through his pale limbs, and passed to its eclipse.

XIII

And others came . . . Desires and Adorations,
110   Wingèd Persuasions and veiled Destinies,
Splendours, and Glooms, and glimmering Incarnations
Of hopes and fears, and twilight Phantasies;
And Sorrow, with her family of Sighs,
And Pleasure, blind with tears, led by the gleam
Of her own dying smile instead of eyes,
Came in slow pomp;—the moving pump might seem
Like pageantry of mist on an autumnal stream.

XIV

All he had loved, and moulded into thought,
From shape, and hue, and odour, and sweet sound,
120   Lamented Adonais. Morning sought
Her eastern watch-tower, and her hair unbound,
Wet with the tears which should adorn the ground,
Dimmed the aereal eyes that kindle day;
Afar the melancholy thunder moaned,
Pale Ocean in unquiet slumber lay,
And the wild Winds flew round, sobbing in their dismay.

XV

Lost Echo sits amid the voiceless mountains,
And feeds her grief with his remembered lay,
And will no more reply to winds or fountains,
130   Or amorous birds perched on the young green spray,
Or herdsman's horn, or bell at closing day;
Since she can mimic not his lips, more dear
Than those for whose disdain she pined away
Into a shadow of all sounds:—a drear
Murmur, between their songs, is all the woodmen hear.

XVI

Grief made the young Spring wild, and she threw down
Her kindling buds, as if she Autumn were,
Or they dead leaves; since her delight is flown,
For whom should she have waked the sullen year?
140   To Phoebus was not Hyacinth so dear
Nor to himself Narcissus, as to both
Thou, Adonais: wan they stand and sere
Amid the faint companions of their youth,
With dew all turned to tears; odour, to sighing ruth.

XVII

Thy spirit's sister, the lorn nightingale
Mourns not her mate with such melodious pain;
Not so the eagle, who like thee could scale
Heaven, and could nourish in the sun's domain
Her mighty youth with morning, doth complain,
150   Soaring and screaming round her empty nest,
As Albion wails for thee: the curse of Cain
Light on his head who pierced thy innocent breast,
And scared the angel soul that was its earthly guest!

XVIII

Ah, woe is me! Winter is come and gone,
But grief returns with the revolving year;
The airs and streams renew their joyous tone;
The ants, the bees, the swallows reappear;
Fresh leaves and flowers deck the dead Seasons' bier;
The amorous birds now pair in every brake,
160   And build their mossy homes in field and brere;
And the green lizard, and the golden snake,
Like unimprisoned flames, out of their trance awake.

XIX

Through wood and stream and field and hill and Ocean
A quickening life from the Earth's heart has burst
As it has ever done, with change and motion,
From the great morning of the world when first
God dawned on Chaos; in its stream immersed,
The lamps of Heaven flash with a softer light;
All baser things pant with life's sacred thirst;
170   Diffuse themselves; and spend in love's delight,
The beauty and the joy of their renewed might.

XX

The leprous corpse, touched by this spirit tender,
Exhales itself in flowers of gentle breath;
Like incarnations of the stars, when splendour
Is changed to fragrance, they illumine death
And mock the merry worm that wakes beneath;
Nought we know, dies. Shall that alone which knows
Be as a sword consumed before the sheath
By sightless lightning?—the intense atom glows
180   A moment, then is quenched in a most cold repose.

XXI

Alas! that all we loved of him should be,
But for our grief, as if it had not been,
And grief itself be mortal! Woe is me!
Whence are we, and why are we? of what scene
The actors or spectators? Great and mean
Meet massed in death, who lends what life must borrow.
As long as skies are blue, and fields are green,
Evening must usher night, night urge the morrow,
Month follow month with woe, and year wake year to sorrow.

XXII

190 *He* will awake no more, oh, never more!
'Wake thou,' cried Misery, 'childless Mother, rise
Out of thy sleep, and slake, in thy heart's core,
A wound more fierce than his, with tears and sighs.'
And all the Dreams that watched Urania's eyes,
And all the Echoes whom their sister's song
Had held in holy silence, cried: 'Arise!'
Swift as a Thought by the snake Memory stung,
From her ambrosial rest the fading Splendour sprung.

XXIII

She rose like an autumnal Night, that springs
200 Out of the East, and follows wild and drear
The golden Day, which, on eternal wings,
Even as a ghost abandoning a bier,
Had left the Earth a corpse. Sorrow and fear
So struck, so roused, so rapt Urania;
So saddened round her like an atmosphere
Of stormy mist; so swept her on her way
Even to the mournful place where Adonais lay.

XXIV

Out of her secret Paradise she sped,
Through camps and cities rough with stone, and steel,
210 And human hearts, which to her aery tread
Yielding not, wounded the invisible
Palms of her tender feet where'er they fell:
And barbèd tongues, and thoughts more sharp than they,
Rent the soft Form they never could repel,
Whose sacred blood, like the young tears of May,
Paved with eternal flowers that undeserving way.

XXV

In the death-chamber for a moment Death,
Shamed by the presence of that living Might,
Blushed to annihilation, and the breath
220   Revisited those lips, and Life's pale light
Flashed through those limbs, so late her dear delight.
'Leave me not wild and dread and comfortless,
As silent lightning leaves the starless night!
Leave me not!' cried Urania; her distress
Roused Death: Death rose and smiled, and met her vain caress.

XXVI

'Stay yet awhile! speak to me once again;
Kiss me, so long but as a kiss may live;
And in my heartless breast and burning brain
That word, that kiss, shall all thoughts else survive,
230   With food of saddest memory kept alive,
Now thou art dead, as if it were a part
Of thee, my Adonais! I would give
All that I am to be as thou now art!
But I am chained to Time, and cannot thence depart!

XXVII

'O gentle child, beautiful as thou wert,
Why didst thou leave the trodden paths of men
Too soon, and with weak hands though mighty heart
Dare the unpastured dragon in his den?
Defenceless as thou wert, oh, where was then
240   Wisdom the mirrored shield, or scorn the spear?
Or hadst thou waited the full cycle, when
Thy spirit should have filled its crescent sphere,
The monsters of life's waste had fled from thee like deer.

XXVIII

'The herded wolves, bold only to pursue;
The obscene ravens, clamorous o'er the dead;
The vultures to the conqueror's banner true
Who feed where Desolation first has fed,
And whose wings rain contagion;—how they fled,
When, like Apollo, from his golden bow
250   The Pythian of the age one arrow sped
And smiled!—The spoilers tempt no second blow,
They fawn on the proud feet that spurn them lying low.

XXIX

The sun comes forth, and many reptiles spawn;
He sets, and each ephemeral insect then
Is gathered into death without a dawn,
And the immortal stars awake again;
So is it in the world of living men:
A godlike mind soars forth, in its delight
Making earth bare and veiling heaven, and when
260   It sinks, the swarms that dimmed or shared its light
Leave to its kindred lamps the spirit's awful night.'

XXX

Thus ceased she: and the mountain shepherds came,
Their garlands sere, their magic mantles rent;
The Pilgrim of Eternity, whose fame
Over his living head like Heaven is bent,
An early but enduring monument,
Came, veiling all the lightnings of his song
In sorrow; from her wilds Ierne sent
The sweetest lyrist of her saddest wrong,
270   And Love taught Grief to fall like music from his tongue.

XXXI

Midst others of less note, came one frail Form,
A phantom among men; companionless
As the last cloud of an expiring storm
Whose thunder is its knell; he, as I guess,
Had gazed on Nature's naked loveliness,
Actaeon-like, and now he fled astray
With feeble steps o'er the world's wilderness,
And his own thoughts, along that rugged way,
Pursued, like raging hounds, their father and their prey.

XXXII

280   A pardlike Spirit beautiful and swift—
A Love in desolation masked;—a Power
Girt round with weakness;—it can scarce uplift
The weight of the superincumbent hour;
It is a dying lamp, a falling shower,
A breaking billow;—even whilst we speak
Is it not broken? On the withering flower
The killing sun smiles brightly: on a cheek
The life can burn in blood, even while the heart may break.

XXXIII

His head was bound with pansies overblown,
And faded violets, white, and pied, and blue;
And a light spear topped with a cypress cone,
Round whose rude shaft dark ivy-tresses grew
Yet dripping with the forest's noonday dew,
Vibrated, as the ever-beating heart
Shook the weak hand that grasped it; of that crew
He came the last, neglected and apart;
A herd-abandoned deer struck by the hunter's dart.

XXXIV

All stood aloof, and at his partial moan
Smiled through their tears; well knew that gentle band
Who in another's fate now wept his own,
As in the accents of an unknown land
He sung new sorrow; sad Urania scanned
The Stranger's mien, and murmured: 'Who art thou?'
He answered not, but with a sudden hand
Made bare his branded and ensanguined brow,
Which was like Cain's or Christ's—oh! that it should be so!

XXXV

What softer voice is hushed over the dead?
Athwart what brow is that dark mantle thrown?
What form leans sadly o'er the white death-bed,
In mockery of monumental stone,
The heavy heart heaving without a moan?
If it be He, who, gentlest of the wise,
Taught, soothed, loved, honoured the departed one,
Let me not vex, with inharmonious sighs,
The silence of that heart's accepted sacrifice.

XXXVI

Our Adonais has drunk poison—oh!
What deaf and viperous murderer could crown
Life's early cup with such a draught of woe?
The nameless worm would now itself disown:
It felt, yet could escape, the magic tone
Whose prelude held all envy, hate, and wrong,
But what was howling in one breast alone,
Silent with expectation of the song,
Whose master's hand is cold, whose silver lyre unstrung.

XXXVII

Live thou, whose infamy is not thy fame!
Live! fear no heavier chastisement from me,
Thou noteless blot on a remembered name!
But be thyself, and know thyself to be!
And ever at thy season be thou free
To spill the venom when thy fangs o'erflow;
Remorse and Self-contempt shall cling to thee;
Hot Shame shall burn upon thy secret brow,
And like a beaten hound tremble thou shalt—as now.

XXXVIII

Nor let us weep that our delight is fled
Far from these carrion kites that scream below;
He wakes or sleeps with the enduring dead;
Thou canst not soar where he is sitting now.—
Dust to the dust! but the pure spirit shall flow
Back to the burning fountain whence it came,
A portion of the Eternal, which must glow
Through time and change, unquenchably the same,
Whilst thy cold embers choke the sordid hearth of shame.

XXXIX

Peace, peace! he is not dead, he doth not sleep—
He hath awakened from the dream of life—
'Tis we, who lost in stormy visions, keep
With phantoms an unprofitable strife,
And in mad trance, strike with our spirit's knife
Invulnerable nothings.—We decay
Like corpses in a charnel; fear and grief
Convulse us and consume us day by day,
And cold hopes swarm like worms within our living clay.

XL

He has outsoared the shadow of our night;
Envy and calumny and hate and pain,
And that unrest which men miscall delight,
Can touch him not and torture not again;
From the contagion of the world's slow stain
He is secure, and now can never mourn
A heart grown cold, a head grown gray in vain;
Nor, when the spirit's self has ceased to burn,
With sparkless ashes load an unlamented urn.

XLI

He lives, he wakes—'tis Death is dead, not he;
Mourn not for Adonais.—Thou young Dawn,
Turn all thy dew to splendour, for from thee
The spirit thou lamentest is not gone;
Ye caverns and ye forests, cease to moan!
Cease, ye faint flowers and fountains, and thou Air,
Which like a mourning veil thy scarf hadst thrown
O'er the abandoned Earth, now leave it bare
Even to the joyous stars which smile on its despair!

XLII

He is made one with Nature: there is heard
His voice in all her music, from the moan
Of thunder, to the song of night's sweet bird;
He is a presence to be felt and known
In darkness and in light, from herb and stone,
Spreading itself where'er that Power may move
Which has withdrawn his being to its own;
Which wields the world with never-wearied love,
Sustains it from beneath, and kindles it above.

XLIII

He is a portion of the loveliness
Which once he made more lovely: he doth bear
His part, while the one Spirit's plastic stress
Sweeps through the dull dense world, compelling there,
All new successions to the forms they wear;
Torturing the unwilling dross that checks its flight
To its own likeness, as each mass may bear;
And bursting in its beauty and its might
From trees and beasts and men into the Heaven's light.

XLIV

The splendours of the firmament of time
May be eclipsed, but are extinguished not;
Like stars to their appointed height they climb,
And death is a low mist which cannot blot
The brightness it may veil. When lofty thought
Lifts a young heart above its mortal lair,
And love and life contend in it, for what
Shall be its earthly doom, the dead live there
And move like winds of light on dark and stormy air.

XLV

The inheritors of unfulfilled renown
Rose from their thrones, built beyond mortal thought,
Far in the Unapparent. Chatterton
400   Rose pale,—his solemn agony had not
Yet faded from him; Sidney, as he fought
And as he fell and as he lived and loved
Sublimely mild, a Spirit without spot,
Arose; and Lucan, by his death approved:
Oblivion as they rose shrank like a thing reproved.

XLVI

And many more, whose names on Earth are dark,
But whose transmitted effluence cannot die
So long as fire outlives the parent spark,
Rose, robed in dazzling immortality.
410   'Thou art become as one of us,' they cry,
'It was for thee yon kingless sphere has long
Swung blind in unascended majesty,
Silent alone amid an Heaven of Song.
Assume thy wingèd throne, thou Vesper of our throng!'

XLVII

Who mourns for Adonais? Oh, come forth,
Fond wretch! and know thyself and him aright.
Clasp with thy panting soul the pendulous Earth;
As from a centre, dart thy spirit's light
Beyond all worlds, until its spacious might
420   Satiate the void circumference: then shrink
Even to a point within our day and night;
And keep thy heart light lest it make thee sink
When hope has kindled hope, and lured thee to the brink.

XLVIII

Or go to Rome, which is the sepulchre,
Oh, not of him, but of our joy: 'tis nought
That ages, empires, and religions there
Lie buried in the ravage they have wrought;
For such as he can lend,—they borrow not
Glory from those who made the world their prey;
430   And he is gathered to the kings of thought
Who waged contention with their time's decay,
And of the past are all that cannot pass away.

XLIX

Go thou to Rome,—at once the Paradise,
The grave, the city, and the wilderness;
And where its wrecks like shattered mountains rise,
And flowering weeds, and fragrant copses dress
The bones of Desolation's nakedness
Pass, till the spirit of the spot shall lead
Thy footsteps to a slope of green access
440   Where, like an infant's smile, over the dead
A light of laughing flowers along the grass is spread;

L

And gray walls moulder round, on which dull Time
Feeds, like slow fire upon a hoary brand;
And one keen pyramid with wedge sublime,
Pavilioning the dust of him who planned
This refuge for his memory, doth stand
Like flame transformed to marble; and beneath,
A field is spread, on which a newer band
Have pitched in Heaven's smile their camp of death,
450   Welcoming him we lose with scarce extinguished breath.

LI

Here pause: these graves are all too young as yet
To have outgrown the sorrow which consigned
Its charge to each; and if the seal is set,
Here, on one fountain of a mourning mind,
Break it not thou! too surely shalt thou find
Thine own well full, if thou returnest home,
Of tears and gall. From the world's bitter wind
Seek shelter in the shadow of the tomb.
What Adonais is, why fear we to become?

LII

460   The One remains, the many change and pass;
Heaven's light forever shines, Earth's shadows fly;
Life, like a dome of many-coloured glass,
Stains the white radiance of Eternity,
Until Death tramples it to fragments.—Die,
If thou wouldst be with that which thou dost seek!
Follow where all is fled!—Rome's azure sky,
Flowers, ruins, statues, music, words, are weak
The glory they transfuse with fitting truth to speak.

LIII

Why linger, why turn back, why shrink, my Heart?
Thy hopes are gone before: from all things here
They have departed; thou shouldst now depart!
A light is passed from the revolving year,
And man, and woman; and what still is dear
Attracts to crush, repels to make thee wither.
The soft sky smiles,—the low wind whispers near:
'Tis Adonais calls! oh, hasten thither,
No more let Life divide what Death can join together.

LIV

That Light whose smile kindles the Universe,
That Beauty in which all things work and move,
That Benediction which the eclipsing Curse
Of birth can quench not, that sustaining Love
Which through the web of being blindly wove
By man and beast and earth and air and sea,
Burns bright or dim, as each are mirrors of
The fire for which all thirst; now beams on me,
Consuming the last clouds of cold mortality.

LV

The breath whose might I have invoked in song
Descends on me; my spirit's bark is driven,
Far from the shore, far from the trembling throng
Whose sails were never to the tempest given;
The massy earth and spherèd skies are riven!
I am borne darkly, fearfully, afar;
Whilst, burning through the inmost veil of Heaven,
The soul of Adonais, like a star,
Beacons from the abode where the Eternal are.

1821   1821

from Hellas

CHORUS

The world's great age begins anew,
The golden years return,
The earth doth like a snake renew
Her winter weeds outworn:

Heaven smiles, and faiths and empires gleam,
Like wrecks of a dissolving dream.

A brighter Hellas rears its mountains
    From waves serener far;
A new Peneus rolls his fountains
    Against the morning star.
1070 Where fairer Tempes bloom, there sleep
Young Cyclads on a sunnier deep.

A loftier Argo cleaves the main,
    Fraught with a later prize;
Another Orpheus sings again,
    And loves, and weeps, and dies.
A new Ulysses leaves once more
Calypso for his native shore.

Oh, write no more the tale of Troy,
    If earth Death's scroll must be!
1080 Nor mix with Laian rage the joy
    Which dawns upon the free:
Although a subtler Sphinx renew
Riddles of death Thebes never knew.

Another Athens shall arise,
    And to remoter time
Bequeath, like sunset to the skies,
    The splendour of its prime;
And leave, if nought so bright may live,
All earth can take or Heaven can give.

1090 Saturn and Love their long repose
    Shall burst, more bright and good
Than all who fell, than One who rose,
    Than many unsubdued:
Not gold, not blood, their altar dowers,
But votive tears and symbol flowers.

Oh, cease! must hate and death return?
    Cease! must men kill and die?
Cease! drain not to its dregs the urn
    Of bitter prophecy.

1100   The world is weary of the past,
        Oh, might it die or rest at last!
        1821   1822

With a Guitar, to Jane

        Ariel to Miranda:—Take
        This slave of Music, for the sake
        Of him who is the slave of thee,
        And teach it all the harmony
        In which thou canst, and only thou,
        Make the delighted spirit glow,
        Till joy denies itself again,
        And, too intense, is turned to pain;
        For by permission and command
10   Of thine own Prince Ferdinand,
        Poor Ariel sends this silent token
        Of more than ever can be spoken;
        Your guardian spirit, Ariel, who,
        From life to life, must still pursue
        Your happiness;—for thus alone
        Can Ariel ever find his own.
        From Prospero's enchanted cell,
        As the mighty verses tell,
        To the throne of Naples, he
20   Lit you o'er the trackless sea,
        Flitting on, your prow before,
        Like a living meteor.
        When you die, the silent Moon,
        In her interlunar swoon,
        Is not sadder in her cell
        Than deserted Ariel.
        When you live again on earth,
        Like an unseen star of birth,
        Ariel guides you o'er the sea
30   Of life from your nativity.
        Many changes have been run
        Since Ferdinand and you begun
        Your course of love, and Ariel still
        Has tracked your steps, and served your will;
        Now, in humbler, happier lot,
        This is all remembered not;

And now, alas! the poor sprite is
Imprisoned, for some fault of his,
In a body like a grave;—
From you he only dares to crave,
For his service and his sorrow,
A smile today, a song tomorrow.
The artist who this idol wrought,
To echo all harmonious thought,
Felled a tree, while on the steep
The woods were in their winter sleep,
Rocked in that repose divine
On the wind-swept Apennine;
And dreaming, some of Autumn past,
And some of Spring approaching fast,
And some of April buds and showers,
And some of songs in July bowers,
And all of love; and so this tree,—
O that such our death may be!—
Died in sleep, and felt no pain,
To live in happier form again:
From which, beneath Heaven's fairest star,
The artist wrought this loved Guitar,
And taught it justly to reply,
To all who question skilfully,
In language gentle as thine own;
Whispering in enamoured tone
Sweet oracles of woods and dells,
And summer winds in sylvan cells;
For it had learned all harmonies
Of the plains and of the skies,
Of the forests and the mountains,
And the many-voicèd fountains;
The clearest echoes of the hills,
The softest notes of falling rills,
The melodies of birds and bees,
The murmuring of summer seas,
And pattering rain, and breathing dew,
And airs of evening; and it knew
That seldom-heard mysterious sound,
Which, driven on its diurnal round,
As it floats through boundless day,
Our world enkindles on its way.—
All this it knows, but will not tell

80   To those who cannot question well
The Spirit that inhabits it;
It talks according to the wit
Of its companions; and no more
Is heard than has been felt before,
By those who tempt it to betray
These secrets of an elder day:
But, sweetly as its answers will
Flatter hands of perfect skill,
It keeps its highest, holiest tone
90   For our belovèd Jane alone.

    1822 1832

Lines Written in the Bay of Lerici

She left me at the silent time
When the moon had ceased to climb
The azure path of Heaven's steep,
And like an albatross asleep,
Balanced on her wings of light,
Hovered in the purple night,
Ere she sought her ocean nest
In the chambers of the West.
She left me, and I stayed alone
10   Thinking over every tone
Which, though silent to the ear,
The enchanted heart could hear,
Like notes which die when born, but still
Haunt the echoes of the hill;
And feeling ever—oh, too much!—
The soft vibration of her touch,
As if her gentle hand, even now,
Lightly trembled on my brow;
And thus, although she absent were,
20   Memory gave me all of her
That even Fancy dares to claim:—
Her presence had made weak and tame
All passions, and I lived alone
In the time which is our own;
The past and future were forgot,
As they had been, and would be, not.
But soon, the guardian angel gone,

The daemon reassumed his throne
In my faint heart. I dare not speak
30   My thoughts, but thus disturbed and weak
I sat and saw the vessels glide
Over the ocean bright and wide,
Like spirit-wingèd chariots sent
O'er some serenest element
For ministrations strange and far;
As if to some Elysian star
Sailed for drink to medicine
Such sweet and bitter pain as mine.
And the wind that winged their flight
40   From the land came fresh and light,
And the scent of wingèd flowers,
And the coolness of the hours
Of dew, and sweet warmth left by day,
Were scattered o'er the twinkling bay.
And the fisher with his lamp
And spear about the low rocks damp
Crept, and struck the fish which came
To worship the delusive flame.
Too happy they, whose pleasure sought
50   Extinguishes all sense and thought
Of the regret that pleasure leaves,
Destroying life alone, not peace!

    1822   1862

The Triumph of Life

Shelley's last poem, left incomplete when he drowned, shows a new severity of impulse and extraordinary purgation of style. Yet it is the most
despairing poem he wrote, even darker in its implications than *Adonais*.
Many readers want to believe that the poem would have ended in some
affirmation, had it been completed, but there is little in the poem to
encourage such speculation. The poem's best critics, from Hazlitt to Yeats,
have seen its bleakness, and the extent to which it constitutes a palinode or
recantation of Shelley's more positive visions, such as *Prometheus
Unbound*. What Yeats called the *antithetical* quest, undertaken against the
natural man and his human affections, which Shelley had begun to pursue in *Alastor*, here attains its shattering climax. The best (and most

restrained) statement of a more hopeful reading of the poem can be found in M. H. Abrams's *Natural Supernaturalism*.

Shelley's poem takes its tone from Dante's *Purgatorio*, but the action and context of *The Triumph of Life* share more with *The Inferno*. Rousseau, prophet of nature, serving as a surrogate for Wordsworth, enters the poem as Vergil, the guide to Shelley's Dante. But Shelley here is no Pilgrim of the Absolute. What he sees in this magnificent fragment is horror, the defeat of all human integrity by life, our life, which is only a lively death. This vision is not nihilistic, for all its hopelessness, not because anything in the text suggests that Shelley will clamber out of the abyss, but because he will not join the dance, will not be seduced by Nature as his precursor Rousseau was. And yet he stands in the hell of life's triumph, and sees around him all men who have lived, save for a sacred few of Athens and Jerusalem, whom he declines to name.

Amid this frightening splendor, two elements stand forth: the chastening of Shelley's idiom and mythic inventiveness, and the provocative distinction between three realms of light—poetry (the stars), nature (the sun), life (the chariot's glare). As nature outshines imagination, so the chariot's horrible splendor outshines nature. In the fragment's closing passages, Shelley writes his final critique of Wordsworthianism. Nature, whether she desires otherwise or not, always does betray the heart that loves her. The "shape all light," Wordsworthian Nature, offers her cup of communion, Rousseau drinks, and his imagination becomes as sand. Shelley, perhaps hours from his death, is at the height of his powers, but gazes out at a universe of death that offers only a mockery of his own vitalism.

The Triumph of Life

Swift as a spirit hastening to his task
  Of glory & of good, the Sun sprang forth
Rejoicing in his splendour, & the mask

  Of darkness fell from the awakened Earth.
The smokeless altars of the mountain snows
  Flamed above crimson clouds, & at the birth

Of light, the Ocean's orison arose
  To which the birds tempered their matin lay.
All flowers in field or forest which unclose

10   Their trembling eyelids to the kiss of day,
     Swinging their censers in the element,
        With orient incense lit by the new ray

     Burned slow & inconsumably, & sent
        Their odorous sighs up to the smiling air,
     And in succession due, did Continent,

        Isle, Ocean, & all things that in them wear
     The form & character of mortal mould
        Rise as the Sun their father rose, to bear

     Their portion of the toil which he of old
20   Took as his own & then imposed on them;
     But I, whom thoughts which must remain untold

        Had kept as wakeful as the stars that gem
     The cone of night, now they were laid asleep,
        Stretched my faint limbs beneath the hoary stem

     Which an old chestnut flung athwart the steep
        Of a green Apennine: before me fled
     The night; behind me rose the day; the Deep

        Was at my feet, & Heaven above my head
     When a strange trance over my fancy grew
30   Which was not slumber, for the shade it spread

     Was so transparent that the scene came through
        As clear as when a veil of light is drawn
     O'er evening hills they glimmer; and I knew

        That I had felt the freshness of that dawn,
     Bathed in the same cold dew my brow & hair
        And sate as thus upon that slope of lawn

     Under the self same bough, & heard as there
        The birds, the fountains & the Ocean hold
     Sweet talk in music through the enamoured air.

40   And then a Vision on my brain was rolled.

_____

As in that trance of wondrous thought I lay
　This was the tenour of my waking dream.
Methought I sate beside a public way

　Thick strewn with summer dust, & a great stream
Of people there was hurrying to & fro
　Numerous as gnats upon the evening gleam,

All hastening onward, yet none seemed to know
　Whither he went, or whence he came, or why
He made one of the multitude, yet so

50　Was born amid the crowd as through the sky
One of the million leaves of summer's bier.—
　Old age & youth, manhood & infancy,

Mixed in one mighty torrent did appear,
　Some flying from the thing they feared & some
Seeking the object of another's fear,

　And others as with steps towards the tomb
Pored on the trodden worms that crawled beneath,
　And others mournfully within the gloom

Of their own shadow walked, and called it death . . .
60　And some fled from it as it were a ghost,
Half fainting in the affliction of vain breath.

　But more with motions which each other crost
Pursued or shunned the shadows the clouds threw
　Or birds within the noonday ether lost,

Upon that path where flowers never grew;
　And weary with vain toil & faint for thirst
Heard not the fountains whose melodious dew

　Out of their mossy cells forever burst
Nor felt the breeze which from the forest told
70　Of grassy paths, & wood lawns interspersed

With overarching elms & caverns cold,
　And violet banks where sweet dreams brood, but they
Pursued their serious folly as of old . . .

And as I gazed methought that in the way
The throng grew wilder, as the woods of June
   When the South wind shakes the extinguished day.—

And a cold glare, intenser than the noon
   But icy cold, obscured with   light
The Sun as he the stars. Like the young moon

80   When on the sunlit limits of the night
Her white shell trembles amid crimson air
   And whilst the sleeping tempest gathers might

Doth, as a herald of its coming, bear
   The ghost of her dead Mother, whose dim form
Bends in dark ether from her infant's chair,

   So came a chariot on the silent storm
Of its own rushing splendour, and a Shape
   So sate within as one whom years deform

Beneath a dusky hood & double cape
90   Crouching within the shadow of a tomb,
And o'er what seemed the head, a cloud like crape,

   Was bent a dun & faint aetherial gloom
Tempering the light; upon the chariot's beam
   A Janus-visaged Shadow did assume

The guidance of that wonder-wingèd team.
   The Shapes which drew it in thick lightnings
Were lost: I heard alone on the air's soft stream

   The music of their ever moving wings,
All the four faces of that charioteer
100   Had their eyes banded . . . little profit brings

Speed in the van & blindness in the rear,
   Nor then avail the beams that quench the Sun
Or that his banded eyes could pierce the sphere

   Of all that is, has been, or will be done.—
So ill was the car guided, but it past
   With solemn speed majestically on . . .

The crowd gave way, & I arose aghast,
   Or seemed to rise, so mighty was the trance,
And saw like clouds upon the thunder blast

110   The million with fierce song and maniac dance
Raging around; such seemed the jubilee
   As when to greet some conqueror's advance

Imperial Rome poured forth her living sea
   From senatehouse & prison & theatre
When Freedom left those who upon the free

   Had bound a yoke which soon they stooped to bear.
Nor wanted here the true similitude
   Of a triumphal pageant, for where'er

The chariot rolled a captive multitude
120   Was driven; all those who had grown old in power
Or misery,—all who have their age subdued,

   By action or by suffering, and whose hour
Was drained to its last sand in weal or woe,
   So that the trunk survived both fruit & flower;

All those whose fame or infamy must grow
   Till the great winter lay the form & name
Of their own earth with them forever low,

   All but the sacred few who could not tame
Their spirits to the Conqueror, but as soon
130   As they had touched the world with living flame

Fled back like eagles to their native noon,
   Or those who put aside the diadem
Of earthly thrones or gems, till the last one

   Were there;—for they of Athens & Jerusalem
Were neither mid the mighty captives seen
   Nor mid the ribald crowd that followed them

Or fled before . . . Now swift, fierce & obscene
   The wild dance maddens in the van, & those
Who lead it, fleet as shadows on the green,

140   Outspeed the chariot & without repose
  Mix with each other in tempestuous measure
   To savage music . . . Wilder as it grows,

  They, tortured by the agonizing pleasure,
   Convulsed & on the rapid whirlwinds spun
  Of that fierce spirit, whose unholy leisure

   Was soothed by mischief since the world begun,
  Throw back their heads & loose their streaming hair,
   And in their dance round her who dims the Sun

  Maidens & youths fling their wild arms in air
150   As their feet twinkle; they recede, and now
  Bending within each other's atmosphere

   Kindle invisibly; and as they glow
  Like moths by light attracted & repelled,
   Oft to new bright destruction come & go.

  Till like two clouds into one vale impelled
   That shake the mountains when their lightnings mingle
  And die in rain,—the fiery band which held

   Their natures, snaps . . . ere the shock cease to tingle
  One falls and then another in the path
160   Senseless, nor is the desolation single,

  Yet ere I can say *where* the chariot hath
   Past over them; nor other trace I find
  But as of foam after the Ocean's wrath

   Is spent upon the desert shore.—Behind,
  Old men, and women foully disarrayed
   Shake their grey hair in the insulting wind.

  Limp in the dance & strain with limbs decayed
   To reach the car of light which leaves them still
  Farther behind & deeper in the shade.

170   But not the less with impotence of will
  They wheel, though ghastly shadows interpose
   Round them & round each other, and fulfill

Their work and to the dust whence they arose
   Sink & corruption veils them as they lie
And frost in these performs what fire in those.

   Struck to the heart by this sad pageantry,
Half to myself I said, 'And what is this?
   Whose shape is that within the car? & why'—

I would have added—'is all here amiss?'
180   But a voice answered . . . 'Life' . . . I turned & knew
(O Heaven have mercy on such wretchedness!)

   That what I thought was an old root which grew
To strange distortion out of the hill side
   Was indeed one of that deluded crew,

And that the grass which methought hung so wide
   And white, was but his thin discoloured hair,
And that the holes it vainly sought to hide

   Were or had been eyes.—'If thou canst forbear
To join the dance, which I had well forborne.'
190   Said the grim Feature, of my thought aware,

'I will now tell that which to this deep scorn
   Led me & my companions, and relate
The progress of the pageant since the morn;

   'If thirst of knowledge doth not thus abate,
Follow it even to the night, but I
   Am weary' . . . Then like one who with the weight

Of his own words is staggered, wearily
   He paused, and ere he could resume, I cried,
'First who art thou?' . . . 'Before thy memory

200   'I feared, loved, hated, suffered, did, & died,
And if the spark with which Heaven lit my spirit
   Earth had with purer nutriment supplied

'Corruption would not now thus much inherit
   Of what was once Rousseau—nor this disguise
Stained that within which still disdains to wear it.—

'If I have been extinguished, yet there rise
A thousand beacons from the spark I bore.'—
'And who are those chained to the car?' 'The Wise,

'The great, the unforgotten: they who wore
210   Mitres & helms & crowns, or wreathes of light,
Signs of thought's empire over thought; their lore

'Taught them not this—to know themselves; their might
Could not repress the mutiny within,
And for the morn of truth they feigned, deep night

'Caught them ere evening.' 'Who is he with chin
Upon his breast and hands crost on his chain?'
'The Child of a fierce hour; he sought to win

'The world, and lost all it did contain
Of greatness, in its hope destroyed; & more
220   Of fame & peace than Virtue's self can gain

'Without the opportunity which bore
Him on its eagle's pinion to the peak
From which a thousand climbers have before

'Fall'n as Napoleon fell.'—I felt my cheek
Alter to see the great form pass away
Whose grasp had left the giant world so weak

That every pigmy kicked it as it lay—
And much I grieved to think how power & will
In opposition rule our mortal day—

230   And why God made irreconcilable
Good & the means of good, and for despair
I half disdained mine eye's desire to fill

With the spent vision of the times that were
And scarce have ceased to be . . . 'Dost thou behold,'
Said then my guide, 'those spoilers spoiled, Voltaire,

'Frederic, & Kant, Catherine, & Leopold,
Chained hoary anarchs, demagogue & sage
Whose name the fresh world thinks already old—

'For in the battle Life & they did wage
240   She remained conqueror—I was overcome
By my own heart alone, which neither age

    'Nor tears nor infamy nor now the tomb
Could temper to its object.'—'Let them pass'—
    I cried—'the world & its mysterious doom

'Is not so much more glorious than it was
    That I desire to worship those who drew
New figures on its false & fragile glass

    'As the old faded.'—'Figures ever new
Rise on the bubble, paint them how you may;
250   We have but thrown, as those before us threw,

'Our shadows on it as it past away.
    But mark, how chained to the triumphal chair
The mighty phantoms of an elder day—

    'All that is mortal of great Plato there
Expiates the joy & woe his master knew not,
    That star that ruled his doom was far too fair—

'And Life, where long that flower of Heaven grew not,
    Conquered the heart by love which gold or pain
Or age or sloth or slavery could subdue not—

260   And near   walk the   twain,
The tutor & his pupil, whom Dominion
    Followed as tame as vulture in a chain.—

'The world was darkened beneath either pinion
    Of him whom from the flock of conquerors
Fame singled as her thunderbearing minion;

    'The other long outlived both woes & wars,
Throned in new thoughts of men, and still had kept
    The jealous keys of truth's eternal doors

'If Bacon's spirit   had not leapt
270   Like lightning out of darkness; he compelled
The Proteus shape of Nature's as it slept

'To wake & to unbar the caves that held
The treasure of the secrets of its reign—
    See the great bards of old who inly quelled

'The passions which they sung, as by their strain
    May well be known: their living melody
Tempers its own contagion to the vein

    'Of those who are infected with it—I
Have suffered what I wrote, or viler pain!—

280   'And so my words were seeds of misery—
Even as the deeds of others.'—'Not as theirs,'
    I said—he pointed to a company

In which I recognized amid the heirs
    Of Caesar's crime from him to Constantine,
The Anarchs old whose force & murderous snares

    Had founded many a sceptre bearing line
And spread the plague of blood & gold abroad,
    And Gregory & John and men divine

Who rose like shadows between Man & god
290   Till that eclipse, still hanging under Heaven,
Was worshipped by the world o'er which they strode

    For the true Sun it quenched.—'Their power was given
But to destroy,' replied the leader—'I
    Am one of those who have created, even

'If it be but a world of agony.'—
    'Whence camest thou & whither goest thou?
How did thy course begin,' I said, '& why?

    'Mine eyes are sick of this perpetual flow
Of people, & my heart of one sad thought.—
300   Speak.' 'Whence I came, partly I seem to know,

'And how & by what paths I have been brought
    To this dread pass, methinks even thou mayst guess;
Why this should be my mind can compass not;

'Whither the conqueror hurries me still less.
But follow thou, & from spectator turn
 Actor or victim in this wretchedness,

'And what thou wouldst be taught I then may learn
 From thee.—Now listen . . . In the April prime
When all the forest tops began to burn

310 'With kindling green, touched by the azure clime
Of the young year, I found myself asleep
 Under a mountain which from unknown time

'Had yawned into a cavern high & deep,
 And from it came a gentle rivulet
Whose water like clear air in its calm sweep

 'Bent the soft grass & kept for ever wet
The stems of the sweet flowers, and filled the grove
 With sound which all who hear must needs forget

'All pleasure & all pain, all hate & love,
320 Which they had known before that hour of rest:
A sleeping mother then would dream not of

 'The only child who died upon her breast
At eventide, a king would mourn no more
 The crown of which his brow was dispossest

'When the sun lingered o'er his ocean floor
 To gild his rival's new prosperity.
Thou wouldst forget thus vainly to deplore

 'Ills, which if ills can find no cure from thee,
The thought of which no other sleep will quell,
330 Nor other music blot from memory,

'So sweet and deep is the oblivious spell;
 And whether life had been before that sleep
The Heaven which I imagine, or a Hell

 'Like this harsh world in which I wake to weep,
I know not. I arose, and for a space
 The scene of woods and waters seemed to keep,

'Though it was now broad day, a gentle trace
    Of light diviner than the common sun
Sheds on the common earth, and all the place

340 'Was filled with magic sounds woven into one
Oblivious melody, confusing sense
    Amid the gliding waves and shadows dun;

'And, as I looked, the bright omnipresence
    Of morning through the orient cavern flowed,
And the sun's image radiantly intense

'Burned on the waters of the well that glowed
Like gold, and threaded all the forest's maze
    With winding paths of emerald fire; there stood

'Amid the sun, as he amid the blaze
350   Of his own glory, on the vibrating
Floor of the fountain, paved with flashing rays,

'A Shape all light, which with one hand did fling
Dew on the earth, as if she were the dawn,
    And the invisible rain did ever sing

'A silver music on the mossy lawn;
    And still before me on the dusky grass,
Iris her many-coloured scarf had drawn:

'In her right hand she bore a crystal glass,
Mantling with bright Nepenthe; the fierce splendour
360   Fell from her as she moved under the mass

'Of the deep cavern, and with palms so tender,
    Their tread broke not the mirror of its billow,
Glided along the river, and did bend her

'Head under the dark boughs, till like a willow
Her fair hair swept the bosom of the stream
    That whispered with delight to be its pillow.

'As one enamoured is upborne in dream
    O'er lily-paven lakes, mid silver mist,
To wondrous music, so this shape might seem

370   'Partly to tread the waves with feet which kissed
The dancing foam; partly to glide along
   The air which roughened the moist amethyst,

'Or the faint morning beams that fell among
   The trees, or the soft shadows of the trees;
And her feet, ever to the ceaseless song

   'Of leaves, and winds, and waves, and birds, and bees,
And falling drops, moved in a measure new
   Yet sweet, as on the summer evening breeze,

'Up from the lake a shape of golden dew
380   Between two rocks, athwart the rising moon,
Dances i' the wind, where never eagle flew;

   'And still her feet, no less than the sweet tune
To which they moved, seemed as they moved to blot
   The thoughts of him who gazed on them; and soon

'All that was, seemed as if it had been not;
   And all the gazer's mind was strewn beneath
Her feet like embers; and she, thought by thought,

   'Trampled its sparks into the dust of death;
As day upon the threshold of the east
390   Treads out the lamps of night, until the breath

'Of darkness re-illumine even the least
   Of heaven's living eyes—like day she came,
Making the night a dream; and ere she ceased

   'To move, as one between desire and shame
Suspended, I said—If, as it doth seem,
   Thou comest from the realm without a name

'Into this valley of perpetual dream,
   Show whence I came, and where I am, and why—
Pass not away upon the passing stream.

400   ' "Arise and quench thy thirst," was her reply.
And as a shut lily, stricken by the wand
   Of dewy morning's vital alchemy,

'I rose; and, bending at her sweet command,
　　Touched with faint lips the cup she raised,
And suddenly my brain became as sand

　　'Where the first wave had more than half erased
The track of deer on desert Labrador,
　　Whilst the fierce wolf from which they fled amazed

'Leaves his stamp visibly upon the shore
410　　Until the second bursts—so on my sight
Burst a new Vision never seen before.—

　　'And the fair shape waned in the coming light
As veil by veil the silent splendour drops
　　From Lucifer, amid the chrysolite

'Of sunrise ere it strike the mountain tops—
　　And as the presence of that fairest planet
Although unseen is felt by one who hopes

　　'That his day's path may end as he began it
In that star's smile, whose light is like the scent
420　　Of a jonquil when evening breezes fan it,

'Or the soft note in which his dear lament
　　The Brescian shepherd breathes, or the caress
That turned his weary slumber to content.—

　　'So knew I in that light's severe excess
The presence of that shape which on the stream
　　Moved, as I moved along the wilderness,

'More dimly than a day appearing dream,
　　The ghost of a forgotten form of sleep,
A light from Heaven whose half extinguished beam

430　　'Through the sick day in which we wake to weep
Glimmers, forever sought, forever lost.—
　　So did that shape its obscure tenour keep

'Beside my path, as silent as a ghost,
　　But the new Vision, and its cold bright car,
With savage music, stunning music, crost

'The forest, and as if from some dread war
Triumphantly returning, the loud million
   Fiercely extolled the fortune of her star.—

'A moving arch of victory the vermilion
440   And green & azure plumes of Iris had
Built high over her wind-winged pavilion,

   'And underneath aetherial glory clad
The wilderness, and far before her flew
   The tempest of the splendour which forbade

'Shadow to fall from leaf or stone;—the crew
   Seemed in that light like atomies that dance
Within a sunbeam.—Some upon the new

   'Embroidery of flowers that did enhance
The grassy vesture of the desert, played,
450   Forgetful of the chariot's swift advance;

'Others stood gazing till within the shade
   Of the great mountain its light left them dim.—
Others outspeeded it, and others made

   'Circles around it like the clouds that swim
Round the high moon in a bright sea of air,
   And more did follow, with exulting hymn,

'The chariot & the captives fettered there,
   But all like bubbles on an eddying flood
Fell into the same track at last & were

460   'Borne onward.—I among the multitude
Was swept; me sweetest flowers delayed not long.
   Me not the shadow nor the solitude,

'Me not the falling stream's Lethean song,
   Me, not the phantom of that early form
Which moved upon its motion,—but among

   'The thickest billows of the living storm
I plunged, and bared my bosom to the clime
   Of that cold light, whose airs too soon deform.—

'Before the chariot had begun to climb
470   The opposing steep of that mysterious dell,
Behold a wonder worthy of the rhyme

    'Of him whom from the lowest depths of Hell
Through every Paradise & through all glory
    Love led serene, & who returned to tell

'In words of hate & awe the wondrous story
    How all things are transfigured, except Love;
For deaf as is a sea which wrath makes hoary

    'The world can hear not the sweet notes that move
The sphere whose light is melody to lovers—
480   A wonder worthy of his rhyme—the grove

'Grew dense with shadows to its inmost covers,
    The earth was grey with phantoms, & the air
Was peopled with dim forms, as when there hovers

    'A flock of vampire-bats before the glare
Of the tropic sun, bringing ere evening
    Strange night upon some Indian isle,—thus were

'Phantoms diffused around, & some did fling
    Shadows of shadows, yet unlike themselves,
Behind them, some like eaglets on the wing

490   'Were lost in the white blaze, others like elves
Danced in a thousand unimagined shapes
    Upon the sunny streams & grassy shelves;

'And others sate chattering like restless apes
    On vulgar paws and voluble like fire.
Some made a cradle of the ermined capes

    'Of kingly mantles, some upon the tiar
Of pontiffs sate like vultures, others played
    Within the crown which girt with empire

'A baby's or an idiot's brow, & made
500   Their nests in it; the old anatomies
Sate hatching their bare brood under the shade

'Of demon wings, and laughed from their dead eyes
To reassume the delegated power
Arrayed in which these worms did monarchize

'Who make this earth their charnel.—Others more
Humble, like falcons sate upon the fist
Of common men, and round their heads did soar,

'Or like small gnats & flies, as thick as mist
On evening marshes, thronged about the brow
510   Of lawyer, statesman, priest & theorist,

'And others like discoloured flakes of snow
On fairest bosoms & the sunniest hair
Fell, and were melted by the youthful glow

'Which they extinguished; for like tears, they were
A veil to those from whose faint lids they rained
In drops of sorrow.—I became aware

'Of whence those forms proceeded which thus stained
The track in which we moved; after brief space
From every form the beauty slowly waned,

520   'From every firmest limb & fairest face
The strength & freshness fell like dust, & left
The action & the shape without the grace

'Of life; the marble brow of youth was cleft
With care, and in the eyes where once hope shone
Desire like a lioness bereft

'Of its last cub, glared ere it died; each one
Of that great crowd sent forth incessantly
These shadows, numerous as the dead leaves blown

'In Autumn evening from a poplar tree—
530   Each, like himself & like each other were,
At first, but soon distorted, seemed to be

'Obscure clouds moulded by the casual air;
And of this stuff the car's creative ray
Wrought all the busy phantoms that were there

'As the sun shapes the clouds—thus, on the way
   Mask after mask fell from the countenance
And form of all, and long before the day

   'Was old, the joy which waked like Heaven's glance
The sleepers in the oblivious valley, died,
540   And some grew weary of the ghastly dance

'And fell, as I have fallen by the way side,
   Those soonest from whose forms most shadows past
And least of strength & beauty did abide.'—

   'Then, what is Life?' I said . . . the cripple cast
His eye upon the car which now had rolled
   Onward, as if that look must be the last,

And answered . . . "Happy those for whom the fold
   Of
1822   1824

| JOHN KEATS |

1795–1821

KEATS WAS BORN October 31, 1795, in London, the first of four children in the family of a prosperous coachman. His father died in a riding accident when the future poet was eight, his mother of tuberculosis when he was fourteen. He grew up, despite the tubercular inheritance, to be pugnacious and handsome, but stunted in size at five feet. Apprenticed to a surgeon by his dishonest guardian, he went on in 1815 to Guy's Hospital, London, as a medical student. His earliest poetry was mawkish, but "Sleep and Poetry" in 1816 demonstrated a genuine voice rising in him, and consolidated his poetic ambitions.

   Haunted, like all his major contemporaries, by the shadow of Milton's splendor, Keats was also both burdened and aided by his perceptive reading of Wordsworth. His long poem *Endymion* rightly seemed a failure even to him, and he probably did not suffer as keenly from its negative reviews as tradition has held. Intellectually, the principal influence upon him was Hazlitt, but, from early 1818 on, his matchless letters show a rugged independence of mind, and a speculative development well in advance of his own poetry. One of the puzzles of Keats's rapid development was that the poet in him did not catch up with the man until the autumn of 1818. In the year between the ages of twenty-three and twenty-four, certainly one of the most fecund ever experienced by any poet, Keats wrote almost all of his major poetry.

Yet this brilliant year was full of sorrows. A summer walking tour, largely in Scotland, ended suddenly in August 1818 with the first signs of the tuberculosis that was to kill him. Autumn 1818, when the glorious year of poetry started, was largely spent nursing his brother Tom, who was dying, with agonizing slowness, of the family disease. In December, Tom died, and soon after Keats fell genuinely in love with Fanny Brawne—a relationship that was never to be fulfilled, as Keats gradually began to realize but naturally could not accept. He worked at his first *Hyperion* fragment, but could not advance in it. In January 1819, surely in tribute to Fanny Brawne, he wrote "The Eve of St. Agnes," his least tragic major poem. The great self-recognition of his imaginative life began in April, with the composition of "Ode to Psyche" and "La Belle Dame Sans Merci." In May, the great odes "On a Grecian Urn," "On Melancholy," and "To a Nightingale" were written. "Lamia," probably his only poem to be overrated consistently in our century, began to be drafted in June and July. Culmination came in August–September, with the superb fragment *The Fall of Hyperion* and the perfect ode "To Autumn." But with the transition to middle and fuller autumn, an ultimate despair followed all these gifts of the spirit, and effectively ended Keats's poetry.

By February 1820, Keats came to understand that he might have only a year or so to live, and consequently had no hope of marriage to Fanny Brawne. After a terrible half-year, he sailed to Italy in September, on the outside chance of improving his health, but he lingered only until February 23, 1821, when he died in Rome, aged twenty-five years and four months.

Of all nineteenth-century poets who wrote in English, Keats has demonstrated the most universal power to move readers in our own time. His effect upon later nineteenth-century poets was extraordinary, from Thomas Hood through Tennyson, Arnold (an unwilling and even unrecognized case of influence), Hopkins, Rossetti, and Morris, but a vast audience did not come to him until the twentieth century. The modern common reader and literary critic have agreed on Keats, for somewhat different reasons, and his influence is still vital in several major twentieth-century poets, particularly in Wallace Stevens. It seems justified to observe that Keats has the most secure and uncontested reputation of any poet since the Renaissance, an astonishing eminence for a unique but flawed artist who did not live long enough to perfect more than a handful of works.

Even the poet's letters, which were viciously deprecated as "unmanly" during the Victorian period, enjoy a prestige today second to none in the language. Keats-idolatry is a benign malady, compared with many other literary disorders, and this editor has no desire to deplore it. But why does Keats appear a more timeless phenomenon than his great contemporaries now seem to be? What accounts for the generous overpraise that consistently links him with Shakespeare in modern criticism? Clearly he is the most sympathetic of modern poets, though he does not compare to Blake in conceptual power or to Wordsworth in originality. To define this power of sympathy is to identify what intrinsically belongs to Keats, what could not have come to us without him.

The prime element is Keats's thoroughgoing naturalistic humanism, in him a tough-minded and healthy doctrine very difficult to parallel in any writer since. Here he stemmed from Wordsworth, particularly the poet of "Home at Grasmere" ("The Recluse" fragment), who, by words which speak of nothing more than what we already are, would rouse us from the sleep of death to show us we are at home in a nature fitted to our minds. But Wordsworth's naturalism, his sense that the earth was enough, remained uneasy. Even in "Tintern Abbey" it wavers at the borders of a theophany, as though the visible world threatened to go out with the light of sense, and only infinity remained as an emblem of the deepest truth. From at least the "Ode to Psyche" on, Keats proclaims a more strenuously naturalistic confidence: "I see, and sing, by my own eyes inspired."

Allied to this heroic priesthood of the visible is Keats's extraordinary detachment, a capacity for disinterestedness so rare in a poet of all men as to be especially refreshing. He himself, in the crucial letter of December 21–27, 1817, to his brothers, developed this gift into the difficult but radiant quality "which Shakespeare possessed so enormously—I mean *Negative Capability*, that is when man is capable of being in uncertainties, Mysteries, doubts, without any irritable reaching after fact and reason—." No better description could be made of the poet-quester of *The Fall of Hyperion*, or of the voice that chants the Great Odes.

Beyond the uncompromising sense that we are completely physical in a physical world, and the allied realization that we are compelled to imagine more than we can know or understand, there is a third quality in Keats more clearly present than in any other poet since Shakespeare. This is the gift of tragic acceptance, which persuades us again that Keats was the least solipsistic of poets, the one most able to grasp the individuality and reality of selves totally distinct from his own, and of an outward world that would survive his perception of it. In his final poems he succeeds miraculously in communicating to us what it would be like if we shared this most uncommon and most gracious of human gifts.

✧ ✧ ✧

On the Sea

It keeps eternal whisperings around
    Desolate shores, and with its mighty swell
    Gluts twice ten thousand Caverns, till the spell
Of Hecate leaves them their old shadowy sound.
Often 'tis in such gentle temper found,
    That scarcely will the very smallest shell
    Be moved for days from where it sometime fell,
When last the winds of Heaven were unbound.
Oh ye! who have your eyeballs vexed and tired,
    Feast them upon the wideness of the Sea;
      Oh ye! whose ears are dinned with uproar rude,
    Or fed too much with cloying melody—
      Sit ye near some old Cavern's Mouth and brood,
Until ye start, as if the sea-nymphs quired!
    1817   1848

La Belle Dame Sans Merci

A Ballad

O, what can ail thee, knight-at-arms,
    Alone and palely loitering?
The sedge has withered from the lake,
    And no birds sing.

O, what can ail thee, knight-at-arms,
    So haggard and so woe-begone?
The squirrel's granary is full,
    And the harvest's done.

I see a lily on thy brow,
10   With anguish moist and fever dew;
And on thy cheeks a fading rose
     Fast withereth too.

I met a lady in the meads,
     Full beautiful—a faery's child,
Her hair was long, her foot was light,
     And her eyes were wild.

I made a garland for her head,
     And bracelets too, and fragrant zone;
She looked at me as she did love,
20   And made sweet moan.

I set her on my pacing steed,
     And nothing else saw all day long;
For sidelong would she bend, and sing
     A faery's song.

She found me roots of relish sweet,
     And honey wild, and manna dew,
And sure in language strange she said—
     'I love thee true.'

She took me to her elfin grot,
30   And there she wept and sighed full sore,
And there I shut her wild wild eyes
     With kisses four.

And there she lullèd me asleep
     And there I dreamed—Ah! woe betide!
The latest dream I ever dreamed
     On the cold hill side.

I saw pale kings and princes too,
     Pale warriors, death-pale were they all;
40   They cried—'La Belle Dame sans Merci
     Hath thee in thrall!'

I saw their starved lips in the gloam,
     With horrid warning gapèd wide,

And I awoke and found me here,
   On the cold hill's side.

And this is why I sojourn here
   Alone and palely loitering,
Though the sedge has withered from the lake,
   And no birds sing.
   1819   1820

Ode to Psyche

O Goddess! hear these tuneless numbers, wrung
   By sweet enforcement and remembrance dear,
And pardon that thy secrets should be sung
   Even into thine own soft-conchèd ear:
Surely I dreamt today, or did I see
   The wingèd Psyche with awakened eyes?
I wandered in a forest thoughtlessly,
   And, on the sudden, fainting with surprise,
Saw two fair creatures, couchèd side by side
10   In deepest grass, beneath the whispering roof
   Of leaves and trembled blossoms, where there ran
       A brooklet, scarce espied:

'Mid hushed, cool-rooted flowers, fragrant-eyed,
   Blue, silver-white, and budded Tyrian,
They lay calm-breathing on the bedded grass;
   Their arms embracèd, and their pinions too;
   Their lips touched not, but had not bade adieu,
As if disjoinèd by soft-handed slumber,
And ready still past kisses to outnumber
20   At tender eye-dawn of aurorean love:
       The wingèd boy I knew;
   But who wast thou, O happy, happy dove?
       His Psyche true!

O latest born and loveliest vision far
   Of all Olympus' faded hierarchy!
Fairer than Phoebe's sapphire-regioned star,
   Or Vesper, amorous glow-worm of the sky;
Fairer than these, though temple thou hast none,

Nor altar heaped with flowers;
30 Nor virgin-choir to make delicious moan
Upon the midnight hours;
No voice, no lute, no pipe, no incense sweet
From chain-swung censer teeming;
No shrine, no grove, no oracle, no heat
Of pale-mouthed prophet dreaming.

O brightest! though too late for antique vows,
Too, too late for the fond believing lyre,
When holy were the haunted forest boughs,
Holy the air, the water, and the fire;
40 Yet even in these days so far retired
From happy pieties, thy lucent fans,
Fluttering among the faint Olympians,
I see, and sing, by my own eyes inspired.
So let me be thy choir, and make a moan
Upon the midnight hours;
Thy voice, thy lute, thy pipe, thy incense sweet
From swingèd censer teeming;
Thy shrine, thy grove, thy oracle, thy heat
Of pale-mouthed prophet dreaming.

50 Yes, I will be thy priest, and build a fane
In some untrodden region of my mind,
Where branchèd thoughts, new grown with pleasant pain,
Instead of pines shall murmur in the wind:
Far, far around shall those dark-clustered trees
Fledge the wild-ridgèd mountains steep by steep;
And there by zephyrs, streams, and birds, and bees,
The moss-lain Dryads shall be lulled to sleep;
And in the midst of this wide quietness
A rosy sanctuary will I dress
60 With the wreathed trellis of a working brain,
With buds, and bells, and stars without a name,
With all the gardener Fancy e'er could feign,
Who breeding flowers, will never breed the same:
And there shall be for thee all soft delight
That shadowy thought can win,
A bright torch, and a casement ope at night,
To let the warm Love in!
1819   1820

Ode to a Nightingale

I

My heart aches, and a drowsy numbness pains
    My sense, as though of hemlock I had drunk,
Or emptied some dull opiate to the drains
    One minute past, and Lethe-wards had sunk:
'Tis not through envy of thy happy lot,
    But being too happy in thine happiness,—
        That thou, light-winged Dryad of the trees,
            In some melodious plot
Of beechen green, and shadows numberless,
10   Singest of summer in full-throated ease.

II

O, for a draught of vintage! that hath been
    Cooled a long age in the deep-delved earth,
Tasting of Flora and the country green,
    Dance, and Provençal song, and sunburnt mirth!
O for a beaker full of the warm South,
    Full of the true, the blushful Hippocrene,
        With beaded bubbles winking at the brim,
            And purple-stainèd mouth;
That I might drink, and leave the world unseen,
20   And with thee fade away into the forest dim:

III

Fade far away, dissolve, and quite forget
    What thou among the leaves hast never known,
The weariness, the fever, and the fret
    Here, where men sit and hear each other groan;
Where palsy shakes a few, sad, last grey hairs,
    Where youth grows pale, and spectre-thin, and dies;
        Where but to think is to be full of sorrow
            And leaden-eyed despairs,
        Where Beauty cannot keep her lustrous eyes,
30   Or new Love pine at them beyond tomorrow.

IV

Away! away! for I will fly to thee,
    Not charioted by Bacchus and his pards,
But on the viewless wings of Poesy,

Though the dull brain perplexes and retards:
Already with thee! tender is the night,
   And haply the Queen-Moon is on her throne,
     Clustered around by all her starry Fays;
       But here there is no light,
   Save what from heaven is with the breezes blown
40   Through verdurous glooms and winding mossy ways.

V

I cannot see what flowers are at my feet,
   Nor what soft incense hangs upon the boughs,
But, in embalmèd darkness, guess each sweet
   Wherewith the seasonable month endows
The grass, the thicket, and the fruit-tree wild;
   White hawthorn, and the pastoral eglantine;
     Fast fading violets covered up in leaves;
       And mid-May's eldest child,
   The coming musk-rose, full of dewy wine,
50   The murmurous haunt of flies on summer eves.

VI

Darkling I listen; and, for many a time
   I have been half in love with easeful Death,
Called him soft names in many a musèd rhyme,
   To take into the air my quiet breath;
Now more than ever seems it rich to die,
   To cease upon the midnight with no pain,
     While thou art pouring forth thy soul abroad
       In such an ecstasy!
   Still wouldst thou sing, and I have ears in vain—
60   To thy high requiem become a sod.

VII

Thou wast not born for death, immortal Bird!
   No hungry generations tread thee down;
The voice I hear this passing night was heard
   In ancient days by emperor and clown:
Perhaps the self-same song that found a path
   Through the sad heart of Ruth, when, sick for home,
     She stood in tears amid the alien corn;
       The same that oft-times hath
   Charmed magic casements, opening on the foam
70   Of perilous seas, in faery lands forlorn.

VIII

Forlorn! the very word is like a bell
 To toll me back from thee to my sole self!
Adieu! the fancy cannot cheat so well
 As she is famed to do, deceiving elf.
Adieu! adieu! thy plaintive anthem fades
 Past the near meadows, over the still stream,
  Up the hill-side; and now 'tis buried deep
   In the next valley-glades:
 Was it a vision, or a waking dream?
80 Fled is that music:—Do I wake or sleep?

1819 1819

Ode on a Grecian Urn

I

Thou still unravished bride of quietness,
 Thou foster-child of silence and slow time,
Sylvan historian, who canst thus express
 A flowery tale more sweetly than our rhyme:
What leaf-fringed legend haunts about thy shape
 Of deities or mortals, or of both,
  In Tempe or the dales of Arcady?
 What men or gods are these? What maidens loth?
What mad pursuit? What struggle to escape?
10 What pipes and timbrels? What wild ecstasy?

II

Heard melodies are sweet, but those unheard
 Are sweeter; therefore, ye soft pipes, play on:
Not to the sensual ear, but, more endeared,
 Pipe to the spirit ditties of no tone:
Fair youth, beneath the trees, thou canst not leave
 Thy song, nor ever can those trees be bare;
  Bold Lover, never, never canst thou kiss,
Though winning near the goal—yet, do not grieve;
 She cannot fade, though thou hast not thy bliss,
20 Forever wilt thou love, and she be fair!

III

Ah, happy, happy boughs! that cannot shed
 Your leaves, nor ever bid the Spring adieu;

And, happy melodist, unwearièd,
    Forever piping songs forever new;
More happy love! more happy, happy love!
    Forever warm and still to be enjoyed,
      Forever panting, and forever young;
All breathing human passion far above,
    That leaves a heart high-sorrowful and cloyed,
30   A burning forehead, and a parching tongue.

IV

Who are these coming to the sacrifice?
    To what green altar, O mysterious priest,
Lead'st thou that heifer lowing at the skies,
    And all her silken flanks with garlands dressed?
What little town by river or sea shore,
    Or mountain-built with peaceful citadel,
      Is emptied of this folk, this pious morn?
And, little town, thy streets for evermore
    Will silent be; and not a soul to tell
40   Why thou art desolate, can e'er return.

V

O Attic shape! Fair attitude! with brede
    Of marble men and maidens overwrought,
With forest branches and the trodden weed;
    Thou, silent form, dost tease us out of thought
As doth eternity: Cold Pastoral!
    When old age shall this generation waste,
      Thou shalt remain, in midst of other woe
Than ours, a friend to man, to whom thou say'st,
    'Beauty is truth, truth beauty,—that is all
50   Ye know on earth, and all ye need to know.'
    1819   1820

Ode on Melancholy

I

No, no, go not to Lethe, neither twist
    Wolf's-bane, tight-rooted, for its poisonous wine;
Nor suffer thy pale forehead to be kissed
    By nightshade, ruby grape of Proserpine;
Make not your rosary of yew-berries,

Nor let the beetle, nor the death-moth be
    Your mournful Psyche, nor the downy owl
A partner in your sorrow's mysteries;
    For shade to shade will come too drowsily,
10   And drown the wakeful anguish of the soul.

II

But when the melancholy fit shall fall
    Sudden from heaven like a weeping cloud,
That fosters the droop-headed flowers all,
    And hides the green hill in an April shroud;
Then glut thy sorrow on a morning rose,
    Or on the rainbow of the salt sand-wave,
        Or on the wealth of globèd peonies;
Or if thy mistress some rich anger shows,
    Emprison her soft hand, and let her rave,
20   And feed deep, deep upon her peerless eyes.

III

She dwells with Beauty—Beauty that must die;
    And Joy, whose hand is ever at his lips
Bidding adieu; and aching Pleasure nigh,
    Turning to poison while the bee-mouth sips:
Ay, in the very temple of Delight
    Veiled Melancholy has her sovereign shrine,
        Though seen of none save him whose strenuous tongue
Can burst Joy's grape against his palate fine;
    His soul shall taste the sadness of her might,
30   And be among her cloudy trophies hung.
    1819 1820

Hyperion

Rejecting the sentimentality of much of his earlier work, including *Endymion*, Keats wrote *Hyperion* in what he called "a more naked and grecian Manner." Though he had abandoned the fragment by April 1819, and it is undeniably an inconsistent work, few more powerful attempts at the Sublime exist. The view taken of the conflict between Olympians and Titans is an original one, and contrasts strongly with those of Shelley and Byron (see headnote to *Prometheus Unbound*). In an atmosphere at once strong and cool, *Hyperion* surveys the fallen condition of the Titans without either a Miltonic didactic emphasis or a Shelleyan personalizing self-dramatization. Here is the first triumph of Keats's earlier idea of poetry as a disinterested mode.

The situation in which the poem begins is that difficult moment in myth when the old gods are departing and the new are not yet securely themselves. In particular, Hyperion, Titan of the sun, uneasily abides in heaven, and the young Apollo, down on earth, is "dying into life," becoming the god of poetry. Though an overt march-of-mind moral, of history as necessary progress, is given to Oceanus, displaced god of the sea, there is a small reason to believe that he speaks for Keats himself. The poem hesitates at the verge of becoming an allegory of the history of imagination, and this hesitation is one of its strengths.

We can surmise that Keats gave up this first *Hyperion* for two reasons: first that the fragment is so complete in itself that any continuation would have meant redundancy, and second that he either could not or more likely would not maintain the beautiful but strained Miltonic high style of the first two books. The brief fragment of Book III shows a return to the subjective, romance style of *Endymion,* which was to be transformed into the harsh, purgatorial style of *The Fall of Hyperion.* Something vital and open in Keats had begun to discover his own personalizing involvement in this magnificent but abortive epic, and he was too honest to go on. But he had made already the most successful single emulation of Miltonic style and procedure in the Romantic tradition. Even the use throughout of sonorous Titanic names is a return of the Miltonic glory of a Sublime cataloguing.

The Fall of Hyperion

This purgatorial fragment is parallel to Shelley's *Triumph of Life,* in that each poem derives its structure and procedure from Dante (by way of the Cary translation, in Keats's case), each has elements of palinode or recantation, and each shows also a new severity of style and firmer discipline of mythopoeic invention. Keats too is writing his vision of judgment, but his vision, though tragic, is not as dark or as deliberately universalizing as Shelley's. Where Shelley passively renders Rousseau's terrifying story, Keats actively confronts his Muse, Moneta, and compels her not only to accept him as a true poet but to modify her harsh and narrow categorizations of poets and of humanist men of action. He does this not by asserting his own identity, but by finding a truer form in the merged, higher identity of a more humanistic poethood than the world has known.

Incomplete as it is (probably Keats did not go on because he was no longer healthy enough, in spirit or in body), *The Fall of Hyperion* shows the start of a different kind of tragic theme and procedure, one that is founded upon a realization that every credence attending literary and spiritual tradition is now dead. Moneta presides over a ruined shrine of all the dead faiths, and the lesson Keats searches out in her countenance is that tragedy is not enough, though he still desires to be a tragic poet. The burden of history, of the fused but broken splendor of past poetic achievements, is heroically taken on by Keats as a necessary prelude to a new level of achievement he believes he can attain. He did not live to do so, but this fragment persuades us that he was the chosen man to make the attempt.

The Fall of Hyperion

A Dream

CANTO I

Fanatics have their dreams, wherewith they weave
A paradise for a sect; the savage too
From forth the loftiest fashion of his sleep
Guesses at Heaven; pity these have not
Traced upon vellum or wild Indian leaf
The shadows of melodious utterance.
But bare of laurel they live, dream, and die;
For Poesy alone can tell her dreams,
With the fine spell of words alone can save
10   Imagination from the sable charm
And dumb enchantment. Who alive can say,
'Thou art no Poet—mayst not tell thy dreams?'
Since every man whose soul is not a clod
Hath visions, and would speak, if he had loved,
And been well nurtured in his mother tongue,
Whether the dream now purposed to rehearse
Be poet's or fanatic's will be known
When this warm scribe my hand is in the grave.

Methought I stood where trees of every clime,
20   Palm, myrtle, oak, and sycamore, and beech,
With plantain, and spice-blossoms, made a screen;
In neighbourhood of fountains (by the noise

Soft-showering in my ears), and (by the touch
Of scent) not far from roses. Turning round
I saw an arbour with a drooping roof
Of trellis vines, and bells, and larger blooms,
Like floral censers, swinging light in air;
Before its wreathèd doorway, on a mound
Of moss, was spread a feast of summer fruits,
30　Which, nearer seen, seemed refuse of a meal
By angel tasted or our Mother Eve;
For empty shells were scattered on the grass,
And grape-stalks but half bare, and remnants more,
Sweet-smelling, whose pure kinds I could not know.
Still was more plenty than the fabled horn
Thrice emptied could pour forth, at banqueting
For Proserpine returned to her own fields,
Where the white heifers low. And appetite
More yearning than on Earth I ever felt
40　Growing within, I ate deliciously;
And, after not long, thirsted, for thereby
Stood a cool vessel of transparent juice
Sipped by the wandered bee, the which I took,
And, pledging all the mortals of the world,
And all the dead whose names are in our lips,
Drank. That full draught is parent of my theme.
No Asian poppy nor elixir fine
Of the soon-fading jealous Caliphat;
No poison gendered in close monkish cell,
50　To thin the scarlet conclave of old men,
Could so have rapt unwilling life away.
Among the fragrant husks and berries crushed,
Upon the grass I struggled hard against
The domineering potion; but in vain:
The cloudy swoon came on, and down I sank,
Like a Silenus on an antique vase.
How long I slumbered 'tis a chance to guess.
When sense of life returned, I started up
As if with wings; but the fair trees were gone,
60　The mossy mound and arbour were no more:
I looked around upon the carvèd sides
Of an old sanctuary with roof august,
Builded so high, it seemed that filmèd clouds
Might spread beneath, as o'er the stars of heaven;

So old the place was, I remembered none
The like upon the Earth: what I had seen
Of grey cathedrals, buttressed walls, rent towers,
The superannuations of sunk realms,
Or Nature's rocks toiled hard in waves and winds,
70 Seemed but the faulture of decrepit things
To that eternal domèd Monument.—
Upon the marble at my feet there lay
Store of strange vessels and large draperies,
Which needs had been of dyed asbestos wove,
Or in that place the moth could not corrupt,
So white the linen, so, in some, distinct
Ran imageries from a sombre loom.
All in a mingled heap confused there lay
Robes, golden tongs, censer and chafing-dish,
80 Girdles, and chains, and holy jewelries.

Turning from these with awe, once more I raised
My eyes to fathom the space every way;
The embossed roof, the silent massy range
Of columns north and south, ending in mist
Of nothing, then to eastward, where black gates
Were shut against the sunrise evermore.—
Then to the west I looked, and saw far off
An image, huge of feature as a cloud,
At level of whose feet an altar slept,
90 To be approached on either side by steps,
And marble balustrade, and patient travail
To count with toil the innumerable degrees.
Towards the altar sober-paced I went,
Repressing haste, as too unholy there;
And, coming nearer, saw beside the shrine
One ministering; and there arose a flame.—
When in mid-May the sickening East wind
Shifts sudden to the south, the small warm rain
Melts out the frozen incense from all flowers,
100 And fills the air with so much pleasant health
That even the dying man forgets his shroud;—
Even so that lofty sacrificial fire,
Sending forth Maian incense, spread around
Forgetfulness of everything but bliss,
And clouded all the altar with soft smoke;

From whose white fragrant curtains thus I heard
Language pronounced: 'If thou canst not ascend
These steps, die on that marble where thou art.
Thy flesh, near cousin to the common dust,
110 Will parch for lack of nutriment—thy bones
Will wither in few years, and vanish so
That not the quickest eye could find a grain
Of what thou now art on that pavement cold.
The sands of thy short life are spent this hour,
And no hand in the universe can turn
Thy hourglass, if these gummed leaves be burnt
Ere thou canst mount up these immortal steps.'
I heard, I looked: two senses both at once,
So fine, so subtle, felt the tyranny
120 Of that fierce threat and the hard task proposed.
Prodigious seemed the toil; the leaves were yet
Burning—when suddenly a palsied chill
Struck from the pavèd level up my limbs,
And was ascending quick to put cold grasp
Upon those streams that pulse beside the throat:
I shrieked, and the sharp anguish of my shriek
Stung my own ears—I strove hard to escape
The numbness; strove to gain the lowest step.
Slow, heavy, deadly was my pace: the cold
130 Grew stifling, suffocating, at the heart;
And when I clasped my hands I felt them not.
One minute before death, my iced foot touched
The lowest stair; and as it touched, life seemed
To pour in at the toes: I mounted up,
As once fair angels on a ladder flew
From the green turf to Heaven—'Holy Power,'
Cried I, approaching near the hornèd shrine,
'What am I that should so be saved from death?
What am I that another death come not
140 To choke my utterance sacrilegious, here?'
Then said the veiled shadow—'Thou hast felt
What 'tis to die and live again before
Thy fated hour, that thou hadst power to do so
Is thy own safety; thou hast dated on
Thy doom.'—'High Prophetess,' said I, 'purge off,
Benign, if so it please thee, my mind's film.'—
'None can usurp this height,' returned that shade,

'But those to whom the miseries of the world
Are misery, and will not let them rest.
150   All else who find a haven in the world,
Where they may thoughtless sleep away their days,
If by a chance into this fane they come,
Rot on the pavement where thou rottedst half.'—
'Are there not thousands in the world,' said I,
Encouraged by the sooth voice of the shade,
'Who love their fellows even to the death,
Who feel the giant agony of the world,
And more, like slaves to poor humanity,
Labour for mortal good? I sure should see
160   Other men here; but I am here alone.'
'Those whom thou spak'st of are no visionaries,'
Rejoined that voice—'They are no dreamers weak,
They seek no wonder but the human face;
No music but a happy-noted voice—
They come not here, they have no thought to come—
And thou art here, for thou art less than they—
What benefit canst thou do, or all thy tribe,
To the great world? Thou art a dreaming thing,
A fever of thyself—think of the Earth;
170   What bliss even in hope is there for thee?
What haven? every creature hath its home;
Every sole man hath days of joy and pain,
Whether his labours be sublime or low—
The pain alone; the joy alone; distinct:
Only the dreamer venoms all his days,
Bearing more woe than all his sins deserve.
Therefore, that happiness be somewhat shared,
Such things as thou art are admitted oft
Into like gardens thou didst pass erewhile,
180   And suffered in these temples: for that cause
Thou standest safe beneath this statue's knees.'
'That I am favoured for unworthiness,
By such propitious parley medicined
In sickness not ignoble, I rejoice,
Aye, and could weep for love of such award.'
So answered I, continuing, 'If it please,
Majestic shadow, tell me: sure not all
Those melodies sung into the World's ear
Are useless: sure a poet is a sage;

190 A humanist, physician to all men.
That I am none I feel, as vultures feel
They are no birds when eagles are abroad.
What am I then: Thou spakest of my tribe:
What tribe?' The tall shade veiled in drooping white
Then spake, so much more earnest, that the breath
Moved the thin linen folds that drooping hung
About a golden censer from the hand
Pendent—'Art thou not of the dreamer tribe?
The poet and the dreamer are distinct,
200 Diverse, sheer opposite, antipodes.
The one pours out a balm upon the World,
The other vexes it.' Then shouted I
Spite of myself, and with a Pythia's spleen,
'Apollo! faded! O far flown Apollo!
Where is thy misty pestilence to creep
Into the dwellings, through the door crannies
Of all mock lyrists, large self worshippers
And careless Hectorers in proud bad verse.
Though I breathe death with them it will be life
210 To see them sprawl before me into graves.
Majestic shadow, tell me where I am,
Whose altar this; for whom this incense curls;
What image this whose face I cannot see,
For the broad marble knees; and who thou art,
Of accent feminine so courteous?'

        Then the tall shade, in drooping linens veiled,
Spoke out, so much more earnest, that her breath
Stirred the thin folds of gauze that drooping hung
About a golden censer from her hand
220 Pendent; and by her voice I knew she shed
Long-treasured tears. 'This temple, sad and lone,
Is all spared from the thunder of a war
Foughten long since by giant hierarchy
Against rebellion: this old image here,
Whose carvèd features wrinkled as he fell,
Is Saturn's; I Moneta, left supreme
Sole Priestess of this desolation,'—
I had no words to answer, for my tongue,
Useless, could find about its roofèd home
230 No syllable of a fit majesty

To make rejoinder to Moneta's mourn.
There was a silence, while the altar's blaze
Was fainting for sweet food: I looked thereon,
And on the pavèd floor, where nigh were piled
Faggots of cinnamon, and many heaps
Of other crispèd spice-wood—then again
I looked upon the altar, and its horns
Whitened with ashes, and its languorous flame,
And then upon the offerings again;
240   And so by turns—till sad Moneta cried,
'The sacrifice is done, but not the less
Will I be kind to thee for thy good will.
My power, which to me is still a curse,
Shall be to thee a wonder; for the scenes
Still swooning vivid through my globèd brain,
With an electral changing misery,
Thou shalt with those dull mortal eyes behold,
Free from all pain, if wonder pain thee not,'
As near as an immortal's spherèd words
250   Could to a mother's soften, were these last:
And yet I had a terror of her robes,
And chiefly of the veils, that from her brow
Hung pale, and curtained her in mysteries,
That made my heart too small to hold its blood.
This saw that Goddess, and with sacred hand
Parted the veils. Then saw I a wan face,
Not pined by human sorrows, but bright-blanched
By an immortal sickness which kills not;
It works a constant change, which happy death
260   Can put no end to; deathwards progressing
To no death was that visage; it had passed
The lily and the snow; and beyond these
I must not think now, though I saw that face—
But for her eyes I should have fled away.
They held me back, with a benignant light,
Soft mitigated by divinest lids
Half-closed, and visionless entire they seemed
Of all external things;—they saw me not,
But in blank splendour, beamed like the mild moon,
270   Who comforts those she sees not, who knows not
What eyes are upward cast. As I had found
A grain of gold upon a mountain side,

And twinged with avarice strained out my eyes
To search its sullen entrails rich with ore,
So at the view of sad Moneta's brow,
I ached to see what things the hollow brain
Behind enwombèd: what high tragedy
In the dark secret chambers of her skull
Was acting, that could give so dread a stress
280 To her cold lips, and fill with such a light
Her planetary eyes; and touch her voice
With such a sorrow—'Shade of Memory!'—
Cried I, with act adorant at her feet,
'By all the gloom hung round thy fallen house,
By this last temple, by the golden age,
By great Apollo, thy dear Foster Child,
And by thyself, forlorn divinity,
The pale Omega of a withered race,
Let me behold, according as thou saidst,
290 What in thy brain so ferments to and fro!'
No sooner had this conjuration passed
My devout lips, than side by side we stood
(Like a stunt bramble by a solemn pine)
Deep in the shady sadness of a vale,
Far sunken from the healthy breath of morn,
Far from the fiery noon and eve's one star.
Onward I looked beneath the gloomy boughs,
And saw, what first I thought an image huge,
Like to the image pedestaled so high
300 In Saturn's temple. Then Moneta's voice
Came brief upon mine ear—'So Saturn sat
When he had lost his Realms—' whereon there grew
A power within me of enormous ken
To see as a god sees, and take the depth
Of things as nimbly as the outward eye
Can size and shape pervade. The lofty theme
At those few words hung vast before my mind,
With half-unraveled web. I sat myself
Upon an eagle's watch, that I might see,
310 And seeing ne'er forget. No stir of life
Was in this shrouded vale, not so much air
As in the zoning of a summer's day
Robs not one light seed from the feathered grass,
But where the dead leaf fell there did it rest:
A stream went voiceless by, still deadened more

By reason of the fallen divinity
Spreading more shade; the Naiad 'mid her reeds
Pressed her cold finger closer to her lips.

    Along the margin-sand large footmarks went
320 No farther than to where old Saturn's feet
Had rested, and there slept, how long a sleep!
Degraded, cold, upon the sodden ground
His old right hand lay nerveless, listless, dead,
Unsceptred; and his realmless eyes were closed,
While his bowed head seemed listening to the Earth,
His ancient mother, for some comfort yet.

    It seemed no force could wake him from his place;
But there came one who, with a kindred hand
Touched his wide shoulders after bending low
330 With reverence, though to one who knew it not.
Then came the grieved voice of Mnemosyne,
And grieved I hearkened. 'That divinity
Whom thou saw'st step from yon forlornest wood,
And with slow pace approach our fallen King,
Is Thea, softest-natured of our Brood.'
I marked the Goddess in fair statuary
Surpassing wan Moneta by the head,
And in her sorrow nearer woman's tears.
There was a listening fear in her regard,
340 As if calamity had but begun;
As if the vanward clouds of evil days
Had spent their malice, and the sullen rear
Was with its storèd thunder labouring up.
One hand she pressed upon that aching spot
Where beats the human heart, as if just there,
Though an immortal, she felt cruel pain;
The other upon Saturn's bended neck
She laid, and to the level of his hollow ear
Leaning with parted lips, some words she spake
350 In solemn tenor and deep organ tune;
Some mourning words, which in our feeble tongue
Would come in this-like accenting; how frail
To that large utterance of the early Gods!

    'Saturn! look up—and for what, poor lost King?
I have no comfort for thee; no not one;

I cannot cry, wherefore thus sleepest thou?
For Heaven is parted from thee, and the Earth
Knows thee not, so afflicted, for a God;
And Ocean too, with all its solemn noise,
360   Has from thy sceptre passed, and all the air
Is emptied of thine hoary majesty:
Thy thunder, captious at the new command,
Rumbles reluctant o'er our fallen house;
And thy sharp lightning, in unpracticed hands,
Scorches and burns our once serene domain.
With such remorseless speed still come new woes,
That unbelief has not a space to breathe.
Saturn! sleep on:—Me thoughtless, why should I
Thus violate thy slumbrous solitude?
370   Why should I ope thy melancholy eyes?
Saturn, sleep on, while at thy feet I weep.'

As when upon a trancèd summer-night
Forests, branch-charmèd by the earnest stars,
Dream, and so dream all night without a noise,
Save from one gradual solitary gust,
Swelling upon the silence; dying off;
As if the ebbing air had but one wave;
So came these words, and went; the while in tears
She pressed her fair large forehead to the earth,
380   Just where her fallen hair might spread in curls,
A soft and silken mat for Saturn's feet.
Long, long those two were postured motionless,
Like sculpture builded-up upon the grave
Of their own power. A long awful time
I looked upon them: still they were the same;
The frozen God still bending to the earth,
And the sad Goddess weeping at his feet,
Moneta silent. Without stay or prop,
But my own weak mortality, I bore
390   The load of this eternal quietude,
The unchanging gloom, and the three fixèd shapes
Ponderous upon my senses, a whole moon.
For by my burning brain I measured sure
Her silver seasons shedded on the night,
And ever day by day methought I grew
More gaunt and ghostly.—Oftentimes I prayed

Intense, that Death would take me from the Vale
And all its burthens—gasping with despair
Of change, hour after hour I cursed myself;
400   Until old Saturn raised his faded eyes,
And looked around and saw his kingdom gone,
And all the gloom and sorrow of the place,
And that fair kneeling Goddess at his feet.
As the moist scent of flowers, and grass, and leaves,
Fills forest dells with a pervading air,
Known to the woodland nostril, so the words
Of Saturn filled the mossy glooms around,
Even to the hollows of time-eaten oaks,
And to the windings of the foxes' hole,
410   With sad low tones, while thus he spake, and sent
Strange musings to the solitary Pan.
'Moan, brethren, moan; for we are swallowed up
And buried from all Godlike exercise
Of influence benign on planets pale,
And peaceful sway above man's harvesting.
And all those acts which Deity supreme
Doth ease its heart of love in. Moan and wail,
Moan, brethren, moan; for lo, the rebel spheres
Spin round, the stars their ancient courses keep,
420   Clouds still with shadowy moisture haunt the earth,
Still suck their fill of light from sun and moon;
Still buds the tree, and still the sea-shores murmur;
There is no death in all the Universe,
No smell of death—there shall be death—Moan, moan,
Moan, Cybele, moan; for thy pernicious Babes
Have changed a god into a shaking Palsy.
Moan, brethren, moan, for I have no strength left,
Weak as the reed—weak—feeble as my voice—
O, O, the pain, the pain of feebleness.
430   Moan, moan, for still I thaw—or give me help;
Throw down those imps, and give me victory.
Let me hear other groans, and trumpets blown
Of triumph calm, and hymns of festival,
From the gold peaks of Heaven's high-pilèd clouds;
Voices of soft proclaim, and silver stir
Of strings in hollow shells; and let there be
Beautiful things made new for the surprise
Of the sky-children.' So he feebly ceased,

With such a poor and sickly sounding pause,
440   Methought I heard some old man of the earth
Bewailing earthly loss; nor could my eyes
And ears act with that pleasant unison of sense
Which marries sweet sound with the grace of form,
And dolorous accent from a tragic harp
With large-limbed visions.—More I scrutinized:
Still fixed he sat beneath the sable trees,
Whose arms spread straggling in wild serpent forms,
With leaves all hushed; his awful presence there
(Now all was silent) gave a deadly lie
450   To what I erewhile heard—only his lips
Trembled amid the white curls of his beard.
They told the truth, though, round, the snowy locks
Hung nobly, as upon the face of heaven
A mid-day fleece of clouds. Thea arose,
And stretched her white arm through the hollow dark,
Pointing some whither: whereat he too rose
Like a vast giant, seen by men at sea
To grow pale from the waves at dull midnight.
They melted from my sight into the woods;
460   Ere I could turn, Moneta cried, 'These twain
Are speeding to the families of grief,
Where roofed in by black rocks they waste, in pain
And darkness, for no hope.'—And she spake on,
As ye may read who can unwearied pass
Onward from the Antechamber of this dream,
Where even at the open doors awhile
I must delay, and glean my memory
Of her high phrase:—perhaps no further dare.

    CANTO II
'Mortal, that thou may'st understand aright,
I humanize my sayings to thine ear,
Making comparisons of earthly things;
Or thou might'st better listen to the wind,
Whose language is to thee a barren noise,
Though it blows legend-laden through the trees.—
In melancholy realms big tears are shed,
More sorrow like to this, and such like woe,
Too huge for mortal tongue, or pen of scribe.
10   The Titans fierce, self hid or prison bound,
Groan for the old allegiance once more,

Listening in their doom for Saturn's voice.
But one of our whole eagle-brood still keeps
His sovereignty, and rule, and majesty;
Blazing Hyperion on his orbèd fire
Still sits, still snuffs the incense teeming up
From Man to the Sun's God: yet unsecure.
For as upon the earth dire prodigies
Fright and perplex, so also shudders he:
20 Nor at dog's howl or gloom-bird's Even screech,
Or the familiar visitings of one
Upon the first toll of his passing bell:
But horrors, portioned to a giant nerve,
Make great Hyperion ache. His palace bright,
Bastioned with pyramids of glowing gold,
And touched with shade of bronzèd obelisks,
Glares a blood-red through all the thousand courts,
Arches, and domes, and fiery galleries:
And all its curtains of Aurorian clouds
30 Flush angerly; when he would taste the wreaths
Of incense breathed aloft from sacred hills,
Instead of sweets, his ample palate takes
Savour of poisonous brass and metals sick.
Wherefore when harboured in the sleepy West,
After the full completion of fair day,
For rest divine upon exalted couch
And slumber in the arms of melody,
He paces through the pleasant hours of ease
With strides colossal, on from hall to hall;
40 While far within each aisle and deep recess
His wingèd minions in close clusters stand
Amazed, and full of fear; like anxious men,
Who on a wide plain gather in sad troops,
When earthquakes jar their battlements and towers.
Even now, while Saturn, roused from icy trance,
Goes, step for step, with Thea from yon woods,
Hyperion, leaving twilight in the rear,
Is sloping to the threshold of the West.—
Thither we tend.'—Now in clear light I stood,
50 Relieved from the dusk vale. Mnemosyne
Was sitting on a square-edged polished stone,
That in its lucid depth reflected pure
Her priestess-garments.—My quick eyes ran on
From stately nave to nave, from vault to vault,

Through bowers of fragrant and enwreathèd light
And diamond-pavèd lustrous long arcades.
Anon rushed by the bright Hyperion;
His flaming robes streamed out beyond his heels,
And gave a roar, as if of earthly fire,
60   That scared away the meek ethereal hours,
And made their dove-wings tremble. On he flared.

    1819 1856

To Autumn

I

Season of mists and mellow fruitfulness,
    Close bosom-friend of the maturing sun;
Conspiring with him how to load and bless
    With fruit the vines that round the thatch-eves run;
To bend with apples the mossed cottage-trees,
    And fill all fruit with ripeness to the core;
        To swell the gourd, and plump the hazel shells
With a sweet kernel; to set budding more,
    And still more, later flowers for the bees,
10   Until they think warm days will never cease,
        For Summer has o'er-brimmed their clammy cells.

II

Who hath not seen thee oft amid thy store?
    Sometimes whoever seeks abroad may find
Thee sitting careless on a granary floor,
    Thy hair soft-lifted by the winnowing wind;
Or on a half-reaped furrow sound asleep,
    Drowsed with the fume of poppies, while thy hook
        Spares the next swath and all its twinèd flowers:
And sometimes like a gleaner thou dost keep
20   Steady thy laden head across a brook;
    Or by a cider-press, with patient look,
        Thou watchest the last oozings hours by hours.

III

Where are the songs of Spring? Aye, where are they?
    Think not of them, thou hast thy music too,—
While barred clouds bloom the soft-dying day,
    And touch the stubble-plains with rosy hue;

Then in a wilful choir the small gnats mourn
  Among the river sallows, borne aloft
    Or sinking as the light wind lives or dies;
30 And full-grown lambs loud bleat from hilly bourn;
  Hedge-crickets sing; and now with treble soft
  The red-breast whistles from a garden-croft;
    And gathering swallows twitter in the skies.

1819   1820

Bright Star

*[Written on a Blank Page in Shakespeare's Poems,
facing 'A Lover's Complaint']*

Bright star, would I were stedfast as thou art—
  Not in lone splendour hung aloft the night
And watching, with eternal lids apart,
  Like nature's patient, sleepless Eremite,
The moving waters at their priestlike task
  Of pure ablution round earth's human shores,
Or gazing on the new soft-fallen mask
  Of snow upon the mountains and the moors—
No—yet still stedfast, still unchangeable,
10   Pillowed upon my fair love's ripening breast,
To feel forever its soft fall and swell,
  Awake forever in a sweet unrest,
Still, still to hear her tender-taken breath,
And so live ever—or else swoon to death.

1819–1820   1838

This Living Hand

This living hand, now warm and capable
Of earnest grasping, would, if it were cold
And in the icy silence of the tomb,
So haunt thy days and chill thy dreaming nights
That thou wouldst wish thine own heart dry of blood
So in my veins red life might stream again,
And thou be conscience-calmed—see here it is—
I hold it towards you.

1819–1820   1898

WALTER SAVAGE LANDOR

1775–1864

LANDOR, who died in Italy near the age of ninety, is a unique figure who was associated first with the Romantic poets, and then with the major Victorian authors. A fierce personality, quarrelsome and turbulent in his life, Landor wrote both classical epigrams and the beautifully restrained prose of his *Imaginary Conversations.*

I give here only three very brief poems by Landor: elegiac, memorable, and polished. Rose Aylmer, a noblewoman four years younger than Landor, and his good friend, died at twenty-one. Dirce, a young classical beauty being ferried across the river Styx to Hades by the boatman Charon, urbanely fears that her spectral beauty may tempt him excessively. Landor himself, turning seventy-five, stoically awaits a death that was not to come for fifteen more years, and charmingly insists that he "strove with none." In fact, his life had been and continued to be an endless series of lawsuits and controversies with parents, wife, children, friends, and strangers.

❧   ❧   ❧

[Rose Aylmer, 1779–1800]

Ah what avails the sceptred race,
   Ah what the form divine!
What every virtue, every grace!
   Rose Aylmer, all were thine.
Rose Aylmer, whom these wakeful eyes
   May weep, but never see,
A night of memories and of sighs
   I consecrate to thee.
   1806

Dirce

Stand close around, ye Stygian set,
   With Dirce in one boat conveyed!

Or Charon, seeing, may forget
    That he is old and she a shade.
1831

On His Seventy-fifth Birthday

I strove with none, for none was worth my strife:
    Nature I loved, and next to Nature, Art:
I warmed both hands before the fire of Life;
    It sinks; and I am ready to depart.
1853

THOMAS LOVE PEACOCK

1785–1866

PEACOCK'S MARVELOUS comic novels, including *Nightmare Abbey* and *Headlong Hall,* still have a substantial audience, though not as numerous as they deserve. We remember Peacock as Shelley's devoted friend, and as George Meredith's father-in-law, and also as the author of a crucial essay, "The Four Ages of Poetry," which prompted Shelley's great reply, "A Defence of Poetry."

An autodidact, Peacock worked much of his life for the East India Company, and was charmingly satirized, in the mode of his *Nightmare Abbey,* a loving satire on Shelley, by George Meredith in his major novel, *The Egoist.*

I include here two delicious mock-songs by Peacock, the first sung by Mr. Cypress (Lord Byron) in *Nightmare Abbey,* as a parody of *Childe Harold's Pilgrimage.* Cypress/Byron is about to go abroad into permanent self-exile from England because, as he explains, he has quarreled with his wife, and a man who has quarreled with his wife is free of any further obligations to his country.

"The War-Song of Dinas Vawr," a minor Welsh king in the era of King Arthur, is from Peacock's novel *The Misfortunes of Elphin.* Peacock himself commented that this song was: ". . . the quintessence of all war-songs

that ever were written, and the sum and substance of all appetencies, ten-
dencies, and consequences of military."

❧   ❧   ❧

Song by Mr. Cypress

There is a fever of the spirit,
   The brand of Cain's unresting doom,
Which in the lone dark souls that bear it
   Glows like the lamp in Tullia's tomb.
Unlike the lamp, its subtle fire
   Burns, blasts, consumes its cell, the heart.
Till, one by one, hope, joy, desire,
   Like dreams of shadowy smoke depart.

When hope, love, life itself, are only
10   Dust—spectral memories—dead and cold—
The unfed fire burns bright and lonely,
   Like that undying lamp of old:
And by that drear illumination,
   Till time its clay-built home has rent,
Thought broods on feeling's desolation—
   The soul is its own monument.
   1818

The War-Song of Dinas Vawr

The mountain sheep are sweeter,
But the valley sheep are fatter;
We therefore deemed it meeter
To carry off the latter,
We made an expedition;
We met a host, and quelled it;
We forced a strong position,
And killed the men who held it.

On Dyfed's richest valley,
10 Where herds of kine were browsing,
We made a mighty sally,
To furnish our carousing.
Fierce warriors rushed to meet us;

We met them, and o'erthrew them:
They struggled hard to beat us;
But we conquered them, and slew them.

As we drove our prize at leisure,
The king marched forth to catch us;
His rage surpassed all measure,
20   But his people could not match us.
He fled to his hall-pillars;
And, ere our force we led off,
Some sacked his house and cellars,
While others cut his head off.

We there, in strife bewildr'ing,
Spilt blood enough to swim in:
We orphaned many children,
And widowed many women.
The eagles and the ravens
30   We glutted with our foemen;
The heroes and the cravens,
The spearmen and the bowmen.

We brought away from battle,
And much their land bemoaned them,
Two thousand head of cattle.
And the head of him who owned them:
Ednyfed, king of Dyfed,
His head was borne before us;
His wine and beasts supplied our feasts,
40   And his overthrow, our chorus.

    1829

| JOHN CLARE |

1793–1864

JOHN CLARE is frequently a major poet, an eminence obscured by the proximity of Blake, Wordsworth, Coleridge, Byron, Shelley, and Keats.

The son of a farm laborer, Clare was an authentic peasant poet, which the more sophisticated Robert Burns both was and was not.

In his long madness, Clare suffered delusions of identity, sometimes believing himself to be Burns, and sometimes Lord Byron. He had achieved an early poetic recognition, but it passed quickly, and most of his life was spent in asylums, since he was caught up perpetually in an acute manic-depressive cycle.

Clare is remarkably free of self-consciousness, a freedom that gives his best poems a superb purity and directness of address. They have an immediacy that is very rare in poetry of any period.

I have included six poems by Clare, starting with "Badger," from which I omit the first and final stanzas, which lessen the effect of the badger's heroic last stance.

The two poems on the "I Am" motif have a kind of involuntary pathos unique to Clare. "An Invite to Eternity," "A Vision," and the "Song: I Hid My Love" are extraordinarily like William Blake, whom Clare had never read. They seem to tap into a visionary realm in which the objects of sense-perception are charged with an intensity we recognize but cannot join.

❦   ❦   ❦

from Badger

When midnight comes a host of dogs and men
Go out and track the badger to his den,
And put a sack within the hole, and lie
Till the old grunting badger passes by.
He comes and hears—they let the strongest loose.
The old fox hears the noise and drops the goose.
The poacher shoots and hurries from the cry,
And the old hare half wounded buzzes by.
They get a forkèd stick to bear him down
And clapt the dogs and bare him to the town,
And bait him all the day with many dogs,
And laugh and shout and fright the scampering hogs.
He runs along and bites at all he meets:
They shout and hollo down the noisy streets.

He turns about to face the loud uproar
And drives the rebels to their very door.
The frequent stone is hurled where 'er they go;

When badgers fight, and every one's a foe.
The dogs are clapt and urged to join the fray;
The badger turns and drives them all away.
Though scarcely half as big, dimute and small,
He fights with dogs for hours and beats them all.
The heavy mastiff, savage in the fray,
Lies down and licks his feet and turns away.
The bulldog knows his match and waxes cold,
The badger grins and never leaves his hold.
He drives the crowd and follows at their heels
And bites them through—the drunkard swears and reels.

The frighted women take the boys away.
The blackguard laughs and hurries on the fray.
He tries to reach the woods, an awkward race,
But sticks and cudgels quickly stop the chase.
He turns agen and drives the noisy crowd
And beats the many dogs in noises loud.
He drives away and beats them every one,
And then they loose them all and set them on.
He falls as dead and kicked by boys and men,
Then starts and grins and drives the crowd agen;
Till kicked and torn and beaten out he lies
And leaves his hold and cackles, groans, and dies.

.   .   .

1835–1837   1920

[John Clare]

I feel I am, I only know I am,
    And plod upon the earth as dull and void:
Earth's prison chilled my body with its dram
    Of dullness, and my soaring thoughts destroyed.
I fled to solitudes from passion's dream,
    But strife pursued—I only know I am.
I was a being created in the race
    Of men, disdaining bounds of place and time,
A spirit that could travel o'er the space
10   Of earth and heaven, like a thought sublime—
Tracing creation, like my Maker free,—
    A soul unshackled—like eternity:

Spurning earth's vain and soul debasing thrall—
But now I only know I am,—that's all.
        AFTER 1842   1935

I Am

I am: yet what I am none cares or knows;
    My friends forsake me like a memory lost;
I am the self-consumer of my woes—
    They rise and vanish in oblivion's host,
Like shadows in love, frenzied, stifled throes:—
And yet I am, and live—like vapours tost

Into the nothingness of scorn and noise,
    Into the living sea of waking dreams,
Where there is neither sense of life or joys,
10   But the vast shipwreck of my life's esteems;
Even the dearest, that I love the best
Are strange—nay, rather stranger than the rest.

I long for scenes, where man hath never trod,
    A place where woman never smiled or wept
There to abide with my Creator God,
    And sleep as I in childhood sweetly slept,
Untroubling and untroubled where I lie,
The grass below, above, the vaulted sky.
        1844? 1865

An Invite to Eternity

Wilt thou go with me, sweet maid
Say, maiden, wilt thou go with me
Through the valley depths of shade,
Of night and dark obscurity,
Where the path hath lost its way,
Where the sun forgets the day,
Where there's nor life nor light to see,
Sweet maiden, wilt thou go with me?

Where stones will turn to flooding streams,
10   Where plains will rise like ocean waves,

Where life will fade like visioned dreams
And mountains darken into caves,
Say, maiden, wilt thou go with me
Through this sad non-identity,
Where parents live and are forgot,
And sisters live and know us not?

Say, maiden, wilt thou go with me
In this strange death of life to be,
To live in death and be the same
20   Without this life, or home, or name,
At once to be and not to be—
That was and is not—yet to see
Things pass like shadows and the sky
Above, below, around us lie?

The land of shadows wilt thou trace,
And look, nor know each other's face;
The present mixed with reasons gone,
And past and present all as one?
Say, maiden, can thy life be led
30   To join the living with the dead?
Then trace thy footsteps on with me;
We're wed to one eternity.

    1844? 1920

A Vision

I lost the love of heaven above,
    I spurned the lust of earth below.
I felt the sweets of fancied love,
    And hell itself my only foe.

I lost earth's joys, but felt the glow
    Of heaven's flame abound in me,
Till loveliness and I did grow
    The bard of immortality.

I loved but woman fell away,
10   I hid me from her faded flame,
I snatched the sun's eternal ray
    And wrote till earth was but a name.

In every language upon earth,
  On every shore, o'er every sea,
I gave my name immortal birth
  And kept my spirit with the free.
  1844   1924

Song [Secret Love]

I hid my love when young while I
Couldn't bear the buzzing of a fly;
I hid my love to my despite
Till I could not bear to look at light:
I dare not gaze upon her face
But left her memory in each place;
Where'er I saw a wild flower lie
I kissed and bade my love good-bye.

I met her in the greenest dells,
Where dewdrops pearl the wood bluebells;
The lost breeze kissed her bright blue eye,
The bee kissed and went singing by,
A sunbeam found a passage there,
A gold chain round her neck so fair;
As secret as the wild bee's song
She lay there all the summer long.

I hid my love in field and town
Till e'en the breeze would knock me down;
The bees seemed singing ballads o'er,
The fly's buss turned a lion's roar;
And even silence found a tongue,
To haunt me all the summer long;
The riddle nature could not prove
Was nothing else but secret love.
  AFTER 1842   1920

GEORGE DARLEY

1795–1846

AN ANGLO-IRISHMAN from Dublin, Darley became the disciple of both Keats and Shelley. In London, Darley eked out a living by literary journalism, while writing Jacobean tragedies like those of other Romantic poets.

A repressed homosexual, Darley progressively augmented a melancholia that made his a borderline case, very close to madness. Dead at fifty from alcoholism, Darley left as legacy a handful of fine lyrics and the rhapsodic longer poem *Nepenthe,* which echoes both Shelley's *Alastor* and Keats's *Endymion.*

I include here Darley's stately lyric "It Is Not Beauty I Demand," which has a seventeenth-century flavor, and provides a touchstone for High Romantic self-destructiveness:

> He who the Syren's hair would win
> Is mostly strangled in the tide.

I have gathered together also three rhapsodic passages from *Nepenthe* that celebrate the Phoenix, mythological bird of beauty and child of the sun. The phoenix burns up every few centuries, and then is resurrected from its ashes.

ψ   ψ   ψ

It Is Not Beauty I Demand

It is not Beauty I demand,
    A crystal brow, the moon's despair,
Nor the snow's daughter, a white hand,
    Nor mermaid's yellow pride of hair.

Tell me not of your starry eyes,
    Your lips that seem on roses fed,
Your breasts where Cupid trembling lies,
    Nor sleeps for kissing of his bed.

A bloomy pair of vermeil cheeks,
10   Like Hebe's in her ruddiest hours,
A breath that softer music speaks
     Than summer winds a-wooing flowers.

These are but gauds; nay, what are lips?
     Coral beneath the ocean-stream,
Whose brink when your adventurer sips
     Full oft he perisheth on them.

And what are cheeks but ensigns oft
     That wave hot youth to fields of blood?
Did Helen's breast though ne'er so soft,
20   Do Greece or Ilium any good?

Eyes can with baleful ardour burn,
     Poison can breath that erst perfumed,
There's many a white hand holds an urn
     With lovers' hearts to dust consumed.

For crystal brows—there's naught within,
     They are but empty cells for pride;
He who the Syren's hair would win
     Is mostly strangled in the tide.

Give me, instead of beauty's bust,
30   A tender heart, a loyal mind,
Which with temptation I could trust,
     Yet never linked with error find.

One in whose gentle bosom I
     Could pour my secret heart of woes,
Like the care-burthened honey-fly
     That hides his murmurs in the rose.

My earthly comforter! whose love
     So indefeasible might be,
That when my spirit won above
40   Hers could not stay for sympathy.
     1828

The Phoenix

I

O blest unfabled Incense Tree,
That burns in glorious Araby,
With red scent chalicing the air,
Till earth-life grow Elysian there!

Half buried to her flaming breast
In this bright tree, she makes her nest,
Hundred-sunned Phoenix! when she must
Crumble at length to hoary dust!

Her gorgeous death-bed! her rich pyre
10   Burnt up with aromatic fire!
Her urn, sight high from spoiler men!
Her birthplace when self-born again!

The mountainless green wilds among,
Here ends she her unechoing song!
With amber tears and odorous sighs
Mourned by the desert where she dies!

II

Laid like the young fawn mossily
In sun-green vales of Araby,
I woke hard by the Phoenix tree
20   That with shadeless boughs flamed over me;
And upward called by a dumb cry
With moonbroad orbs of wonder, I
Beheld the immortal Bird on high
Glassing the great sun in her eye.
Stedfast she gazed upon his fire,
Still her destroyer and her sire!
As if to his her soul of flame
Had flown already, whence it came;
Like those that sit and glare so still,
30   Intense with their death struggle, till
We touch, and curdle at their chill!—
But breathing yet while she doth burn,
    The deathless Daughter of the sun!
Slowly to crimson embers turn
    The beauties of the brightsome one.

O'er the broad nest her silver wings
Shook down their wasteful glitterings;
Her brinded neck high-arched in air
Like a small rainbow faded there;
40 But brighter glowed her plumy crown
Mouldering to golden ashes down;
With fume of sweet woods, to the skies,
Pure as a Saint's adoring sighs,
Warm as a prayer in Paradise,
Her life-breath rose in sacrifice!
The while with shrill triumphant tone
Sounding aloud, aloft, alone
Ceaseless her joyful deathwail she
Sang to departing Araby!
50   Deep melancholy wonder drew
Tears from my heartspring at that view;
Like cresset shedding its last flare
Upon some wistful mariner,
The Bird, fast blending with the sky,
Turned on me her dead-gazing eye
Once—and as surge to shallow spray
Sank down to vapoury dust away!

III
O, fast her amber blood doth flow
    From the heart-wounded Incense Tree,
60 Fast as earth's deep-embosomed woe
    In silent rivulets to the sea!

Beauty may weep her fair first-born,
    Perchance in as resplendent tears,
Such golden dewdrops bow the corn
    When the stern sickleman appears.

But oh! such perfume to a bower
    Never allured sweet-seeking bee,
As to sip fast that nectarous shower
    A thirstier minstrel drew in me!
    1835

THOMAS LOVELL BEDDOES

1803–1849

A DISCIPLE OF SHELLEY, Beddoes is a unique poet, far superior to Poe as a reviver of Gothic morbidities. I memorized a score of his poems in my childhood, and they recite themselves to me still. Like Shelley, Beddoes is superb at songs, but in Beddoes they are grisly in substance while maintaining a tone of controlled delicacy, wonderfully at variance with their burden.

Beddoes was the son of a famous eccentric literary physician who practiced in Bristol. From Oxford, where he wrote strange versions of Jacobean tragedy, Beddoes went to Germany to study medicine, particularly anatomy, at which he became a master. He lived most of his life in Germany and Switzerland, where he participated in revolutionary activities, suffered through unhappy homosexual love affairs, and practiced medicine.

Throughout his last twenty years, Beddoes worked incessantly at composing his masterwork, *Death's Jest-Book; or the Fool's Tragedy,* an apocalyptic parody of the Jacobean dramas of John Webster, John Ford, and Cyril Tourneur. At the age of forty-six, Beddoes committed suicide in Basel, Switzerland, of which he had written: "Down from the Alps Paracelsus came, / To dance with death at Basel."

I have space for only three poems by Beddoes, the first of which is his undergraduate response to the death of his idol, Shelley. "Song: Old Adam the Carrion Crow" is sung in *Death's Jest-Book* by Isbrand the avenger, who disguises himself as a court jester. The exquisite and menacing "Song of the Stygian Naiades" creates river nymphs of the Styx, Hades's river of death, and has them celebrate the abduction and rape of Proserpine by the amorous Pluto, who makes his victim the Queen of Hell. Beelzebub, Lord of the Flies, seems here to be Satan himself, rather than one of his ranking subordinates.

✣   ✣   ✣

Lines

Written in a Blank Leaf of the Prometheus Unbound

Write it in gold—a Spirit of the sun,
An Intellect ablaze with heavenly thoughts,
A Soul with all the dews of pathos shining,
Odorous with love, and sweet to silent woe
With the dark glories of concentrate song,
Was sphered in mortal earth. Angelic sounds
Alive with panting thoughts sunned the dim world.
The bright creations of an human heart
Wrought magic in the bosoms of mankind.
10   A flooding summer burst on Poetry;
Of which the crowning sun, the night of beauty,
The dancing showers, the birds whose anthems wild
Note after note unbind the enchanted leaves
Of breaking buds, eve, and the flow of dawn,
Were centred and condensed in his one name
As in a providence—and that was SHELLEY.

    1822   1851

Song

Old Adam, the carrion crow,
    The old crow of Cairo;
He sat in the shower, and let it flow
Under his tail and over his crest;
      And through every feather
      Leaked the wet weather;
And the bough swung under his nest;
For his beak it was heavy with marrow.
   Is that the wind dying? O no;
10   It's only two devils, that blow
Through a murderer's bones, to and fro,
      In the ghosts' moonshine.

Ho! Eve, my grey carrion wife,
    When we have supped on king's marrow,
Where shall we drink and make merry our life?
Our nest it is queen Cleopatra's skull,
      'Tis cloven and cracked,

And battered and hacked,
But with tears of blue eyes it is full:
20 Let us drink then, my raven of Cairo.
Is that the wind dying? O no;
It's only two devils, that blow
Through a murderer's bones, to and fro,
In the ghosts' moonshine.
1825? 1850

Song of the Stygian Naiades

*What do you think the mermaids of the Styx were singing as I watched
them bathing the other day—*

I

Proserpine may pull her flowers,
Wet with dew or wet with tears,
Red with anger, pale with fears;
Is it any fault of ours,
If Pluto be an amorous king
And come home nightly, laden
Underneath his broad bat-wing
With a gentle earthly maiden?
Is it so, Wind, is it so?
10 All that I and you do know
Is that we saw fly and fix
'Mongst the flowers and reeds of Styx,
Yesterday,
Where the Furies made their hay
For a bed of tiger cubs,
A great fly of Beelzebub's,
The bee of hearts, which mortals name
Cupid, Love, and Fie for shame.

II

Proserpine may weep in rage,
20 But ere I and you have done
Kissing, bathing in the sun,
What I have in yonder cage,
She shall guess and ask in vain,
Bird or serpent, wild or tame;

But if Pluto does't again,
It shall sing out loud his shame.
   What hast caught them? What hast caught?
Nothing but a poet's thought,
   Which so light did fall and fix
30   'Mongst the flowers and reeds of Styx,
          Yesterday,
Where the Furies made their hay
For a bed of tiger cubs,
A great fly of Beelzebub's,
The bee of hearts, which mortals name
Cupid, Love, and Fie for shame.
   1835? 1851

WILLIAM CULLEN BRYANT

1794–1878

A POETIC PRODIGY as a child, William Cullen Bryant was the first distinctively American poet. His two most famous poems, "Thanatopsis" and "To a Waterfowl," given here, were written when he was twenty. A Massachusetts lawyer by profession, Bryant married in 1821, fathered two daughters, and won a strong reputation as a poet with his first volume, *Poems* (1822). In 1825, Bryant abandoned the law for literature.

From 1829 until 1878, when he died, Bryant edited the *Evening Post* in New York City. After 1848, the crusading Bryant was a Free Soil Party member, and joined the Republicans in John Charles Fremont's losing campaign for president in 1856, and then in Abraham Lincoln's victory in 1860. As an Abolitionist, Bryant eulogized Lincoln in 1865. In 1866, he encouraged and aided Garibaldi in Italy. It was appropriate that the aged Bryant died from the effects of a fall after his address celebrating the dedication of the statue of Mazzini in Central Park.

Thanatopsis is Greek for "a view of death," and the poem reflects the influence of William Wordsworth, but with an authentic American difference that can be heard in its eloquent conclusion:

So live, that when thy summons comes to join
The innumerable caravan, that moves
To that mysterious realm, where each shall take
His chamber in the silent halls of death,
Thou go not, like the quarry-slave at night,
Scourged to his dungeon, but sustained and soothed
By an unfaltering trust, approach thy grave,
Like one who wraps the drapery of his couch
About him, and lies down to pleasant dreams.

Even more American in accent, "To a Waterfowl" prophesies the American Sublime from Emerson through Whitman to Hart Crane, whose "Proem: To Brooklyn Bridge" distantly echoes, in its start, a superb stanza of Bryant's lyric invocation:

All day thy wings have fanned,
At that far height, the cold thin atmosphere,
Yet stoop not, weary, to the welcome land,
Though the dark night is near.

ᔕ   ᔕ   ᔕ

To a Waterfowl

Whither, 'midst falling dew,
While glow the heavens with the last steps of day
Far, through their rosy depths, dost thou pursue
Thy solitary way?

Vainly the fowler's eye
Might mark thy distant flight to do thee wrong,
As, darkly painted on the crimson sky,
Thy figure floats along.

Seek'st thou the plashy brink
Of weedy lake, or marge of river wide,
Or where the rocking billows rise and sink
On the chafed ocean side?

There is a Power whose care
Teaches thy way along that pathless coast,—

The desert and illimitable air,—
　　Lone wandering, but not lost.

　　All day thy wings have fanncd,
At that far height, the cold thin atmosphere,
Yet stoop not, weary, to the welcome land,
　　Though the dark night is near.

　　And soon that toil shall end,
Soon shalt thou find a summer home, and rest,
And scream among thy fellows; reeds shall bend,
　　Soon, o'er thy sheltered nest.

　　Thou'rt gone, the abyss of heaven
Hath swallow'd up thy form; yet, on my heart
Deeply hath sunk the lesson thou hast given,
　　And shall not soon depart.

　　He, who, from zone to zone,
Guides through the boundless sky thy certain flight,
In the long way that I must tread alone,
　　Will lead my steps aright.

RALPH WALDO EMERSON

1803–1882

EMERSON, who is the mind of America, necessarily matters most for his prose writings: essays, lectures, notebooks, and journals. No single poem by Emerson is as intricate and powerful as the greatest of the essays: "Self-Reliance," "Circles," "Experience," and almost all of *The Conduct of Life*. And yet Emerson, after Walt Whitman and Emily Dickinson, is the most considerable poet of the nineteenth century in the United States.

I have represented Emerson here by four poems, which together give an accurate impression of his gifts. The relation of his poems to his life is not more intimate than that of the prose, but allows perspectives upon his personality that can be surprising.

Born in Boston on May 25, 1803, Emerson was descended, on both sides of the family, from a long sequence of ministers, first Calvinist, and then Unitarian. His father, William Emerson, pastor of Boston's First Church, died in 1811. The dominant influence upon Waldo (the name he preferred) became his aunt, Mary Moody Emerson, strong-minded and benign.

Emerson entered Harvard in 1817, much the youngest member of his class. After graduation, in 1821, he taught school until he entered Harvard Divinity to study for the Unitarian ministry. Frail (the family curse was tuberculosis) yet amazingly resilient, the twenty-six-year-old Emerson married the beautiful Ellen Tucker in 1829, when she was scarcely eighteen. Unhappily, she died of tuberculosis early in 1831. A year later, he resigned his ministry, and went abroad, meeting Coleridge, Wordsworth, and J. S. Mill, and commencing a lifelong friendship with the stormy Scot, Thomas Carlyle.

From 1835 on, Emerson was a secular lecturer, which became his true profession until old age. Life began for him again with his marriage to Lidian Jackson on September 14, 1835. His public fame was inaugurated by the publication of *Nature* in 1836, but notoriety came with the delivery of the Harvard Divinity School Address in 1838.

A fierce opponent of slavery, Emerson nevertheless tried to avoid taking public stances. His hatred of the South, during the Civil War, was an experience that helped to burn the sage out, prematurely. By 1875, the superb mind was senile, and its final seven years were spent in a kind of psychic twilight.

Emerson was the center of American literary culture in his own era: his disciples included Thoreau, Margaret Fuller, Jones Very, Whitman, and the senior Henry James. Poe, Hawthorne, and Melville defined themselves by their dissent from Emerson, and yet Hester Prynne and Captain Ahab are Emersonians. William James was profoundly Emersonian; his brother Henry tried to hold Emerson off by an affectionate condescension, but Isabel Archer is Emerson's child. In the first half of the twentieth century, Emerson was rejected by the school of Eliot and Pound. "The essays of Emerson," Eliot proclaimed, "are already an encumbrance," and Eliot's followers were more vehement. "Emerson was the Devil," Allen Tate remarked to me, and Robert Penn Warren assured me that Emerson was poison. In 1964, I joined with a few others in sparking an Emerson revival, which is still an ongoing enterprise.

After Emerson, an American writer or scholar can be anti-Emerson if that is desired, but you cannot be non-Emersonian. He usurped the possibilities for the imagination in the United States, and he accomplished this with extraordinary pugnacity. Back in the Eliotic Fifties, there was a general impression (among those who hadn't read Emerson) that he was a sweet fellow. Cure yourself of that by reflecting upon a single sentence of "Self-Reliance": "As men's prayers are a disease of the will, so are their creeds a disease of the intellect." In George W. Bush's America, Emerson could not be elected dogcatcher.

The poems tend to be cognitively stronger than aesthetically quite perfected: there is something abrupt and impatient in Emerson's Muse. Robert Frost, the most overtly Emersonian of major modern poets, judged "Uriel" to be "the greatest Western poem yet." Overpraise aside, Frost heard something we would do well to hear—Emerson's defiance of the old gods:

> "Line in nature is not found;
> Unit and universe are round;
> In vain produced, all rays return;
> Evil will bless, and ice will burn."

One feels Frost himself wrote that quatrain, but "Uriel" is Emerson's satire of the furor that followed his Divinity School Address.

A fiercer, public Emerson writes the Channing Ode, in protest against the American land-grab in the Mexican War, but this is no mere political poem:

> The horseman serves the horse,
> The neatherd serves the neat,
> The merchant serves the purse,
> The eater serves his meat;
> 'Tis the day of the chattel,
> Web to weave, and corn to grind;
> Things are in the saddle,
> And ride mankind.

That can seem to us all too appropriate to 2003, having rushed into war with the Iraqis, continuing to seek the elusive bin Laden, and peering after the vanished economy:

> Things are in the saddle,
> And ride mankind.

Yet Emerson concludes: "The astonished Muse finds thousands at her side," a transcendental intimation, but not likely for us. But then his ideas of poetry are the most strenuous in his nation's tradition, and are primordial and shamanistic:

> The trivial harp will never please
> Or fill my craving ear;
> Its chords should ring as blows the breeze,
> Free, peremptory, clear.
> No jingling serenader's art,
> Nor tinkle of piano strings,
> Can make the wild blood start
> In its mystic springs.
> The kingly bard
> Must smite the chords rudely and hard,
> As with hammer or with mace;
> That they may render back
> Artful thunder, which conveys
> Secrets of the solar track,
> Sparks of the supersolar blaze.

This is from "Merlin" I, and is surpassed by the Dionysian chant, "Bacchus," which seems to me Emerson's strongest poem, and which concludes with a poignant fusion of personal loss and imaginative gain:

> Pour, Bacchus! the remembering wine;
> Retrieve the loss of me and mine!
> Vine for vine be antidote,
> And the grape requite the lote!
> Haste to cure the old despair,—
> Reason in Nature's lotus drenched,
> The memory of ages quenched;
> Give them again to shine;
> Let wine repair what this undid;
> And where the infection slid,
> A dazzling memory revive;
> Refresh the faded tints,
> Recut the aged prints,
> And write my old adventures with the pen
> Which on the first day drew,
> Upon the tablets blue,
> The dancing Pleiads and eternal men.

"The loss of me and mine" had been heavy: his first wife Ellen, his son Waldo, his brother Charles. But there is a force in Emerson always battling the past, personal and cultural. This force, at its strongest, found its form in the other harmony of prose, but frequently enough it achieved splendor in Emerson's poems.

ᕯ   ᕯ   ᕯ

Uriel

It fell in the ancient periods,
    Which the brooding soul surveys,
Or ever the wild Time coined itself
    Into calendar months and days.

This was the lapse of Uriel,
Which in Paradise befell.
Once, among the Pleiads walking,
SAID overheard the young gods talking;
And the treason, too long pent,
To his ears was evident.
The young deities discussed
Laws of form, and metre just,
Orb, quintessence, and sunbeams,
What subsisteth, and what seems.
One, with low tones that decide,
And doubt and reverend use defied,
With a look that solved the sphere,
And stirred the devils everywhere,
Gave his sentiment divine
Against the being of a line.
'Line in nature is not found;
Unit and universe are round;
In vain produced, all rays return;
Evil will bless, and ice will burn.'
As Uriel spoke with piercing eye,
A shudder ran around the sky;
The stern old war-gods shook their heads;
The seraphs frowned from myrtle-beds;
Seemed to the holy festival
The rash word boded ill to all;
The balance-beam of Fate was bent;
The bounds of good and ill were rent;

Strong Hades could not keep his own,
But all slid to confusion.
A sad self-knowledge, withering, fell
On the beauty of Uriel;
In heaven once eminent, the god
Withdrew, that hour, into his cloud;
Whether doomed to long gyration
In the sea of generation,
Or by knowledge grown too bright
To hit the nerve of feebler sight.
Straightway, a forgetting wind
Stole over the celestial kind,
And their lips the secret kept,
If in ashes the fire-seed slept.
But now and then, truth-speaking things
Shamed the angels' veiling wings;
And, shrilling from the solar course,
Or from fruit of chemic force,
Procession of a soul in matter,
Or the speeding change of water,
Or out of the good of evil born,
Came Uriel's voice of cherub scorn,
And a blush tinged the upper sky,
And the gods shook, they knew not why.

Ode, Inscribed to W. H. Channing

Though loath to grieve
The evil time's sole patriot,
I cannot leave
My honied thought
For the priest's cant,
Or statesman's rant.

If I refuse
My study for their politique,
Which at the best is trick,
The angry Muse
Puts confusion in my brain.

But who is he that prates
Of the culture of mankind,

Of better arts and life?
Go, blindworm, go,
Behold the famous States
Harrying Mexico
With rifle and with knife!

Or who, with accent bolder,
Dare praise the freedom-loving mountaineer?
I found by thee, O rushing Contoocook!
And in thy valleys, Agiochook!
The jackals of the negro-holder.

The God who made New Hampshire
Taunted the lofty land
With little men;—
Small bat and wren
House in the oak:—
If earth-fire cleave
The upheaved land, and bury the folk,
The southern crocodile would grieve.
Virtue palters; Right is hence;
Freedom praised, but hid;
Funeral eloquence
Rattles the coffin-lid.

What boots thy zeal,
O glowing friend,
That would indignant rend
The northland from the south?
Wherefore? to what good end?
Boston Bay and Bunker Hill
Would serve things still;—
Things are of the snake.

The horseman serves the horse,
The neatherd serves the neat,
The merchant serves the purse,
The eater serves his meat;
'Tis the day of the chattel,
Web to weave, and corn to grind;
Things are in the saddle,
And ride mankind.

There are two laws discrete,
Not reconciled,—
Law for man, and law for thing;
The last builds town and fleet,
But it runs wild,
And doth the man unking.

'Tis fit the forest fall,
The steep be graded,
The mountain tunnelled,
The sand shaded,
The orchard planted,
The glebe tilled,
The prairie granted,
The steamer built.

Let man serve law for man;
Live for friendship, live for love,
For truth's and harmony's behoof;
The state may follow how it can,
As Olympus follows Jove.

 Yet do not I invite
The wrinkled shopman to my sounding woods,
Nor bid the unwilling senator
Ask votes of thrushes in the solitudes.
Every one to his chosen work;—
Foolish hands may mix and mar;
Wise and sure the issues are.
Round they roll till dark is light,

Sex to sex, and even to odd;—
The over-god
Who marries Right to Might,
Who peoples, unpeoples,—
He who exterminates
Races by stronger races,
Black by white faces,—
Knows to bring honey
Out of the lion;
Grafts gentlest scion
On pirate and Turk.

The Cossack eats Poland,
Like stolen fruit;
Her last noble is ruined,
Her last poet mute:
Straight, into double band
The victors divide;
Half for freedom strike and stand;—
The astonished Muse finds thousands at her side.

Bacchus

Bring me wine, but wine which never grew
In the belly of the grape,
Or grew on vine whose tap-roots, reaching through
Under the Andes to the Cape,
Suffered no savor of the earth to scape.

Let its grapes the morn salute
From a nocturnal root,
Which feels the acrid juice
Of Styx and Erebus;
And turns the woe of Night,
By its own craft, to a more rich delight.

We buy ashes for bread;
We buy diluted wine;
Give me of the true,—
Whose ample leaves and tendrils curled
Among the silver hills of heaven,
Draw everlasting dew;
Wine of wine,
Blood of the world,
Form of forms, and mould of statures,
That I intoxicated,
And by the draught assimilated,
May float at pleasure through all natures;
The bird-language rightly spell,
And that which roses say so well.

Wine that is shed
Like the torrents of the sun
Up the horizon walls,

Or like the Atlantic streams, which run
When the South Sea calls.

Water and bread,
Food which needs no transmuting,
Rainbow-flowering, wisdom-fruiting
Wine which is already man,
Food which teach and reason can.

Wine which Music is,—
Music and wine are one,—
That I, drinking this,
Shall hear far Chaos talk with me;
Kings unborn shall walk with me;
And the poor grass shall plot and plan
What it will do when it is man.
Quickened so, will I unlock
Every crypt of every rock.

I thank the joyful juice
For all I know;—
Winds of remembering
Of the ancient being blow,
And seeming-solid walls of use
Open and flow.

Pour, Bacchus! the remembering wine;
Retrieve the loss of me and mine!
Vine for vine be antidote,
And the grape requite the lote!
Haste to cure the old despair,—
Reason in Nature's lotus drenched,
The memory of ages quenched;
Give them again to shine;
Let wine repair what this undid;
And where the infection slid,
A dazzling memory revive;
Refresh the faded tints,
Recut the aged prints,
And write my old adventures with the pen
Which on the first day drew,
Upon the tablets blue,
The dancing Pleiads and eternal men.

Days

Daughters of Time, the hypocritic Days,
Muffled and dumb like barefoot dervishes,
And marching single in an endless file,
Bring diadems and fagots in their hands.
To each they offer gifts after his will,
Bread, kingdoms, stars, and sky that holds them all.
I, in my pleached garden, watched the pomp,
Forgot my morning wishes, hastily
Took a few herbs and apples, and the Day
Turned and departed silent. I, too late,
Under her solemn fillet saw the scorn.

HENRY WADSWORTH LONGFELLOW

1807–1882

THOUGH SO LONG IN ECLIPSE, Longfellow is a superb lyric poet, as the four poems included here testify. Once overpopular, Longfellow only now begins to be read again with accurate appreciation.

Born in Portland, Maine (then legally part of Massachusetts), Longfellow was a classmate of Nathaniel Hawthorne at Bowdoin College. After three years' study in Europe, Longfellow taught at Bowdoin, and married Mary Potter in 1831, only to lose her to a miscarriage in 1835.

From 1836 on, Longfellow taught at Harvard as professor of modern languages. By the early 1840s, he was widely read and admired as a poet. He married Frances Appleton in 1843, having weathered repeated rejections by the lady. They had six children together, and appear to have been reasonably happy, despite the death of their daughter Fanny in 1848. Unfortunately, Mrs. Longfellow died in 1861, when her dress caught fire: Longfellow himself was seriously burned in trying to save her.

In his own lifetime, Longfellow was best known for his narrative poems, *Evangeline* and *The Song of Hiawatha*. These remain readable, but are little read. His translation of Dante's *Divine Comedy* seems to me undervalued, and compares favorably with the current versions.

Longfellow is a very learned poet, but is subtle in subduing his erudition to his poetic purposes. "Seaweed" is a technical triumph in the transition from its initial four stanzas to its final four, while "My Lost Youth" is a triumph of refined nostalgia, universal in its application.

Even more remarkable is "Snow-Flakes": "This is the poem of the air" hovers always in my memory, as does the superb sonnet, "The Cross of Snow," memorializing Frances Longfellow. As a lyrical poet, Longfellow frequently achieves the purity and only apparent simplicity that his enemy, Poe, scarcely could approach:

> The day returns, but nevermore
> Returns the traveller to the shore,
> And the tide rises, the tide falls.

Few experiences of the Protestant sensibility are as lyrically intense as the magnificent "The Bells of San Blas," with its defiant rejection of a Catholic plea for order.

> O Bells of San Blas, in vain
> Ye call back the Past again!
> The Past is deaf to your prayer:
> Out of the shadows of night
> The world rolls into light;
> It is daybreak everywhere.

Longfellow is not, like Whitman and Dickinson, a great original, and he compares poorly with the rugged Emerson in what Emerson called "meter-making argument." But he remains a permanent poet, replete with grace and his own chastened mode of cognitive music.

↓   ↓   ↓

Snow-Flakes

Out of the bosom of the Air,
    Out of the cloud-folds of her garments shaken,
Over the woodlands brown and bare
    Over the harvest-fields forsaken,
        Silent, and soft, and slow
        Descends the snow.

Even as our cloudy fancies take
    Suddenly shape in some divine expression,
Even as the troubled heart doth make
    In the white countenance confession,
        The troubled sky reveals
        The grief it feels.

This is the poem of the air,
    Slowly in silent syllables recorded;
This is the secret of despair,
    Long in its cloudy bosom hoarded,
        Now whispered and revealed
        To wood and field.

The Cross of Snow

In the long, sleepless watches of the night,
    A gentle face—the face of one long dead—
    Looks at me from the wall, where round its head
    The night-lamp casts a halo of pale light.
Here in this room she died; and soul more white
    Never through martyrdom of fire was led
    To its repose; nor can in books be read
    The legend of a life more benedight.
There is a mountain in the distant West
    That, sun-defying, in its deep ravines
    Displays a cross of snow upon its side.
Such is the cross I wear upon my breast
    These eighteen years, through all the changing scenes
    And seasons, changeless since the day she died.

The Tide Rises, the Tide Falls

The tide rises, the tide falls,
The twilight darkens, the curlew calls;
Along the sea-sands damp and brown
The traveller hastens toward the town,
    And the tide rises, the tide falls.

Darkness settles on roofs and walls,
But the sea, the sea in the darkness calls;

The little waves, with their soft, white hands,
Efface the footprints in the sands,
   And the tide rises, the tide falls.

The morning breaks; the steeds in their stalls
Stamp and neigh, as the hostler calls;
The day returns, but nevermore
Returns the traveller to the shore,
   And the tide rises, the tide falls.

The Bells of San Blas

What say the Bells of San Blas
To the ships that southward pass
    From the harbor of Mazatlan?
To them it is nothing more
Than the sound of surf on the shore,—
    Nothing more to master or man.

But to me, a dreamer of dreams,
To whom what is and what seems
    Are often one and the same,—
The Bells of San Blas to me
Have a strange, wild melody,
    And are something more than a name.

For bells are the voice of the church;
They have tones that touch and search
    The hearts of young and old;
One sound to all, yet each
Lends a meaning to their speech,
    And the meaning is manifold.

They are a voice of the Past,
Of an age that is fading fast,
    Of a power austere and grand;
When the flag of Spain unfurled
Its folds o'er this western world,
    And the Priest was lord of the land.

The chapel that once looked down
On the little seaport town

Has crumbled into the dust;
And on oaken beams below
The bells swing to and fro,
    And are green with mould and rust.

"Is, then, the old faith dead,"
They say, "and in its stead
    Is some new faith proclaimed,
That we are forced to remain
Naked to sun and rain,
    Unsheltered and ashamed?

"Once in our tower aloof
We rang over wall and roof
    Our warnings and our complaints;
And round about us there
The white doves filled the air,
    Like the white souls of the saints.

"The saints! Ah, have they grown
Forgetful of their own?
    Are they asleep, or dead,
That open to the sky
Their ruined Missions lie;
    No longer tenanted?

"Oh, bring us back once more
The vanished days of yore,
    When the world with faith was filled;
Bring back the fervid zeal,
The hearts of fire and steel,
    The hands that believe and build.

"Then from our tower again
We will send over land and main
    Our voices of command,
Like exiled kings who return
To their thrones, and the people learn
    That the Priest is lord of the land!"

O Bells of San Blas, in vain
Ye call back the Past again!
    The Past is deaf to your prayer:

Out of the shadows of night
The world rolls into light;
    It is daybreak everywhere.

EDGAR ALLAN POE

1809–1849

POE IS A BAD POET, a poor critic, and a dreadful prose stylist in his celebrated tales. Poe is also inescapable. No other American writer—Whitman, Emerson, Mark Twain, Henry James, Faulkner—is so widely read, both domestically and abroad. In translation, Poe improves greatly, as French and German versions demonstrate. He dreamed universal nightmares, and still frightens children. The late actor Vincent Price was Poe's true celebrant. Only outrageous overplaying works with Poe.

Poe is not a paradox, but a tribute to the power of myth. Almost anyone can retell "The Fall of the House of Usher" more effectively than Poe does, because Poe's diction is uniquely abominable. As for the most famous Poe lyrics—"The Raven," "The Bells," "Annabel Lee," and the astonishingly dreadful "Ulalume"—you can abandon yourself to them if you want to, but what is it that Poe gives you?

    Here once, through an alley Titanic,
        Of Cypress, I roamed with my Soul—
        Of Cypress, with Psyche, my Soul.
    These were days when my heart was volcanic
        As the scoriac rivers that roll—
        As the lavas that restlessly roll
    Their sulphurous currents down Yaanek,
        In the ultimate climes of the Pole—
    That groan as they roll down Mount Yaanek,
    In the realms of the Boreal Pole.

They groan as they roll; if we were in Edward Lear's *Book of Nonsense*, we might assimilate all this to the great Gromboolian plain, where we listen to the laments of the Dong with a Luminous Nose. In Poe's art of sinking in poetry, every deep conceals a lower deep, a bathos more profound. Perhaps the deepest is reached in the second stanza of Poe's "For Annie":

> Sadly, I know
> I am shorn of my strength,
> And no muscle I move
> As I lie at full length—
> But no matter!—I feel
> I am better at length.

Poe's life itself was mostly nightmare. The child of wandering actors, he was adopted by a wealthy merchant, but left both the University of Virginia and West Point, his lack of discipline being absolute. He married his cousin Virginia when she was thirteen; she died of tuberculosis at twenty-five. Increasingly alcoholic, Poe died two years later, in Baltimore, in rather obscure circumstances.

One cannot dismiss Poe: he always will be there. His poetry, at its rare best, imitates Byron, as in "The City in the Sea," or Shelley, as in "Israfel." The legend or myth of Poe has a vitality that repetition does not stale. I greatly prefer Longfellow (whom Poe falsely accused of plagiarism), but Poe, as I have glumly acknowledged, is inescapable. To dream everyone's nightmare has to be genius, which cannot be denied Poe.

ꙮ   ꙮ   ꙮ

Israfel

In Heaven a spirit doth dwell
    "Whose heart-strings are a lute";
None sing so wildly well
As the angel Israfel,
And the giddy stars (so legends tell)
Ceasing their hymns, attend the spell
    Of his voice, all mute.

Tottering above
    In her highest noon,
    The enamoured moon
Blushes with love,
    While, to listen, the red levin
    (With the rapid Pleiads, even,

Which were seven,)
Pauses in Heaven.

And they say (the starry choir
    And the other listening things)
That Israfeli's fire
Is owing to that lyre
    By which he sits and sings—
The trembling living wire
Of those unusual strings.

But the skies that angel trod,
    Where deep thoughts are a duty—
Where Love's a grown-up God—
    Where the Houri glances are
Imbued with all the beauty
    Which we worship in a star.

Therefore, thou art not wrong,
    Israfeli, who despisest
An unimpassioned song;
To thee the laurels belong,
    Best bard, because the wisest!
Merrily live, and long!

The ecstasies above
    With thy burning measures suit—
Thy grief, thy joy, thy hate, thy love,
With the fervour of thy lure—
Well may the stars be mute!

Yes, Heaven is thine; but this
    Is a world of sweets and sours;
    Our flowers are merely—flowers,
And the shadow of thy perfect bliss
    Is the sunshine of ours.

If I could dwell
Where Israfel
    Hath dwelt, and he where I,
He might not sing so wildly well
    A mortal melody,

While a bolder note than this might swell
 From my lyre within the sky.

The City in the Sea

Lo! Death has reared himself a throne
In a strange city lying alone
Far down within the dim West,
Where the good and the bad and the worst and the best
Have gone to their eternal rest.
There shrines and palaces and towers
(Time-eaten towers that tremble not!)
Resemble nothing that is ours.
Around, by lifting winds forgot,
Resignedly beneath the sky
The melancholy waters lie.

No rays from the holy heaven come down
On the long night-time of that town;
But light from out the lurid sea
Streams up the turrets silently—
Gleams up the pinnacles far and free—
Up domes—up spires—up kingly halls—
Up fanes—up Babylon-like walls—
Up shadowy long-forgotten bowers
Of sculptured ivy and stone flowers—
Up many and many a marvellous shrine
Whose wreathéd friezes intertwine
The viol, the violet, and the vine.

Resignedly beneath the sky
The melancholy waters lie.
So blend the turrets and shadows there
That all seem pendulous in air,
While from a proud tower in the town
Death looks gigantically down.

There open fanes and gaping graves
Yawn level with the luminous waves;
But not the riches there that lie
In each idol's diamond eye—

Not the gaily-jewelled dead
Tempt the waters from their bed;
For no ripples curl, alas!
Along that wilderness of glass—
No swellings tell that winds may be
Upon some far-off happier sea—
No heavings hint that winds have been
On seas less hideously serene.

But lo, a stir is in the air!
The wave—there is a movement there!
As if the towers had thrust aside,
In slightly sinking, the dull tide—
As if their tops had feebly given
A void within the filmy Heaven.
The waves have now a redder glow—

The hours are breathing faint and low—
And when, amid no earthly moans,
Down, down that town shall settle hence,
Hell, rising from a thousand thrones,
Shall do it reverence.

JONES VERY

1813–1880

JONES VERY, teaching Greek at Harvard, had an intense mystical experience in 1837, which stimulated him to write some remarkable sonnets. In 1838, he became a friend and disciple of Emerson. Forced out of Harvard when his sanity was questioned, Very was confined at McLean Asylum for a month in the autumn of 1838.

Ironically, Very's poems and essays declined from 1840 on, as the aura of his mystical "madness" faded away. He became a rather conventional preacher, and abandoned any Transcendental interests. But from 1837 to

1839, he had been an original devotional poet, probably the best the United States has had.

The two sonnets I have included are deftly disquieting. In "The New Birth," dramatic urgency develops from line to line, as the mystical experience triumphs over every recalcitrance in Very. "The Dead" also exploits delayed meaning, as we gradually understand that *we* are the dead.

✤   ✤   ✤

The New Birth

'Tis a new life—thoughts move not as they did
With slow uncertain steps across my mind,
In thronging haste fast pressing on they bid
The portals open to the viewless wind;
That comes not, save when in the dust is laid
The crown of pride that gilds each mortal brow,
And from before man's vision melting fade
The heavens and earth—Their walls are falling now—
Fast crowding on each thought claims utterance strong,
Storm-lifted waves swift rushing to the shore
On from the sea they send their shouts along,
Back through the cave-worn rocks their thunders roar,
And I a child of God by Christ made free
Start from death's slumbers to eternity.

The Dead

I see them crowd on crowd they walk the earth
Dry, leafless trees no Autumn wind laid bare;
And in their nakedness find cause for mirth,
And all unclad would winter's rudeness dare;
No sap doth through their clattering branches flow,
Whence springing leaves and blossoms bright appear;
Their hearts the living God have ceased to know,
Who gives the spring time to th'expectant year;
They mimic life, as if from him to steal
His glow of health to paint the livid cheek;
They borrow words for thoughts they cannot feel,
That with a seeming heart their tongue may speak;
And in their show of life more dead they live
Than those that to the earth with many tears they give.

HENRY DAVID THOREAU

1817–1862

WE REMEMBER THOREAU primarily as the author of *Walden* (1854) and of such influential essays as "Civil Disobedience" and "Life Without Principle." But he was always a poet, with his own voice and vision, who perhaps would have developed his gift had he not died at forty-four from tuberculosis.

Fourteen years younger than Ralph Waldo Emerson, Thoreau began as the great essayist's disciple in 1834, a relationship that faded after 1850. Until then, Thoreau was almost part of Emerson's family, and perhaps was in love with Lidian, the second Mrs. Emerson, in what we can be certain remained a blameless attachment.

An active Abolitionist, Thoreau sheltered fugitive slaves, and met John Brown. After the raid on Harpers Ferry, both Thoreau and Emerson delivered public addresses in support of Brown. Again like Emerson, Thoreau befriended Walt Whitman, whose "Sun-Down Poem" ("Crossing Brooklyn Ferry") he particularly admired.

Thoreau's life seems to me more enigmatic than his writings, and the poems are a welcome path into his complex personality.

↓   ↓   ↓

"My life has been the poem I would have writ,"

My life has been the poem I would have writ,
But I could not both live and utter it.

"I am a parcel of vain strivings tied"

I am a parcel of vain strivings tied
　　By a chance bond together,
　Dangling this way and that, their links
　　Were made so loose and wide,
　　　　Methinks,
　　　For milder weather.

A bunch of violets without their roots,
    And sorrel intermixed,
      Encircled by a wisp of straw
        Once coiled about their shoots,
          The law
        By which I'm fixed.

A nosegay which Time clutched from out
    Those fair Elysian fields,
      With weeds and broken stems, in haste,
        Doth make the rabble rout
          That waste
        The day he yields.

And here I bloom for a short hour unseen,
    Drinking my juices up,
  With no root in the land
    To keep my branches green,
        But stand
      In a bare cup.

Some tender buds were left upon my stem
    In mimicry of life,
  But ah! the children will not know,
    Till time has withered them,
        The woe
      With which they're rife.

But now I see I was not plucked for naught,
    And after in life's vase
  Of glass set while I might survive,
    But by a kind hand brought
        Alive
      To a strange place.

That stock thus thinned will soon redeem its hours,
    And by another year,
  Such as God knows, with freer air,
  More fruits and fairer flowers
        Will bear,
      While I droop here.

"Light-winged Smoke, Icarian bird,"

Light-winged Smoke, Icarian bird,
Melting thy pinions in thy upward flight,
Lark without song, and messenger of dawn,
Circling above the hamlets as thy nest;
Or else, departing dream, and shadowy form
Of midnight vision, gathering up thy skirts;
By night star-veiling, and by day
Darkening the light and blotting out the sun;
Go thou my incense upward from this hearth,
And ask the gods to pardon this clear flame.

| JULIA WARD HOWE |

1819–1910

THE "BATTLE-HYMN OF THE REPUBLIC" was the all-but-official anthem of the Northern Army in the Civil War. Sung to the same tune, and in alternation with, "John Brown's Body," it inspired the ultimate overwhelming Union victory over the outnumbered South. Quite aside from this, it is a superb poem, a "popular" creation equal to all but a few contemporaries, Walt Whitman and Emily Dickinson among the exceptions.

Born into a wealthy New York City banking family, Julia Ward married Samuel Gridley Howe, and joined him in the Abolitionist cause. They moved to Boston, and became the center of its antislavery movement.

Julia Ward Howe's poetry is copious but ignites only in the "Battle-Hymn," published in the *Atlantic Monthly* in April 1862, and immediately taken up by the Northern forces and public.

In her later years, Julia Ward Howe became prominent in feminism, world peace movements, and prison reform, gradually alienating her husband, who felt neglected, but he died in 1876, and so freed her for another third of a century of good works.

↓   ↓   ↓

Battle-Hymn of the Republic

Mine eyes have seen the glory of the coming of the Lord:
He is trampling out the vintage where the grapes of wrath
    are stored;
He hath loosed the fateful lightning of his terrible swift
    sword:
        His truth is marching on.

I have seen Him in the watch-fires of a hundred circling
    camps;
They have builded Him an altar in the evening dews and
    damps;
I can read His righteous sentence by the dim and flaring
    lamps.
        His day is marching on.

I have read a fiery gospel, writ in burnished rows of steel:
"As ye deal with my contemners, so with you my grace shall
    deal;
Let the Hero, born of woman, crush the serpent with his
    heel,
        Since God is marching on."

He has sounded forth the trumpet that shall never call
    retreat;
He is sifting out the hearts of men before his judgment-
    seat:
Oh! be swift, my soul, to answer Him! be jubilant, my feet!
        Our God is marching on.

In the beauty of the lilies Christ was born across the sea,
With a glory in his bosom that transfigures you and me:
As he died to make men holy, let us die to make men free,
        While God is marching on.

WALT WHITMAN

1819–1892

THE CENTRAL AMERICAN POET, Walt Whitman, emerged rather improbably from the family of a Long Island Quaker carpenter, Walter Whitman, Sr., a passionate and angry man, and a follower of the dissident Quaker preacher, Elias Hicks, who was partly black and partly Indian. The poet's spiritual background of Hicksite Quakerism is subtly reflected in "Song of Myself."

Walt Whitman is a difficult poet—complex, evasive, subtle, hermetic—who wants his poetry to look easy. Democratic in ideology, Whitman personally was intensely private and elitest, and his open stance toward his readers is a rhetorical fiction.

The poets who have followed Whitman include overt partisans like D. H. Lawrence and Hart Crane. Yet Whitman's stance, his idea of the poem, deeply infuses T. S. Eliot and Wallace Stevens, elegant formalists who on the surface do not seem Whitmanian. *The Waste Land* is a revision of "When Lilacs Last in the Dooryard Bloom'd," and Stevens's *The Auroras of Autumn* returns one to Walt Whitman walking the beach in "As I Ebb'd With the Ocean of Life."

Whitman's influence upon Spanish poetry (Federico García Lorca) and South American (Pablo Neruda, César Vallejo, Jorge Luis Borges) is matched by the agon waged with Whitman by the great Portuguese modernist Fernando Pessoa. The presence of Walt Whitman is unbounded: our greatest living poet, John Ashbery, seems more and more Whitmanian, and the late A. R. Ammons was close to being a Whitman for the United States of his time.

Whitman, with Emily Dickinson, is one of the two great American poet-originals. He does not have Dickinson's cognitive originality; what is new in Whitman is expressed in gesture, nuance, rhetorical stance, the mythology of the self. No poet since Whitman, in any language I know, has anything like his largeness of being, his enormous consciousness of himself, of his time, and of his nation.

Though Whitman later took to denying it, his starting point was Ralph Waldo Emerson, the sage of "Self-Reliance." The self of "Song of Myself" is an Emersonian construct having little to do with Walter Whitman, Jr. A more authentic Whitman lurks in the poetry as the Real Me or Me Myself, uneasily coping with the enigmatic, mostly unknowable Whitmanian soul.

Whitman, like his poetic descendants, essentially is the elegist of the self, though he purports to be its celebrant. Lawrence saw Whitman as the poet of the Evening Land. Four great images merge into one in Whitman's strongest poems: night, death, the mother, and the sea.

Whitman had little formal schooling; his education came in Brooklyn newspaper offices, where he learned the printer's trade. As compositor and journalist, Whitman became a denizen of Manhattan, until his father's illness brought him back home in 1854. The year 1854–1855 was Whitman's mysterious time of poetic gestation. Very much under the influence of Emerson's *Essays*, Whitman composed the first edition of *Leaves of Grass*, which he dispatched to Emerson. Critics perpetually face the test of the new, and generally they fail it. Emerson triumphed, by seeing immediately the power and full American relevance of the great book that had manifested out of nowhere.

Despite Emerson, Whitman's recognition came slowly. The first edition of *Leaves of Grass* (1855) included what eventually was called "Song of Myself" and "The Sleepers." The second edition, 1856, introduced the majestic poem later called "Crossing Brooklyn Ferry." The 1860 third edition brought forth the two great "Sea-Drift" elegies, known now by their first lines: "Out of the Cradle Endlessly Rocking" and "As I Ebb'd with the Ocean of Life."

Whitman celebrates a pansexualism, clearly tends toward a homoerotic stance (in the ideal, anyway), but is pragmatically rather more autoerotic than not.

Until the Civil War, the poet supported himself by freelance journalism, but the apotheosis of Whitman's life came in 1863–1864 when the poet served as a volunteer nurse and wound-dresser in the military hospitals of Washington, D.C. Toss away any nonsense about homoerotic gratifications amid the dead and dying; Whitman *served*, cadging what funds he could to purchase brandy and ice cream, pencils and paper, clothes for the suffering, bewildered, frequently illiterate soldiers. He read letters from home to them, wrote letters for them, and comforted the suffering and the dying. Try to envision any other American writer of Whitman's eminence acting as he did. The legend of the Good Gray Poet emerges from this with the authority of total persuasiveness.

After the Civil War, Whitman burned out. All his best poetry belongs to the decade 1855–1865, from "Song of Myself" through the elegy for President Lincoln, "When Lilacs Last in the Dooryard Bloom'd." He lived his final years, after a paralyzing stroke, in Camden, New Jersey, cared for by his literary secretary Horace Traubel, and supported by admirers here and abroad, including the naturalist John Burroughs.

I include all five of Whitman's major poems here: "Song of Myself," "Crossing Brooklyn Ferry," "As I Ebb'd with the Ocean of Life," "Out of the Cradle Endlessly Rocking," and "Lilacs." There is a headnote to each poem. Here I desire to conclude with a general characterization of Walt Whitman's poetic achievement.

"Free verse" is an oxymoron, and if Allen Ginsberg wrote free verse, Whitman created something very different. John Hollander has written definitively about Whitman's innovations:

> . . . their formal modes as well as their complex articulations of those modes are all in themselves subtle and powerful formal and metaphoric versions of more traditional ones.

Whitman is far more an allusive poet than generally is realized. Shakespeare, Milton, Shelley, Keats, and Tennyson join Emerson and the Bible as his literary ancestors. The poet-speaker of "Crossing Brooklyn Ferry" identifies himself with Edgar in *King Lear,* and "Lilacs" shapes itself with *Lycidas* and *Adonais* as background. But Hollander's point is subtler: Whitman, a great rhetorician, understood that there are no poetic forms but only the *tropes of form.* The major poems of Whitman invariably sustain a clear metaphoric relation to the tradition. His persistent title—*Leaves of Grass*—is a highly complex metaphor, difficult to work through fully. Isaiah and the Psalms proclaim that all flesh is grass, while there is a persistent secular fiction of the falling leaves of autumn as being emblematic of individual human lives: Homer, Vergil, Dante, Milton, Spenser, Shelley. Whitman intends to merge both images: falling human life in the leaves, all flesh in the grass.

That is the high sense (or part of it) of Whitman's titular metaphor. But he intends something homelier: in nineteenth-century printers' lingo, leaves are bundles of paper as well as our sense of pages, while grass can be just printers' casual junk filling up the page. It is like Whitman to be sublime and throwaway simultaneously.

It is possible that Whitman also means that *his* poems, in particular, are leaves of grass—not a bouquet of lyrical flowers but something far more primal. But the metaphor is endless to meditation, as Whitman intended it to be.

Song of Myself

After almost a century and a half, "Song of Myself" is firmly established as the American epic, the long poem that defines the ethos of the nation. Paradoxes abound in this canonization: Whitman achieves the national, indeed almost the universal, by way of the personal. The fiction, the Whitmanian Self, is idiosyncratic to the highest degree. More than conscious of his myth, Whitman carefully posits two more entities of the spirit that are not easily comprehended: my Soul and the Real Me or Me Myself. Unlike the Whitmanian Self, neither of these is primarily a fiction. Hence, the poem is "Song of Myself" and not "Song of the Soul" or "Song of the Real Me or Me Myself," neither of them a poem that Whitman wanted to write or indeed could have written.

The Self is "Walt Whitman, an American, one of the roughs." This outward Self and the more authentic Real Me or Me Myself are part of nature, while the Whitmanian Soul, like the body in Emerson's "The Over-Soul" (a prime source for Whitman), is defined as "that great nature in which we rest," and the Self of "Self-Reliance" is "the aboriginal Self" (akin to Whitman's Me Myself), preceding Nature and as old as God.

Whitman is estranged from his Soul, or unknown nature: in the sequence of his major poems, she will appear as a great four-fold figure: Night, Death, the Mother, and the Sea.

"Song of Myself," with its eventual division into fifty-two sections, suggests Whitman's comprehensiveness, though the poem is not organized upon the natural or seasonal cycle of the weeks. There is no single structure or story to "Song of Myself"; Walt Whitman is his poem, and holds it together. Broadly it moves between epiphanies or representations of the Whitmanian godhead through crises of identity, before attaining an extraordinarily serene conclusion.

The rough Walt and his unknown Soul can make their own pact, but the Real Me, "the other I am," and the Soul are enemies, and can only abase themselves to one another. One sees why "Walt Whitman," the fictitious Self, is necessary; he holds the antagonists apart. In ancient heresy, the Real Me or Me Myself was called the *pneuma,* the breath-soul or spark, and was the best and oldest part of the individual, akin to the God within. The psyche or soul, part of the natural man or woman, was at enmity with the *pneuma.* Whitman, a religious throwback, achieves a great epiphany in section 5 after a reconciliation between his rough Self and his Soul:

Swiftly arose and spread around me the peace and knowledge
    that pass all the argument of the earth,
And I know that the hand of God is the promise of my own,
And I know that the spirit of God is the brother of my own,
And that all the men ever born are also my brothers, and the
    women my sisters and lovers,
And that a kelson of the creation is love,
And limitless are leaves stiff or drooping in the fields,
And brown ants in the little wells beneath them,
And mossy scabs of the worm fence, heap'd stones, elder,
    mullein and poke-weed.

The form of this is Hicksite Quaker testimony, sublimely extended to the virtual end of being: "And the mossy scabs of the worm fence, heap'd stones, elder, mullein and poke-weed."

There are two crises in "Song of Myself," an autoerotic rape of the Real Me by the rough Walt in sections 28–30, and a far more serious crisis of identity in section 38. Both achieve rapid resolutions, and yield to the majestic prospect of Whitman as resurrected prophet of life and death being absorbed back into reality:

I depart as air, I shake my white locks at the runaway sun,
I effuse my flesh in eddies, and drift it in lacy jags.

I bequeath myself to the dirt to grow from the grass I love,
If you want me again look for me under your boot-soles.

You will hardly know who I am or what I mean,
But I shall be good health to you nevertheless,
And filter and fibre your blood.

Failing to fetch me at first keep encouraged,
Missing me one place search another,
I stop somewhere waiting for you.

✧   ✧   ✧

from Song of Myself

1

I Celebrate myself, and sing myself,
And what I assume you shall assume,
For every atom belonging to me as good belongs to you.

I loafe and invite my soul,
I lean and loafe at my ease observing a spear of summer grass.

My tongue, every atom of my blood, form'd from this soil, this air,
Born here of parents born here from parents the same, and their parents the
same,
I, now thirty-seven years old in perfect health begin,
Hoping to cease not till death.

Creeds and schools in abeyance,
Retiring back a while sufficed at what they are, but never forgotten,
I harbor for good or bad, I permit to speak at every hazard,
Nature without check with original energy.

2

Houses and rooms are full of perfumes, the shelves are crowded with per-
fumes,
I breathe the fragrance myself and know it and like it,
The distillation would intoxicate me also, but I shall not let it.

The atmosphere is not a perfume, it has no taste of the distillation, it is
odorless,
It is for my mouth forever, I am in love with it,
I will go to the bank by the wood and become undisguised and naked,
I am mad for it to be in contact with me.

The smoke of my own breath,
Echoes, ripples, buzz'd whispers, love-root, silk-thread, crotch and vine,
My respiration and inspiration, the beating of my heart, the passing of blood
and air through my lungs,
The sniff of green leaves and dry leaves, and of the shore and dark-color'd
sea-rocks, and of hay in the barn,
The sound of the belch'd words of my voice loos'd to the eddies of the
wind,
A few light kisses, a few embraces, a reaching around of arms,
The play of shine and shade on the trees as the supple boughs wag,
The delight alone or in the rush of the streets, or along the fields and hill-
sides,
The feeling of health, the full-noon trill, the song of me rising from bed and
meeting the sun.

Have you reckon'd a thousand acres much? have you reckon'd the earth
much?

Have you practis'd so long to learn to read?
Have you felt so proud to get at the meaning of poems?

Stop this day and night with me and you shall possess the origin of all poems,
You shall possess the good of the earth and sun, (there are millions of suns
    left,)
You shall no longer take things at second or third hand, nor look through the
    eyes of the dead, nor feed on the spectres in books,
You shall not look through my eyes either, nor take things from me,
You shall listen to all sides and filter them from your self.

    3
I have heard what the talkers were talking, the talk of the beginning and the
    end,
But I do not talk of the beginning or the end.

There was never any more inception than there is now,
Nor any more youth or age than there is now,
And will never be any more perfection than there is now,
Nor any more heaven or hell than there is now.

Urge and urge and urge,
Always the procreant urge of the world.

Out of the dimness opposite equals advance, always substance and increase, always sex,
Always a knit of identity, always distinction, always a breed of life.

To elaborate is no avail, learn'd and unlearn'd feel that it is so.

Sure as the most certain sure, plumb in the uprights, well entretied, braced
    in the beams,
Stout as a horse, affectionate, haughty, electrical,
I and this mystery here we stand.

Clear and sweet is my soul, and clear and sweet is all that is not my soul.

Lack one lacks both, and the unseen is proved by the seen,
Till that becomes unseen and receives proof in its turn.

Showing the best and dividing it from the worst age vexes age,
Knowing the perfect fitness and equanimity of things, while they discuss I
    am silent, and go bathe and admire myself.

Welcome is every organ and attribute of me, and of any man hearty and
    clean,
Not an inch nor a particle of an inch is vile, and none shall be less familiar
    than the rest.

I am satisfied—I see, dance, laugh, sing;
As the hugging and loving bed-fellow sleeps at my side through the night,
    and withdraws at the peep of the day with stealthy tread,
Leaving me baskets cover'd with white towels swelling the house with their
    plenty,
Shall I postpone my acceptation and realization and scream at my eyes,
That they turn from gazing after and down the road,
And forthwith cipher and show me to a cent,
Exactly the value of one and exactly the value of two, and which is ahead?

4
Trippers and askers surround me,
People I meet, the effect upon me of my early life or the ward and city I live
    in, or the nation,
The latest dates, discoveries, inventions, societies, authors old and new,
My dinner, dress, associates, looks, compliments, dues,
The real or fancied indifference of some man or woman I love,
The sickness of one of my folks or of myself, or ill-doing or loss or lack of
    money, or depressions or exaltations,
Battles, the horrors of fratricidal war, the fever of doubtful news, the fitful
    events;
These come to me days and nights and go from me again,
But they are not the Me myself.

Apart from the pulling and hauling stands what I am,
Stands amused, complacent, compassionating, idle, unitary,
Looks down, is erect, or bends an arm on an impalpable certain rest,
Looking with side-curved head curious what will come next,
Both in and out of the game and watching and wondering at it.

Backward I see in my own days where I sweated through fog with linguists
    and contenders,
I have no mockings or arguments, I witness and wait.

5
I believe in you my soul, the other I am must not abase itself to you,
And you must not be abased to the other.

Loafe with me on the grass, loose the stop from your throat,
Not words, not music or rhyme I want, not custom or lecture, not even the
    best,
Only the lull I like, the hum of your valvèd voice.

I mind how once we lay such a transparent summer morning,
How you settled your head athwart my hips and gently turn'd over upon me,
And parted the shirt from my bosom-bone, and plunged your tongue to my
    bare-stript heart,
And reach'd till you felt my beard, and reach'd till you held my feet.

Swiftly arose and spread around me the peace and knowledge that pass all
    the argument of the earth,
And I know that the hand of God is the promise of my own,
And I know that the spirit of God is the brother of my own,
And that all the men ever born are also my brothers, and the women my sis-
    ters and lovers,
And that a kelson of the creation is love,
And limitless are leaves stiff or drooping in the fields,
And brown ants in the little wells beneath them,
And mossy scabs of the worm fence, heap'd stones, elder, mullein and poke-
    weed.

6

A child said What is the grass? fetching it to me with full hands;
How could I answer the child? I do not know what it is any more than he.

I guess it must be the flag of my disposition, out of hopeful green stuff
    woven.

Or I guess it is the handkerchief of the Lord,
A scented gift and remembrancer designedly dropt,
Bearing the owner's name someway in the corners, that we may see and
    remark, and say Whose?

Or I guess the grass is itself a child, the produced babe of the vegetation.

Or I guess it is a uniform hieroglyphic,
And it means, Sprouting alike in broad zones and narrow zones,
Growing among black folks as among white,
Kanuck, Tuckahoe, Congressman, Cuff, I give them the same, I receive them
    the same.

And now it seems to me the beautiful uncut hair of graves.

Tenderly will I use you curling grass,
It may be you transpire from the breasts of young men,
It may be if I had known them I would have loved them,
It may be you are from old people, or from offspring taken soon out of their
　　mothers' laps,
And here you are the mothers' laps.

This grass is very dark to be from the white heads of old mothers,
Darker than the colorless beards of old men,
Dark to come from under the faint red roofs of mouths.

O I perceive after all so many uttering tongues,
And I perceive they do not come from the roofs of mouths for nothing.

I wish I could translate the hints about the dead young men and women,
And the hints about old men and mothers, and the offspring taken soon out
　　of their laps.

What do you think has become of the young and old men?
And what do you think has become of the women and children?

They are alive and well somewhere,
The smallest sprout shows there is really no death,
And if ever there was it led forward life, and does not wait at the end to
　　arrest it,
And ceas'd the moment life appear'd.

All goes onward and outward, nothing collapses,
And to die is different from what any one supposed, and luckier.

　　·　·　·

20
Who goes there? hankering, gross, mystical, nude;
How is it I extract strength from the beef I eat?

What is a man anyhow? what am I? what are you?

All I mark as my own you shall offset it with your own,
Else it were time lost listening to me.

I do not snivel that snivel the world over,
That months are vacuums and the ground but wallow and filth.

Whimpering and truckling fold with powders for invalids, conformity goes to
    the fourth-remov'd,
I wear my hat as I please indoors or out.

Why should I pray? why should I venerate and be ceremonious?

Having pried through the strata, analyzed to a hair, counsel'd with doctors
    and calculated close,
I find no sweeter fat than sticks to my own bones.

In all people I see myself, none more and not one a barleycorn less,
And the good or bad I say of myself I say of them.

I know I am solid and sound,
To me the converging objects of the universe perpetually flow,
All are written to me, and I must get what the writing means.

I know I am deathless,
I know this orbit of mine cannot be swept by a carpenter's compass,
I know I shall not pass like a child's carlacue cut with a burnt stick at
    night.

I know I am august,
I do not trouble my spirit to vindicate itself or be understood,
I see that the elementary laws never apologize,
(I reckon I behave no prouder than the level I plant my house by, after all.)

I exist as I am, that is enough,
If no other in the world be aware I sit content,
And if each and all be aware I sit content.

One world is aware and by far the largest to me, and that is myself,
And whether I come to my own to-day or in ten thousand or ten million
    years,
I can cheerfully take it now, or with equal cheerfulness I can wait.

My foothold is tenon'd and mortis'd in granite,
I laugh at what you call dissolution,
And I know the amplitude of time.

21
I am the poet of the Body and I am the poet of the Soul,
The pleasures of heaven are with me and the pains of hell are with me,

The first I graft and increase upon myself, the latter I translate into a new
   tongue.

I am the poet of the woman the same as the man,
And I say it is as great to be a woman as to be a man,
And I say there is nothing greater than the mother of men.

I chant the chant of dilation or pride,
We have had ducking and deprecating about enough,
I show that size is only development.

Have you outstript the rest? are you the President?
It is a trifle, they will more than arrive there every one, and still pass on.

I am he that walks with the tender and growing night,
I call to the earth and sea half-held by the night.

Press close bare-bosom'd night—press close magnetic nourishing
   night!
Night of south winds—night of the large few stars!
Still nodding night—mad naked summer night.

Smile O voluptuous cool-breath'd earth!
Earth of the slumbering and liquid trees!
Earth of departed sunset—earth of the mountains misty-topt!
Earth of the vitreous pour of the full moon just tinged with blue!
Earth of shine and dark mottling the tide of the river!
Earth of the limpid gray of clouds brighter and clearer for my sake!
Far-swooping elbow'd earth—rich apple-blossom'd earth!
Smile, for your lover comes.

Prodigal, you have given me love—therefore I to you give love!
O unspeakable passionate love.

22
You sea! I resign myself to you also—I guess what you mean,
I behold from the beach your crooked inviting fingers,
I believe you refuse to go back without feeling of me,
We must have a turn together, I undress, hurry me out of sight of the
   land,
Cushion me soft, rock me in billowy drowse,
Dash me with amorous wet, I can repay you.

Sea of stretch'd ground-swells,
Sea breathing broad and convulsive breaths,
Sea of the brine of life and of unshovell'd yet always-ready graves,
Howler and scooper of storms, capricious and dainty sea,
I am integral with you, I too am of one phase and of all phases.

Partaker of influx and efflux I, extoller of hate and conciliation,
Extoller of amies and those that sleep in each others' arms.

I am he attesting sympathy,
(Shall I make my list of things in the house and skip the house that supports
    them?)

I am not the poet of goodness only, I do not decline to be the poet of wicked-
    ness also.

What blurt is this about virtue and about vice?
Evil propels me and reform of evil propels me, I stand indifferent,
My gait is no fault-finder's or rejecter's gait,
I moisten the roots of all that has grown.

Did you fear some scrofula out of the unflagging pregnancy?
Did you guess the celestial laws are yet to be work'd over and rectified?

I find one side a balance and the antipodal side a balance,
Soft doctrine as steady help as stable doctrine,
Thoughts and deeds of the present our rouse and early start.

This minute that comes to me over the past decillions,
There is no better than it and now.

What behaved well in the past or behaves well to-day is not such a wonder,
The wonder is always and always how there can be a mean man or an
    infidel.

.   .   .

27
To be in any form, what is that?
(Round and round we go, all of us, and ever come back thither,)
If nothing lay more develop'd the quahaug in its callous shell were
    enough.

Mine is no callous shell,
I have instant conductors all over me whether I pass or stop,
They seize every object and lead it harmlessly through me.

I merely stir, press, feel with my fingers, and am happy,
To touch my person to some one else's is about as much as I can stand.

28
Is this then a touch? quivering me to a new identity,
Flames and ether making a rush for my veins,
Treacherous tip of me reaching and crowding to help them,
My flesh and blood playing out lightning to strike what is hardly different
    from myself,
On all sides prurient provokers stiffening my limbs,
Straining the udder of my heart for its withheld drip,
Behaving licentious toward me, taking no denial,
Depriving me of my best as for a purpose,
Unbuttoning my clothes, holding me by the bare waist,
Deluding my confusion with the calm of the sunlight and pasture-fields,
Immodestly sliding the fellow-senses away,
They bribed to swap off with touch and go and graze at the edges of me,
No consideration, no regard for my draining strength or my anger,
Fetching the rest of the herd around to enjoy them a while,
Then all uniting to stand on a headland and worry me.

The sentries desert every other part of me,
They have left me helpless to a red marauder,
They all come to the headland to witness and assist against me.

I am given up by traitors,
I talk wildly, I have lost my wits, I and nobody else am the greatest traitor,
I went myself first to the headland, my own hands carried me there.

You villain touch! what are you doing? my breath is tight in its throat,
Unclench your floodgates, you are too much for me.

29
Blind loving wrestling touch, sheath'd hooded sharp-tooth'd touch!
Did it make you ache so, leaving me?

Parting track'd by arriving, perpetual payment of perpetual loan,
Rich showering rain, and recompense richer afterward.

Sprouts take and accumulate, stand by the curb prolific and vital,
Landscapes projected masculine, full-sized and golden.

30
All truths wait in all things,
They neither hasten their own delivery nor resist it,
They do not need the obstetric forceps of the surgeon,
The insignificant is as big to me as any,
(What is less or more than a touch?)

Logic and sermons never convince,
The damp of the night drives deeper into my soul.

(Only what proves itself to every man and woman is so,
Only what nobody denies is so.)

A minute and a drop of me settle my brain,
I believe the soggy clods shall become lovers and lamps,
And a compend of compends is the meat of a man or woman,
And a summit and flower there is the feeling they have for each other,
And they are to branch boundlessly out of that lesson until it becomes
      omnific,
And until one and all shall delight us, and we them.

31
I believe a leaf of grass is no less than the journey-work of the stars,
And the pismire is equally perfect, and a grain of sand, and the egg of the
      wren,
And the tree-toad is a chef-d'œuvre for the highest,
And the running blackberry would adorn the parlors of heaven,
And the narrowest hinge in my hand puts to scorn all machinery,
And the cow crunching with depress'd head surpasses any statue,
And a mouse is miracle enough to stagger sextillions of infidels.

I find I incorporate gneiss, coal, long-threaded moss, fruits, grains, esculent
      roots,
And am stucco'd with quadrupeds and birds all over,
And have distanced what is behind me for good reasons,
But call any thing back again when I desire it.

In vain the speeding or shyness,
In vain the plutonic rocks send their old heat against my approach,

In vain the mastodon retreats beneath its own powder'd bones,
In vain objects stand leagues off and assume manifold shapes,
In vain the ocean settling in hollows and the great monsters lying low,
In vain the buzzard houses herself with the sky,
In vain the snake slides through the creepers and logs,
In vain the elk takes to the inner passes of the woods,
In vain the razor-bill'd auk sails far north to Labrador,
I follow quickly, I ascend to the nest in the fissure of the cliff.

32
I think I could turn and live with animals, they are so placid and self-
    contain'd,
I stand and look at them long and long.

They do not sweat and whine about their condition,
They do not lie awake in the dark and weep for their sins,
They do not make me sick discussing their duty to God,
Not one is dissatisfied, not one is demented with the mania of owning things,
Not one kneels to another, nor to his kind that lived thousands of years ago,
Not one is respectable or unhappy over the whole earth.

So they show their relations to me and I accept them,
They bring me tokens of myself, they evince them plainly in their possession.

I wonder where they get those tokens,
Did I pass that way huge times ago and negligently drop them?

Myself moving forward then and now and forever,
Gathering and showing more always and with velocity,
Infinite and omnigenous, and the like of these among them,
Not too exclusive toward the reachers of my remembrancers,
Picking out here one that I love, and now go with him on brotherly terms.

A gigantic beauty of a stallion, fresh and responsive to my caresses,
Head high in the forehead, wide between the ears,
Limbs glossy and supple, tail dusting the ground,
Eyes full of sparkling wickedness, ears finely cut, flexibly moving.

His nostrils dilate as my heels embrace him,
His well-built limbs tremble with pleasure as we race around and return.

I but use you a minute, then I resign you, stallion,
Why do I need your paces when I myself out-gallop them?
Even as I stand or sit passing faster than you.

33

.   .   .

I am the hounded slave, I wince at the bite of the dogs,
Hell and despair are upon me, crack and again crack the marksmen,
I clutch the rails of the fence, my gore dribs, thinn'd with the ooze of my
    skin,
I fall on the weeds and stones,
The riders spur their unwilling horses, haul close,
Taunt my dizzy ears and beat me violently over the head with whip-stocks.

Agonies are one of my changes of garments,
I do not ask the wounded person how he feels, I myself become the
    wounded person,
My hurts turn livid upon me as I lean on a cane and observe.

I am the mash'd fireman with breast-bone broken,
Tumbling walls buried me in their debris,
Heat and smoke I inspired, I heard the yelling shouts of my comrades,
I heard the distant click of their picks and shovels,
They have clear'd the beams away, they tenderly lift me forth.

I lie in the night air in my red shirt, the pervading hush is for my sake,
Painless after all I lie exhausted but not so unhappy,
White and beautiful are the faces around me, the heads are bared of their
    fire-caps,
The kneeling crowd fades with the light of the torches.

Distant and dead resuscitate,
They show as the dial or move as the hands of me, I am the clock myself.

I am an old artillerist, I tell of my fort's bombardment,
I am there again.

Again the long roll of the drummers,
Again the attacking cannon, mortars,
Again to my listening ears the cannon responsive.

I take part, I see and hear the whole,
The cries, curses, roar, the plaudits for well-aim'd shots,
The ambulanza slowly passing trailing its red drip,
Workmen searching after damages, making indispensable repairs,
The fall of grenades through the rent roof, the fan-shaped explosion,
The whizz of limbs, heads, stone, wood, iron, high in the air.

Again gurgles the mouth of my dying general, he furiously waves with his
    hand,
He gasps through the clot *Mind not me—mind—the entrenchments.*

. . .

37

You laggards there on guard! look to your arms!
In at the conquer'd doors they crowd! I am possess'd!
Embody all presences outlaw'd or suffering,
See myself in prison shaped like another man,
And feel the dull unintermitted pain.

For me the keepers of convicts shoulder their carbines and keep watch,
It is I let out in the morning and barr'd at night.

Not a mutineer walks handcuff'd to jail but I am handcuff'd to him and walk
    by his side,
(I am less the jolly one there, and more the silent one with sweat on my
    twitching lips.)

Not a youngster is taken for larceny but I go up too, and am tried and
    sentenced.

Not a cholera patient lies at the last gasp but I also lie at the last gasp,
My face is ash-color'd, my sinews gnarl, away from me people retreat.

Askers embody themselves in me and I am embodied in them,
I project my hat, sit shame-faced, and beg.

38

Enough! enough! enough!
Somehow I have been stunn'd. Stand back!
Give me a little time beyond my cuff'd head, slumbers, dreams, gaping,
I discover myself on the verge of a usual mistake.

That I could forget the mockers and insults!
That I could forget the trickling tears and the blows of the bludgeons and
    hammers!
That I could look with a separate look on my own crucifixion and bloody
    crowning.

I remember now,
I resume the overstaid fraction,

The grave of rock multiplies what has been confided to it, or to any graves,
Corpses rise, gashes heal, fastenings roll from me.

I troop forth replenish'd with supreme power, one of an average unending
    procession,
Inland and sea-coast we go, and pass all boundary lines,
Our swift ordinances on their way over the whole earth,
The blossoms we wear in our hats the growth of thousands of years.

Eleves, I salute you! come forward!
Continue your annotations, continue your questionings.

.   .   .

44
It is time to explain myself—let us stand up.

What is known I strip away,
I launch all men and women forward with me into the Unknown.

The clock indicates the moment—but what does eternity indicate?

We have thus far exhausted trillions of winters and summers,
There are trillions ahead, and trillions ahead of them.

Births have brought us richness and variety,
And other births will bring us richness and variety.

I do not call one greater and one smaller,
That which fills its period and place is equal to any.

Were mankind murderous or jealous upon you, my brother, my sister?
I am sorry for you, they are not murderous or jealous upon me,
All has been gentle with me, I keep no account with lamentation,
(What have I to do with lamentation?)
I am an acme of things accomplish'd, and I an encloser of things to be.

My feet strike an apex of the apices of the stairs,
On every step bunches of ages, and larger bunches between the steps,
All below duly travel'd, and still I mount and mount.

Rise after rise bow the phantoms behind me,
Afar down I see the huge first Nothing, I know I was even there,

I waited unseen and always, and slept through the lethargic mist,
And took my time, and took no hurt from the fetid carbon.

Long I was hugg'd close—long and long.

Immense have been the preparations for me,
Faithful and friendly the arms that have help'd me.

Cycles ferried my cradle, rowing and rowing like cheerful boatmen,
For room to me stars kept aside in their own rings,
They sent influences to look after what was to hold me.

Before I was born out of my mother generations guided me,
My embryo has never been torpid, nothing could overlay it.

For it the nebula cohered to an orb,
The long slow strata piled to rest it on,
Vast vegetables gave it sustenance,
Monstrous sauroids transported it in their mouths and deposited it with care.

All forces have been steadily employ'd to complete and delight me,
Now on this spot I stand with my robust soul.

.   .   .

48

I have said that the soul is not more than the body,
And I have said that the body is not more than the soul,
And nothing, not God, is greater to one than one's self is,
And whoever walks a furlong without sympathy walks to his own funeral
    drest in his shroud,
And I or you pocketless of a dime may purchase the pick of the earth,
And to glance with an eye or show a bean in its pod confounds the learning
    of all times,
And there is no trade or employment but the young man following it may
    become a hero,
And there is no object so soft but it makes a hub for the wheel'd universe,
And I say to any man or woman, Let your soul stand cool and composed
    before a million universes.

And I say to mankind, Be not curious about God,
For I who am curious about each am not curious about God,
(No array of terms can say how much I am at peace about God and about
    death.)

I hear and behold God in every object, yet understand God not in the
    least,
Nor do I understand who there can be more wonderful than myself.

Why should I wish to see God better than this day?
I see something of God each hour of the twenty-four, and each moment
    then,
In the faces of men and women I see God, and in my own face in the glass,
I find letters from God dropt in the street, and every one is sign'd by God's
    name,
And I leave them where they are, for I know that wheresoe'er I go,
Others will punctually come for ever and ever.

    49
And as to you Death, and you bitter hug of mortality, it is idle to try to alarm
    me.

To his work without flinching the accoucheur comes,
I see the elder-hand pressing receiving supporting,
I recline by the sills of the exquisite flexible doors,
And mark the outlet, and mark the relief and escape.

And as to you Corpse I think you are good manure, but that does not offend
    me,
I smell the white roses sweet-scented and growing,
I reach to the leafy lips, I reach to the polish'd breasts of melons.

And as to you Life I reckon you are the leavings of many deaths,
(No doubt I have died myself ten thousand times before.)

I hear you whispering there O stars of heaven,
O suns—O grass of graves—O perpetual transfers and promotions,
If you do not say any thing how can I say any thing?

Of the turbid pool that lies in the autumn forest,
Of the moon that descends the steeps of the soughing twilight,
Toss, sparkles of day and dusk—toss on the black stems that decay in the
    muck,
Toss to the moaning gibberish of the dry limbs.

I ascend from the moon, I ascend from the night,
I perceive that the ghastly glimmer is noonday sunbeams reflected,
And debouch to the steady and central from the offspring great or small.

50

There is that in me—I do not know what it is—but I know it is in me.

Wrench'd and sweaty—calm and cool then my body becomes,
I sleep—I sleep long.

I do not know it—it is without name—it is a word unsaid,
It is not in any dictionary, utterance, symbol.

Something it swings on more than the earth I swing on,
To it the creation is the friend whose embracing awakes me.

Perhaps I might tell more. Outlines! I plead for my brothers and sisters.

Do you see O my brothers and sisters?
It is not chaos or death—it is form, union, plan—it is eternal life—it is
  Happiness.

51

The past and present wilt—I have fill'd them, emptied them,
And proceed to fill my next fold of the future.

Listener up there! what have you to confide to me?
Look in my face while I snuff the sidle of evening,
(Talk honestly, no one else hears you, and I stay only a minute longer.)

Do I contradict myself?
Very well then I contradict myself,
(I am large, I contain multitudes.)

I concentrate toward them that are nigh, I wait on the door-slab.

Who has done his day's work? who will soonest be through with his supper?
Who wishes to walk with me?

Will you speak before I am gone? will you prove already too late?

52

The spotted hawk swoops by and accuses me, he complains of my gab and
  my loitering.

I too am not a bit tamed, I too am untranslatable,
I sound my barbaric yawp over the roofs of the world.

The last scud of day holds back for me,
It flings my likeness after the rest and true as any on the shadow'd wilds,
It coaxes me to the vapor and the dusk.

I depart as air, I shake my white locks at the runaway sun,
I effuse my flesh in eddies, and drift it in lacy jags.

I bequeath myself to the dirt to grow from the grass I love,
If you want me again look for me under your boot-soles.

You will hardly know who I am or what I mean,
But I shall be good health to you nevertheless,
And filter and fibre your blood.

Failing to fetch me at first keep encouraged,
Missing me one place search another,
I stop somewhere waiting for you.

As Adam Early in the Morning

As Adam early in the morning,
Walking forth from the bower refresh'd with sleep,
Behold me where I pass, hear my voice, approach,
Touch me, touch the palm of your hand to my body as I pass,
Be not afraid of my body.

Crossing Brooklyn Ferry

For the 1856 second edition of *Leaves of Grass,* Whitman composed a wholly new kind of a poem, very different from *Leaves of Grass* 1855, or indeed what was to come in 1860 or 1865 or later. "Crossing Brooklyn Ferry" was one of the inspirations for Hart Crane's *The Bridge* (1930), Brooklyn Bridge having replaced the Brooklyn Ferry. Certainly "Crossing Brooklyn Ferry" and *The Bridge* are the great poems of New York City.

Whitman, with his direct addresses to the reader, attains a new level of directness in "Crossing Brooklyn Ferry":

Closer yet I approach you,
What thought you have of me now, I had as much of you—

> I laid in my stores in advance,
> I consider'd long and seriously of you before you were born.
>
> Who was to know what should come home to me?
> Who knows but I am enjoying this?
> Who knows, for all this distance, but I am as good as looking
>   at you now, for all you cannot see me?

Whitman, no occultist, refers to his poetic rather than literal survival. As his belated readers, we enter "Crossing Brooklyn Ferry" at the close of section 1:

> And you that shall cross from shore to shore years hence are more to
> · me, and more in my meditations, than you might suppose.

What then is he thinking of us? Evidently, that in essentials we will not differ from him, particularly in the dark experiences of personal negativity:

> It is not upon you alone the dark patches fall,
> The dark threw its patches down upon me also,
> The best I had done seem'd to me blank and suspicious,
> My great thoughts as I supposed them, were they not in
>   reality meagre?
> Nor is it you alone who know what it is to be evil,
> I am he who knew what it was to be evil,
> I too knotted the old knot of contrariety,
> Blabb'd, blush'd, resented, lied, stole, grudg'd,
> Had guile, anger, lust, hot wishes I dared not speak,
> Was wayward, vain, greedy, shallow, sly, cowardly, malignant,
> The wolf, the snake, the hog, not wanting in me,
> The cheating look, the frivolous word, the adulterous wish,
>   not wanting,
> Refusals, hates, postponements, meanness, laziness, none of these
>   wanting,

We can surmise that Whitman had been reading *King Lear,* since he echoes Shakespeare's Edgar, disguised as Tom O'Bedlam, telling the old, mad king, out on the heath, of his own supposed past: "False of heart, light of ear, bloody of hand; hog in sloth, fox in stealth, wolf in greediness, dog in madness, lion in prey." Whitman tells us of "the wolf, the snake, the hog, not wanting in me." It is fascinating that, of all Shakespeare's host of persons, Edgar should be so closely echoed by Whitman. Disguising himself to survive, Edgar is the figure who will be king after Lear's death, a rule Edgar assumes reluctantly. Whitman addresses his readers as though they were a composite Lear, suffering all, yet redeemed by Whitman's prophetic thoughts of them:

> We understand then do we not?
> What I promis'd without mentioning it, have you not accepted?
> What the study could not teach—what the preaching could
>   not accomplish is accomplish'd, is it not?

Crossing Brooklyn Ferry

1

Flood-tide below me! I see you face to face!
Clouds of the west—sun there half an hour high—I see you also face to
    face.

Crowds of men and women attired in the usual costumes, how curious you
    are to me!
On the ferry-boats the hundreds and hundreds that cross, returning home,
    are more curious to me than you suppose,
And you that shall cross from shore to shore years hence are more to me, and
    more in my meditations, than you might suppose.

2

The impalpable sustenance of me from all things at all hours of the day,
The simple, compact, well-join'd scheme, myself disintegrated, every one
    disintegrated yet part of the scheme,
The similitudes of the past and those of the future,
The glories strung like beads on my smallest sights and hearings, on the walk
    in the street and the passage over the river,
The current rushing so swiftly and swimming with me far away.
The others that are to follow me, the ties between me and them,
The certainty of others, the life, love, sight, hearing of others.

Others will enter the gates of the ferry and cross from shore to shore,
Others will watch the run of the flood-tide,
Others will see the shipping of Manhattan north and west, and the heights of
    Brooklyn to the south and east,
Others will see the islands large and small;
Fifty years hence, others will see them as they cross, the sun half an hour
    high,

A hundred years hence, or ever so many hundred years hence, others will see
   them,
Will enjoy the sunset, the pouring-in of the flood-tide, the falling-back to the
   sea of the ebb-tide.

3

It avails not, time nor place—distance avails not,
I am with you, you men and women of a generation, or ever so many genera-
   tions hence,
Just as you feel when you look on the river and sky, so I felt,
Just as any of you is one of a living crowd, I was one of a crowd,
Just as you are refresh'd by the gladness of the river and the bright flow, I
   was refresh'd,
Just as you stand and lean on the rail, yet hurry with the swift current, I stood
   yet was hurried,
Just as you look on the numberless masts of ships and the thick-stemm'd
   pipes of steamboats, I look'd.

I too many and many a time cross'd the river of old,
Watched the Twelfth-month sea-gulls, saw them high in the air floating with
   motionless wings, oscillating their bodies,
Saw how the glistening yellow lit up parts of their bodies and left the rest in
   strong shadow,
Saw the slow-wheeling circles and the gradual edging toward the south,
Saw the reflection of the summer sky in the water,
Had my eyes dazzled by the shimmering track of beams,
Look'd at the fine centrifugal spokes of light round the shape of my head in
   the sunlit water,
Look'd on the haze on the hills southward and south-westward,
Look'd on the vapor as it flew in fleeces tinged with violet,
Look'd toward the lower bay to notice the vessels arriving,
Saw their approach, saw aboard those that were near me,
Saw the white sails of schooners and sloops, saw the ships at anchor,
The sailors at work in the rigging or out astride the spars,
The round masts, the swinging motion of the hulls, the slender serpentine
   pennants,
The large and small steamers in motion, the pilots in their pilot-houses,
The white wake left by the passage, the quick tremulous whirl of the wheels,
The flags of all nations, the falling of them at sunset,
The scallop-edged waves in the twilight, the ladled cups, the frolicsome
   crests and glistening,
The stretch afar growing dimmer and dimmer, the gray walls of the granite
   storehouses by the docks,

On the river the shadowy group, the big steam-tug closely flank'd on each
    side by the barges, the hay-boat, the belated lighter,
On the neighboring shore the fires from the foundry chimneys burning high
    and glaringly into the night,
Casting their flicker of black contrasted with wild red and yellow light over
    the tops of houses, and down into the clefts of streets.

4

These and all else were to me the same as they are to you,
I loved well those cities, loved well the stately and rapid river,
The men and women I saw were all near to me,
Others the same—others who look back on me because I look'd forward to
    them,
(The time will come, though I stop here to-day and to-night.)

5

What is it then between us?
What is the count of the scores or hundreds of years between us?

Whatever it is, it avails not—distance avails not, and place avails not,
I too lived, Brooklyn of ample hills was mine,
I too walk'd the streets of Manhattan island, and bathed in the waters
    around it,
I too felt the curious abrupt questionings stir within me,
In the day among crowds of people sometimes they came upon me,
In my walks home late at night or as I lay in my bed they came upon me,
I too had been struck from the float forever held in solution,
I too had receiv'd identity by my body,
That I was I knew was of my body, and what I should be I knew I should be
    of my body.

6

It is not upon you alone the dark patches fall,
The dark threw its patches down upon me also,
The best I had done seem'd to me blank and suspicious,
My great thoughts as I supposed them, were they not in reality meagre?
Nor is it you alone who know what it is to be evil,
I am he who knew what it was to be evil,
I too knotted the old knot of contrariety,
Blabb'd, blush'd, resented, lied, stole, grudg'd,
Had guile, anger, lust, hot wishes I dared not speak,
Was wayward, vain, greedy, shallow, sly, cowardly, malignant,
The wolf, the snake, the hog, not wanting in me,

The cheating look, the frivolous word, the adulterous wish, not wanting,
Refusals, hates, postponements, meanness, laziness, none of these
    wanting,
Was one with the rest, the days and haps of the rest,
Was call'd by my nighest name by clear loud voices of young men as they saw
    me approaching or passing,
Felt their arms on my neck as I stood, or the negligent leaning of their flesh
    against me as I sat,
Saw many I loved in the street or ferry-boat or public assembly, yet never
    told them a word,
Lived the same life with the rest, the same old laughing, gnawing,
    sleeping,
Play'd the part that still looks back on the actor or actress,
The same old role, the role that is what we make it, as great as we like,
Or as small as we like, or both great and small.

7

Closer yet I approach you,
What thought you have of me now, I had as much of you—I laid in my stores
    in advance,
I consider'd long and seriously of you before you were born.

Who was to know what should come home to me?
Who knows but I am enjoying this?
Who knows, for all the distance, but I am as good as looking at you now, for
    all you cannot see me?

8

Ah, what can ever be more stately and admirable to me than mast-hemm'd
    Manhattan?
River and sunset and scallop-edg'd waves of flood-tide?
The sea-gulls oscillating their bodies, the hay-boat in the twilight, and the
    belated lighter?
What gods can exceed these that clasp me by the hand, and with voices I love
    call me promptly and loudly by my nighest name as I approach?
What is more subtle than this which ties me to the woman or man that looks
    in my face?
Which fuses me into you now, and pours my meaning into you?

We understand then do we not?
What I promis'd without mentioning it, have you not accepted?
What the study could not teach—what the preaching could not accomplish is
    accomplish'd, is it not?

9

Flow on, river! flow with the flood-tide, and ebb with the ebb-tide!
Frolic on, crested and scallop-edg'd waves!
Gorgeous clouds of the sunset! drench with your splendor me, or the men
    and women generations after me!
Cross from shore to shore, countless crowds of passengers!
Stand up, tall masts of Mannahatta! stand up, beautiful hills of Brooklyn!
Throb, baffled and curious brain! throw out questions and answers!
Suspend here and everywhere, eternal float of solution!
Gaze, loving and thirsting eyes, in the house or street or public assembly!
Sound out, voices of young men! loudly and musically call me by my nighest
    name!
Live, old life! play the part that looks back on the actor or actress!
Play the old role, the role that is great or small according as one makes it!
Consider, you who peruse me, whether I may not in unknown ways be look-
    ing upon you;
Be firm, rail over the river, to support those who lean idly, yet haste with the
    hasting current;
Fly on, sea-birds! fly sideways, or wheel in large circles high in the air;
Receive the summer sky, you water, and faithfully hold it till all downcast
    eyes have time to take it from you!
Diverge, fine spokes of light, from the shape of my head, or any one's head,
    in the sunlit water!
Come on, ships from the lower bay! pass up or down, white-sail'd schooners,
    sloops, lighters!
Flaunt away, flags of all nations! be duly lower'd at sunset!
Burn high your fires, foundry chimneys! cast black shadows at nightfall! cast
    red and yellow light over the tops of the houses!
Appearances, now or henceforth, indicate what you are,
You necessary film, continue to envelop the soul,
About my body for me, and your body for you, be hung out divinest aromas,
Thrive, cities—bring your freight, bring your shows, ample and sufficient
    rivers,
Expand, being than which none else is perhaps more spiritual,
Keep your places, objects than which none else is more lasting.

You have waited, you always wait, you dumb, beautiful ministers,
We receive you with free sense at last, and are insatiate henceforward,
Not you any more shall be able to foil us, or withhold yourselves from us,
We use you, and do not cast you aside—we plant you permanently within us,
We fathom you not—we love you—there is perfection in you also,
You furnish your parts toward eternity,
Great or small, you furnish your parts toward the soul.

The "Sea-Drift" Elegies

In the winter of 1859–1860, Whitman seems to have experienced a bitter homoerotic relationship—brief, intense, and thwarted—how and why we do not know. In the 1860 *Leaves of Grass*, third edition, appear two powerful new poems, eventually to be titled by their first lines and gathered in the "Sea-Drift" section of the definitive *Leaves of Grass*.

The more popular of the two poems has been "Out of the Cradle Endlessly Rocking," a majestic hymn celebrating what the eighteenth century would have called the incarnation of the poetic character. And yet the poem explicitly returns to the four-fold Muse of "The Sleepers": Night, Death, the Mother, and the Sea. Even more powerful, for me, is Whitman's poignant elegy of poetic disincarnation, "As I Ebb'd with the Ocean of Life," where he identifies his being with the sea-drift, the fragments that mark the shifting borders between shore and sea. Confronted by his Real Me, his mocking dusky demon and brother, Whitman works through an agonized crisis, by no means resolved at the poem's conclusion.

from Sea-Drift

"Out of the cradle endlessly rocking,"

Out of the cradle endlessly rocking,
Out of the mocking-bird's throat, the musical shuttle,
Out of the Ninth-month midnight,
Over the sterile sands and the fields beyond, where the child leaving his bed
    wander'd alone, bareheaded, barefoot,
Down from the shower'd halo,
Up from the mystic play of shadows twining and twisting as if they were
    alive,
Out from the patches of briers and blackberries,
From the memories of the bird that chanted to me,
From your memories sad brother, from the fitful risings and fallings I
    heard,
From under that yellow half-moon late-risen and swollen as if with
    tears,
From those beginning notes of yearning and love there in the mist,
From the thousand responses of my heart never to cease,

From the myriad thence-arous'd words,
From the word stronger and more delicious than any,
From such as now they start the scene revisiting,
As a flock, twittering, rising, or overhead passing,
Borne hither, ere all eludes me, hurriedly,
A man, yet by these tears a little boy again,
Throwing myself on the sand, confronting the waves,
I, chanter of pains and joys, uniter of here and hereafter,
Taking all hints to use them, but swiftly leaping beyond them,
A reminiscence sing.

Once Paumanok,
When the lilac-scent was in the air and Fifth-month grass was growing,
Up this seashore in some briers,
Two feather'd guests from Alabama, two together,
And their nest, and four light-green eggs spotted with brown,
And every day the he-bird to and fro near at hand,
And every day the she-bird crouch'd on her nest, silent, with bright
    eyes,
And every day I, a curious boy, never too close, never disturbing them,
Cautiously peering, absorbing, translating.

Shine! shine! shine!
Pour down your warmth, great sun!
While we bask, we two together.

Two together!
Winds blow south, or winds blow north,
Day come white, or night come black,
Home, or rivers and mountains from home,
Singing all time, minding no time,
While we two keep together.

Till of a sudden,
May-be kill'd, unknown to her mate,
One forenoon the she-bird crouch'd not on the nest,
Nor return'd that afternoon, nor the next,
Nor ever appear'd again.

And thenceforward all summer in the sound of the sea,
And at night under the full of the moon in calmer weather,
Over the hoarse surging of the sea,

Or flitting from brier to brier by day,
I saw, I heard at intervals the remaining one, the he-bird,
The solitary guest from Alabama.

Blow! blow! blow!
Blow up sea-winds along Paumanok's shore;
I wait and I wait till you blow my mate to me.

Yes, when the stars glisten'd,
All night long on the prong of a moss-scallop'd stake,
Down almost amid the slapping waves,
Sat the lone singer wonderful causing tears.

He call'd on his mate,
He pour'd forth the meanings which I of all men know.

Yes my brother I know,
The rest might not, but I have treasur'd every note,
For more than once dimly down to the beach gliding,
Silent, avoiding the moonbeams, blending myself with the shadows,
Recalling now the obscure shapes, the echoes, the sounds and sights after
    their sorts,
The white arms out in the breakers tirelessly tossing,
I, with bare feet, a child, the wind wafting my hair,
Listen'd long and long.

Listen'd to keep, to sing, now translating the notes,
Following you my brother.

Soothe! soothe! soothe!
Close on its wave soothes the wave behind,
And again another behind embracing and lapping, every one close,
But my love soothes not me, not me.

Low hangs the moon, it rose late,
It is lagging—O I think it is heavy with love, with love.

O madly the sea pushes upon the land,
With love, with love.

O night! do I not see my love fluttering out among the breakers?
What is that little black thing I see there in the white?

Loud! loud! loud!
Loud I call to you, my love!

High and clear I shoot my voice over the waves,
Surely you must know who is here, is here,
You must know who I am, my love.

Low-hanging moon!
What is that dusky spot in your brown yellow?
O it is the shape, the shape of my mate!
O moon do not keep her from me any longer.

Land! land! O land!
Whichever way I turn, O I think you could give me my mate back again if
    you only would,
For I am almost sure I see her dimly whichever way I look.

O rising stars!
Perhaps the one I want so much will rise, will rise with some of you.

O throat! O trembling throat!
Sound clearer through the atmosphere!
Pierce the woods, the earth,
Somewhere listening to catch you must be the one I want.

Shake out carols!
Solitary here, the night's carols!
Carols of lonesome love! death's carols!
Carols under that lagging, yellow, waning moon!
O under that moon where she droops almost down into the sea!
O reckless despairing carols.

But soft! sink low!
Soft! let me just murmur,
And do you wait a moment you husky-nois'd sea,
For somewhere I believe I heard my mate responding to me,
So faint, I must be still, be still to listen,
But not altogether still, for then she might not come immediately to me.

Hither my love!
Here I am! here!

With this just-sustain'd note I announce myself to you,
This gentle call is for you my love, for you.

Do not be decoy'd elsewhere,
That is the whistle of the wind, it is not my voice,
That is the fluttering, the fluttering of the spray,
Those are the shadows of leaves.

O darkness! O in vain!
O I am very sick and sorrowful.

O brown halo in the sky near the moon, drooping upon the sea!
O troubled reflection in the sea!
O throat! O throbbing heart!
And I singing uselessly, uselessly all the night.

O past! O happy life! O songs of joy!
In the air, in the woods, over fields,
Loved! loved! loved! loved! loved!
But my mate no more, no more with me!
We two together no more.

The aria sinking,
All else continuing, the stars shining,
The winds blowing, the notes of the bird continuous echoing,
With angry moans the fierce old mother incessantly moaning,
On the sands of Paumanok's shore gray and rustling,
The yellow half-moon enlarged, sagging down, drooping, the face of the sea
    almost touching,
The boy ecstatic, with his bare feet the waves, with his hair the atmosphere
    dallying,
The love in the heart long pent, now loose, now at last tumultuously bursting,
The aria's meaning, the ears, the soul, swiftly depositing,
The strange tears down the cheeks coursing,
The colloquy there, the trio, each uttering,
The undertone, the savage old mother incessantly crying,
To the boy's soul's questions sullenly timing, some drown'd secret hissing,
To the outsetting bard.

Demon or bird! (said the boy's soul,)
Is it indeed toward your mate you sing? or is it really to me?
For I, that was a child, my tongue's use sleeping, now I have heard you,
Now in a moment I know what I am for, I awake,

And already a thousand singers, a thousand songs, clearer, louder and more
    sorrowful than yours,
A thousand warbling echoes have started to life within me, never to die.

O you singer solitary, singing by yourself, projecting me,
O solitary me listening, never more shall I cease perpetuating you,
Never more shall I escape, never more the reverberations,
Never more the cries of unsatisfied love be absent from me,
Never again leave me to be the peaceful child I was before what there in the
    night,
By the sea under the yellow and sagging moon,
The messenger there arous'd, the fire, the sweet hell within,
The unknown want, the destiny of me.

O give me the clew! (it lurks in the night here somewhere,)
O if I am to have so much, let me have more!

A word then, (for I will conquer it,)
The word final, superior to all,
Subtle, sent up—what is it?—I listen;
Are you whispering it, and have been all the time, you sea-waves?
Is that it from your liquid rims and wet sands?
Whereto answering, the sea,
Delaying not, hurrying not,
Whisper'd me through the night, and very plainly before daybreak,
Lisp'd to me the low and delicious word death,
And again death, death, death, death,
Hissing melodious, neither like the bird nor like my arous'd child's heart,
But edging near as privately for me rustling at my feet,
Creeping thence steadily up to my ears and laving me softly all over,
Death, death, death, death, death.

Which I do not forget,
But fuse the song of my dusky demon and brother,
That he sang to me in the moonlight on Paumanok's gray beach,
With the thousand responsive songs at random,
My own songs awaked from that hour,
And with them the key, the word up from the waves,
The word of the sweetest song and all songs,
That strong and delicious word which, creeping to my feet,
(Or like some old crone rocking the cradle, swathed in sweet garments,
    bending aside,)
The sea whisper'd me.

"As I ebb'd with the ocean of life,"

1

As I ebb'd with the ocean of life,
As I wended the shores I know,
As I walk'd where the ripples continually wash you Paumanok,
Where they rustle up hoarse and sibilant,
Where the fierce old mother endlessly cries for her castaways,
I musing late in the autumn day, gazing off southward,
Held by this electric self out of the pride of which I utter poems,
Was seiz'd by the spirit that trails in the lines underfoot,
The rim, the sediment that stands for all the water and all the land of the
    globe.

Fascinated, my eyes reverting from the south, dropt, to follow those slender
    windrows,
Chaff, straw, splinters of wood, weeds, and the sea-gluten,
Scum, scales from shining rocks, leaves of salt-lettuce, left by the tide,
Miles walking, the sound of breaking waves the other side of me,
Paumanok there and then as I thought the old thought of likenesses,
These you presented to me you fish-shaped island,
As I wended the shores I know,
As I walk'd with that electric self seeking types.

2

As I wend to the shores I know not,
As I list to the dirge, the voices of men and women wreck'd,
As I inhale the impalpable breezes that set in upon me,
As the ocean so mysterious rolls toward me closer and closer,
I too but signify at the utmost a little wash'd-up drift,
A few sands and dead leaves to gather,
Gather, and merge myself as part of the sands and drift.

O baffled, balk'd, bent to the very earth,
Oppress'd with myself that I have dared to open my mouth,
Aware now that amid all that blab whose echoes recoil upon me I have not
    once had the least idea who or what I am,
But that before all my arrogant poems the real Me stands yet untouch'd,
    untold, altogether unreach'd,
Withdrawn far, mocking me with mock-congratulatory signs and bows,
With peals of distant ironical laughter at every word I have written,
Pointing in silence to these songs, and then to the sand beneath.

I perceive I have not really understood any thing, not a single object, and
    that no man ever can,
Nature here in sight of the sea taking advantage of me to dart upon me and
    sting me,
Because I have dared to open my mouth to sing at all.

3

You oceans both, I close with you,
We murmur alike reproachfully rolling sands and drift, knowing not why,
These little shreds indeed standing for you and me and all.

You friable shore with trails of debris,
You fish-shaped island, I take what is underfoot,
What is yours is mine my father.

I too Paumanok,
I too have bubbled up, floated the measureless float, and been wash'd on
    your shores,
I too am but a trail of drift and debris,
I too leave little wrecks upon you, you fish-shaped island.

I throw myself upon your breast my father,
I cling to you so that you cannot unloose me,
I hold you so firm till you answer me something.

Kiss me my father,
Touch me with your lips as I touch those I love,
Breathe to me while I hold you close the secret of the murmuring I envy.

4

Ebb, ocean of life, (the flow will return,)
Cease not your moaning you fierce old mother,
Endlessly cry for your castaways, but fear not, deny not me,
Rustle not up so hoarse and angry against my feet as I touch you or gather
    from you.

I mean tenderly by you and all,
I gather for myself and for this phantom looking down where we lead, and
    following me and mine.

Me and mine, loose windrows, little corpses,
Froth, snowy white, and bubbles,
(See, from my dead lips the ooze exuding at last,

See, the prismatic colors glistening and rolling,)
Tufts of straw, sands, fragments,
Buoy'd hither from many moods, one contradicting another,
From the storm, the long calm, the darkness, the swell,
Musing, pondering, a breath, a briny tear, a dab of liquid or soil,
Up just as much out of fathomless workings fermented and thrown,
A limp blossom or two, torn, just as much over waves floating, drifted at
    random,
Just as much for us that sobbing dirge of Nature,
Just as much whence we come that blare of the cloudtrumpets,
We, capricious, brought hither we know not whence, spread out before you,
You up there walking or sitting,
Whoever you are, we too lie in drifts at your feet.

When Lilacs Last in the Dooryard Bloom'd

Whitman's elegy for the martyred Abraham Lincoln seems to me his greatest poem. Edith Wharton records Henry James's total devotion to the poem, as an old man, particularly striking because the young Henry James vehemently attacked this work of Whitman in 1865, when it was published.

If Whitman—more even than Emerson, Dickinson, Hawthorne, Melville, James, Faulkner, Hart Crane—is the strongest American writer, then "Lilacs" is the summit of our imaginative literature to date. It is the American answer to *Lycidas,* Milton's best shorter poem.

Particular attention should be paid to the metaphor of the "tally," here as in "Song of Myself." It is the sprig of lilac that Whitman surrenders to Lincoln's coffin, and is emblematic of the Whitmanian poetic voice, which was never to be so powerful again.

When Lilacs Last in the Dooryard Bloom'd

1
When lilacs last in the dooryard bloom'd,
And the great star early droop'd in the western sky in the night,
I mourn'd, and yet shall mourn with ever-returning spring.

Ever-returning spring, trinity sure to me you bring,
Lilac blooming perennial and drooping star in the west,
And thought of him I love.

2

O powerful western fallen star!
O shades of night—O moody, tearful night!
O great star disappear'd—O the black murk that hides the star!
O cruel hands that hold me powerless—O helpless soul of me!
O harsh surrounding cloud that will not free my soul.

3

In the dooryard fronting an old farm-house near the white-wash'd palings,
Stands the lilac-bush tall-growing with heart-shaped leaves of rich green,
With many a pointed blossom rising delicate, with the perfume strong I love,
With every leaf a miracle—and from this bush in the dooryard,
With delicate-color'd blossoms and heart-shaped leaves of rich green,
A sprig with its flower I break.

4

In the swamp in secluded recesses,
A shy and hidden bird is warbling a song.

Solitary the thrush,
The hermit withdrawn to himself, avoiding the settlements,
Sings by himself a song.

Song of the bleeding throat,
Death's outlet song of life, (for well dear brother I know,
If thou wast not granted to sing thou would'st surely die.)

5

Over the breast of the spring, the land, amid cities,
Amid lanes and through old woods, where lately the violets peep'd from the
    ground, spotting the gray debris,
Amid the grass in the fields each side of the lanes, passing the endless grass,
Passing the yellow-spear'd wheat, every grain from its shroud in the dark-
    brown fields uprisen,
Passing the apple-tree blows of white and pink in the orchards,
Carrying a corpse to where it shall rest in the grave,
Night and day journeys a coffin.

6

Coffin that passes through lanes and streets,
Through day and night with the great cloud darkening the land,
With the pomp of the inloop'd flags with the cities draped in black,
With the show of the States themselves as of crape-veil'd women standing,
With processions long and winding and the flambeaus of the night,
With the countless torches lit, with the silent sea of faces and the unbared
   heads,
With the waiting depot, the arriving coffin, and the sombre faces,
With dirges through the night, with the thousand voices rising strong and
   solemn,
With all the mournful voices of the dirges pour'd around the coffin,
The dim-lit churches and the shuddering organs—where amid these you
   journey,
With the tolling tolling bells' perpetual clang,
Here, coffin that slowly passes,
I give you my sprig of lilac.

7

(Nor for you, for one alone,
Blossoms and branches green to coffins all I bring,
For fresh as the morning, thus would I chant a song for you O sane and
   sacred death.

All over bouquets of roses,
O death, I cover you over with roses and early lilies,
But mostly and now the lilac that blooms the first,
Copious I break, I break the sprigs from the bushes,
With loaded arms I come, pouring for you,
For you and the coffins all of you O death.)

8

O western orb sailing the heaven,
Now I know what you must have meant as a month since I walk'd,
As I walk'd in silence the transparent shadowy night,
As I saw you had something to tell as you bent to me night after night,
As you droop'd from the sky low down as if to my side, (while the other stars
   all look'd on,)
As we wander'd together the solemn night, (for something I know not what
   kept me from sleep,)
As the night advanced, and I saw on the rim of the west how full you were of
   woe,
As I stood on the rising ground in the breeze in the cool transparent night,

As I watch'd where you pass'd and was lost in the netherward black of the
    night,
As my soul in its trouble dissatisfied sank, as where you sad orb,
Concluded, dropt in the night, and was gone.

9

Sing on there in the swamp,
O singer bashful and tender, I hear your notes, I hear your call,
I hear, I come presently, I understand you,
But a moment I linger, for the lustrous star has detain'd me,
The star my departing comrade holds and detains me.

10

O how shall I warble myself for the dead one there I loved?
And how shall I deck my song for the large sweet soul that has gone?
And what shall my perfume be for the grave of him I love?

Sea-winds blown from east and west,
Blown from the Eastern sea and blown from the Western sea, till there on
    the prairies meeting,
These and with these and the breath of my chant,
I'll perfume the grave of him I love.

11

O what shall I hang on the chamber walls?
And what shall the pictures be that I hang on the walls,
To adorn the burial-house of him I love?

Pictures of growing spring and farms and homes,
With the Fourth-month eve at sundown, and the gray smoke lucid and
    bright,
With floods of the yellow gold of the gorgeous, indolent, sinking sun,
    burning, expanding the air,
With the fresh sweet herbage under foot, and the pale green leaves of the
    trees prolific,
In the distance the flowing glaze, the breast of the river, with a wind-dapple
    here and there,
With ranging hills on the banks, with many a line against the sky, and
    shadows,
And the city at hand with dwellings so dense, and stacks of chimneys,
And all the scenes of life and the workshops, and the workmen homeward
    returning.

12

Lo, body and soul—this land,

My own Manhattan with spires, and the sparkling and hurrying tides, and the
    ships,

The varied and ample land, the South and the North in the light, Ohio's
    shores and flashing Missouri,

And ever the far-spreading prairies cover'd with grass and corn.

Lo, the most excellent sun so calm and haughty,

The violet and purple morn with just-felt breezes,

The gentle soft-born measureless light,

The miracle spreading bathing all, the fulfill'd noon,

The coming eve delicious, the welcome night and the stars,

Over my cities shining all, enveloping man and land.

13

Sing on, sing on you gray-brown bird,

Sing from the swamps, the recesses, pour your chant from the bushes,

Limitless out of the dusk, out of the cedars and pines.

Sing on dearest brother, warble your reedy song,

Loud human song, with voice of uttermost woe.

O liquid and free and tender!

O wild and loose to my soul—O wondrous singer!

You only I hear—yet the star holds me, (but will soon depart,)

Yet the lilac with mastering odor holds me.

14

Now while I sat in the day and look'd forth,

In the close of the day with its light and the fields of spring, and the farmers
    preparing their crops,

In the large unconscious scenery of my land with its lakes and forests,

In the heavenly aerial beauty, (after the perturb'd winds and the storms,)

Under the arching heavens of the afternoon swift passing, and the voices of
    children and women,

The many-moving sea-tides, and I saw the ships how they sail'd,

And the summer approaching with richness, and the fields all busy with
    labor,

And the infinite separate houses, how they all went on, each with its meals
    and minutia of daily usages,

And the streets how their throbbings throbb'd, and the cities pent—lo, then
    and there,

Falling upon them all and among them all, enveloping me with the rest,
Appear'd the cloud, appear'd the long black trail,
And I knew death, its thought, and the sacred knowledge of death.

Then with the knowledge of death as walking one side of me,
And the thought of death close-walking the other side of me,
And I in the middle as with companions, and as holding the hands of com-
    panions,
I fled forth to the hiding receiving night that talks not,
Down to the shores of the water, the path by the swamp in the dimness,
To the solemn shadowy cedars and ghostly pines so still.

And the singer so shy to the rest receiv'd me,
The gray-brown bird I know receiv'd us comrades three,
And he sang the carol of death, and a verse for him I love.

From deep secluded recesses,
From the fragrant cedars and the ghostly pines so still,
Came the carol of the bird.

And the charm of the carol rapt me,
As I held as if by their hands my comrades in the night,
And the voice of my spirit tallied the song of the bird.

Come lovely and soothing death,
Undulate round the world, serenely arriving, arriving,
In the day, in the night, to all, to each,
Sooner or later delicate death.

Prais'd be the fathomless universe,
For life and joy, and for objects and knowledge curious,
And for love, sweet love—but praise! praise! praise!
For the sure-enwinding arms of cool-enfolding death.

Dark mother always gliding near with soft feet,
Have none chanted for thee a chant of fullest welcome?
Then I chant it for thee, I glorify thee above all,
I bring thee a song that when thou must indeed come, come unfalteringly.

Approach strong deliveress,
When it is so, when thou hast taken them I joyously sing the dead,
Lost in the loving floating ocean of thee,
Laved in the flood of thy bliss O death.

From me to thee glad serenades,
Dances for thee I propose saluting thee, adornments and feastings for thee,
And the sights of the open landscape and the high-spread sky are fitting,
And life and the fields, and the huge and thoughtful night.

The night in silence under many a star,
The ocean shore and the husky whispering wave whose voice I know,
And the soul turning to thee O vast and well-veil'd death,
And the body gratefully nestling close to thee.

Over the tree-tops I float thee a song,
Over the rising and sinking waves, over the myriad fields and the prairies
    wide,
Over the dense-pack'd cities all and the teeming wharves and ways,
I float this carol with joy, with joy to thee O death.

15

To the tally of my soul,
Loud and strong kept up the gray-brown bird,
With pure deliberate notes spreading filling the night.

Loud in the pines and cedars dim,
Clear in the freshness moist and the swamp-perfume,
And I with my comrades there in the night.

While my sight that was bound in my eyes unclosed,
As to long panoramas of visions.

And I saw askant the armies,
I saw as in noiseless dreams hundreds of battle-flags,
Borne through the smoke of the battles and pierc'd with missiles I saw
    them,
And carried hither and yon through the smoke, and torn and bloody,
And at last but a few shreds left on the staffs, (and all in silence,)
And the staffs all splinter'd and broken.

I saw battle-corpses, myriads of them,
And the white skeletons of young men, I saw them,
I saw the debris and debris of all the slain soldiers of the war,
But I saw they were not as was thought,
They themselves were fully at rest, they suffer'd not,
The living remain'd and suffer'd, the mother suffer'd,

And the wife and the child and the musing comrade suffer'd,
And the armies that remain'd suffer'd.

16

Passing the visions, passing the night,
Passing, unloosing the hold of my comrades' hands,
Passing the song of the hermit bird and the tallying song of my soul,
Victorious song, death's outlet song, yet varying ever-altering song,
As low and wailing, yet clear the notes, rising and falling, flooding the night,
Sadly sinking and fainting, as warning and warning, and yet again bursting
    with joy,
Covering the earth and filling the spread of the heaven,
As that powerful psalm in the night I heard from recesses,
Passing, I leave thee lilac with heart-shaped leaves,
I leave thee there in the door-yard, blooming, returning with spring.

I cease from my song for thee,
From my gaze on thee in the west, fronting the west, communing with thee,
O comrade lustrous with silver face in the night.

Yet each to keep and all, retrievements out of the night,
The song, the wondrous chant of the gray-brown bird,
And the tallying chant, the echo arous'd in my soul,
With the lustrous and drooping star with the countenance full of woe,
With the holders holding my hand nearing the call of the bird,
Comrades mine and I in the midst, and their memory ever to keep, for the
    dead I loved so well,
For the sweetest, wisest soul of all my days and lands—and this for his dear
    sake,
Lilac and star and bird twined with the chant of my soul,
There in the fragrant pines and the cedars dusk and dim.

The Last Invocation

At the last, tenderly,
From the walls of the powerful fortress'd house,
From the clasp of the knitted locks, from the keep of the well-closed doors,
Let me be wafted.

Let me glide noiselessly forth;
With the key of softness unlock the locks—with a whisper,
Set ope the doors O soul.

Tenderly—be not impatient,
(Strong is your hold O mortal flesh,
Strong is your hold O love.)

HERMAN MELVILLE

1819–1891

THE THREE POEMS by Melville included here would be memorable even if they had not been composed by the author of *Moby-Dick,* though they reverberate with particular intensity when we remember Captain Ahab.

Melville's career as a writer began with the commercial success of *Typee* (1846), but after that went poorly. *Moby-Dick* (1851) is one of the essential American books, but its reception was lukewarm, and Melville's life was marked by a series of dangerous depressions. His marriage was difficult: his oldest son was a suicide in 1867. Poetry, in his final years, largely displaced prose fiction for him, except for the posthumously published short novel, *Billy Budd.*

Melville's poetry tends to be rugged, even rough-hewn, in some ways premonitory of Thomas Hardy's poems. Like Hardy, Melville was profoundly influenced by Shelley's life and work. Shakespeare, the prime engenderer of *Moby-Dick,* is also echoed frequently in Melville's poems, and is strikingly characterized in "The Coming Storm":

> No utter surprise can come to him
>   Who reaches Shakspeare's core;
> That which we seek and shun is there—
>   Man's final lore.

As *Moby-Dick* implicitly manifests, Melville's reading of the Shakespeare of the high tragedies essentially was nihilistic. What seems to me Melville's finest poem, "After the Pleasure Party," gives us his darkest view of human sexual relations:

> For, Nature, in no shallow surge
> Against thee either sex may urge,

Why hast thou made us but in halves—
Co-relatives? This makes us slaves.
If these co-relatives never meet
Self-hood itself seems incomplete.
And such the dicing of blind fate
Few matching halves here meet and mate.
What Cosmic jest or Anarch blunder
The human integral clove asunder
And shied the fractions through life's gate?

Gnostic and hermetic sources, known to Melville, adumbrate the fall of the divine androgyne into "love and sleep," sexual division and its consequences. Melville's violent ambivalence is akin to Ahab's fury at having been maimed by Moby-Dick. Once he had written his epic, there was no White Whale for Melville to hunt unless it were Nature herself.

✤   ✤   ✤

The Portent

Hanging from the beam,
    Slowly swaying (such the law),
Gaunt the shadow on your green,
    Shenandoah!
The cut is on the crown
(Lo, John Brown),
And the stabs shall heal no more.

Hidden in the cap
    Is the anguish none can draw;
So your future veils its face,
    Shenandoah!
But the streaming beard is shown
(Weird John Brown),
The meteor of the war.
    1859

Fragments of a Lost Gnostic Poem of the 12th Century

.   .   .

Found a family, build a state,
The pledged event is still the same:

Matter in end will never abate
His ancient brutal claim.

.   .   .

Indolence is heaven's ally here,
And energy the child of hell:
The Good Man pouring from his pitcher clear,
But brims the poisoned well.

The Maldive Shark

About the Shark, phlegmatical one,
Pale sot of the Maldive sea,
The sleek little pilot-fish, azure and slim,
How alert in attendance be.
From his saw-pit of mouth, from his charnel of maw
They have nothing of harm to dread,
But liquidly glide on his ghastly flank
Or before his Gorgonian head;
Or lurk in the port of serrated teeth
In white triple tiers of glittering gates,
And there find a haven when peril's abroad,
An asylum in jaws of the Fates!

They are friends; and friendly they guide him to prey,
Yet never partake of the treat—
Eyes and brains to the dotard lethargic and dull,
Pale ravener of horrible meat.

EMILY DICKINSON

1830–1886

EMILY DICKINSON and Walt Whitman remain the two greatest and most original of American poets, surpassing such major figures of the twentieth century as Robert Frost, Wallace Stevens, T. S. Eliot, and Hart Crane. Unlike the self-printed Whitman, Dickinson rejected publication, which she called "the auction of the Mind of Man."

Like Whitman's, Dickinson's poetry looks simple and is very difficult, though the *kind* of difficulty is very different from that of *Leaves of Grass*. Whitman is nuanced and evasive, and most figurative where he proclaims he is literal. Dickinson is so cognitively original that she challenges William Blake in that regard. William Shakespeare's powers of thought, quite aside from all his other gifts, are unmatchable in literature and in language. Dickinson, at her strongest, has something in her lyrics that recalls the swiftness and compression of Shakespeare's mind.

Dickinson's life is both known and unknown; she has kept some of her secrets, perhaps forever. Her letters are prose-poems, as artful and complex as are her crisis-lyrics. You cannot argue her attachments from her letters, which are high fantastical.

Except for medical sojourns in Boston, and one year at Mount Holyoke, Dickinson lived her fifty-five years of intensely inner life in her father's house in Amherst, Massachusetts. In her later years her life was largely spent indoors.

There were three major instances of Dickinson's actual erotic interests: the Reverend Charles Wadsworth, Samuel Bowles, and Judge Otis Lord. Wadsworth, to some degree, may have reciprocated; Bowles, because of his circumstances, did not. But after Judge Lord became a widower, he and Dickinson were in something close to a secret marriage. Erotic anguish is one of Dickinson's recurrent subjects, and evidently was founded upon her personal experiences.

I find nothing in the poems (or letters) to indicate that Dickinson's bond (frequently strained) to her difficult sister-in-law Sue was sexual, whereas the erotic suffering so common to Dickinson's poetry has much to do with the loss of (or failure to attain) Wadsworth, Bowles, and Lord. Dickinson's spinsterhood, like her sister Lavinia's, could have some relation to the formidable Edward Dickinson, their father, Amherst's leading citizen: lawyer, educational founder, United States congressman. His death, in 1874, was as dreadful a grief for her as the death of Judge Lord a decade later. She survived Lord by only two years.

A nonconformist in religion from her childhood on, Dickinson is not post-Christian like Emerson and Whitman, but rather a sect of one, like Milton and Blake. Though satiric toward Calvinism, she remained its dissenting daughter. In the United States of the twenty-first century, she would not be considered a Christian at all. Emersonian self-reliance is her fundamental principle, and hers is a private religion of the self. She did not accept Jesus as her redeemer; she not did believe in the Resurrection. And yet Jesus to her was the exemplary sufferer who had triumphed over suffering. What are we to make of her "White Election," which attired her perpetually in white? She termed herself "Empress of Calvary," and after the death of Judge Lord, took the Holy Ghost as husband. Had she not written poems of the greatest aesthetic and intellectual eminence, we might feel that these are the fantasies of a high-born spinster of nineteenth-century Amherst. But the poems dismiss any such feeling:

> A word made Flesh is seldom
> And trembling partook
> Nor then perhaps reported
> But have I not mistook
>
> Each one of us has tasted
> With ecstasies of stealth
> The very food debated
> To our specific strength—
>
> A word that breathes distinctly
> Has not the power to die
> Cohesive as the Spirit
> It may expire if He—
>
> "Made Flesh and dwelt among us"
> Could condescension be
> Like this consent of Language
> This loved Philology

It seems appropriate that R. W. Franklin, Dickinson's definitive editor, cannot date this poem, because it is emblematic of the poet's stance, early and late. "Philology" here is poetry itself, the reading of which usurps Christian communion. The theological term "condescension" is ironized, since the poetic word has taken the place of "the word made Flesh," the Christ of the Gospel of John. This poem (with many others) might be called the Gospel of Emily Dickinson.

She has, though, no good news to proclaim. Despair, mourning and melancholia, psychic pain, erotic suffering; these are her *materia poetica*. But where could so extraordinary a spirit hope to have found her equal? Judge Lord, her father's friend, was eighteen years older than Dickinson and a person of considerable distinction, and perhaps came closer to being her consort than anyone else could have been. Franklin dates Poem 1314 as 1874, the year of her father's death, but it burns through me even if it is a negative elegy for Edward Dickinson rather than a lament for Wadsworth or Lord:

> Because that you are going
> And never coming back
> And I, however absolute
> May overlook your Track—
>
> Because that Death is final,
> However first it be
> This instant be suspended
> Above Mortality.
>
> Significance that each has lived
> The other to detect
> Discovery not God himself
> Could now annihilate
>
> Eternity, Presumption
> The instant I perceive
> That you, who were Existence
> Yourself forgot to live—

The biographical mysteries of Dickinson's outer life may never be solved, but it is better that way, just as all we know about Shakespeare are external facts. Dickinson's inner life is her poetry, whereas it cannot be said that the plays and sonnets reveal the Shakespearean inwardness, even in *Hamlet*. Dickinson after all is a High Romantic poet, influenced by Emerson and Wordsworth, Shelley and Keats. Walt Whitman had rethought the relation of the poet's self to his own vision. Dickinson, more radically, rethought the entire content of poetic vision, as the English High Romantics had done before her. But again, Dickinson is even more radical: each of her poems starts out fresh as though it could be a cosmos reimagined:

> Of Bronze—and Blaze—
> The North—tonight—
> So adequate—it forms—
> So preconcerted with itself—
> So distant—to alarms—
> An Unconcern so sovereign—
> To Universe, or me—
> Infects my simple spirit

With Taints of Majesty—
Till I take vaster attitudes—
And strut upon my stem—
Disdaining Men, and Oxygen,
For Arrogance of them—

My Splendours, are Menagerie—
But their Competeless Show
Will entertain the Centuries
When I, am long ago,
An Island in dishonored Grass—
Whom none but Daisies, know—

This is a poem "about" the northern lights, and makes an interesting contrast with Wallace Stevens's *The Auroras of Autumn*. Stevens walks the beach at twilight, as the season changes, and is challenged and appalled by the *aurora borealis* whose power exposes his vulnerability to aging and to death. Dickinson gleefully is inspired by the northern lights "With Taints of Majesty," and has the ambivalent prolepsis of knowing that her poems "Will entertain the Centuries" while knowing also that such immortality is entirely figurative, her personal remains being "An Island, in dishonored Grass." Stevens's auroras are menacing and sublime; Dickinson's are domesticated, and she makes the universe her playpen.

This splendid arrogance is compensated for by terror, not of extinction but of meaninglessness. She is Hamlet-like both in accepting a final silence and in at least approaching nihilism. Again rather like Hamlet, she can win any argument with anyone, except herself.

No Crowd that has occurred
Exhibit—I suppose
That General Attendance
That Resurrection—does—

Circumference be full—
The long restricted Grave
Assert her Vital Privilege—
The Dust—connect—and live—

On Atoms—features place—
All Multitudes that were
Efface in the Comparison—
As Suns—dissolve a star—

Solemnity—prevail—
It's Individual Doom
Possess each—separate Consciousness—
August—Absorbed—Numb—

What Duplicate—exist
What Parallel can be—
Of the Significance of This—
To Universe—and Me?

"Circumference," one of her key figurations, means what she wants it to mean, and changes each time she employs it. If the Bible deals with the Center, then her business is circumference, which essentially is her consciousness at its farthest limits, which are far out indeed. She had pondered, perhaps ironically, Emerson's extraordinary essay "Circles": "There is no outside, no inclosing wall, no circumference to us." That renders us akin to St. Augustine's God, a circle whose center was everywhere, and its circumference nowhere. Not a believer in Resurrection, Dickinson plays with it here before ambiguously dismissing it as being too large in significance both for the universe and for herself.

I have chosen twenty poems by Emily Dickinson, aside from the three I have quoted entire in this headnote. Anthologizing Dickinson is a frustration, as there are 1,789 poems in Franklin's great edition, and perhaps a third of them are of permanent aesthetic value. Though I read and teach her constantly, I remain a bewildered idolator, struggling to understand her enigmatic sublimities. With Emerson, Whitman, and Henry James, she seems to me our highest national achievement in thought and the arts.

❧ ❧ ❧

"There's a certain Slant of light,"

There's a certain Slant of light,
Winter Afternoons—
That oppresses, like the Heft
Of Cathedral Tunes—

Heavenly Hurt, it gives us—
We can find no scar,
But internal difference,
Where the Meanings, are—

None may teach it—Any—
'Tis the Seal Despair—
An imperial affliction
Sent us of the Air—

When it comes, the Landscape listens—
Shadows—hold their breath—
When it goes, 'tis like the Distance
On the look of Death—

"I felt a Funeral, in my Brain,"

I felt a Funeral, in my Brain,
And Mourners to and fro
Kept treading—treading—till it seemed
That Sense was breaking through—

And when they all were seated,
A Service, like a Drum—
Kept beating—beating—till I thought
My Mind was going numb—

And then I heard them lift a Box
And creak across my Soul
With those same Boots of Lead, again,
Then Space—began to toll,

As all the Heavens were a Bell,
And Being, but an Ear,
And I, and Silence, some strange Race
Wrecked, solitary, here—

And then a Plank in Reason, broke,
And I dropped down, and down—
And hit a World, at every plunge,
And Finished knowing—then—

"From Blank to Blank—"

From Blank to Blank—
A Threadless Way

I pushed Mechanic feet—
To stop—or perish—or advance—
Alike indifferent—

If end I gained
It ends beyond
Indefinite disclosed—
I shut my eyes—and groped as well
'Twas lighter—to be Blind—

"After great pain, a formal feeling comes—"

After great pain, a formal feeling comes—
The Nerves sit ceremonious, like Tombs—
The stiff Heart questions was it He, that bore,
And Yesterday, or Centuries before?

The Feet, mechanical, go round—
Of Ground, or Air, or Ought—
A Wooden way
Regardless grown,
A Quartz contentment, like a stone—

This is the Hour of Lead—
Remembered, if outlived,
As Freezing persons, recollect the Snow—
First—Chill—then Stupor—then the letting go—

"I started Early—Took my Dog—"

I started Early—Took my Dog—
And visited the Sea—
The Mermaids in the Basement
Came out to look at me—

And Frigates—in the Upper Floor
Extended Hempen Hands—
Presuming Me to be a Mouse—
Aground—upon the Sands—

But no Man moved Me—till the Tide
Went past my simple Shoe—
And past my Apron—and my Belt
And past my Bodice—too—

And made as He would eat me up—
As wholly as a Dew
Upon a Dandelion's Sleeve—
And then—I started—too—

And He—He followed—close behind—
I felt His Silver Heel
Upon my Ankle—Then my Shoes
Would overflow with Pearl—

Until We met the Solid Town—
No One He seemed to know—
And bowing—with a Mighty look—
At me—The Sea withdrew—

"This Consciousness that is aware"

This Consciousness that is aware
Of Neighbors and the Sun
Will be the one aware of Death
And that itself alone

Is traversing the interval
Experience between
And most profound experiment
Appointed unto Men—

How adequate unto itself
Its properties shall be
Itself unto itself and None
Shall make discovery.

Adventure most unto itself
The Soul condemned to be—
Attended by a single Hound
Its own identity.

"Our journey had advanced—"

Our journey had advanced—
Our feet were almost come
To that odd Fork in Being's Road—
Eternity—by Term—

Our pace took sudden awe—
Our feet—reluctant—led—
Before—were Cities—but Between—
The Forest of the Dead—

Retreat—was out of Hope—
Behind—a Sealed Route—
Eternity's White Flag—Before—
And God—at every Gate—

"The Tint I cannot take—is best—"

The Tint I cannot take—is best
The Color too remote
That I could show it in Bazaar—
A Guinea at a sight—

The fine—impalpable Array—
That swaggers on the eye
Like Cleopatra's Company—
Repeated—in the sky—

The Moments of Dominion
That happen on the Soul
And leave it with a Discontent
Too exquisite—to tell—

The eager look—on Landscapes—
As if they just repressed
Some Secret—that was pushing
Like Chariots—in the Vest—

The Pleading of the Summer—
That other Prank—of Snow—
That Cushions Mystery with Tulle,
For fear the Squirrels—know.

Their Graspless manners—mock us—
Until the Cheated Eye
Shuts arrogantly—in the Grave—
Another way—to see—

"Because I could not stop for Death—"

Because I could not stop for Death—
He kindly stopped for me—
The Carriage held but just Ourselves—
And Immortality.

We slowly drove—He knew no haste
And I had put away
My labor and my leisure too,
For His Civility—

We passed the School, where Children strove
At Recess—in the Ring—
We passed the Fields of Gazing Grain—
We passed the Setting Sun—

Or rather—He passed Us—
The Dews drew quivering and Chill—
For only Gossamer, my Gown—
My Tippet—only Tulle—

We paused before a House that seemed
A Swelling of the Ground—
The Roof was scarcely visible—
The Cornice—in the Ground—

Since then—'tis Centuries—and yet
Feels shorter than the Day
I first surmised the Horses' Heads
Were toward Eternity—

"My Life had stood—a Loaded Gun—"

My Life had stood—a Loaded Gun—
In Corners—till a Day

The Owner passed—identified—
And carried Me away—

And now We roam in Sovereign Woods—
And now We hunt the Doe—
And every time I speak for Him—
The Mountains straight reply—

And do I smile, such cordial light
Upon the Valley glow—
It is as a Vesuvian face
Had let its pleasure through—

And when at Night—Our good Day done—
I guard My Master's Head—
'Tis better than the Eider-Duck's
Deep Pillow—to have shared—

To foe of His—I'm deadly foe—
None stir the second time—
On whom I lay a Yellow Eye—
Or an emphatic Thumb—

Though I than He—may longer live
He longer must—than I—
For I have but the power to kill,
Without—the power to die—

"A Light exists in Spring"

A Light exists in Spring
Not present on the Year
At any other period—
When March is scarcely here

A Color stands abroad
On Solitary Fields
That Science cannot overtake
But Human Nature feels.

It waits upon the Lawn,
It shows the furthest Tree

Upon the furthest Slope you know
It almost speaks to you.

Then as Horizons step
Or Noons report away
Without the Formula of sound
It passes and we stay—

A quality of loss
Affecting our Content
As Trade had suddenly encroached
Upon a Sacrament.

"Tell all the Truth but tell it slant—"

Tell all the Truth but tell it slant—
Success in Circuit lies
Too bright for our infirm Delight
The Truth's superb surprise
As Lightning to the Children eased
With explanation kind
The Truth must dazzle gradually
Or every man be blind—

"In Winter in my Room"

In Winter in my Room
I came upon a Worm—
Pink, lank and warm—
But as he was a worm
And worms presume
Not quite with him at home—
Secured him by a string
To something neighboring
And went along.

A Trifle afterward
A thing occurred
I'd not believe it if I heard
But state with creeping blood—
A snake with mottles rare

Surveyed my chamber floor
In feature as the worm before
But ringed with power—
The very string with which
I tied him—too
When he was mean and new
That string was there—

I shrank—"How fair you are"!
Propitiation's claw—
"Afraid," he hissed
"Of me"?
"No cordiality"—
He fathomed me—

"Because that you are going"

Because that you are going
And never coming back
And I, however absolute
May overlook your Track—

Because that Death is final,
However first it be
This instant be suspended
Above Mortality.

Significance that each has lived
The other to detect
Discovery not God himself
Could now annihilate

Eternity, Presumption
The instant I perceive
That you, who were Existence
Yourself forgot to live—

The "Life that is" will then have been
A Thing I never knew—
As Paradise fictitious
Until the Realm of you—

The "Life that is to be," to me,
A Residence too plain
Unless in my Redeemer's Face
I recognize your own.

Of Immortality who doubts
He may exchange with me
Curtailed by your obscuring Face
Of Everything but He—

Of Heaven and Hell I also yield
The Right to reprehend
To whoso would commute this Face
For his less priceless Friend.

If "God is Love" as he admits
We think that he must be
Because he is a "jealous God"
He tells us certainly

If "All is possible with" him
As he besides concedes
He will refund us finally
Our confiscated Gods—

"A Pit—but Heaven over it—"

A Pit—but Heaven over it—
And Heaven beside, and Heaven abroad,
And yet a Pit—
With Heaven over it.

To stir would be to slip—
To look would be to drop—
To dream—to sap the Prop
That holds my chances up.
Ah! Pit! With Heaven over it!

The depth is all my thought—
I dare not ask my feet—
'Twould start us where we sit
So straight you'd scarce suspect
It was a Pit—with fathoms under it—
Its Circuit just the same.

Seed—summer—tomb—
Whose Doom to whom?

"By a departing light"

By a departing light
We see acuter, quite,
Than by a wick that stays.
There's something in the flight
That clarifies the sight
And decks the rays.

"I dwell in Possibility—"

I dwell in Possibility—
A fairer House than Prose—
More numerous of Windows—
Superior—for Doors—

Of Chambers as the Cedars—
Impregnable of Eye—
And for an Everlasting Roof
The Gambrels of the Sky—

Of Visitors—the fairest—
For Occupation—This—
The spreading wide my narrow Hands
To gather Paradise—

"Through what transports of Patience"

Through what transports of Patience
I reached the stolid Bliss
To breathe my Blank without thee
Attest me this and this—
By that bleak exultation
I won as near as this
Thy privilege of dying
Abbreviate me this

"We grow accustomed to the Dark—"

We grow accustomed to the Dark—
When Light is put away—

As when the Neighbor holds the Lamp
To witness her Good bye—

A Moment—We uncertain step
For newness of the night—
Then—fit our Vision to the Dark—
And meet the Road—erect—

And so of larger—Darknesses—
Those Evenings of the Brain—
When not a Moon disclose a sign—
Or Star—come out—within—

The Bravest—grope a little—
And sometimes hit a Tree
Directly in the Forehead—
But as they learn to see—

Either the Darkness alters—
Or something in the sight
Adjusts itself to Midnight—
And Life steps almost straight.

"No man saw awe, nor to his house"

No man saw awe, nor to his house
Admitted he a man
Though by his awful residence
Has human nature been.

Not deeming of his dread abode
Till laboring to flee
A grasp on comprehension laid
Detained vitality.

Returning is a different route
The Spirit could not show
For breathing is the only work
To be enacted now.

"Am not consumed," old Moses wrote,
"Yet saw Him face to face"—
That very physiognomy
I am convinced was this

ALFRED, LORD TENNYSON

1809–1892

TENNYSON, the most accomplished artist of all English poets since Milton and Pope, was born and raised at Somersby in Lincolnshire, where his father was the unhappy rector. Two of his elder brothers, Frederick and Charles, were also poets of talent, but afflicted by melancholia, like Alfred. Himself a natural poet, Tennyson began writing at five, and continued until he entered Trinity College, Cambridge, in 1827, where he befriended Arthur Henry Hallam, who became the true Muse of all Tennyson's work. The friendship between the two was the most important experience of Tennyson's life, and if it had a repressed sexual element, neither Tennyson nor Hallam (nor anyone else) seems ever to have been aware of this. Under Hallam's inspiration, Tennyson became a Keatsian poet, which he always remained.

In 1827, together with his brothers Frederick and Charles, Tennyson published the mistitled *Poems by Two Brothers,* but his first real book was *Poems, Chiefly Lyrical* in 1830, followed by *Poems* late in 1832. Both volumes received some severe reviews, and the oversensitive poet did not publish again before the British public until 1842, when he attained fame and financial rewards unknown since Byron, by bringing out *Poems* in two volumes. Meanwhile, between 1830 and 1842, the crucial events of Tennyson's life occurred. His father died in 1831, and subsequently the poet left Cambridge without taking his degree. On September 15, 1833, Arthur Hallam died suddenly at twenty-two, in Vienna, of a brain seizure. Tennyson had met Emily Sellwood and reached an understanding with her as early as 1830; they became engaged in 1838, but did not marry until 1850. Biographers explain this twenty-year delay as financial in nature, but that seems mildly preposterous. Tennyson would not marry until then, and surely it is significant that his marriage took place only after the first publication (anonymous) of *In Memoriam,* his elegies for Hallam.

In 1850 Tennyson succeeded Wordsworth as Poet Laureate, and became an English institution. From 1853 on, he lived on an estate on the Isle of Wight, cultivating close relationships with the other major figures of the age, cared for faithfully by Mrs. Tennyson, who bore him two sons, Hallam and Lionel. In 1884, he accepted a barony, having declined the offer twice previously. His reputation remained high until his death in 1892, declined in the earlier twentieth century, and is rightly very high again today. Looking back, his life had one event only, and that was the death of Hallam. Most of his best poetry, quite aside from *In Memoriam*, is elegiac, and the subject of the sense of loss is always Hallam. "Ulysses," "Tithonus," *Morte d'Arthur*, "Tears, Idle Tears," much of *Idylls of the King*, the late "Merlin and the Gleam," all mourn Hallam (sometimes obliquely), just as the living Hallam directly inspired the best poems of the 1830 and 1832 volumes. This matter hardly can be overemphasized in considering Tennyson's poetry. He became the perfect model of a poet who is a bereaved lover, and the largest clue we can have as to the meaning of his poetry is in its relationship to Hallam. Hallam represented Romanticism to Tennyson, and the later Tennyson would have been more of a High Romantic and less of a societal spokesman if Hallam had lived.

Hallam had reviewed Tennyson's *Poems, Chiefly Lyrical* in 1831, and characterized his friend's poetry as belonging to the Romantic school of Keats and Shelley as opposed to that of Wordsworth. William Butler Yeats, who said that Hallam's review was crucial for his own early work, summarized Hallam's distinction between the two schools: "Keats and Shelley, unlike Wordsworth, intermixed into their poetry no elements from the general thought, but wrote out of the impression made by the world upon their delicate senses." Yeats was remembering one of Hallam's most acute sentences about Keats and Shelley: "So vivid was the delight attending the simple exertions of eye and ear, that it became mingled more and more with trains of active thought, and tended to absorb their whole being into the energy of sense." This marks the young Tennyson under Hallam's influence (1828–1833), and the necessary link between the Keats of "The Eve of St. Agnes" and the Great Odes, and the Pre-Raphaelite and Aesthetic poets later in the century. While Hallam lived, Tennyson did not mix into his poetry "elements from the general thought" without taking that thought up into the highly original context of his own imagination. He remembered an admonition of Hallam's, also included in the invaluable review of 1830: "That delicate sense of fitness which grows with the growth of artist feelings, and strengthens with their strength, until it acquires a celerity and weight of decision hardly inferior to the correspondent judgments of conscience, is weakened by every indulgence of heterogeneous aspirations, however pure they may be, however lofty, however suitable to human nature." Tennyson retreated from this, particularly after 1850, and perhaps he delayed his marriage and consequent domestication and institutionalization because something in him accurately feared that he would forget Hallam's instruction.

Tennyson always feared his own imagination, and distrusted its tendency to assert autonomy. Hallam's gift to Tennyson was to give the poet enough confidence in the value of his own imagination to allow him to indulge it, for a time. The best early poems—"Mariana," "The Lady of Shalott," "The Palace of Art," "The Lotos-Eaters" (all except the magical "The Hesperides")—manifest an uneasiness at their own Spenserian-Keatsian luxuriance, but in all of them the poetry is at work celebrating itself, so that as readers we believe the song and not the singer. What stays with us is the embowered, self-delighting consciousness in the sensuous prison-paradise, and not the societal censor that disapproves of such delight. If we follow a distinction of D. H. Lawrence's and say that a daemon wrote what is most valuable in Tennyson's early poems, we can be glad that this daemon, fortunately, never vanished entirely from the later poetry, so long as Hallam continued to haunt it.

Tennyson wrote in praise of Vergil and (very powerfully) in unfair dispraise of Lucretius, because he was at peace with the Vergilian strain in his own poetry, and feared the Lucretian, which he knew secretly he possessed also. This Epicurean tendency, which was to triumph in Pater, in much of Yeats, and in some of Yeats's friends of the 1890s, made no intellectual appeal to Tennyson, yet moved him deeply. *In Memoriam* is so troubled by the materialistic metaphysical implications of Victorian geology because Tennyson's imagination responded naturally and even buoyantly to speculations which his moral intellect could not tolerate.

If Tennyson is something of a poetic split personality, this does not make his work less powerful, nor does it affect his poetry where it is strongest, in style, by which more than diction and metric is meant. Tennyson's style, the most flawless in English poetry after Milton's and Pope's, is itself a sensibility, a means of apprehending both the internal and the external world. Intuitively, Tennyson understood what poetry was; argument that could not be separated from song, gesture, dance, and the rhythms of a unique but representative individual's breath-soul. Browning and Yeats, and the High Romantics before Tennyson, were all more powerful and original conceptualizers than Tennyson, and all of them mastered a great style, but none of them wrote so well so consistently as he did. A reader who knows no Latin and so cannot read Vergil has lost a great

deal, but it is Tennyson's triumph that any such reader can remedy the loss
by reading Tennyson, who richly sustains the comparison.

ᴠ   ᴠ   ᴠ

Mariana

Mariana in the moated grange
MEASURE FOR MEASURE

With blackest moss the flower-plots
　　Were thickly crusted, one and all:
The rusted nails fell from the knots
　　That held the pear to the gable-wall.
The broken sheds looked sad and strange:
　　Unlifted was the clinking latch;
　　Weeded and worn the ancient thatch
Upon the lonely moated grange.
　　　　She only said, 'My life is dreary,
10　　　　　　He cometh not,' she said;
　　　　She said, 'I am aweary, aweary,
　　　　　　I would that I were dead!'

Her tears fell with the dews at even;
　　Her tears fell ere the dews were dried;
She could not look on the sweet heaven,
　　Either at morn or eventide.
After the flitting of the bats,
　　When thickest dark did trance the sky,
　　She drew her casement-curtain by,
20　And glanced athwart the glooming flats.
　　　　She only said, 'The night is dreary,
　　　　　　He cometh not,' she said;
　　　　She said, 'I am aweary, aweary,
　　　　　　I would that I were dead!'

Upon the middle of the night,
　　Waking she heard the night-fowl crow:
The cock sung out an hour ere light:
　　From the dark fen the oxen's low
Came to her: without hope of change,
30　　In sleep she seemed to walk forlorn,
　　Till cold winds woke the gray-eyed morn

About the lonely moated grange.
    She only said, 'The day is dreary,
      He cometh not,' she said;
    She said, 'I am aweary, aweary,
      I would that I were dead!'

About a stone-cast from the wall
    A sluice with blackened waters slept,
And o'er it many, round and small,
40   The clustered marish-mosses crept.
Hard by a poplar shook alway,
    All silver-green with gnarlèd bark:
    For leagues no other tree did mark
The level waste, the rounding gray.
    She only said, 'My life is a dreary,
      He cometh not,' she said;
    She said, 'I am aweary, aweary,
      I would that I were dead!'

And ever when the moon was low,
50   And the shrill winds were up and away,
In the white curtain, to and fro,
    She saw the gusty shadow sway.
But when the moon was very low,
    And wild winds bound within their cell,
    The shadow of the poplar fell
Upon her bed, across her brow.
    She only said, 'The night is dreary,
      He cometh not,' she said;
    She said, 'I am aweary, aweary,
60   I would that I were dead!'

All day within the dreamy house,
    The doors upon their hinges creaked;
The blue fly sung in the pane; the mouse
    Behind the mouldering wainscot shrieked,
Or from the crevice peered about.
    Old faces glimmered through the doors,
    Old footsteps trod the upper floors,
Old voices called her from without.
    She only said, 'My life is dreary.
70   He cometh not,' she said;

> She said, 'I am aweary, aweary,
>   I would that I were dead!'

The sparrow's chirrup on the roof,
    The slow clock ticking, and the sound
Which to the wooing wind aloof
    The poplar made, did all confound
Her sense; but most she loathed the hour
    When the thick-moted sunbeam lay
    Athwart the chambers, and the day
80 Was sloping toward his western bower.
        Then, said she, 'I am very dreary,
            He will not come,' she said;
        She wept, 'I am aweary, aweary,
            Oh God, that I were dead!'

    1830

The Eagle

FRAGMENT

He clasps the crag with crookèd hands;
Close to the sun in lonely lands,
Ringed with the azure world, he stands.

The wrinkled sea beneath him crawls;
He watches from his mountain walls,
And like a thunderbolt he falls.

    1851

Ulysses

This equivocal dramatic monologue was written in the autumn of 1833, when Tennyson's despairing grief for Hallam was most oppressive. Later, the poet insisted that it stated his "feeling about the need of going forward, and braving the struggle of life perhaps more simply than anything in *In Memoriam*." Yet the monologue is founded more upon the evil counselor Ulysses of Dante's *Inferno* XXVI (whom nevertheless Dante in some sense admired) than on the hero of the prophecy of Tiresias in the *Odyssey* (XI, 1,003–1,037). Dante's Trojan sympathies stem from his nationality and from his guide Vergil, who sang the flight of Aeneas from fallen Troy, and the hero's subsequent founding of Rome. In *The Inferno,* Ulysses goes forth again on a last voyage, to "explore the world, and search the ways of life, / Man's evil and his virtue" (Cary's translation, which Tennyson probably used); when the Ithacans' ship comes to the Pillars of Hercules, "the boundaries not to be o'erstepped by man," the wily Ulysses urges his "small faithful band / That yet cleaved to me" to attempt a breakthrough into forbidden realms: "Ye were not formed to live the life of brutes, / But virtue to pursue and knowledge high." His men obey him, and are washed down with Ulysses in the forbidden gulfs when they sight the Mount of Purgatory. Though Tennyson takes a High Romantic view of Ulysses as a quester animated by heroic humanism and a sustained drive for knowledge, the poem persistently qualifies our admiration for its speaker. He appears to lack a capacity for loving other human beings, scorns his son's sense of responsibility, and in his final lines echoes the defiant Satan of Milton's *Paradise Lost* I–II.

Ulysses

It little profits that an idle king,
By this still hearth, among these barren crags,
Matched with an agèd wife, I mete and dole
Unequal laws unto a savage race,
That hoard, and sleep, and feed, and know not me.

I cannot rest from travel: I will drink
Life to the lees: all times I have enjoyed
Greatly, have suffered greatly, both with those
That loved me, and alone; on shore, and when
10   Through scudding drifts the rainy Hyades
Vexed the dim sea: I am become a name;
For always roaming with a hungry heart
Much have I seen and known; cities of men
And manners, climates, councils, governments,
Myself not least, but honoured of them all;
And drunk delight of battle with my peers,
Far on the ringing plains of windy Troy.
I am a part of all that I have met;
Yet all experience is an arch wherethrough
20   Gleams that untravelled world, whose margin fades
For ever and for ever when I move.
How dull it is to pause, to make an end,

To rust unburnished, not to shine in use!
As though to breathe were life. Life piled on life
Were all too little, and of one to me
Little remains: but every hour is saved
From that eternal silence, something more,
A bringer of new things; and vile it were
For some three suns to store and hoard myself,
30   And this grey spirit yearning in desire
To follow knowledge like a sinking star,
Beyond the utmost bound of human thought.

      This is my son, mine own Telemachus,
To whom I leave the sceptre and the isle—
Well-loved of me, discerning to fulfil
This labour, by slow prudence to make mild
A rugged people, and through soft degrees
Subdue them to the useful and the good.
Most blameless is he, centred in the sphere
40   Of common duties, decent not to fail
In offices of tenderness, and pay
Meet adoration to my household gods, ·
When I am gone. He works his work, I mine.

      There lies the port; the vessel puffs her sail:
There gloom the dark broad seas. My mariners,
Souls that have toiled, and wrought, and thought with me—
That ever with a frolic welcome took
The thunder and the sunshine, and opposed
Free hearts, free foreheads—you and I are old;
50   Old age hath yet his honour and his toil;
Death closes all: but something ere the end,
Some work of noble note, may yet be done,
Not unbecoming men that strove with Gods.
The lights begin to twinkle from the rocks:
The long day wanes: the slow moon climbs: the deep
Moans round with many voices. Come, my friends,
'Tis not too late to seek a newer world.
Push off, and sitting well in order smite
The sounding furrows; for my purpose holds
60   To sail beyond the sunset, and the baths
Of all the western stars, until I die.
It may be that the gulfs will wash us down:
It may be we shall touch the Happy Isles,

And see the great Achilles, whom we knew.
Though much is taken, much abides; and though
We are not now that strength which in old days
Moved earth and heaven; that which we are, we are;
One equal temper of heroic hearts,
Made weak by time and fate, but strong in will
70   To strive, to seek, to find, and not to yield.

    1833   1842

Morte d'Arthur

So all day long the noise of battle rolled
Among the mountains by the winter sea;
Until King Arthur's table, man by man,
Had fallen in Lyonnesse about their Lord,
King Arthur: then, because his wound was deep,
The bold Sir Bedivere uplifted him,
Sir Bedivere, the last of all his knights,
And bore him to a chapel nigh the field,
A broken chancel with a broken cross,
10   That stood on a dark strait of barren land.
On one side lay the Ocean, and on one
Lay a great water, and the moon was full.

    Then spake King Arthur to Sir Bedivere:
'The sequel of today unsolders all
The goodliest fellowship of famous knights
Whereof this world holds record. Such a sleep
They sleep—the men I loved. I think that we
Shall never more, at any future time,
Delight our souls with talk of knightly deeds,
20   Walking about the gardens and the halls
Of Camelot, as in the days that were.
I perish by this people which I made,—
Though Merlin sware that I should come again
To rule once more—but let what will be, be,
I am so deeply smitten through the helm
That without help I cannot last till morn.
Thou therefore take my brand Excalibur,
Which was my pride: for thou rememberest how
In those old days, one summer noon, an arm
30   Rose up from out the bosom of the lake,

Clothed in white samite, mystic, wonderful,
Holding the sword—and how I rowed across
And took it, and have worn it, like a king:
And, wheresoever I am sung or told
In aftertime, this also shall be known:
But now delay not: take Excalibur,
And fling him far into the middle mere:
Watch what thou seest, and lightly bring me word.'

    To him replied the bold Sir Bedivere:
40 'It is not meet, Sir King, to leave thee thus,
Aidless, alone, and smitten through the helm.
A little thing may harm a wounded man.
Yet I thy hest will all perform at full,
Watch what I see, and lightly bring thee word.'

    So saying, from the ruined shrine he stepped
And in the moon athwart the place of tombs,
Where lay the mighty bones of ancient men,
Old knights, and over them the sea-wind sang
Shrill, chill, with flakes of foam. He, stepping down
50 By zig-zag paths, and juts of pointed rock,
Came on the shining levels of the lake.

    There drew he forth the brand Excalibur,
And o'er him, drawing it, the winter moon,
Brightening the skirts of a long cloud, ran forth
And sparkled keen with frost against the hilt:
For all the haft twinkled with diamond sparks,
Myriads of topaz-lights, and jacinth-work
Of subtlest jewellery. He gazed so long
That both his eyes were dazzled, as he stood,
60 This way and that dividing the swift mind,
In act to throw: but at the last it seemed
Better to leave Excalibur concealed
There in the many-knotted waterflags,
That whistled stiff and dry about the marge.
So strode he back slow to the wounded King.

    Then spake King Arthur to Sir Bedivere:
'Hast thou performed my mission which I gave?
What is it thou hast seen? or what hast heard?'

And answer made the bold Sir Bedivere:
'I heard the ripple washing in the reeds,
And the wild water lapping on the crag.'

To whom replied King Arthur, faint and pale:
'Thou hast betrayed thy nature and thy name,
Not rendering true answer, as beseemed
Thy fealty, nor like a noble knight:
For surer sign had followed, either hand,
Or voice, or else a motion of the mere.
This is a shameful thing for men to lie.
Yet now, I charge thee, quickly go again
80 As thou art lief and dear, and do the thing
I bad thee, watch, and lightly bring me word.'

Then went Sir Bedivere the second time
Across the ridge, and paced beside the mere,
Counting the dewy pebbles, fixed in thought;
But when he saw the wonder of the hilt,
How curiously and strangely chased, he smote
His palms together, and he cried aloud,

'And if indeed I cast the brand away,
Surely a precious thing, one worthy note,
90 Should thus be lost for ever from the earth,
Which might have pleased the eyes of many men.
What good should follow this, if this were done?
What harm, undone? deep harm to disobey,
Seeing obedience is the bond of rule.
Were it well to obey then, if a king demand
An act unprofitable, against himself?
The King is sick, and knows not what he does.
What record, or what relic of my lord
Should be to aftertime, but empty breath
100 And rumours of a doubt? but were this kept,
Stored in some treasure-house of mighty kings,
Some one might show it at a joust of arms,
Saying, "King Arthur's sword, Excalibur,
Wrought by the lonely maiden of the Lake.
Nine years she wrought it, sitting in the deeps
Upon the hidden bases of the hills."

So might some old man speak in the aftertime
To all the people, winning reverence.
But now much honour and much fame were lost.'

110   So spake he, clouded with his own conceit,
And hid Excalibur the second time,
And so strode back slow to the wounded King.

Then spoke King Arthur, breathing heavily:
'What is it thou hast seen? or what hast heard?'

And answer made the bold Sir Bedivere:
'I heard the water lapping on the crag,
And the long ripple washing in the reeds.'

To whom replied King Arthur, much in wrath:
'Ah, miserable and unkind, untrue,
120   Unknightly, traitor-hearted! Woe is me!
Authority forgets a dying king,
Laid widowed of the power in his eye
That bowed the will. I see thee what thou art,
For thou, the latest-left of all my knights,
In whom should meet the offices of all,
Thou wouldst betray me for the precious hilt;
Either from lust of gold, or like a girl
Valuing the giddy pleasure of the eyes.
Yet, for a man may fail in duty twice,
130   And the third time may prosper, get thee hence:
But, if thou spare to fling Excalibur,
I will arise and slay thee with my hands.'

Then quickly rose Sir Bedivere, and ran,
And, leaping down the ridges lightly, plunged
Among the bulrush-beds, and clutched the sword,
And strongly wheeled and threw it. The great brand
Made lightnings in the splendour of the moon,
And flashing round and round, and whirled in an arch,
Shot like a streamer of the northern morn,
140   Seen where the moving isles of winter shock
By night, with noises of the northern sea.
So flashed and fell the brand Excalibur:
But ere he dipped the surface, rose an arm
Clothed in white samite, mystic, wonderful,

And caught him by the hilt, and brandished him
Three times, and drew him under in the mere.
And lightly went the other to the King.

Then spoke King Arthur, drawing thicker breath:
'Now see I by thine eyes that this is done.
150   Speak out: what is it thou hast heard, or seen?'

And answer made the bold Sir Bedivere:
'Sir King, I closed mine eyelids, lest the gems
Should blind my purpose, for I never saw,
Nor shall see, here or elsewhere, till I die,
Not though I live three lives of mortal men,
So great a miracle as yonder hilt.
Then with both hands I flung him, wheeling him;
But when I looked again, behold an arm,
Clothed in white samite, mystic, wonderful,
160   That caught him by the hilt, and brandished him
Three times, and drew him under in the mere.'

And answer made King Arthur, breathing hard:
'My end draws nigh; 'tis time that I were gone.
Make broad thy shoulders to receive my weight,
And bear me to the margin; yet I fear
My wound hath taken cold, and I shall die.'

So saying, from the pavement he half rose,
Slowly, with pain, reclining on his arm,
And looking wistfully with wide blue eyes
170   As in a picture. Him Sir Bedivere
Remorsefully regarded through his tears,
And would have spoken, but he found not words,
Then took with care, and kneeling on one knee,
O'er both his shoulders drew the languid hands,
And rising bore him through the place of tombs.

But, as he walked, King Arthur panted hard,
Like one that feels a nightmare on his bed
When all the house is mute. So sighed the King,
Muttering and murmuring at his ear, 'Quick, quick!
180   I fear it is too late, and I shall die.'
But the other swiftly strode from ridge to ridge,
Clothed with his breath, and looking, as he walked,

Larger than human on the frozen hills.
He heard the deep behind him, and a cry
Before. His own thought drove him, like a goad.
Dry clashed his harness in the icy caves
And barren chasms, and all to left and right
The bare black cliff clanged round him, as he based
His feet on juts of slippery crag that rang
190   Sharp-smitten with the dint of armèd heels—
And on a sudden, lo! the level lake,
And the long glories of the winter moon.

    Then saw they how there hove a dusky barge,
Dark as a funeral scarf from stem to stern,
Beneath them; and descending they were ware
That all the decks were dense with stately forms
Black-stoled, black-hooded, like a dream—by these
Three Queens with crowns of gold—and from them rose
A cry that shivered to the tingling stars,
200   And, as it were one voice, an agony
Of lamentation, like a wind, that shrills
All night in a waste land, where no one comes,
Or hath come, since the making of the world.

    Then murmured Arthur, 'Place me in the barge,'
And to the barge they came. There those three Queens
Put forth their hands, and took the King, and wept.
But she, that rose the tallest of them all
And fairest, laid his head upon her lap,
And loosed the shattered casque, and chafed his hands,
210   And called him by his name, complaining loud,
And dropping bitter tears against his brow
Striped with dark blood: for all his face was white
And colourless, and like the withered moon
Smote by the fresh beam of the springing east;
And all his greaves and cuisses dashed with drops
Of onset; and the light and lustrous curls—
That made his forehead like a rising sun
High from the dais-throne—were parched with dust;
Or, clotted into points and hanging loose,
220   Mixed with the knightly growth that fringed his lips.
So like a shattered column lay the King;
Not like that Arthur who, with lance in rest,
From spur to plume a star of tournament,

Shot through the lists at Camelot, and charged
Before the eyes of ladies and of kings.

   Then loudly cried the bold Sir Bedivere,
'Ah! my Lord Arthur, whither shall I go?
Where shall I hide my forehead and my eyes?
For now I see the true old times are dead,
230 When every morning brought a noble chance,
And every chance brought out a noble knight.
Such times have been not since the light that led
The holy Elders with the gift of myrrh.
But now the whole ROUND TABLE is dissolved
Which was an image of the mighty world;
And I, the last, go forth companionless,
And the days darken round me, and the years,
Among new men, strange faces, other minds.'

   And slowly answered Arthur from the barge:
240 'The old order changeth, yielding place to new,
And Cod fulfils Himself in many ways,
Lest one good custom should corrupt the world.
Comfort thyself: what comfort is in me?
I have lived my life, and that which I have done
May He within Himself make pure! but thou,
If thou shouldst never see my face again,
Pray for my soul. More things are wrought by prayer
Than this world dreams of. Wherefore, let thy voice
Rise like a fountain for me night and day.
250 For what are men better than sheep or goats
That nourish a blind life within the brain,
If, knowing God, they lift not hands of prayer
Both for themselves and those who call them friend?
For so the whole round earth is every way
Bound by gold chains about the feet of God.
But now farewell. I am going a long way
With these thou seest—if indeed I go—
(For all my mind is clouded with a doubt)
To the island-valley of Avilion;
260 Where falls not hail, or rain, or any snow,
Nor ever wind blows loudly; but it lies
Deep-meadowed, happy, fair with orchard-lawns
And bowery hollows crowned with summer sea,
Where I will heal me of my grievous wound.'

So said he, and the barge with oar and sail
Moved from the brink, like some full-breasted swan
That, fluting a wild carol ere her death,
Ruffles her pure cold plume, and takes the flood
With swarthy webs. Long stood Sir Bedivere
270   Revolving many memories, till the hull
Looked one black dot against the verge of dawn,
And on the mere the wailing died away.

1833–1834   1842

from The Princess

The Splendour Falls

The splendour falls on castle walls
    And snowy summits old in story:
The long light shakes across the lakes,
    And the wild cataract leaps in glory.
Blow, bugle, blow, set the wild echoes flying,
Blow, bugle; answer, echoes, dying, dying, dying.

O hark, O hear! how thin and clear,
    And thinner, clearer, farther going!
O sweet and far from cliff and scar
10   The horns of Elfland faintly blowing!
Blow, let us hear the purple glens replying:
Blow, bugle; answer, echoes, dying, dying, dying.
    O love, they die in yon rich sky,
        They faint on hill or field or river:
Our echoes roll from soul to soul,
    And grow for ever and for ever.
Blow, bugle, blow, set the wild echoes flying,
And answer, echoes, answer, dying, dying, dying.

1850

Tears, Idle Tears

'Tears, idle tears, I know not what they mean,
Tears from the depth of some divine despair
Rise in the heart, and gather to the eyes,

In looking on the happy Autumn-fields,
And thinking of the days that are no more.

    'Fresh as the first beam glittering on a sail,
That brings our friends up from the underworld,
Sad as the last which reddens over one
That sinks with all we love below the verge;
10   So sad, so fresh, the days that are no more.

    'Ah, sad and strange as in dark summer dawns
The earliest pipe of half-awakened birds
To dying ears, when unto dying eyes
The casement slowly grows a glimmering square;
So sad, so strange, the days that are no more.

    'Dear as remembered kisses after death,
And sweet as those by hopeless fancy feigned
On lips that are for others; deep as love,
Deep as first love, and wild with all regret;
20   O Death in Life, the days that are no more.'
    1847

In Memoriam A. H. H.

This is Tennyson's most ambitious poem, and as much the defining work of its time as Eliot's *Waste Land* was of the 1920s and 1930s. "It happens now and then that a poet by some strange accident expresses the mood of his generation, at the same time that he is expressing a mood of his own which is quite removed from that of his generation." Eliot shrewdly links *In Memoriam* with *The Waste Land* in this remark. Both seem to me to be poems of repressed passions, presumably of a man for a man. Eliot notes again, in Tennyson, "emotion so deeply suppressed, even from himself, as to tend rather towards the blackest melancholia." Though critics both Victorian and modern have seen these poems as celebrations of the necessity for Christianity, neither of them (discontinuous sequences both) is very convincing when it argues against modern doubt and materialism. Both poems are violently personal, eccentric, High Romantic at the core, and the quest in each is yet another version of what Yeats called "the antithetical" and accurately traced back to Shelley's *Alastor.*

A. C. Bradley gave the best account of the structure of *In Memoriam*. Following Tennyson's own statement that the poem's divisions are made by the Christmas sections (XXVIII, LXXVIII, CIV) Bradley sees *In Memoriam* as a three-year cycle (though written, of course, over many other years). The turning point for Bradley is the second Christmas poem, LXXVIII, after which deeper sorrow has passed. I myself would urge attention to sections XCV and CIII, as being not only the best poems in the sequence, but as showing the deeper enterprise of Tennyson's imagination in the poem. Section XCV is Tennyson's extreme version of Wordsworth's "Intimations" Ode, while section CIII is a variation upon the concluding love voyage of Shelley's *Epipsychidion*. Also remarkable is the apotheosis of Hallam in sections CXXVI to CXXX, a version of the transfiguration of Keats in the closing stanzas of *Adonais,* and about as Christian in its vision as Shelley's poem was.

from In Memoriam A. H. H.

Obiit MDCCCXXXIII
[PROLOGUE]
Strong Son of God, immortal Love,
    Whom we, that have not seen thy face,
    By faith, and faith alone, embrace,
Believing where we cannot prove;

Thine are these orbs of light and shade;
    Thou madest Life in man and brute;
    Thou madest Death; and lo, thy foot
Is on the skull which thou hast made.

Thou wilt not leave us in the dust:
10   Thou madest man, he knows not why,
    He thinks he was not made to die;
And thou hast made him: thou art just.

Thou seemest human and divine,
    The highest, holiest manhood, thou:
    Our wills are ours, we know not how;
Our wills are ours, to make them thine.

Our little systems have their day;
    They have their day and cease to be:

They are but broken lights of thee,
20   And thou, O Lord, art more than they.

We have but faith: we cannot know;
    For knowledge is of things we see;
    And yet we trust it comes from thee,
A beam in darkness: let it grow.

Let knowledge grow from more to more,
    But more of reverence in us dwell;
    That mind and soul, according well,
May make one music as before,

But vaster. We are fools and slight;
30   We mock thee when we do not fear:
    But help thy foolish ones to bear;
Help thy vain worlds to bear thy light.

Forgive what seemed my sin in me;
    What seemed my worth since I began;
    For merit lives from man to man,
And not from man, O Lord, to thee.

Forgive my grief for one removed,
    Thy creature, whom I found so fair.
    I trust he lives in thee, and there
40   I find him worthier to be loved.

Forgive these wild and wandering cries,
    Confusions of a wasted youth;
    Forgive them where they fail in truth,
And in thy wisdom make me wise.
    1849

    I
I held it truth, with him who sings
    To one clear harp in divers tones,
    That men may rise on stepping-stones
Of their dead selves to higher things.

But who shall so forecast the years
    And find in loss a gain to match?
    Or reach a hand through time to catch
The far-off interest of tears?

Let Love clasp Grief lest both be drowned,
   Let darkness keep her raven gloss:
   Ah, sweeter to be drunk with loss,
To dance with death, to beat the ground,

Than that the victor Hours should scorn
   The long result of love, and boast,
   'Behold the man that loved and lost,
But all he was is overworn.'

    ·   ·   ·

V

I sometimes hold it half a sin
   To put in words the grief I feel;
   For words, like Nature, half reveal
And half conceal the Soul within.

But, for the unquiet heart and brain,
   A use in measured language lies;
   The sad mechanic exercise,
Like dull narcotics, numbing pain.

In words, like weeds, I'll wrap me o'er,
   Like coarsest clothes against the cold:
   But that large grief which these enfold
Is given in outline and no more.

    ·   ·   ·

VII

Dark house, by which once more I stand
   Here in the long unlovely street,
   Doors, where my heart was used to beat
So quickly, waiting for a hand,

A hand that can be clasped no more—
   Behold me, for I cannot sleep,
   And like a guilty thing I creep
At earliest morning to the door.

He is not here; but far away
   The noise of life begins again,

And ghastly through the drizzling rain
On the bald street breaks the blank day.

   •   •   •

IX

Fair ship, that from the Italian shore
   Sailest the placid ocean-plains
   With my lost Arthur's loved remains,
Spread thy full wings, and waft him o'er.

So draw him home to those that mourn
   In vain; a favourable speed
   Ruffle thy mirrored mast, and lead
Through prosperous floods his holy urn.

All night no ruder air perplex
   Thy sliding keel, till Phosphor, bright
   As our pure love, through early light
Shall glimmer on the dewy decks.

Sphere all your lights around, above;
   Sleep, gentle heavens, before the prow;
   Sleep, gentle winds, as he sleeps now,
My friend, the brother of my love;

My Arthur, whom I shall not see
   Till all my widowed race be run;
   Dear as the mother to the son,
More than my brothers are to me.

   •   •   •

XV

Tonight the winds begin to rise
   And roar from yonder dropping day:
   The last red leaf is whirled away,
The rooks are blown about the skies;

The forest cracked, the waters curled,
   The cattle huddled on the lea;
   And wildly dashed on tower and tree
The sunbeam strikes along the world:

And but for fancies, which aver
   That all thy motions gently pass
   Athwart a plane of molten glass,
I scarce could brook the strain and stir

That makes the barren branches loud;
   And but for fear it is not so,
   The wild unrest that lives in woe
Would dote and pore on yonder cloud

That rises upward always higher,
   And onward drags a labouring breast,
   And topples round the dreary west,
A looming bastion fringed with fire.

     ·   ·   ·

XXIV

And was the day of my delight
   As pure and perfect as I say?
   The very source and fount of Day
Is dashed with wandering isles of night.

If all was good and fair we met,
   This earth had been the Paradise
   It never looked to human eyes
Since our first Sun arose and set.

And is it that the haze of grief
   Makes former gladness loom so great?
   The lowness of the present state,
That sets the past in this relief?

Or that the past will always win
   A glory from its being far;
   And orb into the perfect star
We saw not, when we moved therein?

     ·   ·   ·

XXVII

I envy not in any moods
   The captive void of noble rage,

The linnet born within the cage,
That never knew the summer woods:

I envy not the beast that takes
   His license in the field of time,
   Unfettered by the sense of crime,
To whom a conscience never wakes;

Nor, what may count itself as blest,
   The heart that never plighted troth
   But stagnates in the weeds of sloth;
Nor any want-begotten rest.

I hold it true, whate'er befall;
   I feel it, when I sorrow most;
   'Tis better to have loved and lost
Than never to have loved at all.

XXVIII

The time draws near the birth of Christ:
   The moon is hid; the night is still;
   The Christmas bells from hill to hill
Answer each other in the mist.

Four voices of four hamlets round,
   From far and near, on mead and moor,
   Swell out and fail, as if a door
Were shut between me and the sound:

Each voice four changes on the wind,
   That now dilate, and now decrease,
   Peace and goodwill, goodwill and peace,
Peace and goodwill, to all mankind.

This year I slept and woke with pain,
   I almost wished no more to wake,
   And that my hold on life would break
Before I heard those bells again:

But they my troubled spirit rule,
   For they controlled me when a boy;
   They bring me sorrow touched with joy,
The merry merry bells of Yule.

. . .

XXX

With trembling fingers did we weave
    The holly round the Christmas hearth;
    A rainy cloud possessed the earth,
And sadly fell our Christmas-eve.

At our old pastimes in the hall
    We gambolled, making vain pretence
    Of gladness, with an awful sense
Of one mute Shadow watching all.

We paused: the winds were in the beech:
    We heard them sweep the winter land;
    And in a circle hand-in-hand
Sat silent, looking each at each.

Then echo-like our voices rang;
    We sung, though every eye was dim,
    A merry song we sang with him
Last year: impetuously we sang:

We ceased: a gentler feeling crept
    Upon us: surely rest is meet:
    'They rest,' we said, 'their sleep is sweet,'
And silence followed, and we wept.

Our voices took a higher range;
    Once more we sang: They do not die
    Nor lose their mortal sympathy,
Nor change to us, although they change;

'Rapt from the fickle and the frail
    With gathered power, yet the same,
    Pierces the keen seraphic flame
From orb to orb, from veil to veil.'

Rise, happy morn, rise, holy morn,
    Draw forth the cheerful day from night:
    O Father, touch the east, and light
The light that shone when Hope was born.

.   .   .

XXXIV

My own dim life should teach me this,
    That life shall live for evermore,
    Else earth is darkness at the core,
And dust and ashes all that is;

This round of green, this orb of flame,
    Fantastic beauty; such as lurks
    In some wild Poet, when he works
Without a conscience or an aim.

What then were God to such as I?
    'Twere hardly worth my while to choose
    Of things all mortal, or to use
A little patience ere I die;

'Twere best at once to sink to peace,
    Like birds the charming serpent draws,
    To drop head-foremost in the jaws
Of vacant darkness and to cease.

XXXV

Yet if some voice that man could trust
    Should murmur from the narrow house,
    'The cheeks drop in; the body bows;
Man dies: nor is there hope in dust:'

Might I not say? 'Yet even here,
    But for one hour, O Love, I strive
    To keep so sweet a thing alive:'
But I should turn mine ears and hear

The moanings of the homeless sea,
    The sound of streams that swift or slow
    Draw down Aeonian hills, and sow
The dust of continents to be;

And Love would answer with a sigh,
    'The sound of that forgetful shore
    Will change my sweetness more and more,
Half-dead to know that I shall die.'

O me, what profits it to put
   An idle case? If Death were seen
   At first as Death, Love had not been,
Or been in narrowest working shut,

Mere fellowship of sluggish moods,
   Or in his coarsest Satyr-shape
   Had bruised the herb and crushed the grape,
And basked and battened in the woods.

   XXXVI
Though truths in manhood darkly join,
   Deep-seated in our mystic frame,
   We yield all blessing to the name
Of Him that made them current coin;

For Wisdom dealt with mortal powers,
   Where truth in closest words shall fail,
   When truth embodied in a tale
Shall enter in at lowly doors.

And so the Word had breath, and wrought
   With human hands the creed of creeds
   In loveliness of perfect deeds,
More strong than all poetic thought;

Which he may read that binds the sheaf,
   Or builds the house, or digs the grave,
   And those wild eyes that watch the wave
In roarings round the coral reef.

   XXXVII
Urania speaks with darkened brow:
   'Thou pratest here where thou art least;
   This faith has many a purer priest,
And many an abler voice than thou.

'Go down beside thy native rill,
   On thy Parnassus set thy feet,
   And hear thy laurel whisper sweet
About the ledges of the hill.'

And my Melpomene replies,
    A touch of shame upon her cheek:
    'I am not worthy even to speak
Of thy prevailing mysteries;

'For I am but an earthly Muse,
    And owning but a little art
    To lull with song an aching heart,
And render human love his dues;

'But brooding on the dear one dead,
    And all he said of things divine,
    (And dear to me as sacred wine
To dying lips is all he said),

'I murmured, as I came along,
    Of comfort clasped in truth revealed;
    And loitered in the master's field,
And darkened sanctities with song.'

    .   .   .

XLIX
From art, from nature, from the schools,
    Let random influences glance,
    Like light in many a shivered lance
That breaks about the dappled pools:

The lightest wave of thought shall lisp,
    The fancy's tenderest eddy wreathe,
    The slightest air of song shall breathe
To make the sullen surface crisp.

And look thy look, and go thy way,
    But blame not thou the winds that make
    The seeming-wanton ripple break,
The tender-pencilled shadow play,

Beneath all fancied hopes and fears
    Ay me, the sorrow deepens down,
    Whose muffled motions blindly drown
The bases of my life in tears.

L

Be near me when my light is low,
　　When the blood creeps, and the nerves prick
　　And tingle; and the heart is sick,
And all the wheels of Being slow.

Be near me when the sensuous frame
　　Is racked with pangs that conquer trust;
　　And Time, a maniac scattering dust,
And Life, a Fury slinging flame.

Be near me when my faith is dry,
　　And men the flies of latter spring,
　　That lay their eggs, and sting and sing
And weave their petty cells and die.

Be near me when I fade away,
　　To point the term of human strife,
　　And on the low dark verge of life
The twilight of eternal day.

LI

Do we indeed desire the dead
　　Should still be near us at our side?
　　Is there no baseness we would hide?
No inner vileness that we dread?

Shall he for whose applause I strove,
　　I had such reverence for his blame,
　　See with clear eye some hidden shame
And I be lessened in his love?

I wrong the grave with fears untrue:
　　Shall love be blamed for want of faith?
　　There must be wisdom with great Death:
The dead shall look me through and through.

Be near us when we climb or fall:
　　Ye watch, like God, the rolling hours
　　With larger other eyes than ours,
To make allowance for us all.

　　　·　　·　　·

LIV

Oh yet we trust that somehow good
   Will be the final goal of ill,
   To pangs of nature, sins of will,
Defects of doubt, and taints of blood;

That nothing walks with aimless feet;
   That not one life shall be destroyed,
   Or cast as rubbish to the void,
When God hath made the pile complete;

That not a worm is cloven in vain;
   That not a moth with vain desire
   Is shrivelled in a fruitless fire,
Or but subserves another's gain.

Behold, we know not anything;
   I can but trust that good shall fall
   At last—far off—at last, to all,
And every winter change to spring.

So runs my dream: but what am I?
   An infant crying in the night:
   An infant crying for the light:
And with no language but a cry.

LV

The wish, that of the living whole
   No life may fail beyond the grave,
   Derives it not from what we have
The likest God within the soul?

Are God and Nature then at strife,
   That Nature lends such evil dreams?
   So careful of the type she seems,
So careless of the single life;

That I, considering everywhere
   Her secret meaning in her deeds,
   And finding that of fifty seeds
She often brings but one to bear,

I falter where I firmly trod,
    And falling with my weight of cares
    Upon the great world's altar-stairs
That slope through darkness up to God,

I stretch lame hands of faith, and grope,
    And gather dust and chaff, and call
    To what I feel is Lord of all,
And faintly trust the larger hope.

LVI

'So careful of the type?' but no.
    From scarpèd cliff and quarried stone
    She cries, 'A thousand types are gone:
I care for nothing, all shall go.

'Thou makest thine appeal to me:
    I bring to life, I bring to death:
    The spirit does but mean the breath:
I know no more.' And he, shall he,

Man, her last work, who seemed so fair,
    Such splendid purpose in his eyes,
    Who rolled the psalm to wintry skies,
Who built him fanes of fruitless prayer,

Who trusted God was love indeed
    And love Creation's final law—
    Though Nature, red in tooth and claw
With ravine, shrieked against his creed—

Who loved, who suffered countless ills.
    Who battled for the True, the Just,
    Be blown about the desert dust,
Or sealed within the iron hills?

No more? A monster then, a dream,
    A discord. Dragons of the prime,
    That tare each other in their slime,
Were mellow music matched with him.

O life as futile, then, as frail!
    O for thy voice to soothe and bless!

What hope of answer, or redress?
Behind the veil, behind the veil.

. . .

LXVII

When on my bed the moonlight falls,
   I know that in thy place of rest
   By that broad water of the west,
There comes a glory on the walls;

Thy marble bright in dark appears,
   As slowly steals a silver flame
   Along the letters of thy name,
And o'er the number of thy years.

The mystic glory swims away;
   From off my bed the moonlight dies;
   And closing eaves of wearied eyes
I sleep till dusk is dipped in grey:

And then I know the mist is drawn
   A lucid veil from coast to coast,
   And in the dark church like a ghost
Thy tablet glimmers to the dawn.

. . .

LXXVII

What hope is here for modern rhyme
   To him, who turns a musing eye
   On songs, and deeds, and lives, that lie
Foreshortened in the tract of time?

These mortal lullabies of pain
   May bind a book, may line a box,
   May serve to curl a maiden's locks;
Or when a thousand moons shall wane

A man upon a stall may find,
   And, passing, turn the page that tells
   A grief, then changed to something else,
Sung by a long-forgotten mind.

But what of that? My darkened ways
    Shall ring with music all the same;
    To breathe my loss is more than fame,
To utter love more sweet than praise.

LXXVIII

Again at Christmas did we weave
    The holly round the Christmas hearth;
    The silent snow possessed the earth,
And calmly fell our Christmas-eve:

The yule-clog sparkled keen with frost,
    No wing of wind the region swept,
    But over all things brooding slept
The quiet sense of something lost.

As in the winters left behind,
    Again our ancient games had place,
    The mimic picture's breathing grace,
And dance and song and hoodman-blind.

Who showed a token of distress?
    No single tear, no mark of pain:
    O sorrow, then can sorrow wane?
O grief, can grief be changed to less?

O last regret, regret can die!
    No—mixed with all this mystic frame,
    Her deep relations are the same,
But with long use her tears are dry.

LXXIX

'More than my brothers are to me,'—
    Let this not vex thee, noble heart!
    I know thee of what force thou art
To hold the costliest love in fee.

But thou and I are one in kind,
    As moulded like in Nature's mint;
    And hill and wood and field did print
The same sweet forms in either mind.

For us the same cold streamlet curled
    Through all his eddying coves; the same

All winds that roam the twilight came
In whispers of the beauteous world.

At one dear knee we proffered vows,
    One lesson from one book we learned,
    Ere childhood's flaxen ringlet turned
To black and brown on kindred brows.

And so my wealth resembles thine,
    But he was rich where I was poor,
    And he supplied my want the more
As his unlikeness fitted mine.

.   .   .

XCV

By night we lingered on the lawn,
    For underfoot the herb was dry;
    And genial warmth; and o'er the sky
The silvery haze of summer drawn;

And calm that let the tapers burn
    Unwavering: not a cricket chirred:
    The brook alone far-off was heard,
And on the board the fluttering urn:

And bats went round in fragrant skies,
    And wheeled or lit the filmy shapes
    That haunt the dusk, with ermine capes
And woolly breasts and beaded eyes;

While now we sang old songs that pealed
    From knoll to knoll, where, couched at ease,
    The white kine glimmered, and the trees
Laid their dark arms about the field.

But when those others, one by one,
    Withdrew themselves from me and night,
    And in the house light after light
Went out, and I was all alone,

A hunger seized my heart; I read
    Of that glad year which once had been,

In those fallen leaves which kept their green,
The noble letters of the dead:

And strangely on the silence broke
    The silent-speaking words, and strange
    Was love's dumb cry defying change
To test his worth; and strangely spoke

The faith, the vigour, bold to dwell
    On doubts that drive the coward back,
    And keen through wordy snares to track
Suggestion to her inmost cell.

So word by word, and line by line,
    The dead man touched me from the past,
    And all at once it seemed at last
The living soul was flashed on mine,

And mine in this was wound, and whirled
    About empyreal heights of thought,
    And came on that which is, and caught
The deep pulsations of the world,

Aeonian music measuring out
    The steps of Time—the shocks of Chance—
    The blows of Death. At length my trance
Was cancelled, stricken through with doubt.

Vague words! but ah, how hard to frame
    In matter-moulded forms of speech,
    Or even for intellect to reach
Through memory that which I became:

Till now the doubtful dusk revealed
    The knolls once more where, couched at ease,
    The white kine glimmered, and the trees
Laid their dark arms about the field:

And sucked from out the distant gloom
    A breeze began to tremble o'er
    The large leaves of the sycamore,
And fluctuate all the still perfume,

And gathering freshlier overhead,
    Rocked the full-foliaged elms, and swung
    The heavy-folded rose, and flung
The lilies to and fro, and said

'The dawn, the dawn,' and died away;
    And East and West, without a breath,
    Mixed their dim lights, like life and death,
To broaden into boundless day.

.   .   .

CIII

On that last night before we went
    From out the doors where I was bred,
    I dreamed a vision of the dead,
Which left my after-morn content.

Methought I dwelt within a hall,
    And maidens with moi distant hills
    From hidden summits fed with rills
A river sliding by the wall.

The hall with harp and carol rang.
    They sang of what is wise and good
    And graceful. In the centre stood
A statue veiled, to which they sang;

And which, though veiled, was known to me,
    The shape of him I loved, and love
    For ever: then flew in a dove
And brought a summons from the sea:

And when they learnt that I must go
    They wept and wailed, but led the way
    To where a little shallop lay
At anchor in the flood below;

And on by many a level mead,
    And shadowing bluff that made the banks,
    We glided winding under ranks
Of iris, and the golden reed;

And still as vaster grew the shore
   And rolled the floods in grander space,
   The maidens gathered strength and grace
And presence, lordlier than before;

And I myself, who sat apart
   And watched them, waxed in every limb;
   I felt the thews of Anakim,
The pulses of a Titan's heart;

As one would sing the death of war,
   And one would chant the history
   Of that great race, which is to be,
And one the shaping of a star;

Until the forward-creeping tides
   Began to foam, and we to draw
   From deep to deep, to where we saw
A great ship lift her shining sides.

The man we loved was there on deck,
   But thrice as large as man he bent
   To greet us. Up the side I went,
And fell in silence on his neck:

Whereat those maidens with one mind
   Bewailed their lot; I did them wrong:
   'We served thee here,' they said, 'so long,
And wilt thou leave us now behind?'

So rapt I was, they could not win
   An answer from my lips, but he
   Replying, 'Enter likewise ye
And go with us'; they entered in.

And while the wind began to sweep
   A music out of sheet and shroud,
   We steered her toward a crimson cloud
That landlike slept along the deep.

CIV

The time draws near the birth of Christ;
   The moon is hid, the night is still;

A single church below the hill
Is pealing, folded in the mist.

A single peal of bells below,
    That wakens at this hour of rest
    A single murmur in the breast,
That these are not the bells I know.

Like strangers' voices here they sound,
    In lands where not a memory strays,
    Nor landmark breathes of other days,
But all is new unhallowed ground.

CV

Tonight ungathered let us leave
    This laurel, let this holly stand:
    We live within the stranger's land,
And strangely falls our Christmas-eve.

Our father's dust is left alone
    And silent under other snows:
    There in due time the woodbine blows,
The violet comes, but we are gone.

No more shall wayward grief abuse
    The genial hour with mask and mine;
    For change of place, like growth of time,
Has broke the bond of dying use.

Let cares that petty shadows cast,
    By which our lives are chiefly proved,
    A little spare the night I loved,
And hold it solemn to the past.

But let no footstep beat the floor,
    Nor bowl of wassail mantle warm;
    For who would keep an ancient form
Through which the spirit breathes no more?

Be neither song, nor game, nor feast;
    Nor harp be touched, nor flute be blown;
    No dance, no motion, save alone
What lightens in the lucid east

Of rising worlds by yonder wood.
   Long sleeps the summer in the seed;
   Run out your measured arcs, and lead
The closing cycle rich in good.

CVI

Ring out, wild bells, to the wild sky,
   The flying cloud, the frosty light:
   The year is dying in the night;
Ring out, wild bells, and let him die.

Ring out the old, ring in the new,
   Ring, happy bells, across the snow:
   The year is going, let him go;
Ring out the false, ring in the true.

Ring out the grief that saps the mind,
   For those that here we see no more;
   Ring out the feud of rich and poor,
Ring in redress to all mankind.

Ring out a slowly dying cause,
   And ancient forms of party strife;
   Ring in the nobler modes of life,
With sweeter manners, purer laws.

Ring out the want, the care, the sin,
   The faithless coldness of the times;
   Ring out, ring out my mournful rhymes,
But ring the fuller minstrel in.

Ring out false pride in place and blood,
   The civic slander and the spite;
   Ring in the love of truth and right,
Ring in the common love of good.

Ring out old shapes of foul disease;
   Ring out the narrowing lust of gold;
   Ring out the thousand wars of old,
Ring in the thousand years of peace.

Ring in the valiant man and free,
   The larger heart, the kindlier hand;

Ring out the darkness of the land,
Ring in the Christ that is to be.

.   .   .

CXVIII
Contemplate all this work of Time,
   The giant labouring in his youth;
   Nor dream of human love and truth,
As dying Nature's earth and lime;

But trust that those we call the dead
   Are breathers of an ampler day
   For ever nobler ends. They say,
The solid earth whereon we tread

In tracts of fluent heat began,
   And grew to seeming-random forms,
   The seeming prey of cyclic storms,
Till at the last arose the man;

Who throve and branched from clime to clime,
   The herald of a higher race,
   And of himself in higher place,
If so he type this work of time

Within himself, from more to more;
   Or, crowned with attributes of woe
   Like glories, move his course, and show
That life is not as idle ore,

But iron dug from central gloom,
   And heated hot with burning fears,
   And dipped in baths of hissing tears,
And battered with the shocks of doom

To shape and use. Arise and fly
   The reeling Faun, the sensual feast;
   Move upward, working out the beast,
And let the ape and tiger die.

.   .   .

CXX

I trust I have not wasted breath:
   I think we are not wholly brain,
   Magnetic mockeries; not in vain,
Like Paul with beasts, I fought with Death;

Not only cunning casts in clay:
   Let Science prove we are, and then
   What matters Science unto men,
At least to me? I would not stay.

Let him, the wiser man who springs
   Hereafter, up from childhood shape
   His action like the greater ape,
But I was *born* to other things.

.   .   .

CXXIII

There rolls the deep where grew the tree.
   O earth, what changes hast thou seen!
   There where the long street roars, hath been
The stillness of the central sea.

The hills are shadows, and they flow
   From form to form, and nothing stands;
   They melt like mist, the solid lands,
Like clouds they shape themselves and go.

But in my spirit will I dwell,
   And dream my dream, and hold it true;
   For though my lips may breathe adieu,
I cannot think the thing farewell.

CXXIV

That which we dare invoke to bless;
   Our dearest faith; our ghastliest doubt;
   He, They, One, All; within, without;
The Power in darkness whom we guess;

I found Him not in world or sun,
   Or eagle's wing, or insect's eye;

Nor through the questions men may try,
The petty cobwebs we have spun:

If e'er when faith had fallen asleep,
    I heard a voice 'believe no more'
    And heard an ever-breaking shore
That tumbled in the Godless deep;

A warmth within the breast would melt
    The freezing reason's colder part,
    And like a man in wrath the heart
Stood up and answered 'I have felt.'

No, like a child in doubt and fear:
    But that blind clamour made me wise;
    Then was I as a child that cries,
But, crying, knows his father near;

And what I am beheld again
    What is, and no man understands;
    And out of darkness came the hands
That reach through nature, moulding men.

   •   •   •

CXXVII
And all is well, though faith and form
    Be sundered in the night of fear;
    Well roars the storm to those that hear
A deeper voice across the storm,

Proclaiming social truth shall spread,
    And justice, even though thrice again
    The red fool-fury of the Seine
Should pile her barricades with dead.

But ill for him that wears a crown,
    And him, the lazar, in his rags:
    They tremble, the sustaining crags;
The spires of ice are toppled down,

And molten up, and roar in flood;
    The fortress crashes from on high,

The brute earth lightens to the sky,
And the great Aeon sinks in blood,

And compassed by the fires of Hell;
    While thou, dear spirit, happy star,
    O'erlook'st the tumult from afar,
And smilest, knowing all is well.

.   .   .

CXXIX

Dear friend, far off, my lost desire,
    So far, so near in woe and weal;
    O loved the most, when most I feel
There is a lower and a higher;

Known and unknown; human, divine;
    Sweet human hand and lips and eye;
    Dear heavenly friend that canst not die,
Mine, mine, for ever, ever mine;

Strange friend, past, present, and to be;
    Loved deeplier, darklier understood;
    Behold, I dream a dream of good,
And mingle all the world with thee.

CXXX

Thy voice is on the rolling air;
    I hear thee where the waters run;
    Thou standest in the rising sun,
And in the setting thou art fair.

What art thou then? I cannot guess;
    But though I seem in star and flower
    To feel thee some diffusive power,
I do not therefore love thee less:

My love involves the love before;
    My love is vaster passion now;
    Though mixed with God and Nature thou,
I seem to love thee more and more.

Far off thou art, but ever nigh;
    I have thee still, and I rejoice;

I prosper, circled with thy voice;
I shall not lose thee though I die.

CXXXI

O living will that shalt endure
  When all that seems shall suffer shock,
  Rise in the spiritual rock,
Flow through our deeds and make them pure,

That we may lift from out of dust
  A voice as unto him that hears,
  A cry above the conquered years
To one that with us works, and trust,

With faith that comes of self-control,
  The truths that never can be proved
  Until we close with all we loved,
And all we flow from, soul in soul.

———

[EPILOGUE]
O true and tried, so well and long,
  Demand not thou a marriage lay;
  In that it is thy marriage day
Is music more than any song.

.   .   .

And touch with shade the bridal doors,
  With tender gloom the roof, the wall;
  And breaking let the splendour fall
To spangle all the happy shores

By which they rest, and ocean sounds,
  And, star and system rolling past,
  A soul shall draw from out the vast
And strike his being into bounds,

And, moved through life of lower phase,
  Result in man, be born and think,
  And act and love, a closer link
Betwixt us and the crowning race

Of those that, eye to eye, shall look
  On knowledge; under whose command

Is Earth and Earth's, and in their hand
Is Nature like an open book;

No longer half-akin to brute,
   For all we thought and loved and did,
   And hoped, and suffered, is but seed
Of what in them is flower and fruit;

Whereof the man, that with me trod
   This planet, was a noble type
   Appearing ere the times were ripe,
That friend of mine who lives in God,

That God, which ever lives and loves,
   One God, one law, one element,
   And one far-off divine event,
To which the whole creation moves.
   1833–1850   1850

from Maud: A Monodrama

from Part I

XXII

I

850 Come into the garden, Maud,
   For the black bat, night, has flown,
Come into the garden, Maud,
   I am here at the gate alone;
And the woodbine spices are wafted abroad,
   And the musk of the rose is blown.

II

For a breeze of morning moves,
   And the planet of Love is on high,
Beginning to faint in the light that she loves
   On a bed of daffodil sky,
860 To faint in the light of the sun she loves,
   To faint in his light, and to die.

III

All night have the roses heard
   The flute, violin, bassoon;

All night has the casement jessamine stirred
    To the dancers dancing in tune;
Till a silence fell with the waking bird,
    And a hush with the setting moon.

IV

I said to the lily, 'There is but one
    With whom she has heart to be gay.
870   When will the dancers leave her alone?
    She is weary of dance and play.'
Now half to the setting moon are gone,
    And half to the rising day;
Low on the sand and loud on the stone
    The last wheel echoes away.

V

I said to the rose, 'The brief night goes
    In babble and revel and wine.
O young lord-lover, what sighs are those,
    For one that will never be thine?
880   But mine, but mine,' so I swore to the rose,
    'For ever and ever, mine.'

VI

And the soul of the rose went into my blood,
    As the music clashed in the hall;
And long by the garden lake I stood,
    For I heard your rivulet fall
From the lake to the meadow and on to the wood,
    Our wood, that is dearer than all;

VII

From the meadow your walks have left so sweet
    That whenever a March-wind sighs
890   He sets the jewel-print of your feet
    In violets blue as your eyes,
To the woody hollows in which we meet
    And the valleys of Paradise.

VIII

The slender acacia would not shake
    One long milk-bloom on the tree;
The white lake-blossom fell into the lake

As the pimpernel dozed on the lea;
But the rose was awake all night for your sake,
    Knowing your promise to me;
900 The lilies and roses were all awake,
    They sighed for the dawn and thee.

IX

Queen rose of the rosebud garden of girls,
    Come hither, the dances are done,
In gloss of satin and glimmer of pearls,
    Queen lily and rose in one;
Shine out, little head, sunning over with curls,
    To the flowers, and be their sun.

X

There has fallen a splendid tear
    From the passion-flower at the gate.
910 She is coming, my dove, my dear;
    She is coming, my life, my fate;
The red rose cries, 'She is near, she is near;'
    And the white rose weeps, 'She is late;'
The larkspur listens, 'I hear, I hear;'
    And the lily whispers, 'I wait.'

XI

She is coming, my own, my sweet;
    Were it ever so airy a tread,
My heart would hear her and beat,
    Were it earth in an earthy bed;
920 My dust would hear her and beat,
    Had I lain for a century dead;
Would start and tremble under her feet,
    And blossom in purple and red.

    •   •   •

from Part II

IV

I

O that 'twere possible
After long grief and pain

To find the arms of my true love
Round me once again!

II

When I was wont to meet her
In the silent woody places
By the home that gave me birth,
We stood tranced in long embraces
Mixed with kisses sweeter sweeter
150 Than anything on earth.

III

A shadow flits before me,
Not thou, but like to thee:
Ah Christ, that it were possible
For one short hour to see
The souls we loved, that they might tell us
What and where they be.

.   .   .

V

I

Dead, long dead,
240 Long dead!
And my heart is a handful of dust,
And the wheels go over my head,
And my bones are shaken with pain,
For into a shallow grave they are thrust,
Only a yard beneath the street,
And the hoofs of the horses beat, beat,
The hoofs of the horses beat,
Beat into my scalp and my brain,
With never an end to the stream of passing feet,
250 Driving, hurrying, marrying, burying,
Clamour and rumble, and ringing and clatter,
And here beneath it is all as bad,
For I thought the dead had peace, but it is not so;
To have no peace in the grave, is that not sad?
But up and down and to and fro,
Ever about me the dead men go;
And then to hear a dead man chatter
Is enough to drive one mad.

II

Wretchedest age, since Time began,
They cannot even bury a man;
And though we paid our tithes in the days that are gone,
Not a bell was rung, not a prayer was read;
It is that which makes us loud in the world of the dead;
There is none that does his work, not one;
A touch of their office might have sufficed,
But the churchmen fain would kill their church,
As the churches have killed their Christ.

.   .   .

Crossing the Bar

Sunset and evening star,
    And one clear call for me!
And may there be no moaning of the bar,
    When I put out to sea,

But such a tide as moving seems asleep,
    Too full for sound and foam,
When that which drew from out the boundless deep
    Turns again home.

Twilight and evening bell,
    And after that the dark!
And may there be no sadness of farewell,
    When I embark;

For though from out our bourne of Time and Place
    The flood may bear me far,
I hope to see my Pilot face to face
    When I have crossed the bar.
    1889   1889

EDWARD FITZGERALD

1809–1883

WE REMEMBER FITZGERALD for only one work, but that remains the most popular poem in the English language, incessantly read by people who do not read poetry. *The Rubáiyát of Omar Khayyám* (1859) probably will go on, since it is a startling fusion of high and popular art.

A great eccentric, fortunately endowed with private means, Fitzgerald made a dreadful mistake in 1856 by marrying the daughter of a deceased friend, the Quaker poet Bernard Barton. After a year of quarrels, the couple separated, and Fitzgerald solaced himself by composing his *Rubáiyát.*

The historical Omar Khayyám (1048–1131) was a renowned astronomer and mathematician but only a minor poet, content to write many epigrams. *Rubáiyát* simply means quatrains, following a rhyme scheme (*aaba*). A close friend, a scholar of Persian, made the manuscripts of Omar available to Fitzgerald. Published by an antiquarian bookseller and soon remaindered, Fitzgerald's *Rubáiyát* would have vanished utterly except that a copy reached Dante Gabriel Rossetti, who fell in love with the poem. Rossetti introduced it to his circle, including Algernon Charles Swinburne, William Morris, and George Meredith, and these enthusiasts made it known to a soon enthralled general reading public.

The poem became a transatlantic cult, and continues to be a part of Anglo-American literary culture. A close friend of Alfred, Lord Tennyson, the Epicurean pagan Fitzgerald composes his *Rubáiyát* with one eye (at least) upon Tennyson's *In Memoriam,* the antithesis of Fitzgerald's nihilistic vision.

✤   ✤   ✤

The Rubáiyát of Omar Khayyám

1

WAKE! For the Sun, who scatter'd into flight
The Stars before him from the Field of Night,
    Drives Night along with them from Heav'n, and strikes
The Sultán's Turret with a Shaft of Light.

2

Before the phantom of False morning died,
Methought a Voice within the Tavern cried,
    "When all the Temple is prepared within,
Why nods the drowsy Worshipper outside?"

3

And, as the Cock crew, those who stood before
The Tavern shouted—"Open then the Door!
    You know how little while we have to stay,
And, once departed, may return no more."

4

Now the New Year reviving old Desires,
The thoughtful Soul to Solitude retires,
    Where the WHITE HAND OF MOSES on the Bough
Puts out, and Jesus from the Ground suspires.

5

Iram indeed is gone with all his Rose,
And Jamshýd's Sev'n-ring'd Cup where no one knows;
    But still a Ruby kindles in the Vine,
And many a Garden by the Water blows.

6

And David's lips are lockt; but in divine
High-piping Pehleví, with "Wine! Wine! Wine!
    Red Wine!"—the Nightingale cries to the Rose
That sallow cheek of hers t' incarnadine.

7

Come, fill the Cup, and in the fire of Spring
Your Winter-garment of Repentance fling:
    The Bird of Time has but a little way
To flutter—and the Bird is on the Wing.

8

Whether at Naishápúr or Babylon,
Whether the Cup with sweet or bitter run,
    The Wine of Life keeps oozing drop by drop,
The Leaves of Life keep falling one by one.

9

Each Morn a thousand Roses brings, you say;
Yes, but where leaves the Rose of Yesterday?
    And this first Summer month that brings the Rose
Shall take Jamshýd and Kaikobád away.

10

Well, let it take them! What have we to do
With Kaikobád the Great, or Kaikhosrú?
    Let Zál and Rustum bluster as they will,
Or Hátim call to Supper—heed not you.

11

With me along the strip of Herbage strown
That just divides the desert from the sown,
    Where name of Slave and Sultán is forgot—
And Peace to Mahmúd on his golden Throne!

12

A Book of Verses underneath the Bough,
A Jug of Wine, a Loaf of Bread—and Thou
    Beside me singing in the Wilderness—
Oh, Wilderness were Paradise enow!

13

Some for the Glories of This World; and some
Sigh for the Prophet's Paradise to come;
    Ah, take the Cash, and let the Credit go,
Nor heed the rumble of a distant Drum!

14

Look to the blowing Rose about us—"Lo,
Laughing," she says, "into the world I blow,
    At once the silken tassel of my Purse
Tear, and its Treasure on the Garden throw."

15

And those who husbanded the Golden grain,
And those who flung it to the winds like Rain,
    Alike to no such aureate Earth are turn'd
As, buried once, Men want dug up again.

16

The Worldly Hope men set their Hearts upon
Turns Ashes—or it prospers; and anon,
    Like Snow upon the Desert's dusty Face,
Lighting a little hour or two—is gone.

17

Think, in this batter'd Caravanserai
Whose Portals are alternate Night and Day,
    How Sultán after Sultán with his Pomp
Abode his destined Hour, and went his way.

18

They say the Lion and the Lizard keep
The Courts where Jamshýd gloried and drank deep:
    And Bahrám, that great Hunter—the Wild Ass
Stamps o'er his Head, but cannot break his Sleep.

19

I sometimes think that never blows so red
The Rose as where some buried Cæsar bled;
    That every Hyacinth the Garden wears
Dropt in her Lap from some once lovely Head.

20

And this reviving Herb whose tender Green
Fledges the River-Lip on which we lean—
    Ah, lean upon it lightly! for who knows
From what once lovely Lip it springs unseen!

21

Ah, my Belovéd, fill the Cup that clears
TO-DAY of Past Regrets and Future Fears:
    To-morrow!—Why, To-morrow I may be
Myself with Yesterday's Sev'n Thousand Years.

22

For some we loved, the loveliest and the best
That from his Vintage rolling Time hath prest,
    Have drunk their Cup a Round or two before,
And one by one crept silently to rest.

23

And we, that now make merry in the Room
They left, and Summer dresses in new bloom
    Ourselves must we beneath the Couch of Earth
Descend—ourselves to make a Couch—for whom?

24

Ah, make the most of what we yet may spend,
Before we too into the Dust descend;
    Dust into Dust, and under Dust to lie
Sans Wine, sans Song, sans Singer, and—sans End!

25

Alike for those who for TO-DAY prepare,
And those that after some TO-MORROW stare,
    A Muezzín from the Tower of Darkness cries
"Fools! your Reward is neither Here nor There."

26

Why, all the Saints and Sages who discuss'd
Of the Two Worlds so wisely—they are thrust
    Like foolish Prophets forth; their Words to Scorn
Are scatter'd, and their Mouths are stopt with Dust.

27

Myself when young did eagerly frequent
Doctor and Saint, and heard great argument
    About it and about: but evermore
Came out by the same door where in I went.

28

With them the seed of Wisdom did I sow,
And with mine own hand wrought to make it grow;
    And this was all the Harvest that I reap'd—
"I came like Water, and like Wind I go."

29

Into this Universe, and *Why* not knowing
Nor *Whence,* like Water willy-nilly flowing;
    And out of it, as Wind along the Waste,
I know not *Whither,* willy-nilly blowing.

30

What, without asking, hither hurried *Whence?*
And, without asking, *Whither* hurried hence!
   Oh, many a Cup of this forbidden Wine
Must drown the memory of that insolence!

31

Up from Earth's Centre through the Seventh Gate
I rose, and on the Throne of Saturn sate;
   And many a Knot unravel'd by the Road;
But not the Master-knot of Human Fate.

32

There was the Door to which I found no Key;
There was the Veil through which I might not see:
   Some little talk awhile of ME and THEE
There was—and then no more of THEE and ME.

33

Earth could not answer; nor the Seas that mourn
In flowing Purple, of their Lord forlorn;
   Nor rolling Heaven, with all his Signs reveal'd
And hidden by the sleeve of Night and Morn.

34

Then of the THEE in ME who works behind
The Veil, I lifted up my hands to find
   A Lamp amid the Darkness; and I heard,
As from Without—"THE ME WITHIN THEE BLIND!"

35

Then to the lip of this poor earthen Urn
I lean'd, the Secret of my Life to learn:
   And Lip to Lip it murmur'd—"While you live
Drink!—for, once dead, you never shall return."

36

I think the Vessel, that with fugitive
Articulation answer'd, once did live,
   And drink; and Ah! the passive Lip I kiss'd,
How many Kisses might it take—and give!

37

For I remember stopping by the way
To watch a Potter thumping his wet Clay:
    And with its all-obliterated Tongue
It murmur'd—"Gently, Brother, gently, pray!"

38

And has not such a Story from of Old
Down Man's successive generations roll'd
    Of such a clod of saturated Earth
Cast by the Maker into Human mould?

39

And not a drop that from our Cups we throw
For Earth to drink of, but may steal below
    To quench the fire of Anguish in some Eye
There hidden—far beneath, and long ago.

40

As then the Tulip for her morning sup
Of Heav'nly Vintage from the soil looks up,
    Do you devoutly do the like, till Heav'n
To Earth invert you—like an empty Cup.

41

Perplext no more with Human or Divine,
To-morrow's tangle to the winds resign,
    And lose your fingers in the tresses of
The Cypress-slender Minister of Wine.

42

And if the Wine you drink, the Lip you press
End in what All begins and ends in—Yes;
    Think then you are TO-DAY what YESTERDAY
You were—TO-MORROW you shall not be less.

43

So when that Angel of the darker Drink
At last shall find you by the river-brink,
    And, offering his Cup, invite your Soul
Forth to your Lips to quaff—you shall not shrink.

44

Why, if the Soul can fling the Dust aside,
And naked on the Air of Heaven ride,
    Were't not a Shame—were't not a Shame for him
In this clay carcase crippled to abide?

45

'Tis but a Tent where takes his one day's rest
A Sultán to the realm of Death addrest;
    The Sultán rises, and the dark Ferrásh
Strikes, and prepares it for another Guest.

46

And fear not lest Existence closing your
Account, and mine, should know the like no more;
    The Eternal Sákí from that Bowl has pour'd
Millions of Bubbles like us, and will pour.

47

When You and I behind the Veil are past,
Oh, but the long, long while the World shall last,
    Which of our Coming and Departure heeds
As the Sea's self should heed a pebble-cast.

48

A Moment's Halt—a momentary taste
Of BEING from the Well amid the Waste—
    And Lo!—the phantom Caravan has reach'd
The NOTHING it set out from—Oh, make haste!

49

Would you that spangle of Existence spend
About THE SECRET—quick about it. Friend!
    A Hair perhaps divides the False and True—
And upon what, prithee, may life depend?

50

A Hair perhaps divides the False and True;
Yes; and a single Alif were the clue—
    Could you but find it—to the Treasure-house,
And peradventure to THE MASTER too;

51

Whose secret Presence, through Creation's veins
Running Quicksilver-like eludes your pains;
    Taking all shapes from Máh to Máhi; and
They change and perish all—but He remains;

52

A moment guess'd—then back behind the Fold
Immerst of Darkness round the Drama roll'd
    Which, for the Pastime of Eternity,
He doth Himself contrive, enact, behold.

53

But if in vain, down on the stubborn floor
Of Earth, and up to Heav'n's unopening Door
    You gaze TO-DAY, while You are You—how then
TO-MORROW, You when shall be You no more?

54

Waste not your Hour, nor in the vain pursuit
Of This and That endeavour and dispute;
    Better be jocund with the fruitful Grape
Than sadden after none, or bitter, Fruit.

55

You know, my Friends, with what a brave Carouse
I made a Second Marriage in my house;
    Divorced old barren Reason from my Bed
And took the Daughter of the Vine to Spouse.

56

For "Is" and "Is-NOT" though with Rule and Line
And "UP-AND-DOWN" by Logic I define,
    Of all that one should care to fathom, I
Was never deep in anything but—Wine.

57

Ah, but my Computations, People say,
Reduced the Year to better reckoning?—Nay
    'Twas only striking from the Calendar
Unborn To-morrow, and dead Yesterday.

58

And lately, by the Tavern Door agape,
Came shining through the Dusk an Angel Shape
    Bearing a Vessel on his Shoulder; and
He bid me taste of it; and 'twas—the Grape!

59

The Grape that can with Logic absolute
The Two-and-Seventy jarring Sects confute:
    The sovereign Alchemist that in a trice
Life's leaden metal into Gold transmute:

60

The mighty Mahmúd, Allah-breathing Lord
That all the misbelieving and black Horde
    Of Fears and Sorrows that infest the Soul
Scatters before him with his whirlwind Sword.

61

Why, be this Juice the growth of God, who dare
Blaspheme the twisted tendril as a Snare?
    A Blessing, we should use it, should we not?
And if a Curse—why, then, Who set it there?

62

I must abjure the Balm of Life, I must,
Scared by some After-reckoning ta'en on trust,
    Or lured with Hope of some Diviner Drink,
To fill the Cup—when crumbled into Dust!

63

Oh, threats of Hell and Hopes of Paradise!
One thing at least is certain—*This* Life flies;
    One thing is certain and the rest is Lies;
The Flower that once has blown for ever dies.

64

Strange, is it not? that of the myriads who
Before us pass'd the door of Darkness through,
    Not one returns to tell us of the Road,
Which to discover we must travel too.

65

The Revelations of Devout and Learn'd
Who rose before us, and as Prophets burn'd
    Are all but Stories, which, awoke from Sleep,
They told their comrades, and to Sleep return'd.

66

I sent my Soul through the Invisible,
Some letter of that After-life to spell:
    And by and by my Soul return'd to me,
And answer'd "I Myself am Heav'n and Hell:"

67

Heav'n but the Vision of fulfill'd Desire,
And Hell the Shadow from a Soul on fire,
    Cast on the Darkness into which Ourselves,
So late emerged from, shall so soon expire.

68

We are no other than a moving row
Of Magic Shadow-shapes that come and go
    Round with the Sun-illumined Lantern held
In Midnight by the Master of the Show;

69

But helpless Pieces of the Game He plays
Upon this Chequer-board of Nights and Days;
    Hither and thither moves, and checks, and slays,
And one by one back in the Closet lays.

70

The Ball no question makes of Ayes and Noes,
But Here or There as strikes the Player goes;
    And He that toss'd you down into the Field,
He knows about it all—HE knows—HE knows!

71

The Moving Finger writes; and, having writ,
Moves on: nor all your Piety nor Wit
    Shall lure it back to cancel half a Line,
Nor all your Tears wash out a Word of it.

72

And that inverted Bowl they call the Sky,
Whereunder crawling coop'd we live and die,
   Lift not your hands to *It* for help—for It
As impotently moves as you or I.

73

With Earth's first Clay They did the Last Man knead,
And there of the Last Harvest sow'd the Seed:
   And the first Morning of Creation wrote
What the Last Dawn of Reckoning shall read.

74

YESTERDAY *This* Day's Madness did prepare;
TO-MORROW'S Silence, Triumph, or Despair:
   Drink! for you know not whence you came, nor why:
Drink! for you know not why you go, nor where.

75

I tell you this—When, started from the Goal,
Over the flaming shoulders of the Foal
   Of Heav'n Parwín and Mushtarí they flung
In my predestined Plot of Dust and Soul

76

The Vine had struck a fibre: which about
If clings my being—let the Dervish flout;
   Of my Base metal may be filed a Key,
That shall unlock the Door he howls without.

77

And this I know: whether the one True Light
Kindle to Love, or Wrath-consume me quite,
   One Flash of It within the Tavern caught
Better than in the Temple lost outright.

78

What! out of senseless Nothing to provoke
A conscious Something to resent the yoke
   Of unpermitted Pleasure, under pain
Of Everlasting Penalties, if broke!

79

What! from his helpless Creature be repaid
Pure Gold for what he lent him dross-allay'd—
    Sue for a Debt he never did contract,
And cannot answer—Oh, the sorry trade!

80

Oh, Thou, who didst with pitfall and with gin
Beset the Road I was to wander in,
    Thou wilt not with Predestined Evil round
Enmesh, and then impute my Fall to Sin!

81

Oh, Thou, who Man of baser Earth didst make,
And ev'n with Paradise devise the Snake:
    For all the Sin wherewith the Face of Man
Is blacken'd—Man's forgiveness give—and take!

82

As under cover of departing Day
Slunk hunger-stricken Ramazán away,
    Once more within the Potter's house alone
I stood, surrounded by the Shapes of Clay.

83

Shapes of all Sorts and Sizes, great and small,
That stood along the floor and by the wall;
    And some loquacious Vessels were; and some
Listen'd perhaps, but never talk'd at all.

84

Said one among them—"Surely not in vain
My substance of the common Earth was ta'en
    And to this Figure moulded, to be broke,
Or trampled back to shapeless Earth again."

85

Then said a Second—"Ne'er a peevish Boy
Would break the Bowl from which he drank in joy,
    And He that with his hand the Vessel made
Will surely not in after Wrath destroy."

86

After a momentary silence spake
Some Vessel of a more ungainly Make;
    "They sneer at me for leaning all awry:
What! did the Hand then of the Potter shake?"

87

Whereat some one of the loquacious Lot—
I think a Súfi pipkin—waxing hot—
    "All this of Pot and Potter—Tell me then,
Who is the Potter, pray, and who the Pot?"

88

"Why," said another, "Some there are who tell
Of one who threatens he will toss to Hell
    The luckless Pots he marr'd in making—Pish!
He's a Good Fellow, and 'twill all be well."

89

"Well," murmur'd one, "Let whose make or buy,
My Clay with long Oblivion is gone dry:
    But fill me with the old familiar Juice,
Methinks I might recover by and by."

90

So while the Vessels one by one were speaking,
The little Moon look'd in that all were seeking:
    And then they jogg'd each other, "Brother! Brother!
Now for the Porter's shoulder-knot a-creaking!"

91

Ah, with the Grape my fading Life provide,
And wash the Body whence the Life has died,
    And lay me, shrouded in the living Leaf,
By some not unfrequented Garden-side.

92

That ev'n my buried Ashes such a snare
Of Vintage shall fling up into the Air
    As not a True-believer passing by
But shall be overtaken unaware.

93

Indeed the Idols I have loved so long
Have done my credit in this World much wrong:
    Have drown'd my Glory in a shallow Cup
And sold my Reputation for a Song.

94

Indeed, indeed, Repentance oft before
I swore—but was I sober when I swore?
    And then and then came Spring, and Rose-in-hand
My thread-bare Penitence apieces tore.

95

And much as Wine has play'd the Infidel,
And robb'd me of my Robe of Honour—Well,
    I wonder often what the Vintners buy
One half so precious as the stuff they sell.

96

Yet Ah, that Spring should vanish with the Rose!
That Youth's sweet-scented manuscript should close!
    The Nightingale that in the branches sang,
Ah, whence, and whither flown again, who knows!

97

Would but the Desert of the Fountain yield
One glimpse—if dimly, yet indeed, reveal'd,
    To which the fainting Traveller might spring,
As springs the trampled herbage of the field!

98

Would but some wingèd Angel ere too late
Arrest the yet unfolded Roll of Fate,
    And make the stern Recorder otherwise
Enregister, or quite obliterate!

99

Ah, Love! could you and I with Him conspire
To grasp this sorry Scheme of Things entire,
    Would not we shatter it to bits—and then
Re-mould it nearer to the Heart's Desire!

100

Yon rising Moon that looks for us again—
How oft hereafter will she wax and wane;
  How oft hereafter rising look for us
Through this same Garden—and for *one* in vain!

101

And when like her, oh, Sákí, you shall pass
Among the Guests Star-scatter'd on the Grass,
  And in your joyous errand reach the spot
Where I made One—turn down an empty Glass!

TAMÁM

[1859, 1868, 1872, 1879]

ROBERT BROWNING

1812–1889

BROWNING WAS BORN on May 7, 1812, in an outlying district of London. He was the firstborn child of his wealthy parents. His father worked for the Bank of England but had intense artistic and scholarly interests. The young Browning was raised surrounded by the six thousand volumes of a superb library. Browning's mother was an evangelical Protestant, and her religious stance, in greatly altered form, remained alive in Browning's consciousness.

Educated mostly at home after fourteen, Browning made up his mind to be a poet, and pursuaded his reluctant family. Emotionally very close to his mother, Browning partly overcame his own Oedipal anxieties in regard to her, but there was a lasting effect upon his life and work. In 1826, when Browning was fourteen, he received a small, pirated edition of Shelley's lyrics, and this major influence upon his poetry began with some violence. Under Shelley's initial impact, Browning denied his mother's religion. His first important poem, *Pauline,* clearly based on Shelley's *Alastor,* tells the sorrow of the battle and the lasting shame of the boy's defeat. His love for his mother was stronger than his esteem for his own integrity, and so he gave up. Something crucial in him never forgot.

Pauline had no sale, but the young John Stuart Mill read a review copy, and his written comments reached and affected Browning. Mill, a great authority on self-consciousness, saw clearly that *Pauline* did not purge the young poet of that condition, and that Browning was free neither of Shelleyanism nor of the psychological consequences of having given up his rebellion against mother and religion. Attempting to resolve his conflicts, Browning wrote two more verse romances in the Shelleyan mode, *Paracelsus* (1835) and *Sordello* (1840). Neither is a success, yet each is remarkable and difficult, particularly *Sordello*, which baffled whoever read it. His quest had induced Browning to create a nightmare of history mixed with personal reflections that is repeated by his poetic disciple, Ezra Pound, in the *Cantos*. Between 1840 and 1842, when *Dramatic Lyrics* appeared, Browning accomplished a superb metamorphosis of his Shelleyan heritage, and emerged with his characteristic and triumphant form, the dramatic monologue.

In 1844 Browning revisited Italy, and decided it was his true home. He returned lonesomely to England, and began in January 1845 a correspondence with the invalid poet Elizabeth Barrett. This notorious and difficult courtship continued for almost two years, as the thirty-three-year-old Browning attempted to persuade the thirty-nine-year-old Elizabeth. The lovers did not meet until May 1845, and a reading of the correspondence both fascinates and troubles, as Browning wavered continually, desiring the lady, but wishing her to be the stronger and make the final decision. On September 19, 1846, these two demanding beings somehow managed to elope together to Italy.

The Brownings' life together was reasonably happy, though it had its hidden difficulties, and some open conflicts. Unfortunately, it lasted only fifteen years, until Mrs. Browning suddenly died on June 29, 1861, in Florence, where they had lived for some years. Browning was left with a son, born in 1849, the year also of Browning's mother's death, which affected him almost as deeply as his wife's, twelve years later. For many reasons, including his wariness at yielding up his new freedom but also because in a way he had become the prisoner of his own myth of perfect married love, Browning never remarried, but he became a social lion both in London and in Italy, and experienced some passionate involvements. His caution fell away once, in 1869, when he proposed marriage to Lady Ashburton, but he suffered the pain of being rejected.

When Browning fell in love with Elizabeth Barrett, she had a more considerable poetical reputation than he did, despite the *Dramatic Lyrics* of 1842 and the *Dramatic Romances* of 1845. Indeed, throughout even the

1850s, Browning was better known as a husband than as a poet. But in 1855 Browning published his first masterpiece, the fifty magnificent monologues of the two-volume *Men and Women,* and though only a few discerning poets and critics at first realized his achievement, the book's fame increased over a decade. In 1864, *Dramatis Personae,* a collection almost as powerful, appeared, to be followed by his culminating work and second masterpiece, the long poem *The Ring and the Book,* in 1868. After that, and until his death, Browning at last achieved an audience and critical reputation almost equal to Tennyson's. For the final twenty years, there was a falling off in Browning's poetry. There are, however, some remarkable lyrics in his last volume, *Asolando: Fancies and Facts,* published in London on December 12, 1889, the day that Browning died in Venice, at the house of his son.

Browning is the most considerable poet in English since the major Romantics, surpassing his great contemporary rival Tennyson and the principal twentieth-century poets, including even Yeats, Hardy, and Wallace Stevens. But Browning is a very difficult poet, notoriously badly served by criticism, and ill-served also by his own accounts of what he was doing as a poet. His public statements and letters, his conversational asides, and the implicit polemic of his one important essay (inevitably on Shelley) all work together to emphasize the dramatic and objective elements in his poetry. Thus, his essay on Shelley implicitly claims kinship for himself with Shakespeare, classified as the supreme objective poet, as against Shelley, who is judged (with reverence) the outstanding example of the subjective poet. In the advertisement to the original *Dramatic Lyrics* of 1842, Browning insisted that the poems were, "though for the most part Lyric in expression, always Dramatic in principle, and so many utterances of so many imaginary persons, not mine." This insistence he maintained until the end.

Clearly, Browning himself could not be the varied group that included Johannes Agricola, the tomb-ordering Bishop, Fra Lippo Lippi, Childe Roland, Andrea del Sarto, Cleon, Abt Vogler, Caliban, the Pope of *The Ring and the Book,* and dozens more, but just as clearly his relation to them is not that of Shakespeare to Antony, Lear, Hamlet, Falstaff, Prospero, and the rest, or of Chaucer to his fellow pilgrims. Browning's form is dramatic, but his imaginative procedure is not. His company of ruined questers, imperfect poets, self-sabotaged artists, failed lovers, inspired fanatics, charlatans, monomaniacs, and self-deceiving confidence men all have a certain family resemblance. We harm Browning by comparing his work to Shakespeare's or Chaucer's, not because his range and depth of characterization are narrow and shallow compared with theirs, but because his poems are neither dramatic nor monologues, but something else. They are not dramatic, but lyrical and subjective, despite their coverings and gestures, and they are not monologues, but antiphons in which many voices speak, including several that belong to Browning himself. Browning, in his uncanny greatness, is a kind of psychological atomist, like Blake, Balzac, Proust, Kafka, Lawrence, Yeats, and some other modern innovators. In his work, older conceptions of personality disappear, and a more incoherent individual continuity is allowed to express the truths of actual existence. Whether Browning ever understood how wide the chasm between his own inner and outer selves had become, his art constantly explores the multiplicity of selves that inhabit apparently single, unitary personalities, some of them not at all unlike some of his own. Each of his men and women is at least several men and women, and his lovers learn that we can never embrace any one person at a time, but only the whole of an incoherence, the cluster of voices and beings that jostles in any separate self.

Browning had swerved away from the remorseless, questing, lyrical art of Shelley, where the poet seeks to fulfill desire by associating desire with the Intellectual Beauty that manifests itself just beyond the range of the senses. In Browning's vision the family resemblance to Shelley remains very strong, for all of his beings suffer from a quester's temperament, are self-deceived, and seek a sensuous fulfillment, yet manage all too frequently to turn aside from any fate as being inadequate to the contradictory desires of their own crowded selves.

The uniqueness of Browning's art might have dismayed him, if he could see it in the perspective of a hundred years after, for he meant his speakers to give us their involuntary self-revelations, and just as strongly he did *not* mean them to give us his. Yet when you read your way into his world, precisely his largest gift to you is his involuntary unfolding of one of the largest, most enigmatic, and most multipersoned literary and human selves you can hope to encounter. In a brilliant monologue by the contemporary poet Richard Howard, "November, 1889," Browning is made to observe: "I am not interested in art, but in the obstacles to art." His poems, obsessed with those obstacles, do more to remove them than any others of the last century.

✢   ✢   ✢

My Last Duchess

Ferrara

That's my last Duchess painted on the wall,
Looking as if she were alive. I call
That piece a wonder, now: Frà Pandolf's hands
Worked busily a day, and there she stands.
Will't please you sit and look at her? I said
'Fra Pandolf' by design, for never read
Strangers like you that pictured countenance,
The depth and passion of its earnest glance,
But to myself they turned (since none puts by
10   The curtain I have drawn for you, but I)
And seemed as they would ask me, if they durst,
How such a glance came there; so, not the first
Are you to turn and ask thus. Sir, 'twas not
Her husband's presence only, called that spot
Of joy into the Duchess' cheek: perhaps
Frà Pandolf chanced to say 'Her mantle laps
Over my lady's wrist too much,' or 'Paint
Must never hope to reproduce the faint
Half-flush that dies along her throat:' such stuff
20   Was courtesy, she thought, and cause enough
For calling up that spot of joy. She had
A heart—how shall I say?—too soon made glad,
Too easily impressed; she liked whate'er
She looked on, and her looks went everywhere.
Sir, 'twas all one! My favour at her breast,
The dropping of the daylight in the West,
The bough of cherries some officious fool
Broke in the orchard for her, the white mule
She rode with round the terrace—all and each
30   Would draw from her alike the approving speech,
Or blush, at least. She thanked men,—good! but thanked
Somehow—I know not how—as if she ranked
My gift of a nine-hundred-years-old name
With anybody's gift. Who'd stoop to blame
This sort of trifling? Even had you skill
In speech—(which I have not)—to make your will
Quite clear to such an one, and say, 'Just this
Or that in you disgusts me; here you miss,
Or there exceed the mark'—and if she let
40   Herself be lessoned so, nor plainly set

Her wits to yours, forsooth, and made excuse,
—E'en then would be some stooping; and I choose
Never to stoop. Oh sir, she smiled, no doubt,
Whene'er I passed her; but who passed without
Much the same smile? This grew; I gave commands;
Then all smiles stopped together. There she stands
As if alive. Will't please you rise? We'll meet
The company below, then. I repeat,
The Count your master's known munificence
50 Is ample warrant that no just pretence
Of mine for dowry will be disallowed;
Though his fair daughter's self, as I avowed
At starting, is my object. Nay, we'll go
Together down, sir. Notice Neptune, though,
Taming a sea-horse, thought a rarity,
Which Claus of Innsbruck cast in bronze for me!

    1842   1842

Fra Lippo Lippi

I am poor brother Lippo, by your leave!
You need not clap your torches to my face.
Zooks, what's to blame? you think you see a monk!
What, 'tis past midnight, and you go the rounds,
And here you catch me at an alley's end
Where sportive ladies leave their doors ajar?
The Carmine's my cloister: hunt it up,
Do,—harry out, if you must show your zeal,
Whatever rat, there, haps on his wrong hole,
10 And nip each softling of a wee white mouse,
Weke, weke, that's crept to keep him company!
Aha, you know your betters? Then, you'll take
Your hand away that's fiddling on my throat,
And please to know me likewise. Who am I?
Why, one, sir, who is lodging with a friend
Three streets off—he's a certain . . . how d'ye call?
Master—a . . . Cosimo of the Medici,
In the house that caps the corner. Boh! you were best!
Remember and tell me, the day you're hanged,
20 How you affected such a gullet's-gripe!
But you, sir, it concerns you that your knaves
Pick up a manner nor discredit you:

Zooks, are we pilchards, that they sweep the streets
And count fair prize what comes into their net?
He's Judas to a tittle, that man is!
Just such a face! Why, sir, you make amends.
Lord, I'm not angry! Bid your hangdogs go
Drink out this quarter-florin to the health
Of the munificent House that harbours me
30   (And many more beside, lads! more beside!)
And all's come square again. I'd like his face—
His, elbowing on his comrade in the door
With the pike and lantern,—for the slave that holds
John Baptist's head a-dangle by the hair
With one hand ('Look you, now,' as who should say)
And his weapon in the other, yet unwiped!
It's not your chance to have a bit of chalk,
A wood-coal or the like? or you should see!
Yes, I'm the painter, since you style me so.
40   What, brother Lippo's doings, up and down,
You know them and they take you? like enough!
I saw the proper twinkle in your eye—
'Tell you, I liked your looks at very first.
Let's sit and set things straight now, hip to haunch.
Here's spring come, and the nights one makes up bands
To roam the town and sing out carnival,
And I've been three weeks shut within my mew,
A-painting for the great man, saints and saints
And saints again. I could not paint all night—
50   Ouf! I leaned out of window for fresh air.
There came a hurry of feet and little feet,
A sweep of lute-strings, laughs, and whifts of song,—
Flower o' the broom,
Take away love, and our earth is a tomb!
Flower o' the quince,
I let Lisa go, and what good in life since?
Flower o' the thyme—and so on. Round they went.
Scarce had they turned the corner when a titter
Like the skipping of rabbits by moonlight,—three slim shapes,
60   And a face that looked up . . . zooks, sir, flesh and blood,
That's all I'm made of! Into shreds it went,
Curtain and counterpane and coverlet,
All the bed furniture—a dozen knots,
There was a ladder! Down I let myself,
Hands and feet, scrambling somehow, and so dropped,

And after them. I came up with the fun
Hard by St. Laurence, hail fellow, well met.—
Flower o' the rose,
If I've been merry, what matter who knows?
70 And so as I was stealing back again
To get to bed and have a bit of sleep
Ere I rise up to-morrow and go work
On Jerome knocking at his poor old breast
With his great round stone to subdue the flesh,
You snap me of the sudden. Ah, I see!
Though your eye twinkles still, you shake your head—
Mine's shaved,—a monk, you say—the sting's in that!
If Master Cosimo announced himself,
Mum's the word naturally; but a monk!
80 Come, what am I a beast for? tell us, now!
I was a baby when my mother died
And father died and left me in the street.
I starved there, God knows how, a year or two
On fig-skins, melon-parings, rinds and shucks,
Refuse and rubbish. One fine frosty day,
My stomach being empty as your hat,
The wind doubled me up and down I went.
Old Aunt Lapaccia trussed me with one hand,
(Its fellow was a stinger as I knew)
90 And so along the wall, over the bridge,
By the straight cut to the convent. Six words there,
While I stood munching my first bread that month:
'So, boy, you're minded,' quoth the good fat father
Wiping his own mouth, 'twas refection-time,—
'To quit this very miserable world?
Will you renounce' . . . 'the mouthful of bread?' thought I;
By no means! Brief, they made a monk of me;
I did renounce the world, its pride and greed,
Palace, farm, villa, shop and banking-house,
100 Trash, such as these poor devils of Medici
Have given their hearts to—all at eight years old.
Well, sir, I found in time, you may be sure,
'Twas not for nothing—the good bellyful,
The warm serge and the rope that goes all round,
And day-long blessed idleness beside!
'Let's see what the urchin's fit for'—that came next.
Not overmuch their way, I must confess.
Such a to-do! they tried me with their books:

Lord, they'd have taught me Latin in pure waste!
110   *Flower o' the clove,*
All the Latin I construe is, 'amo' I love!
But, mind you, when a boy starves in the streets
Eight years together, as my fortune was,
Watching folk's faces to know who will fling
The bit of half-stripped grape-bunch he desires,
And who will curse or kick him for his pains,—
Which gentleman processional and fine,
Holding a candle to the Sacrament,
Will wink and let him lift a plate and catch
120   The droppings of the wax to sell again,
Or holla for the Eight and have him whipped,—
How say I?—nay, which dog bites, which lets drop
His bone from the heap of offal in the street,—
Why, soul and sense of him grow sharp alike,
He learns the look of things, and none the less
For admonition from the hunger-pinch.
I had a store of such remarks, be sure,
Which, after I found leisure, turned to use.
I drew men's faces on my copy-books,
130   Scrawled them within the antiphonary's marge,
Joined legs and arms to the long music-notes,
Found eyes and nose and chin for A's and B's,
And made a string of pictures of the world
Betwixt the ins and outs of verb and noun,
On the wall, the bench, the door. The monks looked black.
'Nay,' quoth the Prior, 'turn him out, d'ye say?
In no wise. Lose a crow and catch a lark.
What if at last we get our man of parts,
We Carmelites, like those Camaldolese
140   And Preaching Friars, to do our church up fine
And put the front on it that ought to be!'
And hereupon he bade me daub away.
Thank you! my head being crammed, the walls a blank,
Never was such prompt disemburdening.
First, every sort of monk, the black and white,
I drew them, fat and lean: then, folk at church,
From good old gossips waiting to confess
Their cribs of barrel-droppings, candle-ends,—
To the breathless fellow at the altar-foot,
150   Fresh from his murder, safe and sitting there
With the little children round him in a row

Of admiration, half for his beard and half
For that white anger of his victim's son
Shaking a fist at him with one fierce arm,
Signing himself with the other because of Christ
(Whose sad face on the cross sees only this
After the passion of a thousand years)
Till some poor girl, her apron o'er her head,
(Which the intense eyes looked through) came at eve
160 On tiptoe, said a word, dropped in a loaf,
Her pair of earrings and a bunch of flowers
(The brute took growling), prayed, and so was gone.
I painted all, then cried, ' 'Tis ask and have;
Choose, for more's ready!'—laid the ladder flat,
And showed my covered bit of cloister-wall.
The monks closed in a circle and praised loud
Till checked, taught what to see and not to see,
Being simple bodies,—'That's the very man!
Look at the boy who stoops to pat the dog!
170 That woman's like the Prior's niece who comes
To care about his asthma: it's the life!
But there my triumph's straw-fire flared and funked;
Their betters took their turn to see and say:
The Prior and the learnèd pull a face
And stopped all that in no time. 'How? what's here?
Quite from the mark of painting, bless us all!
Faces, arms, legs and bodies like the true
As much as pea and pea! it's devil's-game!
Your business is not to catch men with show,
180 With homage to the perishable clay,
But lift them over it, ignore it all,
Make them forget there's such a thing as flesh.
Your business is to paint the souls of men—
Man's soul, and it's a fire, smoke . . . no, it's not . . .
It's vapour done up like a new-born babe—
(In that shape when you die it leaves your mouth)
It's . . . well, what matters talking, it's the soul!
Give us no more of body than shows soul!
Here's Giotto, with his Saint a-praising God,
190 That sets up praising,—why not stop with him?
Why put all thoughts of praise out of our head
With wonder at lines, colours, and what not?
Paint the soul, never mind the legs and arms!
Rub all out, try at it a second time.

Oh, that white smallish female with the breasts,
She's just my niece . . . Herodias, I would say,—
Who went and danced and got men's heads cut off!
Have it all out!' Now, is this sense, I ask?
A fine way to paint soul, by painting body
So ill, the eye can't stop there, must go further
And can't fare worse! Thus, yellow does for white
When what you put for yellow's simply black,
And any sort of meaning looks intense
When all beside itself means and looks nought.
Why can't a painter lift each foot in turn,
Left foot and right foot, go a double step,
Make his flesh liker and his soul more like,
Both in their order? Take the prettiest face,
The Prior's niece . . . patron-saint—is it so pretty
You can't discover if it means hope, fear,
Sorrow or joy? won't beauty go with these?
Suppose I've made her eyes all right and blue,
Can't I take breath and try to add life's flash,
And then add soul and heighten them threefold?
Or say there's beauty with no soul at all—
(I never saw it—put the case the same—)
If you get simple beauty and nought else,
You get about the best thing God invents:
That's somewhat: and you'll find the soul you have missed,
Within yourself, when you return him thanks.
'Rub all out!' Well, well, there's my life, in short,
And so the thing has gone on ever since.
I'm grown a man no doubt, I've broken bounds:
You should not take a fellow eight years old
And make him swear to never kiss the girls.
I'm my own master, paint now as I please—
Having a friend, you see, in the Corner-house!
Lord, it's fast holding by the rings in front—
Those great rings serve more purposes than just
To plant a flag in, or tie up a horse!
And yet the old schooling sticks, the old grave eyes
Are peeping o'er my shoulder as I work,
The heads shake still—'It's art's decline, my son!
You're not of the true painters, great and old;
Brother Angelico's the man, you'll find;
Brother Lorenzo stands his single peer:
Fag on at flesh, you'll never make the third!'

Flower o' the pine,
You keep your mistr . . . manners, and I'll stick to mine!

240 I'm not the third, then: bless us, they must know!
Don't you think they're the likeliest to know.
They with their Latin? So, I swallow my rage,
Clench my teeth, suck my lips in tight, and paint
To please them—sometimes do and sometimes don't;
For, doing most, there's pretty sure to come
A turn, some warm eve finds me at my saints—
A laugh, a cry, the business of the world—
(*Flower o' the peach,*
Death for us all, and his own life for each!)
250 And my whole soul revolves, the cup runs over,
The world and life's too big to pass for a dream,
And I do these wild things in sheer despite,
And play the fooleries you catch me at,
In pure rage! The old mill-horse, out at grass
After hard years, throws up his stiff heels so,
Although the miller does not preach to him
The only good of grass is to make chaff.
What would men have? Do they like grass or no—
May they or mayn't they? all I want's the thing
260 Settled for ever one way. As it is,
You tell too many lies and hurt yourself:
You don't like what you only like too much,
You do like what, if given you at your word,
You find abundantly detestable.
For me, I think I speak as I was taught;
I always see the garden and God there
A-making man's wife: and, my lesson learned,
The value and significance of flesh,
I can't unlearn ten minutes afterwards.

270   You understand me: I'm a beast, I know.
But see, now—why, I see as certainly
As that the morning-star's about to shine,
What will hap some day. We've a youngster here
Comes to our convent, studies what I do,
Slouches and stares and lets no atom drop:
His name is Guidi—he'll not mind the monks—
They call him Hulking Tom, he lets them talk—
He picks my practice up—he'll paint apace,
I hope so—though I never live so long,

280 I know what's sure to follow. You be judge!
     You speak no Latin more than I, belike,
     However, you're my man, you've seen the world
     —The beauty and the wonder and the power,
     The shapes of things, their colours, lights and shades,
     Changes, surprises,—and God made it all!
     —For what? Do you feel thankful, ay or no,
     For this fair town's face, yonder river's line,
     The mountain round it and the sky above,
     Much more the figures of man, woman, child,
290 These are the frame to? What's it all about?
     To be passed over, despised? or dwelt upon,
     Wondered at? oh, this last of course!—you say.
     But why not do as well as say,—paint these
     Just as they are, careless what comes of it?
     God's works—paint anyone, and count it crime
     To let a truth slip. Don't object, 'His works
     Are here already; nature is complete:
     Suppose you reproduce her—(which you can't)
     There's no advantage! you must beat her, then.'
300 For, don't you mark? we're made so that we love
     First when we see them painted, things we have passed
     Perhaps a hundred times nor cared to see;
     And so they are better, painted—better to us,
     Which is the same thing. Art was given for that;
     God uses us to help each other so,
     Lending our minds out. Have you noticed, now,
     Your cullion's hanging face? A bit of chalk,
     And trust me but you should, though! How much more,
     If I drew higher things with the same truth!
310 That were to take the Prior's pulpit-place,
     Interpret God to all of you! Oh, oh,
     It makes me mad to see what men shall do
     And we in our graves! This world's no blot for us,
     Nor blank; it means intensely, and means good:
     To find its meaning is my meat and drink.
     'Ay, but you don't so instigate to prayer!'
     Strikes in the Prior: 'when your meaning's plain
     It does not say to folk—remember matins,
     Or, mind you fast next Friday!' Why, for this
320 What need of art at all? A skull and bones,
     Two bits of stick nailed crosswise, or, what's best,
     A bell to chime the hour with, does as well.

I painted a Saint Laurence six months since
At Prato, splashed the fresco in fine style:
'How looks my painting, now the scaffold's down?'
I ask a brother: 'Hugely,' he returns—
'Already not one phiz of your three slaves
Who turn the Deacon off his toasted side,
But's scratched and prodded to our heart's content,
330 The pious people have so eased their own
With coming to say prayers there in a rage:
We get on fast to see the bricks beneath.
Expect another job this time next year,
For piety and religion grow in the crowd—
Your painting serves its purpose!' Hang the fools!
—That is—you'll not mistake an idle word
Spoke in a huff by a poor monk, God wot,
Tasting the air this spicy night which turns
The unaccustomed head like Chianti wine!
340 Oh, the church knows! don't misreport me, now!
It's natural a poor monk out of bounds
Should have his apt word to excuse himself:
And hearken how I plot to make amends.
I have bethought me: I shall paint a piece
. . . There's for you! Give me six months, then go, see
Something in Sant' Ambrogio's! Bless the nuns!
They want a cast o' my office I shall paint
God in the midst, Madonna and her babe,
Ringed by a bowery flowery angel-brood,
350 Lilies and vestments and white faces, sweet
As puff on puff of grated orris-root
When ladies crowd to Church at midsummer.
And then in the front, of course a saint or two—
Saint John, because he saves the Florentines,
Saint Ambrose, who puts down in black and white
The convent's friends and gives them a long day,
And Job, I must have him there past mistake,
The man of Uz (and Us without the z,
Painters who need his patience). Well, all these
360 Secured at their devotion, up shall come
Out of a corner when you least expect,
As one by a dark stair into a great light,
Music and talking, who but Lippo! I!—
Mazed, motionless and moonstruck—I'm the man!
Back I shrink—what is this I see and hear?

I, caught up with my monk's things by mistake,
My old serge gown and rope that goes all round,
I, in this presence, this pure company!
Where's a hole, where's a corner for escape?
370 Then steps a sweet angelic slip of a thing
Forward, puts out a soft palm—'Not so fast!'
—Addresses the celestial presence, 'nay—
He made you and devised you, after all,
Though he's none of you! Could Saint John there draw—
His camel-hair make up a painting-brush?
We come to brother Lippo for all that,
Isle perfecit opus!' So, all smile—
I shuffle sideways with my blushing face
Under the cover of a hundred wings
380 Thrown like a spread of kirtles when you're gay
And play hot cockles, all the doors being shut,
Till, wholly unexpected, in there pops
The hothead husband! Thus I scuttle off
To some safe bench behind, not letting go
The palm of her, the little lily thing
That spoke the good word for me in the nick,
Like the Prior's niece . . . Saint Lucy, I would say.
And so all's saved for me, and for the church
A pretty picture gained. Go, six months hence!
390 Your hand, sir, and good-bye: no lights, no lights!
The street's hushed, and I know my own way back,
Don't fear me! There's the grey beginning. Zooks!

     1853   1855

A Toccata of Galuppi's

I

Oh Galuppi, Baldassaro, this is very sad to find!
I can hardly misconceive you; it would prove me deaf and blind;
But although I take your meaning, 'tis with such a heavy mind!

II

Here you come with your old music, and here's all the good it brings.
What, they lived once thus at Venice where the merchants were the kings,
Where Saint Mark's is, where the Doges used to wed the sea with rings?

III

Ay, because the sea's the street there; and 'tis arched by . . . what you call
. . . Shylock's bridge with houses on it, where they kept the carnival:
I was never out of England—it's as if I saw it all.

IV

10   Did young people take their pleasure when the sea was warm in May?
Balls and masks begun at midnight, burning ever to mid-day,
When they made up fresh adventures for the morrow, do you say?

V

Was a lady such a lady, cheeks so round and lips so red,—
On her neck the small face buoyant, like a bell-flower on its bed,
O'er the breast's superb abundance where a man might base his head?

VI

Well, and it was graceful of them—they'd break talk off and afford
—She, to bite her mask's black velvet—he, to finger on his sword,
While you sat and played Toccatas, stately at the clavichord?

VII

What? Those lesser thirds so plaintive, sixths diminished, sigh on sigh,
20   Told them something? Those suspensions, those solutions—'Must we die?'
Those commiserating sevenths—'Life might last! we can but try!'

VIII

'Were you happy?'—'Yes.'—'And are you still as happy?'—'Yes. And you?'
—'Then, more kisses!'—'Did I stop them, when a million seemed so few?'
Hark, the dominant's persistence till it must be answered to!

IX

So, an octave struck the answer. Oh, they praised you, I dare say!
'Brave Galuppi! that was music! good alike at grave and gay!
I can always leave off talking when I hear a master play!'

X

Then they left you for their pleasure: till in due time, one by one,
Some with lives that came to nothing, some with deeds as well undone,
30   Death stepped tacitly and took them where they never see the sun.

XI

But when I sit down to reason, think to take my stand nor swerve,
While I triumph o'er a secret wrung from nature's close reserve,
In you come with your cold music till I creep through every nerve.

XII

Yes, you, like a ghostly cricket, creaking where a house was burned:
'Dust and ashes, dead and done with, Venice spent what Venice earned.
The soul, doubtless, is immortal—where a soul can be discerned.

XIII

'Yours for instance: you know physics, something of geology,
Mathematics are your pastime; souls shall rise in their degree;
Butterflies may dread extinction,—you'll not die, it cannot be!

XIV

40   'As for Venice and her people, merely born to bloom and drop,
Here on earth they bore their fruitage, mirth and folly were the crop:
What of soul was left, I wonder, when the kissing had to stop?

XV

'Dust and ashes!' So you creak it, and I want the heart to scold.
Dear dead women, with such hair, too—what's become of all the gold
Used to hang and brush their bosoms? I feel chilly and grown old.

1847   1855

"Childe Roland to the Dark Tower Came"

This nightmare poem, according to Browning, had no overt allegorical purpose, but the phantasmagoria is so powerful as to invite many allegorizings. W. C. DeVane traced much of the landscape to one chapter of a book Browning had memorized as a boy, Gerard de Lairesse's *The Art of Painting in All Its Branches*. The chapter's title, "Of Things Deformed and Broken," might be a motto to the poem. However the poem is interpreted, its universal appeal seems to center upon its vision of a willfully ruined quester, whose own strength of imagination has become a deforming and breaking agent, and who calls into question the meaningfulness of all premeditated human action. The relation of Childe Roland to his band of brothers, the questers who failed one by one before him, may suggest the relation of Browning to his own poetic precursors, and prefigures the relation between the hero and the cowards in Yeats's death-poem, "Cuchulain Comforted."

The title is taken from Shakespeare's *King Lear* (III.iv.173). A "childe" is a wellborn youth who is still a candidate for knighthood.

"Childe Roland to the Dark Tower Came"

(See Edgar's Song in Lear*)*

I

My first thought was, he lied in every word.
   That hoary cripple, with malicious eye
   Askance to watch the working of his lie
On mine, and mouth scarce able to afford
Suppression of the glee, that pursed and scored
   Its edge, at one more victim gained thereby.

II

What else should he be set for, with his staff?
   What, save to waylay with his lies, ensnare
   All travellers who might find him posted there,
10 And ask the road? I guessed what skull-like laugh
Would break, what crutch 'gin write my epitaph
   For pastime in the dusty thoroughfare.

III

If at his counsel I should turn aside
   Into that ominous tract which, all agree,
   Hides the Dark Tower. Yet acquiescingly
I did turn as he pointed: neither pride
Nor hope rekindling at the end descried,
   So much as gladness that some end might be.

IV

For, what with my whole world-wide wandering,
20   What with my search drawn out through years, my hope
   Dwindled into a ghost not fit to cope
With that obstreperous joy success would bring,—
I hardly tried now to rebuke the spring
   My heart made, finding failure in its scope.

V

As when a sick man very near to death
  Seems dead indeed, and feels begin and end
  The tears and takes the farewell of each friend,
And hears one bid the other go, draw breath
Freelier outside, ('since all is o'er,' he saith.
30   'And the blow fallen no grieving can amend');

VI

While some discuss if near the other graves
  Be room enough for this, and when a day
  Suits best for carrying the corpse away,
With care about the banners, scarves and staves:
And still the man hears all, and only craves
  He may not shame such tender love and stay.

VII

Thus, I had so long suffered in this quest,
  Heard failure prophesied so oft, been writ
  So many times among 'The Band'—to wit,
40 The knights who to the Dark Tower's search addressed
Their steps—that just to fail as they, seemed best,
  And all the doubt was now—should I be fit?

VIII

So, quiet as despair, I turned from him,
  That hateful cripple, out of his highway
  Into the path he pointed. All the day
Had been a dreary one at best, and dim
Was settling to its close, yet shot one grim
  Red leer to see the plain catch its estray.

IX

For mark! no sooner was I fairly found
50   Pledged to the plain, after a pace or two,
  Than, pausing to throw backward a last view
O'er the safe road, 'twas gone; grey plain all round:
Nothing but plain to the horizon's bound.
  I might go on; nought else remained to do.

X

So, on I went. I think I never saw
  Such starved ignoble nature; nothing throve:

For flowers—as well expect a cedar grove!
But cockle, spurge, according to their law
Might propagate their kind, with none to awe,
You'd think; a burr had been a treasure-trove.

XI

No! penury, inertness and grimace,
    In some strange sort, were the land's portion. 'See
    Or shut your eyes,' said Nature peevishly,
'It nothing skills: I cannot help my case:
'Tis the Last Judgment's fire must cure this place,
    Calcine its clods and set my prisoners free.'

XII

If there pushed any ragged thistle-stalk
    Above its mates, the head was chopped; the bents
    Were jealous else. What made those holes and rents
In the dock's harsh swarth leaves, bruised as to baulk
All hope of greenness? 'tis a brute must walk
    Pashing their life out, with a brute's intents.

XIII

As for the grass, it grew as scant as hair
    In leprosy; thin dry blades pricked the mud
    Which underneath looked kneaded up with blood.
One stiff blind horse, his every bone a-stare,
Stood stupefied, however he came there:
    Thrust out past service from the devil's stud!

XIV

Alive? he might be dead for aught I know,
    With that red gaunt and colloped neck a-strain,
    And shut eyes underneath the rusty mane;
Seldom went such grotesqueness with such woe;
I never saw a brute I hated so;
    He must be wicked to deserve such pain.

XV

I shut my eyes and turned them on my heart.
    As a man calls for wine before he fights,
    I asked one draught of earlier, happier sights,
Ere fitly I could hope to play my part.
Think first, fight afterwards—the soldier's art:
    One taste of the old time sets all to rights.

XVI

Not it! I fancied Cuthbert's reddening face
    Beneath its garniture of curly gold,
    Dear fellow, till I almost felt him fold
An arm in mine to fix me to the place,
That way he used. Alas, one night's disgrace!
    Out went my heart's new fire and left it cold.

XVII

Giles then, the soul of honour—there he stands
    Frank as ten years ago when knighted first.
    What honest men should dare (he said) he durst.
100 Good—but the scene shifts—faugh! what hangman-hands
Pin to his breast a parchment? his own bands
    Read it. Poor traitor, spit upon and curst!

XVIII

Better this present than a past like that;
    Back therefore to my darkening path again!
    No sound, no sight as far as eye could strain.
Will the night send a howlet or a bat?
I asked: when something on the dismal flat
    Came to arrest my thoughts and change their train.

XIX

A sudden little river crossed my path
110   As unexpected as a serpent comes.
    No sluggish tide congenial to the glooms;
This, as it frothed by, might have been a bath
For the fiend's glowing hoof—to see the wrath
    Of its black eddy bespate with flakes and spumes.

XX

So petty yet so spiteful! All along,
    Low scrubby alders kneeled down over it;
    Drenched willows flung them headlong in a fit
Of mute despair, a suicidal throng:
The river which had done them all the wrong,
120   Whate'er that was, rolled by, deterred no whit.

XXI

Which, while I forded,—good saints, how I feared
    To set my foot upon a dead man's cheek,

Each step, or feel the spear I thrust to seek
For hollows, tangled in his hair or beard!
—It may have been a water-rat I speared,
    But, ugh! it sounded like a baby's shriek.

XXII

Glad was I when I reached the other bank.
    Now for a better country. Vain presage!
    Who were the strugglers, what war did they wage,
130 Whose savage trample thus could pad the dank
Soil to a plash? Toads in a poisoned tank,
    Or wild cats in a red-hot iron cage—

XXIII

The fight must so have seemed in that fell cirque.
    What penned them there, with all the plain to choose?
    No foot-print leading to the horrid mews,
None out of it. Mad brewage set to work
Their brains, no doubt, like galley-slaves the Turk
    Pits for his pastime, Christians against Jews.

XXIV

And more than that—a furlong on—why, there!
140   What bad use was that engine for, that wheel,
    Or brake, not wheel—that harrow fit to reel
Men's bodies out like silk? with all the air
Of Tophet's tool, on earth left unaware,
    Or brought to sharpen its rusty teeth of steel.

XXV

Then came a bit of stubbed ground, once a wood,
    Next a marsh, it would seem, and now mere earth
    Desperate and done with; (so a fool finds mirth,
Makes a thing and then mars it, till his mood
Changes and off he goes!) within a rood—
150   Bog, clay and rubble, sand and stark black dearth.

XXVI

Now blotches ranking, coloured gay and grim,
    Now patches where some leanness of the soil's
    Broke into moss or substances like boils;
Then came some palsied oak, a cleft in him

Like a distorted mouth that splits its rim
    Gaping at death, and dies while it recoils.

XXVII

And just as far as ever from the end!
    Nought in the distance but the evening, nought
    To point my footstep further! At the thought,
A great black bird, Apollyon's bosom-friend,
Sailed past, nor beat his wide wing dragon-penned
    That brushed my cap—perchance the guide I sought.

XXVIII

For, looking up, aware I somehow grew,
    'Spite of the dusk, the plain had given place
    All round to mountains—with such name to grace
Mere ugly heights and heaps now stolen in view.
How thus they had surprised me,—solve it, you!
    How to get from them was no clearer case.

XXIX

Yet half I seemed to recognize some trick
    Of mischief happened to me, God knows when—
    In a bad dream perhaps. Here ended, then,
Progress this way. When, in the very nick
Of giving up, one time more, came a click
    As when a trap shuts—you're inside the den!

XXX

Burningly it came on me all at once,
    This was the place! those two hills on the right,
    Crouched like two bulls locked horn in horn in fight;
While to the left, a tall scalped mountain . . . Dunce,
Dotard, a-dozing at the very nonce,
    After a life spent training for the sight!

XXXI

What in the midst lay but the Tower itself?
    The round squat turret, blind as the fool's heart,
    Built of brown stone, without a counterpart
In the whole world. The tempest's mocking elf
Points to the shipman thus the unseen shelf
    He strikes on, only when the timbers start.

XXXII

Not see? because of night perhaps?—why, day
 Came back again for that! before it left,
 ·The dying sunset kindled through a cleft:
190 The hills, like giants at a hunting, lay,
Chin upon hand, to see the game at bay,—
 'Now stab and end the creature—to the heft!'

XXXIII

Not hear? when noise was everywhere! it tolled
 Increasing like a bell. Names in my ears
 Of all the lost adventurers my peers,—
How such a one was strong, and such was bold.
And such was fortunate, yet each of old
 Lost, lost! one moment knelled the woe of years.

XXXIV

There they stood, ranged along the hill-sides, met
200 To view the last of me, a living frame
 For one more picture! in a sheet of flame
I saw them and I knew them all. And yet
Dauntless the slug-horn to my lips I set,
 And blew. *'Childe Roland to the Dark Tower Came.'*
 1852 1855

Andrea del Sarto

(Called 'The Faultless Painter')

But do not let us quarrel any more,
No, my Lucrezia; bear with me for once;
Sit down and all shall happen as you wish.
You turn your face, but does it bring your heart?
I'll work then for your friend's friend, never fear,
Treat his own subject after his own way,
Fix his own time, accept too his own price,
And shut the money into this small hand
When next it takes mine. Will it? tenderly?
10 Oh, I'll content him,—but tomorrow, Love!
I often am much wearier than you think,
This evening more than usual, and it seems
As if—forgive now—should you let me sit

Here by the window with your hand in mine
And look a half-hour forth on Fiesole,
Both of one mind, as married people use,
Quietly, quietly the evening through,
I might get up tomorrow to my work
Cheerful and fresh as ever. Let us try.
20 Tomorrow, how you shall be glad for this!
Your soft hand is a woman of itself,
And mine the man's bared breast she curls inside.
Don't count the time lost, neither; you must serve
For each of the five pictures we require:
It saves a model. So! keep looking so—
My serpentining beauty, rounds on rounds!
—How could you ever prick those perfect ears,
Even to put the pearl there! oh, so sweet—
My face, my moon, my everybody's moon,
30 Which everybody looks on and calls his,
And, I suppose, is looked on by in turn,
While she looks—no one's: very dear, no less.
You smile? why, there's my picture ready made,
There's what we painters call our harmony!
A common greyness silvers everything,—
All in a twilight, you and I alike
—You, at the point of your first pride in me
(That's gone you know),—but I, at every point;
My youth, my hope, my art, being all toned down
40 To yonder sober pleasant Fiesole.
There's the bell clinking from the chapel-top;
That length of convent-wall across the way
Holds the trees safer, huddled more inside;
The last monk leaves the garden; days decrease,
And autumn grows, autumn in everything.
Eh? the whole seems to fall into a shape
As if I saw alike my work and self
And all that I was born to be and do,
A twilight-piece. Love, we are in God's hand.
50 How strange now, looks the life he makes us lead;
So free we seem, so fettered fast we are!
I feel he laid the fetter: let it lie!
This chamber for example—turn your head—
All that's behind us! You don't understand
Nor care to understand about my art,
But you can hear at least when people speak:

And that cartoon, the second from the door
—It is the thing, Love! so such things should be—
Behold Madonna!—I am bold to say.
60   I can do with my pencil what I know,
What I see, what at bottom of my heart
I wish for, if I ever wish so deep—
Do easily, too—when I say, perfectly,
I do not boast, perhaps: yourself are judge,
Who listened to the Legate's talk last week,
And just as much they used to say in France.
At any rate 'tis easy, all of it!
No sketches first, no studies, that's long past:
I do what many dream of, all their lives,
70   —Dream? strive to do, and agonize to do,
And fail in doing. I could count twenty such
On twice your fingers, and not leave this town,
Who strive—you don't know how the others strive
To paint a little thing like that you smeared
Carelessly passing with your robes afloat,—
Yet do much less, so much less, Someone says,
(I know his name, no matter)—so much less!
Well, less is more, Lucrezia: I am judged.
There burns a truer light of God in them.
80   In their vexed beating stuffed and stopped-up brain,
Heart, or whate'er else, than goes on to prompt
This low-pulsed forthright craftsman's hand of mine.
Their works drop groundward, but themselves, I know,
Reach many a time a heaven that's shut to me,
Enter and take their place there sure enough,
Though they come back and cannot tell the world.
My works are nearer heaven, but I sit here.
The sudden blood of these men! at a word—
Praise them, it boils, or blame them, it boils too.
90   I, painting from myself and to myself,
Know what I do, am unmoved by men's blame
Or their praise either. Somebody remarks
Morello's outline there is wrongly traced,
His hue mistaken; what of that? or else,
Rightly traced and well ordered; what of that?
Speak as they please, what does the mountain care?
Ah, but a man's reach should exceed his grasp,
Or what's a heaven for? All is silver-grey
Placid and perfect with my art: the worse!

100 I know both what I want and what might gain,
And yet how profitless to know, to sigh
'Had I been two, another and myself,
Our head would have o'erlooked the world!' No doubt.
Yonder's a work now, of that famous youth
The Urbinate who died five years ago.
('Tis copied, George Vasari sent it me.)
Well, I can fancy how he did it all,
Pouring his soul, with kings and popes to see,
Reaching, that heaven might so replenish him,
110 Above and through his art—for it gives way;
That arm is wrongly put—and there again—
A fault to pardon in the drawing's lines,
Its body, so to speak; its soul is right,
He means right—that, a child may understand.
Still, what an arm! and I could alter it:
But all the play, the insight and the stretch—
Out of me, out of me! And wherefore out?
Had you enjoined them on me, given me soul,
We might have risen to Rafael, I and you!
120 Nay, Love, you did give all I asked, I think—
More than I merit, yes, by many times.
But had you—oh, with the same perfect brow,
And perfect eyes, and more than perfect mouth,
And the low voice my soul hears, as a bird
The fowler's pipe, and follows to the snare—
Had you, with these the same, but brought a mind!
Some women do so. Had the mouth there urged
'God and the glory! never care for gain.
The present by the future, what is that?
130 Live for fame, side by side with Agnolo!
Rafael is waiting: up to God, all three!'
I might have done it for you. So it seems:
Perhaps not. All is as God over-rules.
Besides, incentives come from the soul's self;
The rest avail not. Why do I need you?
What wife had Rafael, or has Agnolo?
In this world, who can do a thing, will not:
And who would do it, cannot, I perceive:
Yet the will's somewhat—somewhat, too, the power—
140 And thus we half-men struggle. At the end,
God, I conclude, compensates, punishes.
'Tis safer for me, if the award be strict,

That I am something underrated here,
Poor this long while, despised, to speak the truth.
I dared not, do you know, leave home all day,
For fear of chancing on the Paris lords.
The best is when they pass and look aside;
But they speak sometimes; I must bear it all.
Well may they speak! That Francis, that first time,
150 And that long festal year at Fontainebleau!
I surely then could sometimes leave the ground,
Put on the glory, Rafael's daily wear,
In that humane great monarch's golden look,—
One finger in his beard or twisted curl
Over his mouth's good mark that made the smile,
One arm about my shoulder, round my neck,
The jingle of his gold chain in my ear,
I painting proudly with his breath on me,
All his court round him, seeing with his eyes,
160 Such frank French eyes, and such a fire of souls
Profuse, my hand kept plying by those hearts,—
And, best of all, this, this, this face beyond,
This in the background, waiting on my work,
To crown the issue with a last reward!
A good time, was it not, my kingly days?
And had you not grown restless . . . but I know—
'Tis done and past; 'twas right, my instinct said;
Too live the life grew, golden and not grey,
And I'm the weak-eyed bat no sun should tempt
170 Out of the grange whose four walls make his world.
How could it end in any other way?
You called me, and I came home to your heart.
The triumph was—to reach and stay there; since
I reached it ere the triumph, what is lost?
Let my hands frame your face in your hair's gold,
You beautiful Lucrezia that are mine!
'Rafael did this, Andrea painted that;
The Roman's is the better when you pray,
But still the other's Virgin was his wife—'
180 Men will excuse me. I am glad to judge
Both pictures in your presence; clearer grows
My better fortune, I resolve to think.
For, do you know, Lucrezia, as God lives,
Said one day Agnolo, his very self,
To Rafael . . . I have known it all these years . . .

(When the young man was flaming out his thoughts
Upon a palace-wall for Rome to see,
Too lifted up in heart because of it)
'Friend, there's a certain sorry little scrub
190   Goes up and down our Florence, none cares how,
Who, were he set to plan and execute
As you are, pricked on by your popes and kings,
Would bring the sweat into that brow of yours!'
To Rafael's!—And indeed the arm is wrong.
I hardly dare . . . yet, only you to see,
Give the chalk here—quick, thus the line should go!
Ay, but the soul! he's Rafael! rub it out!
Still, all I care for, if he spoke the truth,
(What he? why, who but Michel Agnolo?
200   Do you forget already words like those?)
If really there was such a chance, so lost,—
Is, whether you're—not grateful—but more pleased.
Well, let me think so. And you smile indeed!
This hour has been an hour! Another smile?
If you would sit thus by me every night
I should work better, do you comprehend?
I mean that I should earn more, give you more.
See, it is settled dusk now; there's a star;
Morello's gone, the watch-lights show the wall,
210   The cue-owls speak the name we call them by.
Come from the window, love,—come in, at last,
Inside the melancholy little house
We built to be so gay with. God is just.
King Francis may forgive me: oft at nights
When I look up from painting, eyes tired out,
The walls become illumined, brick from brick
Distinct, instead of mortar, fierce bright gold,
That gold of his I did cement them with!
Let us but love each other. Must you go?
220   That Cousin here again? he waits outside?
Must see you—you, and not with me? Those loans?
More gaming debts to pay? you smiled for that?
Well, let smiles buy me! have you more to spend?
While hand and eye and something of a heart
Are left me, work's my ware, and what's it worth?
I'll pay my fancy. Only let me sit
The grey remainder of the evening out,
Idle, you call it, and muse perfectly

How I could paint, were I but back in France,
230   One picture, just one more—the Virgin's face,
Not yours this time! I want you at my side
To hear them—that is, Michel Agnolo—
Judge all I do and tell you of its worth.
Will you? Tomorrow, satisfy your friend.
I take the subjects for his corridor,
Finish the portrait out of hand—there, there.
And throw him in another thing or two
If he demurs; the whole should prove enough
To pay for this same Cousin's freak. Beside,
240   What's better and what's all I care about,
Get you the thirteen scudi for the ruff!
Love, does that please you? Ah, but what does he,
The Cousin! what does he to please you more?

    I am grown peaceful as old age tonight.
I regret little, I would change still less.
Since there my past life lies, why alter it?
The very wrong to Francis!—it is true
I took his coin, was tempted and complied,
And built this house and sinned, and all is said.
250   My father and my mother died of want.
Well, had I riches of my own? you see
How one gets rich! Let each one bear his lot.
They were born poor, lived poor, and poor they died:
And I have laboured somewhat in my time
And not been paid profusely. Some good son
Paint my two hundred pictures—let him try!
No doubt, there's something strikes a balance. Yes,
You loved me quite enough, it seems tonight.
This must suffice me here. What would one have?
260   In heaven, perhaps, new chances, one more chance—
Four great walls in the New Jerusalem,
Meted on each side by the angel's reed,
For Leonard, Rafael, Agnolo and me
To cover—the three first without a wife,
While I have mine! So—still they overcome
Because there's still Lucrezia,—as I choose.

    Again the Cousin's whistle! Go, my Love.
      1853   1855

MATTHEW ARNOLD

1822–1888

ARNOLD, long admired both for his poetry and for his literary criticism, was not particularly good at either. I am aware that mine is not a popular judgment, among scholars.

I have included only one poem by Arnold: the famous "Dover Beach." The elegiac monuments, "The Scholar-Gipsy" and "Thyrsis," a pastoral lament for Arnold's close friend, the poet Arthur Hugh Clough (1819–1861), disconcertingly are echo chambers for the Great Odes of John Keats. I emphasize the "disconcertingly" because Arnold had nothing good to say about Keats, and evidently was unaware that Keats had contaminated the professedly anti-Romantic Arnold's diction, metric, and imagistic procedures.

Matthew Arnold was the son of Thomas Arnold, headmaster of Rugby School. After Oxford, Matthew worked in London in government, and then became an inspector of schools. Vacationing in Switzerland in the autumn of 1848, he fell in love with "Marguerite," to whom he addressed poems but then fled, evidently because of erotic timidity. He then proceeded to marry the daughter of a judge, in 1851.

After his *Poems* of 1853, Arnold wrote mostly prose, becoming what we now call a "cultural critic," the Lionel Trilling of his day. This role of oracle is prefigured in "Dover Beach," upon which the best commentary is Anthony Hecht's poem, "The Dover Bitch," which revises Arnold from the young woman's point of view.

❧   ❧   ❧

Dover Beach

The sea is calm tonight.
The tide is full, the moon lies fair
Upon the straits;—on the French coast the light
Gleams and is gone; the cliffs of England stand,
Glimmering and vast, out in the tranquil bay.
Come to the window, sweet is the night-air!

Only, from the long line of spray
Where the sea meets the moon-blanched land,
Listen! you hear the grating roar
10 Of pebbles which the waves draw back, and fling,
At their return, up the high strand,
Begin, and cease, and then again begin,
With tremulous cadence slow, and bring
The eternal note of sadness in.

Sophocles long ago
Heard it on the Ægæan, and it brought
Into his mind the turbid ebb and flow
Of human misery; we
Find also in the sound a thought,
20 Hearing it by this distant northern sea.

The Sea of Faith
Was once, too, at the full, and round earth's shore
Lay like the folds of a bright girdle furled.
But now I only hear
Its melancholy, long, withdrawing roar,
Retreating, to the breath
Of the night-wind, down the vast edges drear
And naked shingles of the world.

Ah, love, let us be true
30 To one another! for the world, which seems
To lie before us like a land of dreams,
So various, so beautiful, so new,
Hath really neither joy, nor love, nor light,
Nor certitude, nor peace, nor help for pain;
And we are here as on a darkling plain
Swept with confused alarms of struggle and flight,
Where ignorant armies clash by night.

?1848 1867

GERARD MANLEY HOPKINS

1844–1889

THE JESUIT POET, Gerard Manley Hopkins, is akin to Emily Dickinson only in having avoided publication in his own lifetime. In my youth, Hopkins was regarded as a great innovator, and as an anti-Romantic throwback to such seventeenth-century devotional poets as John Donne, with whom he shares neither style nor vision. He is a Keatsian poet, but with the difference of converting Keats's naturalistic humanism into the language of Catholic orthodoxy. His aesthetic is that of his Oxford tutor, Walter Pater, but he returns Pater's secular "privileged moments" to their source in the Christian epiphany, the manifestation of the Christ child in the manger. The Pre-Raphaelite diction and coloring is reappropriated by him for the Christian context of a natural world strengthened and sanctified by grace.

At its best, Father Hopkins's counter-Romanticism produced great poetry, as in the four included here. They have a complex relation to Hopkins's repressed life and religious vocation. Born into a very devout High Anglican family, Hopkins found himself at Balliol College, in the midst of the Oxford Movement of Christian revival. Under the sponsorship of Cardinal Newman, Hopkins converted to Roman Catholicism and then entered the Society of Jesus. A personal element in this conversion was Hopkins's intense though chaste attachment to a young religious poet, Digby Dolben, who drowned in 1867, aged nineteen. In a letter to his friend, the poet Robert Bridges (who was to edit Hopkins posthumously), Hopkins confessed a deep empathy with Walt Whitman. Though he meant Whitman's mode of metrical breakthrough, homoerotic elements certainly formed part of the attraction of the rough Walt for the withdrawn Jesuit professor of Greek.

Hopkins's rhythms frequently return to Old English examples, and yet can seem (as he saw) akin to Whitman's innovations. My favorite poem by Hopkins, the sonnet "To R. B." (Bridges), seeks to confess poetic failure, as the Jesuit poet confronts death, but is a brilliant success, worthy of one of Keats's true heirs.

❧   ❧   ❧

No Worst, There Is None

No worst, there is none. Pitched past pitch of grief,
More pangs will, schooled at forepangs, wilder wring.
Comforter, where, where is your comforting?
Mary, mother of us, where is your relief?
My cries heave, herds-long; huddle in a main, a chief-
woe, world-sorrow; on an age-old anvil wince and sing—
Then lull, then leave off. Fury had shrieked 'No ling-
ering! Let me be fell: force I must be brief.'
O the mind, mind has mountains; cliffs of fall
10   Frightful, sheer, no-man-fathomed. Hold them cheap
May who ne'er hung there. Nor does long our small
Durance deal with that steep or deep. Here! creep,
Wretch, under a comfort serves in a whirlwind: all
Life death does end and each day dies with sleep.

    1885   1918

I Wake and Feel the Fell of Dark

I wake and feel the fell of dark, not day.
What hours, O what black hoürs we have spent
This night! what sights you, heart, saw; ways you went!
And more must, in yet longer light's delay.

With witness I speak this. But where I say
Hours I mean years, mean life. And my lament
Is cries countless, cries like dead letters sent
To dearest him that lives alas! away.

I am gall, I am heartburn. God's most deep decree
10   Bitter would have me taste: my taste was me;
Bones built in me, flesh filled, blood brimmed the curse.

Selfyeast of spirit a dull dough sours. I see
The lost are like this, and their scourge to be
As I am mine, their sweating selves; but worse.

    1885   1918

Thou Art Indeed Just, Lord

*Justus quidem tu es, Domine, si disputem tecum; verumtamen
justa loquar ad te: Quare via impiorum prosperatur? &c.*

Thou art indeed just, Lord, if I contend
With thee; but, sir, so what I plead is just.
Why do sinners' ways prosper? and why must
Disappointment all I endeavour end?

Wert thou my enemy, O thou my friend.
How wouldst thou worse, I wonder, than thou dost
Defeat, thwart me? Oh, the sots and thralls of lust
Do in spare hours more thrive than I that spend.

Sir, life upon thy cause. See, banks and brakes
10   Now, leavèd how thick! lacèd they are again
With fretty chervil, look, and fresh wind shakes

Them; birds build—but not I build; no, but strain,
Time's eunuch, and not breed one work that wakes.
Mine, O thou lord of life, send my roots rain.

    1889   1918

To R.B.

The fine delight that fathers thought; the strong
Spur, live and lancing like the blowpipe flame,
Breathes once and, quenchèd faster than it came,
Leaves yet the mind a mother of immortal song.

Nine months she then, nay years, nine years she long
Within her wears, bears, cares and combs the same:
The widow of an insight lost she lives, with aim
Now known and hand at work now never wrong.

Sweet fire the sire of muse, my soul needs this;
10   I want the one rapture of an inspiration
O then if in my lagging lines you miss

The roll, the rise, the carol, the creation,
My winter world, that scarcely breathes that bliss
Now, yields you, with some sighs, our explanation.

    1889   1918

DANTE GABRIEL ROSSETTI

1828–1882

ROSSETTI IS RECALLED more frequently for his troubled life (brilliantly depicted in a Ken Russell short film, with Oliver Reed as Rossetti) or for his disturbing, imperfect paintings, than for his powerfully intellectualized and sensually troubling poetry. And yet he was a great poet, surpassed only by Browning and Tennyson in his own time, a judgment that I am aware is unfashionable these days.

Since he was both erotically obsessive and paranoid in relation to any criticism of his work and life, it is surprising that Rossetti lasted into his fifty-fourth year. The London-born son of a refugee scholar from Naples and a mother half-English, Rossetti was trained as a painter and always considered that his primary identity. As a poet, Rossetti stylistically derives wholly from Keats, with Dante a principal external influence. From both poets, he learned how *to think in verse,* and he needs to be read very closely.

Rossetti's erotic life was a perpetual disaster, including his marriage to his model, Elizabeth Siddal, after a decade's relationship. Two years later, she killed herself. In grief and guilt, Rossetti buried his manuscripts with her, but had to dig them up again in 1869, in order to prepare his *Poems* (1870).

After the death of Elizabeth Siddal, Rossetti lived with his model, the splendidly fleshy Fanny Cornforth. But in 1857 Rossetti also began the fatal relationship of his life, to Jane Burden, who married William Morris in 1859, which scarcely affected her destructive and passionate affair with Rossetti. Increasingly, he lived on drugs and alcohol, until his death at fifty-four.

Rossetti's poetic masterpiece is *The Stream's Secret,* a direct reflection of his ambiguous love for Jane Burden, but it is too long to print here. Instead, I have selected "Willowwood" from the unique sonnet sequence, *The House of Life,* and "The Blessed Damozel" and the eloquent translation of Dante's "stony sestina," which are central to Rossetti. I include also the dark fragment, "The Orchard-Pit," in which Jane Burden appears as Proserpina, Queen of Hell.

The sonnet here from *The House of Life* might have fascinated Dante himself. Where is it set: in actual nature or in a phantasmagoria that might be Hell? It was accurate that Ken Russell entitled his film *Dante's Inferno*.

✤   ✤   ✤

The Blessed Damozel

The blessed damozel leaned out
   From the gold bar of heaven;
Her eyes were deeper than the depth
   Of waters stilled at even;
She had three lilies in her hand,
   And the stars in her hair were seven.

Her robe, ungirt from clasp to hem,
   No wrought flowers did adorn,
But a white rose of Mary's gift,
10   For service meetly worn;
Her hair that lay along her back
   Was yellow like ripe corn.

Herseemed she scarce had been a day
   One of God's choristers;
The wonder was not yet quite gone
   From that still look of hers;
Albeit, to them she left, her day
   Had counted as ten years.

(To one, it is ten years of years.
20   . . . Yet now, and in this place,
Surely she leaned o'er me—her hair
   Fell all about my face. . . .
Nothing: the autumn-fall of leaves.
   The whole year sets apace.)

It was the rampart of God's house
   That she was standing on;
By God built over the sheer depth
   The which is Space begun;
So high, that looking downward thence
30   She scarce could see the sun.

It lies in Heaven, across the flood
    Of ether, as a bridge.
Beneath, the tides of day and night
    With flame and darkness ridge
The void, as low as where this earth
    Spins like a fretful midge.

Around her, lovers, newly met
    'Mid deathless love's acclaims,
Spoke evermore among themselves
40   Their heart-remembered names;
And the souls mounting up to God
    Went by her like thin flames.

And still she bowed herself and stooped
    Out of the circling charm;
Until her bosom must have made
    The bar she leaned on warm,
And the lilies lay as if asleep
    Along her bended arm.

From the fixed place of Heaven she saw
50   Time like a pulse shake fierce
Through all the worlds. Her gaze still strove
    Within the gulf to pierce
Its path; and now she spoke as when
    The stars sang in their spheres.

The sun was gone now; the curled moon
    Was like a little feather
Fluttering far down the gulf; and now
    She spoke through the still weather.
Her voice was like the voice the stars
60   Had when they sang together.

(Ah sweet! Even now, in that bird's song,
    Strove not her accents there,
Fain to be hearkened? When those bells
    Possessed the mid-day air,
Strove not her steps to reach my side
    Down all the echoing stair?)

'I wish that he were come to me,
    For he will come,' she said,
'Have I not prayed in Heaven?—on earth,
70   Lord, Lord, has he not prayed?
Are not two prayers a perfect strength?
    And shall I feel afraid?

'When round his head the aureole clings,
    And he is clothed in white,
I'll take his hand and go with him
    To the deep wells of light;
As unto a stream we will step down,
    And bathe there in God's sight.

'We two will stand beside that shrine,
80   Occult, withheld, untrod,
Whose lamps are stirred continually
    With prayer sent up to God;
And see our old prayers, granted, melt
    Each like a little cloud.

'We two will lie in the shadow of
    That living mystic tree
Within whose secret growth the Dove
    Is sometimes felt to be,
While every leaf that His plumes touch
90   Saith His Name audibly.

'And I myself will teach to him,
    I myself, lying so,
The songs I sing here; which his voice
    Shall pause in, hushed and slow,
And find some knowledge at each pause,
    Or some new thing to know.'

(Alas! We two, we two, thou say'st!
    Yea, one wast thou with me
That once of old. But shall God lift
100   To endless unity
The soul whose likeness with thy soul
    Was but its love for thee?)

'We two,' she said, 'will seek the groves
   Where the lady Mary is,
With her five handmaidens, whose names
   Are five sweet symphonies,
Cecily, Gertrude, Magdalen,
   Margaret and Rosalys.

110   'Circlewise sit they, with bound locks
   And foreheads garlanded;
Into the fine cloth white like flame
   Weaving the golden thread,
To fashion the birth-robes for them
   Who are just born, being dead.

'He shall fear, haply, and be dumb:
   Then will I lay my cheek
To his, and tell about our love,
   Not once abashed or weak:
And the dear Mother will approve
120   My pride, and let me speak.

'Herself shall bring us, hand in hand,
   To Him round whom all souls
Kneel, the clear-ranged unnumbered heads
   Bowed with their aureoles:
And angels meeting us shall sing
   To their citherns and citoles.

'There will I ask of Christ the Lord
   Thus much for him and me:—
Only to live as once on earth
130   With Love,—only to be,
As then awhile, for ever now
   Together, I and he.'

She gazed and listened and then said,
   Less sad of speech than mild,—
'All this is when he comes.' She ceased.
   The light thrilled towards her, filled
With angels in strong level flight.
   Her eyes prayed, and she smiled.

(I saw her smile.) But soon their path
140　　Was vague in distant spheres:
And then she cast her arms along
　　The golden barriers,
And laid her face between her hands,
　　And wept. (I heard her tears.)
　　1847　1850

Sestina (after Dante)

Of the Lady Pietra degli Scrovigni

To the dim light and the large circle of shade
I have clomb, and to the whitening of the hills,
There where we see no colour in the grass.
Natheless my longing loses not its green,
It has so taken root in the hard stone
Which talks and hears as though it were a lady.

Utterly frozen is this youthful lady,
Even as the snow that lies within the shade;
For she is no more moved than is the stone
10　By the sweet season which makes warm the hills
And alters them afresh from white to green,
Covering their sides again with flowers and grass.

When on her hair she sets a crown of grass
The thought has no more room for other lady,
Because she weaves the yellow with the green
So well that Love sits down there in the shade,—
Love who has shut me in among low hills
Faster than between walls of granite-stone.

She is more bright than is a precious stone;
20　The wound she gives may not be healed with grass:
I therefore have fled far o'er plains and hills
For refuge from so dangerous a lady;
But from her sunshine nothing can give shade,—
Not any hill, nor wall, nor summer-green.

A while ago, I saw her dressed in green,—
So fair, she might have wakened in a stone

This love which I do feel even for her shade;
And therefore, as one woos a graceful lady,
I wooed her in a field that was all grass
30   Girdled about with very lofty hills.

Yet shall the streams turn back and climb the hills
Before Love's flame in this damp wood and green
Burn, as it burns within a youthful lady,
For my sake, who would sleep away in stone
My life, or feed like beasts upon the grass,
Only to see her garments cast a shade.

How dark soe'er the hills throw out their shade,
Under her summer-green the beautiful lady
Covers it, like a stone covered in grass.
    1861

from The House of Life

Willowwood

XLIX

I sat with Love upon a woodside well,
    Leaning across the water, I and he;
    Nor ever did he speak nor looked at me,
But touched his lute wherein was audible
The certain secret thing he had to tell:
    Only our mirrored eyes met silently
    In the low wave; and that sound came to be
The passionate voice I knew; and my tears fell.

And at their fall, his eyes beneath grew hers;
10   And with his foot and with his wing-feathers
    He swept the spring that watered my heart's drouth.
Then the dark ripples spread to waving hair,
And as I stooped, her own lips rising there
    Bubbled with brimming kisses at my mouth.

The Orchard-Pit

A Fragment

Piled deep below the screening apple branch
   They lie with bitter apples in their hands:
And some are only ancient bones that blanch,
And some had ships that last year's wind did launch,
   And some were yesterday the lords of lands.

In the soft dell, among the apple trees,
   High up above the hidden pit she stands,
And there forever sings, who gave to these,
That lie below, her magic hour of ease,
10   And those her apples holden in their hands.

This in my dreams is shown me; and her hair
   Crosses my lips and draws my burning breath;
Her song spreads golden wings upon the air,
Life's eyes are gleaming from her forehead fair,
   And from her breasts the ravishing eyes of Death.

Men say to me that sleep hath many dreams,
   Yet I knew never but this dream alone:
There, from a dried-up channel, once the stream's,
The glen slopes up; even such in sleep it seems
As to my waking sight the place well known.

My love I call her, and she loves me well:
   But I love her as in the maelstrom's cup
The whirled stone loves the leaf inseparable
That clings to it round all the circling swell,
   And that the same last eddy swallows up.
   1869   1886

CHRISTINA ROSSETTI

1830–1894

TWO YEARS YOUNGER than her brother, Dante Gabriel, Christina Rossetti is a very different but scarcely lesser poet: devotional, subtly erotic, endlessly skilled in diction and metric. An independent theologian, Anglican but also Adventist, she is unlike the other great religious poets in the language: George Herbert and Gerard Manley Hopkins. And her gift for fantasy, triumphant in the disturbing long poem *Goblin Market*, establishes her as a visionary romancer unlike any other.

Feminists usefully point out that the only males in *Goblin Market* are goblins, but I am wary of extending that into a general principle as to Christina Rossetti's vision of Eros. We know that she declined at least two marriage proposals, perhaps because of religious differences, but she was fiercely independent and presumably did not care to dwindle into a wife. And yet her lyrics, like "A Birthday," "Remember," and "Song: When I Am Dead," convey accents of erotic ecstasy, and not the negations of renunciation.

It may be that her great poem is "Passing Away," which seems to me both a declaration of aesthetic autonomy and of spiritual ecstasy. She has affinities with Emily Dickinson and with Emily Brontë, three creators who knew their own power, and guarded it from encroachment.

❧ ❧ ❧

Goblin Market

Morning and evening
Maids heard the goblins cry:
"Come buy our orchard fruits,
Come buy, come buy:
Apples and quinces,
Lemons and oranges,
Plump unpecked cherries,
Melons and raspberries,
Bloom-down-cheeked peaches,

Swart-headed mulberries,
Wild free-born cranberries,
Crab-apples, dewberries,
Pine-apples, blackberries,
Apricots, strawberries;—
All ripe together
In summer weather,—
Morns that pass by,
Fair eves that fly;
Come buy, come buy:
Our grapes fresh from the vine,
Pomegranates full and fine,
Dates and sharp bullaces,
Rare pears and greengages,
Damsons and bilberries,
Taste them and try:
Currants and gooseberries,
Bright-fire-like barberries,
Figs to fill your mouth,
Citrons from the South,
Sweet to tongue and sound to eye;
Come buy, come buy."

Evening by evening
Among the brookside rushes,
Laura bowed her head to hear,
Lizzie veiled her blushes:
Crouching close together
In the cooling weather,
With clasping arms and cautioning lips,
With tingling cheeks and finger tips,
"Lie close," Laura said,
Pricking up her golden head:
"We must not look at goblin men,
We must not buy their fruits:
Who knows upon what soil they fed
Their hungry thirsty roots?"
"Come buy," call the goblins
Hobbling down the glen.
"Oh," cried Lizzie, "Laura, Laura,
You should not peep at goblin men."
Lizzie covered up her eyes,
Covered close lest they should look;

Laura reared her glossy head,
And whispered like the restless brook:
"Look, Lizzie, look, Lizzie,
Down the glen tramp little men.
One hauls a basket,
One bears a plate,
One lugs a golden dish
Of many pounds weight.
How fair the vine must grow
Whose grapes are so luscious;
How warm the wind must blow
Thro' those fruit bushes."
"No," said Lizzie: "No, no, no;
Their offers should not charm us,
Their evil gifts would harm us."
She thrust a dimpled finger
In each ear, shut eyes and ran:
Curious Laura chose to linger
Wondering at each merchant man.
One had a cat's face,
One whisked a tail,
One tramped at a rat's pace,
One crawled like a snail,
One like a wombat prowled obtuse and furry,
One like a ratel tumbled hurry skurry.
She heard a voice like voice of doves
Cooing all together:
They sounded kind and full of loves
In the pleasant weather.

Laura stretched her gleaming neck
Like a rush-imbedded swan,
Like a lily from the beck,
Like a moonlit poplar branch,
Like a vessel at the launch
When its last restraint is gone.

Backwards up the mossy glen
Turned and trooped the goblin men,
With their shrill repeated cry,
"Come buy, come buy."
When they reached where Laura was
They stood stock still upon the moss,

Leering at each other,
Brother with queer brother;
Signalling each other,
Brother with sly brother.
One set his basket down,
One reared his plate;
One began to weave a crown
Of tendrils, leaves and rough nuts brown
(Men sell not such in any town);
One heaved the golden weight
Of dish and fruit to offer her:
"Come buy, come buy," was still their cry,
Laura stared but did not stir,
Longed but had no money:
The whisk-tailed merchant bade her taste
In tones as smooth as honey,
The cat-faced purr'd,
The rat-paced spoke a word
Of welcome, and the snail-paced even was heard;
One parrot-voiced and jolly
Cried "Pretty Goblin" still for "Pretty Polly;"—
One whistled like a bird.

But sweet-tooth Laura spoke in haste:
"Good folk, I have no coin;
To take were to purloin:
I have no copper in my purse,
I have no silver either,
And all my gold is on the furze
That shakes in windy weather
Above the rusty heather."
"You have much gold upon your head,"
They answered all together:
"Buy from us with a golden curl."
She clipped a precious golden lock,
She dropped a tear more rare than pearl,
Then sucked their fruit globes fair or red:
Sweeter than honey from the rock,
Stronger than man-rejoicing wine,
Clearer than water flowed that juice;
She never tasted such before,
How should it cloy with length of use?
She sucked and sucked and sucked the more

Fruits which that unknown orchard bore;
She sucked until her lips were sore;
Then flung the emptied rinds away
But gathered up one kernel-stone,
And knew not was it night or day
As she turned home alone.
Lizzie met her at the gate
Full of wise upbraidings:
"Dear, you should not stay so late,
Twilight is not good for maidens;
Should not loiter in the glen
In the haunts of goblin men.
Do you not remember Jeanie,
How she met them in the moonlight,
Took their gifts both choice and many,
Ate their fruits and wore their flowers
Plucked from bowers
Where summer ripens at all hours?
But ever in the moonlight
She pined and pined away;
Sought them by night and day,
Found them no more but dwindled and grew grey;
Then fell with the first snow,
While to this day no grass will grow
Where she lies low:
I planted daisies there a year ago
That never blow.
You should not loiter so."
"Nay, hush," said Laura:
"Nay, hush, my sister:
I ate and ate my fill,
Yet my mouth waters still;
Tomorrow night I will
Buy more:" and kissed her:
"Have done with sorrow;
I'll bring you plums tomorrow
Fresh on their mother twigs,
Cherries worth getting;
You cannot think what figs
My teeth have met in,
What melons icy-cold
Piled on a dish of gold
Too huge for me to hold,

What peaches with a velvet nap,
Pellucid grapes without one seed:
Odorous indeed must be the mead
Whereon they grow, and pure the wave they drink
With lilies at the brink,
And sugar-sweet their sap."
Golden head by golden head,
Like two pigeons in one nest
Folded in each other's wings,
They lay down in their curtained bed:
Like two blossoms on one stem,
Like two flakes of new-fall'n snow,
Like two wands of ivory
Tipped with gold for awful kings.
Moon and stars gazed in at them,
Wind sang to them lullaby,
Lumbering owls forbore to fly,
Not a bat flapped to and fro
Round their rest:
Cheek to cheek and breast to breast
Locked together in one nest.

Early in the morning
When the first cock crowed his warning,
Neat like bees, as sweet and busy,
Laura rose with Lizzie:
Fetched in honey, milked the cows,
Aired and set to rights the house,
Kneaded cakes of whitest wheat,
Cakes for dainty mouths to eat,
Next churned butter, whipped up cream,
Fed their poultry, sat and sewed;
Talked as modest maidens should:
Lizzie with an open heart,
Laura in an absent dream,
One content, one sick in part;
One warbling for the mere bright day's delight,
One longing for the night.

At length slow evening came:
They went with pitchers to the reedy brook;
Lizzie most placid in her look,
Laura most like a leaping flame.

They drew the gurgling water from its deep;
Lizzie plucked purple and rich golden flags,
Then turning homewards said: "The sunset flushes
Those furthest loftiest crags;
Come, Laura, not another maiden lags,
No wilful squirrel wags,
The beasts and birds are fast asleep."
But Laura loitered still among the rushes
And said the bank was steep.

And said the hour was early still,
The dew not fall'n, the wind not chill:
Listening ever, but not catching
The customary cry,
"Come buy, come buy,"
With its iterated jingle
Of sugar-baited words:
Not for all her watching
Once discerning even one goblin
Racing, whisking, tumbling, hobbling;
Let alone the herds
That used to tramp along the glen,
In groups or single,
Of brisk fruit-merchant men.
Till Lizzie urged, "O Laura, come;
I hear the fruit-call but I dare not look:
You should not loiter longer at this brook:
Come with me home.
The stars rise, the moon bends her arc,
Each glowworm winks her spark,
Let us get home before the night grows dark:
For clouds may gather
Tho' this is summer weather,
Put out the lights and drench us thro';
Then if we lost our way what should we do?"

Laura turned cold as stone
To find her sister heard that cry alone,
That goblin cry,
"Come buy our fruits, come buy."
Must she then buy no more such dainty fruit?
Must she no more such succous pasture find,
Gone deaf and blind?

Her tree of life drooped from the root:
She said not one word in her heart's sore ache;
But peering thro' the dimness, nought discerning,
Trudged home, her pitcher dripping all the way;
So crept to bed, and lay
Silent till Lizzie slept;
Then sat up in a passionate yearning,
And gnashed her teeth for baulked desire, and wept
As if her heart would break.

Day after day, night after night,
Laura kept watch in vain
In sullen silence of exceeding pain.
She never caught again the goblin cry:
"Come buy, come buy;"—
She never spied the goblin men
Hawking their fruits along the glen:
But when the noon waxed bright
Her hair grew thin and grey;
She dwindled, as the fair full moon doth turn
To swift decay and burn
Her fire away.

One day remembering her kernel-stone
She set it by a wall that faced the south;
Dewed it with tears, hoped for a root,
Watched for a waxing shoot,
But there came none;
It never saw the sun,
It never felt the trickling moisture run:
While with sunk eyes and faded mouth
She dreamed of melons, as a traveller sees
False waves in desert drouth
With shade of leaf-crowned trees,
And burns the thirstier in the sandful breeze.
She no more swept the house,
Tended the fowls or cows,
Fetched honey, kneaded cakes of wheat,
Brought water from the brook:
But sat down listless in the chimney-nook
And would not eat.

Tender Lizzie could not bear
To watch her sister's cankerous care

Yet not to share.
She night and morning
Caught the goblins' cry:
"Come buy our orchard fruits,
Come buy, come buy:"—
Beside the brook, along the glen,
She heard the tramp of goblin men,
The voice and stir
Poor Laura could not hear;
Longed to buy fruit to comfort her,
But feared to pay too dear.
She thought of Jeanie in her grave,
Who should have been a bride;
But who for joys brides hope to have
Fell sick and died
In her gay prime,
In earliest Winter time,
With the first glazing rime,
With the first snow-fall of crisp Winter time.
Till Laura dwindling
Seemed knocking at Death's door:
Then Lizzie weighed no more
Better and worse;
But put a silver penny in her purse,
Kissed Laura, crossed the heath with clumps of furze
At twilight, halted by the brook:
And for the first time in her life
Began to listen and look.

Laughed every goblin
When they spied her peeping:
Came towards her hobbling,
Flying, running, leaping,
Puffing and blowing,
Chuckling, clapping, crowing,
Clucking and gobbling,
Mopping and mowing,
Full of airs and graces,
Pulling wry faces,
Demure grimaces,
Cat-like and rat-like,
Ratel- and wombat-like,
Snail-paced in a hurry,

Parrot-voiced and whistler,
Helter skelter, hurry skurry,
Chattering like magpies,
Fluttering like pigeons,
Gliding like fishes,—
Hugged her and kissed her,
Squeezed and caressed her:
Stretched up their dishes,
Panniers, and plates:
"Look at our apples
Russet and dun,
Bob at our cherries,
Bite at our peaches,
Citrons and dates,
Grapes for the asking,
Pears red with basking
Out in the sun,
Plums on their twigs;
Pluck them and suck them,
Pomegranates, figs."—
"Good folk," said Lizzie,
Mindful of Jeanie:
"Give me much and many:"—
Held out her apron,
Tossed them her penny.
"Nay, take a seat with us,
Honour and eat with us,"
They answered grinning:
"Our feast is but beginning.
Night yet is early,
Warm and dew-pearly,
Wakeful and starry:
Such fruits as these
No man can carry;
Half their bloom would fly,
Half their dew would dry,
Half their flavour would pass by.
Sit down and feast with us,
Be welcome guest with us,
Cheer you and rest with us."—
"Thank you," said Lizzie: "But one waits
At home alone for me:
So without further parleying,

If you will not sell me any
Of your fruits tho' much and many,
Give me back my silver penny
I tossed you for a fee."—
They began to scratch their pates,
No longer wagging, purring,
But visibly demurring,
Grunting and snarling.
One called her proud,
Cross-grained, uncivil;
Their tones waxed loud,
Their looks were evil.
Lashing their tails
They trod and hustled her,
Elbowed and jostled her,
Clawed with their nails,
Barking, mewing, hissing, mocking,
Tore her gown and soiled her stocking,
Twitched her hair out by the roots,
Stamped upon her tender feet,
Held her hands and squeezed their fruits
Against her mouth to make her eat.
White and golden Lizzie stood,
Like a lily in a flood,—
Like a rock of blue-veined stone
Lashed by tides obstreperously,—
Like a beacon left alone
In a hoary roaring sea,
Sending up a golden fire,—
Like a fruit-crowned orange-tree
White with blossoms honey-sweet
Sore beset by wasp and bee,—
Like a royal virgin town
Topped with gilded dome and spire
Close beleaguered by a fleet
Mad to tug her standard down.

One may lead a horse to water,
Twenty cannot make him drink.
Tho' the goblins cuffed and caught her,
Coaxed and fought her,
Bullied and besought her,
Scratched her, pinched her black as ink,

Kicked and knocked her,
Mauled and mocked her,
Lizzie uttered not a word;
Would not open lip from lip
Lest they should cram a mouthful in:
But laughed in heart to feel the drip
Of juice that syrupped all her face,
And lodged in dimples of her chin,
And streaked her neck which quaked like curd.
At last the evil people
Worn out by her resistance
Flung back her penny, kicked their fruit
Along whichever road they took,
Not leaving root or stone or shoot;
Some writhed into the ground,
Some dived into the brook
With ring and ripple,
Some scudded on the gale without a sound,
Some vanished in the distance.

In a smart ache, tingle,
Lizzie went her way;
Knew not was it night or day;
Sprang up the bank, tore thro' the furze,
Threaded copse and dingle,
And heard her penny jingle
Bouncing in her purse,
Its bounce was music to her ear.
She ran and ran
As if she feared some goblin man
Dogged her with gibe or curse
Or something worse:
But not one goblin skurried after,
Nor was she pricked by fear;
The kind heart made her windy-paced
That urged her home quite out of breath with haste
And inward laughter.

She cried "Laura," up the garden,
"Did you miss me?
Come and kiss me.
Never mind my bruises,
Hug me, kiss me, suck my juices

Squeezed from goblin fruits for you,
Goblin pulp and goblin dew.
Eat me, drink me, love me;
Laura, make much of me:
For your sake I have braved the glen
And had to do with goblin merchant men."

Laura started from her chair,
Flung her arms up in the air,
Clutched her hair:
"Lizzie, Lizzie, have you tasted
For my sake the fruit forbidden?
Must your light like mine be hidden,
Your young life like mine be wasted,
Undone in mine undoing
And ruined in my ruin,
Thirsty, cankered, goblin-ridden?"—
She clung about her sister,
Kissed and kissed and kissed her:
Tears once again
Refreshed her shrunken eyes,
Dropping like rain
After long sultry drouth;
Shaking with aguish fear, and pain,
She kissed and kissed her with a hungry mouth.
Her lips began to scorch,
That juice was wormwood to her tongue,
She loathed the feast:
Writhing as one possessed she leaped and sung,
Rent all her robe, and wrung
Her hands in lamentable haste,
And beat her breast.
Her locks streamed like the torch
Borne by a racer at full speed,
Or like the mane of horses in their flight,
Or like an eagle when she stems the light
Straight toward the sun,
Or like a caged thing freed,
Or like a flying flag when armies run.

Swift fire spread thro' her veins, knocked at her heart,
Met the fire smouldering there,
And overbore its lesser flame;

She gorged on bitterness without a name:
Ah! fool, to choose such part
Of soul-consuming care!
Sense failed in the mortal strife:
Like the watch-tower of a town
Which an earthquake shatters down,
Like a lightning-stricken mast,
Like a wind-uprooted tree
Spun about,
Like a foam-topped waterspout
Cast down headlong in the sea,
She fell at last;
Pleasure past and anguish past,
Is it death or is it life?
Life out of death.
That night long Lizzie watched by her,
Counted her pulse's flagging stir,
Felt for her breath,
Held water to her lips, and cooled her face
With tears and fanning leaves:
But when the first birds chirped about their eaves,
And early reapers plodded to the place
Of golden sheaves,
And dew-wet grass
Bowed in the morning winds so brisk to pass,
And new buds with new day
Opened of cup-like lilies on the stream,
Laura awoke as from a dream,
Laughed in the innocent old way,
Hugged Lizzie but not twice or thrice;
Her gleaming locks showed not one thread of grey,
Her breath was sweet as May
And light danced in her eyes.
Days, weeks, months, years
Afterwards, when both were wives
With children of their own;
Their mother-hearts beset with fears,
Their lives bound up in tender lives;
Laura would call the little ones
And tell them of her early prime,
Those pleasant days long gone
Of not-returning time:
Would talk about the haunted glen,

The wicked, quaint fruit-merchant men,
Their fruits like honey to the throat
But poison in the blood;
(Men sell not such in any town:)
Would tell them how her sister stood
In deadly peril to do her good,
And win the fiery antidote:
Then joining hands to little hands
Would bid them cling together,
"For there is no friend like a sister
In calm or stormy weather;
To cheer one on the tedious way,
To fetch one if one goes astray,
To lift one if one totters down,
To strengthen whilst one stands."

Song

When I am dead, my dearest,
    Sing no sad songs for me;
Plant thou no roses at my head,
    Nor shady cypress tree:
Be the green grass above me
    With showers and dewdrops wet:
And if thou wilt, remember,
    And if thou wilt, forget.

I shall not see the shadows,
    I shall not feel the rain;
I shall not hear the nightingale
    Sing on as if in pain:
And dreaming through the twilight
    That doth not rise nor set,
Haply I may remember,
    And haply may forget.
    1848 1862

Remember

Remember me when I am gone away,
    Gone far away into the silent land;

When you can no more hold me by the hand,
Nor I half turn to go yet turning stay.
Remember me when no more day by day
    You tell me of our future that you planned:
    Only remember me; you understand
It will be late to counsel then or pray.
Yet if you should forget me for a while
10   And afterwards remember, do not grieve:
    For if the darkness and corruption leave
    A vestige of the thoughts that once I had,
Better by far you should forget and smile
    Than that you should remember and be sad.
    1849   1862

Passing Away

Passing away, saith the World, passing away:
Chances, beauty, and youth, sapped day by day:
Thy life never continueth in one stay.
Is the eye waxen dim, is the dark hair changing to grey
That hath won neither laurel nor bay?
I shall clothe myself in Spring and bud in May:
Thou, root-stricken, shalt not rebuild thy decay
On my bosom for aye.
Then I answered: Yea.

10 Passing away, saith my Soul, passing away:
With its burden of fear and hope, of labour and play,
Hearken what the past doth witness and say:
Rust in thy gold, a moth is in thine array,
A canker is in thy bud, thy leaf must decay.
A midnight, at cockcrow, at morning, one certain day
Lo the Bridegroom shall come and shall not delay;
Watch thou and pray.
Then I answered: Yea.

Passing away, saith my God, passing away:
20 Winter passeth after the long delay:
New grapes on the vine, new figs on the tender spray,
Turtle calleth turtle in Heaven's May.
Though I tarry, wait for Me, trust Me, watch and pray:
Arise, come away, night is past and lo it is day,

My love, My sister, My spouse, thou shalt hear Me say.
Then I answered: Yea.

1860   1862

A Birthday

My heart is like a singing bird
   Whose nest is in a watered shoot:
My heart is like an apple-tree
   Whose boughs are bent with thickset fruit;
My heart is like a rainbow shell
   That paddles in a halcyon sea;
My heart is gladder than all these
   Because my love is come to me.

Raise me a dais of silk and down;
10   Hang it with vair and purple dyes;
Carve it in doves and pomegranates,
   And peacocks with a hundred eyes;
Work it in gold and silver grapes,
   In leaves and silver fleurs-de-lys;
Because the birthday of my life
   Is come, my love is come to me.

1857   1862

Up-Hill

Does the road wind up-hill all the way?
   Yes, to the very end.
Will the day's journey take the whole long day?
   From morn to night, my friend.

But is there for the night a resting-place?
   A roof for when the slow dark hours begin.
May not the darkness hide it from my face?
   You cannot miss that inn.

Shall I meet other wayfarers at night?
10   Those who have gone before.
Then must I knock, or call when just in sight?
   They will not keep you standing at that door.

Shall I find comfort, travel-sore and weak?
   Of labour you shall find the sum.
Will there be beds for me and all who seek?
   Yea, beds for all who come.
1858   1862

| WILLIAM MORRIS |

1834–1896

MORRIS WAS A GIFTED lyrical and narrative poet: his now unread *Sigurd the Volsung* remains a superbly readable long poem. I regret that his poetry has been obscured by his fame as a socialist activist, and by his attempt to reform all of British decorative art: wallpaper, tapestries, furniture, carpets, bookbindings, what you will.

I give only two poems by Morris here, but they show his realistic medievalism (most unlike Tennyson's) and the elegiac sturdiness of his lyric gifts. "A Garden by the Sea" is particularly beautiful, and its incantatory verve makes it readily available for possession by memory. Its contrast with Swinburne's "A Forsaken Garden" is salutary, and shows how normative and populist Morris's vision always remained.

✵   ✵   ✵

Near Avalon

A ship with shields before the sun,
Six maidens round the mast,
A red-gold crown on every one,
A green gown on the last.

The fluttering green banners there
Are wrought with ladies' heads most fair,
And a portraiture of Guenevere
The middle of each sail doth bear.

A ship with sails before the wind,
And round the helm six knights,

Their heaumes are on, whereby, half blind,
They pass by many sights.

The tattered scarlet banners there,
Right soon will leave the spear-heads bare,
Those six knights sorrowfully bear
In all their heaumes some yellow hair.
    1858

A Garden by the Sea

I know a little garden-close,
Set thick with lily and red rose,
Where I would wander if I might
From dewy dawn to dewy night,
And have one with me wandering.

And though within it no birds sing,
And though no pillared house is there,
And though the apple-boughs are bare
Of fruit and blossom, would to God
10   Her feet upon the green grass trod,
And I beheld them as before.

There comes a murmur from the shore,
And in the place two fair streams are,
Drawn from the purple hills afar,
Drawn down unto the restless sea:
Dark hills whose heath-bloom feeds no bee,
Dark shore no ship has ever seen,
Tormented by the billows green
Whose murmur comes unceasingly
20   Unto the place for which I cry.

For which I cry both day and night,
For which I let slip all delight,
Whereby I grow both deaf and blind,
Careless to win, unskilled to find,
And quick to loose what all men seek.
Yet tottering as I am and weak,
Still have I left a little breath
To seek within the jaws of death

An entrance to that happy place,
30   To seek the unforgotten face,
Once seen, once kissed, once reft from me
Anigh the murmuring of the sea.

1867   1891

ALGERNON CHARLES SWINBURNE

1837–1909

SWINBURNE, the son of an admiral in the British navy and an earl's daughter, incongruously became the most outrageous poet of the age of Tennyson. Raised on the Isle of Wight, Swinburne grew up obsessed with the shifting borders between beach and sea, rather like Walt Whitman, whom Swinburne, for a while, came to champion.

A brilliant student of the classics at Oxford, Swinburne took no degree, and went off to London and a poetic career. Always Shelley's disciple, Swinburne denounced Christianity, and agitated for the liberation of Italy. His personal life featured alcoholism and, frequently, dominatrixes. His health collapsing at forty-two, Swinburne lived on another thirty years, essentially broken.

His poetry is now neglected, almost forgotten, but the two poems given here are extraordinary, and not at all well known. "August" is a superbly nostalgic celebration of Swinburne's youthful, unfulfilled love for his cousin Mary Gordon, with whom he grew up like a brother on the Isle of Wight. I urge the reader to chant "August" aloud; its cumulative force and poignance is overwhelming.

"At a Month's End" is a superbly stately march to the death of love, memorializing Swinburne's doomed relationship with the formidable Adah Isaacs Menken, notorious actress-poet-courtesan, of Memphis, Tennessee.

One can name all of Swinburne's best poetry a forsaken garden, poised on the verge, like much of Whitman, of falling into the abyss of night, death, the mother, and the sea.

✤   ✤   ✤

August

There were four red apples on the bough,
Half gold half red, that one might know
The blood was ripe inside the core;
The colour of the leaves was more
Like stems of yellow corn that grow
Through all the gold June meadow's floor.

The warm smell of the fruit was good
To feed on, and the split green wood,
With all its bearded lips and stains
Of mosses in the cloven veins,
Most pleasant, if one lay or stood
In sunshine or in happy rains.

There were four apples on the tree,
Red stained through gold, that all might see
The sun went warm from core to rind;
The green leaves made the summer blind
In that soft place they kept for me
With golden apples shut behind.

The leaves caught gold across the sun,
And where the bluest air begun
Thirsted for song to help the heat;
As I to feel my lady's feet
Draw close before the day were done
Both lips grew dry with dreams of it.

In the mute August afternoon
They trembled to some undertune
Of music in the silver air;
Great pleasure was it to be there
Till green turned duskier and the moon
Coloured the corn-sheaves like gold hair.

That August time it was delight
To watch the red moons wane to white
'Twixt grey seamed stems of apple-trees;
A sense of heavy harmonies

Grew on the growth of patient night,
More sweet than shapen music is.

But some three hours before the moon
The air, still eager from the noon,
Flagged after heat, not wholly dead;
Against the stem I leant my head;
The colour soothed me like a tune,
Green leaves all round the gold and red.

I lay there till the warm smell grew
More sharp, when flecks of yellow dew
Between the round ripe leaves that blurred
The rind with stain and wet; I heard
A wind that blew and breathed and blew,
Too weak to alter its one word.

The wet leaves next the gentle fruit
Felt smoother, and the brown tree-root
Felt the mould warmer: I too felt
(As water feels the slow gold melt
Right through it when the day burns mute)
The peace of time wherein love dwelt.

There were four apples on the tree,
Gold stained on red that all might see
The sweet blood filled them to the core:
The colour of her hair is more
Like stems of fair faint gold, that be
Mown from the harvest's middle floor.

At a Month's End

The night last night was strange and shaken:
    More strange the change of you and me.
Once more, for the old love's love forsaken,
    We went out once more toward the sea.

For the old love's love-sake dead and buried,
    One last time, one more and no more,
We watched the waves set in, the serried
    Spears of the tide storming the shore.

Hardly we saw the high moon hanging,
10   Heard hardly through the windy night
Far waters ringing, low reefs clanging,
      Under wan skies and waste white light.

With chafe and change of surges chiming,
      The clashing channels rocked and rang
Large music, wave to wild wave timing,
      And all the choral water sang.

Paint lights fell this way, that way floated,
      Quick sparks of sea-fire keen like eyes
From the rolled surf that flashed, and noted
20   Shores and faint cliffs and bays and skies.

The ghost of sea that shrank up sighing
      At the sand's edge, a short sad breath
Trembling to touch the goal, and dying
      With weak heart heaved up once in death—

The rustling sand and shingle shaken
      With light sweet touches and small sound—
These could not move us, could not waken
      Hearts to look forth, eyes to look round.

Silent we went an hour together,
30   Under grey skies by waters white.
Our hearts were full of windy weather,
      Clouds and blown stars and broken light.

Full of cold clouds and moonbeams drifted
      And streaming storms and straying fires,
Our souls in us were stirred and shifted
      By doubts and dreams and foiled desires.

Across, aslant, a scudding sea-mew
      Swam, dipped, and dropped, and grazed the sea:
And one with me I could not dream you;
40   And one with you I could not be.

As the white wing the white wave's fringes
      Touched and slid over and flashed past—

As a pale cloud a pale flame tinges
    From the moon's lowest light and last—

As a star feels the sun and falters,
    Touched to death by diviner eyes—
As on the old gods' untended altars
    The old fire of withered worship dies—

(Once only, once the shrine relighted
50   Sees the last fiery shadow shine,
Last shadow of flame and faith benighted,
    Sees falter and flutter and fail the shrine)

So once with fiery breath and flying
    Your winged heart touched mine and went,
And the swift spirits kissed, and sighing,
    Sundered and smiled and were content.

That only touch, that feeling only,
    Enough we found, we found too much;
For the unlit shrine is hardly lonely
60   As one the old fire forgets to touch.

Slight as the sea's sight of the sea-mew,
    Slight as the sun's sight of the star:
Enough to show one must not deem you
    For love's sake other than you are.

Who snares and tames with fear and danger
    A bright beast of a fiery kin,
Only to mar, only to change her
    Sleek supple soul and splendid skin?

Easy with blows to mar and maim her,
70   Easy with bonds to bind and bruise;
What profit, if she yield her tamer
    The limbs to mar, the soul to lose?

Best leave or take the perfect creature,
    Take all she is or leave complete;
Transmute you will not form or feature,
    Change feet for wings or wings for feet.

Strange eyes, new limbs, can no man give her;
    Sweet is the sweet thing as it is.
No soul she hath, we see, to outlive her;
80   Hath she for that no lips to kiss?

So may one read his weird, and reason,
    And with vain drugs assuage no pain.
For each man in his loving season
    Fools and is fooled of these in vain.

Charms that allay not any longing,
    Spells that appease not any grief,
Time brings us all by handfuls, wronging
    All hurts with nothing of relief.

Ah, too soon shot, the fool's bolt misses!
90   What help? the world is full of loves;
Night after night of running kisses,
    Chirp after chirp of changing doves.

Should Love disown or disesteem you
    For loving one man more or less?
You could not tame your light white sea-mew,
    Nor I my sleek black pantheress.

For a new soul let whoso please pray,
    We are what life made us, and shall be.
For you the jungle and me the sea-spray,
100   And south for you and north for me.

But this one broken foam-white feather
    I throw you off the hither wing.
Splashed stiff with sea-scurf and salt weather,
    This song for sleep to learn and sing—

Sing in your ear when, daytime over,
    You couched at long length on hot sand
With some sleek sun-discoloured lover,
    Wince from his breath as from a brand:

Till the acrid hour aches out and ceases,
110   And the sheathed eyeball sleepier swims,

The deep flank smoothes its dimpling creases,
   And passion loosens all the limbs:

Till dreams of sharp grey north-sea weather
   Fall faint upon your fiery sleep,
As on strange sands a strayed bird's feather
   The wind may choose to lose or keep.

But I, who leave my queen of panthers,
   As a tired honey-heavy bee
Gilt with sweet dust from gold-grained anthers
120   Leaves the rose-chalice, what for me?

From the ardours of the chaliced centre,
   From the amorous anthers' golden grime.
That scorch and smutch all wings that enter,
   I fly forth hot from honey-time.

But as to a bee's gilt thighs and winglets
   The flower-dust with the flower-smell clings;
As a snake's mobile rampant ringlets
   Leave the sand marked with print of rings;

So to my soul in surer fashion
130   Your savage stamp and savour hangs;
The print and perfume of old passion,
   The wild-beast mark of panther's fangs.

EMILY BRONTË

1818–1848

THE AUTHOR OF *Wuthering Heights* (1847) died of tuberculosis, the family malady, a year after it was published. Two older sisters, Maria and Elizabeth, died of tuberculosis in 1825. Branwell, the only brother, died the same year as Emily. The youngest sister, Anne, died in 1849, but she had published two enduring novels, *Agnes Grey* (1847) and *The Tenant of*

Wildfell Hall (1848). Charlotte survived to marry, but died of toxemia during her pregnancy in 1855, at thirty-nine. Her monument remains *Jane Eyre* (1847), but she wrote three other authentic novels: *Shirley* (1849), *Villette* (1853), and the posthumously published *The Professor* (1857, but actually written as her first work, completed in 1846).

In 1846, *Poems by Currer, Ellis, and Acton Bell* appeared, Currer being Charlotte; Ellis, Emily; and Acton, Anne. There is a rough vigor to Charlotte's poems, and a lyric sensibility is at work in Anne's, but Emily's are the thing itself, strong poetry, of a wholly original kind.

The three Brontë sisters (and Branwell) had written childhood cycles of poems, including *The Gondal Saga,* in which some of Emily's best work was embedded. The Byronism of *Jane Eyre, Wuthering Heights,* and *Agnes Grey* is prefigured in these ardent early cycles.

I include here two poems by Emily Brontë, both of them worthy of the visionary of *Wuthering Heights.* The "Stanzas" ("Often rebuked, yet always back returning") might take as their motto the admonition of Nietzsche's Zarathustra: "Think of the earth!" Emily Brontë celebrates her own recalcitrance to yield to "high morality," history, or theology.

"Last Lines" exalts the "God within my breast," the spark that is the oldest and best element of the self. A natural Gnostic (I am aware that is an oxymoron), she denies all creeds as diseases of the intellect, and avoids prayer, knowing it to be a disease of the will. Emily Brontë did not derive her Gnosticism from ancient texts and traditions, as Herman Melville did. She did not require anything that was not already her own.

❧   ❧   ❧

Stanzas

Often rebuked, yet always back returning
    To those first feelings that were born with me,
And leaving busy chase of wealth and learning
    For idle dreams of things which cannot be:

Today, I will seek not the shadowy region;
    Its unsustaining vastness waxes drear;
And visions rising, legion after legion,
    Bring the unreal world too strangely near.

I'll walk, but not in old heroic traces,
    And not in paths of high morality,

And not among the half-distinguished faces,
    The clouded forms of long-past history.

I'll walk where my own nature would be leading—
    It vexes me to choose another guide—
Where the grey flocks in ferny glens are feeding,
    Where the wild wind blows on the mountainside.

What have those lonely mountains worth revealing?
    More glory and more grief than I can tell:
The earth that wakes one human heart to feeling
20   Can centre both the worlds of Heaven and Hell.
      1850

Last Lines

    No coward soul is mine,
No trembler in the world's storm-troubled sphere;
    I see Heaven's glories shine,
And faith shines equal, arming me from fear.

    O God within my breast,
Almighty, ever-present Deity!
    Life—that in me has rest,
As I—undying Life—have power in Thee!

    Vain are the thousand creeds
10 That move men's hearts—unutterably vain;
    Worthless as withered weeds,
Or idlest froth amid the boundless main,

    To waken doubt in one
Holding so fast by Thine infinity;
    So surely anchored on
The steadfast rock of immortality.

    With wide-embracing love
Thy spirit animates eternal years,
    Pervades and broods above,
20 Changes, sustains, dissolves, creates, and rears.

    Though earth and man were gone,
And suns and universes ceased to be,

And Thou were left alone,
Every existence would exist in Thee.

There is not room for Death,
Nor atom that his might could render void;
  Thou—Thou art Being and Breath,
And what that Thou art may never be destroyed.

  1846   1850

ELIZABETH BARRETT BROWNING

1806–1861

FEMINIST CRITICISM HAS focused attention upon the poetry of Elizabeth Barrett, rather at the expense of her husband, Robert Browning, who nevertheless abides as one of the greatest poets in the language. I venture that academic fashion will wane (it always does) and the aesthetic inadequacies of Barrett Browning's long poem, *Aurora Leigh* (1856), and of the famous *Sonnets from the Portuguese* (addressed to Robert, who thought she looked Portuguese) again will be apparent. Very bad also is Barrett Browning's "The Cry of the Children," where the sentiments are admirable but the expression is wearisome. In an occasional lyric, like "A Musical Instrument," given here, Elizabeth Barrett catches fire.

An inexplicable malady kept her an invalid from 1838 to 1846, when she and Browning eloped to the Continent, escaping whatever it was that animated her father's possessiveness. For two such difficult personalities, the Brownings got on reasonably well, though Elizabeth's right-wing politics (she adored Napoleon III) and her credulity in regard to spiritualism provoked Robert. They had one son, who settled down in Venice as an indifferent painter, but the fame of both parents must have been a burden for him.

Elizabeth Barrett Browning died in Florence, at fifty-five, to her husband's enormous grief. He survived her for twenty-four years, and never remarried, though he was surrounded by the admiring women of the Browning Society.

✤   ✤   ✤

A Musical Instrument

What was he doing, the great god Pan,
    Down in the reeds by the river?
Spreading ruin and scattering ban,
Splashing and paddling with hoofs of a goat,
And breaking the golden lilies afloat
    With the dragon-fly on the river.

He tore out a reed, the great god Pan,
    From the deep cool bed of the river;
The limpid water turbidly ran,
10 And the broken lilies a-dying lay,
And the dragon-fly had fled away,
    Ere he brought it out of the river.

High on the shore sat the great god Pan
    While turbidly flowed the river;
And hacked and hewed as a great god can,
With his hard bleak steel at the patient reed,
Till there was not a sign of the leaf indeed
    To prove it fresh from the river.

He cut it short, did the great god Pan
20   (How tall it stood in the river!),
Then drew the pith, like the heart of a man.
Steadily from the outside ring,
And notched the poor dry empty thing
    In holes, as he sat by the river.

'This is the way,' laughed the great god Pan
    (Laughed while he sat by the river),
'The only way, since gods began
To make a sweet music, they could succeed.'
Then, dropping his mouth to a hole in the reed,
30   He blew in power by the river.

Sweet, sweet, sweet, O Pan!
    Piercing sweet by the river!
Blinding sweet, O great god Pan!
The sun on the hill forgot to die,

And the lilies revived, and the dragon-fly
    Came back to dream on the river.

Yet half a beast is the great god Pan,
    To laugh as he sits by the river,
Making a poet out of a man;
40   The true gods sigh for the cost and pain
For the reed which grows nevermore again
    As a reed with the reeds in the river.

    1860

EDWARD LEAR

1812–1888

A LANDSCAPE PAINTER by profession, Edward Lear would seem to have had a very happy life, with travels in search of subjects in Sinai and Albania, but primarily in Italy, where he died at seventy-six, cheerfully at work illustrating the poems of Tennyson, his close friend.

Lear's masterwork is his first volume, *A Book of Nonsense* (1846), replete with his unique limericks and his mysterious lyrics of visionary nonsense that fuse Shelley and Tennyson in quest-poems that are at once laments for lost love and yet weirdly boisterous.

I include three of these that still enthrall extremely intelligent children of all ages, and give also one of the most effective of the limericks.

❧   ❧   ❧

The Owl and the Pussy-Cat

I

The Owl and the Pussy-cat went to sea
    In a beautiful pea-green boat,
They took some honey, and plenty of money,
    Wrapped up in a five-pound note.
The Owl looked up to the stars above,
    And sang to a small guitar,

"O lovely Pussy! O Pussy, my love,
  What a beautiful Pussy you are,
    You are,
    You are!
What a beautiful Pussy you are!"

II

Pussy said to the Owl, "You elegant fowl!
  How charmingly sweet you sing!
O let us be married! too long we have tarried:
  But what shall we do for a ring?"
They sailed away, for a year and a day,
  To the land where the Bong-tree grows
And there in a wood a Piggy-wig stood
  With a ring at the end of his nose,
    His nose,
    His nose,
With a ring at the end of his nose.

III

"Dear Pig, are you willing to sell for one shilling
  Your ring?" Said the Piggy, "I will."
So they took it away, and were married next day
  By the Turkey who lives on the hill.
They dined on mince, and slices of quince,
  Which they ate with a runcible spoon;
And hand in hand, on the edge of the sand,
  They danced by the light of the moon,
    The moon,
    The moon,
They danced by the light of the moon.

The Jumblies

I

They went to sea in a Sieve, they did,
  In a Sieve they went to sea:
In spite of all their friends could say,
On a winter's morn, on a stormy day,
  In a Sieve they went to sea!
And when the Sieve turned round and round,
And every one cried, "You'll all be drowned!"

They called aloud, "Our Sieve ain't big,
But we don't care a button! we don't care a fig!
    In a Sieve we'll go to sea!"
        Far and few, far and few,
            Are the lands where the Jumblies live;
            Their heads are green, and their hands are blue,
                And they went to sea in a Sieve.

        II

They sailed away in a Sieve, they did,
    In a Sieve they sailed so fast,
With only a beautiful pea-green veil
Tied with a riband by way of a sail,
    To a small tobacco-pipe mast;
And every one said, who saw them go,
"O won't they be soon upset, you know!
For the sky is dark, and the voyage is long,
And happen what may, it's extremely wrong
    In a Sieve to sail so fast!"
        Far and few, far and few,
            Are the lands where the Jumblies live;
            Their heads are green, and their hands are blue,
                And they went to sea in a Sieve.

        III

The water it soon came in, it did,
    The water it soon came in;
So to keep them dry, they wrapped their feet
In a pinky paper all folded neat,
    And they fastened it down with a pin.
And they passed the night in a crockery-jar,
And each of them said, "How wise we are!
Though the sky be dark, and the voyage be long,
Yet we never can think we were rash or wrong,
    While round in our Sieve we spin!"
        Far and few, far and few,
            Are the lands where the Jumblies live;
            Their heads are green, and their hands are blue,
                And they went to sea in a Sieve.

        IV

And all night long they sailed away;
    And when the sun went down,

They whistled and warbled a moony song
To the echoing sound of a coppery gong,
    In the shade of the mountains brown.
"O Timballo! How happy we are,
When we live in a sieve and a crockery-jar,
And all night long in the moonlight pale,
We sail away with a pea-green sail,
    In the shade of the mountains brown!"
        Far and few, far and few,
            Are the lands where the Jumblies live;
        Their heads are green, and their hands are blue,
            And they went to sea in a Sieve.

        V

They sailed to the Western Sea, they did,
    To a land all covered with trees,
And they bought an Owl, and a useful Cart,
And a pound of Rice, and a Cranberry Tart,
    And a hive of silvery Bees.
And they bought a Pig, and some green Jack-daws,
And a lovely Monkey with lollipop paws,
And forty bottles of Ring-Bo-Ree,
    And no end of Stilton Cheese.
        Far and few, far and few,
            Are the lands where the Jumblies live;
        Their heads are green, and their hands are blue,
            And they went to sea in a Sieve.

    VI

And in twenty years they all came back,
    In twenty years or more,
And every one said, "How tall they've grown!
For they've been to the Lakes, and the Torrible Zone,
    And the hills of the Chankly Bore";
And they drank their health, and gave them a feast
Of dumplings made of beautiful yeast;
And every one said, "If we only live,
We too will go to sea in a Sieve,—
    To the hills of the Chankly Bore!"
        Far and few, far and few,
            Are the lands where the Jumblies live;
        Their heads are green, and their hands are blue,
            And they went to sea in a Sieve.

The Courtship of the Yonghy-Bonghy-Bò

I

On the Coast of the Coromandel
Where the early pumpkins blow,
In the middle of the woods
   Lived the Yonghy-Bonghy-Bò.
Two old chairs, and half a candle,—
One old jug without a handle,—
     These were all his wordly goods:
     In the middle of the woods,
     These were all the wordly goods,
   Of the Yonghy-Bonghy-Bò,
   Of the Yonghy-Bonghy-Bò.

II

Once, among the Bong-trees walking
   Where the early pumpkins blow,
     To a little heap of stones
   Came the Yonghy-Bonghy-Bò.
There he heard a Lady talking,
To some milk-white Hens of Dorking,—
     "'Tis the Lady Jingly Jones!
     "On that little heap of stones
     "Sits the Lady Jingly Jones!"
   Said the Yonghy-Bonghy-Bò,
   Said the Yonghy-Bonghy-Bò.

III

"Lady Jingly! Lady Jingly!
   Sitting where the pumpkins blow,
     "Will you come and be my wife?"
   Said the Yonghy-Bonghy-Bò.
"I am tired of living singly,—
"On this coast so wild and shingly,—
     "I'm a-weary of my life:
     "If you'll come and be my wife,
     "Quite serene would be my life!"—
   Said the Yonghy-Bonghy-Bò,
   Said the Yonghy-Bonghy-Bò.

IV

"On this Coast of Coromandel,
   "Shrimps and watercresses grow,

"Prawns are plentiful and cheap,"
    Said the Yonghy-Bonghy-Bò.
"You shall have my Chairs and candle,
"And my jug without a handle!—
        "Gaze upon the rolling deep
        ("Fish is plentiful and cheap)
        "As the sea, my love is deep!"
    Said the Yonghy-Bonghy-Bò,
    Said the Yonghy-Bonghy-Bò.

        v

Lady Jingly answered sadly,
    And her tears began to flow,—
        "Your proposal comes too late,
        "Mr. Yonghy-Bonghy-Bò!
"I would be your wife most gladly!"
(Here she twirled her fingers madly,)
        "But in England I've a mate!
        "Yes! you've asked me far too late,
        "For in England I've a mate,
        "Mr. Yonghy-Bonghy-Bò!
        "Mr. Yonghy-Bonghy-Bò!"

        VI

"Mr. Jones—(his name is Handel,—
    "Handel Jones, Esquire, & Co.)
        "Dorking fowls delights to send,
        "Mr. Yonghy-Bonghy-Bò!
"Keep, oh! keep your chairs and candle,
"And your jug without a handle,—
        "I can merely be your friend!
        "—Should my Jones more Dorkings send,
        "I will give you three, my friend!
        "Mr. Yonghy-Bonghy-Bò!
        "Mr. Yonghy-Bonghy-Bò!"

        VII

"Though you've such a tiny body,
    "And your head so large doth grow,—
        "Though your hat may blow away,
        "Mr. Yonghy-Bonghy-Bò!
"Though you're such a Hoddy Doddy—

"Yet I wish that I could modi-
    "fy the words I needs must say!
    "Will you please to go away?
    "That is all I have to say—
  "Mr. Yonghy-Bonghy-Bò!
  "Mr. Yonghy-Bonghy-Bò!"

VIII
Down the slippery slopes of Myrtle,
    Where the early pumpkins blow,
        To the calm and silent sea
    Fled the Yonghy-Bonghy-Bò.
There, beyond the Bay of Gurtle,
Lay a large and lively Turtle;—
        "You're the Cove," he said, "for me
        "On your back beyond the sea,
        "Turtle, you shall carry me!"
    Said the Yonghy-Bonghy-Bò,
    Said the Yonghy-Bonghy-Bò.

IX
Through the silent-roaring ocean
    Did the Turtle swiftly go;
        Holding fast upon his shell
    Rode the Yonghy-Bonghy-Bò.
With a sad primæval motion
Towards the sunset isles of Boshen
        Still the Turtle bore him well.
        Holding fast upon his shell,
        "Lady Jingly Jones, farewell!"
    Sang the Yonghy-Bonghy-Bò,
    Sang the Yonghy-Bonghy-Bò.

X
From the Coast of Coromandel,
    Did that Lady never go;
        On that heap of stones she mourns
    For the Yonghy-Bonghy-Bò.
On the Coast of Coromandel,
In his jug without a handle
        Still she weeps, and daily moans;
        On that little heap of stones

To her Dorking Hens she moans,
For the Yonghy-Bonghy-Bò,
For the Yonghy-Bonghy-Bò.

The Floating Old Man

There was an Old Man in a boat,
Who said, "I'm afloat! I'm afloat!"
When they said, "No! you ain't!" he was ready to faint,
That unhappy Old Man in a boat.

LEWIS CARROLL

1832–1898

I AM DELIGHTED to reprint here all of Lewis Carroll's sublime *The Hunting of the Snark*, as well as three of my favorite short poems: "The Man Gardener's Song," "A Pig-Tale," and "The Walrus and the Carpenter." The fame of Carroll's prose in *Alice's Adventures in Wonderland* (1865) and *Through the Looking-Glass and What Alice Found There* (1871) has perhaps obscured Carroll's equal originality and hilarity as a poet, whether in the lyrics interpolated in the *Alice* books or in the outrageous *The Hunting of the Snark: An Agony in Eight Fits*.

Having survived a serious heart operation, I have retired from polemic, as the stress might be fatal. I remain however in wonderment that there are hosts of *Harry Potter* readers for every reader of the *Alice* books. Time will settle this: they will be reading Carroll in the twenty-second century, long after cliché-laden period pieces will crowd up the dustbins.

Charles Lutwidge Dodgson, enigmatic genius, might be termed the Humbert Humbert of his day, except that he never touched any of his eleven-year-old enchantresses, whether Alice Liddell, or Mary Badcock, or Alice Raikes, or Gertrude Chataway. His blameless correspondence with an entire range of eleven-year-old beauties went on forever. He was fortunate in his era: one fears that a lecturer in mathematics at Christ Church College, Oxford, might now have to confront the Sexual Harassment committee (whatever these covens of harpies are now called in Britain).

The Hunting of the Snark sustains comparison with Coleridge's *Rime of the Ancient Mariner* or Rimbaud's "Le Bateau ivre," let alone with Yeats's *The Wanderings of Oisin.* Its opening is magnificent:

> "Just the place for a Snark!" the Bellman cried,
>   As he landed his crew with care;
> Supporting each man on the top of the tide
>   By a finger entwined in his hair.

> "Just the place for a Snark! I have said it twice:
>   That alone should encourage the crew.
> Just the place for a Snark! I have said it thrice:
>   What I tell you three times is true."

The Bellman, a town crier turned captain, is the Ahab who will lead his lunatic crew upon their real quest to ensnare the Moby-Dick of the Boojum. But our sacrificed hero is the Baker (who can only bake wedding cake) and who immolates himself at the poem's close:

> Erect and sublime, for one moment of time,
> In the next, that wild figure they saw
>   (As if stung by a spasm) plunge into a chasm . . .

The Baker discerns that every Snark turns out to be a devouring Boojum. Boojums are clearly horrid, but what are snarks? Our best clue is a stanza that Carroll keeps repeating:

> They sought it with thimbles, they sought it with care;
>   They pursued it with forks and hope;
> They threatened its life with a railway-share;
>   They charmed it with smiles and soap.

If "it" is the snark or eleven-year-old enchantresses, then there is something wrong with this stanza. Boojums cannot simply represent mature female sexuality, and we feel a missing element. I think you have to turn to some of Carroll's major lyrics for clues, as here in the unmatchable "Mad Gardener's Song":

> He thought he saw an Elephant,
>   That practiced on a fife:

He looked again, and found it was
A letter from his wife.
"At length I realize," he said,
"The bitterness of Life!"

That presumably unopened letter starts the Gardener off on a series of hallucinations, the most harrowing of which is the last:

He thought he saw an Argument
That proved he was the Pope;
He looked again, and found it was
A Bar of Mottled Soap.
"A fact so dread," he faintly said,
"Extinguishes all hope!"

As pontiff, he would be unmarried: the dread letter will have to be opened. There is an aura of sadistic charm in Lewis Carroll that provokes some pondering. The pathetic fate of the poor pig in "A Pig-Tale" is unnervingly hilarious, but how should we react to the doom of those amiable little oysters who will be devoured by the Walrus and the Carpenter:

But four young Oysters hurried up,
All eager for the treat;
Their coats were brushed, their faces washed,
Their shoes were clean and neat—

"The treat" is dreadfully ambiguous, and while, as readers, we enjoy ourselves almost as much as the Walrus and the Carpenter do, we are left deliciously uneasy.

✤   ✤   ✤

The Hunting of the Snark

Fit the First

The Landing

"Just the place for a Snark!" the Bellman cried,
    As he landed his crew with care;
Supporting each man on the top of the tide
    By a finger entwined in his hair.

"Just the place for a Snark! I have said it twice:
　　That alone should encourage the crew.
Just the place for a Snark! I have said it thrice:
　　What I tell you three times is true."

The crew was complete: it included a Boots—
　　A maker of Bonnets and Hoods—
A Barrister, brought to arrange their disputes—
　　And a Broker, to value their goods.

A Billiard-marker, whose skill was immense,
　　Might perhaps have won more than his share—
But a Banker, engaged at enormous expense,
　　Had the whole of their cash in his care.

There was also a Beaver, that paced on the deck,
　　Or would sit making lace in the bow:
And had often (the Bellman said) saved them from wreck
　　Though none of the sailors knew how.

There was one who was famed for the number of things
　　He forgot when he entered the ship:
His umbrella, his watch, all his jewels and rings,
　　And the clothes he had bought for the trip.

He had forty-two boxes, all carefully packed,
　　With his name painted clearly on each:
But, since he omitted to mention the fact,
　　They were all left behind on the beach.

The loss of his clothes hardly mattered, because
　　He had seven coats on when he came,
With three pair of boots—but the worst of it was,
　　He had wholly forgotten his name.

He would answer to "Hi!" or to any loud cry,
　　Such as "Fry me!" or "Fritter my wig!"
To "What-you-may-call-um!" or "What-was-his-name!"
　　But especially "Thing-um-a-jig!"

While, for those who preferred a more forcible word,
　　He had different names from these:

His intimate friends called him "Candle-ends",
  And his enemies "Toasted-cheese".

"His form is ungainly—his intellect small—"
  (So the Bellman would often remark)—
"But his courage is perfect! And that, after all,
  Is the thing that one needs with a Snark."

He would joke with hyænas, returning their stare
  With an impudent wag of the head:
And he once went a walk, paw-in-paw, with a bear,
  "Just to keep up its spirits," he said.

He came as a Baker: but owned, when too late—
  And it drove the poor Bellman half-mad—
He could only bake Bridecake—for which, I may state,
  No materials were to be had.

The last of the crew needs especial remark,
  Though he looked an incredible dunce:
He had just one idea—but, that one being "Snark",
  The good Bellman engaged him at once.

He came as a Butcher: but gravely declared,
  When the ship had been sailing a week,
He could only kill Beavers. The Bellman looked scared,
  And was almost too frightened to speak:

But at length he explained, in a tremulous tone,
  There was only one Beaver on board;
And that was a tame one he had of his own,
  Whose death would be deeply deplored.

The Beaver, who happened to hear the remark,
  Protested, with tears in its eyes,
That not even the rapture of hunting the Snark
  Could atone for that dismal surprise!

It strongly advised that the Butcher should be
  Conveyed in a separate ship:
But the Bellman declared that would never agree
  With the plans he had made for the trip:

Navigation was always a difficult art,
    Though with only one ship and one bell:
And he feared he must really decline, for his part,
    Undertaking another as well.

The Beaver's best course was, no doubt, to procure
    A second-hand dagger-proof coat—
So the Baker advised it—and next, to insure
    Its life in some Office of note:

This the Baker suggested, and offered for hire
    (On moderate terms), or for sale,
Two excellent Policies, one Against Fire
    And one Against Damage From Hail.

Yet still, ever after that sorrowful day,
    Whenever the Butcher was by,
The Beaver kept looking the opposite way,
    And appeared unaccountably shy.

Fit the Second

The Bellman's Speech

The Bellman himself they all praised to the skies—
    Such a carriage, such ease and such grace!
Such solemnity, too! One could see he was wise,
    The moment one looked in his face!

He had bought a large map representing the sea,
    Without the least vestige of land:
And the crew were much pleased when they found it to be
    A map they could all understand.

"What's the good of Mercator's North Poles and Equators,
    Tropics, Zones, and Meridian Lines?"
So the Bellman would cry: and the crew would reply
    "They are merely conventional signs!

"Other maps are such shapes, with their islands and capes!
    But we've got our brave Captain to thank"
(So the crew would protest) "that he's bought *us* the best—
    A perfect and absolute blank!"

This was charming, no doubt: but they shortly found out
    That the Captain they trusted so well
Had only one notion for crossing the ocean,
    And that was to tingle his bell.

He was thoughtful and grave—but the orders he gave
    Were enough to bewilder a crew.
When he cried "Steer to starboard, but keep her head larboard!"
    What on earth was the helmsman to do?

Then the bowsprit got mixed with the rudder sometimes;
    A thing, as the Bellman remarked,
That frequently happens in tropical climes,
    When a vessel is, so to speak, "snarked".

But the principal failing occurred in the sailing,
    And the Bellman, perplexed and distressed,
Said he *had* hoped, at least, when the wind blew due East,
    That the ship would *not* travel due West!

But the danger was past—they had landed at last,
    With their boxes, portmanteaus, and bags:
Yet at first sight the crew were not pleased with the view
    Which consisted of chasms and crags.

The Bellman perceived that their spirits were low,
    And repeated in musical tone
Some jokes he had kept for a season of woe—
    But the crew would do nothing but groan.

He served out some grog with a liberal hand,
    And bade them sit down on the beach:
And they could not but own that their Captain looked grand,
    As he stood and delivered his speech.

"Friends, Romans, and countrymen, lend me your ears!"
    (They were all of them fond of quotations:
So they drank to his health, and they gave him three cheers,
    While he served out additional rations).

"We have sailed many months, we have sailed many weeks,
    (Four weeks to the month you may mark),

But never as yet ('tis your Captain who speaks)
    Have we caught the least glimpse of a Snark!

"We have sailed many weeks, we have sailed many days,
    (Seven days to the week I allow),
But a Snark, on the which we might lovingly gaze,
    We have never beheld till now!

"Come, listen, my men, while I tell you again
    The five unmistakable marks
By which you may know, wheresoever you go,
    The warranted genuine Snarks.

"Let us take them in order. The first is the taste,
    Which is meagre and hollow, but crisp:
Like a coat that is rather too tight in the waist,
    With a flavour of Will-o'-the-Wisp.

"Its habit of getting up late you'll agree
    That it carries too far, when I say
That it frequently breakfasts at five-o'clock tea,
    And dines on the following day.

"The third is its slowness in taking a jest.
    Should you happen to venture on one.
It will sigh like a thing that is deeply distressed:
    And it always looks grave at a pun.

"The fourth is its fondness for bathing-machines,
    Which it constantly carries about,
And believes that they add to the beauty of scenes—
    A sentiment open to doubt.

"The fifth is ambition. It next will be right
    To describe each particular batch:
Distinguishing those that have feathers, and bite,
    From those that have whiskers, and scratch.

"For, although common Snarks do no manner of harm,
    Yet I feel it my duty to say
Some are Boojums——" The Bellman broke off in alarm,
    For the Baker had fainted away.

Fit the Third

The Baker's Tale

They roused him with muffins—they roused him with ice—
   They roused him with mustard and cress—
They roused him with jam and judicious advice—
   They set him conundrums to guess.

When at length he sat up and was able to speak,
   His sad story he offered to tell;
And the Bellman cried "Silence! Not even a shriek!"
   And excitedly tingled his bell.

There was silence supreme! Not a shriek, not a scream,
   Scarcely even a howl or a groan,
As the man they called "Ho!" told his story of woe
   In an antediluvian tone.

"My father and mother were honest, though poor——"
   "Skip all that!" cried the Bellman in haste.
"If it once becomes dark, there's no chance of a Snark—
   We have hardly a minute to waste!"

"I skip forty years," said the Baker in tears,
   "And proceed without further remark
To the day when you took me aboard of your ship
   To help you in hunting the Snark.

"A dear uncle of mine (after whom I was named)
   Remarked, when I bade him farewell——"
"Oh, skip your dear uncle!" the Bellman exclaimed,
   As he angrily tingled his bell.

"He remarked to me then," said that mildest of men,
   " 'If your Snark be a Snark, that is right:
Fetch it home by all means—you may serve it with greens
   And it's handy for striking a light.

" 'You may seek it with thimbles—and seek it with care—
   You may hunt it with forks and hope;
You may threaten its life with a railway-share;
   You may charm it with smiles and soap——' "

("That's exactly the method," the Bellman bold
    In a hasty parenthesis cried.
"That's exactly the way I have always been told
    That the capture of Snarks should be tried!")

" 'But oh, beamish nephew, beware of the day,
    If your Snark be a Boojum! For then
You will softly and suddenly vanish away,
    And never be met with again!'

"It is this, it is this that oppresses my soul,
    When I think of my uncle's last words:
And my heart is like nothing so much as a bowl
    Brimming over with quivering curds!

"It is this, it is this——" "We have had that before!"
    The Bellman indignantly said.
And the Baker replied "Let me say it once more.
    It is this, it is this that I dread!

"I engage with the Snark—every night after dark—
    In a dreamy delirious fight:
I serve it with greens in those shadowy scenes,
    And I use it for striking a light:

"But if ever I meet with a Boojum, that day,
    In a moment (of this I am sure),
I shall softly and suddenly vanish away—
    And the notion I cannot endure!"

Fit the Fourth

The Hunting

The Bellman looked uffish, and wrinkled his brow.
    "If only you'd spoken before!
It's excessively awkward to mention it now,
    With the Snark, so to speak, at the door!

"We should all of us grieve, as you well may believe,
    If you never were met with again—
But surely, my man, when the voyage began,
    You might have suggested it then?

"It's excessively awkward to mention it now—
    As I think I've already remarked."
And the man they called "Hi!" replied, with a sigh,
    "I informed you the day we embarked.

"You may charge me with murder—or want of sense—
    (We are all of us weak at times):
But the slightest approach to a false pretence
    Was never among my crimes!

"I said it in Hebrew—I said it in Dutch—
    I said it in German and Greek:
But I wholly forgot (and it vexes me much)
    That English is what you speak!"

" 'Tis a pitiful tale," said the Bellman, whose face
    Had grown longer at every word:
"But, now that you've stated the whole of your case,
    More debate would be simply absurd.

"The rest of my speech" (he exclaimed to his men)
    "You shall hear when I've leisure to speak it.
But the Snark is at hand, let me tell you again!
    'Tis your glorious duty to seek it!

"To seek it with thimbles, to seek it with care;
    To pursue it with forks and hope;
To threaten its life with a railway-share:
    To charm it with smiles and soap!

"For the Snark's a peculiar creature, that wo'n't
    Be caught in a commonplace way.
Do all that you know, and try all that you don't:
    Not a chance must be wasted to-day!

"For England expects—I forbear to proceed:
    'Tis a maxim tremendous, but trite:
And you'd best be unpacking the things that you need
    To rig yourselves out for the fight."

Then the Banker endorsed a blank cheque (which he crossed),
    And changed his loose silver for notes:

The Baker with care combed his whiskers and hair,
  And shook the dust out of his coats:

The Boots and the Broker were sharpening a spade—
  Each working the grindstone in turn:
But the Beaver went on making lace, and displayed
  No interest in the concern:

Though the Barrister tried to appeal to its pride,
  And vainly proceeded to cite
A number of cases, in which making laces
  Had been proved an infringement of right.

The maker of Bonnets ferociously planned
  A novel arrangement of bows:
While the Billiard-marker with quivering hand
  Was chalking the tip of his nose.

But the Butcher turned nervous, and dressed himself fine,
  With yellow kid gloves and a ruff
Said he felt it exactly like going to dine,
  Which the Bellman declared was all "stuff".

"Introduce me, now there's a good fellow," he said,
  "If we happen to meet it together!"
And the Bellman, sagaciously nodding his head,
  Said "That must depend on the weather."

The Beaver went simply galumphing about,
  At seeing the Butcher so shy:
And even the Baker, though stupid and stout,
  Made an effort to wink with one eye.

"Be a man!" said the Bellman in wrath, as he heard
  The Butcher beginning to sob.
"Should we meet with a Jubjub, that desperate bird,
  We shall need all our strength for the job!"

Fit the Fifth

The Beaver's Lesson

They sought it with thimbles, they sought it with care;
  They pursued it with forks and hope;

They threatened its life with a railway-share;
    They charmed it with smiles and soap.

Then the Butcher contrived an ingenious plan
    For making a separate sally;
And had fixed on a spot unfrequented by man,
    A dismal and desolate valley.

But the very same plan to the Beaver occurred:
    It had chosen the very same place:
Yet neither betrayed, by a sign or a word,
    The disgust that appeared in his face.

Each thought he was thinking of nothing but "Snark"
    And the glorious work of the day;
And each tried to pretend that he did not remark
    That the other was going that way.

But the valley grew narrower and narrower still,
    And the evening got darker and colder,
Till (merely from nervousness, not from good will)
    They marched along shoulder to shoulder.

Then a scream, shrill and high, rent the shuddering sky
    And they knew that some danger was near:
The Beaver turned pale to the tip of its tail,
    And even the Butcher felt queer.

He thought of his childhood, left far behind—
    That blissful and innocent state—
The sound so exactly recalled to his mind
    A pencil that squeaks on a slate!

"'Tis the voice of the Jubjub!" he suddenly cried.
    (This man, that they used to call "Dunce".)
"As the Bellman would tell you," he added with pride,
    "I have uttered that sentiment once.

"'Tis the note of the Jubjub! Keep count, I entreat.
    You will find I have told it you twice.
'Tis the song of the Jubjub! The proof is complete.
    If only I've stated it thrice."

The Beaver had counted with scrupulous care,
    Attending to every word:
But it fairly lost heart, and outgrabe in despair,
    When the third repetition occurred.

It felt that, in spite of all possible pains,
    It had somehow contrived to lose count,
And the only thing now was to rack its poor brains
    By reckoning up the amount.

"Two added to one—if that could but be done,"
    It said, "with one's fingers and thumbs!"
Recollecting with tears how, in earlier years,
    It had taken no pains with its sums.

"The thing can be done," said the Butcher, "I think.
    The thing must be done, I am sure.
The thing shall be done! Bring me paper and ink.
    The best there is time to procure."

The Beaver brought paper, portfolio, pens,
    And ink in unfailing supplies:
While strange creepy creatures came out of their dens,
    And watched them with wondering eyes.

So engrossed was the Butcher, he heeded them not,
    As he wrote with a pen in each hand,
And explained all the while in a popular style
    Which the Beaver could well understand.

"Taking Three as the subject to reason about—
    A convenient number to state—
We add Seven, and Ten, and then multiply out
    By One Thousand diminished by Eight.

"The result we proceed to divide, as you see,
    By Nine Hundred and Ninety and Two:
Then subtract Seventeen, and the answer must be
    Exactly and perfectly true.

"The method employed I would gladly explain,
    While I have it so clear in my head,

If I had but the time and you had but the brain—
    But much yet remains to be said.

"In one moment I've seen what has hitherto been
    Enveloped in absolute mystery,
And without extra charge I will give you at large
    A Lesson in Natural History."

In his genial way he proceeded to say
    (Forgetting all laws of propriety,
And that giving instruction, without introduction,
    Would have caused quite a thrill in Society),

"As to temper the Jubjub's a desperate bird,
    Since it lives in perpetual passion;
Its taste in costume is entirely absurd—
    It is ages ahead of the fashion:

"But it knows any friend it has met once before:
    It never will look at a bribe:
And in charity-meetings it stands at the door,
    And collects—though it does not subscribe.

"Its flavour when cooked is more exquisite far
    Than mutton, or oysters, or eggs:
(Some think it keeps best in an ivory jar,
    And some, in mahogany kegs:)

"You boil it in sawdust; you salt it in glue:
    You condense it with locusts and tape.
Still keeping one principal object in view—
    To preserve its symmetrical shape."

The Butcher would gladly have talked till next day,
    But he felt that the Lesson must end,
And he wept with delight in attempting to say
    He considered the Beaver his friend:

While the Beaver confessed, with affectionate looks
    More eloquent even than tears,
It had learned in ten minutes far more than all books
    Would have taught it in seventy years.

They returned hand-in-hand, and the Bellman, unmanned
   (For a moment) with noble emotion,
Said "This amply repays all the wearisome days
   We have spent on the billowy ocean!"

Such friends, as the Beaver and Butcher became,
   Have seldom if ever been known;
In winter or summer, 'twas always the same—
   You could never meet either alone.

And when quarrels arose—as one frequently finds
   Quarrels will, spite of every endeavour—
The song of the Jubjub recurred to their minds,
   And cemented their friendship for ever!

Fit the Sixth

The Barrister's Dream

They sought it with thimbles, they sought it with care;
   They pursued it with forks and hope;
They threatened its life with a railway-share;
   They charmed it with smiles and soap.

But the Barrister, weary of proving in vain
   That the Beaver's lace-making was wrong,
Fell asleep, and in dreams saw the creature quite plain
   That his fancy had dwelt on so long.

He dreamed that he stood in a shadowy Court,
   Where the Snark, with a glass in its eye,
Dressed in gown, bands, and wig, was defending a pig
   On the charge of deserting its sty.

The Witnesses proved, without error or flaw,
   That the sty was deserted when found:
And the Judge kept explaining the state of the law
   In a soft under-current of sound.

The indictment had never been clearly expressed,
   And it seemed that the Snark had begun,
And had spoken three hours, before any one guessed
   What the pig was supposed to have done.

The Jury had each formed a different view
    (Long before the indictment was read),
And they all spoke at once, so that none of them knew
    One word that the others had said.

"You must know——" said the Judge: but the Snark exclaimed "Fudge!
    That statute is obsolete quite!
Let me tell you, my friends, the whole question depends
    On an ancient manorial right.

"In the matter of Treason the pig would appear
    To have aided, but scarcely abetted:
While the charge of Insolvency fails, it is clear,
    If you grant the plea 'never indebted'.

"The fact of Desertion I will not dispute:
    But its guilt, as I trust, is removed
(So far as relates to the costs of this suit)
    By the Alibi which has been proved.

"My poor client's fate now depends on your votes."
    Here the speaker sat down in his place,
And directed the Judge to refer to his notes
    And briefly to sum up the case.

But the Judge said he never had summed up before;
    So the Snark undertook it instead,
And summed it so well that it came to far more
    Than the Witnesses ever had said!

When the verdict was called for, the Jury declined,
    As the word was so puzzling to spell;
But they ventured to hope that the Snark wouldn't mind
    Undertaking that duty as well.

So the Snark found the verdict, although, as it owned,
    It was spent with the toils of the day:
When it said the word "GUILTY!" the Jury all groaned
    And some of them fainted away.

Then the Snark pronounced sentence, the Judge being quite
    Too nervous to utter a word:

When it rose to its feet, there was silence like night,
　　And the fall of a pin might be heard.

"Transportation for life" was the sentence it gave,
　　"And *then* to be fined forty pound."
The Jury all cheered, though the Judge said he feared
　　That the phrase was not legally sound.

But their wild exultation was suddenly checked
　　When the jailer informed them, with tears,
Such a sentence would have not the slightest effect,
　　As the pig had been dead for some years.

The Judge left the Court, looking deeply disgusted,
　　But the Snark, though a little aghast,
As the lawyer to whom the defence was intrusted,
　　Went bellowing on to the last.

Thus the Barrister dreamed, while the bellowing seemed
　　To grow every moment more clear:
Till he woke to the knell of a furious bell,
　　Which the Bellman rang close at his ear.

Fit the Seventh

The Banker's Fate

They sought it with thimbles, they sought it with care;
　　They pursued it with forks and hope;
They threatened its life with a railway-share,
　　They charmed it with smiles and soap.

And the Banker, inspired with a courage so new
　　It was matter for general remark,
Rushed madly ahead and was lost to their view
　　In his zeal to discover the Snark.

But while he was seeking with thimbles and care,
　　A Bandersnatch swiftly drew nigh
And grabbed at the Banker, who shrieked in despair,
　　For he knew it was useless to fly.

He offered large discount—he offered a cheque
　　(Drawn "to bearer") for seven-pounds-ten:

But the Bandersnatch merely extended its neck
    And grabbed at the Banker again.

Without rest or pause—while those frumious jaws
    Went savagely snapping around—
He skipped and he hopped, and he floundered and flopped,
    Till fainting he fell to the ground.

The Bandersnatch fled as the others appeared
    Led on by that fear-stricken yell:
And the Bellman remarked "It is just as I feared!"
    And solemnly tolled on his bell.

He was black in the face, and they scarcely could trace
    The least likeness to what he had been:
While so great was his fright that his waistcoat turned white—
    A wonderful thing to be seen!

To the horror of all who were present that day,
    He uprose in full evening dress,
And with senseless grimaces endeavoured to say
    What his tongue could no longer express.

Down he sank in a chair—ran his hands through his hair—
    And chanted in mimsiest tones
Words whose utter inanity proved his insanity,
    While he rattled a couple of bones.

"Leave him here to his fate—it is getting so late!"
    The Bellman exclaimed in a fright.
"We have lost half the day. Any further delay,
    And we sha'n't catch a Snark before night!"

Fit the Eight

The Vanishing

They sought it with thimbles, they sought it with care;
    They pursued it with forks and hope;
They threatened its life with a railway-share;
    They charmed it with smiles and soap.

They shuddered to think that the chase might fail,
    And the Beaver, excited at last,

Went bounding along on the tip of its tail,
    For the daylight was nearly past.

"There is Thingumbob shouting!" the Bellman said.
    "He is shouting like mad, only hark!
He is waving his hands, he is wagging his head,
    He has certainly found a Snark!"

They gazed in delight, while the Butcher exclaimed
    "He was always a desperate wag!"
They beheld him—their Baker—their hero unnamed—
    On the top of a neighbouring crag,

Erect and sublime, for one moment of time,
    In the next, that wild figure they saw
(As if stung by a spasm) plunge into a chasm,
    While they waited and listened in awe.

"It's a Snark!" was the sound that first came to their ears,
    And seemed almost too good to be true.
Then followed a torrent of laughter and cheers:
    Then the ominous words "It's a Boo—"

Then, silence. Some fancied they heard in the air
    A weary and wandering sigh
That sounded like "—jum!" but the others declare
    It was only a breeze that went by.

They hunted till darkness came on, but they found
    Not a button, or feather, or mark,
By which they could tell that they stood on the ground
    Where the Baker had met with the Snark.

In the midst of the word he was trying to say,
    In the midst of his laughter and glee,
He had softly and suddenly vanished away—
    For the Snark *was* a Boojum, you see.

The Mad Gardener's Song

He thought he saw an Elephant,
    That practised on a fife:

He looked again, and found it was
    A letter from his wife.
"At length I realize," he said,
    "The bitterness of Life!"

He thought he saw a Buffalo
    Upon the chimney-piece;
He looked again, and found it was
    His Sister's Husband's Niece,
"Unless you leave this house," he said,
    "I'll send for the Police!"

He thought he saw a Rattlesnake
    That questioned him in Greek:
He looked again, and found it was
    The Middle of Next Week.
"The one thing I regret," he said,
    "Is that it cannot speak!"

He thought he saw a Banker's Clerk
    Descending from the 'bus:
He looked again, and found it was
    A Hippopotamus.
"If this should stay to dine," he said
    "There won't be much for us!"

He thought he saw a Kangaroo
    That worked a coffee-mill:
He looked again, and found it was
    A Vegetable-Pill.
"Were I to swallow this," he said,
    "I should be very ill!"

He thought he saw a Coach-and-Four
    That stood beside his bed:
He looked again, and found it was
    A Bear without a Head.
"Poor thing," he said, "poor silly thing!
    It's waiting to be fed!"

He thought he saw an Albatross
    That fluttered around the lamp:
He looked again, and found it was

A Penny-Postage-Stamp.
"You'd best be getting home," he said,
    "The nights are very damp!"

He thought he saw a Garden-Door
    That opened with a key:
He looked again, and found it was
    A Double Rule of Three:
"And all its mystery," he said
    "Is clear as day to me!"

He thought he saw an Argument
    That proved he was the Pope:
He looked again, and found it was
    A Bar of Mottled Soap.
"A fact so dread," he faintly said,
    "Extinguishes all hope!"

A Pig-Tale

There was a Pig that sat alone
    Beside a ruined Pump:
By day and night he made his moan—
It would have stirred a heart of stone
To see him wring his hoofs and groan,
    Because he could not jump.

A certain Camel heard him shout—
    A Camel with a hump.
"Oh, is it Grief, or is it Gout?
What is this bellowing about?"
That Pig replied, with quivering snout,
    "Because I cannot jump!"

That Camel scanned him, dreamy-eyed.
    "Methinks you are too plump.
I never knew a Pig so wide—
That wobbled so from side to side—
Who could, however much he tried,
    Do such a thing as jump!

"Yet mark those trees, two miles away,
    All clustered in a clump:

If you could trot there twice a day,
Not ever pause for rest or play,
In the far future—Who can say?—
    You may be fit to jump."

That Camel passed, and left him there,
    Beside the ruined Pump.
Oh, horrid was that Pig's despair!
His shrieks of anguish filled the air.
He wrung his hoofs, he rent his hair,
    Because he could not jump.

There was a Frog that wandered by—
    A sleek and shinning lump:
Inspected him with fishy eye,
And said "O Pig, what makes you cry?"
And bitter was that Pig's reply,
    "Because I cannot jump!"

That Frog he grinned a grin of glee,
    And hit his chest a thump.
"O Pig," he said, "be ruled by me,
And you shall see what you shall see.
This minute, for a trifling fee,
    I'll teach you how to jump!

"You may be faint from many a fall,
    And bruised by many a bump:
But, if you persevere through all,
And practise first on something small,
Concluding with a ten-foot wall,
    You'll find that you can jump!"

That Pig looked up with joyful start:
    "Oh Frog, you are a thump!
Your words have healed my inward smart—
Come, name your fee and do your part:
Bring comfort to a broken heart,
    By teaching me to jump!"

"My fee shall be a mutton-chop,
    My goal this ruined Pump.

Observe with what an airy flop
I plant myself upon the top!
Now bend your knees and take a hop,
    For that's the way to jump!"

Uprose that Pig, and rushed, full whack,
    Against the ruined Pump:
Rolled over like an empty sack,
And settled down upon his back,
While all his bones at once went "Crack!"
    It was a fatal jump.

That Camel passed, as Day grew dim
    Around the ruined Pump.
"O broken heart! O broken limb!
It needs," that Camel said to him,
"Something more fairy-like and slim,
    To execute a jump!"

That Pig lay still as any stone,
    And could not stir a stump:
Nor ever, if the truth were known,
Was he again observed to moan,
Nor ever wring his hoofs and groan,
    Because he could not jump.

That Frog made no remark, for he
    Was dismal as a dump:
He knew the consequence must be
That he would never get his fee—
And still he sits, in miserie,
    Upon that ruined Pump!

The Walrus and the Carpenter

"The sun was shining on the sea,
    Shining with all his might:
He did his very best to make
    The billows smooth and bright—
And this was odd, because it was
    The middle of the night.

The moon was shining sulkily,
 Because she thought the sun
Had got no business to be there
 After the day was done—
'It's very rude of him,' she said,
 'To come and spoil the fun!'

The sea was wet as wet could be,
 The sands were dry as dry.
You could not see a cloud, because
 No cloud was in the sky:
No birds were flying overhead—
 There were no birds to fly.

The Walrus and the Carpenter
 Were walking close at hand:
They wept like anything to see
 Such quantities of sand:
'If this were only cleared away,'
 They said, 'it would be grand!'

'If seven maids with seven mops
 Swept it for half a year,
Do you suppose,' the Walrus said,
 'That they could get it clear?'
'I doubt it,' said the Carpenter,
 And shed a bitter tear.

'O Oysters, come and walk with us!'
 The Walrus did beseech.
'A pleasant walk, a pleasant talk,
 Along the briny beach:
We cannot do with more than four,
 To give a hand to each.'

The eldest Oyster looked at him,
 But never a word he said:
The eldest Oyster winked his eye,
 And shook his heavy head—
Meaning to say he did not choose
 To leave the oyster-bed.

But four young Oysters hurried up,
     All eager for the treat:
Their coats were brushed, their faces washed,
     Their shoes were clean and neat—
And this was odd, because, you know,
     They hadn't any feet.

Four other Oysters followed them,
     And yet another four;
And thick and fast they came at last,
     And more, and more, and more—
All hopping through the frothy waves,
     And scrambling to the shore.

The Walrus and the Carpenter
     Walked on a mile or so,
And then they rested on a rock
     Conveniently low:
And all the little Oysters stood
     And waited in a row.

'The time has come,' the Walrus said,
     'To talk of many things:
Of shoes—and ships—and sealing wax—
     Of cabbages—and kings—
And why the sea is boiling hot—
     And whether pigs have wings.'

'But wait a bit,' the Oysters cried,
     'Before we have our chat;
For some of us are out of breath,
     And all of us are fat!'
'No hurry!' said the Carpenter.
     They thanked him much for that.

'A loaf of bread,' the Walrus said,
     'Is what we chiefly need:
Pepper and vinegar besides
     Are very good indeed—
Now, if you're ready, Oysters dear,
     We can begin to feed.'

'But not on us!' the Oysters cried,
    Turning a little blue.
'After such kindness, that would be
    A dismal thing to do!'
'The night is fine,' the Walrus said.
    'Do you admire the view?

'It was so kind of you to come!
    And you are very nice!'
The Carpenter said nothing but
    'Cut us another slice.
I wish you were not quite so deaf—
    I've had to ask you twice!'

'It seems a shame,' the Walrus said,
    'To play them such a trick.
After we've brought them out so far,
    And made them trot so quick!'
The Carpenter said nothing but
'The butter's spread too thick!'

'I weep for you,' the Walrus said:
    'I deeply sympathize.'
With sobs and tears he sorted out
    Those of the largest size,
Holding his pocket-handkerchief
Before his streaming eyes.

'O Oysters,' said the Carpenter,
    'You've had a pleasant run!
Shall we be trotting home again?'
    But answer came there none—
And this was scarcely odd, because
    They'd eaten every one."

GEORGE MEREDITH

1828–1909

MEREDITH IS NOW remembered more as a novelist than as a poet, though his poetry is of a high order. I would like to have represented him copiously here, with the longish erotic hymn "Love in the Valley," five sonnets from the tragic sequence *Modern Love,* and I wish there were room for "The Lark Ascending" and selections from "The Woods of Westermain," since Meredith, like John Clare, is one of the best neglected poets in the language.

Readers are likelier now to have read some of Meredith's novels, particularly *The Ordeal of Richard Feverel* (1859), *The Egoist* (1879), and *Diana of the Crossways* (1885). *The Egoist* is a comic masterpiece, worthy of Meredith's own very useful *Essay on Comedy.*

As a poet, Meredith began as Rossetti's disciple, but with a Wordsworthian tempering that helped preserve him from Rossetti's fierce idiosyncracies. With no formal education, Meredith became a literary journalist. He married the tempestuous daughter of the poet-novelist Thomas Love Peacock. After nine terrible years, she sensibly ran off with a painter. Meredith intrepidly moved in with Rossetti and Swinburne, a perfectly mad household, from which he was rescued by his happy second marriage.

"Love in the Valley" is one of the happiest poems in the language, while the *Modern Love* sequence of quasi-sonnets (sixteen lines each) is one of the saddest. "A Ballad of Past Meridian" is both eloquently macabre and resolute.

❧   ❧   ❧

from Modern Love

L

Thus piteously Love closed what he begat:
The union of this ever-diverse pair!
These two were rapid falcons in a snare,
Condemned to do the flitting of the bat.
Lovers beneath the singing sky of May,
They wandered once; clear as the dew on flowers:

But they fed not on the advancing hours:
Their hearts held cravings for the buried day.
Then each applied to each that fatal knife,
10   Deep questioning, which probes to endless dole.
Ah, what a dusty answer gets the soul
When hot for certainties in this our life!—
In tragic hints here see what evermore
Moves dark as yonder midnight ocean's force,
Thundering like ramping hosts of warrior horse,
To throw that faint thin line upon the shore!

    1862   1892

A Ballad of Past Meridian

Last night returning from my twilight walk
I met the grey mist Death, whose eyeless brow
Was bent on me, and from his hand of chalk
He reached me flowers as from a withered bough.
O Death, what bitter nosegays givest thou!

Death said, 'I gather,' and pursued his way.
Another stood by me, a shape in stone,
Sword-hacked and iron-stained, with breasts of clay,
And metal veins that sometimes fiery shone.
10   O Life, how naked and how hard when known!

Life said, 'As thou hast carved me, such am I.'
Then Memory, like the nightjar on the pine,
And sightless Hope, a woodlark in night sky,
Joined notes of Death and Life till night's decline.
Of Death, of Life, those inwound notes are mine.

    1876

RUDYARD KIPLING

1865–1936

KIPLING WAS A SUPERB STORY WRITER, and composed an enduring novel in *Kim,* much under the influence of Mark Twain. His two *Jungle Books* also do not wear out. As a verse writer, he has become something of a special case. The *Barrack-Room Ballads* of 1892 are authentic "popular poetry," and persist. Here I have contrasted two antithetical poems, the popular "The Vampire" and the lyrical "The Way Through the Woods."

"The Vampire" works with men, and not at all with women. Kipling, born in Bombay, was unhappy during his English education, but prospered as a journalist and writer of stories and verses, when he returned to India. His subsequent marriage, to an American, proved unfortunate, and its demise returned him from Vermont to England. His views on women-as-vampires do not appear to have undergone much change.

Yet "The Way Through the Woods" is always reciting itself in my head. Its hint of a lost eros may be the largest clue to Kipling's many enigmas.

❦   ❦   ❦

The Vampire

A fool there was and he made his prayer
(Even as you and I!)
To a rag and a bone and a hank of hair
(We called her the woman who did not care)
But the fool he called her his lady fair—
(Even as you and I!)

Oh, the years we waste and the tears we waste
And the work of our head and hand
Belong to the woman who did not know
(And now we know that she never could know)
And did not understand!

A fool there was and his goods he spent
(Even as you and I!)

Honour and faith and a sure intent
(And it wasn't the least what the lady meant)
But a fool must follow his natural bent
(Even as you and I!)

Oh, the toil we lost and the spoil we lost
And the excellent things we planned
Belong to the woman who didn't know why
(And now we know that she never knew why)
And did not understand!

The fool was stripped to his foolish hide
(Even as you and I!)
Which she might have seen when she threw him aside—
(But it isn't on record the lady tried)
So some of him lived but the most of him died—
(Even as you and I!)

And it isn't the shame and it isn't the blame
That stings like a white hot brand—
It's coming to know that she never knew why
(Seeing, at last, she could never know why)
And never could understand!

The Way Through the Woods

They shut the road through the woods
Seventy years ago.
Weather and rain have undone it again,
And now you would never know
There was once a road through the woods
Before they planted the trees.
It is underneath the coppice and heath,
And the thin anemones.
Only the keeper sees
That, where the ring-dove broods,
And the badgers roll at ease,
There was once a road through the woods.

Yet, if you enter the woods
Of a summer evening late,
When the night-air cools on the trout-ringed pools

Where the otter whistles his mate
(They fear not men in the woods,
Because they see so few),
You will hear the beat of a horse's feet
And the swish of a skirt in the dew,
Steadily cantering through
The misty solitudes,
As though they perfectly knew
The old lost road through the woods . . .
But there is no road through the woods!

WILLIAM BUTLER YEATS

1865–1939

THE ANGLO-IRISH POET W. B. Yeats probably was the major poet in English of the twentieth century, surpassing even Thomas Hardy, Robert Frost, Wallace Stevens, T. S. Eliot, and Hart Crane. One might have to turn to William Wordsworth to find a more eminent poet.

Yeats was an enthusiastic occultist, like Victor Hugo before him and like our late contemporary James Merrill. One cannot dismiss Yeats's occultism as a side issue: it is frequently central to his poetry. Mrs. Yeats was a medium, and the spirits spoke through her to her husband on 450 visitations.

In 1917, only a few months before he married Bertha George Hyde-Lees (she was twenty-five to his fifty-two), Yeats composed the most beautiful of his prose reveries, *Per Amica Silentia Lunae* ("in the moon's friendly silence"). This marmoreal meditation, much influenced by Walter Pater's style, centers in a passage that will forever stay with me:

> He only can create the greatest imaginable beauty who has endured all imaginable pangs, for only when we have seen and foreseen what we dread shall we be rewarded by that dazzling, unforeseen, wing-footed wanderer. We could not find him if he were not in some sense of our being, and yet of our own being but

as water with fire, a noise with silence. He is of all things not impossible the most difficult, for that which comes easily can never be a portion of our being; soon got, soon gone, as the proverb says. I shall find the dark grown luminous, the void fruitful when I understand I have nothing, that the ringers in the tower have appointed for the hymen of the soul a passing bell.

That is Yeats's truest and most passionate conviction, and while for him it was occult, it is universal in its implications.

Born in Dublin on June 13, 1865, Yeats was descended from a line of Protestant clergymen, a tradition broken by his exuberant father, the painter John Butler Yeats. W. B. Yeats's brother, Jack Butler Yeats, became one of the most respected of Irish painters, and W. B. himself began as a student in the Dublin School of Art. But soon his literary powers manifested themselves with his long poem *The Wanderings of Oisin* (1889). During this same time he met and fell desperately in love with Maud Gonne, whom he was to court fruitlessly for twenty-eight years.

Yeats's life was turbulent, centered upon the Abbey Theatre in Dublin, for which he wrote a sequence of remarkable verse-dramas. Meanwhile, the violent revolutionary Maud Gonne married Major John MacBride, a gunman who was to be one of the executed leaders of the Easter Rising in Dublin against the British in 1916.

After his marriage, that taking place the next year, Yeats entered upon his major phase in a superb volume of lyrics, *The Wild Swans at Coole* (1918). His later works culminate in *The Tower* (1928), *The Winding Stair* (1933), and the posthumous *Last Poems* (1939).

I have represented Yeats here by the ever-popular "The Song of Wandering Aengus," by the wisdom-meditation "Adam's Curse," by the perfect lyric "The Wild Swans at Coole," and by three visionary poems that emerge from his "system": "The Cold Heaven," "The Second Coming," and "The Double Vision of Michael Robartes." My separate headnote on "The Second Coming" is also a brief introduction to the occult Yeats.

❧   ❧   ❧

The Song of Wandering Aengus

I went out to the hazel wood,
Because a fire was in my head,
And cut and peeled a hazel wand,
And hooked a berry to a thread;

And when white moths were on the wing,
And moth-like stars were flickering out,
I dropped the berry in a stream
And caught a little silver trout.

When I had laid it on the floor
I went to blow the fire aflame,
But something rustled on the floor,
And some one called me by my name:
It had become a glimmering girl
With apple blossom in her hair
Who called me by my name and ran
And faded through the brightening air.

Though I am old with wandering
Through hollow lands and hilly lands,
I will find out where she has gone,
And kiss her lips and take her hands;
And walk among long dappled grass,
And pluck till time and times are done
The silver apples of the moon,
The golden apples of the sun.

Adam's Curse

We sat together at one summer's end,
That beautiful mild woman, your close friend,
And you and I, and talked of poetry.
I said, 'A line will take us hours maybe;
Yet if it does not seem a moment's thought,
Our stitching and unstitching has been naught.

Better go down upon your marrow-bones
And scrub a kitchen pavement, or break stones
Like an old pauper, in all kinds of weather;
For to articulate sweet sounds together
Is to work harder than all these, and yet
Be thought an idler by the noisy set
Of bankers, schoolmasters, and clergymen
The martyrs call the world.'

                    And thereupon
That beautiful mild woman for whose sake

There's many a one shall find out all heartache
On finding that her voice is sweet and low
Replied, 'To be born woman is to know—
Although they do not talk of it at school—
20   That we must labour to be beautiful.'

I said, 'It's certain there is no fine thing
Since Adam's fall but needs much labouring.
There have been lovers who thought love should be
So much compounded of high courtesy
That they would sigh and quote with learned looks
Precedents out of beautiful old books;
Yet now it seems an idle trade enough.'

We sat grown quiet at the name of love;
We saw the last embers of daylight die,
30   And in the trembling blue-green of the sky
A moon, worn as if it had been a shell
Washed by time's waters as they rose and fell
About the stars and broke in days and years.

I had a thought for no one's but your ears:
That you were beautiful, and that I strove
To love you in the old high way of love;
That it had all seemed happy, and yet we'd grown
As weary-hearted as that hollow moon.

    1902? 1902

The Cold Heaven

Suddenly I saw the cold and rook-delighting heaven
That seemed as though ice burned and was but the more ice,
And thereupon imagination and heart were driven
So wild that every casual thought of that and this
Vanished, and left but memories, that should be out of season
With the hot blood of youth, of love crossed long ago;
And I took all the blame out of all sense and reason,
Until I cried and trembled and rocked to and fro,
Riddled with light. Ah! when the ghost begins to quicken,
10   Confusion of the death-bed over, is it sent
Out naked on the roads, as the books say, and stricken
By the injustice of the skies for punishment?

    1910   1910

The Second Coming

In January 1919, Yeats began to write an apocalyptic poem that initially he titled "The Second Birth." Politically a partisan of the extreme Right, Yeats was horrified by the Russian Revolution, and his first draft celebrated the coming of the proto-Fascist German *Freikorps* to Russia, as part of the attempt to end the Revolution. But "The Second Coming," as Yeats came to call it, was purged in revision of most of its merely political elements.

Why is the poem called "The Second Coming"? Yeats, fiercely not a Christian, did not believe in the first coming of Christ. This extraordinary chant celebrates the Second Birth (ironically, the Second Coming) of the Egyptian Sphinx of Memphis, one-eyed God of the Sun. This Sphinx is male, and for Yeats represents the spirit of counterrevolutionary violence. Shelley's "Ozymandias" and Blake's *The Book of Urizen* are alluded to by Yeats, but he seeks to turn their radical visions into a fable for the Right.

In *A Vision,* Christ represents a false myth of *primary* salvation, while the *antithetical* Beast, the Sphinx, incarnates the truth. In this great poem of *antithetical* influx, Yeats brilliantly suggests both intellectual welcome and emotional revulsion toward the "rough beast" who is coming. "The ceremony of innocence" for Yeats is necessarily an aristocratic matter; elsewhere he asked, rhetorically: "How but in custom and in ceremony / Are innocence and beauty born?"

I cannot think of any other modern poem with this overt rhetorical power. The falcon, emblem of royal sport, breaks loose, and things fall apart. In the poem's draft, Yeats had complained: "And there's no Burke to cry aloud, no Pitt," referring to Edmund Burke and William Pitt the Younger, fiercely eloquent denouncers of the French Revolution. Instead, Yeats looks at his allies and finds them inadequate compared to the advocates of revolution:

> The best lack all conviction, while the worst
> Are full of passionate intensity.

What can Yeats mean when he cries out: "Surely the Second Coming is at hand"? We know he means the Egyptian Sphinx and not Jesus, and yet he ends the poem with: "Slouches towards Bethlehem to be born." Are we to imagine the rough beast as devouring the Christ child in the cradle? We do not know, and we are left with Yeats's final, equivocal word, "born," which must have an ironical meaning in relation to the Sphinx. "The Second Coming" may not be a poem to love, but it distinctly is not a poem to be forgotten.

The Second Coming

Turning and turning in the widening gyre
The falcon cannot hear the falconer;
Things fall apart; the centre cannot hold;
Mere anarchy is loosed upon the world,
The blood-dimmed tide is loosed, and everywhere
The ceremony of innocence is drowned;
The best lack all conviction, while the worst
Are full of passionate intensity.

Surely some revelation is at hand;
10   Surely the Second Coming is at hand.
The Second Coming! Hardly are those words out
When a vast image out of *Spiritus Mundi*
Troubles my sight: somewhere in sands of the desert
A shape with lion body and the head of a man,
A gaze blank and pitiless as the sun,
Is moving its slow thighs, while all about it
Reel shadows of the indignant desert birds.
The darkness drops again; but now I know
That twenty centuries of stony sleep
20   Were vexed to nightmare by a rocking cradle,
And what rough beast, its hour come round at last,
Slouches towards Bethlehem to be born?

      1919   1921

The Wild Swans at Coole

The trees are in their autumn beauty,
The woodland paths are dry,
Under the October twilight the water
Mirrors a still sky;
Upon the brimming water among the stones
Are nine-and-fifty swans.

The nineteenth autumn has come upon me
Since I first made my count;
I saw, before I had well finished,

All suddenly mount
And scatter wheeling in great broken rings
Upon their clamorous wings.

I have looked upon those brilliant creatures,
And now my heart is sore.
All's changed since I, hearing at twilight,
The first time on this shore,
The bell-beat of their wings above my head,
Trod with a lighter tread.

Unwearied still, lover by lover,
They paddle in the cold
Companionable streams or climb the air;
Their hearts have not grown old;
Passion or conquest, wander where they will,
Attend upon them still.

But now they drift on the still water,
Mysterious, beautiful;
Among what rushes will they build,
By what lake's edge or pool
Delight men's eyes when I awake some day
To find they have flown away?

The Double Vision of Michael Robartes

I

On the grey rock of Cashel the mind's eye
Has called up the cold spirits that are born
When the old moon is vanished from the sky
And the new still hides her horn.

Under blank eyes and fingers never still
The particular is pounded till it is man.
When had I my own will?
O not since life began.

Constrained, arraigned, baffled, bent and unbent
By these wire-jointed jaws and limbs of wood,
Themselves obedient,
Knowing not evil and good;

Obedient to some hidden magical breath.
They do not even feel, so abstract are they,
So dead beyond our death,
Triumph that we obey.

II

On the grey rock of Cashel I suddenly saw
A Sphinx with woman breast and lion paw,
A Buddha, hand at rest,
Hand lifted up that blest;

And right between these two a girl at play
That, it may be, had danced her life away,
For now being dead it seemed
That she of dancing dreamed.

Although I saw it all in the mind's eye
There can be nothing solider till I die;
I saw by the moon's light
Now at its fifteenth night.

One lashed her tail; her eyes lit by the moon
Gazed upon all things known, all things unknown,
In triumph of intellect
With motionless head erect.

That other's moonlit eyeballs never moved,
Being fixed on all things loved, all things unloved,
Yet little peace he had,
For those that love are sad.

O little did they care who danced between,
And little she by whom her dance was seen
So she had outdanced thought.
Body perfection brought,

For what but eye and ear silence the mind
With the minute particulars of mankind?
Mind moved yet seemed to stop
As 'twere a spinning-top.

In contemplation had those three so wrought
Upon a moment, and so stretched it out

That they, time overthrown,
Were dead yet flesh and bone.

   III
I knew that I had seen, had seen at last
That girl my unremembering nights hold fast
Or else my dreams that fly
If I should rub an eye,

And yet in flying fling into my meat
A crazy juice that makes the pulses beat
As though I had been undone
By Homer's Paragon

Who never gave the burning town a thought;
To such a pitch of folly I am brought,
Being caught between the pull
Of the dark moon and the full,

The commonness of thought and images
That have the frenzy of our western seas.
Thereon I made my moan,
And after kissed a stone,

And after that arranged it in a song
Seeing that I, ignorant for so long,
Had been rewarded thus
In Cormac's ruined house.

| LIONEL JOHNSON |

1867–1902

LIKE HIS FRIENDS Ernest Dowson and the young W. B. Yeats, Johnson represented the poetry of the 1890s at its rare best. Although he came from an English military family, Johnson joined Yeats's Irish literary movement. Unable to accept his own homosexuality, Johnson converted to

Roman Catholicism in 1891. Dead of alcoholism at thirty-five, Johnson left one masterpiece, "The Dark Angel."

The Dark Angel is a fusion of Satan, Johnson's shadow self, and his homosexuality, but also his precursor Shelley, who had urged us to cast out penitence, holding that remorse was only "the dark idolatry of self." A forerunner closer in time, the critic Walter Pater is also an aspect of the Dark Angel, since Pater argued that an intensity of aesthetic experience was all that mattered. Pater's "gem-like flame" becomes the morally unacceptable (by Johnson) "flames of evil ecstasy." At his poem's conclusion, Johnson quotes the most famous passage in Plotinus, founder of Neo-Platonism: "a flight of the alone to the alone," of the liberated spirit to the gods.

❧   ❧   ❧

The Dark Angel

Dark Angel, with thine aching lust
To rid the world of penitence:
Malicious Angel, who still dost
My soul such subtile violence!

Because of thee, no thought, no thing
Abides for me undesecrate:
Dark Angel, ever on the wing,
Who never reachest me too late!

When music sounds, then changest thou
10   Its silvery to a sultry fire:
Nor will thine envious heart allow
Delight untortured by desire.

Through thee, the gracious Muses turn
To Furies, O mine Enemy!
And all the things of beauty burn
With flames of evil ecstasy.

Because of thee, the land of dreams
Becomes a gathering-place of fears:
Until tormented slumber seems
20   One vehemence of useless tears.

When sunlight glows upon the flowers,
Or ripples down the dancing sea:

Thou, with thy troop of passionate powers,
Beleaguerest, bewilderest me.

Within the breath of autumn woods,
Within the winter silences:
Thy venomous spirit stirs and broods,
O master of impieties!

The ardour of red flames is thine,
30 And thine the steely soul of ice:
Thou poisonest the fair design
Of nature, with unfair device.

Apples of ashes, golden bright;
Waters of bitterness, how sweet!
O banquet of a foul delight,
Prepared by thee, dark Paraclete.

Thou art the whisper in the gloom,
The lilting tone, the haunting laugh:
Thou art the adorner of my tomb,
40 The minstrel of mine epitaph.

I fight thee, in the Holy Name!
Yet, what thou dost, is what God saith:
Tempter! should I escape thy flame,
Thou wilt have helped my soul from Death:

The second Death, that never dies,
That cannot die, when time is dead:
Live Death, wherein the lost soul cries,
Eternally uncomforted.

Dark Angel, with thine aching lust!
50 Of two defeats, of two despairs:
Less dread, a change to drifting dust,
Than thine eternity of cares.

Do what thou wilt, thou shalt not so,
Dark Angel! triumph over me:
Lonely, unto the Lone I go;
Divine, to the Divinity.
        1893

ERNEST DOWSON

1867–1900

DOWSON WAS THE ARCHETYPAL poet of the 1890s, of what W. B. Yeats named the "Tragic Generation," which also included Lionel Johnson, poet-critic, as well as Oscar Wilde and Arthur Symons.

Raised mostly in France, Ernest Dowson left Oxford without a degree and lived hand-to-mouth as a translator, addicted to alcohol and drugs. As the century closed, Dowson died in Paris, aged thirty-three.

"*Non sum qualis eram bonae sub regno Cynarae*" is a line from Horace, *Odes* IV, 1: "I am not what once I was under the reign of the kind Cynara." Dowson's irony is fierce in this allusion, and his poem, despite its abandoned rhetoric, remains surprisingly effective, including even the phrase "gone with the wind," made overfamiliar through its appropriation by Margaret Mitchell for her popular novel about the American Civil War.

❧   ❧   ❧

Non sum qualis eram bonae sub regno Cynarae

Last night, ah, yesternight, betwixt her lips and mine
There fell thy shadow, Cynara! thy breath was shed
Upon my soul between the kisses and the wine;
And I was desolate and sick of an old passion,
    Yea, I was desolate and bowed my head:
I have been faithful to thee, Cynara! in my fashion.

All night upon mine heart I felt her warm heart beat,
Night-long within mine arms in love and sleep she lay;
Surely the kisses of her bought red mouth were sweet;
But I was desolate and sick of an old passion,
    When I awoke and found the dawn was gray:
I have been faithful to thee, Cynara! in my fashion.

I have forgot much, Cynara! gone with the wind.
Flung roses, roses riotously with the throng.
Dancing, to put thy pale, lost lilies out of mind;

But I was desolate and sick of an old passion,
    Yea, all the time, because the dance was long:
I have been faithful to thee, Cynara! in my fashion.

I cried for madder music and for stronger wine,
20   But when the feast is finished and the lamps expire,
Then falls thy shadow, Cynara! the night is thine;
And I am desolate and sick of an old passion,
    Yea, hungry for the lips of my desire:
I have been faithful to thee, Cynara! in my fashion.

    1896

THOMAS HARDY

1840–1928

THE FIVE POEMS I have chosen for this great poet-novelist are each remarkable as an aesthetic splendor, but scarcely can represent Hardy's poetic strength. Hardy's poems, like his prose fiction, enact a paradox: how can the imagination be so free when Hardy himself is passionately convinced that no freedom for the individual self is possible?

Hardy, like the philosopher Arthur Schopenhauer, believed that the rapacious Will to Live subsumed all individual will. Our desires are repetitious, and not openings to permanent love nor to possibilities of transcendence. Renunciation, negativity, tragedies of circumstance: these are the essence of Hardy.

Hardy began as an architect, and triumphed as a novelist, until in 1896 his last novel, *Jude the Obscure,* provoked a great deal of stupidity and malice. From 1896 until his death in 1928, Hardy concentrated upon his poetry, under the lasting influence of Shelley, whose final poems were more despairing of human nature than Hardy's own.

Hardy's long, very unhappy marriage to Emma Gifford was one element in his experiential sadness, but a consciousness as rugged and dark as Hardy's was never destined for contentment. In "Neutral Tones," a great hymn to the death of love, the reader encounters about as persuasive a vision of erotic destruction as even Shakespeare affords. Hymning the turn into the twentieth century, "The Darkling Thrush" recalls the ecstasy of Keats's nightingale and of Whitman's hermit thrush (in "Lilacs"), but suggests an unnegotiated distance between the song's "blessed Hope" and Hardy's unawareness.

My own favorite among Hardy's poems is the post-Shelleyan "During Wind and Rain," which makes a deliberate contrast with Shelley's apocalyptic "Ode to the West Wind." "How the sick leaves reel down in throngs!," Hardy cries out, while remembering that Shelley's "dead leaves" will quicken a new birth. Hardy has no such hopes, or yearnings.

❧   ❧   ❧

Neutral Tones

We stood by a pond that winter day,
And the sun was white, as though chidden of God,
And a few leaves lay on the starving sod;
        —They had fallen from an ash, and were grey.

Your eyes on me were as eyes that rove
Over tedious riddles of years ago;
And some words played between us to and fro
        On which lost the more by our love.

The smile on your mouth was the deadest thing
10 Alive enough to have strength to die;
And a grin of bitterness swept thereby
        Like an ominous bird a-wing. . . .

Since then, keen lessons that love deceives,
And wrings with wrong, have shaped to me
Your face, and the God-curst sun, and a tree.
        And a pond edged with greyish leaves.
    1867   1898

The Darkling Thrush

I leant upon a coppice gate
        When Frost was spectre-grey,
And Winter's dregs made desolate
        The weakening eye of day.

The tangled bine-stems scored the sky
    Like strings of broken lyres.
And all mankind that haunted nigh
    Had sought their household fires.

The land's sharp features seemed to be
    The Century's corpse outleant,
His crypt the cloudy canopy,
    The wind his death-lament.
The ancient pulse of germ and birth
    Was shrunken hard and dry,
And every spirit upon earth
    Seemed fervourless as I.

At once a voice arose among
    The bleak twigs overhead
In a full-hearted evensong
    Of joy illimited;
An agèd thrush, frail, gaunt, and small,
    In blast-beruffled plume,
Had chosen thus to fling his soul
    Upon the growing gloom.

So little cause for carolings
    Of such ecstatic sound
Was written on terrestrial things
    Afar or nigh around,
That I could think there trembled through
    His happy good-night air
Some blessèd Hope, whereof he knew
    And I was unaware.

    1900   1902

During Wind and Rain

    They sing their dearest songs—
    He, she, all of them—yea,
    Treble and tenor and bass,
        And one to play;
    With the candles mooning each face. . . .
        Ah, no; the years O!
How the sick leaves reel down in throngs!

They clear the creeping moss—
Elders and juniors—aye,
Making the pathways neat
   And the garden gay;
And they build a shady seat. . . .
    Ah, no; the years, the years;
See, the white storm-birds wing across!

They are blithely breakfasting all—
Men and maidens—yea,
Under the summer tree,
   With a glimpse of the bay,
While pet fowl come to the knee. . . .
    Ah, no: the years O!
And the rotten rose is ript from the wall.

They change to a high new house,
He, she, all of them—aye,
Clocks and carpets and chairs
   On the lawn all day,
And brightest things that are theirs. . . .
    Ah, no; the years, the years;
Down their carved names the rain-drop ploughs.

   1917

Moments of Vision

   That mirror
Which makes of men a transparency,
   Who holds that mirror
And bids us such a breast-bare spectacle see
   Of you and me?

   That mirror
Whose magic penetrates like a dart,
   Who lifts that mirror
And throws our mind back on us, and our heart,
   Until we start?

   That mirror
Works well in these night hours of ache;
   Why in that mirror

Are tincts we never see ourselves once take
    When the world is awake?

    That mirror
Can test each mortal when unaware;
    Yea, that strange mirror
May catch his last thoughts, whole life foul or fair,
20   Glassing it—where?

Afterwards

When the Present has latched its postern behind my tremulous stay,
    And the May month flaps its glad green leaves like wings,
Delicate-filmed as new-spun silk, will the neighbours say,
    'He was a man who used to notice such things'?

If it be in the dusk when, like an eyelid's soundless blink,
    The dewfall-hawk comes crossing the shades to alight
Upon the wind-warped upland thorn, a gazer may think,
    'To him this must have been a familiar sight.'

If I pass during some nocturnal blackness, mothy and warm,
10   When the hedgehog travels furtively over the lawn,
One may say, 'He strove that such innocent creatures should come to no harm,
    But he could do little for them; and now he is gone.'

If, when hearing that I have been stilled at last, they stand at the door,
    Watching the full-starred heavens that winter sees,
Will this thought rise on those who will meet my face no more,
    'He was one who had an eye for such mysteries'?

And will any say when my bell of quittance is heard in the gloom,
    And a crossing breeze cuts a pause in its outrollings,
Till they rise again, as they were a new bell's boom,
20   'He hears it not now, but used to notice such things?'

1917   1917

ROBERT BRIDGES

1844–1930

NOW NEGLECTED, Bridges was a lyric poet of genius, though of narrow range. The reclusive Jesuit and unpublished poet, Gerard Manley Hopkins, was a close friend, and a clear influence upon the metrics of the wonderful "London Snow."

Bridges gave up medical practice for literature, and ended with a long poem *The Testament of Beauty,* now wholly unread, though I enjoy it as a special case. I commend also his obscure but pungent "Poor Poll," a satire upon Eliot's *The Waste Land.*

"Nightingales" is a brilliant reply to Keats's great ode, with Bridges's songbirds refusing Keats's beautiful idealization, and lamenting their own sorrows.

✧   ✧   ✧

London Snow

When men were all asleep the snow came flying,
In large white flakes falling on the city brown,
Stealthily and perpetually settling and loosely lying,
　　Hushing the latest traffic of the drowsy town;
Deadening, muffling, stiffling its murmurs failing;
Lazily and incessantly floating down and down;
　　Silently sifting and veiling road, roof and railing;
Hiding difference, making unevenness even,
Into angles and crevices softly drifting and sailing.
10　　All night it fell, and when full inches seven
It lay in the depth of its uncompacted lightness,
The clouds blew off from a high and frosty heaven;
　　And all woke earlier for the unaccustomed brightness
Of the winter dawning, the strange unheavenly glare:
The eye marvelled—marvelled at the dazzling whiteness;
　　The ear hearkened to the stillness of the solemn air;
No sound of wheel rumbling nor of foot falling,
And the busy morning cries came thin and spare.
　　Then boys I heard, as they went to school, calling,

20 They gathered up the crystal manna to freeze
    Their tongues with tasting, their hands with snowballing;
        Or rioted in a drift, plunging up to the knees;
    Or peering up from under the white-mossed wonder,
    'O look at the trees!' they cried, 'O look at the trees!'
        With lessened load a few carts creak and blunder,
    Following along the white deserted way,
    A country company long dispersed asunder:
        When now already the sun, in pale display
    Standing by Paul's high dome, spread forth below
30 His sparkling beams, and awoke the stir of the day.
        For now doors open, and war is waged with the snow;
    And trains of somber men, past tale of number,
    Tread long brown paths, as toward their toil they go:
        But even for them awhile no cares encumber
    Their minds diverted; the daily word is unspoken,
    The daily thoughts of labour and sorrow slumber
    At the sight of the beauty that greets them, for the charm they have broken.
        1880

Nightingales

    Beautiful must be the mountains whence ye come,
    And bright in the fruitful valleys the streams, wherefrom
        Ye learn your song:
    Where are those starry woods? O might I wander there,
    Among the flowers, which in that heavenly air
        Bloom the year long!

    Nay, barren are those mountains and spent the streams;
    Our song is the voice of desire, that haunts our dreams,
        A throe of the heart,
10 Whose pining visions dim, forbidden hopes profound,
    No dying cadence nor long sigh can sound,
        For all our art.

    Alone, aloud in the raptured ear of men
    We pour our dark nocturnal secret; and then,
        As night is withdrawn
    From these sweet-springing meads and bursting boughs of May,
    Dream, while the innumerable choir of day
        Welcome the dawn.
        1893

D. H. LAWRENCE

1885–1930

DAVID HERBERT LAWRENCE, dead of tuberculosis at forty-four, is still underappreciated as a poet and as a story writer. He thought of himself primarily as a novelist, and achieved a precarious greatness in two extended narrative fictions, *The Rainbow* (1915) and *Women in Love* (1921). His later novels, including the once notorious *Lady Chatterley's Lover*, are flawed, but his poetry and stories constantly strengthened, and his travel writings, polemics, and prophecies remain vital.

I give seven superb poems here by Lawrence, all of them ultimately emanating from the influence of Walt Whitman. Lawrence's earlier poetry (some of it very good) stemmed from Thomas Hardy's work, just as Lawrence's first novels were Hardyesque. Whitman induced enormous ambivalences in Lawrence, but that seems to me a frequent element in the drama of poetic influence. Lawrence was furious at Whitman's excesses in representing the democratic merging of his own identity with others, and yet: "Whitman, the great poet, has meant so much to me. Whitman, the one man breaking a way ahead."

Lawrence was born the son of a coal miner and of a woman who aspired after gentility. The story of the poet-novelist's Oedipal relation to his mother is told in his early novel *Sons and Lovers* (1913), which remains very readable. It tells a story already concluded, since Lawrence's mother died in 1910.

In May 1912, Lawrence eloped with the formidable Frieda von Richthofen Weekley, the wife of one of his former professors at Nottingham University College. The stormy marriage to Frieda lasted until Lawrence's death. After November 1919, the Lawrences rarely were in England, favoring Italy, Sicily, Sardinia, Ceylon, Australia, Mexico, and finally the American Southwest, all partly in flight from the tuberculosis that ended him so early.

Of the seven poems by Lawrence I have given here, the first four are from his middle period, while the other three are majestic death-poems. In "Medlars and Sorb-Apples," Lawrence invokes the myth of Orpheus but reimagines it, centering upon the Orphic loneliness, after the permanent separation from Eurydice. But Lawrence strikingly celebrates a merging of Orpheus into Dionysos, and sees this as an exaltation of artistic freedom, as though solitude could be completion:

> Orphic farewell, and farewell, and farewell
> And the *ego sum* of Dionysos
> The *sono io* of perfect drunkenness
> Intoxication of final loneliness.

In "The Song of a Man Who Has Come Through," Lawrence overtly celebrates sexual completion with Frieda (including the liberation of anal intercourse):

> The rock will split, and we shall come at the wonder, we shall find the
> Hesperides.

"Tortoise Shout" and "Snake" evidence Lawrence's preternatural awareness of nonhuman modes of life, while "The Ship of Death" opens his extraordinary sequence of death-poems:

> Now it is autumn and the falling fruit
> and the long journey towards oblivion.
>
> The apples falling like great drops of dew
> to bruise themselves an exit from themselves.

In "Bavarian Gentians," Lawrence discovers in the dark flowers, with their mysterious blue-violet coloring, an image of Proserpina carried off to become Persephone, queen of the underworld. "Shadows," Lawrence's farewell, goes from the despair of "My wrists seem broken and my heart seems dead" to a final, poignant affirmation:

> Then I most knew that still
> I am in the hands of the unknown God,
> He is breaking me down to his own oblivion
> To send me forth on a new morning, a new man.

Lawrence evolved his own prophetic religion (fiercely denounced by the churchwardenly T. S. Eliot in *After Strange Gods*) in which Christ and Lawrence merge as an image of resurrection (see the late novella *The Man Who Died*). Nonconformist Protestant without being Christian, Lawrence belongs to the English prophetic tradition, with Milton, Blake, and Shelley. His art, he insisted, was for the sake of life, and it is.

❧   ❧   ❧

Medlars and Sorb-Apples

I love you, rotten,
Delicious rottenness.

I love to suck you out from your skins
So brown and soft and coming suave,
So morbid, as the Italians say.

What a rare, powerful, reminiscent flavour
Comes out of your falling through the stages of decay:
Stream within stream.

Something of the same flavour as Syracusan muscat wine
10   Or vulgar Marsala.

Though even the word Marsala will smack of preciosity
Soon in the pussyfoot West.

What is it?
What is it, in the grape turning raisin,
In the medlar, in the sorb-apple,

Wineskins of brown morbidity,
Autumnal excrementa;
What is it that reminds us of white gods?

Gods nude as blanched nut-kernels,
20   Strangely, half-sinisterly flesh-fragrant
As if with sweat,
And drenched with mystery.

Sorb-apples, medlars with dead crowns.
I say, wonderful are the hellish experiences,
Orphic, delicate
Dionysos of the Underworld.

A kiss, and a spasm of farewell, a moment's orgasm of rupture,
Then along the damp road alone, till the next turning.
And there, a new partner, a new parting, a new unfusing into twain,

30   A new gasp of further isolation,
A new intoxication of loneliness, among decaying, frost-cold leaves.

Going down the strange lanes of hell, more and more intensely alone,
The fibres of the heart parting one after the other
And yet the soul continuing, naked-footed, ever more vividly embodied
Like a flame blown whiter and whiter
In a deeper and deeper darkness
Ever more exquisite, distilled in separation.

So, in the strange retorts of medlars and sorb-apples
The distilled essence of hell.
40   The exquisite odour of leave-taking.
      Jamque vale!
Orpheus, and the winding, leaf-clogged, silent lanes of hell.

Each soul departing with its own isolation,
Strangest of all strange companions,
And best.

Medlars, sorb-apples,
More than sweet
Flux of autumn
Sucked out of your empty bladders
50   And sipped down, perhaps, with a sip of Marsala
So that the rambling, sky-dropped grape can add its savour to yours,
Orphic farewell, and farewell, and farewell
And the *ego sum* of Dionysos
The *sono io* of perfect drunkenness
Intoxication of final loneliness.
    1921

The Song of a Man Who Has Come Through

Not I, not I, but the wind that blows through me!
A fine wind is blowing the new direction of Time.
If only I let it bear me, carry me, if only it carry me!
If only I am sensitive, subtle, oh, delicate, a winged gift!
If only, most lovely of all, I yield myself and am borrowed
By the fine, fine wind that takes its course through the
    chaos of the world
Like a fine, an exquisite chisel, a wedge-blade inserted;

If only I am keen and hard like the sheer tip of a wedge
Driven by invisible blows,
The rock will split, we shall come at the wonder, we shall
     find the Hesperides.

Oh, for the wonder that bubbles into my soul,
I would be a good fountain, a good well-head,
Would blur no whisper, spoil no expression.

What is the knocking?
What is the knocking at the door in the night?
It is somebody wants to do us harm.

No, no, it is the three strange angels.
Admit them, admit them.

Tortoise Shout

I thought he was dumb,
I said he was dumb,
Yet I've heard him cry.

First faint scream,
Out of life's unfathomable dawn,
Far off, so far, like a madness, under the horizon's dawning rim,
Far, far off, far scream.

Tortoise *in extremis.*

Why were we crucified into sex?
Why were we not left rounded off, and finished in ourselves,
As we began,
As he certainly began, so perfectly alone?

A far, was-it-audible scream,
Or did it sound on the plasm direct?

Worse than the cry of the new-born,
A scream,
A yell,
A shout,

A pæan,
A death-agony,
A birth-dry,
A submission,
All, tiny, far away, reptile under the first dawn.

War-cry, triumph, acute-delight, death-scream reptilian,
Why was the veil torn?
The silken shriek of the soul's torn membrane?
The male soul's membrane
Torn with a shriek half music, half horror.

Crucifixion.
Male tortoise, cleaving behind the hovel-wall of that dense female,
Mounted and tense, spread-eagle, out-reaching out of the shell
In tortoise-nakedness,
Long neck, and long vulnerable limbs extruded, spread-eagle over her
    house-roof,
And the deep, secret, all-penetrating tail curved beneath her walls,
Reaching and gripping tense, more reaching anguish in uttermost tension
Till suddenly, in the spasm of coition, tupping like a jerking leap, and oh!
Opening its clenched face from his outstretched neck
And giving that fragile yell, that scream,
Super-audible,
From his pink, cleft, old-man's mouth,
Giving up the ghost,
Or screaming in Pentecost, receiving the ghost.

His scream, and his moment's subsidence,
The moment of eternal silence,
Yet unreleased, and after the moment, the sudden, startling jerk of coition,
    and at once
The inexpressible faint yell—
And so on, till the last plasm of my body was melted back
To the primeval rudiments of life, and the secret.

So he tups, and screams
Time after time that frail, torn scream
After each jerk, the longish interval,
The tortoise eternity,
Age-long, reptilian persistence,
Heart-throb, slow heart-throb, persistent for the next spasm.

I remember, when I was a boy,
I heard the scream of a frog, which was caught with his foot in the mouth of
    an up-starting snake;
I remember when I first heard bull-frogs break into sound in the spring;
I remember hearing a wild goose out of the throat of night
Cry loudly, beyond the lake of waters;
I remember the first time, out of a bush in the darkness, a nightingale's
    piercing cries and gurgles startled the depths of my soul;
I remember the scream of a rabbit as I went through a wood at midnight;
I remember the heifer in her heat, blorting and blorting through the hours,
    persistent and irrepressible;
I remember my first terror hearing the howl of weird, amorous cats;
I remember the scream of a terrified, injured horse, the sheet-lightning,
And running away from the sound of a woman in labour, something like an
    owl whooing,
And listening inwardly to the first bleat of a lamb,
The first wail of an infant,
And my mother singing to herself,
And the first tenor singing of the passionate throat of a young collier, who has
    long since drunk himself to death,
The first elements of foreign speech
On wild dark lips.

And more than all these,
And less than all these,
This last,
Strange, faint coition yell
Of the male tortoise at extremity,
Tiny from under the very edge of the farthest far-off horizon of life.

The cross,
The wheel on which our silence first is broken,
Sex, which breaks up our integrity, our single inviolability, our deep silence,
Tearing a cry from us.

Sex, which breaks us into voice, sets us calling across the deeps, calling, call-
    ing for the complement,
Singing, and calling, and singing again, being answered, having found.

Torn, to become whole again, after long seeking for what is lost,
The same cry from the tortoise as from Christ, the Osiris-cry of abandon-
    ment,
That which is whole, torn asunder,
That which is in part, finding its whole again throughout the universe.

Snake

A snake came to my water-trough
On a hot, hot day, and I in pyjamas for the heat,
To drink there.

In the deep, strange-scented shade of the great dark carob tree
I came down the steps with my pitcher
And must wait, must stand and wait, for there he was at the trough before
　　me.

He reached down from a fissure in the earth-wall in the gloom
And trailed his yellow-brown slackness soft-bellied down, over the edge of
　　the stone trough

And rested his throat upon the stone bottom,
10　And where the water had dripped from the tap, in a small clearness,
He sipped with his straight mouth,
Softly drank through his straight gums, into his slack long body,
Silently.

Someone was before me at my water-trough,
And I, like a second comer, waiting.

He lifted his head from his drinking, like cattle do,
And looked at me vaguely, as drinking cattle do,
And flickered his two-forked tongue from his lips, and mused a moment,
And stooped and drank a little more,
20　Being earth-brown, earth-golden from the burning bowels of the earth
On the day of Sicilian July, with Etna smoking.

The voice of my education said to me
He must be killed,
For in Sicily the black, black snakes are innocent, the gold are venomous.

And voices in me said, if you were a man
You would take a stick and break him now, and finish him off.
But I must confess how I liked him,
How glad I was he had come like a guest in quiet, to drink at my water-
　　trough
And depart peaceful, pacified, and thankless,
30　Into the burning bowels of this earth.

Was it cowardice, that I dared not kill him?
Was it perversity, that I longed to talk to him?
Was it humility, to feel so honoured?
I felt so honoured.

And yet those voices:
If you were not afraid, you would kill him!

And truly I was afraid, I was most afraid,
But even so, honoured still more
That he should seek my hospitality
40   From out the dark door of the secret earth.

He drank enough
And lifted his head, dreamily, as one who has drunken,
And flickered his tongue like a forked night on the air, so black,
Seeming to lick his lips,
And looking around like a god, unseeing, into the air,
And slowly turned his head,
And slowly, very slowly, as if thrice adream,
Proceeded to draw his slow length curving round
And climb again the broken bank of my wall-face.

50   And as he put his head into that dreadful hole,
And as he slowly drew up, snake-easing his shoulders, and entered farther,
A sort of horror, a sort of protest against his withdrawing into that horrid
      black hole,
Deliberately going into the blackness, and slowly drawing himself after,
Overcame me now his back was turned.

I looked around, I put down my pitcher,
I picked up a clumsy log
And threw it at the water-trough with a clatter.

I think I did not hit him,
But suddenly that part of him that was left behind convulsed in undignified
      haste,
60   Writhed like lightning, and was gone
Into the black hole, the earth-lipped fissure in the wall-front,
At which, in the intense still noon, I stared with fascination.

And immediately I regretted it.
I thought how paltry, how vulgar, what a mean act!

I despised myself and the voices of my accursed human education.
And I thought of the albatross,
And I wished he would come back, my snake.

For he seemed to me again like a king,
Like a king in exile, uncrowned in the underworld,
70   Now due to be crowned again.

And so, I missed my chance with one of the lords
Of life.
And I have something to expiate;
A pettiness.
   1923

The Ship of Death

I

Now it is autumn and the falling fruit
and the long journey towards oblivion.

The apples falling like great drops of dew
to bruise themselves an exit from themselves.

And it is time to go, to bid farewell
to one's own self, and find an exit
from the fallen self.

II

Have you built your ship of death, O have you?
O build your ship of death, for you will need it.

10   The grim forest is at hand, when the apples will fall
thick, almost thunderous, on the hardened earth.

And death is on the air like a smell of ashes!
Ah! can't you smell it?

And in the bruised body, the frightened soul
finds itself shrinking, wincing from the cold
that blows upon it through the orifices.

III

And can a man his own quietus make
with a bare bodkin?

With daggers, bodkins, bullets, man can make
20   a bruise or break of exit for his life;
but is that a quietus, O tell me, is it quietus?

Surely not so! for how could murder, even self-murder
ever a quietus make?

IV

O let us talk of quiet that we know,
that we can know, the deep and lovely quiet
of a strong heart at peace!

How can we this, our own quietus, make?

V

Build then the ship of death, for you must take
the longest journey, to oblivion.

30   And die the death, the long and painful death
that lies between the old self and the new.

Already our bodies are fallen, bruised, badly bruised,
already our souls are oozing through the exit
of the cruel bruise.

Already the dark and endless ocean of the end
is washing in through the breaches of our wounds,
already the flood is upon us.

O build your ship of death, your little ark
and furnish it with food, with little cakes, and wine
40   for the dark flight down oblivion.

VI

Piecemeal the body dies, and the timid soul
has her footing washed away, as the dark flood rises.

We are dying, we are dying, we are all of us dying
and nothing will stay the death-flood rising within us
and soon it will rise on the world, on the outside world.

We are dying, we are dying, piecemeal our bodies are dying
and our strength leaves us,
and our soul cowers naked in the dark rain over the flood,
cowering in the last branches of the tree of our life.

VII
50 We are dying, we are dying, so all we can do
is now to be willing to die, and to build the ship
of death to carry the soul on the longest journey.

A little ship, with oars and food
and little dishes, and all accoutrements
fitting and ready for the departed soul.

Now launch the small ship, now as the body dies
and life departs, launch out, the fragile soul
in the fragile ship of courage, the ark of faith
with its store of food and little cooking pans
60 and change of clothes,
upon the flood's black waste
upon the waters of the end
upon the sea of death, where still we sail
darkly, for we cannot steer, and have no port.

There is no port, there is nowhere to go
only the deepening blackness darkening still
blacker upon the soundless, ungurgling flood
darkness at one with darkness, up and down
and sideways utterly dark, so there is no direction any more,
70 and the little ship is there; yet she is gone.
She is not seen, for there is nothing to see her by.
She is gone! gone! and yet
somewhere she is there.

Nowhere!

VIII
And everything is gone, the body is gone
completely under, gone, entirely gone.
The upper darkness is heavy as the lower,
between them the little ship
is gone
80 she is gone
It is the end, it is oblivion.

IX

And yet out of eternity a thread
separates itself on the blackness,
a horizontal thread
that fumes a little with pallor upon the dark.

Is it illusion? or does the pallor fume
a little higher?
Ah wait, wait, for there's the dawn,
the cruel dawn of coming back to life
90   out of oblivion.

Wait, wait, the little ship
drifting, beneath the deadly ashy grey
of a flood-dawn.

Wait, wait! even so, a flush of yellow
and strangely, O chilled wan soul, a flush of rose.

A flush of rose, and the whole thing starts again.

X

The flood subsides, and the body, like a worn sea-shell
emerges strange and lovely.
And the little ship wings home, faltering and lapsing
on the pink flood,
100   and the frail soul steps out, into her house again
filling the heart with peace.

Swings the heart renewed with peace
even of oblivion.

Oh build your ship of death. Oh build it!
for you will need it.
For the voyage of oblivion awaits you.

    1929–30   1932

Bavarian Gentians

(final version)

Not every man has gentians in his house
In Soft September, at slow, Sad Michaelmas.

Bavarian gentians, big and dark, only dark
Darkening the day-time torch-like with the smoking blueness of Pluto's
    gloom,
Ribbed and torch-like with their blaze of darkness spread blue
Down flattening into points, flattened under the sweep of white day
Torch-flower of the blue-smoking darkness, Pluto's dark-blue daze,
Black lamps from the halls of Dis, burning dark blue,
Giving off darkness, blue darkness, as Demeter's pale lamps give off light,
Lead me then, lead me the way.

Reach me a gentian, give me a torch
Let me guide myself with the blue, forked torch of this flower
Down the darker and darker stairs, where blue is darkened on blueness,
Even where Persephone goes, just now, from the frosted September
To the sightless realm where darkness is awake upon the dark
And Persephone herself is but a voice
Or a darkness invisible enfolded in the deeper dark
Of the arms Plutonic, and pierced with the passion of dense gloom,
Among the splendour of torches of darkness, shedding darkness on the lost
    bride and her groom.
    1929   1932

Shadows

And if tonight my soul may find her peace
in sleep, and sink in good oblivion,
and in the morning wake like a new-opened flower
then I have been dipped again in God, and new-created.
And if, as weeks go round, in the dark of the moon
my spirit darkens and goes out, and soft strange gloom
pervades my movements and my thoughts and words
then I shall know that I am walking still
with God, we are close together now the moon's in shadow.

And if, as autumn deepens and darkens
I feel the pain of falling leaves, and stems that break in storms
and trouble and dissolution and distress
and then the softness of deep shadows folding, folding
around my soul and spirit, around my lips
so sweet, like a swoon, or more like the drowse of a low, sad song
singing darker than the nightingale, on, on to the solstice
and the silence of short days, the silence of the year, the shadow,

then I shall know that my life is moving still
with the dark earth, and drenched
with the deep oblivion of earth's lapse and renewal.

And if, in the changing phases of man's life
I fall in sickness and in misery
my wrists seem broken and my heart seems dead
and strength is gone, and my life
is only the leavings of a life:

and still, among it all, snatches of lovely oblivion, and snatches of renewal
odd, wintry flowers upon the withered stem, yet new, strange flowers
such as my life has not brought forth before, new blossoms of me—

then I must know that still
I am in the hands [of] the unknown God,
he is breaking me down to his own oblivion
to send me forth on a new morning, a new man.

A. E. HOUSMAN

1859–1936

A. E. HOUSMAN, whose poetry I have loved for sixty years, persists despite much critical abuse, ranging from Edmund Wilson's to Tom Stoppard's negative view in his brilliant play *The Invention of Love*. And yet Housman's best poems are worthy of their models: the border ballads, Shakespeare's songs, Heinrich Heine.

The half dozen poems I give here are perfectly representative of Housman, of his strengths and his deliberate limits. His massive classical scholarship, which brought him a professorship of Latin at University College, London, affects his poetry only obliquely. Determined to be minor, Housman's best work transcends its own intentions.

Housman's unhappiness stems from unfulfilled homoeroticism, but I am not persuaded that his negative poetics would have been greatly different had his sexual nature been fulfilled. The poetry meshes its refusal to rejoice with a devastating apparent simplicity:

> Into my heart an air that kills
> From yon far country blows.

This is the epitome of Housman: an air that kills. A genius for memorability sustains that negative intensity.

❦   ❦   ❦

from A Shropshire Lad

II

Loveliest of trees, the cherry now
Is hung with bloom along the bough,
And stands about the woodland ride
Wearing white for Eastertide.

Now, of my threescore years and ten,
Twenty will not come again,
And take from seventy springs a score,
It only leaves me fifty more.

And since to look at things in bloom
10   Fifty springs are little room,
About the woodlands I will go
To see the cherry hung with snow.

XL

Into my heart an air that kills
    From yon far country blows:
What are those blue remembered hills,
    What spires, what farms are those?

That is the land of lost content,
    I see it shining plain,
The happy highways where I went.
    And cannot come again.

from Last Poems

III

Her strong enchantments failing,
    Her towers of fear in wreck,

Her limbecks dried of poisons
   And the knife at her neck,

The Queen of air and darkness
   Begins to shrill and cry,
'O young man, O my slayer,
   To-morrow you shall die.'

O Queen of air and darkness,
   I think 'tis truth you say,
And I shall die to-morrow;
   But you will die to-day.

XXXVI

Here dead lie we because we did not choose
   To live and shame the land from which we sprung.
Life, to be sure, is nothing much to lose,
   But young men think it is, and we were young.

XXXVII
EPITAPH ON AN ARMY OF MERCENARIES

These, in the day when heaven was falling,
   The hour when earth's foundations fled,
Followed their mercenary calling
   And took their wages and are dead.

Their shoulders held the sky suspended;
   They stood, and earth's foundations stay;
What God abandoned, these defended,
   And saved the sum of things for pay.

XL

Tell me not here, it needs not saying,
   What tune the enchantress plays
In aftermaths of soft September
   Or under blanching mays,
For she and I were long acquainted
   And I knew all her ways.

On russet floors, by waters idle,
   The pine lets fall its cone;
The cuckoo shouts all day at nothing
   In leafy dells alone;

And traveller's joy beguiles in autumn
   Hearts that have lost their own.

On acres of the seeded grasses
   The changing burnish heaves;
Or marshalled under moons of harvest
   Stand still all night the sheaves;
Or beeches strip in storms for winter
   And stain the wind with leaves.

Possess, as I possessed a season,
   The countries I resign,
Where over elmy plains the highway
   Would mount the hills and shine,
And full of shade the pillared forest
   Would murmur and be mine.

For nature, heartless, witless nature,
   Will neither care nor know
What stranger's feet may find the meadow
   And trespass there and go,
Nor ask amid the dews of morning
   If they are mine or no.

WILFRED OWEN

1893–1918

OWEN HAS REMAINED the archetypal War Poet, a major figure killed in action just before the World War I Armistice. A passionate enemy of war, Owen nevertheless acted with heroism in combat, exposing his Keatsian sensibility and his repressed homoeroticism to all the horrors of Western Front trench warfare.

    After a childhood in Shropshire and attendance at the University of London, Owen became a teacher in France until he enlisted in 1915.

    It is immensely sad to contemplate what Owen would have written had he not died on the battlefield. The three poems I give here far tran-

scend the pathos of their occasion, and touch the sublime through original
vision, perfection of form and of diction, and Owen's innovation in slant
rhyme or pararhyme, which conveys an effect of baffled expectation, beautifully suited to the burden of his work.

✦   ✦   ✦

Futility

Move him into the sun—
Gently its touch awoke him once,
At home, whispering of fields unsown.
Always it woke him, even in France,
Until this morning and this snow.
If anything might rouse him now
The kind old sun will know.

Think how it wakes the seeds,—
Woke, once, the clays of a cold star.
Are limbs, so dear-achieved, are sides,
Full-nerved—still warm—too hard to stir?
Was it for this the clay grew tall?
—O what made fatuous sunbeams toil
To break earth's sleep at all?

Strange Meeting

It seemed that out of battle I escaped
Down some profound dull tunnel, long since scooped
Through granites which titanic wars had groined.
Yet also there encumbered sleepers groaned,
Too fast in thought or death to be bestirred.
Then, as I probed them, one sprang up, and stared
With piteous recognition in fixed eyes,
Lifting distressful hands as if to bless.
And by his smile, I knew that sullen hall,
By his dead smile I knew we stood in Hell.
With a thousand pains that vision's face was grained;
Yet no blood reached there from the upper ground,
And no guns thumped, or down the flues made moan.
"Strange friend," I said, "here is no cause to mourn."

"None," said that other, "save the undone years,
The hopelessness. Whatever hope is yours,
Was my life also; I went hunting wild
After the wildest beauty in the world,
Which lies not calm in eyes, or braided hair,
But mocks the steady running of the hour,
And if it grieves, grieves richlier than here.
For of my glee might many men have laughed,
And of my weeping something had been left,
Which must die now. I mean the truth untold,
The pity of war, the pity war distilled.
Now men will go content with what we spoiled,
Or, discontent, boil bloody, and be spilled.
They will be swift with swiftness of the tigress.
None will break ranks, though nations trek from progress.
Courage was mine, and I had mystery,
Wisdom was mine, and I had mastery:
To miss the march of this retreating world
Into vain citadels that are not walled.
Then, when much blood had clogged their chariot-wheels,
I would go up and wash them from sweet wells,
Even with truths that lie too deep for taint.
I would have poured my spirit without stint
But not through wounds; not on the cess of war.
Foreheads of men have bled where no wounds were.
I am the enemy you killed, my friend.
I knew you in this dark: for so you frowned
Yesterday through me as you jabbed and killed.
I parried; but my hands were loath and cold.
Let us sleep now. . . ."

Anthem for Doomed Youth

What passing-bells for these who die as cattle?
    Only the monstrous anger of the guns.
    Only the stuttering rifles' rapid rattle
Can patter out their hasty orisons.
No mockeries now for them; no prayers nor bells,
    Nor any voice of mourning save the choirs,—
The shrill, demented choirs of wailing shells;
    And bugles calling for them from sad shires.

What candles may be held to speed them all?
   Not in the hands of boys, but in their eyes
Shall shine the holy glimmers of good-byes.
   The pallor of girls' brows shall be their pall;
Their flowers the tenderness of patient minds,
And each slow dusk a drawing-down of blinds.

EDWARD THOMAS

1878–1917

UNLIKE WILFRED OWEN and Isaac Rosenberg, one does not think
of Edward Thomas as a War Poet, though he died fighting at Arras in 1917.
A professional man of letters, he was so awed by poetry that he was reluctant to begin writing it. The catalyst of a friendship with Robert Frost
helped him to begin a poetic career in 1914, only three years before his
death.

   Thomas and Frost exchanged influences, but remained very different
poets, partly because of national traditions. What Emerson and Dickinson
were to Frost, Wordsworth and John Clare were to Thomas.

   The three poems I give here by Edward Thomas all seem to me
extraordinary. His death at thirty-nine cost England a major poet.

❧   ❧   ❧

Liberty

The last light has gone out of the world, except
This moonlight lying on the grass like frost
Beyond the brink of the tall elm's shadow.
It is as if everything else had slept
Many an age, unforgotten and lost—
The men that were, the things done, long ago,
All I have thought; and but the moon and I
Live yet and here stand idle over a grave
Where all is buried. Both have liberty

To dream what we could do if we were free
To do some thing we had desired long,
The moon and I. There's none less free than who
Does nothing and has nothing else to do,
Being free only for what is not to his mind,
And nothing is to his mind. If every hour
Like this one passing that I have spent among
The wiser others when I have forgot
To wonder whether I was free or not,
Were piled before me, and not lost behind,
And I could take and carry them away
I should be rich; or if I had the power
To wipe out every one and not again
Regret, I should be rich to be so poor.
And yet I still am half in love with pain,
With what is imperfect, with both tears and mirth,
With things that have an end, with life and earth,
And this moon that leaves me dark within the door.

The Owl

Downhill I came, hungry, and yet not starved;
Cold, yet had heat within me that was proof
Against the North wind; tired, yet so that rest
Had seemed the sweetest thing under a roof.

Then at the inn I had food, fire, and rest,
Knowing how hungry, cold, and tired was I.
All of the night was quite barred out except
An owl's cry, a most melancholy cry

Shaken out long and clear upon the hill,
No merry note, nor cause of merriment,
But one telling me plain what I escaped
And others could not, that night, as in I went.

And salted was my food, and my repose,
Salted and sobered, too, by the bird's voice
Speaking for all who lay under the stars,
Soldiers and poor, unable to rejoice.

The Gallows

There was a weasel lived in the sun
With all his family,
Till a keeper shot him with his gun
And hung him up on a tree,
Where he swings in the wind and rain,
In the sun and in the snow,
Without pleasure, without pain,
On the dead oak tree bough.

There was a crow who was no sleeper,
But a thief and a murderer
Till a very late hour; and this keeper
Made him one of the things that were,
To hang and flap in rain and wind,
In the sun and in the snow.
There are no more sins to be sinned
On the dead oak tree bough.

There was a magpie, too,
Had a long tongue and a long tail;
He could both talk and do—
But what did that avail?
He, too, flaps in the wind and rain
Alongside weasel and crow,
Without pleasure, without pain,
On the dead oak tree bough.

And many other beasts
And birds, skin, bone, and feather,
Have been taken from their feasts
And hung up there together,
To swing and have endless leisure
In the sun and in the snow,
Without pain, without pleasure,
On the dead oak tree bough.

ISAAC ROSENBERG

1890–1918

RAISED IN LONDON'S East End Jewish community, Isaac Rosenberg possessed considerable talent as a painter, and studied art at the Slade School. But he was more gifted at poetry, and might have achieved major status had he not become part of the meaningless slaughter on the Western Front.

The visionary influence of William Blake is manifest in the superb fragment "A Worm Fed on the Heart of Corinth," where a Satanic future is prophesied for England. "Returning, We Hear the Larks" shows Rosenberg's fine fusion of passion and detachment throughout his trench poems.

❧   ❧   ❧

Returning, We Hear the Larks

Sombre the night is:
And, though we have our lives, we know
What sinister threat lurks there.

Dragging these anguished limbs, we only know
This poison-blasted track opens on our camp—
On a little safe sleep.

But hark! Joy—joy—strange joy.
Lo! Heights of night ringing with unseen larks:
Music showering on our upturned listening faces.

10 Death could drop from the dark
As easily as song—
But song only dropped,
Like a blind man's dreams on the sand
By dangerous tides;
Like a girl's dark hair, for she dreams no ruin lies there,
Or her kisses where a serpent hides.

1922

A Worm Fed on the Heart of Corinth

A worm fed on the heart of Corinth,
Babylon and Rome:
Not Paris raped tall Helen,
But this incestuous worm,
Who lured her vivid beauty
To his amorphous sleep.
England! famous as Helen
Is thy betrothal sung
To him the shadowless,
More amorous than Solomon.

1917   1922

EDWIN ARLINGTON
ROBINSON

1869–1935

ROBINSON, just five years older than Robert Frost, shared a mutual admiration with him, but they are very different poets. I wish that Robinson had more readers these days, and am puzzled that he doesn't. I have possessed "Luke Havergal" and "Eros Turannos" by memory since my childhood, and they still recite themselves to me. The critic Yvor Winters spoke of the impersonal greatness of Robinson's style, a judgment I admire but do not understand. Greatness there certainly is, but the three poems I include here seem to me intensely personal in their balked but fervent heterosexual passion.

Born in a small Maine village, Robinson grew up in Gardiner, lived at home with his parents, and was fiercely determined to be a poet. He spent two years at Harvard as a special student, and remained a solitary. Most of his life, he lived a marginal existence in New York City.

Robinson's luck changed when President Theodore Roosevelt had the good taste to enjoy his poems, and gave him a sinecure in the New York Custom House. Unfortunately, this vanished under President William Howard Taft.

Robinson was partly saved by long summers at the MacDowell Colony for artists, and partly by his friends. By 1921, when his *Collected Poems* appeared, he had acquired a public. His lifelong, unrequited love for his sister-in-law Emma continued.

When he died in the spring of 1935, Robinson was a famous and a solvent poet. His life had been bleak, but wholly dedicated to his superb art.

"Luke Havergal," composed when Robinson was very young, is one of those rare incantations that are inevitable and overwhelming. It prophesies the erotic longing that marked Robinson all his life, transferred in this poem to a ghostly dimension.

"For a Dead Lady" is a flawless elegy for Robinson's mother, as delicate as it is dark. Robinson's masterpiece, to me, is "Eros Turannos," where love is a tyrant, a god of destruction:

> Meanwhile we do no harm; for they
>   That with a god have striven,
> Not hearing much of what we say,
>   Take what the god has given;
> Though like waves breaking it may be,
> Or like a changed familiar tree,
> Or like a stairway to the sea
>   Where down the blind are driven.

✔   ✔   ✔

Luke Havergal

Go to the western gate, Luke Havergal,
There where the vines cling crimson on the wall,
And in the twilight wait for what will come.
The leaves will whisper there of her, and some,
Like flying words, will strike you as they fall;
But go, and if you listen she will call.
Go to the western gate, Luke Havergal—
Luke Havergal.

No, there is not a dawn in eastern skies
To rift the fiery night that's in your eyes;
But there, where western glooms are gathering,
The dark will end the dark, if anything:
God slays Himself with every leaf that flies,
And hell is more than half of paradise.

No, there is not a dawn in eastern skies—
In eastern skies.

Out of a grave I come to tell you this,
Out of a grave I come to quench the kiss
That flames upon your forehead with a glow
That blinds you to the way that you must go.
Yes, there is yet one way to where she is,
Bitter, but one that faith may never miss.
Out of a grave I come to tell you this—
To tell you this.

There is the western gate, Luke Havergal,
There are the crimson leaves upon the wall.
Go, for the winds are tearing them away,—
Nor think to riddle the dead words they say,
Nor any more to feel them as they fall;
But go, and if you trust her she will call.
There is the western gate, Luke Havergal—
Luke Havergal.

For a Dead Lady

No more with overflowing light
Shall fill the eyes that now are faded,
Nor shall another's fringe with night
Their woman-hidden world as they did.
No more shall quiver down the days
The flowing wonder of her ways,
Whereof no language may require
The shifting and the many-shaded.

The grace, divine, definitive,
Clings only as a faint forestalling;
The laugh that love could not forgive
Is hushed, and answers to no calling;
The forehead and the little ears
Have gone where Saturn keeps the years;
The breast where roses could not live
Has done with rising and with falling.

The beauty, shattered by the laws
That have creation in their keeping,

No longer trembles at applause,
Or over children that are sleeping;
And we who delve in beauty's lore
Know all that we have known before
Of what inexorable cause
Makes Time so vicious in his reaping.

Eros Turannos

She fears him, and will always ask
   What fated her to choose him;
She meets in his engaging mask
   All reasons to refuse him;
But what she meets and what she fears
Are less than are the downward years,
Drawn slowly to the foamless weirs
   Of age, were she to lose him.

Between a blurred sagacity
   That once had power to sound him,
And Love, that will not let him be
   The Judas that she found him,
Her pride assuages her almost,
As if it were alone the cost.—
He sees that he will not be lost,
   And waits and looks around him.

A sense of ocean and old trees
   Envelops and allures him;
Tradition, touching all he sees,
   Beguiles and reassures him;
And all her doubts of what he says
Are dimmed with what she knows of days—
Till even prejudice delays
   And fades, and she secures him.

The falling leaf inaugurates
   The reign of her confusion;
The pounding wave reverberates
   The dirge of her illusion;
And home, where passion lived and died,
Becomes a place where she can hide,

While all the town and harbor side
   Vibrate with her seclusion.

We tell you, tapping on our brows,
   The story as it should be,—
As if the story of a house
   Were told, or ever could be;
We'll have no kindly veil between
Her visions and those we have seen,—
As if we guessed what hers have been,
   Or what they are or would be.

Meanwhile we do no harm; for they
   That with a god have striven,
Not hearing much of what we say,
   Take what the god has given;
Though like waves breaking it may be,
Or like a changed familiar tree,
Or like a stairway to the sea
   Where down the blind are driven.

STEPHEN CRANE

1871–1900

WE REMEMBER STEPHEN CRANE primarily for his novel *The Red Badge of Courage* (1895) and for three superb short stories: "The Bride Comes to Yellow Sky," "The Open Boat," and "The Blue Hotel." His poems, very original for his time, are uneven, but the best of them are economical and memorable. The ironies of *War Is Kind* are rather too overt, but still effective.

Crane's life was turbulent, and provided a paradigm for later journalist-novelists, Ernest Hemingway in particular. The youngest of fourteen children, Crane made an early entrance into journalism, at the age of twenty. He had never seen a battle when he wrote *The Red Badge of Courage,* an instant best-seller. But soon enough he remedied that, serving as a war correspondent who covered the Cuban Revolution, the Greek-Turkish War, and finally the Spanish-American War.

With his companion, Cora, Crane lived in England for much of 1897, and then for 1899–1900, where they were in the company of Henry James, Joseph Conrad, and H. G. Wells. Crane died at twenty-eight, at a tuberculosis sanatorium in Germany.

↓   ↓   ↓

from War Is Kind

Do not weep, maiden, for war is kind.
Because your lover threw wild hands toward the sky
And the affrighted steed ran on alone,
Do not weep.
War is kind.

      Hoarse, booming drums of the regiment
      Little souls who thirst for fight,
      These men were born to drill and die
      The unexplained glory flies above them
      Great is the battle-god, great, and his kingdom—
      A field where a thousand corpses lie.

Do not weep, babe, for war is kind.
Because your father rumbled in the yellow trenches,
Raged at his breast, gulped and died,
Do not weep.
War is kind.

      Swift, blazing flag of the regiment
      Eagle with crest of red and gold,
      These men were born to drill and die
      Point for them the virtue of slaughter
      Make plain to them the excellence of killing
      And a field where a thousand corpses lie.

Mother whose heart hung humble as a button
On the bright splendid shroud of your son,
Do not weep.
War is kind.

TRUMBULL STICKNEY

1874–1904

TRAGICALLY DEAD AT THIRTY of brain cancer, Trumbull Stickney had no time to develop his marvelous poetic gift. A classicist in the old Harvard mode, he can be regarded as the best American Pre-Raphaelite poet before the young Wallace Stevens, who wrote his way out of the style of "Sunday Morning" into the austere sublimity of *The Auroras of Autumn.* Something similar could have happened had Stickney lived.

I have given only two poems by Stickney, but they suffice to show what was lost with his early death. "Mnemosyne" is a perfect exemplification of American nostalgia, and an anticipation of the "slant rhyme" of Wilfred Owen:

> I had a sister lovely in my sight:
> Her hair was dark, her eyes were very sombre;
> We sang together in the woods at night.
>
> It's lonely in the country I remember.

ψ   ψ   ψ

Mnemosyne

It's autumn in the country I remember.

How warm a wind blew here about the ways!
And shadows on the hillside lay to slumber
During the long sun-sweetened summer-days.

It's cold abroad the country I remember.

The swallows veering skimmed the golden grain
At midday with a wing aslant and limber;
And yellow cattle browsed upon the plain.

It's empty down the country I remember.

I had a sister lovely in my sight:
Her hair was dark, her eyes were very sombre;
We sang together in the woods at night.

It's lonely in the country I remember.

The babble of our children fills my ears,
And on our hearth I stare the perished ember
To flames that show all starry thro' my tears.

It's dark about the country I remember.

There are the mountains where I lived. The path
Is slushed with cattle-tracks and fallen timber,
The stumps are twisted by the tempests' wrath.

But that I knew these places are my own,
I'd ask how came such wretchedness to cumber
The earth, and I to people it alone.

It rains across the country I remember.

Eride, V

Now in the palace gardens warm with age,
On lawn and flower-bed this afternoon
The thin November-coloured foliage
Just as last year unfastens lilting down,

And round the terrace in gray attitude
The very statues are becoming sere
With long presentiment of solitude.
Most of the life that I have lived is here,

Here by the path and autumn's earthy grass
And chestnuts standing down the breadths of sky:
Indeed I know not how it came to pass,
The life I lived here so unhappily.

Yet blessing over all! I do not care
What wormwood I have ate to cups of gall;

I care not what despairs are buried there
Under the ground, no, I care not at all.

Nay, if the heart have beaten, let it break!
I have not loved and lived but only this
Betwixt my birth and grave. Dear Spirit, take
The gratitude that pains, so deep it is.

When Spring shall be again, and at your door
You stand to feel the mellower evening wind,
Remember if you will my heart is pure,
Perfectly pure and altogether kind;

That not an aftercry of all our strife
Troubles the love I give you and the faith:
Say to yourself that at the ends of life
My arms are open to you, life and death.—

How much it aches to linger in these things!
I thought the perfect end of love was peace
Over the long-forgiven sufferings,
But something else, I know not what it is,

The words that came so nearly and then not,
The vanity, the error of the whole,
The strong cross-purpose, oh, I know not what
Cries dreadfully in the distracted soul.

The evening fills the garden, hardly red;
And autumn goes away, like one alone.
Would I were with the leaves that thread by thread
Soften to soil, I would that I were one.

ROBERT FROST

1874–1963

ROBERT FROST was an extraordinary American phenomenon: a great poet who was also immensely popular. Though he exulted in his fame, he was also wary of the audience's effect upon his art. He learned to write between the lines (as it were) and became a subtle master, far more difficult than he appears to be.

The archetypal New England poet (a mountain in Vermont is named for him) was born in San Francisco but raised in New Hampshire. Frost married Elinor White in 1895. The marriage endured until Mrs. Frost's death in 1938, but seems to have been difficult. Two children died in childhood; of the remaining four, a daughter died young, another had to be institutionalized, while a son committed suicide.

Frost survived, laden with well-merited honors, and augmented in ironic power, not so much defensive as inventive. Of poetry, Frost remarked: "Why not have it imply everything?" Poetic implication became his characteristic mode. "The Oven Bird" gives us Frost's surrogate, a builder of an oven-shaped nest, also known as "the teacher bird":

> The bird would cease and be as other birds
> But that he knows in singing not to sing.
> The question that he frames in all but words
> Is what to make of a diminished thing.

Frost, like the later Emerson of *The Conduct of Life,* makes a cosmos of a reductive or nihilistic vision. Much of that cosmos emerges in "Never Again Would Birds' Song Be the Same":

> Never again would birds' song be the same.

> And to do that to birds was why she came.

"She" is Eve, fallen into language and into nature. Implication is everything here, and tone is very difficult to interpret. Frost is a kind of mourning Adam, yet what should we make of his final line? Was *that* why Eve came into the world, to feminize bird song? Something recalcitrant in

Frost, a knowing maleness that accepts things as they are, asserts itself with characteristic irony.

✦ ✦ ✦

After Apple-Picking

My long two-pointed ladder's sticking through a tree
Toward heaven still,
And there's a barrel that I didn't fill
Beside it, and there may be two or three
Apples I didn't pick upon some bough.
But I am done with apple-picking now.
Essence of winter sleep is on the night,
The scent of apples: I am drowsing off.
I cannot rub the strangeness from my sight
I got from looking through a pane of glass
I skimmed this morning from the drinking trough
And held against the world of hoary grass.
It melted, and I let it fall and break.
But I was well
Upon my way to sleep before it fell,
And I could tell
What form my dreaming was about to take.
Magnified apples appear and disappear,
Stem end and blossom end,
And every fleck of russet showing clear.
My instep arch not only keeps the ache,
It keeps the pressure of a ladder-round.
I feel the ladder sway as the boughs bend.
And I keep hearing from the cellar bin
The rumbling sound
Of load on load of apples coming in.
For I have had too much
Of apple-picking: I am overtired
Of the great harvest I myself desired.
There were ten thousand thousand fruit to touch,
Cherish in hand, lift down, and not let fall.
For all
That struck the earth,
No matter if not bruised or spiked with stubble,
Went surely to the cider-apple heap
As of no worth.

One can see what will trouble
This sleep of mine, whatever sleep it is.
Were he not gone,
The woodchuck could say whether it's like his
Long sleep, as I describe its coming on,
Or just some human sleep.

The Wood-Pile

Out walking in the frozen swamp one gray day,
I paused and said, 'I will turn back from here.
No, I will go on farther—and we shall see.'
The hard snow held me, save where now and then
One foot went through. The view was all in lines
Straight up and down of tall slim trees
Too much alike to mark or name a place by
So as to say for certain I was here
Or somewhere else: I was just far from home.
A small bird flew before me. He was careful
To put a tree between us when he lighted,
And say no word to tell me who he was
Who was so foolish as to think what *he* thought.
He thought that I was after him for a feather—
The white one in his tail; like one who takes
Everything said as personal to himself.
One flight out sideways would have undeceived him.
And then there was a pile of wood for which
I forgot him and let his little fear
Carry him off the way I might have gone,
Without so much as wishing him good-night.
He went behind it to make his last stand.
It was a cord of maple, cut and split
And piled—and measured, four by four by eight.
And not another like it could I see.
No runner tracks in this year's snow looped near it.
And it was older sure than this year's cutting,
Or even last year's or the year's before.
The wood was gray and the bark warping off it
And the pile somewhat sunken. Clematis
Had wound strings round and round it like a bundle.
What held it though on one side was a tree
Still growing, and on one a stake and prop,

These latter about to fall. I thought that only
Someone who lived in turning to fresh tasks
Could so forget his handiwork on which
He spent himself, the labor of his ax,
And leave it there far from a useful fireplace
To warm the frozen swamp as best it could
With the slow smokeless burning of decay.

The Oven Bird

There is a singer everyone has heard,
Loud, a mid-summer and a mid-wood bird,
Who makes the solid tree trunks sound again.
He says that leaves are old and that for flowers
Mid-summer is to spring as one to ten.
He says the early petal-fall is past
When pear and cherry bloom went down in showers
On sunny days a moment overcast;
And comes that other fall we name the fall.
He says the highway dust is over all.
The bird would cease and be as other birds
But that he knows in singing not to sing.
The question that he frames in all but words
Is what to make of a diminished thing.

Birches

When I see birches bend to left and right
Across the lines of straighter darker trees,
I like to think some boy's been swinging them.
But swinging doesn't bend them down to stay
As ice-storms do. Often you must have seen them
Loaded with ice a sunny winter morning
After a rain. They click upon themselves
As the breeze rises, and turn many-colored
As the stir cracks and crazes their enamel.
Soon the sun's warmth makes them shed crystal shells
Shattering and avalanching on the snow-crust—
Such heaps of broken glass to sweep away
You'd think the inner dome of heaven had fallen.
They are dragged to the withered bracken by the load,
And they seem not to break; though once they are bowed
So low for long, they never right themselves:

You may see their trunks arching in the woods
Years afterwards, trailing their leaves on the ground
Like girls on hands and knees that throw their hair
Before them over their heads to dry in the sun.
But I was going to say when Truth broke in
With all her matter-of-fact about the ice-storm
I should prefer to have some boy bend them
As he went out and in to fetch the cows—
Some boy too far from town to learn baseball,
Whose only play was what he found himself,
Summer or winter, and could play alone.
One by one he subdued his father's trees
By riding them down over and over again
Until he took the stiffness out of them,
And not one but hung limp, not one was left
For him to conquer. He learned all there was
To learn about not launching out too soon
And so not carrying the tree away
Clear to the ground. He always kept his poise
To the top branches, climbing carefully
With the same pains you use to fill a cup
Up to the brim, and even above the brim.
Then he flung outward, feet first, with a swish,
Kicking his way down through the air to the ground.
So was I once myself a swinger of birches.
And so I dream of going back to be.
It's when I'm weary of considerations,
And life is too much like a pathless wood
Where your face burns and tickles with the cobwebs
Broken across it, and one eye is weeping
From a twig's having lashed across it open.
I'd like to get away from earth awhile
And then come back to it and begin over.
May no fate willfully misunderstand me
And half grant what I wish and snatch me away
Not to return. Earth's the right place for love:
I don't know where it's likely to go better.
I'd like to go by climbing a birch tree,
And climb black branches up a snow-white trunk
Toward heaven, till the tree could bear no more,
But dipped its top and set me down again.
That would be good both going and coming back.
One could do worse than be a swinger of birches.

Putting in the Seed

You come to fetch me from my work tonight
When supper's on the table, and we'll see
If I can leave off burying the white
Soft petals fallen from the apple tree
(Soft petals, yes, but not so barren quite,
Mingled with these, smooth bean and wrinkled pea;)
And go along with you ere you lose sight
Of what you came for and become like me,
Slave to a springtime passion for the earth.
How Love burns through the Putting in the Seed
On through the watching for that early birth
When, just as the soil tarnishes with weed,
The sturdy seedling with arched body comes
Shouldering its way and shedding the earth crumbs.

Design

I found a dimpled spider, fat and white,
On a white heal-all, holding up a moth
Like a white piece of rigid satin cloth—
Assorted characters of death and blight
Mixed ready to begin the morning right,
Like the ingredients of a witches' broth—
A snow-drop spider, a flower like a froth,
And dead wings carried like a paper kite.

What had that flower to do with being white,
The wayside blue and innocent heal-all?
What brought the kindred spider to that height,
Then steered the white moth thither in the night?
What but design of darkness to appall?—
If design govern in a thing so small.

Never Again Would Birds' Song Be the Same

He would declare and could himself believe
That the birds there in all the garden round
From having heard the daylong voice of Eve
Had added to their own an oversound,

Her tone of meaning but without the words.
Admittedly an eloquence so soft
Could only have had an influence on birds
When call or laughter carried it aloft.
Be that as may be, she was in their song.
Moreover her voice upon their voices crossed
Had now persisted in the woods so long
That probably it never would be lost.
Never again would birds' song be the same.
And to do that to birds was why she came.

Directive

Back out of all this now too much for us,
Back in a time made simple by the loss
Of detail, burned, dissolved, and broken off
Like graveyard marble sculpture in the weather,
There is a house that is no more a house
Upon a farm that is no more a farm
And in a town that is no more a town.
The road there, if you'll let a guide direct you
Who only has at heart your getting lost,
May seem as if it should have been a quarry—
Great monolithic knees the former town
Long since gave up pretense of keeping covered,
And there's a story in a book about it:
Besides the wear of iron wagon wheels
The ledges show lines ruled southeast northwest,
The chisel work of an enormous Glacier
That braced his feet against the Arctic Pole.
You must not mind a certain coolness from him
Still said to haunt this side of Panther Mountain.
Nor need you mind the serial ordeal
Of being watched from forty cellar holes
As if by eye pairs out of forty firkins.
As for the woods' excitement over you
That sends light rustle rushes to their leaves,
Charge that to upstart inexperience.
Where were they all not twenty years ago?
They think too much of having shaded out
A few old pecker-fretted apple trees.
Make yourself up a cheering song of how

Someone's road home from work this once was,
Who may be just ahead of you on foot
Or creaking with a buggy load of grain.
The height of the adventure is the height
Of country where two village cultures faded
Into each other. Both of them are lost.
And if you're lost enough to find yourself
By now, pull in your ladder road behind you
And put a sign up CLOSED to all but me.
Then make yourself at home. The only field
Now left's no bigger than a harness gall.
First there's the children's house of make believe,
Some shattered dishes underneath a pine,
The playthings in the playhouse of the children.
Weep for what little things could make them glad.
Then for the house that is no more a house,
But only a belilaced cellar hole,
Now slowly closing like a dent in dough.
This was no playhouse but a house in earnest.
Your destination and your destiny's
A brook that was the water of the house,
Cold as a spring as yet so near its source,
Too lofty and original to rage.
(We know the valley streams that when aroused
Will leave their tatters hung on barb and thorn.)
I have kept hidden in the instep arch
Of an old cedar at the waterside
A broken drinking goblet like the Grail
Under a spell so the wrong ones can't find it,
So can't get saved, as Saint Mark says they mustn't.
(I stole the goblet from the children's playhouse.)
Here are your waters and your watering place.
Drink and be whole again beyond confusion.

WALLACE STEVENS

1879–1955

IN THIS EDITOR'S LIFELONG JUDGMENT, Wallace Stevens is the principal American poet since Walt Whitman and Emily Dickinson. A poetic and human paradox, Stevens has come very slowly into the general esteem he merits. He is at once the poet of "the hum of thoughts evaded in the mind" and the visionary of "the plain sense of things."

Stevens was an undergraduate poet at Harvard, and then gave up the art for insurance law and marriage. He began again with the meditation "Sunday Morning," written in 1915, when he was thirty-six. His first volume, *Harmonium* (1922), vies with Hart Crane's *White Buildings* (1926) as the most original first book of poems by an American since Walt Whitman's *Leaves of Grass* (1855).

After *Harmonium,* Stevens retreated into poetic silence until he wrote "The Idea of Order at Key West" (1934). From then, until his death in 1955, he was continuously fecund, writing a remarkable series of longer poems: *The Man with the Blue Guitar* (1937), *Notes Toward a Supreme Fiction* (1942), *The Auroras of Autumn* (1947), and *An Ordinary Evening in New Haven* (1949).

When Stevens gathered his *Collected Poems,* his personal choice (overruled by editors) was to call the book *The Whole of Harmonium.* He would have been right, for the essential Stevens is in the hedonistic humanism and mingled skepticisms and assertions of his grand first book.

The woman of "Sunday Morning" is what Stevens eventually was to call his "interior paramour," the internalized figure of the Muse in the tradition between Milton and Tennyson. She speaks for Stevens, who then speaks for himself in the poem's closing lines:

> And, in the isolation of the sky,
> At evening, casual flocks of pigeons make
> Ambiguous undulations as they sink,
> Downward to darkness, on extended wings.

This is the world of "Domination of Black," the vision of reality as a dominant blank. And it is the cosmos of another famous poem by Stevens, "The Snow Man," which critics delight in misreading. Stevens subtly argues with himself in "The Snow Man." The "mind of winter" dominates the poem, but there is an undersong of rich figuration throughout: the shift from "regard" to "behold," the "crusted" and "shagged" and "distant glitter" by which metaphor returns to a poem that says it wants a listener, "nothing himself," who "beholds / Nothing that is not there and the nothing that is." The "nothing that is" is alive with sensory observation, and the reduction and negation are never final.

The antithesis to "The Snow Man" is the great chant of affirmation that concludes "Tea at the Palaz of Hoon":

> Out of my mind the golden ointment rained,
> And my ears made the blowing hymns they heard.
> I was myself the compass of that sea:
>
> I was the world in which I walked, and what I saw
> Or heard or felt came not but from myself;
> And there I found myself more truly and more strange.

This prophesies the singing girl at Key West thirteen years later, and is a Whitmanian declaration. Though Stevens sought to deny Whitman, he is a profoundly Whitmanian poet. Like Whitman's, Stevens's affirmations were qualified, but a qualified assertion is not an asserted qualification. As profoundly as Whitman's, Stevens's poetry ultimately is celebratory.

✔   ✔   ✔

Sunday Morning

I

Complacencies of the peignoir, and late
Coffee and oranges in a sunny chair,
And the green freedom of a cockatoo
Upon a rug mingle to dissipate
The holy hush of ancient sacrifice.
She dreams a little, and she feels the dark
Encroachment of that old catastrophe,
As a calm darkens among water-lights.
The pungent oranges and bright, green wings
Seem things in some procession of the dead,
Winding across wide water, without sound.
The day is like wide water, without sound,
Stilled for the passing of her dreaming feet

Over the seas, to silent Palestine,
Dominion of the blood and sepulchre.

II

Why should she give her bounty to the dead?
What is divinity if it can come
Only in silent shadows and in dreams?
Shall she not find in comforts of the sun,
In pungent fruit and bright, green wings, or else
In any balm or beauty of the earth,
Things to be cherished like the thought of heaven?
Divinity must live within herself:
Passions of rain, or moods in falling snow;
Grievings in loneliness, or unsubdued
Elations when the forest blooms; gusty
Emotions on wet roads on autumn nights;
All pleasures and all pains, remembering
The bough of summer and the winter branch.
These are the measures destined for her soul.

III

Jove in the clouds had his inhuman birth.
No mother suckled him, no sweet land gave
Large-mannered motions to his mythy mind.
He moved among us, as a muttering king,
Magnificent, would move among his hinds,
Until our blood, commingling, virginal,
With heaven, brought such requital to desire
The very hinds discerned it, in a star.
Shall our blood fail? Or shall it come to be
The blood of paradise? And shall the earth
Seem all of paradise that we shall know?
The sky will be much friendlier then than now,
A part of labor and a part of pain,
And next in glory to enduring love,
Not this dividing and indifferent blue.

IV

She says, "I am content when wakened birds,
Before they fly, test the reality
Of misty fields, by their sweet questionings;
But when the birds are gone, and their warm fields
Return no more, where, then, is paradise?"

There is not any haunt of prophesy,
Nor any old chimera of the grave,
Neither the golden underground, nor isle
Melodious, where spirits gat them home,
Nor visionary south, nor cloudy palm
Remote on heaven's hill, that has endured
As April's green endures; or will endure
Like her remembrance of awakened birds,
Or her desire for June and evening, tipped
By the consummation of the swallow's wings.

V

She says, "But in contentment I still feel
The need of some imperishable bliss."
Death is the mother of beauty; hence from her,
Alone, shall come fulfilment to our dreams
And our desires. Although she strews the leaves
Of sure obliteration on our paths,
The path sick sorrow took, the many paths
Where triumph rang its brassy phrase, or love
Whispered a little out of tenderness,
She makes the willow shiver in the sun
For maidens who were wont to sit and gaze
Upon the grass, relinquished to their feet.
She causes boys to pile new plums and pears
On disregarded plate. The maidens taste
And stray impassioned in the littering leaves.

VI

Is there no change of death in paradise?
Does ripe fruit never fall? Or do the boughs
Hang always heavy in that perfect sky,
Unchanging, yet so like our perishing earth,
With rivers like our own that seek for seas
They never find, the same receding shores
That never touch with inarticulate pang?
Why set the pear upon those river-banks
Or spice the shores with odors of the plum?
Alas, that they should wear our colors there,
The silken weavings of our afternoons,
And pick the strings of our insipid lutes!
Death is the mother of beauty, mystical,
Within whose burning bosom we devise
Our earthly mothers waiting, sleeplessly.

VII

Supple and turbulent, a ring of men
Shall chant in orgy on a summer morn
Their boisterous devotion to the sun,
Not as a god, but as a god might be,
Naked among them, like a savage source.
Their chant shall be a chant of paradise,
Out of their blood, returning to the sky;
And in their chant shall enter, voice by voice,
The windy lake wherein their lord delights,
The trees, like serafin, and echoing hills,
That choir among themselves long afterward.
They shall know well the heavenly fellowship
Of men that perish and of summer morn.
And whence they came and whither they shall go
The dew upon their feet shall manifest.

VIII

She hears, upon that water without sound,
A voice that cries, "The tomb in Palestine
Is not the porch of spirits lingering.
It is the grave of Jesus, where he lay."
We live in an old chaos of the sun,
Or old dependency of day and night,
Or island solitude, unsponsored, free,
Of that wide water, inescapable.
Deer walk upon our mountains, and the quail
Whistle about us their spontaneous cries;
Sweet berries ripen in the wilderness;
And, in the isolation of the sky,
At evening, casual flocks of pigeons make
Ambiguous undulations as they sink,
Downward to darkness, on extended wings.

Domination of Black

At night, by the fire,
The colors of the bushes
And of the fallen leaves,
Repeating themselves,
Turned in the room,
Like the leaves themselves
Turning in the wind.

Yes; but the color of the heavy hemlocks
Came striding.
And I remembered the cry of the peacocks.

The colors of their tails
Were like the leaves themselves
Turning in the wind,
In the twilight wind.
They swept over the room,
Just as they flew from the boughs of the hemlocks
Down to the ground.
I heard them cry—the peacocks.
Was it a cry against the twilight
Or against the leaves themselves
Turning in the wind,
Turning as the flames
Turned in the fire,
Turning as the tails of the peacocks
Turned in the loud fire,
Loud as the hemlocks
Full of the cry of the peacocks?
Or was it a cry against the hemlocks?

Out of the window,
I saw how the planets gathered
Like the leaves themselves
Turning in the wind.
I saw how the night came,
Came striding like the color of the heavy hemlocks.
I felt afraid.
And I remembered the cry of the peacocks.

Nomad Exquisite

As the immense dew of Florida
Brings forth
The big-finned palm
And green vine angering for life,

As the immense dew of Florida
Brings forth hymn and hymn
From the beholder,

Beholding all these green sides
And gold sides of green sides,

And blessed mornings,
Meet for the eye of the young alligator,
And lightning colors
So, in me, come flinging
Forms, flames, and the flakes of flames.

The Man Whose Pharynx Was Bad

The time of year has grown indifferent.
Mildew of summer and the deepening snow
Are both alike in the routine I know.
I am too dumbly in my being pent.

The wind attendant on the solstices
Blows on the shutters of the metropoles,
Stirring no poet in his sleep, and tolls
The grand ideas of the villages.

The malady of the quotidian. . . .
Perhaps, if winter once could penetrate
Through all its purples to the final slate,
Persisting bleakly in an icy haze,

One might in turn become less diffident,
Out of such mildew plucking neater mould
And spouting new orations of the cold.
One might. One might. But time will not relent.

The Snow Man

One must have a mind of winter
To regard the frost and the boughs
Of the pine-trees crusted with snow;

And have been cold a long time
To behold the junipers shagged with ice,
The spruces rough in the distant glitter

Of the January sun; and not to think
Of any misery in the sound of the wind,
In the sound of a few leaves,

Which is the sound of the land
Full of the same wind
That is blowing in the same bare place

For the listener, who listens in the snow,
And, nothing himself, beholds
Nothing that is not there and the nothing that is.

Tea at the Palaz of Hoon

Not less because in purple I descended
The western day through what you called
The loneliest air, not less was I myself.

What was the ointment sprinkled on my beard?
What were the hymns that buzzed beside my ears?
What was the sea whose tide swept through me there?

Out of my mind the golden ointment rained,
And my ears made the blowing hymns they heard.
I was myself the compass of that sea:

I was the world in which I walked, and what I saw
Or heard or felt came not but from myself;
And there I found myself more truly and more strange.

The Idea of Order at Key West

She sang beyond the genius of the sea.
The water never formed to mind or voice,
Like a body wholly body, fluttering
Its empty sleeves; and yet its mimic motion
Made constant cry, caused constantly a cry,
That was not ours although we understood,
Inhuman, of the veritable ocean.

The sea was not a mask. No more was she.
The song and water were not medleyed sound

Even if what she sang was what she heard,
Since what she sang was uttered word by word.
It may be that in all her phrases stirred
The grinding water and the gasping wind;
But it was she and not the sea we heard.

For she was the maker of the song she sang.
The ever-hooded, tragic-gestured sea
Was merely a place by which she walked to sing.
Whose spirit is this? we said, because we knew
It was the spirit that we sought and knew
That we should ask this often as she sang.

If it was only the dark voice of the sea
That rose, or even colored by many waves;
If it was only the outer voice of sky
And cloud, of the sunken coral water-walled,
However clear, it would have been deep air,
The heaving speech of air, a summer sound
Repeated in a summer without end
And sound alone. But it was more than that,
More even than her voice, and ours, among
The meaningless plungings of water and the wind,
Theatrical distances, bronze shadows heaped
On high horizons, mountainous atmospheres
Of sky and sea.
                    It was her voice that made
The sky acutest at its vanishing.
She measured to the hour its solitude.
She was the single artificer of the world
In which she sang. And when she sang, the sea,
Whatever self it had, became the self
That was her song, for she was the maker. Then we,
As we beheld her striding there alone,
Knew that there never was a world for her
Except the one she sang and, singing, made.

Ramon Fernandez, tell me, if you know,
Why, when the singing ended and we turned
Toward the town, tell why the glassy lights,
The lights in the fishing boats at anchor there,
As the night descended, tilting in the air,

Mastered the night and portioned out the sea,
Fixing emblazoned zones and fiery poles,
Arranging, deepening, enchanting night.

Oh! Blessed rage for order, pale Ramon,
The maker's rage to order words of the sea,
Words of the fragrant portals, dimly-starred,
And of ourselves and of our origins,
In ghostlier demarcations, keener sounds.

The Poems of Our Climate

I

Clear water in a brilliant bowl,
Pink and white carnations. The light
In the room more like a snowy air,
Reflecting snow. A newly-fallen snow
At the end of winter when afternoons return.
Pink and white carnations—one desires
So much more than that. The day itself
Is simplified: a bowl of white,
Cold, a cold porcelain, low and round,
With nothing more than the carnations there.

II

Say even that this complete simplicity
Stripped one of all one's torments, concealed
The evilly compounded, vital I
And made it fresh in a world of white,
A world of clear water, brilliant-edged,
Still one would want more, one would need more,
More than a world of white and snowy scents.

III

There would still remain the never-resting mind,
So that one would want to escape, come back
To what had been so long composed.
The imperfect is our paradise.
Note that, in this bitterness, delight,
Since the imperfect is so hot in us,
Lies in flawed words and stubborn sounds.

The Auroras of Autumn

I

This is where the serpent lives, the bodiless.
His head is air. Beneath his tip at night
Eyes open and fix on us in every sky.

Or is this another wriggling out of the egg,
Another image at the end of the cave,
Another bodiless for the body's slough?

This is where the serpent lives. This is his nest,
These fields, these hills, these tinted distances,
And the pines above and along and beside the sea.

This is form gulping after formlessness,
Skin flashing to wished-for disappearances
And the serpent body flashing without the skin.

This is the height emerging and its base
These lights may finally attain a pole
In the midmost midnight and find the serpent there,

In another nest, the master of the maze
Of body and air and forms and images,
Relentlessly in possession of happiness.

This is his poison: that we should disbelieve
Even that. His meditations in the ferns,
When he moved so slightly to make sure of sun,

Made us no less as sure. We saw in his head,
Black beaded on the rock, the flecked animal,
The moving grass, the Indian in his glade.

II

Farewell to an idea . . . A cabin stands,
Deserted, on a beach. It is white,
As by a custom or according to

An ancestral theme or as a consequence
Of an infinite course. The flowers against the wall
Are white, a little dried, a kind of mark

Reminding, trying to remind, of a white
That was different, something else, last year
Or before, not the white of an aging afternoon,

Whether fresher or duller, whether of winter cloud
Or of winter sky, from horizon to horizon.
The wind is blowing the sand across the floor.

Here, being visible is being white,
Is being of the solid of white, the accomplishment
Of an extremist in an exercise . . .

The season changes. A cold wind chills the beach.
The long lines of it grow longer, emptier,
A darkness gathers though it does not fall

And the whiteness grows less vivid on the wall.
The man who is walking turns blankly on the sand.
He observes how the north is always enlarging the change,

With its frigid brilliances, its blue-red sweeps
And gusts of great enkindlings, its polar green,
The color of ice and fire and solitude.

III

Farewell to an idea . . . The mother's face,
The purpose of the poem, fills the room.
They are together, here, and it is warm,

With none of the prescience of oncoming dreams.
It is evening. The house is evening, half dissolved.
Only the half they can never possess remains,

Still-starred. It is the mother they possess,
Who gives transparence to their present peace.
She makes that gentler that can gentle be.

And yet she too is dissolved, she is destroyed.
She gives transparence. But she has grown old.
The necklace is a carving not a kiss.

The soft hands are a motion not a touch.
The house will crumble and the books will burn.
They are at ease in a shelter of the mind

And the house is of the mind and they and time,
Together, all together. Boreal night
Will look like frost as it approaches them   .

And to the mother as she falls asleep
And as they say good-night, good-night. Upstairs
The windows will be lighted, not the rooms.

A wind will spread its windy grandeurs round
And knock like a rifle-butt against the door.
The wind will command them with invincible sound.

IV

Farewell to an idea . . . The cancellings,
The negations are never final. The father sits
In space, wherever he sits, of bleak regard,

As one that is strong in the bushes of his eyes.
He says no to no and yes to yes. He says yes
To no; and in saying yes he says farewell.

He measures the velocities of change.
He leaps from heaven to heaven more rapidly
Than bad angels leap from heaven to hell in flames.

But now he sits in quiet and green-a-day.
He assumes the great speeds of space and flutters them
From cloud to cloudless, cloudless to keen clear

In flights of eye and ear, the highest eye
And the lowest ear, the deep ear that discerns,
At evening, things that attend it until it hears

The supernatural preludes of its own,
At the moment when the angelic eye defines
Its actors approaching, in company, in their masks.

Master O master seated by the fire
And yet in space and motionless and yet
Of motion the ever-brightening origin,

Profound, and yet the king and yet the crown,
Look at this present throne. What company,
In masks, can choir it with the naked wind?

V

The mother invites humanity to her house
And table. The father fetches tellers of tales
And musicians who mute much, muse much, on the tales.

The father fetches negresses to dance,
Among the children, like curious ripenesses
Of pattern in the dance's ripening.

For these the musicians make insidious tones,
Clawing the sing-song of their instruments.
The children laugh and jangle a tinny time.

The father fetches pageants out of air,
Scenes of the theatre, vistas and blocks of woods
And curtains like a naive pretence of sleep.

Among these the musicians strike the instinctive poem.
The father fetches his unherded herds,
Of barbarous tongue, slavered and panting halves

Of breath, obedient to his trumpet's touch.
This then is Chatillon or as you please.
We stand in the tumult of a festival.

What festival? This loud, disordered mooch?
These hospitaliers? These brute-like guests?
These musicians dubbing at a tragedy,

A-dub, a-dub, which is made up of this:
That there are no lines to speak? There is no play.
Or, the persons act one merely by being here.

VI

It is a theatre floating through the clouds,
Itself a cloud, although of misted rock
And mountains running like water, wave on wave,

Through waves of light. It is of cloud transformed
To cloud transformed again, idly, the way
A season changes color to no end,

Except the lavishing of itself in change,
As light changes yellow into gold and gold
To its opal elements and fire's delight,

Splashed wide-wise because it likes magnificence
And the solemn pleasures of magnificent space.
The cloud drifts idly through half-thought-of forms.

The theatre is filled with flying birds,
Wild wedges, as of a volcano's smoke, palm-eyed
And vanishing, a web in a corridor

Or massive portico. A capitol,
It may be, is emerging or has just
Collapsed. The denouement has to be postponed . . .

This is nothing until in a single man contained,
Nothing until this named thing nameless is
And is destroyed. He opens the door of his house

On flames. The scholar of one candle sees
An Arctic effulgence flaring on the frame
Of everything he is. And he feels afraid.

VII

Is there an imagination that sits enthroned
As grim as it is benevolent, the just
And the unjust, which in the midst of summer stops

To imagine winter? When the leaves are dead,
Does it take its place in the north and enfold itself,
Goat-leaper, crystalled and luminous, sitting

In highest night? And do these heavens adorn
And proclaim it, the white creator of black, jetted
By extinguishings, even of planets as may be,

Even of earth, even of sight, in snow,
Except as needed by way of majesty,
In the sky, as crown and diamond cabala?

It leaps through us, through all our heavens leaps,
Extinguishing our planets, one by one,
Leaving, of where we were and looked, of where

We knew each other and of each other thought,
A shivering residue, chilled and foregone,
Except for that crown and mystical cabala.

But it dare not leap by chance in its own dark.
It must change from destiny to slight caprice.
And thus its jetted tragedy, its stele

And shape and mournful making move to find
What must unmake it and, at last, what can,
Say, a flippant communication under the moon.

VIII

There may be always a time of innocence.
There is never a place. Or if there is no time,
If it is not a thing of time, nor of place,

Existing in the idea of it, alone,
In the sense against calamity, it is not
Less real. For the oldest and coldest philosopher,

There is or may be a time of innocence
As pure principle. Its nature is its end,
That it should be, and yet not be, a thing

That pinches the pity of the pitiful man,
Like a book at evening beautiful but untrue,
Like a book on rising beautiful and true.

It is like a thing of ether that exists
Almost as predicate. But it exists,
It exists, it is visible, it is, it is.

So, then, these lights are not a spell of light,
A saying out of a cloud, but innocence.
An innocence of the earth and no false sign

Or symbol of malice. That we partake thereof,
Lie down like children in this holiness,
As if, awake, we lay in the quiet of sleep,

As if the innocent mother sang in the dark
Of the room and on an accordion, half-heard,
Created the time and place in which we breathed . . .

IX

And of each other thought—in the idiom
Of the work, in the idiom of an innocent earth,
Not of the enigma of the guilty dream.

We were as Danes in Denmark all day long
And knew each other well, hale-hearted landsmen,
For whom the outlandish was another day

Of the week, queerer than Sunday. We thought alike
And that made brothers of us in a home
In which we fed on being brothers, fed

And fattened as on a decorous honeycomb.
This drama that we live—We lay sticky with sleep.
This sense of the activity of fate—

The rendezvous, when she came alone,
By her coming became a freedom of the two,
An isolation which only the two could share.

Shall we be found hanging in the trees next spring?
Of what disaster in this the imminence:
Bare limbs, bare trees and a wind as sharp as salt?

The stars are putting on their glittering belts.
They throw around their shoulders cloaks that flash
Like a great shadow's last embellishment.

It may come tomorrow in the simplest word,
Almost as part of innocence, almost,
Almost as the tenderest and the truest part.

    x
An unhappy people in a happy world—
Read, rabbi, the phases of this difference.
An unhappy people in an unhappy world—

Here are too many mirrors for misery.
A happy people in an unhappy world—
It cannot be. There's nothing there to roll

On the expressive tongue, the finding fang.
A happy people in a happy world—
Buffo! A ball, an opera, a bar.

Turn back to where we were when we began:
An unhappy people in a happy world.
Now, solemnize the secretive syllables.

Read to the congregation, for today
And for tomorrow, this extremity,
This contrivance of the spectre of the spheres,

Contriving balance to contrive a whole,
The vital, the never-failing genius,
Fulfilling his meditations, great and small.

In these unhappy he meditates a whole,
The full of fortune and the full of fate,
As if he lived all lives, that he might know,

In hall harridan, not hushful paradise,
To a haggling of wind and weather, by these lights
Like a blaze of summer straw, in winter's nick.

The Course of a Particular

Today the leaves cry, hanging on branches swept by wind,
Yet the nothingness of winter becomes a little less.
It is still full of icy shades and shapen snow.

The leaves cry . . . One holds off and merely hears the cry.
It is a busy cry, concerning someone else.
And though one says that one is part of everything,

There is a conflict, there is a resistance involved;
And being part is an exertion that declines:
One feels the life of that which gives life as it is.

The leaves cry. It is not a cry of divine attention,
Nor the smoke-drift of puffed-out heroes, nor human cry.
It is the cry of leaves that do not transcend themselves,

In the absence of fantasia, without meaning more
Than they are in the final finding of the ear, in the thing
Itself, until, at last, the cry concerns no one at all.

Of Mere Being

The palm at the end of the mind,
Beyond the last thought, rises
In the bronze decor,

A gold-feathered bird
Sings in the palm, without human meaning,
Without human feeling, a foreign song.

You know then that it is not the reason
That makes us happy or unhappy.
The bird sings. Its feathers shine.

The palm stands on the edge of space.
The wind moves slowly in the branches.
The bird's fire-fangled feathers dangle down.

WILLIAM CARLOS WILLIAMS

1883–1963

A NEW JERSEYAN ALL HIS LIFE, William Carlos Williams spoke Spanish as a child, his mother being from Puerto Rico. At the University of Pennsylvania, Williams formed lasting friendships with Ezra Pound and H. D. (Hilda Doolittle). After medical school and internship in New York City hospitals, he went abroad to study pediatrics at Leipzig. On his return, he settled in Rutherford, New Jersey, his birth-city, and married Flossie Herman, by whom he had two sons.

Williams published copiously in verse and prose, while keeping up his pediatric career. His long poem *Paterson* (1946–1958) is rightly considered his masterwork. I give here two superb early lyrics, "Queen-Anne's Lace" and "The Widow's Lament in Springtime," and three grand meditations from *Spring and All* (1923).

In his critical biography *William Carlos Williams: A New World Naked*, Paul Mariani wisely asserts the lasting influence of John Keats's poetry upon even the late phases of Williams:

> The voice he *was* listening to, and the voice that struck paydirt for
> him, was a matter of a complex crossing with Keats, especially the

Keats of the *Hyperion* fragments and the odes. Why this should have been so is difficult to say with any exactness, for Williams himself probably did not understand why. What *he* thought he was "capturing" was the voice of the classics—the stately rhythms and sharp straightforward idiom of the Greeks as he thought they must sound should they be discovered walking the streets of his Paterson. But there was something more, a kinship Williams had felt with Keats for over half a century, the plight of the romantic poet who would have spoken as the gods speak if only he had had the power to render their speech in the accents of his own debased language. *Hyperion* is in part the portrait of the dying of the ephebe into the life of the major poet, and Keats had aborted it at the very moment that his poet was undergoing that transformation.

And so with Williams, opting for the step-down line as his "classic" signature as he surfaced from the realization of his mortality, the new rhythm providing a stately, slow saraband to echo Keats's Miltonic and Dantesque phase with a difference. The crossing with Keats is there too in the nature of Williams's late iconography, in the stasis of his late images, frozen for eternity in the realized artifact, as in Williams's translation from Theocritus's first idyl, with its images limned on a "two-eared bowl / of ivy-wood," a girl and two young men, an ancient fisherman, and a small boy preoccupied with "plaiting a pretty / cage of locust stalks and asphodel." The images of *Asphodel* too belong to the same strain: sharply realized but without Williams's earlier breathlessness and jagged line cuttings.

Poetic influence, an intensely problematical process, normally brings together a strong poet's earliest and final phases. Williams's true precursor, necessarily composite and in some sense imaginary, was a figure that fused Keats with Walt Whitman. Such a figure has in it the potential for a serious splitting of the poetic ego in its defense against the poetic past. The "negative capability" of Keats sorts oddly with Whitman's rather positive capability for conveying the powerful press of himself. "Memory is a kind / of accomplishment," Williams wrote in "The Descent," a crucial poem in his *The Desert Music* (1954). The descent to dying beckons to a return of the dead precursors in one's own colors, even as Keats and Whitman beckoned Williams to ascend into his own poetry. But the poem "The Descent" Williams shrewdly quarried from Book II of his own major long poem, *Paterson,* a quarrying that suggests his pride in his own continuities.

Those continuities are massive throughout Williams's best work, which can be catalogued (against the numerous Williams idolators) as a limited yet still remarkably diverse canon: *Paterson* (Book I), *Kora in Hell, Spring and All*, "Queen-Anne's-Lace," "The Widow's Lament in Spring-time," "To Waken an Old Lady," "The Trees," "The Yachts," "A Coronal," "These," "The Poor," "A Marriage Ritual," "Raleigh Was Right," "Burning the Christmas Greens," "A Unison," and the grand return of Keats-as-Williams in *Asphodel, That Greeny Flower.* Intense admirers of Williams would select more, much more, but I am of the school of Wallace Stevens, rather than of Williams, and the Williams I honor is the author of about a dozen shorter poems, and four remarkable long poems and prose or verse sequences. I write this not to dissent, but as an experiment. If you believe—as I do—that Williams is not of the eminence of Stevens and Robert Frost, of Hart Crane and even of T. S. Eliot, then what is the irreducible achievement that survives even an extreme skepticism as to Williams's poetic greatness?

Of the volumes that collect Williams, I return most often to *Imaginations*, edited by Webster Schott (1979), which gathers together four weird American originals—*Kora in Hell, Spring and All, The Great American Novel, The Descent of Winter*—as well as some miscellaneous prose. *Kora in Hell* was subtitled *Improvisations* by Williams, who had a particular fondness for it. He analogized its astonishing "Prologue" to *On the Sublime* by the pseudo-Longinus, a comparison not so far-fetched as he himself asserted it to be. Essentially it, and all of *Kora*, is a collection of what Emerson (following Plutarch and Cudworth) called "lustres" (Ezra Pound's *lustra*), aphoristic impressions drawn either from others or from the self. Its center is in Williams's characteristic polemic against Pound and Eliot, with an ironizing boost from Stevens:

> E. P. is the best enemy United States verse has. He is interested, passionately interested—even if he doesn't know what he is talking about. But of course he does know what he is talking about. He does not, however, know everything, not by more than half. The accordances of which Americans have the parts and the colors but not the completions before them pass beyond the attempts of his thought. It is a middle-aging blight of the imagination.
>
> I praise those who have the wit and courage, and the conventionality, to go direct toward their vision of perfection in an objective world where the signposts are clearly marked, viz., to London. But confine them in hell for their paretic assumption that there is no alternative but their own groove.
>
> Dear fat Stevens, thawing out so beautifully at forty! I was one

day irately damning those who run to London when Stevens caught me up with his mild: "But where in the world will you have them run to?"

The shrewd link to *On the Sublime* is that Williams (admirably and accurately) shares the conviction of Longinus that the Sublime or strong poetry either is agonistic or it is nothing. Williams too seeks to persuade the reader to forsake easier pleasures (Eliot and Pound) for more difficult pleasures (*Kora in Hell*). And his quest is frankly Emersonian, an overt instance of American cultural nationalism. Unfortunately, *Kora*'s considerable verve and vivacity is shadowed by the immense power of James Joyce's *Ulysses,* still incomplete then, but appearing in magazine installments even as Williams wrote and read. Williams's use of mythology is essentially Joyce's, and to fight Joyce on any ground, let alone his prepared killing field, was beyond Williams's talents:

> Giants in the dirt. The gods, the Greek gods, smothered in filth and ignorance. The race is scattered over the world. Where is its home? Find it if you've the genius. Here Hebe with a sick jaw and a cruel husband,—her mother left no place for a brain to grow. Herakles rowing boats on Berry's Creek! Zeus is a country doctor without a taste for coin jingling. Supper is of a bastard nectar on rare nights for they will come—the rare nights! The ground lifts and out sally the heroes of Sophokles, of Aeschylus. They go seeping down into our hearts, they rain upon us and in the bog they sink again down through the white roots, down—to a saloon back of the railroad switch where they have that girl, you know, the one that should have been Venus by the lust that's in her. They've got her down there among the railroad men. A crusade couldn't rescue her. Up to jail—or call it down to Limbo—the Chief of Police our Pluto. It's all of the gods, there's nothing else worth writing of. They are the same men they always were—but fallen. Do they dance now, they that danced beside Helicon? They dance much as they did then, only, few have an eye for it, through the dirt and fumes.

The question becomes: who shall describe the dance of the gods as it is danced now in America? The answer is: Dr. Williams, who brings American babies into the world, and who sees exquisitely what we cannot see without him, which is how differently the gods come to dance here in America.

This is a slight stiff dance to a waking baby whose arms have been lying curled back above his head upon the pillow, making a flower—the eyes closed. Dead to the world! Waking is a little hand brushing away dreams. Eyes open. Here's a new world.

This dance figures again in the concluding improvisation of *Kora in Hell*, as an American seasonal rhythm akin to the natural year of Stevens's "Credences of Summer" and Emerson's "Experience":

> *Seeing the leaves dropping from the high and low branches the thought rises: this day of all others is the one chosen, all other days fall away from it on either side and only itself remains in perfect fullness. It is its own summer, of its leaves as they scrape on the smooth ground it must build its perfection. The gross summer of the year is only a halting counterpart of those fiery days of secret triumph which in reality themselves paint the year as if upon a parchment, giving each season a mockery of the warmth or frozenness which is within ourselves. The true seasons blossom or wilt not in fixed order but so that many of them may pass in a few weeks or hours whereas sometimes a whole life passes and the season remains of a piece from one end to the other.*

The world is largest in the American summer, for Williams and Stevens, even as it was for their forefather, Emerson. *Spring and All* celebrates not this world, but the more difficult American skepticism of a hard spring, imperishably rendered in its magnificent opening lyric, "By the road to the contagious hospital," with its harsh splendor of inception, at once of vegetation, infants, and of Whitmanian or American poems:

> Lifeless in appearance, sluggish
> dazed spring approaches—
>
> They enter the new world naked,
> cold, uncertain of all
> save that they enter. All about them
> the cold, familiar wind—
>
> Now the grass, tomorrow
> the stiff curl of wildcarrot leaf
> One by one objects are defined—
> It quickens: clarity, outline of leaf

> But now the stark dignity of
> entrance—Still, the profound change
> has come upon them: rooted, they
> grip down and begin to awaken

The ancient fiction of the leaves, a continuous tradition from Homer and Vergil, through Dante, and on to Spenser and Milton, Shelley and Whitman, receives one culmination in Stevens, and a very different apotheosis here in Williams. In the prose of *Spring and All*, Williams protests too emphatically that: "THE WORLD IS NEW," a protest that has been taken too much at its own self-mystifying evaluation by the most distinguished of the deconstructive critics of Williams, J. Hillis Miller and Joseph Riddel. But when the best poems in *Spring and All* unfold themselves, the reader can be persuaded that Williams has invented freshly the accurate metaphors for our American sense of imaginative belatedness: "There is / an approach with difficulty from / the dead—," and: "The rose is obsolete / but each petal ends in / an edge." Except for "By the road to the contagious hospital," the best poems in *Spring and All* are the justly famous ones: "The pure products of America / go crazy—," and "so much depends / upon / a red wheel / barrow."

More problematical are *The Great American Novel* and *The Descent of Winter*, pugnacious assaults upon Williams's own formal limits, yet assaults masked as ironies directed against the literary conventionalities of others. I prefer *The Descent of Winter*, where the authentic anxiety of belatedness, the only legitimate point of origin for any American literature, is expressed in relation to that most impossible of all influences, Shakespeare:

> By writing he escaped from the world into the natural world of his mind. The unemployable world of his fine head was unnaturally useless in the gross exterior of his day—or any day. By writing he made this active. He melted himself into that grossness, and colored it with his powers. The proof that he was right and they passing, being that he continues always and naturally while their artificiality destroyed them. A man unable to employ himself in his world.
>
> Therefore his seriousness and his accuracies, because it was not his play but the drama of his life. It is his anonymity that is baffling to nitwits and so they want to find an involved explanation—to defeat the plainness of the evidence.

When he speaks of fools he is one; when of kings he is one, doubly so in misfortune.

He is a woman, a pimp, a prince Hal—

Such a man is a prime borrower and standardizer—No inventor. He lives because he sinks back, does not go forward, sinks back into the mass—

He is Hamlet plainer than a theory—and in everything.

You can't buy a life again after it's gone, that's the way I mean.

He drinks awful bad and he beat me up every single month while I was carrying this baby, pretty nearly every week.

As an overview of Shakespeare, this is unquestionably the weakest commentary available since Tolstoy; but as a representation of Williams's dilemmas, it has a curious force, including the weird parody of Hemingway's agonistic stance in the last sentence I have just quoted. Despite his army of hyperbolic exegetes, Williams's nakedness in relation to the literary past is not so much that of "a new world naked" as it is that of a no longer so very new world awkwardly wrapped round by too many fine rags.

The best lyrics and Book I of *Paterson* are of a higher order, though they also betray darker anxieties of influence than even Williams's defiances dared to confront. They display also another kind of agon, the anxiety as to contemporary rivals, not so much Pound and Eliot as Wallace Stevens and Hart Crane, heirs to Keats and to Whitman, even as Williams was. No two readers are likely to agree upon just which shorter poems by Williams are his strongest, but one that impresses and moves me is "A Unison," where the title seems to comprehend most of the dictionary meanings of "unison": an identity of pitch in music; the same words spoken simultaneously by two or more speakers; musical parts combined in octaves; a concord, agreement, harmony. Thomas R. Whitaker, one of Williams's best and most sympathetic critics but no idolator, gives the best introduction to "A Unison":

It is like an improvisation from *Kora in Hell*—but one with the quiet maturity of vision and movement that some three decades have brought. . . . As the implicit analogies and contrasts accumulate, we discover (long before the speaker tells us) that we are attending a "unison and a dance." This "death's festival"— *memento mori* and celebration of the "*Undying*"—evades neither the mystery of transience nor that of organic continuance, though neither can be "parsed" by the analytical mind. . . . In this composed testament of acceptance, Williams's saxifrage ("through metaphor to reconcile / the people and the stones") quietly does its work. . . . Not since Wordsworth has this natural piety been rendered so freshly and poignantly.

I would not wish to quarrel with Whitaker's judgment, yet there is very little Wordsworth and (inevitably) much Whitman and considerable Keats in "A Unison." Indeed, the poem opens with what must be called an echo from Whitman, in what I assume was a controlled allusion:

> The grass is very green, my friend,
> And tousled, like the head of—
> your grandson, yes?

We hear one of the uncanniest passages in Whitman, from *Song of Myself* 6:

> This grass is very dark to be from the white heads of old mothers,
> Darker than the colorless beards of old men,
> Dark to come from under the faint red roofs of mouths.

Whitman's great fantasia answers a child's question: "*What is the grass?*" As an Epicurean materialist, Whitman believed that the *what* was unknowable, but his remarkable troping on the grass takes a grand turn after his Homeric line: "And now it seems to me the beautiful uncut hair of graves." Williams simply borrows the trope, and even his "very green" merely follows Whitman's hint that a "very green" becomes a "very dark" color, in the shadow of mortality. "A Unison" insists upon:

> what cannot be escaped: the
> mountain riding the afternoon as
> it does, the grass matted green,
> green underfoot and the air—
> rotten wood. *Hear! Hear them!*
> *the Undying.* The hill slopes away,
> then rises in the middleground,
> you remember, with a grove of gnarled
> maples centering the bare pasture,
> sacred, surely—for what reason?

Williams does not know whether he can or cannot say the reason, but the allusion is to Keats's characteristic, Saturnian shrine in *Hyperion.* For Williams it is "a shrine cinctured there by / the trees," the girdling effect suggested by the natural sculpture of Keats's shrine. Where Keats as the quester in *The Fall of Hyperion* pledges "all the mortals of the world, / And all the dead whose names are in our lips," and where Whitman insists, "The smallest sprout shows there is really no death," Williams neither salutes the living and the dead nor folds the two into a single figuration. Rather, he *hears* and urges us to *"Hear the unison of their voices. . . . "* How are we to interpret such an imaginative gesture? Are we hearing more, or enough more, than the unison of the voices of John Keats and Walt Whitman? Devoted Williamsites doubtless would reject the question, but it always retains its force, nevertheless. It is not less true of *The Waste Land* than it is of Williams. Eliot revises Whitman's "When Lilacs Last in the Dooryard Bloom'd" by fusing it with Tennyson (among others, but prime among those others). Image of voice or the trope of poetic identity then becomes a central problem.

Whitman once contrasted himself to Keats by rejecting negative capability and insisting instead that the great poet gave us the "powerful press of himself." Admirable as *Paterson* is (particularly its first book), does even it resolve the antithesis in Williams between his "objectivism" or negative capability, and his own, agonistic, powerful press of himself? Mariani ends his vast, idealizing biography by asserting that Williams established "an American poetic based on a new measure and a primary regard for the living, protean shape of the language as it was actually used." Hillis Miller, even more generously, tells us that Williams gave us a concept of poetry transcending both Homer and Wordsworth, both Aristotle and Coleridge:

> The word is given reality by the fact it names, but the independence of the fact from the word frees the word to be a fact in its own right and at the same time "dynamizes" it with meaning. The word can then carry the facts named in a new form into the realm of imagination.

Mariani and Miller are quite sober compared to more apocalyptic Williamsites. Not even Whitman gave us "a new measure," and not Shakespeare himself freed a single word "to be a fact in its own right." William Carlos Williams was, at his best, a strong American poet, far better than his hordes of imitators. Like Ezra Pound's, Williams's remains a fairly problematical achievement in the traditions of American poetry. Some generations hence, it will become clear whether his critics have canonized him permanently, or subverted him by taking him too much at his own intentions. For now he abides, a live influence, and perhaps with even more fame to come.

✴ ✴ ✴

Queen-Anne's-Lace

Her body is not so white as
anemone petals nor so smooth—nor
so remote a thing. It is a field
of the wild carrot taking
the field by force; the grass
does not raise above it.
Here is no question of whiteness,
white as can be, with a purple mole
at the center of each flower.
Each flower is a hand's span
of her whiteness. Wherever
his hand has lain there is
a tiny purple blemish. Each part
is a blossom under his touch
to which the fibres of her being
stem one by one, each to its end,
until the whole field is a
white desire, empty, a single stem,
a cluster, flower by flower,
a pious wish to whiteness gone over—
or nothing.

The Widow's Lament in Springtime

Sorrow is my own yard
where the new grass
flames as it has flamed
often before but not
with the cold fire
that closes round me this year.
Thirtyfive years
I lived with my husband.
The plumtree is white today
with masses of flowers.
Masses of flowers
load the cherry branches
and color some bushes

yellow and some red
but the grief in my heart
is stronger than they
for though they were my joy
formerly, today I notice them
and turn away forgetting.
Today my son told me
that in the meadows,
at the edge of the heavy woods
in the distance, he saw
trees of white flowers.
I feel that I would like
to go there
and fall into those flowers
and sink into the marsh near them.

from Spring and All

By the road to the contagious hospital
under the surge of the blue
mottled clouds driven from the
northeast—a cold wind. Beyond, the
waste of broad, muddy fields
brown with dried weeds, standing and fallen

patches of standing water
the scattering of tall trees

All along the road the reddish
purplish, forked, upstanding, twiggy
stuff of bushes and small trees
with dead, brown leaves under them
leafless vines—

Lifeless in appearance, sluggish
dazed spring approaches—

They enter the new world naked,
cold, uncertain of all
save that they enter. All about them
the cold, familiar wind—

Now the grass, tomorrow
the stiff curl of wildcarrot leaf

One by one objects are defined—
It quickens: clarity, outline of leaf

But now the stark dignity of
entrance—Still, the profound change
has come upon them: rooted, they
grip down and begin to awaken

     .   .   .

The rose is obsolete
but each petal ends in
an edge, the double facet
cementing the grooved
columns of air—The edge
cuts without cutting

meets—nothing—renews
itself in metal or porcelain—

whither? It ends—

But if it ends
the start is begun
so that to engage roses
becomes a geometry—

Sharper, neater, more cutting
figured in majolica—
the broken plate
glazed with a rose

Somewhere the sense
makes copper roses
steel roses—

The rose carried weight of love
but love is at an end—of roses

It is at the edge of the
petal that love waits

Crisp, worked to defeat
laboredness—fragile
plucked, moist, half-raised
cold, precise, touching

What

The place between the petal's
edge and the

From the petal's edge a line starts
that being of steel
infinitely fine, infinitely
rigid penetrates
the Milky Way
without contact—lifting
from it—neither hanging
nor pushing—

The fragility of the flower
unbruised
penetrates space

.   .   .

The pure products of America
go crazy—
mountain folk from Kentucky

or the ribbed north end of
Jersey
with its isolate lakes and

valleys, its deaf-mutes, thieves
old names
and promiscuity between

devil-may-care men who have taken
to railroading
out of sheer lust of adventure—

and young slatterns, bathed
in filth
from Monday to Saturday

to be tricked out that night
with gauds
from imaginations which have no

peasant traditions to give them
character
but flutter and flaunt

sheer rags—succumbing without
emotion
save numbed terror

under some hedge of choke-cherry
or viburnum—
which they cannot express—

Unless it be that marriage
perhaps
with a dash of Indian blood

will throw up a girl so desolate
so hemmed round
with disease or murder

that she'll be rescued by an
agent—
reared by the state and

sent out at fifteen to work in
some hard pressed
house in the suburbs—

some doctor's family, some Elsie—
voluptuous water
expressing with broken

brain the truth about us—
her great
ungainly hips and flopping breasts

addressed to cheap
jewelry
and rich young men with fine eyes

as if the earth under our feet
were
an excrement of some sky

and we degraded prisoners
destined
to hunger until we eat filth

while the imagination strains
after deer
going by fields of goldenrod in

the stifling heat of September
Somehow
it seems to destroy us

It is only in isolate flocks that
something
is given off

No one
to witness
and adjust, no one to drive the car

EZRA POUND

1885–1972

I

BORN IN IDAHO, Pound grew up in Philadelphia, met William Carlos Williams (a lifelong friend) at the University of Pennsylvania, where he also knew Hilda Doolittle (H. D.), with whom briefly he was engaged to be married. After living in Italy, Pound resided in London, where he became the center of a literary matrix that included the poet William Butler Yeats, the novelist Ford Maddox Ford, and the painter-novelist Wyndham Lewis. Already a promoter of James Joyce, Pound joined Lewis in founding the magazine *BLAST: A Review of the Great English Vortex.*

In April 1914, Pound married Dorothy Shakespear, the daughter of Yeats's mistress, the novelist Olivia Shakespear. Soon after, Pound and T. S. Eliot met and became close friends. After three years in France, Pound moved to Italy in 1924. A son was born to Pound and Dorothy in 1926, a year after Pound's mistress, American violinist Olga Rudge, gave birth to their daughter, Mary.

Immensely active as poet-critic, and head of the Modernist literary movement, Pound unfortunately became a Fascist, and was received by Benito Mussolini in 1933. In 1940, Mussolini declared war on Britain and France, and Pound became a radio propagandist for the Axis. His broadcasts ought to be read by admirers of his poetry, since they feature virulent anti-Semitic diatribes, exactly contemporary with Hitler's Holocaust in his Death Camps. A federal grand jury indicted Pound for treason (in absentia). In May 1945, Italian partisans captured Pound, and turned him over to the FBI in Genoa.

For a while, Pound was confined to a military stockade, until he was taken to Washington, D.C., for a treason hearing. The jury judged him to be mentally unfit for trial. Kept in a psychiatric hospital until 1958, Pound was released on a petition signed by Hemingway and Robert Frost, among others. Pound returned to Italy, and lived there until his death in 1972, at the age of eighty-seven.

Pound's major poetic work is *The Cantos,* which seem to me to anthologize badly, nor do I have much esteem for them, or for Pound, whether as a person or poet. Like Dante Gabriel Rossetti, who, with Robert Browning and Walt Whitman, was a crucial precursor, Pound excelled as a translator. I give here a version of a lament by the Provençal poet Bertrans de Born, and of the Old English *The Seafarer.*

2

I have brought the great ball of crystal;
who can lift it?

—CANTO CXVI

POUND'S PRIME EXPLAINER, Hugh Kenner, commenting on *The Cantos,* writes of "the paradox that an intensely topical poem has become archaic without ever having been contemporary: archaic in an honorific sense." Kenner accounts for the paradox by insisting: "There is no substitute for critical tradition: a continuum of understanding, early commenced. . . . Precisely because William Blake's contemporaries did not know what to make of him, we do not know either. . . . " Kenner was the greatest of antiquarian Modernists, and his authority in these judgments is doubtless unassailable. His Pound may well be *the* Pound, even if his Joyce somehow seems less Dublin's Joyce than T. S. Eliot's Joyce. I, in any case, would not care to dispute any critic's Pound. They have their reward, and he has them.

I do not know many readers who have an equal affection for *The Cantos* and for say, Wallace Stevens's *An Ordinary Evening in New Haven* or *The Auroras of Autumn.* Doubtless, again, such differences in poetic taste belong to the accidents of sensibility, or to irreconcilable attitudes concerning the relation of poetry to belief. They may indeed belong to more profound distinctions in judgments as to value that transcend literary preferences. I do not desire to address myself to such matters here. Nor will I consider Pound's politics. *The Cantos* contain material that is not humanly acceptable to me, and if that material is acceptable to others, then they themselves are thereby less acceptable, at least to me.

My subject here, in necessarily curtailed terms, is Pound's relation to poetic tradition in his own language, and to Whitman in particular. Pound's critics have taken him at his word in this regard, but no poet whatsoever can be trusted in his or her own story of poetic origins, even as no man or woman can be relied on to speak with dispassionate accuracy of his or her parents. Perhaps Pound triumphed in his agon with poetic tradition, which is the invariable assertion of all of his critical partisans. But the triumph, if it occurred, was a very qualified one. My own experience as a reader of *The Cantos,* across many years, is that the long poem or sequence is marred throughout by Pound's relative failure to transume or transcend his precursors. Their ancestral voices abound, and indeed become more rather than less evident as the sequence continues. Nor is this invariably a controlled allusiveness. Collage, which is handled as metaphor by Marianne Moore and by the Eliot of *The Waste Land,* is a much more literal process in Pound, is more scheme than trope, as it were. The allusive triumph over tradition in Moore's "Marriage" or *The Waste Land* is fairly problematical, yet nowhere near so dubious as it is in *The Cantos.* Confronted by a past poetic wealth in figuration, Pound tends to resort to baroque elaborations of the anterior metaphors. What he almost never manages is to achieve an ellipsis of further troping by his own inventiveness at metaphor. He cannot make the voices of Whitman and Browning seem belated, while his own voice manifests what Stevens called an "ever early candor."

I am aware that I am in apparent defiance of the proud Poundian dictum: *Make It New.* Whitman made it new in one way, and Browning in another, but Pound's strength was elsewhere. Anglo-American Poetic "Modernism" was Ezra Pound's revolution, but it seems now only another continuity in the long history of Romanticism. Literary history may or may not someday regard Pound as it now regards Abraham Cowley, John Cleveland, and Edmund Waller, luminaries of one era who faded into the common light of another age. But, as a manneristic poet, master of a period style, Pound has his deep affinities to Cowley, Cleveland, and above all Waller. He has affinities also, though, to Dante Gabriel Rossetti, an enduring poet who suffered from belatedness in a mode strikingly akin to that of Pound. Poundian critics tend to regard Rossetti as a kind of embarrassing prelude to their hero, but I certainly intend only a tribute to Pound in comparing him to Rossetti. It is, after all, far better to be called the Dante Gabriel Rossetti than the Edmund Waller of your era.

3

> *Mr. Eliot and I are in agreement, or "belong to the same school of critics,"*
> *in so far as we both believe that existing works form a complete order*
> *which is changed by the introduction of the "really new" work.*
> —POUND, *ACTIVE ANTHOLOGY*

TIMELESS, OR COMPLETE, orders are beautiful idealizations, and have not the slightest relevance to the actual sorrows of literary influence. Time's disorders are the truth of poetic tradition. Eliot, child of Whitman and Tennyson, preferred to see himself in the timeless order of Vergil and Dante, Pascal and Baudelaire. Pound, brash and natural child of Whitman and Browning, found his idealized forerunners in Arnaut Daniel and Cavalcanti, Villon, and Landor. Oedipal ambivalence, which marks Pound's stance toward Whitman, never surfaces in his observations on Cavalcanti and Villon, safely remote not only in time and language, but more crucially isolated from the realities of Pound's equivocal relation to his country and compatriots.

I find Whitman quite unrecognizable in nearly every reference Pound makes to him. Our greatest poet and our most elusive, because most figurative, Whitman consistently is literalized by Pound, as though the Whitmanian self could be accepted as a machine rather than as a metaphor. What can be construed in the weird piece of 1909, "What I Feel about Walt Whitman," is a transference so ambivalent that the positive and negative elements defy disentanglement:

From this side of the Atlantic I am for the first time able to read Whitman, and from the vantage of my education and—if it be permitted a man of my scant years—my world citizenship: I see him America's poet. The only Poet before the artists of the Carmen-Hovey period, or better, the only one of the conventionally recognised 'American Poets' who is worth reading.

He *is* America. His crudity is an exceeding great stench, but it *is* America. He is the hollow place in the rock that echoes with his time. He *does* 'chant the crucial stage' and he is the 'voice triumphant.' He is disgusting. He is an exceedingly nauseating pill, but he accomplishes his mission.

Entirely free from the renaissance humanist ideal of the complete man or from the Greek idealism, he is content to be what he is, and he is his time and his people. He is a genius because he has vision of what he is and of his function. He knows that he is a beginning and not a classically finished work.

I honour him for he prophesied me while I can only recognise him as a forebear of whom I ought to be proud.

In America there is much for the healing of the nations, but woe unto him of the cultured palate who attempts the dose.

As for Whitman, I read him (in many parts) with acute pain, but when I write of certain things I find myself using his rhythms. The expression of certain things related to cosmic consciousness seems tainted with this marasmus.

I am (in common with every educated man) an heir of the ages and I demand my birth-right. Yet if Whitman represented his time in language acceptable to one accustomed to my standard of intellectual-artistic living he would belie his time and nation. And yet I am but one of his 'ages and ages encrustations' or to be exact an encrustation of the next age. The vital part of my message, taken from the sap and fibre of America, is the same as his.

Mentally I am a Walt Whitman who has learned to wear a collar and a dress shirt (although at times inimical to both). Personally I might be very glad to conceal my relationship to my spiritual father and brag about my more congenial ancestry—Dante, Shakespeare, Theocritus, Villon, but the descent is a bit difficult to establish. And, to be frank, Whitman is to my fatherland (*Patriam quam odi et amo* for no uncertain reasons) what Dante is to Italy and I at my best can only be a strife for a renaissance in America of all the lost or temporarily mislaid beauty, truth, valour, glory of Greece, Italy, England and all the rest of it.

And yet if a man has written lines like Whitman's to the *Sunset Breeze* one has to love him. I think we have not yet paid enough attention to the deliberate artistry of the man, not in details but in the large.

I am immortal even as he is, yet with a lesser vitality as I am the more in love with beauty (if I really do love it more than he did). Like Dante he wrote in the 'vulgar tongue,' in a new metric. The first great man to write in the language of his people.

Et ego Petrarca in lingua vetera scribo, and in a tongue my people understood not.

It seems to me I should like to drive Whitman into the old world. I sledge, he drill—and to scourge America with all the old beauty. (For Beauty *is* an accusation) and with a thousand thongs from Homer to Yeats, from Theocritus to Marcel Schwob. This desire is because I am young and impatient, were I old and wise I should content myself in seeing and saying that these things will come. But now, since I am by no means sure it would be true prophecy, I am fain set my own hand to the labour.

It is a great thing, reading a man to know, not 'His Tricks are not as yet my Tricks, but I can easily make them mine' but 'His message is my message. We will see that men hear it.'

Whitman is at once crude, disgusting, nauseating, and to be read with acute pain, but also America's poet, indeed America itself, a genius more vital than the equally immortal Pound, and a father one has to love. Let us read this Oedipal fragment just a touch more closely. Its subject is hardly Whitman at all, but rather the United States in 1909, viewed as a country that does not acknowledge its self-exiled bard, Ezra Pound, who had taken up residence in London the year before. As a country that needs to be scourged with/by beauty (a conceit perhaps more Sacher-Masoch than Whitman), the United States (or Whitman) becomes a castrated father, even as the passionate Pound assumes the male function of driving the American vitality into the old world. If this seems crude, it is, but the crudity is certainly not Walt Whitman's.

Though he once assured the world that "Whitman goes bail for the nation," Pound seems to have meant that no one could bail out the nation. Many Poundians have quoted as evidence of their hero's esteem of Whitman a bad little poem of 1913:

A Pact

I make a pact with you, Walt Whitman—
I have detested you long enough.

> I come to you as a grown child
> Who has had a pig-headed father;
> I am old enough now to make friends.
> It was you that broke the new wood,
> Now is a time for carving.
> We have one sap and one root—
> Let there be commerce between us.

"Truce," the original word in the first line, is more accurate than "pact," because truly there was a failure in commerce between Whitman and Pound. Whether Pound remembered that Whitman's father was a carpenter, and that Whitman himself had worked, with his father, at the trade, is beyond surmise. The root, as Pound perhaps knew, was Emerson. It is no accident that Whitman and Emerson return to Pound together in *The Pisan Cantos*, with Whitman central in the eighty-second and Emerson in the eighty-third of *The Cantos*. Emerson, I think, returns in his own trope of self-identification, the Transparent Eyeball, yet in Pound's voice, since Emerson was at most Pound's American grandfather. But Whitman returns in Whitman's own voice, and even in his own image of voice, the "tally," because the obstinate old father's voice remains strong enough to insist upon itself:

> "Fvy! in Tdaenmarck efen dh' beasantz gnow him,"
>   meaning Whitman, exotic, still suspect
>   four miles from Camden
>   "O troubled reflection
>   "O Throat, O throbbing heart"
>   How drawn, O GEA TERRA,
>   what draws as thou drawest
>   till one sink into thee by an arm's width
>   embracing thee. Drawest,
>   truly thou drawest.
>   Wisdom lies next thee,
>   simply, past metaphor.
>
>   Where I lie let the thyme rise
>
>   .   .   .
>
>   fluid ΧΘΟΝΣ, strong as the undertow
>   of the wave receding
>   but that a man should live in that further terror, and live
>   the loneliness of death came upon me

(at 3 P.M., for an instant)   βακρύων
                                          `εντεῦθεν

three solemn half notes
        their white downy chests black-rimmed
on the middle wire
periplum

Pound begins by recalling his German teacher at the University of
Pennsylvania, forty years before, one Richard Henry Riethmuller, author
of *Walt Whitman and the Germans,* an identification I owe to Roy Harvey
Pearce. Riethmuller (Pound got the spelling wrong) had contrasted Whitman's fame in the professor's native Denmark to the bard's supposed
obscurity in the America of 1905, a contrast that leads Pound to a recall of
Whitman's "Out of the Cradle Endlessly Rocking." Whitman's poem is an
elegy for the poetic self so powerful that any other poet ought to be wary
of invoking so great a hymn of poetic incarnation and disincarnation. Whitman's "O troubled reflection in the sea! / O throat! O throbbing heart!" is
revised by Pound into "O troubled reflection / O throat, O throbbing
heart," with "in the sea" omitted. These are the last two lines of the penul-
timate stanza of the song of the bird lamenting his lost mate:

> *O darkness! O in vain!*
> *O I am very sick and sorrowful.*
> *O brown halo in the sky near the moon, drooping upon the sea!*
> *O troubled reflection in the sea!*
> *O throat! O throbbing heart!*
> *And I singing uselessly, uselessly all the night.*

Canto LXXXII rather movingly has shown the incarcerated poet studying the nostalgias of his early literary life, while meditating upon the
unrighteousness of all wars. A vision of the earth now comes to him, in
response to his partly repressed recall of Whitman's vision of the sea. Marrying the earth is Pound's counterpart to Whitman's marrying the sea, both
in "Out of the Cradle Endlessly Rocking" and in "When Lilacs Last in the
Dooryard Bloom'd," and both brides are at once death and the mother.
"Where I lie let the thyme rise," perhaps repeating William Blake's similar
grand pun on "thyme" and "time," is a profound acceptance of the reality
principle, with no more idealization of a timeless order. Whitman returns
from the dead even more strongly in the closing lines of Canto LXXXII,
where Pound lies down in a fluid time "strong as the undertow / of the wave
receding," which invokes another great elegiac triumph of Whitman's, "As I

Ebb'd with the Ocean of Life." The two songbirds of "Out of the Cradle,"
with Whitman, their brother, making a third, utter "three solemn half
notes" even as the loneliness of death came, for an instant, upon Whitman's
son, Pound. Most powerful, to me, is Pound's recall of Whitman's great
image of voice, the tally, from "Lilacs," *Song of Myself,* and other contexts
in the poet of night, death, the mother, and the sea. In Whitman, the tally
counts up the poet's songs as so many wounds, so many autoerotic gratifications that yet, somehow, do not exclude otherness. Pound, marrying the
earth, realizes his terrible solitude: "man, earth: two halves of the tally / but
I will come out of this knowing no one / either they me."

Kenner is able to read this as commerce between Whitman and
Pound, and insists that "the resources in the Canto are Pound's, as are
those of Canto I." But Homer, ultimate ancestor in Canto I, was safely distant. Whitman is very close in Canto LXXXII, and the resources are clearly
his. Pound does better at converting Emerson to his own purposes, a canto
later, than he is able to do with Whitman here. Would the following judgment seem valid to a fully informed and dispassionate reader?

> Pound's faults are superficial, he does convey an image of his time,
> he has written histoire morale, as Montaigne wrote the history of
> his epoch. You can learn more of 20th-century America from
> Pound than from any of the writers who either refrained from per-
> ceiving, or limited their record to what they had been taught to
> consider suitable literary expression. The only way to enjoy Pound
> thoroughly is to concentrate on his fundamental meaning.

This is Pound on Whitman from the *ABC of Reading,* with Pound sub-
stituted for Whitman, and the twentieth for the nineteenth century. Pound
was half right about Whitman; Whitman does teach us his country in his
century, but his form and his content are not so split as Pound says, and his
fundamental meaning resides in nuance, beautifully shaped in figurative
language. Pound's faults are not superficial, and absolutely nothing about
our country in this century can be learned from him. He conveys an image
only of himself, and the only way to enjoy him is not to seek a fundamental meaning that is not there, but to take his drafts and fragments one by
one, shattered crystals, but crystalline nevertheless. He had brought the
great ball of crystal, of poetic tradition, but it proved too heavy for him
to lift.

↓   ↓   ↓

Planh for the Young English King

That is, Prince Henry Plantagenet, elder brother to Richard "Cœur de Lion."
From the Provençal of Bertrans de Born "Si tuit li dol elh plor elh marrimen."

If all the grief and woe and bitterness,
All dolour, ill and every evil chance
That ever came upon this grieving world
Were set together they would seem but light
Against the death of the young English King.
Worth lieth riven and Youth dolorous,
The world o'ershadowed, soiled and overcast,
Void of all joy and full of ire and sadness.

Grieving and sad and full of bitterness
Are left in teen the liegemen courteous,
The joglars supple and the troubadours.
O'er much hath ta'en Sir Death that deadly warrior
In taking from them the young English King,
Who made the freest hand seem covetous.
'Las! Never was nor will be in this world
The balance for this loss in ire and sadness!

O skilful Death and full of bitterness,
Well mayst thou boast that thou the best chevalier
That any folk e'er had, hast from us taken;
Sith nothing is that unto worth pertaineth
But had its life in the young English King,
And better were it, should God grant his pleasure
That he should live than many a living dastard
That doth but wound the good with ire and sadness.

From this faint world, how full of bitterness
Love takes his way and holds his joy deceitful,
Sith no thing is but turneth unto anguish
And each to-day 'vails less than yestere'en,
Let each man visage this young English King
That was most valiant mid all worthiest men!
Gone is his body fine and amorous,
Whence have we grief, discord and deepest sadness.

Him, whom it pleased for our great bitterness
To come to earth to draw us from misventure,
Who drank of death for our salvacioun,

Him do we pray as to a Lord most righteous
And humble eke, that the young English King
He please to pardon, as true pardon is,
And bid go in with honouréd companions
There where there is no grief, nor shall be sadness.

ELINOR WYLIE

1885–1928

AFTER GRADUATING FROM BRYN MAWR, Elinor Hoyt lived in Washington, D.C. She married three times to: Philip Hickborn, Horace Wylie, and the poet William Rose Benét. After living in England with Wylie, she returned to the United States in 1915, and lived in New York City and Washington, D.C. She served as literary editor of *Vanity Fair*, and moved with Benét to Connecticut, and then lived in New York City again until she died of a stroke at forty-three.

Elinor Wylie was obsessed with Shelley, whose influence is manifest in much of her poetry, and in her novel, *The Orphan Angel* (1926). *Nets to Catch the Wind* (1921) and *Trivial Breath* (1928) contain her most memorable poems.

I include here the buoyant sequence of four sonnets, "Wild Peaches," which show Wylie at her best, initially brimming with life and love, celebrating a natural sweetness and abundance. There is a wonderful turn in the seven-line "octave" from our expectations ("We shall live well—we shall live very well") in the third sonnet, and a marvelous shock in the Puritan austerity of the final sonnet.

✧   ✧   ✧

Wild Peaches

1

When the world turns completely upside down
You say we'll emigrate to the Eastern Shore
Aboard a river-boat from Baltimore;

We'll live among wild peach trees, miles from town.
You'll wear a coonskin cap, and I a gown
Homespun, dyed butternut's dark gold color.
Lost, like your lotus-eating ancestor,
We'll swim in milk and honey till we drown.

The winter will be short, the summer long,
The autumn amber-hued, sunny and hot,
Tasting of cider and of scuppernong;
All seasons sweet, but autumn best of all.
The squirrels in their silver fur will fall
Like falling leaves, like fruit, before your shot.

2

The autumn frosts will lie upon the grass
Like bloom on grapes of purple-brown and gold.
The misted early mornings will be cold;
The little puddles will be roofed with glass.
The sun, which burns from copper into brass,
Melts these at noon, and makes the boys unfold
Their knitted mufflers; full as they can hold,
Fat pockets dribble chestnuts as they pass.

Peaches grow wild, and pigs can live in clover;
A barrel of salted herrings lasts a year;
The spring begins before the winter's over.
By February you may find the skins
Of garter snakes and water moccasins
Dwindled and harsh, dead-white and cloudy-clear.

3

When April pours the colors of a shell
Upon the hills, when every little creek
Is shot with silver from the Chesapeake
In shoals new-minted by the ocean swell,
When strawberries go begging, and the sleek
Blue plums lie open to the blackbird's beak,
We shall live well—we shall live very well.

The months between the cherries and the peaches
Are brimming cornucopias which spill
Fruits red and purple, somber-bloomed and black;
Then, down rich fields and frosty river beaches

We'll trample bright persimmons, while we kill
Bronze partridge, speckled quail, and canvasback.

4

Down to the Puritan marrow of my bones
There's something in this richness that I hate.
I love the look, austere, immaculate,
Of landscapes drawn in pearly monotones.
There's something in my very blood that owns
Bare hills, cold silver on a sky of slate,
A thread of water, churned to milky spate
Streaming through slanted pastures fenced with stones.

I love those skies, thin blue or snowy gray,
Those fields sparse-planted, rendering meager sheaves;
That spring, briefer than apple-blossom's breath,
Summer, so much too beautiful to stay,
Swift autumn, like a bonfire of leaves,
And sleepy winter, like the sleep of death.

H. D. (HILDA DOOLITTLE)

1886–1961

I

BROUGHT UP IN A MORAVIAN COMMUNITY in Pennsylvania, H. D. formed early and enduring friendships with Ezra Pound and William Carlos Williams. After moving to London in 1911 to join Pound's literary circle, she married the poet-novelist Richard Aldington, an unhappy venture for her. After a relationship with D. H. Lawrence, she became pregnant by the composer Cecil Gray.

Rescued from a grave illness during this pregnancy by Annie Ellerman (who wrote novels under the name Bryher), H. D. gave birth to a daughter, Perdita. With Bryher and Perdita, H. D. lived in Switzerland. From

1931 onward, she underwent extensive psychoanalysis, most crucially with Sigmund Freud himself.

After wartime residence in London, H. D. lived in Switzerland again, and in Italy. Her poetry, originally imagistic and very clear, to me seems blurred in her later phases and longer works. Here I give only two shorter, early poems, "Orchard" and "Garden," which have been universally popular.

2

LIKE EZRA POUND, her close friend and colleague, H. D. seems to me essentially an American Pre-Raphaelite poet, a naming that I intend as a compliment since I deeply love the poetry of the Rossettis, Morris, Meredith, and Swinburne. Even as Pound assimilates Dante Gabriel Rossetti to Walt Whitman, so H. D. compounds Christina Rossetti with Emily Dickinson, and both together with the male sequence of Dante Gabriel Rossetti, William Morris, Pound, and D. H. Lawrence.

Louis L. Martz, in his "Introduction" to H. D.'s *The Collected Poems 1912–1944*, sensitively sketches the relation between the psychosexual and the poetic crises that kept her from publishing any volumes of poetry between 1931 and 1944. Her brief analysis with Freud himself (about three months in 1933, and some five weeks in 1934) issued not only in her *Tribute to Freud* but in a number of fairly strong if problematic poems, three in particular, which Martz reports she grouped in the order of "The Dancer," "The Master," and "The Poet." "The Dancer" is the most problematic of these and perhaps would not matter much, except that it informs a powerful return of its central trope in the midst of "The Master," which is a moving tribute to Freud. Martz shrewdly calls "The Poet" a calm and measured tribute to D. H. Lawrence, and while it is not as distinguished a poem as "The Master," it has its own value and place in H. D.'s achievement.

Tribute to Freud is a rather overpraised book, particularly dear to Freudian literalists from Ernest Jones to the present since it is a kind of hagiography. H. D. herself chats on rapturously, while the old Professor somehow never does get to say anything remotely memorable. Precisely how he clarifies either the poet's bisexuality or her creative inhibitions may escape even the most assiduous and skilled reader. Section 10 of "Writing on the Wall," the first part of the *Tribute,* is both famous and typical:

So much for the Princess, Hans Sachs, and Walter Schmideberg,
the one-time Rittmeister of the 15th Imperial Austro-Hungarian

Hussars of His Royal Highness, Archduke Francis Salvator. For myself, I veer round, uncanonically seated stark upright with my feet on the floor. The Professor himself is uncanonical enough; he is beating with his hand, with his fist, on the head-piece of the old-fashioned horsehair sofa that had heard more secrets than the confession box of any popular Roman Catholic father-confessor in his heyday. This was the homely historical instrument of the original scheme of psychotherapy, of psychoanalysis, the science of the unravelling of the tangled skeins of the unconscious mind and the healing implicit in the process. *Consciously,* I was not aware of having said anything that might account for the Professor's outburst. And even as I veered around, facing him, my mind was detached enough to wonder if this was some idea of *his* for speeding up the analytic content or redirecting the flow of associated images. The Professor said, "The trouble is—I am an old man— *you do not think it worth your while to love me.*"

Presumably such a shock tactic was intended to speed up the transference, but if Freud actually said anything like this, then he was mistaken, as clearly H. D. loved him beyond measure. "But the Professor insisted I myself wanted to be Moses; not only did I want to be a boy but I wanted to be a hero." That certainly sounds like Freud, or by now like a self-parody on his part.

There is something quaintly archaic about H. D.'s *Tribute to Freud,* where the Professor's interventions are so accurate, his spiritual efficacy so instantaneous, as to suggest the advent of a new age of faith, the Freud era. A prose memorial provokes our resistance when it seems too pious or too amiably earnest. The Pre-Raphaelite aura, hieratic and isolated, with its characteristic effect of a hard-edged phantasmagoria, rescues "The Master" from the cloying literalism of the *Tribute.* "The old man" of the poem is God's prophet, since "the dream is God," and Freud therefore is heard as one who speaks with authority: "his command / was final" and "his tyranny was absolute, / for I had to love him then." The command, at least as H. D. interpreted it, was to accept her own bisexuality as being one with her poethood:

> I do not know what to say to God,
> for the hills
> answer his nod,
> and the sea
> when he tells his daughter,

white Mother
of green
leaves
and green rills
and silver,
to still
tempest
or send peace
and surcease of peril
when a mountain has spit fire:

I did not know how to differentiate
between volcanic desire,
anemones like embers
and purple fire
of violets
like red heat,
and the cold
silver
of her feet:
I had two loves separate;
God who loves all mountains,
alone knew why
and understood
and told the old man
to explain

the impossible,

which he did.
            —"The Master"

The phallic or volcanic is evidently preferred by this male God, at least rhetorically, but of the "two loves separate" the "cold / silver / of her feet" triumphs with the reentry of the dancer in section 5. The force that comes with celebration of the dancer depends upon H. D.'s vision of herself as wrestling Jacob, arguing till daybreak, and of Freud as God or His angel, giving further rhetorical primacy to "the man-strength" rather than to the dancer's leapings:

I was angry with the old man
with his talk of the man-strength,

I was angry with his mystery,
his mysteries,
I argued till day-break;

O, it was late,
and God will forgive me, my anger,
but I could not accept it.

I could not accept from wisdom
what love taught,
woman is perfect.
                    —"The Dancer"

That would appear to have meant that a woman's bisexuality or her perfection (in the sense of completeness) was of a different and more acceptable order than a man's bisexuality. The ecstasy of section 5 gently mocks the Freudian "man-strength" even as it salutes the dancer for needing no male, since at least as dancer (or poet) woman is indeed pragmatically perfect. Section 5 has a kind of uncanny force, akin to Yeatsian celebrations of the dancer as image. But the authentic strength of the poem centers elsewhere, in its elegiac identifications of the dead father, Freud, with the earth, and with all the dead fathers. Freud is Saturn, ancient wisdom, and the rock that cannot be broken—a new earth. His temples will be everywhere, yet H. D. cries out: "only I, I will escape," an escape sanctioned by Freud as the freedom of the woman poet. Though D. H. Lawrence is not even alluded to in "The Master," he enters the poem by negation, since it is transformed into a fierce hymn against Lawrence's vision of sexual release:

no man will be present in those mysteries,
yet all men will kneel,
no man will be potent,
important,
yet all men will feel
what it is to be a woman,
will yearn,
burn,
turn from easy pleasure
to hardship
of the spirit,

men will see how long they have been blind,
poor men

poor man-kind
how long
how long
this thought of the man-pulse has tricked them,
has weakened them,
shall see woman, perfect.

—"The Master"

The blindness is precisely Lawrence's in H. D.'s judgment, and it is
hinted at, in muted form, in "The Poet," not so much an elegy for
Lawrence as for her failed friendship with him. What seems clear is that
her sexual self-acceptance, whether Freudian or not, gave her the creative
serenity that made possible the wonderfully controlled, hushed resigna-
tion of her wisely limited farewell to Lawrence:

No,
I don't pretend, in a way, to understand,
nor know you,
nor even see you;

I say,
"I don't grasp his philosophy,
and I don't understand,"

but I put out a hand, touch a cold door,
(we have both come from so far);
I touch something imperishable;
I think,
why should he stay there?
why should he guard a shrine so alone,
so apart,
on a path that leads nowhere?

he is keeping a candle burning in a shrine
where nobody comes,
there must be some mystery
in the air
about him,

he couldn't live alone in the desert,
without vision to comfort him,
there must be voices somewhere.

—"The Poet"

The wistfulness of that tribute, if it is a tribute, veils the harshness of the critique. A woman can be perfect, but a man cannot, though Lawrence would not learn this. One can imagine his response to H. D.; it would have been violent, but that perhaps would have confirmed her stance, whether sanctioned or unsanctioned by her father and master, Freud.

ꙮ   ꙮ   ꙮ

Orchard

I saw the first pear
as it fell—
the honey-seeking, golden-banded,
the yellow swarm
was not more fleet than I,
(spare us from loveliness)
and I fell prostrate
crying:
you have flayed us
with your blossoms,
spare us the beauty
of fruit-trees.

The honey-seeking
paused not,
the air thundered their song,
and I alone was prostrate.

O rough-hewn
god of the orchard,
I bring you an offering—
do you, alone unbeautiful,
son of the god,
spare us from loveliness:

these fallen hazel-nuts,
stripped late of their green sheaths,
grapes, red-purple,
their berries
dripping with wine,
pomegranates already broken,
and shrunken figs

and quinces untouched,
I bring you as offering.

Garden

I
You are clear
O rose, cut in rock,
hard as the descent of hail.

I could scrape the colour
from the petals
like spilt dye from a rock.

If I could break you
I could break a tree.

If I could stir
I could break a tree—
I could break you.

II
O wind, rend open the heat,
cut apart the heat,
rend it to tatters.

Fruit cannot drop
through this thick air—
fruit cannot fall into heat

that presses up and blunts
the points of pears
and rounds the grapes.

Cut the heat—
plough through it,
turning it on either side
of your path.

ROBINSON JEFFERS

1887–1962

JEFFERS ALWAYS SEEMED to me a potentially strong but problematical poet, a kind of dark footnote to our father, Walt Whitman. The poet of *Leaves of Grass* possessed not only vitalistic exuberance but also astonishing variety, while Jeffers invariably was a mass of negations and could fall into what might be termed a noble monotony.

Still, a poem like "Shine, Perishing Republic" retains its force and relevance more than half a century after its composition, and the rugged "Apology for Bad Dreams" is an acrid defense of Jeffers's stance as poet-prophet.

Jeffers lived the High Romantic myth of his life, dwelling with his wife Una and their twin sons in a stone tower built with his own hands at Carmel, on the California coast.

❧   ❧   ❧

Shine, Perishing Republic

While this America settles in the mould of its vulgarity,
    heavily thickening to empire,
And protest, only a bubble in the molten mass, pops and
    sighs out, and the mass hardens,

I sadly smiling remember that the flower fades to make fruit,
    the fruit rots to make earth.
Out of the mother; and through the spring exultances,
    ripeness and decadence; and home to the mother.

You making haste haste on decay; not blameworthy; life is
    good, be it stubbornly long or suddenly
A mortal splendor: meteors are not needed less than
    mountains; shine, perishing republic.

But for my children, I would have them keep their distance
    from the thickening center; corruption

Never has been compulsory, when the cities lie at the
    monster's feet there are left the mountains.

And boys, be in nothing so moderate as in love of man, a
    clever servant, insufferable master.
There is the trap that catches noblest spirits, that caught—
    they say—God, when he walked on earth.

Apology for Bad Dreams

   I

In the purple light, heavy with redwood, the slopes drop
    seaward,
Headlong convexities of forest, drawn in together to the
    steep ravine. Below, on the sea-cliff,
A lonely clearing; a little field of corn by the streamside; a
    roof under spared trees. Then the ocean
Like a great stone someone has cut to a sharp edge and
    polished to shining. Beyond it, the fountain
And furnace of incredible light flowing up from the sunk sun.
    In the little clearing a woman
Is punishing a horse; she had tied the halter to a sapling at the
    edge of the wood, but when the great whip
Clung to the flanks the creature kicked so hard she feared he
    would snap the halter, she called from the house
The young man her son; who fetched a chain tie-rope, they
    working together
Noosed the small rusty links round the horse's tongue
And tied him by the swollen tongue to the tree.
Seen from this height they are shrunk to insect size,
Out of all human relation. You cannot distinguish
The blood dripping from where the chain is fastened,
The beast shuddering; but the thrust neck and the legs
Far apart. You can see the whip fall on the flanks . . .
The gesture of the arm. You cannot see the face of the
    woman.
The enormous light beats up out of the west across the
    cloud-bars of the trade-wind. The ocean
Darkens, the high clouds brighten, the hills darken together.
    Unbridled and unbelievable beauty
Covers the evening world . . . not covers, grows apparent
    out of it, as Venus down there grows out

From the lit sky. What said the prophet? "I create good: and I
    create evil: I am the Lord."

II

This coast crying out for tragedy like all beautiful places,
(The quiet ones ask for quieter suffering; but here the granite
    cliff the gaunt cypresses crown
Demands what victim? The dykes of red lava and black what
    Titan? The hills like pointed flames
Beyond Soberanes, the terrible peaks of the bare hills under
    the sun, what immolation?)
This coast crying out for tragedy like all beautiful places: and
    like the passionate spirit of humanity
Pain for its bread: God's, many victims', the painful deaths,
    the horrible transfigurements: I said in my heart,
"Better invent than suffer: imagine victims
Lest your own flesh be chosen the agonist, or you
Martyr some creature to the beauty of the place." And I said,
"Burn sacrifices once a year to magic
Horror away from the house, this little house here
You have built over the ocean with your own hands
Beside the standing boulders: for what are we,
The beast that walks upright, with speaking lips
And little hair, to think we should always be fed,
Sheltered, intact, and self-controlled? We sooner more liable
Than the other animals. Pain and terror, the insanities of
    desire; not accidents but essential,
And crowd up from the core": I imagined victims for those
    wolves, I made them phantoms to follow,
They have hunted the phantoms and missed the house. It is
    not good to forget over what gulfs the spirit
Of the beauty of humanity, the petal of a lost flower blown
    seaward by the night-wind, floats to its quietness.

III

Boulders blunted like an old bear's teeth break up from the
    headland; below them
All the soil is thick with shells, the tide-rock feasts of a dead
    people.
Here the granite flanks are scarred with ancient fire, the
    ghosts of the tribe
Crouch in the nights beside the ghost of a fire, they try to
    remember the sunlight,
Light has died out of their skies. These have paid something

for the future
Luck of the country, while we living keep old griefs in
    memory: though God's
Envy is not a likely fountain of ruin, to forget evils calls down
Sudden reminders from the cloud: remembered deaths be our
    redeemers;
Imagined victims our salvation: white as the half moon at
    midnight
Someone flamelike passed me, saying, "I am Tamar
    Cauldwell, I have my desire,"
Then the voice of the sea returned, when she had gone by,
    the stars to their towers.
. . . Beautiful country burn again, Point Pinos down to the
    Sur Rivers
Burn as before with bitter wonders, land and ocean and the
    Carmel water.

IV

He brays humanity in a mortar to bring the savor
From the bruised root: a man having bad dreams, who
    invents victims, is only the ape of that God.
He washes it out with tears and many waters, calcines it with
    fire in the red crucible,
Deforms it, makes it horrible to itself: the spirit flies out and
    stands naked, he sees the spirit,
He takes it in the naked ecstasy; it breaks in his hand, the
    atom is broken, the power that massed it
Cries to the power that moves the stars, "I have come home
    to myself, behold me.
I bruised myself in the flint mortar and burnt me
In the red shell, I tortured myself, I flew forth,
Stood naked of myself and broke me in fragments,
And here am I moving the stars that are me."
I have seen these ways of God: I know of no reason
For fire and change and torture and the old returnings.
He being sufficient might be still. I think they admit no
    reason; they are the ways of my love.
Unmeasured power, incredible passion, enormous craft: no
    thought apparent but burns darkly
Smothered with its own smoke in the human brain-vault: no
    thought outside: a certain measure in phenomena:
The fountains of the boiling stars, the flowers on the
    foreland, the ever-returning roses of dawn.

MARIANNE MOORE

1887–1972

BORN IN MISSOURI, Marianne Moore was raised in Pennsylvania, after her father's collapse and early death. A biology major at Bryn Mawr, she came to Greenwich Village and then Brooklyn, living with her mother. As editor of *The Dial,* she had an authentic influence upon American literature in her time.

Moore's *Collected Poems* (1953) received general acclaim. Her translation of *The Fables of La Fontaine* (1954) remains an extraordinary feat.

I have represented Marianne Moore in this anthology by one extended poem, the allusive, collage-like "Marriage," which seems to me her finest work.

> For Plato the only reality that mattered is exemplified best for us in the principles of mathematics. The aim of our lives should be to draw ourselves away as much as possible from the unsubstantial, fluctuating facts of the world about us and establish some communion with the objects which are apprehended by thought and not sense. This was the source of Plato's asceticism. To the extent that Miss Moore finds only allusion tolerable she shares that asceticism. While she shares it she does so only as it may be necessary for her to do so in order to establish a particular reality or, better, a reality of her own particulars.
>
> —WALLACE STEVENS

Allusion was Marianne Moore's method, a method that was her self. One of the most American of all poets, she was fecund in her progeny— Elizabeth Bishop, May Swenson, and Richard Wilbur being the most gifted among them. Her own American precursors were not Emily Dickinson and Walt Whitman—still our two greatest poets—but the much slighter Stephen Crane, who is echoed in her earliest poems, and in an oblique way Edgar Poe, whom she parodied. I suspect that her nearest poetic father, in English, was Thomas Hardy, who seems to have taught her lessons in the mastery of incongruity, and whose secularized version of biblical irony is not far from her own. If we compare her with her major poetic contemporaries—Frost, Stevens, Eliot, Pound, Williams, Aiken,

Ransom, Cummings, H. D., Hart Crane—she is clearly the most original American poet of her era, though not quite of the eminence of Frost, Stevens, and Crane. A curious kind of devotional poet, with some authentic affinities to George Herbert, she reminds us implicitly but constantly that any distinction between sacred and secular poetry is only a shibboleth of cultural politics. Someday she will remind us also of what current cultural politics obscure: that any distinction between poetry written by women or poetry by men is a mere polemic, unless it follows upon an initial distinction between good and bad poetry. Moore, like Bishop and Swenson, is an extraordinary poet-as-poet. The issue of how gender enters into her vision should arise only after the aesthetic achievement is judged as such.

Moore, as all her readers know, to their lasting delight, is the visionary of natural creatures: the jerboa, frigate pelican, buffalo, monkeys, fish, snakes, mongooses, the octopus (actually a trope for a mountain), snail, peacock, whale, pangolin, wood-weasel, elephants, racehorses, chameleon, jellyfish, arctic ox (or goat), giraffe, blue bug (another trope, this time for a pony), all of La Fontaine's bestiary, not to mention sea and land unicorns, basilisks, and all the weird fabulous roster that perhaps only Borges also, among crucial modern writers, celebrates so consistently. There is something of Blake and of the Christopher Smart of *Jubilate Agno* in Moore, though the affinity does not result from influence, but rather is the consequence of election. Moore's famous eye, like that of Bishop after her, is not so much a visual gift as it is visionary, for the beasts in her poems are charged with a spiritual intensity that doubtless they possess, but which I myself cannot see without the aid of Blake, Smart, and Moore.

I remember always in reading Moore again that her favorite poem was the Book of Job. Just as I cannot read Ecclesiastes without thinking of Dr. Johnson, I cannot read certain passages in Job without recalling Marianne Moore:

> But ask now the beasts, and they shall teach thee; and the fowls of
> the air, and they shall tell thee:
> Or speak to the earth, and it shall teach thee: and the fishes of
> the sea shall declare unto thee.
> Who knoweth not in all these that the hand of the Lord hath
> wrought this? In whose hand is the soul of every living thing.

This, from Chapter 12, is the prelude to the great chant of Yahweh, the Voice out of the Whirlwind that sounds forth in the frightening magnificence of Chapters 38 through 41, where the grand procession of beasts comprehends lions, ravens, wild goats, the wild ass, the unicorn, peacocks, the ostrich, the sublime battle-horse who "saith among the trumpets, Ha, ha," the hawk, the eagle, and at last Behemoth and Leviathan. Gorgeously celebrating his own creation, Yahweh through the poet of Job engendered another strong poet in Marianne Moore. Of the Book of Job, she remarked that its agony was veracious and its fidelity of a force "that contrives glory for ashes."

"Glory for ashes" might be called Moore's ethical motto, the basis for the drive of her poetic will toward a reality of her own particulars. Her poetry, as befitted the translator of La Fontaine, and the heir of George Herbert, would be in some danger of dwindling into moral essays, an impossible form for our time, were it not for her wild allusiveness, her zest for quotations, and her essentially anarchic stance, the American and Emersonian insistence upon seeing everything in her own way, with "conscientious inconsistency." When her wildness or freedom subsided, she produced an occasional poetic disaster like the patriotic war poems "In Distrust of Merits" and " 'Keeping Their World Large.' " But her greatest poems are at just the opposite edge of consciousness: "A Grave," "Novices," "Marriage," "An Octopus," "He 'Digesteth Harde Yron,' " "Elephants," the deceptively light "Tom Fool at Jamaica."

Those seven poems by themselves have an idiosyncratic splendor that restores my faith, as a critic, in what the language of the poets truly is: diction, or choice of words, playing endlessly upon the dialectic of denotation and connotation, a dialectic that simply vanishes in all Structuralist and post-Structuralist ruminations upon the supposed priority of "language" over meaning. "The arbitrariness of the signifier" loses its charm when one asks a Gallic psycholinguistifier whether denotation or connotation belongs to the signifier, as opposed to the signified, and one beholds blank incredulity as one's only answer. Moore's best poems give the adequate reply: the play of the signifier is answered always by the play of the signified, because the play of diction, or the poet's will over language, is itself constituted by the endless interchanges of denotation and connotation. Moore, with her rage to order allusion, echo, and quotation in ghostlier demarcations, keener sounds, helps us to realize that the belated Modernism of the Gallic proclamation of the death of the author was no less premature than it was, always already, belated.

> Marriage, through which thought does not penetrate, appeared to
> Miss Moore a legitimate object for art, an art that would not halt

from using thought about it, however, as it might want to. Against marriage, "this institution, perhaps one should say enterprise"— Miss Moore launched her thought not to have it appear arsenaled as in a textbook on psychology, but to stay among apples and giraffes in a poem.

—William Carlos Williams

If I had to cite a single poem by Moore as representing all of her powers working together, it would be "Marriage" (1923), superficially an outrageous collage but profoundly a poignant comic critique of every society's most sacred and tragic institution. As several critics have ventured, this is Moore's *The Waste Land,* a mosaic of fragments from Francis Bacon, the *Scientific American,* Baxter's *The Saint's Everlasting Rest,* Hazlitt on Burke, William Godwin, Trollope, *The Tempest,* a book on *The Syrian Christ,* the Bible, Ezra Pound, and even Daniel Webster (from an inscription on a statue!), and twenty sources more. Yet it is a poem, and perhaps is more ruggedly unified than any other poem of such ambition by Moore.

The poet's own headnote to "Marriage" could not be more diffident: "Statements that took my fancy which I tried to arrange plausibly." The arrangement is more than plausible; it is quite persuasive, though it begins with a parody of the societal apologia for marriage:

> This institution,
> perhaps one should say enterprise
> out of respect for which
> one says one need not change one's mind
> about a thing one has believed in,
> requiring public promises
> of one's intention
> to fulfill a private obligation.

No one, I believe, could interpret that opening stance with any exactitude. The substitution of "enterprise" for "institution" qualifies the wryness of "public promises / of one's intention / to fulfill a private obligation," but adds a note both of commerce and of the human virtue of taking an initiative. Who could have anticipated that the next movement of the poem would be this?

> I wonder what Adam and Eve
> think of it by this time,
> this fire-gilt steel
> alive with goldenness;

how bright it shows—
"of circular traditions and impostures,
committing many spoils,"
requiring all one's criminal ingenuity
to avoid!

Like nearly every other quotation in this poem, the two lines from Sir Francis Bacon gain nothing for Moore's own text by being restored to their own context. Steel burned by fire does not exactly brighten into a golden bough, so the "gilt" is there partly as anticipation of "criminal ingenuity." Yet "gilt" is in cognitive sequence with "goldenness" and "bright," even if we rightly expect to behold blackened steel. All who have known marriage (as Moore declined to do) will register an unhappy shudder at the force the Baconian phrases take on when Moore appropriates them. Traditions as treasons become circular, and together with impostures can be read here either as performing many despoilments or as investing many gains of previous despoilments. Either way, it might seem as though an ingenuity avoiding this equivocal enterprise could only be taken as criminal by some dogmatist, whether societal or theological.

The poem proceeds to dismiss psychology, since to explain everything is to explain nothing, and then meditates upon the beauty, talents, and contrariness of Eve, a meditation that suddenly achieves Paterian intensity:

Below the incandescent stars
below the incandescent fruit,
the strange experience of beauty;
its existence is too much;
it tears one to pieces
and each fresh wave of consciousness
is poison.

The detachment of Moore as watcher is not totally lost, but seems (by design) never fully recovered again in the poem. A woman's fine bitterness against the West's endless assault upon Eve is felt in Moore's description of the universal mother as "the central flaw" in the experiment of Eden, itself "an interesting impossibility" ecstatically described by Richard Baxter as "the choicest piece of my life." If Baxter's ecstasy (though not his eloquence) is qualified shrewdly by Moore's contextualizations, Eden is nowhere near so scaled down by her as is Adam, whose male pomp is altogether undermined. He is pretty well identified with Satan, and like Satan is: "alive with words, / vibrating like a cymbal / touched before it has been struck."

Moore's genius at her method allows her the joy of exemplifying her borrowings even as she employs them in a corrective polemic against male slanderings of women:

> "Treading chasms
> on the uncertain footing of a spear,"
> forgetting that there is in woman
> a quality of mind
> which as an instinctive manifestation
> is unsafe,
> he goes on speaking,
> in a formal customary strain.

In the first quotation, Hazlitt is praising his precursor Edmund Burke for a paradoxically certain footing: for power, energy, truth set forth in the Sublime style. Burke is a chasm-treader, surefooted as he edges near the abyss. But men less given to truth than Burke have very uncertain footing indeed, whether they forget or remember their characteristic brutalities in regard to a woman's "quality of mind." The poem's "he" therefore goes on speaking of marriage in Richard Baxter's ecstatic terms, as though marriage itself somehow could become "the saints' everlasting rest." Fatuously joyous, the male is ready to suffer the most exquisite passage in the poem, and perhaps in all of Moore:

> Plagued by the nightingale
> in the new leaves,
> with its silence—
> not its silence but its silences,
> he says of it:
> "It clothes me with a shirt of fire."
> "He dares not clap his hands to make it go on lest it should fly off;
> if he does nothing, it will sleep;
> if he cries out, it will not understand."
> Unnerved by the nightingale
> and dazzled by the apple,
> impelled by "the illusion of a fire
> effectual to extinguish fire,"
> compared with which
> the shining of the earth
> is but deformity—a fire
> "as high as deep
> as bright as broad

as long as life itself,"
he stumbles over marriage,
"a very trivial object indeed"
to have destroyed the attitude
in which he stood—.

I hardly know of a more unnerving representation of the male fear and distrust of the female, uncannily combined with the male quandary of being obsessed with, fascinated by, not only the female but the enterprise of marriage as well. Moore imperishably catches the masterpiece of male emotive ambivalence toward the female, which is the male identification of woman and the taboo. Here the nightingale, perhaps by way of Keats's erotic allusions, becomes an emblem of the female, while the male speaker, ravished by the silences of the emblem, becomes Hercules suicidally aflame with the shirt of Nessus. The poor male, "unnerved by the nightingale / and dazzled by the apple," stumbles over the enterprise that is Adam's experiment, marriage:

its fiddlehead ferns,
lotus flowers, opuntias, white dromedaries,
its hippopotamus—
nose and mouth combined
in one magnificent hopper—
its snake and the potent apple.

We again receive what might be called Moore's Paradox: marriage, considered from either the male or the female perspective, is a dreadful disaster, but as a poetic trope gorgeously shines forth its barbaric splendors. The male, quoting Trollope's *Barchester Towers*, returns us to the image of Hercules, and commends marriage "as a fine art, as an experiment, / a duty or as merely recreation." I myself will never get out of my memory Moore's subsequent deadpan definition of marriage as "the fight to be affectionate." With a fine impartiality, the poet has a vision of the agonists in this eternal dispute:

The blue panther with black eyes,
the basalt panther with blue eyes,
entirely graceful—
one must give them the path—.

But this mutual splendor abates quickly, and a rancorous humor emerges:

He says, "What monarch would not blush
to have a wife
with hair like a shaving brush?"
The fact of woman
is "not the sound of the flute
but very poison."
She says, "Men are monopolists
of 'stars, garters, buttons
and other shining baubles'—
unfit to be the guardians
of another person's happiness."
He says, "These mummies
must be handled carefully—
'the crumbs from a lion's meal,
a couple of shins and the bit of an ear';
turn to the letter M and
you will find that 'a wife is a coffin.'

This marvelous exchange of diatribes is weirdly stitched together from outrageously heterogeneous "sources," ranging from a parody of *The Rape of the Lock* (in which Moore herself took a hand) to a women's college president's denunciation of the male love of awards and medals on to a surprising misappropriation of a great moment in the prophet Amos, which is then juxtaposed to a brutal remark of Ezra Pound's. Amos associates the lion with Yahweh:

> The lion hath roared, who will not fear? the Lord GOD hath spoken, who can but prophesy?
> Thus saith the LORD; As the shepherd taketh out of the mouth of the lion two legs, or a piece of an ear; so shall the children of Israel be taken out that dwell in Samaria in the corner of a bed, and in Damascus in a couch.

Moore slyly revises the roaring prophet, making the lion every male, and the children of Israel every woman. Pound's dictum, that "a wife is a coffin" is presumably placed under the letter M for "male," and sorts well with Moore's unfair but strong revision of Amos, since the revision suggests that a wife is a corpse. In order to show that her revisionary zeal is savagely if suavely directed against both sexes (or rather their common frailties), Moore proceeds to dissect the narcissism of men and women alike, until she concludes with the most ironic of her visions in the poem:

"I am such a cow,
if I had a sorrow
I should feel it a long time;
I am not one of those
who have a great sorrow
in the morning
and a great joy at noon";

which says: "I have encountered it
among those unpretentious
protégés of wisdom,
where seeming to parade
as the debater and the Roman,
the statesmanship
of an archaic Daniel Webster
persists to their simplicity of temper
as the essence of the matter:

'Liberty and union
now and forever';

the Book on the writing table;
the hand in the breast pocket."

Webster, hardly unpretentious, and wise only in his political cunning, is indeed the message inscribed upon his statue: "Liberty and union / now and forever." As a judgment upon marriage, it would be a hilarious irony, if we did not wince so much under Moore's not wholly benign tutelage. That Book on the writing table, presumably the Bible, is precisely like Webster's hand in the breast pocket, an equivocal emblem, in this context, of the societal benediction upon marriage. Moore's own *The Waste Land*, "Marriage," may outlast Eliot's poem as a permanent vision of the West in its long, ironic decline.

✤   ✤   ✤

Marriage

This institution,
perhaps one should say enterprise
out of respect for which
one says one need not change one's mind
about a thing one has believed in,

requiring public promises
of one's intention
to fulfil a private obligation:
I wonder what Adam and Eve
think of it by this time,
this fire-gilt steel
alive with goldenness;
how bright it shows—
"of circular traditions and impostures,
committing many spoils,"
requiring all one's criminal ingenuity
to avoid!
Psychology which explains everything
explains nothing,
and we are still in doubt.
Eve: beautiful woman—
I have seen her
when she was so handsome
she gave me a start,
able to write simultaneously
in three languages—
English, German and French—
and talk in the meantime;
equally positive in demanding a commotion
and in stipulating quiet:
"*I* should like to be alone";
to which the visitor replies,
"I should like to be alone;
why not be alone together?"
Below the incandescent stars
below the incandescent fruit,
the strange experience of beauty;
its existence is too much;
it tears one to pieces
and each fresh wave of consciousness
is poison.
"See her, see her in this common world,"
the central flaw
in that first crystal-fine experiment,
this amalgamation which can never be more
than an interesting impossibility,
describing it
as "that strange paradise

unlike flesh, stones,
50   gold or stately buildings,
the choicest piece of my life:
the heart rising
in its estate of peace
as a boat rises
with the rising of the water";
constrained in speaking of the serpent—
shed snakeskin in the history of politeness
not to be returned to again—
that invaluable accident
60   exonerating Adam.
And he has beauty also;
it's distressing—the O thou
to whom from whom,
without whom nothing—Adam;
"something feline,
something colubrine"—how true!
a crouching mythological monster
in that Persian miniature of emerald mines,
raw silk—ivory white, snow white,
70   oyster white and six others—
that paddock full of leopards and giraffes—
long lemon-yellow bodies
sown with trapezoids of blue.
Alive with words,
vibrating like a cymbal
touched before it has been struck,
he has prophesied correctly—
the industrious waterfall,
"the speedy stream
80   which violently bears all before it,
at one time silent as the air
and now as powerful as the wind."
"Treading chasms
on the uncertain footing of a spear,"
forgetting that there is in woman
a quality of mind
which as an instinctive manifestation
is unsafe,
he goes on speaking
90   in a formal customary strain,
of "past states, the present state,

seals, promises,
the evil one suffered,
the good one enjoys,
hell, heaven,
everything convenient
to promote one's joy."
In him a state of mind
perceives what it was not
100   intended that he should;
"he experiences a solemn joy
in seeing that he has become an idol."
Plagued by the nightingale
in the new leaves,
with its silence—
not its silence but its silences,
he says of it:
"It clothes me with a shirt of fire."
"He dares not clap his hands
110   to make it go on
lest it should fly off;
if he does nothing, it will sleep;
if he cries out, it will not understand."
Unnerved by the nightingale
and dazzled by the apple,
impelled by "the illusion of a fire
effectual to extinguish fire,"
compared with which
the shining of the earth
120   is but deformity—a fire
"as high as deep
as bright as broad
as long as life itself,"
he stumbles over marriage,
"a very trivial object indeed"
to have destroyed the attitude
in which he stood—
the ease of the philosopher
unfathered by a woman.
130   Unhelpful Hymen!
a kind of overgrown cupid
reduced to insignificance
by the mechanical advertising
parading as involuntary comment,

by that experiment of Adam's
with ways out but no way in—
the ritual of marriage,
augmenting all its lavishness;
its fiddle-head ferns,
140   lotus flowers, opuntias, white dromedaries,
its hippopotamus—
nose and mouth combined
in one magnificent hopper—
its snake and the potent apple.
He tells us
that "for love that will
gaze an eagle blind,
that is with Hercules
climbing the trees
150   in the garden of the Hesperides,
from forty-five to seventy
is the best age,"
commending it
as a fine art, as an experiment,
a duty or as merely recreation.
One must not call him ruffian
nor friction a calamity—
the fight to be affectionate:
"no truth can be fully known
160   until it has been tried
by the tooth of disputation."
The blue panther with black eyes,
the basalt panther with blue eyes,
entirely graceful—
one must give them the path—
the black obsidian Diana
who "darkeneth her countenance
as a bear doth,"
the spiked hand
170   that has an affection for one
and proves it to the bone,
impatient to assure you
that impatience is the mark of independence,
not of bondage.
"Married people often look that way"—
"seldom and cold, up and down,
mixed and malarial

with a good day and a bad."
We Occidentals are so unemotional,
180   self lost, the irony preserved
in "the Ahasuerus *tête-à-tête* banquet"
with its small orchids like snakes' tongues,
with its "good monster, lead the way,"
with little laughter
and munificence of humor
in that quixotic atmosphere of frankness
in which "four o'clock does not exist,
but at five o'clock
the ladies in their imperious humility
190   are ready to receive you";
in which experience attests
that men have power
and sometimes one is made to feel it.
He says, "What monarch would not blush
to have a wife
with hair like a shaving-brush?"
The fact of woman
is "not the sound of the flute
but very poison."
200   She says, "Men are monopolists
of 'stars, garters, buttons
and other shining baubles'—
unfit to be the guardians
of another person's happiness."
He says, "These mummies
must be handled carefully—
'the crumbs from a lion's meal,
a couple of shins and the bit of an ear';
turn to the letter M
210   and you will find
that 'a wife is a coffin,'
that severe object
with the pleasing geometry
stipulating space not people,
refusing to be buried
and uniquely disappointing,
revengefully wrought in the attitude
of an adoring child
to a distinguished parent."
220   She says, "This butterfly,

this waterfly, this nomad
that has 'proposed
to settle on my hand for life'—
What can one do with it?
There must have been more time
in Shakespeare's day
to sit and watch a play.
You know so many artists who are fools."
He says, "You know so many fools
230   who are not artists."
The fact forgot
that "some have merely rights
while some have obligations,"
he loves himself so much,
he can permit himself
no rival in that love.
She loves herself so much,
she cannot see herself enough—
a statuette of ivory on ivory,
240   the logical last touch
to an expansive splendor
earned as wages for work done:
one is not rich but poor
when one can always seem so right.
What can one do for them—
these savages
condemned to disaffect
all those who are not visionaries
alert to undertake the silly task
250   of making people noble?
This model of petrine fidelity
who "leaves her peaceful husband
only because she has seen enough of him"—
that orator reminding you,
"I am yours to command."
"Everything to do with love is mystery;
it is more than a day's work
to investigate this science."
One sees that it is rare—
260   that striking grasp of opposites
opposed each to the other, not to unity,
which in cycloid inclusiveness
has dwarfed the demonstration

of Columbus with the egg—
a triumph of simplicity—
that charitive Euroclydon
of frightening disinterestedness
which the world hates,
admitting:

270   "I am such a cow,
        if I had a sorrow
        I should feel it a long time;
        I am not one of those
        who have a great sorrow
        in the morning
        and a great joy at noon";
        which says: "I have encountered it
        among those unpretentious
        protégés of wisdom,
280   where seeming to parade
        as the debater and the Roman,
        the statesmanship
        of an archaic Daniel Webster
        persists to their simplicity of temper
        as the essence of the matter:

            'Liberty and union
            now and forever';

        the Book on the writing-table;
        the hand in the breast-pocket."

T. S. (THOMAS STEARNS) ELIOT

1888–1965

I CONFESS A LIFELONG HOSTILITY to T. S. Eliot, whose literary criticism did real harm, and whose cultural criticism showed, at times, a vicious proto-Fascism. But from 1911 to 1925, Eliot was a great poet, pub-

lishing his masterpiece in 1922, *The Waste Land,* certainly the most influential poem in English in the twentieth century. Fortunately, I need consider Eliot only at his best here, in "The Love Song of J. Alfred Prufrock,"
"Preludes," "La Figlia Che Piange," and *The Waste Land.*

Eliot was an anti-Semite, though his variety of that spiritual illness
never achieved the obsessive intensity of his close friend Ezra Pound. I
mention this matter so as to get it out of the way, although I believe it was
central to Eliot's cultural polemic. The Anglo-Catholicism to which he
converted in 1927 somehow had, for Eliot, an authorization for his anti-
Semitism. Even the revelations of the Nazi Death Camps, after the fall of
Germany in 1945, had little or no effect upon Eliot's idea that too many
"free-thinking" Jews would jeopardize an idealized Christian society.

Eliot, born in St. Louis, studied philosophy at Harvard and Oxford,
worked in a London bank, and married his first wife in 1915. The marriage
was a disaster, and its failure led to the poet's breakdown in 1921. Much of
The Waste Land resulted from this personal crisis.

From 1925 on, Eliot worked at the London publishing house Faber,
and became a British subject in 1927, the year of his conversion to the
Church of England. A second marriage, in 1957, was a happy one and sustained Eliot until his death.

Eliot asserted poetic descent from Dante and Baudelaire, and from
Jacobean dramatists and metaphysical poets. The actual deep influences
upon his poetry are Whitman and Tennyson. Against his will, Eliot (rather
like Matthew Arnold) was a belated Romantic poet, strongest as an incantatory master of phantasmagoria.

The Love Song of J. Alfred Prufrock

This impressive dramatic monologue has a clear debt to Browning, but
takes many of its surface procedures from the minor French poet Jules
Laforgue, who died in 1887. Laforgue's personages, like Prufrock, have no
inwardness, unlike the great charlatan-questers of Browning. Prufrock is
erotically timid, Hamlet-haunted (as Laforgue was), and only too aware of
his own comic debasement. As an ironic study of crippling self-
consciousness, this is perhaps the slyest and oddest "Love Song" in the
language.

✦   ✦   ✦

The Love Song of J. Alfred Prufrock

S'io credesse che mia risposta fosse
A persona che mai tornasse al mondo,
Questa fiamma staria senza piu scosse.
Ma perciocche giammai di questo fondo
Non torno vivo alcun, s'i'odo il vero,
Senza tema d'infamia ti rispondo.

Let us go then, you and I,
When the evening is spread out against the sky
Like a patient etherized upon a table;
Let us go, through certain half-deserted streets,
The muttering retreats
Of restless nights in one-night cheap hotels
And sawdust restaurants with oyster-shells:
Streets that follow like a tedious argument
Of insidious intent
To lead you to an overwhelming question.
Oh, do not ask, "What is it?"
Let us go and make our visit.

In the room the women come and go
Talking of Michelangelo.

The yellow fog that rubs its back upon the window-panes,
The yellow smoke that rubs its muzzle on the window-panes,
Licked its tongue into the corners of the evening,
Lingered upon the pools that stand in drains,
Let fall upon its back the soot that falls from chimneys,
Slipped by the terrace, made a sudden leap,
And seeing that it was a soft October night,
Curled once about the house, and fell asleep.

And indeed there will be time
For the yellow smoke that slides along the street,
Rubbing its back upon the window-panes;
There will be time, there will be time
To prepare a face to meet the faces that you meet;
There will be time to murder and create,
And time for all the works and days of hands
That lift and drop a question on your plate;
Time for you and time for me,
And time yet for a hundred indecisions,

And for a hundred visions and revisions,
Before the taking of a toast and tea.

In the room the women come and go
Talking of Michelangelo.

And indeed there will be time
To wonder, "Do I dare?" and, "Do I dare?"
Time to turn back and descend the stair,
With a bald spot in the middle of my hair—
(They will say: "How his hair is growing thin!")
My morning coat, my collar mounting firmly to the chin,
My necktie rich and modest, but asserted by a simple pin—
(They will say: "But how his arms and legs are thin!")
Do I dare
Disturb the universe?
In a minute there is time
For decisions and revisions which a minute will reverse.

For I have known them all already, known them all:
Have known the evenings, mornings, afternoons,
I have measured out my life with coffee spoons;
I know the voices dying with a dying fall
Beneath the music from a farther room.
     So how should I presume?

And I have known the eyes already, known them all—
The eyes that fix you in a formulated phrase,
And when I am formulated, sprawling on a pin,
When I am pinned and wriggling on the wall,
Then how should I begin
To spit out all the butt-ends of my days and ways?
     And how should I presume?

And I have known the arms already, known them all—
Arms that are braceleted and white and bare
(But in the lamplight, downed with light brown hair!)
Is it perfume from a dress
That makes me so digress?
Arms that lie along a table, or wrap about a shawl.
     And should I then presume?
     And how should I begin?

.   .   .

Shall I say, I have gone at dusk through narrow streets
And watched the smoke that rises from the pipes
Of lonely men in shirt-sleeves, leaning out of windows? . . .

I should have been a pair of ragged claws
Scuttling across the floors of silent seas.

.   .   .

And the afternoon, the evening, sleeps so peacefully!
Smoothed by long fingers,
Asleep . . . tired . . . or it malingers,
Stretched on the floor, here beside you and me.
Should I, after tea and cakes and ices,
Have the strength to force the moment to its crisis?
But though I have wept and fasted, wept and prayed,
Though I have seen my head (grown slightly bald) brought in upon a platter,
I am no prophet—and here's no great matter;
I have seen the moment of my greatness flicker,
And I have seen the eternal Footman hold my coat, and snicker,
And in short, I was afraid.

And would it have been worth it, after all,
After the cups, the marmalade, the tea,
Among the porcelain, among some talk of you and me,
Would it have been worth while,
To have bitten off the matter with a smile,
To have squeezed the universe into a ball
To roll it toward some overwhelming question,
To say: "I am Lazarus, come from the dead,
Come back to tell you all, I shall tell you all"—
If one, settling a pillow by her head,
    Should say: "That is not what I meant at all;
    That is not it, at all."

And would it have been worth it, after all,
Would it have been worth while,
After the sunsets and the dooryards and the sprinkled streets,
After the novels, after the teacups, after the skirts that trail along the floor—
And this, and so much more?—
It is impossible to say just what I mean!
But as if a magic lantern threw the nerves in patterns on a screen:

Would it have been worth while
If one, settling a pillow or throwing off a shawl,
And turning toward the window, should say:
   "That is not it at all,
   That is not what I meant, at all."

    .   .   .

No! I am not Prince Hamlet, nor was meant to be;
Am an attendant lord, one that will do
To swell a progress, start a scene or two,
Advise the prince; no doubt, an easy tool,
Deferential, glad to be of use,
Politic, cautious, and meticulous;
Full of high sentence, but a bit obtuse;
At times, indeed, almost ridiculous—
Almost, at times, the Fool.

I grow old . . . I grow old . . .
I shall wear the bottoms of my trousers rolled.

Shall I part my hair behind? Do I dare to eat a peach?
I shall wear white flannel trousers, and walk upon the beach.
I have heard the mermaids singing, each to each.

I do not think that they will sing to me.

I have seen them riding seaward on the waves
Combing the white hair of the waves blown back
When the wind blows the water white and black.

We have lingered in the chambers of the sea
By sea-girls wreathed with seaweed red and brown
Till human voices wake us, and we drown.

Preludes and *La Figlia Che Piange*

La Figlia Che Piange (the young girl who weeps) is an exquisite, Vergilian
lyric of erotic longing and betrayal. *Preludes*, at the other extreme of Eliot's
rhetorical genius, prophesies Hart Crane's visions of a demonic New York
City in *White Buildings* and *The Bridge*.

Preludes

I

The winter evening settles down
With smell of steaks in passageways.
Six o'clock.
The burnt-out ends of smoky days.
And now a gusty shower wraps
The grimy scraps
Of withered leaves about your feet
And newspapers from vacant lots;
The showers beat
On broken blinds and chimney-pots,
And at the corner of the street
A lonely cab-horse steams and stamps.
And then the lighting of the lamps.

II

The morning comes to consciousness
Of faint stale smells of beer
From the sawdust-trampled street
With all its muddy feet that press
To early coffee-stands.

With the other masquerades
That time resumes,
One thinks of all the hands
That are raising dingy shades
In a thousand furnished rooms.

III

You tossed a blanket from the bed,
You lay upon your back, and waited;
You dozed, and watched the night revealing
The thousand sordid images
Of which your soul was constituted;
They flickered against the ceiling.
And when all the world came back
And the light crept up between the shutters,
And you heard the sparrows in the gutters,
You had such a vision of the street
As the street hardly understands;
Sitting along the bed's edge, where

You curled the papers from your hair,
Or clasped the yellow soles of feet
In the palms of both soiled hands.

IV

His soul stretched tight across the skies
That fade behind a city block,
Or trampled by insistent feet
At four and five and six o'clock;
And short square fingers stuffing pipes,
And evening newspapers, and eyes
Assured of certain certainties,
The conscience of a blackened street
Impatient to assume the world.

I am moved by fancies that are curled
Around these images, and cling:
The notion of some infinitely gentle
Infinitely suffering thing.

Wipe your hand across your mouth, and laugh;
The worlds revolve like ancient women
Gathering fuel in vacant lots.

La Figlia Che Piange

Stand on the highest pavement of the stair—
Lean on a garden urn—
Weave, weave the sunlight in your hair—
Clasp your flowers to you with a pained surprise—
Fling them to the ground and turn
With a fugitive resentment in your eyes:
But weave, weave the sunlight in your hair.

So I would have had him leave,
So I would have had her stand and grieve,
So he would have left
As the soul leaves the body torn and bruised,
As the mind deserts the body it has used.
I should find
Some way incomparably light and deft,
Some way we both should understand,
Simple and faithless as a smile and shake of the hand.

She turned away, but with the autumn weather
Compelled my imagination many days,
Many days and many hours:
Her hair over her arms and her arms full of flowers.
And I wonder how they should have been together!
I should have lost a gesture and a pose.
Sometimes these cogitations still amaze
The troubled midnight and the noon's repose.

The Waste Land

Eliot never asserted that his major poem was a vision of a world stricken by the absence of Christian culture, but the Eliotic critics always interpreted the poem as a voice in the wilderness, crying out for the return of Christian, classical, and conservative ideas of order. Northrop Frye, reviewing the Eliotic poet-critic Allen Tate, charmingly called this interpretation the myth of the Great Western Butterslide.

Manifestly, *The Waste Land* is a poem of "mourning and melancholia," to appropriate the title of a great essay by Sigmund Freud (whom Eliot loathed). But the lament is personal, founded upon the premature fear that poetic creativity is waning in its author. Lingering in the poem (and unmentioned in Eliot's "Notes") are traces of Tennyson's monodrama, *Maud*, where the neurasthenic young narrator-protagonist is reduced to complaining: "And my heart is a handful of dust." "I will show you fear in a handful of dust," Eliot proclaims, and the fear is the loss of potency, both sexual and poetic.

The major paradigm for *The Waste Land* is Walt Whitman's majestic elegy, "When Lilacs Last in the Dooryard Bloom'd," though most of Eliot's critics fail to see this. And yet all the major images and thematic clusters of *The Waste Land* derive from the "Lilacs" lament: the lilacs themselves that begin Eliot's poem, the "unreal city," the doubling of the self, the "dear brother," the "murmur of maternal lamentation," faces peering at us, and the hermit thrush's song. Even Eliot's "third who always walks beside you" is hardly the risen Christ, as *The Waste Land*'s notes assert, but is closer to Whitman's companions as he walks down to the hermit thrush's abode, the "thought of death" and the "knowledge of death." Eliot's song of death, or of death-in-life, follows closely the pattern of Whitman's.

Not until 1953, when he acknowledged his deep affinity to Walt Whitman, did Eliot give up his uneasiness in regard to the father of almost all subsequent American poetry. I urge the reader to set "When Lilacs Last in the Dooryard Bloom'd" and *The Waste Land* side by side. The family resemblance is uncanny, though Whitman might have been as unhappy about it as Eliot evidently was.

The Waste Land

Nam Sibyllam quidem Cumis ego ipse oculis meis
vidi in ampulla pendere, et cum illi pueri dicerent;
Σίβυλλα τί θ'έλεις; *respondebut illa:* 'αποθανεîν θ'έλω.

THE BURIAL OF THE DEAD I

April is the cruellest month, breeding
Lilacs out of the dead land, mixing
Memory and desire, stirring
Dull roots with spring rain.
Winter kept us warm, covering
Earth in forgetful snow, feeding
A little life with dried tubers.
Summer surprised us, coming over the Starnbergersee
With a shower of rain; we stopped in the colonnade,
And went on in sunlight, into the Hofgarten,
And drank coffee, and talked for an hour.
Bin gar keine Russin, stamm' aus Litauen, echt deutsch.
And when we were children, staying at the archduke's,
My cousin's, he took me out on a sled,
And I was frightened. He said, Marie,
Marie, hold on tight. And down we went.
In the mountains, there you feel free.
I read, much of the night, and go south in the winter.

What are the roots that clutch, what branches grow
Out of this stony rubbish? Son of man,
You cannot say, or guess, for you know only
A heap of broken images, where the sun beats,
And the dead tree gives no shelter, the cricket no relief,
And the dry stone no sound of water. Only
There is shadow under this red rock,
(Come in under the shadow of this red rock),
And I will show you something different from either
Your shadow at morning striding behind you
Or your shadow at evening rising to meet you;
I will show you fear in a handful of dust.

Frisch weht der Wind
Der Heimat zu.
Mein Irisch Kind,
Wo weilest du?

'You gave me hyacinths first a year ago;
'They called me the hyacinth girl.'
—Yet when we came back, late, from the Hyacinth garden,
Your arms full, and your hair wet, I could not
Speak, and my eyes failed, I was neither
Living nor dead, and I knew nothing,
Looking into the heart of light, the silence.
Oed' und leer das Meer.

Madame Sosostris, famous clairvoyante,
Had a bad cold, nevertheless
Is known to be the wisest woman in Europe,
With a wicked pack of cards. Here, said she,
Is your card, the drowned Phoenician Sailor,
(Those are pearls that were his eyes. Look!)
Here is Belladonna, the Lady of the Rocks,
The lady of situations.
Here is the man with three staves, and here the Wheel,
And here is the one-eyed merchant, and this card,
Which is blank, is something he carries on his back,
Which I am forbidden to see. I do not find
The Hanged Man. Fear death by water.
I see crowds of people, walking round in a ring.
Thank you. If you see dear Mrs. Equitone,
Tell her I bring the horoscope myself:
One must be so careful these days.

Unreal City,
Under the brown fog of a winter dawn,
A crowd flowed over London Bridge, so many,
I had not thought death had undone so many.
Sighs, short and infrequent, were exhaled,
And each man fixed his eyes before his feet.
Flowed up the hill and down King William Street,
To where Saint Mary Woolnoth kept the hours
With a dead sound on the final stroke of nine.
There I saw one I knew, and stopped him, crying 'Stetson!
'You who were with me in the ships at Mylae!

'That corpse you planted last year in your garden,
'Has it begun to sprout? Will it bloom this year?
'Or has the sudden frost disturbed its bed?
'Oh keep the Dog far hence, that's friend to men,
'Or with his nails he'll dig it up again!
'You! hypocrite lecteur!—mon semblable,—mon frère!'

A GAME OF CHESS II

The Chair she sat in, like a burnished throne,
Glowed on the marble, where the glass
Held up by standards wrought with fruited vines
From which a golden Cupidon peeped out
(Another hid his eyes behind his wing)
Doubled the flames of sevenbranched candelabra
Reflecting light upon the table as
The glitter of her jewels rose to meet it,
From satin cases poured in rich profusion;
In vials of ivory and coloured glass
Unstoppered, lurked her strange synthetic perfumes,
Unguent, powdered, or liquid—troubled, confused
And drowned the sense in odours; stirred by the air
That freshened from the window, these ascended
In fattening the prolonged candle-flames,
Flung their smoke into the laquearia,
Stirring the pattern on the coffered ceiling.
Huge sea-wood fed with copper
Burned green and orange, framed by the coloured stone,
In which sad light a carvèd dolphin swam.
Above the antique mantel was displayed
As though a window gave upon the sylvan scene
The change of Philomel, by the barbarous king
So rudely forced; yet there the nightingale
Filled all the desert with inviolable voice
And still she cried, and still the world pursues,
'Jug Jug' to dirty ears.

And other withered stumps of time
Were told upon the walls; staring forms
Leaned out, leaning, hushing the room enclosed.
Footsteps shuffled on the stair.
Under the firelight, under the brush, her hair
Spread out in fiery points
Glowed into words, then would be savagely still.

'My nerves are bad to-night. Yes, bad. Stay with me.
'Speak to me. Why do you never speak? Speak.
'What are you thinking of? What thinking? What?
'I never know what you are thinking. Think.'

I think we are in rats' alley
Where the dead men lost their bones.

'What is that noise?'
                    The wind under the door.
'What is that noise now? What is the wind doing?'
                    Nothing again nothing.
                                   'Do
'You know nothing? Do you see nothing? Do you remember
'Nothing?'
                    I remember
Those are pearls that were his eyes.
'Are you alive, or not? Is there nothing in your head?'

                                                   But
O O O O that Shakespeherian Rag—
It's so elegant
So intelligent
'What shall I do now? What shall I do?'
'I shall rush out as I am, and walk the street
'With my hair down, so. What shall we do to-morrow?
'What shall we ever do?'
                    The hot water at ten.
And if it rains, a closed car at four.
And we shall play a game of chess,
Pressing lidless eyes and waiting for a knock upon the door.

When Lil's husband got demobbed, I said—
I didn't mince my words, I said to her myself,
HURRY UP PLEASE IT'S TIME
Now Albert's coming back, make yourself a bit smart.
He'll want to know what you done with that money he gave you
To get yourself some teeth. He did, I was there.
You have them all out, Lil, and get a nice set,
He said, I swear, I can't bear to look at you.
And no more can't I, I said, and think of poor Albert,
He's been in the army four years, he wants a good time,
And if you don't give it him, there's others will, I said.
Oh is there, she said. Something o' that, I said.

Then I'll know who to thank, she said, and give me a straight look.
HURRY UP PLEASE IT'S TIME
If you don't like it you can get on with it, I said.
Others can pick and choose if you can't.
But if Albert makes off, it won't be for lack of telling.
You ought to be ashamed, I said, to look so antique.
(And her only thirty-one.)
I can't help it, she said, pulling a long face,
It's them pills I took, to bring it off, she said.
(She's had five already, and nearly died of young George.)
The chemist said it would be alright, but I've never been the same.
You *are* a proper fool, I said.
Well, if Albert won't leave you alone, there it is, I said,
What you get married for if you don't want children?
HURRY UP PLEASE IT'S TIME
Well, that Sunday Albert was home, they had a hot gammon,
And they asked me in to dinner, to get the beauty of it hot—
HURRY UP PLEASE IT'S TIME
HURRY UP PLEASE IT'S TIME
Goonight Bill. Goonight Lou. Goonight May. Goonight.
Ta ta. Goonight. Goonight.
Good night, ladies, good night, sweet ladies, good night, good night.

    THE FIRE SERMON III
The river's tent is broken: the last fingers of leaf
Clutch and sink into the wet bank. The wind
Crosses the brown land, unheard. The nymphs are departed.
Sweet Thames, run softly, till I end my song.
The river bears no empty bottles, sandwich papers,
Silk handkerchiefs, cardboard boxes, cigarette ends
Or other testimony of summer nights. The nymphs are departed.
And their friends, the loitering heirs of city directors;
Departed, have left no addresses.
By the waters of Leman I sat down and wept . . .
Sweet Thames, run softly till I end my song,
Sweet Thames, run softly, for I speak not loud or long.
But at my back in a cold blast I hear
The rattle of the bones, and chuckle spread from ear to ear.

A rat crept softly through the vegetation
Dragging its slimy belly on the bank
While I was fishing in the dull canal
On a winter evening round behind the gashouse

Musing upon the king my brother's wreck
And on the king my father's death before him.
White bodies naked on the low damp ground
And bones cast in a little low dry garret,
Rattled by the rat's foot only, year to year.
But at my back from time to time I hear
The sound of horns and motors, which shall bring
Sweeney to Mrs. Porter in the spring.
O the moon shone bright on Mrs. Porter
And on her daughter
They wash their feet in soda water
Et, O ces voix d'enfants, chantant dans la coupole!

Twit twit twit
Jug jug jug jug jug jug
So rudely forc'd.
Tereu
Unreal City
Under the brown fog of a winter noon
Mr. Eugenides, the Smyrna merchant
Unshaven, with a pocket full of currants
C.i.f. London: documents at sight,
Asked me in demotic French
To luncheon at the Cannon Street Hotel
Followed by a weekend at the Metropole.

At the violet hour, when the eyes and back
Turn upward from the desk, when the human engine waits
Like a taxi throbbing waiting,
I Tiresias, though blind, throbbing between two lives,
Old man with wrinkled female breasts, can see
At the violet hour, the evening hour that strives
Homeward, and brings the sailor home from sea,
The typist home at teatime, clears her breakfast, lights
Her stove, and lays out food in tins.
Out of the window perilously spread
Her drying combinations touched by the sun's last rays,
On the divan are piled (at night her bed)
Stockings, slippers, camisoles, and stays.
I Tiresias, old man with wrinkled dugs
Perceived the scene, and foretold the rest—
I too awaited the expected guest.

He, the young man carbuncular, arrives,
A small house agent's clerk, with one bold stare,
One of the low on whom assurance sits
As a silk hat on a Bradford millionaire.
The time is now propitious, as he guesses,
The meal is ended, she is bored and tired,
Endeavours to engage her in caresses
Which still are unreproved, if undesired.
Flushed and decided, he assaults at once;
Exploring hands encounter no defence;
His vanity requires no response,
And makes a welcome of indifference.
(And I Tiresias have foresuffered all
Enacted on this same divan or bed;
I who have sat by Thebes below the wall
And walked among the lowest of the dead.)
Bestows one final patronising kiss,
And gropes his way, finding the stairs unlit . . .

She turns and looks a moment in the glass,
Hardly aware of her departed lover;
Her brain allows one half-formed thought to pass:
'Well now that's done: and I'm glad it's over.'
When lovely woman stoops to folly and
Paces about her room again, alone,
She smoothes her hair with automatic hand,
And puts a record on the gramophone.

'This music crept by me upon the waters'
And along the Strand, up Queen Victoria Street.

O City city, I can sometimes hear
Beside a public bar in Lower Thames Street,
The pleasant whining of a mandoline
And a clatter and a chatter from within
Where fishmen lounge at noon: where the walls
Of Magnus Martyr hold
Inexplicable splendour of Ionian white and gold.

        The river sweats
        Oil and tar
        The barges drift

With the turning tide
Red sails
Wide
To leeward, swing on the heavy spar.
The barges wash
Drifting logs
Down Greenwich reach
Past the Isle of Dogs.
      Weialala leia
      Wallala leialala

Elizabeth and Leicester
Beating oars
The stern was formed
A gilded shell
Red and gold
The brisk swell
Rippled both shores
Southwest wind
Carried down stream
The peal of bells
White towers
      Weialala leia
      Wallala leialala

'Trams and dusty trees.
Highbury bore me. Richmond and Kew
Undid me. By Richmond I raised my knees
Supine on the floor of a narrow canoe.'

'My feet are at Moorgate, and my heart
Under my feet. After the event
He wept. He promised "a new start".
I made no comment. What should I resent?'
'On Margate Sands.
I can connect
Nothing with nothing.
The broken fingernails of dirty hands.
My people humble people who expect
Nothing.'

    la la

To Carthage then I came

Burning burning burning burning
O Lord Thou pluckest me out
O Lord Thou pluckest

burning

DEATH BY WATER IV

Phlebas the Phoenician, a fortnight dead,
Forgot the cry of gulls, and the deep sea swell
And the profit and loss.
                          A current under sea
Picked his bones in whispers. As he rose and fell
He passed the stages of his age and youth
Entering the whirlpool.
                          Gentile or Jew
O you who turn the wheel and look to windward,
Consider Phlebas, who was once handsome and tall as you.

WHAT THE THUNDER SAID V

After the torchlight red on sweaty faces
After the frosty silence in the gardens
After the agony in stony places
The shouting and the crying
Prison and place and reverberation
Of thunder of spring over distant mountains
He who was living is now dead
We who were living are now dying
With a little patience

Here is no water but only rock
Rock and no water and the sandy road
The road winding above among the mountains
Which are mountains of rock without water
If there were water we should stop and drink
Amongst the rock one cannot stop or think
Sweat is dry and feet are in the sand
If there were only water amongst the rock
Dead mountain mouth of carious teeth that cannot spit
Here one can neither stand nor lie nor sit
There is not even silence in the mountains
But dry sterile thunder without rain

There is not even solitude in the mountains
But red sullen faces sneer and snarl
From doors of mudcracked houses
                        If there were water
    And no rock
    If there were rock
    And also water
    And water
    A spring
    A pool among the rock
    If there were the sound of water only
    Not the cicada
    And dry grass singing
    But sound of water over a rock
    Where the hermit-thrush sings in the pine trees
    Drip drop drip drop drop drop drop
    But there is no water

Who is the third who walks always beside you?
When I count, there are only you and I together
But when I look ahead up the white road
There is always another one walking beside you
Gliding wrapt in a brown mantle, hooded
I do not know whether a man or a woman
—But who is that on the other side of you?

What is that sound high in the air
Murmur of maternal lamentation
Who are those hooded hordes swarming
Over endless plains, stumbling in cracked earth
Ringed by the flat horizon only
What is the city over the mountains
Cracks and reforms and bursts in the violet air
Falling towers
Jerusalem Athens Alexandria
Vienna London
Unreal

A woman drew her long black hair out tight
And fiddled whisper music on those strings
And bats with baby faces in the violet light
Whistled, and beat their wings
And crawled head downward down a blackened wall

And upside down in air were towers
Tolling reminiscent bells, that kept the hours
And voices singing out of empty cisterns and exhausted wells.

In this decayed hole among the mountains
In the faint moonlight, the grass is singing
Over the tumbled graves, about the chapel
There is the empty chapel, only the wind's home.
It has no windows, and the door swings,
Dry bones can harm no one.
Only a cock stood on the rooftree
Co co rico co co rico
In a flash of lightning. Then a damp gust
Bringing rain

Ganga was sunken, and the limp leaves
Waited for rain, while the black clouds
Gathered far distant, over Himavant.
The jungle crouched, humped in silence.
Then spoke the thunder
DA
Datta: what have we given?
My friend, blood shaking my heart
The awful daring of a moment's surrender
Which an age of prudence can never retract
By this, and this only, we have existed
Which is not to be found in our obituaries
Or in memories draped by the beneficent spider
Or under seals broken by the lean solicitor
In our empty rooms
DA
Dayadhvam: I have heard the key
Turn in the door once and turn once only
We think of the key, each in his prison
Thinking of the key, each confirms a prison
Only at nightfall, aetherial rumours
Revive for a moment a broken Coriolanus
DA
Damyata: The boat responded
Gaily, to the hand expert with sail and oar
The sea was calm, your heart would have responded
Gaily, when invited, beating obedient
To controlling hands

           I sat upon the shore
Fishing, with the arid plain behind me
Shall I at least set my lands in order?

London Bridge is falling down falling down falling down

Poi s'ascose nel foco che gli affina
Quando fiam ceu chelidon—O swallow swallow
Le Prince d'Aquitaine à la tour abolie
These fragments I have shored against my ruins
Why then Ile fit you. Hieronymo's mad againe.
Datta. Dayadhvam. Damyata.

      Shantih shantih shantih

JOHN CROWE RANSOM

1888–1974

AN ACCOMPLISHED POET–CRITIC, Ransom was a native Tennessean, son of a Methodist minister. After graduating from Vanderbilt University, Ransom went to Oxford as a Rhodes scholar, and then taught at Vanderbilt before serving two years in the field artillery during World War I. He returned to Vanderbilt and stayed there until the end of the 1930s, when he went to Kenyon College, where he edited *The Kenyon Review.*

While at Vanderbilt, Ransom married, and was closely associated with *The Fugitives,* the crucial magazine for the Southern literary movement that included Allen Tate and Robert Penn Warren.

Ransom's poetry, always toughly elegant, was partly obscured by his eminence as a New Critic, a prime follower of T. S. Eliot. But the poetry always remained Ransom's own, a highly original blend of seventeenth-century Cavalier and Eliotic Modernism.

Of his three poems included here, I observe that they have held up for me through a half-century of rereading. "Here Lies a Lady" beautifully evades its own emotions, concealing grief beneath ironies of apprehension. One of my favorites, "Captain Carpenter" is a Tennessean Don Quixote, dismantled with outrageous stylization and lyric grace. The charming "Blue Girls" comes back to me at various moments when, an old and contrary teacher, I admire undergraduate women traveling the sward under the towers of Yale.

❧   ❧   ❧

Here Lies a Lady

Here lies a lady of beauty and high degree.
Of chills and fever she died, of fever and chills,
The delight of her husband, her aunts, an infant of three,
And of medicos marvelling sweetly on her ills.

For either she burned, and her confident eyes would blaze,
And her fingers fly in a manner to puzzle their heads—
What was she making? Why, nothing; she sat in a maze
Of old scraps of laces, snipped into curious shreds—

Or this would pass, and the light of her fire decline
Till she lay discouraged and cold as a thin stalk white and blown,
And would not open her eyes, to kisses, to wine;
The sixth of these states was her last; the cold settled down.

Sweet ladies, long may ye bloom, and toughly I hope ye may thole,
But was she not lucky? In flowers and lace and mourning,
In love and great honour we bade God rest her soul
After six little spaces of chill, and six of burning.

Captain Carpenter

Captain Carpenter rose up in his prime
Put on his pistols and went riding out
But had got wellnigh nowhere at that time
Till he fell in with ladies in a rout.

It was a pretty lady and all her train
That played with him so sweetly but before
An hour she'd taken a sword with all her main
And twined him of his nose for evermore.

Captain Carpenter mounted up one day
And rode straightway into a stranger rogue
That looked unchristian but be that as may
The Captain did not wait upon prologue.

But drew upon him out of his great heart
The other swung against him with a club
And cracked his two legs at the shinny part
And let him roll and stick like any tub.

Captain Carpenter rode many a time
From male and female took he sundry harms
He met the wife of Satan crying "I'm
The she-wolf bids you shall bear no more arms."

Their strokes and counters whistled in the wind
I wish he had delivered half his blows
But where she should have made off like a hind
The bitch bit off his arms at the elbows.

And Captain Carpenter parted with his ears
To a black devil that used him in this wise
O Jesus ere his threescore and ten years
Another had plucked out his sweet blue eyes.

Captain Carpenter got up on his roan
And sallied from the gate in hell's despite
I heard him asking in the grimmest tone
If any enemy yet there was to fight?

"To any adversary it is fame
If he risk to be wounded by my tongue
Or burnt in two beneath my red heart's flame
Such are the perils he is cast among.

"But if he can he has a pretty choice
From an anatomy with little to lose
Whether he cut my tongue and take my voice
Or whether it be my round red heart he choose."

It was the neatest knave that ever was seen
Stepping in perfume from his lady's bower

Who at this word put in his merry mien
And fell on Captain Carpenter like a tower.

I would not knock old fellows in the dust
But there lay Captain Carpenter on his back
His weapons were the old heart in his bust
And a blade shook between rotten teeth alack.

The rogue in scarlet and grey soon knew his mind
He wished to get his trophy and depart
With gentle apology and touch refined
He pierced him and produced the Captain's heart.

God's mercy rest on Captain Carpenter now
I thought him Sirs an honest gentleman
Citizen husband soldier and scholar enow
Let jangling kites eat of him if they can.

But God's deep curses follow after those
That shore him of his goodly nose and ears
His legs and strong arms at the two elbows
And eyes that had not watered seventy years.

The curse of hell upon the sleek upstart
Who got the Captain finally on his back
And took the red red vitals of his heart
And made the kites to whet their beaks clack clack.

Blue Girls

Twirling your blue skirts, travelling the sward
Under the towers of your seminary,
Go listen to your teachers old and contrary
Without believing a word.

Tie the white fillets then about your lustrous hair
And think no more of what will come to pass
Than bluebirds that go walking on the grass
And chattering on the air.

Practice your beauty, blue girls, before it fail;
And I will cry with my loud lips and publish

Beauty which all our power shall never establish,
It is so frail.

For I could tell you a story which is true;
I know a lady with a terrible tongue,
Blear eyes fallen from blue,
All her perfections tarnished—and yet it is not long
Since she was lovelier than any of you.

CONRAD AIKEN

1889–1973

THIS REMARKABLE AMERICAN POET is now much neglected, a sorrow I contend against in my introduction to a new, augmented edition of his *Selected Poems* (2003). Aiken seems resented by some for his continuous eloquence, the superb "music" of his poetic voice and stance. This prejudice will vanish, and Aiken's permanent place in American poetic tradition will be reestablished.

Aiken, the oldest of four children, was eleven years old when his father shot his mother, and then killed himself. Only a very strong consciousness could have survived the experience of first discovering the bodies, as Aiken did. Adopted by an uncle, which moved the future poet from Savannah, Georgia, to Cambridge, Massachusetts, he attended Harvard, where he formed a lifelong friendship with T. S. Eliot.

The poet's first two marriages failed, but the third prospered, and was still ongoing when he died in Savannah, having returned full circle to his birthplace in 1962. His friendship with the novelist Malcolm Lowry, author of *Under the Volcano,* did much to foster Lowry's achievement.

Aiken's own work included a remarkable autobiography, *Ushant* (1952), and his vast *Collected Poems* (1953), which was followed by six more volumes of poetry before his death. The first of his several novels, *Blue Voyage* (1927) still sustains rereading.

I have included five poems by Aiken, all of which have haunted me, and stayed in my memory, for many years. "Morning Song of Senlin" could be termed Aiken's archetypal poem: intensely lyrical, Romantic, assured in its nihilism. "And in the Hanging Gardens," a particular favorite, strikes me as what Trumbull Stickney, a Harvard poet long before Aiken, might have written had he survived.

"Sea Holly" is an exquisitely harsh confrontation of the barren or wasted beauty of an old woman and the wave-lashed rocks, showing Aiken at his subtlest. It is followed here by the first of Aiken's "Preludes," in which the poet's own consciousness sharply meditates upon its sense of mortality.

ᛣ   ᛣ   ᛣ

from Morning Song of Senlin

2

It is morning, Senlin says, and in the morning
When the light drips through the shutters like the dew,
I arise, I face the sunrise,
And do the things my fathers learned to do.
Stars in the purple dusk above the rooftops
Pale in a saffron mist and seem to die,
And I myself on a swiftly tilting planet
Stand before a glass and tie my tie.

Vine leaves tap my window,
Dew-drops sing to the garden stones,
The robin chirps in the chinaberry tree
Repeating three clear tones.

It is morning, I stand by the mirror
And tie my tie once more.
While waves far off in a pale rose twilight
Crash on a coral shore.
I stand by a mirror and comb my hair:
How small and white my face!—
The green earth tilts through a sphere of air
And bathes in a flame of space.

There are houses hanging above the stars
And stars hung under a sea.

And a sun far off in a shell of silence
Dapples my walls for me.

It is morning, Senlin says, and in the morning
Should I not pause in the light to remember god?
Upright and firm I stand on a star unstable,
He is immense and lonely as a cloud.
I will dedicate this moment before my mirror
To him alone, for him I will comb my hair.
Accept these humble offerings, cloud of silence!
I will think of you as I descend the stair.

Vine leaves tap my window,
The snail-track shines on the stones,
Dew-drops flash from the chinaberry tree
Repeating two clear tones.

It is morning, I awake from a bed of silence,
Shining I rise from the starless waters of sleep.
The walls are about me still as in the evening,
I am the same, and the same name still I keep.
The earth revolves with me, yet makes no motion,
The stars pale silently in a coral sky.
In a whistling void I stand before my mirror,
Unconcerned, and tie my tie.

There are horses neighing on far-off hills
Tossing their long white manes,
And mountains flash in the rose-white dusk,
Their shoulders black with rains.
It is morning. I stand by the mirror
And surprise my soul once more;
The blue air rushes above my ceiling.
There are suns beneath my floor.

. . . It is morning, Senlin says, I ascend from darkness
And depart on the winds of space for I know not where,
My watch is wound, a key is in my pocket,
And the sky is darkened as I descend the stair.
There are shadows across the windows, clouds in heaven,
And a god among the stars; and I will go
Thinking of him as I might think of daybreak
And humming a tune I know.

Vine leaves tap at the window,
Dew-drops sing to the garden stones,
The robin chirps in the chinaberry tree
Repeating three clear tones.

And in the Hanging Gardens

And in the hanging gardens there is rain
From midnight until one, striking the leaves
And bells of flowers, and stroking boles of planes,
And drawing slow arpeggios over pools,
And stretching strings of sound from eaves to ferns.
The princess reads. The knave of diamonds sleeps.
The king is drunk, and flings a golden goblet
Down from the turret window (curtained with rain)
Into the lilacs.

        And at one o'clock
The vulcan under the garden wakes and beats
The gong upon his anvil. Then the rain
Ceases, but gently ceases, dripping still,
And sound of falling water fills the dark
As leaves grow bold and upright, and as eaves
Part with water. The princess turns the page
Beside the candle, and between two braids
Of golden hair. And reads: 'From there I went
Northward a journey of four days, and came
To a wild village in the hills, where none
Was living save the vulture and the rat,
And one old man, who laughed, but could not speak.
The roofs were fallen in; the well grown over
With weed; and it was there my father died.
Then eight days further, bearing slightly west,
The cold wind blowing sand against our faces,
The food tasting of sand. And as we stood
By the dry rock that marks the highest point
My brother said: "Not too late is it yet
To turn, remembering home." And we were silent
Thinking of home.' The princess shuts her eyes
And feels the tears forming beneath her eyelids
And opens them, and tears fall on the page.
The knave of diamonds in the darkened room

Throws off his covers, sleeps, and snores again.
The king goes slowly down the turret stairs
To find the goblet.

And at two o'clock
The vulcan in his smithy underground
Under the hanging gardens, where the drip
Of rain among the clematis and ivy
Still falls from sipping flower to purple flower,
Smites twice his anvil, and the murmur comes
Among the roots and vines. The princess reads:
'As I am sick, and cannot write you more,
Nor have not long to live, I give this letter
To him, my brother, who will bear it south
And tell you how I died. Ask how it was,
There in the northern desert, where the grass
Was withered, and the horses, all but one,
Perished' . . . The princess drops her golden head
Upon the page between her two white arms
And golden braids. The knave of diamonds wakes
And at his window in the darkened room
Watches the lilacs tossing, where the king
Seeks for the goblet.

And at three o'clock
The moon inflames the lilac heads, and thrice
The vulcan, in his root-bound smithy, clangs
His anvil; and the sounds creep softly up
Among the vines and walls. The moon is round,
Round as a shield above the turret top.
The princess blows her candle out, and weeps
In the pale room, where scent of lilac comes,
Weeping, with hands across her eyelids, thinking
Of withered grass, withered by sandy wind.
The knave of diamonds, in his darkened room,
Holds in his hands a key, and softly steps
Along the corridor, and slides the key
Into the door that guards her. Meanwhile, slowly,
The king, with raindrops on his beard and hands,
And dripping sleeves, climbs up the turret stairs,
Holding the goblet upright in one hand;
And pauses on the midmost step, to taste
One drop of wine, wherewith wild rain has mixed.

Sea Holly

Begotten by the meeting of rock with rock,
The mating of rock and rock, rocks gnashing together;
Created so, and yet forgetful, walks
The seaward path, puts up her left hand, shades
Blue eyes, the eyes of rock, to see better
In slanting light the ancient sheep (which kneels
Biting the grass) the while her other hand,
Hooking the wicker handle, turns the basket
Of eggs. The sea is high to-day. The eggs
Are cheaper. The sea is blown from the southwest,
Confused, taking up sand and mud in waves,
The waves break, sluggish, in brown foam, the wind
Disperses (on the sheep and hawthorn) spray,—
And on her cheeks, the cheeks engendered of rock,
And eyes, the colour of rock. The left hand
Falls from the eyes, and undecided slides
Over the left breast on which muslin lightly
Rests, touching the nipple, and then down
The hollow side, virgin as rock, and bitterly
Caresses the blue hip.

       It was for this,
This obtuse taking of the seaward path,
This stupid hearing of larks, this hooking
Of wicker, this absent observation of sheep
Kneeling in harsh sea-grass, the cool hand shading
The spray-stung eyes—it was for this the rock
Smote itself. The sea is higher to-day,
And eggs are cheaper. The eyes of rock take in
The seaward path that winds toward the sea,
The thistle-prodder, old woman under a bonnet,
Forking the thistles, her back against the sea,
Pausing, with hard hands on the handle, peering
With rock eyes from her bonnet.

       It was for this,
This rock-lipped facing of brown waves, half sand
And half water, this tentative hand that slides
Over the breast of rock, and into the hollow
Soft side of muslin rock, and then fiercely
Almost as rock against the hip of rock—

It was for this in midnight the rocks met,
And dithered together, cracking and smoking.

            It was for this
Barren beauty, barrenness of rock that aches
On the seaward path, seeing the fruitful sea,
Hearing the lark of rock that sings, smelling
The rock-flower of hawthorn, sweetness of rock—
It was for this, stone pain in the stony heart,
The rock loved and laboured; and all is lost.

Preludes for Memnon

or Preludes to Attitude

I

Winter for a moment takes the mind; the snow
Falls past the arclight; icicles guard a wall;
The wind moans through a crack in the window;
A keen sparkle of frost is on the sill.
Only for a moment; as spring too might engage it,
With a single crocus in the loam, or a pair of birds;
Or summer with hot grass; or autumn with a yellow leaf.
Winter is there, outside, is here in me:
Drapes the planets with snow, deepens the ice on the moon,
Darkens the darkness that was already darkness.
The mind too has its snows, its slippery paths,
Walls bayonetted with ice, leaves ice-encased.
Here is the in-drawn room, to which you return
When the wind blows from Arcturus: here is the fire
At which you warm your hands and glaze your eyes;
The piano, on which you touch the cold treble;
Five notes like breaking icicles; and then silence.

The alarm-clock ticks, the pulse keeps time with it,
Night and the mind are full of sounds. I walk
From the fire-place, with its imaginary fire,
To the window, with its imaginary view.
Darkness, and snow ticking the window: silence,
And the knocking of chains on a motor-car, the tolling
Of a bronze bell, dedicated to Christ.
And then the uprush of angelic wings, the beating
Of wings demonic, from the abyss of the mind:

The darkness filled with a feathery whistling, wings
Numberless as the flakes of angelic snow,
The deep void swarming with wings and sound of wings,
The winnowing of chaos, the aliveness
Of depth and depth and depth dedicated to death.

Here are the bickerings of the inconsequential,
The chatterings of the ridiculous, the iterations
Of the meaningless. Memory, like a juggler,
Tosses its colored balls into the light, and again
Receives them into darkness. Here is the absurd,
Grinning like an idiot, and the omnivorous quotidian,
Which will have its day. A handful of coins,
Tickets, items from the news, a soiled handkerchief,
A letter to be answered, notice of a telephone call,
The petal of a flower in a volume of Shakspere,
The program of a concert. The photograph, too,
Propped on the mantel, and beneath it a dry rosebud;
The laundry bill, matches, an ash-tray, Utamaro's
Pearl-fishers. And the rug, on which are still the crumbs
Of yesterday's feast. These are the void, the night,
And the angelic wings that make it sound.

What is the flower? It is not a sigh of color,
Suspiration of purple, sibilation of saffron,
Nor aureate exhalation from the tomb.
Yet it is these because you think of these,
An emanation of emanations, fragile
As light, or glisten, or gleam, or coruscation,
Creature of brightness, and as brightness brief.
What is the frost? It is not the sparkle of death,
The flash of time's wing, seeds of eternity;
Yet it is these because you think of these.
And you, because you think of these, are both
Frost and flower, the bright ambiguous syllable
Of which the meaning is both no and yes.

Here is the tragic, the distorting mirror
In which your gesture becomes grandiose;
Tears form and fall from your magnificent eyes,
The brow is noble, and the mouth is God's.
Here is the God who seeks his mother, Chaos,—
Confusion seeking solution, and life seeking death.

Here is the rose that woos the icicle; the icicle
That woos the rose. Here is the silence of silences
Which dreams of becoming a sound, and the sound
Which will perfect itself in silence. And all
These things are only the uprush from the void,
The wings angelic and demonic, the sound of the abyss
Dedicated to death. And this is you.

  II

Two coffees in the Español, the last
Bright drops of golden Barsac in a goblet,
Fig paste and candied nuts . . . Hardy is dead,
And James and Conrad dead, and Shakspere dead,
And old Moore ripens for an obscene grave,
And Yeats for an arid one; and I, and you—
What winding sheet for us, what boards and bricks,
What mummeries, candles, prayers, and pious frauds?
You shall be lapped in Syrian scarlet, woman,
And wear your pearls, and your bright bracelets, too,
Your agate ring, and round your neck shall hang
Your dark blue lapis with its specks of gold.
And I, beside you—ah! but will that be?
For there are dark streams in this dark world, lady,
Gulf Streams and Arctic currents of the soul;
And I may be, before our consummation
Beds us together, cheek by jowl, in earth,
Swept to another shore, where my white bones
Will lie unhonored, or defiled by gulls.

What dignity can death bestow on us,
Who kiss beneath a streetlamp, or hold hands
Half hidden in a taxi, or replete
With coffee, figs and Barsac make our way
To a dark bedroom in a wormworn house?
The aspidistra guards the door; we enter,
Per aspidistra—then—*ad astra*—is it?—
And lock ourselves securely in our gloom
And loose ourselves from terror . . . Here's my hand,
The white scar on my thumb, and here's my mouth

EDNA ST. VINCENT MILLAY

1892–1950

MILLAY WAS STILL a highly popular poet in my youth, but by the time of her apparently accidental death she had suffered an eclipse. Some of her work currently is being revived, but I confess to finding her more interesting as a life story than as a poet. The strongest defense of the value of her verse has been made by the brilliant poet-critic J. D. McClatchy, in his introduction to a *Selected Poems* that he edited in 2003 for the American Poets Project of the Library of America.

I include only her early sonnet, "If I should learn, in some quite casual way," which McClatchy accurately praises for its "brutal and elegant immediacy." Certainly this sonnet has a kind of casual force and authentic skill in playing through its single-sentence structure.

Millay was the female version of Lord Byron in the 1920s, with such celebrated lovers as the critic Edmund Wilson, the novelist Floyd Dell, and a platoon of poets including John Peale Bishop, Arthur Davison Ficke, and George Dillon.

A happy marriage to Eugen Boissevain in 1923 did not much alter Millay's amorous career, and she became drug-addicted in reaction to a car accident in the mid-1930s. Whether her death in 1950 was accidental or a suicide is not clear, as she fell downstairs after a mixture of wine and drugs. Her husband had died in 1949, and she could not survive long without him.

❧   ❧   ❧

"If I should learn, in some quite casual way,"

If I should learn, in some quite casual way,
    That you were gone, not to return again—
Read from the back-page of a paper, say,
    Held by a neighbor in a subway train,
How at the corner of this avenue
    And such a street (so are the papers filled)
A hurrying man—who happened to be you—

At noon to-day had happened to be killed,
I should not cry aloud—I could not cry
    Aloud, or wring my hands in such a place—
I should but watch the station lights rush by
    With a more careful interest on my face,
Or raise my eyes and read with greater care
Where to store furs and how to treat the hair.

LOUISE BOGAN

1897–1970

LOUISE BOGAN, a New Englander by birth and upbringing, spent much of her life in New York City, Boston, and New Mexico, until she moved to Hillsdale, New York, with her second husband, the poet Raymond Holden, in 1929. Bogan served as poetry editor for *The New Yorker* for the better part of forty years.

A strong, passionate personality, Bogan had close friendships with the critic Edmund Wilson and with several poets, including Rolfe Humphries and Theodore Roethke. Believing in psychoanalysis, she underwent it from the early 1920s until the end of her life.

Though Bogan is usually categorized as a metaphysical poet, influenced by John Donne, T. S. Eliot, and John Crowe Ransom, her poetry actually was haunted by William Butler Yeats's powerful work, with overtones also of Emily Dickinson.

I have included two poems by Bogan here, while holding on to the realization that she needs to be read in the wider context of her *Collected Poems*.

"Women" is a wry, strong poem that finds appropriate metaphors for the different ways in which women and men love. The even fiercer "Men Loved Wholly Beyond Wisdom" is a gnomic parable, with overtones of the William Blake of "Ah Sunflower!" and the Yeats of "Never Give All the Heart." A contrary statement rises in the sixth line, implicitly disputing the undoubtedly wise counsel not to love so intensely. The final figure of the cricket is a striking emblem akin to those of Blake's state of Experience.

❧   ❧   ❧

Women

Women have no wilderness in them,
They are provident instead,
Content in the tight hot cell of their hearts
To eat dusty bread.

They do not see cattle cropping red winter grass,
They do not hear
Snow water going down under culverts
Shallow and clear.

They wait, when they should turn to journeys,
They stiffen, when they should bend.
They use against themselves that benevolence
To which no man is friend.

They cannot think of so many crops to a field
Or of clean wood cleft by an axe.
Their love is an eager meaninglessness
Too tense, or too lax.

They hear in every whisper that speaks to them
A shout and a cry.
As like as not, when they take life over their door-sills
They should let it go by.

Men Loved Wholly Beyond Wisdom

Men loved wholly beyond wisdom
Have the staff without the banner.
Like a fire in a dry thicket
Rising within women's eyes
Is the love men must return.
Heart, so subtle now, and trembling,
What a marvel to be wise,
To love never in this manner!
To be quiet in the fern
Like a thing gone dead and still,
Listening to the prisoned cricket
Shake its terrible, dissembling
Music in the granite hill.

JOHN BROOKS WHEELWRIGHT

1897–1940

A GRAND POETIC ORIGINAL, now largely forgotten, Wheelwright lived a highly individual life, unfortunately terminated by a Boston drunk driver, soon after the poet's forty-third birthday.

Expelled from Harvard in 1920 (he rarely manifested himself there), Wheelwright worked in architecture for a time, but his passion for poetry led him to a literary career. A fierce Trotskyite, Wheelwright was purged from the Socialist Party in 1937, and was one of the founders of the Socialist Workers Party.

Influenced by William Blake and Walt Whitman, Wheelwright's best poems are dithyrambic. Their high, incantatory style suggests an affinity to Hart Crane, for whom Wheelwright composed an extraordinary elegy, included here. With it, I also reprint the wonderful rhapsody "Come Over and Help Us," written in the characteristic fourteeners of William Blake. The title ironically alludes to St. Paul, but this is a New England Trotskyite lament for American spiritual decline, as relevant now as it was in the revolutionary 1930s.

Readers attracted to Wheelwright are urged to seek out his *Collected Poems* (1972).

✤   ✤   ✤

Fish Food

An Obituary to Hart Crane

As you drank deep as Thor, did you think of milk or wine?
Did you drink blood, while you drank the salt deep?
Or see through the film of light, that sharpened your rage with its stare,
a shark, dolphin, turtle? Did you not see the Cat
who, when Thor lifted her, unbased the cubic ground?
You would drain fathomless flagons to be slaked with vacuum—
The sea's teats have suckled you, and you are sunk far
in bubble-dreams, under swaying translucent vines

of thundering interior wonder. Eagles can never now
carry parts of your body, over cupped mountains
as emblems of their anger, embers to fire self-hate
to other wonders, unfolding white, flaming vistas.

Fishes now look upon you, with eyes which do not gossip.
Fishes are never shocked. Fishes will kiss you, each
fish tweak you; every kiss take bits of you away,
till your bones alone will roll, with the Gulf Stream's swell.
So has it been already, so have the carpers and puffers
nibbled your carcass of fame, each to his liking. Now
in tides of noon, the bones of your thought-suspended structures
gleam as you intended. Noon pulled your eyes with small
magnetic headaches; the will seeped from your blood. Seeds
of meaning popped from the pods of thought. And you fall.
        And the unseen
churn of Time changes the pearl-hued ocean;
like a pearl-shaped drop, in a huge water-clock
falling; from *came* to *go*, from *come* to *went*. And you fell.

Waters received you. Waters of our Birth in Death dissolve you.
Now you have willed it, may the Great Wash take you.
As the Mother-Lover takes your woe away, and cleansing
grief and you away, you sleep, you do not snore.
Lie still. Your rage is gone on a bright flood
away; as, when a bad friend held out his hand
you said, "Do not talk any more. I know you meant no harm."
What was the soil whence your anger sprang, who are deaf
as the stones to the whispering flight of the Mississippi's rivers?
What did you see as you fell? What did you hear as you sank?
Did it make you drunken with hearing?
I will not ask any more. You saw or heard no evil.

Come Over and Help Us

A Rhapsody

I

Our masks are gauze / and screen our faces for those unlike us only,
Who are easily deceived. / Pierce through these masks to our unhidden
    tongues
And watch us scold, / scold with intellectual lust; / scold
Ourselves, our foes, our friends; / Europe, America, Boston; and all that is
    not

Boston; / till we reach a purity, fierce as the love of God;— / Hate.
Hate, still fed by the shadowed source; / but fallen, stagnant fallen;
Sunk low between thin channels; rises, rises; / swells to burst
Its walls; and rolls out deep and wide. / Hate rules our drowning Race.
Any freed from our Tyrant; / abandon their farms, forsake their Country,
    become American.

We, the least subtle of Peoples, / lead each only one life at a time,—
Being never, never anything but sincere; / yet we trust our honesty
So little that we dare not depart from it,— / knowing it to need habitual stim-
    ulation.
And living amid a world of Spooks, / we summon another to us
Who is (in some sort) our Clown,— / as he affords us amusement.
O! sweet tormentor, Doubt! longed-for and human, / leave us some plausible
Evil motive, however incredible. / The Hate in the World outside our World
(Envious, malicious, vindictive) / makes our Hate gleam in the splendor
Of a Castrate / who with tongue plucked out; / arms, legs sawed off;
Eyes and ears, pierced through; / still thinks / thinks
By means of all his nutriment, / with intense, exacting Energy, terrible, con-
    suming.
Madness, we so politely placate / as an every-day inconvenience
We shun in secret. / Madness is sumptuous; Hate, ascetic.
Those only who remain sane, / taste the flavor of Hate.
Strong Joy, we forbid ourselves / and deny large pleasurable objects,
But, too shrewd to forego amusement, / we enjoy all joys which, dying, leave
    us teased.
So spare us, sweet Doubt, our tormentor, / the Arts, our concerts, and novels;
The theater, sports, the exotic Past; / to use to stave off Madness,
To use as breathing spells, / that our drug's tang may not die.
We are not tireless; / distract us from thin ecstasy, that we may hate
If with less conviction, / with some result, some end,—
So pure ourselves; so clear our passion; / *pure, clear, alone.*

II

The New Englander leaves New England / to flaunt his drab person
Before Latin decors / and Asiatic back-drops.
Wearies. / Returns to life,—life tried for a little while.
A poor sort of thing / (filling the stomach; emptying the bowels;
Bothering to speak to friends on the street; / filling the stomach again;
Dancing, drinking, whoring) / forms the tissue of this fabric.—
(Marriage; society; business; charity;— / *Life, and life refused.*)

The New Englander appraises sins, / finds them beyond his means, / and
    hoards.

Likewise, he seldom spends his goodness / on someone ignoble as he,
But, to make an occasion, he proves himself / that he is equally ignoble.
Then he breaks his fast! / Then he ends his thirsting!
He censors the Judge. / He passes judgment on the Censor. / No language is
    left.
His lone faculty, Condemnation,—condemned. / Nothing is left to say.
Proclaim an Armistice / Through Existence, livid, void, / *let silence flood.*

Ask the Silent One your question. / (He is stupid in misery
No more than the talkative man, who talks through his hat.) / Ask the question.
If he replied at all, / it would be to remark that he never could despise
Anyone so much as himself / should he once give way to Self-pity.
A different act of faith is his,— / the white gesture of Humility.
He knows his weakness. / He is well-schooled / and he never forgets the
    shortest
Title of his Knowledge. / The jailer of his Soul sees Pride. / He sees
Tears, never. / The Silent One is so eaten away
He cannot make that little effort / which surrender to external Fact
Requires, / but looks out always only with one wish,— / *to realize he exists.*

Lo! a Desire! / A Faint motive! / A motive (however faint) beyond disinter-
    estedness.
Faint. / It is faint. / But the boundary is clear. / Desire, oh desire further!
Past that boundary lies Annihilation / where the Soul
Breaks the monotonous-familiar / and man wakes to the shocking
Unastounded company of other men. / But the Silent One would not pass
Where the Redmen have gone. / He would live without end. That,— / *the
    ultimate nature of Hell.*

| LÉONIE ADAMS |

1899–1988

LÉONIE ADAMS, in my judgment, was an authentic lyric poet, second
in her generation only to Hart Crane, whose great death-poem, "The Broken Tower," uses Adams's "Bell Tower" as one of its starting points: "The
voice has its tower."

Born in Brooklyn, she graduated from Barnard College, and then
worked as an editor in publishing. Her first volume of poems, *Those Not*

Elect, came out in 1925. Subsequently she held a position at the Metropolitan Museum of Art, and went abroad on a Guggenheim fellowship to Paris, where she lived with Allen Tate's family, Tate having introduced her to Hart Crane.

A second book of poems, *High Falcon,* appeared in 1929. After teaching at New York University, Adams married the critic William Troy, and taught with him at Sarah Lawrence and at Bennington. For twenty years, after that, she was a lecturer at Columbia. Her *Poems: A Selection* (1954) earned her the Bollingen Prize, and remains one of my favorite volumes in my library.

I am unable to understand why Léonie Adams is not more read and discussed than she now is. Four of her best poems are given here, but I wish I had space for more, including "Ghostly Tree," "The Moon and Spectator," "Fragmentary Stars," and "The Figurehead."

"April Mortality," a poem of bittersweet Eros, has the close, finely wrought texture utterly characteristic of Adams. In "The Horn," the poet again subtly both celebrates and deplores the heart's unwisdom.

Adams's stylistic firmness sustains the beautiful "Grapes Making," a remarkably indirect juxtapositioning of natural abundance and the human intimation of mortality ("You whose all-told is still no sum.").

My favorite poem by Léonie Adams was also her friend Hart Crane's favorite: "Bell Tower," beautifully echoed in Crane's self-elegy. "Bell Tower" is a perfect lyric, with Adams's signature mingling of celebration and lament, counting the "secret cost" of being a poet.

❧　　❧　　❧

April Mortality

Rebellion shook an ancient dust,
And bones, bleached dry of rottenness,
Said: Heart, be bitter still, nor trust
The earth, the sky, in their bright dress.

Heart, heart, dost thou not break to know
This anguish thou wilt bear alone?
We sang of it an age ago,
And traced it dimly upon stone.

With all the drifting race of men
Thou also art begot to mourn

That she is crucified again,
The lonely Beauty yet unborn.

And if thou dreamest to have won
Some touch of her in permanence,
'Tis the old cheating of the sun,
The intricate lovely play of sense.

Be bitter still, remember how
Four petals, when a little breath
Of wind made stir the pear-tree bough,
Blew delicately down to death.

The Horn

While coming to the feast I found
A venerable silver-throated horn,
Which were I brave enough to sound,
Then all, as from that moment born,
Would breathe the honey of this clime,
And three times merry in their time
Would praise the virtue of the horn.

The mist is risen like thin breath;
The young leaves of the ground smell chill,
So faintly are they strewn on death,
The road I came down a west hill;
But none can name as I can name
A little golden-bright thing, flame,
Since bones have caught their marrow chill.

And in a thicket passed me by,
In the black brush, a running hare,
Having a spectre in his eye,
That sped in darkness to the snare;
And who but I can know in pride
The heart, set beating in the side,
Has but the wisdom of a hare?

Grapes Making

Noon sun beats down the leaf; the noon
Of summer burns along the vine
And thins the leaf with burning air,
Till from the underleaf is fanned,
And down the woven vine, the light.
Still the pleached leaves drop layer on layer
To wind the sun on either hand,
And echoes of the light are bound,
And hushed the blazing cheek of light,
The hurry of the breathless noon,
And from the thicket of the vine
The grape has pressed into its round.

The grape has pressed into its round,
And swings, aloof chill green, clean won
Of light, between the sky and ground;
Those hid, soft-flashing lamps yet blind,
Which yield an apprehended sun.
Fresh triumph in a courteous kind,
Having more ways to be, and years,
And easy, countless treasuries,
You whose all-told is still no sum,
Like a rich heart, well-said in sighs,
The careless autumn mornings come,
The grapes drop glimmering to the shears.

Now shady sod at heel piles deep,
An overarching shade, the vine
Across the fall of noon is flung;
And here beneath the leaves is cast
A light to colour noonday sleep,
While cool, bemused the grape is swung
Beneath the eyelids of the vine;
And deepening like a tender thought
Green moves along the leaf, and bright
The leaf above, and leaf has caught,
And emerald pierces day, and last
The faint leaf vanishes to light.

Bell Tower

I have seen, desolate one, the voice has its tower;
The voice also, builded at secret cost,
Its temple of precious tissue. Not silent then
Forever—casting silence in your hour.

There marble boys are leant from the light throat,
Thick locks that hang with dew and eyes dewlashed,
Dazzled with morning, angels of the wind,
With ear a-point for the enchanted note.

And these at length shall tip the hanging bell,
And first the sound must gather in deep bronze,
Till, clearer than ice, purer than a bubble of gold,
It beat in the sky and the air and the ear's remorseless well.

| ALLEN TATE |

1899–1979

A FIRM NEW CRITIC, Tate poetically was caught between two powerful influences, T. S. Eliot and Hart Crane. The first of the two poems I
include here, "Aeneas at Washington" has the accent of Eliot:

> The singular passion
> Abides its object and consumes desire
> In the circling shadow of its appetite

"The Mediterranean," to me Tate's best poem, has a strong touch of
Hart Crane's "The River" section of *The Bridge*:

> Let us lie down once more by the breathing side
> Of Ocean, where our live forefathers sleep
> As if the Known sea still were a month wide—
> Atlantis howls but is no longer steep!

And yet Tate was more than a derivative poet, though necessarily not the equal of T. S. Eliot or Hart Crane. "Aeneas at Washington" has savage energy, while "The Mediterranean" is an elegiac splendor.

A Kentuckian, Allen Tate studied at Vanderbilt with John Crowe Ransom and joined the Fugitives, which included Ransom and Robert Penn Warren. His first marriage was to the novelist Caroline Gordon, and for a number of years Hart Crane was all but a member of the Tate family. After living in Paris, Allen Tate was a faculty member at the University of Minnesota for more than two decades.

Besides his *Collected Poems* (1977), Tate's works included a Faulknerian novel, *The Fathers* (1938), and the brilliant if dogmatic *Reactionary Essays on Poetry and Ideas* (1936).

❦   ❦   ❦

Aeneas at Washington

I myself saw furious with blood
Neoptolemus, at his side the black Atridae,
Hecuba and the hundred daughters, Priam
Cut down, his filth drenching the holy fires.
In that extremity I bore me well,
A true gentleman, valorous in arms,
Disinterested and honourable. Then fled:
That was a time when civilization
Run by the few fell to the many, and
Crashed to the shout of men, the clang of arms:
Cold victualing I seized, I hoisted up
The old man my father upon my back,
In the smoke made by sea for a new world
Saving little—a mind imperishable
If time is, a love of past things tenuous
As the hesitation of receding love.

(To the reduction of uncitied littorals
We brought chiefly the vigor of prophecy
Our hunger breeding calculation
And fixed triumphs)

The thirsty dove I saw
In the glowing fields of Troy, hemp ripening
And tawny corn, the thickening Blue Grass

All lying rich forever in the green sun.
I see all things apart, the towers that men
Contrive I too contrived long, long ago.
Now I demand little. The singular passion
Abides its object and consumes desire
In the circling shadow of its appetite.
There was a time when the young eyes were slow,
Their flame steady beyond the firstling fire,
I stood in the rain, far from home at nightfall
By the Potomac, the great Dome lit the water,
The city my blood had built I knew no more
While the screech-owl whistled his new delight
Consecutively dark.

        Stuck in the wet mire
Four thousand leagues from the ninth buried city
I thought of Troy, what we had built her for.

The Mediterranean

Quem das finem, rex magne, dolorum?

Where we went in the boat was a long bay
A slingshot wide, walled in by towering stone—
Peaked margin of antiquity's delay,
And we went there out of time's monotone:

Where we went in the black hull no light moved
But a gull white-winged along the feckless wave,
The breeze, unseen but fierce as a body loved,
That boat drove onward like a willing slave:

Where we went in the small ship the seaweed
Parted and gave to us the murmuring shore,
And we made feast and in our secret need
Devoured the very plates Aeneas bore:

Where derelict you see through the low twilight
The green coast that you, thunder-tossed, would win,
Drop sail, and hastening to drink all night
Eat dish and bowl—to take that sweet land in!

Where we feasted and caroused on the sandless
Pebbles, affecting our day of piracy,

What prophecy of eaten plates could landless
Wanderers fulfill by the ancient sea?

We for that time might taste the famous age
Eternal here yet hidden from our eyes
When lust of power undid its stuffless rage;
They, in a wineskin, bore earth's paradise.

Let us lie down once more by the breathing side
Of Ocean, where our live forefathers sleep
As if the Known Sea still were a month wide—
Atlantis howls but is no longer steep!

What country shall we conquer, what fair land
Unman our conquest and locate our blood?
We've cracked the hemispheres with careless hand!
Now, from the Gates of Hercules we flood

Westward, westward till the barbarous brine
Whelms us to the tired land where tasseling corn,
Fat beans, grapes sweeter than muscadine
Rot on the vine: in that land were we born.

| HART CRANE |

1899–1932

SOMETHING VISIONARY and authentically exalted ended with Hart
Crane, which is why he is the last poet included in this book. Together with
William Blake (an influence upon him), Hart Crane was my first love
among the great poets, and like Blake he gave me a lifelong addiction to
high poetry. I have represented Crane as fully as I could here: "Repose of
Rivers," the *Voyages* sequence, and "At Melville's Tomb" are from his first
volume, *White Buildings* (1926). "Proem: To Brooklyn Bridge," "The Tunnel," and "Atlantis" are sections of *The Bridge* (1930), Hart Crane's sublime epic. "The Broken Tower," written in Mexico in 1932, can be called
his death-poem.

Harold Hart Crane was born in Garrettsville, Ohio, on July 21, 1899, the only child of Clarence Arthur Crane, the candy maker who inaugurated the Life Saver, and Grace Hart Crane. The marriage was a very difficult one, and the poet's mother suffered a breakdown in 1908. He lived with his maternal grandmother in Cleveland, attended high school there in a desultory way, educating himself by deep reading, and by sixteen had developed his highly original style. At seventeen, Crane left high school without graduating and went to live in New York City, vowing to have a poetic career.

The poet's parents divorced in 1917, and Crane spent four years alternately in New York City and in Cleveland, working at various jobs. In 1921, he quarreled fiercely with his father, and returned definitively to New York City, where he worked in advertising until he received the patronage of the philanthropist Otto Kahn.

In the spring of 1927, Crane moved to a building in Columbia Heights, Brooklyn, with a superb view of the Brooklyn Bridge, which helped stimulate the writing of his epic, *The Bridge*. Long confirmed in homosexual identity, Crane, in April of 1924, fell ecstatically in love with an equally young Danish sailor, Emil Oppfer. The marvelous *Voyages* II, analyzed fully in my essay "The Art of Reading Poetry," introducing this book, was first drafted in the early days of the poet's relationship with Oppfer. *White Buildings* was published in 1926 and, together with Wallace Stevens's *Harmonium,* seems to me the finest "first volume" of American poetry in the twentieth century. In April 1926, subsidized again by Otto Kahn, Crane went back to the Isle of Pines, near Cuba in the Caribbean, where he had spent several summers in his childhood. *The Bridge*, which Crane had begun in 1923, was composed mostly on the Isle of Pines in 1926–1927. In 1929, Crane lived in Paris, under the patronage of Harry Crosby, who published the first edition of *The Bridge* in 1930. A first American edition appeared a few months later in New York City. Alcoholic and driven by desperate fears of losing his poetic gift, Crane went to Mexico on a Guggenheim fellowship in 1931, intending to write an epic on Cortés and Montezuma. Instead, he composed some remarkable lyrics and fragments, the most vital being "The Broken Tower," which both laments his life and work, and celebrates his only heterosexual love affair, with Peggy Baird, divorced wife of Crane's friend, the poet-autobiographer Malcolm Cowley. Returning with her from Mexico on a voyage to New York City, Crane jumped overboard to his death on April 27, 1932, three months shy of what would have been his thirty-third birthday.

"Repose of Rivers," written in 1926, was the most recently composed poem to be included in *White Buildings*. It is Crane's tally (in Walt Whitman's sense) of the cost of confirmation of the poetical character in him, and its fusion with homoerotic self-realization.

Voyages I have discussed earlier, while the elegy for Herman Melville is a prophecy of Crane's own fate:

> High in the azure steeps
> Monody shall not wake the mariner.
> This fabulous shadow only the sea keeps.

The Bridge, in its composition, actually began with the turbulent "Atlantis," now its final section. "Proem: To Brooklyn Bridge" is one of the transcendent American poems of the last century, and addresses the "leap" and "vaulting" of that still marvelous structure almost as a hymn to the Gnostic heresy's Stranger or Alien God. In "The Tunnel," an epic descent into the Hell of New York City's subway, Crane most directly struggles with (and against) the influence of Eliot's *The Waste Land*.

"The Broken Tower" is Hart Crane's farewell to poetry and to life, and yet it achieves an exultant despair more eloquent than anything else in his career:

> And so it was I entered the broken world
> To trace the visionary company of love, its voice
> An instant in the wind (I know not whither hurled)
> But not for long to hold each desperate choice.

✤   ✤   ✤

Repose of Rivers

The willows carried a slow sound,
A sarabande the wind mowed on the mead.
I could never remember
That seething, steady leveling of the marshes
Till age had brought me to the sea.

Flags, weeds. And remembrance of steep alcoves
Where cypresses shared the noon's
Tyranny; they drew me into hades almost.
And mammoth turtles climbing sulphur dreams

Yielded, while sun-silt rippled them
Asunder . . .

How much I would have bartered! the black gorge
And all the singular nestings in the hills
Where beavers learn stitch and tooth.
The pond I entered once and quickly fled—
I remember now its singing willow rim.

And finally, in that memory all things nurse;
After the city that I finally passed
With scalding unguents spread and smoking darts
The monsoon cut across the delta
At gulf gates . . . There, beyond the dykes

I heard wind flaking sapphire, like this summer,
And willows could not hold more steady sound.

Voyages

I

Above the fresh ruffles of the surf
Bright striped urchins flay each other with sand.
They have contrived a conquest for shell shucks,
And their fingers crumble fragments of baked weed
Gaily digging and scattering.

And in answer to their treble interjections
The sun beats lightning on the waves,
The waves fold thunder on the sand;
And could they hear me I would tell them:

O brilliant kids, frisk with your dog,
Fondle your shells and sticks, bleached
By time and the elements; but there is a line
You must not cross nor ever trust beyond it
Spry cordage of your bodies to caresses
Too lichen-faithful from too wide a breast.
The bottom of the sea is cruel.

II

—And yet this great wink of eternity,
Of rimless floods, unfettered leewardings,

Samite sheeted and processioned where
Her undinal vast belly moonward bends,
Laughing the wrapt inflections of our love;

Take this Sea, whose diapason knells
On scrolls of silver snowy sentences,
The sceptred terror of whose sessions rends
As her demeanors motion well or ill,
All but the pieties of lovers' hands.

And onward, as bells off San Salvador
Salute the crocus lustres of the stars,
In these poinsettia meadows of her tides,—
Adagios of islands, O my Prodigal,
Complete the dark confessions her veins spell.

Mark how her turning shoulders wind the hours,
And hasten while her penniless rich palms
Pass superscription of bent foam and wave,—
Hasten, while they are true,—sleep, death, desire,
Close round one instant in one floating flower.

Bind us in time, O Seasons clear, and awe.
O minstrel galleons of Carib fire,
Bequeath us to no earthly shore until
Is answered in the vortex of our grave
The seal's wide spindrift gaze toward paradise.

III

Infinite consanguinity it bears—
This tendered theme of you that light
Retrieves from sea plains where the sky
Resigns a breast that every wave enthrones;
While ribboned water lanes I wind
Are laved and scattered with no stroke
Wide from your side, whereto this hour
The sea lifts, also, reliquary hands.

And so, admitted through black swollen gates
That must arrest all distance otherwise,—
Past whirling pillars and lithe pediments,
Light wrestling there incessantly with light,
Star kissing star through wave on wave unto
Your body rocking!

and where death, if shed,
Presumes no carnage, but this single change,—
Upon the steep floor flung from dawn to dawn
The silken skilled transmemberment of song;

Permit me voyage, love, into your hands . . .

IV

Whose counted smile of hours and days, suppose
I know as spectrum of the sea and pledge
Vastly now parting gulf on gulf of wings
Whose circles bridge, I know, (from palms to the severe
Chilled albatross's white immutability)
No stream of greater love advancing now
Than, singing, this mortality alone
Through clay aflow immortally to you.

All fragrance irrefragibly, and claim
Madly meeting logically in this hour
And region that is ours to wreathe again,
Portending eyes and lips and making told
The chancel port and portion of our June—

Shall they not stem and close in our own steps
Bright staves of flowers and quills to-day as I
Must first be lost in fatal tides to tell?

In signature of the incarnate word
The harbor shoulders to resign in mingling
Mutual blood, transpiring as foreknown
And widening noon within your breast for gathering
All bright insinuations that my years have caught
For islands where must lead inviolably
Blue latitudes and levels of your eyes,—

In this expectant, still exclaim receive
The secret oar and petals of all love.

V

Meticulous, past midnight in clear rime,
Infrangible and lonely, smooth as though cast
Together in one merciless white blade—
The bay estuaries fleck the hard sky limits.

—As if too brittle or too clear to touch!
The cables of our sleep so swiftly filed,
Already hang, shred ends from remembered stars.
One frozen trackless smile . . . What words
Can strangle this deaf moonlight? For we

Are overtaken. Now no cry, no sword
Can fasten or deflect this tidal wedge,
Slow tyranny of moonlight, moonlight loved
And changed. . . "There's

Nothing like this in the world," you say,
Knowing I cannot touch your hand and look
Too, into that godless cleft of sky
Where nothing turns but dead sands flashing.

"—And never to quite understand!" No,
In all the argosy of your bright hair I dreamed
Nothing so flagless as this piracy.

                    But now
Draw in your head, alone and too tall here.
Your eyes already in the slant of drifting foam;
Your breath sealed by the ghosts I do not know:
Draw in your head and sleep the long way home.

     VI
Where icy and bright dungeons lift
Of swimmers their lost morning eyes,
And ocean rivers, churning, shift
Green borders under stranger skies,

Steadily as a shell secretes
Its beating leagues of monotone,
Or as many waters trough the sun's
Red kelson past the cape's wet stone;

O rivers mingling toward the sky
And harbor of the phoenix' breast—
My eyes pressed black against the prow,
—Thy derelict and blinded guest

Waiting, afire, what name, unspoke,
I cannot claim: let thy waves rear
More savage than the death of kings,
Some splintered garland for the seer.

Beyond siroccos harvesting
The solstice thunders, crept away,
Like a cliff swinging or a sail
Flung into April's inmost day—

Creation's blithe and petalled word
To the lounged goddess when she rose
Conceding dialogue with eyes
That smile unsearchable repose—

Still fervid covenant, Belle Isle,
—Unfolded floating dais before
Which rainbows twine continual hair—
Belle Isle, white echo of the oar!

The imaged Word, it is, that holds
Hushed willows anchored in its glow.
It is the unbetrayable reply
Whose accent no farewell can know.

At Melville's Tomb

Often beneath the wave, wide from this ledge
The dice of drowned men's bones he saw bequeath
An embassy. Their numbers as he watched,
Beat on the dusty shore and were obscured.

And wrecks passed without sound of bells,
The calyx of death's bounty giving back
A scattered chapter, livid hieroglyph,
The portent wound in corridors of shells.

Then in the circuit calm of one vast coil,
Its lashings charmed and malice reconciled,
Frosted eyes there were that lifted altars;
And silent answers crept across the stars.

Compass, quadrant and sextant contrive
No farther tides . . . High in the azure steeps
Monody shall not wake the mariner.
This fabulous shadow only the sea keeps.

from The Bridge

> *From going to and fro in the earth,*
> *and from walking up and down in it.*
> THE BOOK OF JOB

To Brooklyn Bridge

How many dawns, chill from his rippling rest
The seagull's wings shall dip and pivot him,
Shedding white rings of tumult, building high
Over the chained bay waters Liberty—

Then, with inviolate curve, forsake our eyes
As apparitional as sails that cross
Some page of figures to be filed away;
—Till elevators drop us from our day . . .

I think of cinemas, panoramic sleights
With multitudes bent toward some flashing scene
Never disclosed, but hastened to again,
Foretold to other eyes on the same screen;

And Thee, across the harbor, silver-paced
As though the sun took step of thee, yet left
Some motion ever unspent in thy stride,—
Implicitly thy freedom staying thee!

Out of some subway scuttle, cell or loft
A bedlamite speeds to thy parapets,
Tilting there momently, shrill shirt ballooning,
A jest falls from the speechless caravan.

Down Wall, from girder into street noon leaks,
A rip-tooth of the sky's acetylene;
All afternoon the cloud-flown derricks turn . . .
Thy cables breathe the North Atlantic still.

And obscure as that heaven of the Jews,
Thy guerdon . . . Accolade thou dust bestow
Of anonymity time cannot raise:
Vibrant reprieve and pardon thou dost show.

O harp and altar, of the fury fused,
(How could mere toil align thy choiring strings!)
Terrific threshold of the prophet's pledge,
Prayer of pariah, and the lover's cry,—

Again the traffic lights that skim thy swift
Unfractioned idiom, immaculate sigh of stars,
Beading thy path—condense eternity:
And we have seen night lifted in thine arms.

Under thy shadow by the piers I waited;
Only in darkness is thy shadow clear.
The City's fiery parcels all undone,
Already snow submerges an iron year . . .

O Sleepless as the river under thee,
Vaulting the sea, the prairies' dreaming sod,
Unto us lowliest sometime sweep, descend
And of the curveship lend a myth to God.

VII
The Tunnel

> To Find the Western path
> Right thro' the Gates of Wrath.
> —BLAKE

Performances, assortments, résumés—
Up Times Square to Columbus Circle lights
Channel the congresses, nightly sessions,
Refractions of the thousand theatres, faces—
Mysterious kitchens. . . . You shall search them all.
Someday by heart you'll learn each famous sight
And watch the curtain lift in hell's despite;
You'll find the garden in the third act dead,
Finger your knees—and wish yourself in bed
With tabloid crime-sheets perched in easy sight.

> Then let you reach your hat
> and go.

As usual, let you—also
walking down—exclaim
to twelve upward leaving
a subscription praise
for what time slays.

Or can't you quite make up your mind to ride;
A walk is better underneath the L a brisk
Ten blocks or so before? But you find yourself
Preparing penguin flexions of the arms,—
As usual you will meet the scuttle yawn:
The subway yawns the quickest promise home.

Be minimum, then, to swim the hiving swarms
Out of the Square, the Circle burning bright—
Avoid the glass doors gyring at your right,
Where boxed alone a second, eyes take fright
—Quite unprepared rush naked back to light:
And down beside the turnstile press the coin
Into the slot. The gongs already rattle.

And so
of cities you bespeak
subways, rivered under streets
and rivers. . . . In the car
the overtone of motion
underground, the monotone
of motion is the sound
of other faces, also underground—

"Let's have a pencil Jimmy—living now
at Floral Park
Flatbush—on the fourth of July—
like a pigeon's muddy dream—potatoes
to dig in the field—travlin the town—too—
night after night—the Culver line—the
girls all shaping up—it used to be—"

Our tongues recant like beaten weather vanes.
This answer lives like verdigris, like hair
Beyond extinction, surcease of the bone;
And repetition freezes—"What

"what do you want? getting weak on the links?
fandaddle daddy don't ask for change—IS THIS
FOURTEENTH? it's half past six she said—if
you don't like my gate why did you
swing on it, why *didja*
swing on it
anyhow—"

And somehow anyhow swing—

The phonographs of hades in the brain
Are tunnels that re-wind themselves, and love
A burnt match skating in a urinal—
Somewhere above Fourteenth TAKE THE EXPRESS
To brush some new presentiment of pain—

"But I want service in this office SERVICE
I said—after
the show she cried a little afterwards but—"

Whose head is swinging from the swollen strap?
Whose body smokes along the bitten rails,
Bursts from a smoldering bundle far behind
In back forks of the chasms of the brain,—
Puffs from a riven stump far out behind
In interborough fissures of the mind . . . ?

And why do I often meet your visage here,
Your eyes like agate lanterns—on and on
Below the toothpaste and the dandruff ads?
—And did their riding eyes right through your side,
And did their eyes like unwashed platters ride?
And Death, aloft,—gigantically down
Probing through you—toward me, O evermore!
And when they dragged your retching flesh,
Your trembling hands that night through Baltimore—
That last night on the ballot rounds, did you,
Shaking, did you deny the ticket, Poe?

For Gravesend Manor change at Chambers Street.
The platform hurries along to a dead stop.

The intent escalator lifts a serenade
Stilly
Of shoes, umbrellas, each eye attending its shoe, then
Bolting outright somewhere above where streets
Burst suddenly in rain. . . . The gongs recur:
Elbows and levers, guard and hissing door.
Thunder is galvothermic here below. . . . The car
Wheels off. The train rounds, bending to a scream,
Taking the final level for the dive
Under the river—
And somewhat emptier than before,
Demented, for a hitching second, humps; then
Lets go. . . . Toward corners of the floor
Newspapers wing, revolve and wing.
Blank windows gargle signals through the roar.

And does the Daemon take you home, also,
Wop washerwoman, with the bandaged hair?
After the corridors are swept, the cuspidors—
The gaunt sky-barracks cleanly now, and bare,
O Genoese, do you bring mother eyes and hands
Back home to children and to golden hair?

Daemon, demurring and eventful yawn!
Whose hideous laughter is a bellows mirth
—Or the muffled slaughter of a day in birth—
O cruelly to inoculate the brinking dawn
With antennae toward worlds that glow and sink;—
To spoon us out more liquid than the dim
Locution of the eldest star, and pack
The conscience navelled in the plunging wind,
Umbilical to call—and straightway die!

O caught like pennies beneath soot and steam,
Kiss of our agony thou gatherest;
Condensed, thou takest all—shrill ganglia
Impassioned with some song we fail to keep.
And yet, like Lazarus, to feel the slope,
The sod and billow breaking,—lifting ground,
—A sound of waters bending astride the sky
Unceasing with some Word that will not die . . . !

A tugboat, wheezing wreaths of steam,
Lunged past, with one galvanic blare stove up the River.
I counted the echoes assembling, one after one,
Searching, thumbing the midnight on the piers.
Lights, coasting, left the oily tympanum of waters;
The blackness somewhere gouged glass on a sky.
And this thy harbor, O my City, I have driven under,
Tossed from the coil of ticking towers. . . . Tomorrow,
And to be. . . . Here by the River that is East—
Here at the waters' edge the hands drop memory;
Shadowless in that abyss they unaccounting lie.
How far away the star has pooled the sea—
Or shall the hands be drawn away, to die?

Kiss of our agony Thou gatherest,
                    O Hand of Fire
                              gatherest—

VIII
Atlantis

> *Music is then the knowledge of that which*
> *relates to love in harmony and system.*
>   —PLATO

Through the bound cable strands, the arching path
Upward, veering with light, the flight of strings,—
Taut miles of shuttling moonlight syncopate
The whispered rush, telepathy of wires.
Up the index of night, granite and steel—
Transparent meshes—fleckless the gleaming staves—
Sibylline voices flicker, waveringly stream
As though a god were issue of the strings. . . .

And through that cordage, threading with its call
One arc synoptic of all tides below—
Their labyrinthine mouths of history
Pouring reply as though all ships at sea
Complighted in one vibrant breath made cry,—
"Make thy love sure—to weave whose song we ply!"
—From black embankments, moveless soundings hailed,
So seven oceans answer from their dream.

And on, obliquely up bright carrier bars
New octaves trestle the twin monoliths
Beyond whose frosted capes the moon bequeaths
Two worlds of sleep (O arching strands of song!)—
Onward and up the crystal-flooded aisle
White tempest nets file upward, upward ring
With silver terraces the humming spars,
The loft of vision, palladium helm of stars.

Sheerly the eyes, like seagulls stung with rime—
Slit and propelled by glistening fins of light—
Pick biting way up towering looms that press
Sidelong with flight of blade on tendon blade
—Tomorrows into yesteryear—and link
What cipher-script of time no traveller reads
But who, through smoking pyres of love and death,
Searches the timeless laugh of mythic spears.

Like hails, farewells—up planet-sequined heights
Some trillion whispering hammers glimmer Tyre:
Serenely, sharply up the long anvil cry
Of inchling aeons silence rivets Troy.
And you, aloft there—Jason! hesting Shout!
Still wrapping harness to the swarming air!
Silvery the rushing wake, surpassing call,
Beams yelling Aeolus! splintered in the straits!

From gulfs unfolding, terrible of drums,
Tall Vision-of-the-Voyage, tensely spare—
Bridge, lifting night to cycloramic crest
Of deepest day—O Choir, translating time
Into what multitudinous Verb the suns
And synergy of waters ever fuse, recast
In myriad syllables,—Psalm of Cathay!
O Love, thy white, pervasive Paradigm . . . !

We left the haven hanging in the night—
Sheened harbor lanterns backward fled the keel.
Pacific here at time's end, bearing corn,—
Eyes stammer through the pangs of dust and steel.
And still the circular, indubitable frieze
Of heaven's meditation, yoking wave

To kneeling wave, one song devoutly binds—
The vernal strophe chimes from deathless strings!

O Thou steeled Cognizance whose leap commits
The agile precincts of the lark's return;
Within whose lariat sweep encinctured sing
In single chrysalis the many twain,—
Of stars Thou art the stitch and stallion glow
And like an organ, Thou, with sound of doom—
Sight, sound and flesh Thou leadest from time's realm
As love strikes clear direction for the helm.

Swift peal of secular light, intrinsic Myth
Whose fell unshadow is death's utter wound,—
O River-throated—iridescently unborne
Through the bright drench and fabric of our veins;
With white escarpments swinging into light,
Sustained in tears the cities are endowed
And justified conclamant with ripe fields
Revolving through their harvests in sweet torment.

Forever Deity's glittering Pledge, O Thou
Whose canticle fresh chemistry assigns
To wrapt inception and beatitude,—
Always through blinding cables, to our joy,
Of thy white seizure springs the prophecy:
Always through spiring cordage, pyramids
Of silver sequel, Deity's young name
Kinetic of white choiring wings . . . ascends.

Migrations that must needs void memory,
Inventions that cobblestone the heart,—
Unspeakable Thou Bridge to Thee, O Love.
Thy pardon for this history, whitest Flower,
O Answerer of all,—Anemone,—
Now while thy petals spend the suns about us, hold—
(O Thou whose radiance doth inherit me)
Atlantis,—hold thy floating singer late!

So to thine Everpresence, beyond time,
Like spears ensanguined of one tolling star
That bleeds infinity—the orphic strings,

Sidereal phalanxes, leap and converge:
—One Song, one Bridge of Fire! Is it Cathay,
Now pity steeps the grass and rainbows ring
The serpent with the eagle in the leaves . . . ?
Whispers antiphonal in azure swing.

The Broken Tower

The bell-rope that gathers God at dawn
Dispatches me as though I dropped down the knell
Of a spent day—to wander the cathedral lawn
From pit to crucifix, feet chill on steps from hell.

Have you not heard, have you not seen that corps
Of shadows in the tower, whose shoulders sway
Antiphonal carillons launched before
The stars are caught and hived in the sun's ray?

The bells, I say, the bells break down their tower;
And swing I know not where. Their tongues engrave
Membrane through marrow, my long-scattered score
Of broken intervals . . . And I, their sexton slave!

Oval encyclicals in canyons heaping
The impasse high with choir. Banked voices slain!
Pagodas, campaniles with reveilles outleaping—
O terraced echoes prostrate on the plain! . . .

And so it was I entered the broken world
To trace the visionary company of love, its voice
An instant in the wind (I know not whither hurled)
But not for long to hold each desperate choice.

My word I poured. But was it cognate, scored
Of that tribunal monarch of the air
Whose thigh embronzes earth, strikes crystal Word
In wounds pledged once to hope,—cleft to despair?

The steep encroachments of my blood left me
No answer (could blood hold such a lofty tower
As flings the question true?)—or is it she
Whose sweet mortality stirs latent power?—

And through whose pulse I hear, counting the strokes
My veins recall and add, revived and sure
The angelus of wars my chest evokes:
What I hold healed, original now, and pure . . .

And builds, within, a tower that is not stone
(Not stone can jacket heaven)—but slip
Of pebbles,—visible wings of silence sown
In azure circles, widening as they dip

The matrix of the heart, lift down the eye
That shrines the quiet lake and swells a tower . . .
The commodious, tall decorum of that sky
Unseals her earth, and lifts love in its shower.

INDEX OF POETS

INDEX OF POEM TITLES

PERMISSIONS

ABOUT THE AUTHOR

HAROLD BLOOM is Sterling Professor of Humanities at Yale University and a former Charles Eliot Norton Professor at Harvard. His more than twenty-five books include *Genius*; *How to Read and Why*; *Shakespeare: The Invention of the Human*; *The Western Canon*; *The Book of J*; and *The Anxiety of Influence*. He is a MacArthur Prize Fellow, a member of the American Academy of Arts and Letters, and the recipient of many awards and honorary degrees, including the Academy's Gold Medal for Belles Lettres and Criticism, the International Prize of Catalonia, and the Alfonso Reyes Prize of Mexico.